P9-BZO-672

ANDREA SCHULTE-PEEVERS

BERLIN
CITY GUIDE

INTRODUCING BERLIN

The dramatic canopy of the Sony Center (p111)

Berlin is a scene-stealing, head-turning combo of glamour and grit, teeming with top museums and galleries, grand opera and guerrilla clubs, gourmet temples and ethnic snack shacks.

Over the past decade, Berlin's become a pillar of the fashion, art, design and music worlds, not just keeping up with but setting new trends. A global influx of creatives has turned it into a cauldron of cultural cool that's often compared to New York in the '80s. What draws them is Berlin's legendary climate of tolerance, openness and experimentation infused with an edgy undercurrent that gives this 'eternally unfinished' city its street cred.

All this trendiness is a triumph for a town that's long been in the crosshairs of history: Berlin staged a revolution, was headquartered by fascists, bombed to bits, ripped in half and finally reunited – and that was just in the 20th century! Famous landmarks such as the Reichstag, the Brandenburg Gate, Checkpoint Charlie and what's left of the Berlin Wall are like a virtual 3-D textbook in a city where you'll find history staring you in the face every time you turn a corner.

Perhaps it's because of its heavy historical burden that Berlin is throwing itself into tomorrow with such contagious energy. At times the entire city seems to be bubbling over into one huge party. Cafes are jammed at all hours, drinking is a religious rite and clubs host their scenes of frenzy and hedonism until the wee hours. Sleep? Fuhgeddabout it!

BERLIN LIFE

Berlin is a sprawling city but key areas are pleasingly compact and human-scale. Traffic flows freely, public transportation is brilliant, you can walk without fear at night, clubs have no velvet ropes and your restaurant bill would only buy you a starter back home.

'Where New York might be the Big Apple, Berlin is the Big Appetite'

But try to put your finger on the pulse of Berlin and you'll find that, much like the mysterious movements on a Ouija board, that pulse is already moving on to another location. Today's downtrodden neighbourhood becomes tomorrow's dream of wide-eyed students and artists, young entrepreneurs and, eventually, developers. The city's famously low rents are slowly disappearing, office buildings displace beloved riverside party venues, and 'loft-living' is the new buzzword. Well-established nightlife spots are being forced into closing by noise-sensitive new neighbours lacking the tolerance that attracted them to Berlin in the first place.

On the economic front, there are some slivers of sunlight on the horizon. Between 2005 and 2010 almost 500 companies moved to Berlin, creating 21,000 new jobs while investing €1.7 billion. Still, the dreams of those who shape the future collide with one inescapable fact: the city is broke. The unemployment rate is among the highest in Germany, the city debt hovers at a staggering €60 billion and the ambitious reconstruction of the royal city palace had to be postponed by at least four years for lack of funds.

Still, the band plays on. In a city that is truly 24/7, the creativity, sensory overload and hedonism roar with unapologetic abandon. Where New York might be the Big Apple, Berlin is the Big Appetite and the hunger for experimentation and challenge is rarely sated. It's a city where you can fairly hear and feel the collision between past and future, what is possible and what is realistic, the cultural hopes and the culture clashes between people who've joined together from around the globe in one big experiment.

Berlin may be losing some of its famously raw edge, but at least for now, it's in no danger of selling its soul.

Enjoy the outdoors at Mauerpark (p196), with dining, drinking, entertainment and Berlin's best flea market

HIGHLIGHTS

1

MARTIN MOOS

ICONIC BERLIN

In Berlin, the past is always present. Strolling around, you can't help but pass by legendary sights that take you back to the days of Prussian glory, the Nazi-era nadir, the Cold War chill or the euphoria of reunification. Like a 3-D textbook, only better.

2

3

BERLINER MAUER
BERLIN WALL

JAN HALÁSKA/ALAMY

DAVID PEEVERS

1 Brandenburger Tor Take in the famous Brandenburg Gate, a backdrop for presidential speeches, Pink Floyd concerts and World Cup soccer public viewing parties (p81)

2 Reichstag Stand in awe of history at Germany's political power nexus (p75)

3 Berlin Wall Don't miss the most famous Berlin landmark. Only, where is it? (p82)

4 Fernsehturm Get high at Germany's tallest structure, the TV Tower (p95)

5 Schloss Charlottenburg Try to avoid palace envy at this pretty Prussian power display (p122)

6 Neue Synagoge Visit the beautiful beacon of Berlin's Jewish renaissance (p102)

1 Beate Uhse Erotikmuseum
Learn a trick or two at this arty and educational space (p130)

2 Legendary liberalism Get ready for the classic 'boy meets girl' story. Or maybe *The Crying Game*? (p260)

3 Christopher Street Day Join the throngs out and about at Berlin's gay party of the year (p262)

RICHARD NEBESKY

NAUGHTY BERLIN

Las Vegas may hold the title as the world's 'sin city' but Berlin is no slouch in the libido department. Dive in and be as nice or nasty as you want, pretend to be someone else entirely or live out your most frisky fantasies.

DAVID PEEVERS

DAVID PEEVERS

ON THE WATERFRONT

Boasting more bridges than Venice, Berlin is shaped by water and there are plenty of opportunities for taking a cooling dip, sipping cocktails on a sandy beach or going on an aquatic sightseeing tour.

KRZYSZTOF DYDYNSKI

2 Boat cruises Soak up the sun as you drift gently past Berlin's finest landmarks (p311)

3 Beach bars Enjoy a cold drink at an urban beach – summers wouldn't be the same without them (p224)

3 Badeschiff Cool off in summer, heat up in winter at this unique barge-turned-pool (p147)

DAVID PEEVERS

DAVID PEEVERS

KARL JOHAENTGES/LOOK-FOTO

AFTER DARK

Berlin's your oyster when the moon's high in the sky. Knock back tasty libations at dive bars or designer dens, hobnob with hipsters at hot-stepping clubs, get your kicks in a coterie of cabarets or point your highbrow compass towards the opera.

RICHARD NEBESKY

KRZYSZTOF DYDYNSKI

4

DAVID PEEVERS

5

RICHARD NEBESKY

1 **Freischwimmer** Grab a cocktail and catch a cool evening breeze at this boathouse-turned-bar (p225)

2 **Clubs** Put on your dancing shoes and party till dawn and beyond (p231)

3 **Berliner Philharmonie** Indulge your ears with symphonic strains in an iconic venue (p250)

4 **Life is a cabaret** Flash back to Roaring Twenties glamour at Bar Jeder Vernunft (p238)

5 **Drinking dens** From trashy dives to cocktail temples, explore the endless variety of booze parlours to reach an altered state (p219)

6 **Tempodrom** Take in a rock concert or sporting event at this tent-shaped temple of entertainment (p237)

6

KRZYSZTOF DYDYNSKI

1 **East Side Gallery** Check out the longest Berlin Wall remnant – it's also the world's biggest outdoor canvas (p149)

2 **Luftbrückendenkmal** Pay tribute to a true 'triumph of the will' in the age of democracy (p145)

3 **Checkpoint Charlie** Stand in a hot spot of the Cold War (p144)

GUY MOBERLY

RED BERLIN

Soviet spies, CIA operatives, border guards, spectacular escapes, military standoffs – Berlin was ground zero of the Cold War, the Wall a tangible metaphor for a world divided by politics and ideology. Prepare for goose bumps when facing the ghosts of the past.

LEE FOSTER

MARTIN MOOS

GREEN BERLIN

It's a jungle out there, with parks, forests, lakes and rivers swathed across one third of the metropolis. Fantastic outdoor spots lurk in every neighbourhood, making it a snap to take a break from the tourist track and get a dose of asphalt-free exercise.

1 **Wannsee** Opt for a natural high while lying low at the Wannsee (p165)

2 **Tiergarten** Picnic among beech trees, rhododendrons and statues in Berlin's central park (p117)

BERNHARD LIMBERGER/GETTY

DAVID BORLAND

BERLIN RITUALS

You too can be 'ein Berliner'! Get that wicked little tattoo, spend hours over breakfast, watch the world on parade while perched in a cafe or beer garden, or scarf up Euro icons at a fabulous flea market. C'mon, join Team Berlin.

1 **Cafe scene in Prenzlauer Berg** Watch the world on parade over cakes and cappuccinos (p228)

2 **Flohmarkt am Mauerpark** Indulge in a spot of urban archaeology at Berlin's best flea market (p196)

GUY MOBERLY

DAVID PEEVERS

DIVINE DINING

Berlin's cuisine scene is as varied, fun and adventurous as the city itself. Hunker down for plates of hearty German food, report to top toques for the latest in concept cuisine, sample global plates in exotic locales or simply get your doner kebab fast-food fix.

IMAGE BROKER

DAVID PEEVERS

1 **Currywurst** Take a bite! If there ever was a fast food with cult status, this would be it (p199)

2 **Top doners** Scratch your fast-food itch… And the *Döner* Oscar goes to: Schlemmerbuffet! Applause! (p205)

3 **Grill Royal** Rub shoulders with the rich and famous at this elegant waterside fine-diner (p203)

ANDRES LABES

CONTENTS

Andrea Schulte-Peevers

Andrea has travelled the distance to the moon and back in her visits to over 60 countries and carries her dog-eared passport like a badge of honour. Her fascination with Berlin's mystique goes back to her first stay in the summer of 1989, a few months shy of the Wall's collapse. During many return trips she has watched Berlin shed its Cold-War-era brooding and blossom into a vibrant, creative, seductive and confident metropolis. Born and raised in Germany and educated in London and at UCLA, Andrea has built a career on writing about her native country for nearly two decades. She's authored or contributed to more than 40 Lonely Planet titles, including the first edition of this guide as well as the *Berlin* Encounter and *Germany* country guides. After this trip she's seriously considering permanently trading her house in Los Angeles for a sunny apartment in Berlin.

ANDREA'S TOP BERLIN DAY

As a child I hated Sundays because there was nothing to do but stay home and watch TV. Boring! These days, I love Sundays, at least in Berlin and provided I'm not hung over from the night before… But let's say I got a good night's sleep and have been tickled awake by bright sunshine – perfect! I wake up my husband David, we hop on our bikes and head down to Anna Blume (p228) for a leisurely breakfast. I kiss him goodbye, then pedal through beautiful Prenzlauer Berg to meet up with my best friend Uli and her eight-year-old boy Matt. We've promised to take him to Legoland Discovery Centre (p111), where we spend an hour getting acquainted with giant giraffes, dragons and knights all made from those little plastic pieces. Matt loves it. And strangely, we do too. Matt needs his nap, so I head back to Prenzlauer Berg, stopping at W-Imbiss (p217) for a quick naan pizza for lunch. I spend the early part of the afternoon foraging for treasure at the Flohmarkt am Mauerpark (Mauerpark flea market; p196), then break for cappuccino at Mauersegler (p228) before ambling over to the park's little amphitheatre where the insanely popular Bearpit Karaoke (p159) is already in full swing. For an hour or two I cheer and clap along with the other 2000 folks as Detlev croons and Maurizio moonwalks. The place always puts me in a happy mood, so I arrive with a big smile at the Prater beer garden (p228), where I join some friends for a quick beer and bratwurst before winding down the day in style with a classical concert in the Spiegelsaal (p250) at Clärchens Ballhaus. Sundays don't get much better than this!

No matter whether you're a backpacker, a three-button suit, a cocky jetsetter, a trendy urban nomad or travelling with the tots, you'll find all your needs and expectations met in Berlin. Room and travel reservations are a good idea between June and early September and around major holidays and trade fairs year-round, but otherwise you can keep your advance planning to a minimum (but do have a look at the boxed text on p21). Whatever you do, don't overbook yourself. Berlin is definitely a city that rewards spontaneity.

WHEN TO GO

Berlin has a continental climate, which generally translates into scorching summers and freezing winters, although in recent years global warming has turned such time-tested rules on their heads. In other words: the weather is unpredictable. So whenever you visit, check the forecast and pack accordingly. Rain or shine, May, June, September and October are generally the months to see the city at its best and sop up local colour by the bucketful. That's when festivals, street fairs and cultural events of all stripes are in full swing and temps are pleasant enough for chilling in outdoor cafes and beer gardens or for skipping around Berlin's many parks, forests and other natural assets.

Summers essentially bring a major population exchange: Berliners leave town for hotter climes, while tourists, especially from southern Europe, flock to Berlin to escape the heat. This is the time of outdoor anything: concerts, plays, opera, parties, beach bars, cinema and so on.

In winter, days are short (the December sun, if there is any, sets around 3.30pm) and the entire city is often gloomy and cold, so life moves pretty much indoors. This is the time to slow down and make an in-depth study of museums and galleries, attend concerts and plays or warm up for a couple of hours over hot latte in a cosy cafe. The best winter month by far is December, when the city is bathed in a decorative sea of lights and the air is redolent of mulled wine and gingerbread scents wafting from the city's many Christmas markets. Hotel rates are pretty much constant year-round.

FESTIVALS & EVENTS

Berlin is very much a party town with a busy year-round calendar of concerts, street parties, sports events, trade shows and festivals celebrating everything from film to fetish, music

top picks

BEST FESTIVALS

- Berlinale (opposite)
- Ber-Mu-Da (p20)
- Christopher Street Day (p262)
- Internationale Tourismus Börse (opposite)
- Karneval der Kulturen (p18)

to fashion, porn to travel. Major events such as Christopher Street Day (p262), Karneval der Kulturen (Carnival of Cultures) and New Year's Eve bring hundreds of thousands of revellers to town, filling hotels, restaurants and venues to capacity. Berlin's tourist office (www.visitberlin.de) has an events calendar and can also help you book tickets. The listings magazines *Tip* (www.tip-berlin.de, in German) and *Zitty* (www.zitty.de, in German) are the best sources for up-to-the-minute events listings. For events primarily geared towards the GLBT community, see the Gay & Lesbian Berlin chapter, p257.

January

BERLIN FASHION WEEK
☎ 6290 0850; www.berlin-fashionweek.de
Designers, buyers and media descend upon Berlin to check out the latest streetwear, green fashions and bodywear at such fashion fairs as Mercedes-Benz Fashion Week, Bread & Butter, Premium and Bright. Some events are open to the public.

INTERNATIONALE GRÜNE WOCHE
☎ 303 80; www.gruenewoche.de
The week-long International Green Week, which is a consumer fair for food, agriculture and gardening, is a great excuse for gorging on exotic morsels from around the world.

LANGE NACHT DER MUSEEN
☎ 283 973; www.lange-nacht-der-museen.de
Culture meets entertainment on the last Saturday of January when up to 100 museums keep their doors open until at least midnight. Shuttle buses ferry people between venues. It's a truly sociable affair and fun for the entire family.

TRANSMEDIALE
☎ 2474 9761; www.transmediale.de
Digital media art gets full bandwidth at this progressive festival that also investigates how digital technologies shape today's society and artistic endeavours.

February
BERLINALE
☎ 259 200; www.berlinale.de
Berlin's international film festival draws stars, starlets, directors, critics and the world's A-to-Z-list celebrities for two weeks of screenings and glamour parties around town. The lucky ones go home with a Golden or Silver Bear, while top lesbigay flicks are awarded the Teddy. Screenings often sell out, so book early.

March
INTERNATIONALE TOURISMUS BÖRSE
☎ 303 80; www.itb-berlin.de
Take a virtual trip around the globe at the world's largest international travel expo (more than 10,000 exhibitors); it's trade-only during the week but open to the public at the weekend.

MAERZMUSIK
☎ 2548 9100; www.maerzmusik.de
'Music' or 'soundscapes'? You decide after a day at March Music, a contemporary festival celebrating a boundary-pushing palette of sounds, from full orchestral symphonies to experimental recitals, many of them new or commissioned.

April
ACHTUNG BERLIN
www.achtungberlin.de
About 70 flicks about Berlin and at least partially produced in the city compete for the New Berlin Film Award at this

festival. Screenings take place at Babylon (p252) and other locations, with many writers, directors, producers and actors in attendance.

FESTTAGE
☎ 2035 4555; www.staatsoper-berlin.org
Staatsoper (p253) boss Daniel Barenboim brings the world's finest conductors, soloists and orchestras to Berlin for this 10-day, highbrow hoedown of gala concerts and operas, with an emphasis on that brilliant 'bad boy' composer Richard Wagner.

GALLERY WEEKEND
☎ 2838 6464; www.gallery-weekend-berlin.de
Join art collectors, critics and other fellow art-ficionados in keeping tabs on the Berlin art scene on a free hop around 40 of the city's best galleries. Held over a three-day weekend, usually in late April or early May.

SEHSÜCHTE
☎ 0331-620 2780; www.sehsuechte.de
Berlin's international student film festival, now based in Potsdam (p282), provides five days of the most random, experimental, alternative and occasionally pretentious cinematic efforts around.

May
BRITSPOTTING
www.britspotting.de
It's hard to imagine the Brits returning the compliment, but this small festival of Brit and Irish flicks that never made it into the multiplexes is a huge hit with Berlin art-house buffs.

MAY DAY MADNESS
Not for those of a nervous disposition, May Day (1 May) sees Berlin's central districts (Kreuzberg and Prenzlauer Berg especially) become the venue of large-scale anti-capitalist, anti-globalisation, anti-whatever demonstrations. Traditionally, right-wing groups schedule their marches for the same day, the police turn out in force and within a couple of hours there's chaos. That means violence, vandalism and burning vehicles – we only mention this at all so you can stay out of the way.

KARNEVAL DER KULTUREN
☎ 6097 7022; www.karneval-berlin.de
Berlin's answer to London's Notting Hill Carnival celebrates the city's multicultural tapestry with parties, exotic nosh and a fun parade of flamboyantly dressed dancers, DJs, artists and musicians shimmying through the streets of Kreuzberg.

THEATERTREFFEN BERLIN
☎ 2548 9269; www.theatertreffen-berlin.de
The Berlin Theatre Gathering is a three-week showcase of new productions by emerging and established German-language ensembles from Germany, Austria and Switzerland.

June
See p262 for details about Christopher Street Day.

ALL NATIONS FESTIVAL
☎ 250 025; www.allnationsfestival.de, in German
Take a trip around the world on a single day when a dozen or so Berlin-based foreign embassies open their doors to promote their respective countries with food, drink, music and talks.

BERLIN AIR SHOW (ILA)
☎ 3038 6006; www.ila-berlin.com
Zeppelins to fighter planes, gliders to balloons and jet liners – if it flies, it'll probably be at this huge international aerospace exhibition and air show held every two years (next time in 2012).

BERLIN BIENNALE
☎ 243 4590; www.berlinbiennale.de
This biennial curated forum for contemporary art explores international artistic trends and invites young artists to showcase their work in various locations around town for about eight weeks. One of the main venues is the KW Institute for Contemporary Art (p105), which originated the first Biennale back in 1998.

DMY INTERNATIONAL DESIGN FESTIVAL
☎ 5301 4888; www.dmy-berlin.com
As Unesco-designated 'City of Design', it's only natural that Berlin should host this annual design festival, which brings renowned, young and experimental creatives together to present new products and discuss future trends.

FÊTE DE LA MUSIQUE   21 Jun
☎ 4171 5289; www.lafetedelamusique.com, in German
Summer starts with good vibrations thanks to hundreds of free concerts during this global music festival that first came online in Paris in 1982.

SANDSATION
☎ 0176-9688 6279; www.sandsation.de
A fantasy world built from sand takes shape for eight summer weeks starting in early June. At more than 6m high, these ain't your little brother's sandcastles! Music, cocktails and children's events keep things dynamic.

July
BERLIN FASHION WEEK
☎ 6290 0850; www.berlin-fashionweek.de
Local and international designers present next year's spring fashions during the summer edition of Berlin's fashion fair.

CLASSIC OPEN AIR GENDARMENMARKT
☎ 01805-600 121; www.classicopenair.de
Five days, five alfresco concerts – from opera to pop – delight an adoring crowd hunkered on bleachers before the regal backdrop of the Konzerthaus. No ticket? No problem. Just bring a beer and eavesdrop with the penniless masses outside the flimsy canvas enclosure.

August
BERLINER BIERFESTIVAL
☎ 6576 3560; www.bierfestival-berlin.de, in German
Who needs Oktoberfest when you can have the 'world's longest beer garden'? Pick your poison from over 300 breweries from nearly 100 countries along 2km of Karl-Marx-Allee.

BERLINER GAUKLERFEST
☎ 206 2673; www.gauklerfest.de, in German
Comedians, magicians, puppeteers, artistes, clowns, dancers, jugglers and other *Gaukler* (cabaret-type artists) take over

Schinkelplatz on Unter den Linden for 10 merry days in early August.

FUCKPARADE
www.fuckparade.org
Relax! It's not what you think but simply your average antifascist demonstration. Make sure to wear black or risk not fitting in.

INTERNATIONALE FUNKAUSSTELLUNG
☎ 3069 6924; www.ifa-berlin.de
Find out what gadgets everyone will want for Christmas at this huge international consumer electronics fair at ICC Messe.

LANGE NACHT DER MUSEEN
☎ 283 973; www.lange-nacht-der-museen.de
The summer edition of the January event; see p17.

TANZ IM AUGUST
☎ 2474 9777; www.tanzimaugust.de, in German
Step out gracefully to this international dance festival that attracts loose-limbed talent and highly experimental choreography from around the globe.

September

BERLIN MARATHON
☎ 3012 8810; www.berlin-marathon.com
Sweat it out with the other 50,000 runners or just cheer 'em on during Germany's biggest street race, which has seen nine world records set since 1977.

BERLIN MUSIC WEEK
www.berlin-music-week.de
Catch tomorrow's headliners during this week-long celebration of global music. The Popkomm trade show and the Berlin Festival line-up of DJs and bands are the main events. Bring serious stamina for *Clubnacht* (Club Night), when €14 buys entry to 40 dance clubs.

INTERNATIONALES LITERATURFESTIVAL
☎ 2787 8620; www.literaturfestival.com
Dozens of authors from all corners of the world celebrate the power of the pen with the literary public through readings, workshops and events.

MUSIKFEST BERLIN
☎ 2548 9100; www.berlinerfestspiele.de
World-renowned orchestras, choirs, conductors and soloists come together for two weeks of concerts at the Philharmonie (p250) and other venues around town.

October

ART FORUM BERLIN
☎ 3038 2076; www.art-forum-berlin.com
Find out what's hot in art at this well-established international contemporary art fair that brings together leading galleries, collectors and the merely curious.

BERLINER LISTE
☎ 2809 6115; www.berliner-liste.org
Held around the same time as the Art Forum (above), the Berliner Liste brings together young galleries and emerging artists with the hot shots of the international scene.

FESTIVAL OF LIGHTS
☎ 3186 0114; www.festival-of-lights.de
For two weeks, Berlin isn't only about sightseeing but also about 'lightseeing'. Historic landmarks such as the Fernsehturm (TV Tower), the Berliner Dom and the Brandenburg Gate sparkle with illuminations, projections and fireworks.

JAZZ IN DEN MINISTERGÄRTEN
☎ 01805-4470; www.jazzland.de, in German
Once a year in October, the permanent representations (offices) of seven German *Länder* (states) in the Ministerial Gardens area near Potsdamer Platz open their doors to the public for a night of jazz.

PORN FILM FESTIVAL
www.pornfilmfestivalberlin.de
Vintage porn, Japanese porn, indie porn, sci-fi porn – the 'Berlinale' of sex brings alternative skin flicks out of the smut corner and onto the big screen.

TAG DER DEUTSCHEN EINHEIT   3 Oct
Raise a toast to reunification on the German national holiday celebrated with street parties across town – from the Brandenburger Tor (Brandenburg Gate) to the Rotes Rathaus (town hall).

YOU BERLIN
www.you.de, in German
Stay ahead of the fashion, sports, beauty and lifestyle curves at Europe's largest youth fair, complete with concerts, live TV tapings and roving casting agents.

November & December

BER-MU-DA
www.bermuda-berlin.de
A celebration of electronic dance music, BerMuDa (Berlin Music Days) is a new club festival that brings the world's best DJs to the best of Berlin clubs (Berghain, Cookies, Watergate, Weekend etc – see the Nightlife chapter p231) for wild and sweaty dance parties. It will all culminate with a huge festival at Tempelhof airport.

CHRISTMAS MARKETS
www.visitberlin.de
Pick up shimmering ornaments or get smashed on mulled wine at dozens of yuletide markets held throughout December in such locales as Breitscheidplatz (Map p128) and Alexanderplatz (Map p96).

JAZZFEST BERLIN
☎ 2548 9100; www.jazzfest-berlin.de
This top-rated jazz festival has doo-wopped in Berlin since 1964 and presents fresh and big-time talent in dozens of performances all over town.

NIKOLAUS
6 Dec
On St Nicholas' Day children leave their shoes outside their door to receive sweets if they've been nice, and a stone if they've been naughty. Eventually this custom developed into Father Christmas' more international yearly rounds, but in Germany they seem pretty attached to the original – all kinds of clubs hold Nikolaus parties, complete with costumed St Nicks.

SILVESTER
31 Dec
Ring in the new year hugging complete strangers, cooing at fireworks, guzzling bubbly straight from the bottle and generally misbehaving. The main action is at Brandenburger Tor, but pros and purists may prefer watching the city light up from atop the Kreuzberg hill in Viktoriapark or from Breitscheidplatz (Map pp140-1).

COSTS & MONEY

If you're used to £5 pints, $12 glasses of cabernet or €8 lattes, you're in for a pleasant surprise when visiting Berlin, the Western European capital where you can get the most bang for your euro. Your average Berlin hotel room costs €76 compared to €108 in London and €111 in Paris. In restaurants, the price of a main course would merely buy an appetiser in Moscow or Vienna. And getting around is a snap with the excellent and easy-to-understand public transportation system and reasonably priced and plentiful cabs.

Of course, how much you end up spending depends on what kind of traveller you are and what experiences you wish to have. The daily tab for a stay in a midrange hotel, two sit-down meals, using public transportation, spending some money on sightseeing and going to bars and clubs should be somewhere between €90 and €140 (per person, travelling as an adult couple). For mere survival, you'll need to budget €30 to €60 per day, but this will have you sleeping in hostel dorms, eating in cafes or at fast-food stands or preparing your own meals, and limiting your entertainment. Of course, if you're a high roller, Berlin has no shortage of luxury hotels, Michelin-starred restaurants and fancy bars to help you part with your money.

INTERNET RESOURCES

Do your homework and check out the following sites so you can hit the ground running when you get to Berlin. Websites with events listings are covered on p230.

HOW MUCH?
Bottle of water at supermarket €0.40
Cinema ticket €6-8
Currywurst €1.50
Glass of beer (0.3L) €2.80
Latte macchiato €3
Nightclub entry €5-15
Petrol (1L) €1.38
Public-transport day pass €6.30
Souvenir T-shirt €15
Watermelon Man €7-10

ADVANCE PLANNING

About two or three months ahead, check the website of Berlin's tourist office (www.visitberlin.de), which comes with a searchable database of major upcoming special events and also gives you the option of buying tickets using a credit card. Performing-arts venues usually have their own online calendars and booking facilities.

Tickets to the Berliner Philharmonie (p250), Staatsoper Unter den Linden (p253), Sammlung Boros (p79), Chorin Monastery's summer concerts (p289) and Historisches Grünes Gewölbe (p293) and Semperoper (p294) in Dresden, and for major musical touring acts often sell out and should be booked as early as possible. The same is true for key soccer games such as the German soccer league final in late May. Tickets to regular season matches, though, are usually available on game day.

One week before you go, check the online versions of the listings magazines *Tip* (www.tip-berlin.de, in German) and *Zitty* (www.zitty.de, in German) for the latest openings, festivals and events in Berlin. One week should also be enough time for weekend dinner reservations at trendy or upmarket restaurants such as Cookies Cream (p201), Grill Royal (p203) or Reinstoff (p203). For other restaurants, calling a day ahead or even earlier in the day is usually sufficient.

3D Stadtmodell (www.3d-stadtmodell-berlin.de) Take a virtual journey through central Berlin with this Google Earth-powered 3-D model of 44,000 buildings; the top 40 are covered in greater detail and four of them (the Reichstag, Hauptbahnhof, Sony Center and Olympic Stadium) can even be 'entered'.

Berlin Hidden Places (www.berlin-hidden-places.com) Ideas for getting off the tourist track.

Berlin Tourism (www.visitberlin.de) Excellent, jam-packed, official tourist-office site; also lets you make room and ticket reservations in all major languages.

Berlin Unlike (http://berlin.unlike.net) Hip guide with up-to-the-minute reviews and happenings.

City of Berlin (www.berlin.de) Official government site with information on culture, transport, the economy and politics.

ExBerliner (www.exberliner.net) Online version of Berlin's savvy English-language mag to help you get plugged right into the scene.

Lonely Planet (lonelyplanet.com) The Thorn Tree travel forum is a great place to pick the brains of other travellers.

Museumsportal Berlin (www.museumsportal-berlin.de) Awesome searchable site that lists every museum in town along with handy lists on which ones are open on Monday, which are free and which are open late.

SUSTAINABLE BERLIN

Since our inception in 1973, Lonely Planet has encouraged readers to tread lightly, travel responsibly and enjoy the magic of independent travel. Travel is growing at a jaw-dropping rate, and we still firmly believe in the benefits it can bring. But we also encourage you to consider the impact of your visit on both the global environment and local economies, cultures and ecosystems.

There are few major cities with as many green and open spaces as Berlin. Parks, gardens, lakes, rivers, nature reserves and forests characterise its landscape and contribute to the high quality of life. Keeping Berlin green isn't just about sorting your trash or refilling that water bottle (the tap water here is perfectly fine); there are plenty of ways to make your entire visit more sustainable. For suggestions on how to get to Berlin without hopping on an aeroplane, check out the boxed text on p302.

Getting around Berlin is a snap thanks to the city's well-developed and comprehensive public transportation system, which is cheap, efficient and clean. So don't even think about coming here by car, especially since parking is expensive and scarce. Since 1 January 2008 you also need a special sticker to prove that your car is not a polluting klunker (see p304 for more). Even better, if in Berlin, do as Berliners do and get around by bicycle. Double brownie points: it's good for your heart *and* the environment. Turn to p303 to get the lowdown on renting two-wheelers.

When it comes to sightseeing, build your itinerary around more than the major sites and impacted hot spots. Get out into the leafy suburbs, swim in a lake, cycle the course of the Berlin Wall, hit the trail in a forest or pack a picnic and head to a park. There are also several attractions with an eco-angle. The southwestern suburb of Dahlem, for instance, has the Freilichtmuseum Domäne Dahlem (p163), a working farm that grows only organic produce. Nearby is the Museumsdorf Düppel (p164), a recreated medieval village where staff breed endangered sheep and pig species and grow historic strains of rye. In the Grunewald Forest is the Ökowerk (p132),

BASIC ETIQUETTE

DOS

Say 'Guten Tag' when entering a business.

State your name at the start of a phone call.

Keep your hands above the table when eating.

Bring a small gift, a bottle of wine or flowers when invited to dinner.

Bag your own groceries in supermarkets. And quickly!

DON'TS

Talk about WWII with a victor's mentality.

Be late for meetings and dinner invitations.

Expect the bill to arrive automatically in a restaurant; you have to ask for it.

Assume you can pay by credit card, especially when eating out.

Immediately call people by their first name.

a nature conservation and educational centre. This book is full of such ideas to get you off the beaten path. You might even want to put it away sometimes and simply get lost. (Tell us if you find a great new place.)

When it comes to food, Berlin offers several approaches to eating more sustainably. The German word for organic is *bio* and you'll see it everywhere these days. In fact, *bio* food stores have of late been proliferating faster than hothouse mushrooms. Heck, even budget supermarket chains like Netto and Aldi sell *bio* fruit and vegetables, albeit at slightly higher prices. Nearly every *Kiez* (neighbourhood) has its own weekly farmers market, with a growing number of vendors specialising in pesticide-free produce (see p207). Cafes and restaurants too have jumped on the green bandwagon and reviews in our Eating chapter often point out if chefs are putting organic veggies or fish, seafood and meats from sustainable sources onto the plates. In fact, the most aware chefs try to go locavore whenever possible, meaning they'll buy their lamb, asparagus, berries and other ingredients from small regional farms rather than importing them from goodness-knows-where. Fair-trade products have also been catching on fast, especially when it comes to tea and coffee, so get your java jolt from an ethically minded local cafe and not a global fast-food outlet.

BACKGROUND

HISTORY

MEDIEVAL BERLIN

Berlin is very much an accidental capital, whose birth was a mere blip on the map of history. Sometime in the 13th century, itinerant merchants founded a pair of trading posts called Berlin and Cölln on the banks of the Spree River just southwest of today's Alexanderplatz. It was a profitable spot along a natural east–west trade route, about halfway between the fortified towns of Köpenick to the southeast and Spandau to the northwest, the origins of which date back to the 8th century. The tiny settlements grew in leaps and bounds and, in 1307, merged into a single town for reasons of power and security. As the centre of the March (duchy) of Brandenburg, the twin town continued to assert its political and economic independence and even became a player in the Hanseatic League in 1360.

Such confidence was a thorn in the side of the Holy Roman Emperor who, in 1411, put Friedrich von Hohenzollern, burgrave of Nuremberg, in charge of Brandenburg, ushering in five centuries of uninterrupted rule by the House of Hohenzollern.

REFORMATION & THE THIRTY YEARS' WAR

The Reformation, kick-started in 1517 by Martin Luther in nearby Wittenberg, was slow to arrive in Berlin. Eventually, though, the wave of reform reached Brandenburg, leaving Elector Joachim II (ruled 1535–71) no choice but to subscribe to Protestantism. On 1 November 1539 the court celebrated the first Lutheran-style service in the Nikolaikirche in Spandau (p167). The event is still celebrated as an official holiday in Brandenburg, the German state that surrounds Berlin, although not in the city state of Berlin itself.

Berlin prospered for the ensuing decades until drawn into the Thirty Years' War (1618–48), a conflict between Catholics and Protestants that left Europe's soil drenched with the blood of millions. Elector Georg Wilhelm (ruled 1620–40) tried to maintain a policy of neutrality, only to see his territory repeatedly pillaged and plundered by both sides. By the time the war ended, Berlin lay largely in shambles – broke, ruined and decimated by starvation, murder and disease.

ROAD TO A KINGDOM

Stability finally returned during the long reign of Georg Wilhelm's son, Friedrich Wilhelm (ruled 1640–88). Also known as the Great Elector, he took several steps that helped chart Brandenburg's rise to the status of a European powerhouse. His first order of business was to increase Berlin's safety by turning it into a garrison town encircled by fortifications with 13 bastions. He also levied a new sales tax, using the money to build three new neighbourhoods (Friedrichswerder, Dorotheenstadt and Friedrichstadt), a canal linking the Spree and the Oder rivers (thereby cementing Berlin's position as a trading hub), as well as the Lustgarten (p92) and Unter den Linden (p84).

TIMELINE

1244	1360	1415
Berlin appears for the first time in recorded history, but the city's birthday is pegged to the first mention of its sister settlement Cölln seven years earlier in 1237.	The twin town of Berlin-Cölln joins the Hanseatic League but never plays a major role in the alliance and quits its membership in 1518.	Friedrich von Hohenzollern's grip on power solidifies when German King Sigismund promotes him to elector and margrave of Brandenburg at the Council of Constance.

- Population: 3.43 million, including 480,000 non-Germans
- Gross domestic product: 90.1 billion
- Unemployment: 14.2%
- Percentage of one-person households: 53
- Mean monthly net income: €1525
- Time a Berliner must work to pay for a Big Mac: 19 minutes
- Total annual visitors: 8.263 million, including 2.88 million from abroad
- Total annual overnight stays: 18.87 million
- Number of museums: 175
- Number of dogs: 108,800
- Average daily temperature: 10.4°C

But the Great Elector's most lasting legacy was replenishing Berlin's population by encouraging the settlement of refugees. In 1671, 50 Jewish families arrived from Vienna, followed after 1685 by thousands of Protestant Huguenots – many of them highly skilled – who had been expelled from France by Louis XIV. The Französischer Dom (French Cathedral, p86) on Gendarmenmarkt serves as a tangible reminder of Huguenot influence. Between 1680 and 1710, Berlin saw its population nearly triple to 56,000, making it one of the largest cities in the Holy Roman Empire.

The Great Elector's son, Friedrich III, was a man of great ambition and with a penchant for the arts and sciences. Together with his beloved wife, Sophie-Charlotte, he presided over a lively and intellectual court, founding the Academy of Arts in 1696 and the Academy of Sciences in 1700. One year later, he advanced his career by promoting himself to King Friedrich I (elector 1688–1701, king 1701–13) of Prussia, making Berlin a royal residence and the capital of the new state of Brandenburg-Prussia.

THE AGE OF PRUSSIA

All cultural and intellectual life screeched to a halt under Friedrich's son, Friedrich Wilhelm I (ruled 1713–40), who laid the groundwork for Prussian military might. Soldiers were this king's main obsession and he dedicated much of his life to building up an army of 80,000, partly by instituting the draft (highly unpopular even then, and eventually repealed) and by persuading his fellow rulers to trade him men for treasure. History quite appropriately knows him as the *Soldatenkönig* (soldier king).

Ironically, these soldiers didn't see action until his son and successor Friedrich II (aka Frederick the Great; ruled 1740–86) came to power. Friedrich fought tooth and nail for two decades to wrest Silesia (in today's Poland) from Austria and Saxony. When not busy on the battlefield 'Old Fritz', as he was also called, sought greatness through building. His Forum Fridericianum, a grand architectural master plan for Unter den Linden, although never completed, gave Berlin the Staatsoper Unter den Linden (State Opera House, p92), Sankt-Hedwigs-Kathedrale (p85), a former palace now housing the Humboldt Universität (Humboldt University, p92) and other major attractions.

Frederick also embraced the ideas of the Enlightenment, abolishing torture, guaranteeing religious freedom and introducing legal reforms. With some of the leading thinkers in town (Moses Mendelssohn, Voltaire and Gotthold Ephraim Lessing, among them), Berlin blossomed into a great cultural centre that some even called 'Athens on the Spree'.

NAPOLEON & REFORMS

Old Fritz's death sent Prussia into a downward spiral, culminating in a serious trouncing of its army by Napoleon at Jena-Auerstedt in 1806. The French marched triumphantly into Berlin

1443	1539	1618
Construction of the Berlin Stadtschloss (City Palace) on the Spree island begins and becomes the electors' permanent residence in 1486. Continually enlarged and altered until 1716, the barely war-damaged palace is blown up in 1951 by the GDR.	Elector Joachim II embraces the Reformation by celebrating the first service according to the rites of Protestantism and a year later passes a church ordinance making the new religion binding throughout Brandenburg.	Religious conflict and territorial power struggles escalate into the bloody Thirty Years' War, devastating Berlin financially and decimating its population by half, to a mere 6000 people.

top picks

HISTORICAL READS

- Berlin Rising: Biography of a City (Anthony Read and David Fisher; 1994) An excellent social history, tracing the life of the city from its beginnings to post-Wall times.
- Berlin (David Clay Large; 2001) A smooth and engaging narrative history of Berlin, framed by the two unifications in 1871 and 1990.
- Berlin Diary: Journal of a Foreign Correspondent 1934–41 (William Shirer; 1941) One of the most powerful works of reportage ever written. Shirer's portrait of the city he loved, grew to fear and eventually fled is a giant of the genre.
- Stasiland (Anna Funder; 2003) Australian writer Funder documents the Stasi's vast domestic spying apparatus by letting both the victims and the perpetrators tell their stories.
- The Berlin Wall: 13 August 1961–9 November 1989 (Frederick Taylor; 2006) Highly readable account of the construction of the Wall and its effects on the people and the city.

on 27 October and left two years later, their coffers bursting with loot. Among the pint-sized conqueror's favourite souvenirs was the *Quadriga* sculpture from atop the Brandenburger Tor (Brandenburg Gate; p81).

The post-Napoleonic period saw Berlin caught up in the reform movement sweeping through Europe. Public servants, academics and merchants now questioned the right of the nobility to rule. Friedrich Wilhelm III (ruled 1797–1840) instituted a few token reforms (easing guild regulations, abolishing bonded labour and granting Jews civic equality), but meaningful constitutional reform was not forthcoming. Power continued to be centred in the Prussian state.

The ensuing period of political stability was paired with an intellectual flourishing in Berlin's cafes and salons. The newly founded Universität zu Berlin (Humboldt Universität) was helmed by the philosopher Johann Gottlieb Fichte and, as it grew in status, attracted other leading thinkers of the day, including Hegel and Ranke. This was also the age of Karl Friedrich Schinkel, whose many projects – from the Neue Wache (New Guardhouse; p85) to the Altes Museum (Old Museum; p89) – still beautify Berlin.

REVOLUTION(S)

The Industrial Revolution snuck up on Berliners in the second quarter of the 19th century, with companies like Siemens and Borsig vastly spurring the city's growth. In 1838, trains began chuffing between Berlin and Potsdam, giving birth to the Prussian railway system and spurring the founding of more than 1000 factories, including electrical giants AEG and Siemens. In 1841, August Borsig built the world's fastest locomotive, besting even the British in a race.

Tens of thousands of people now streamed into Berlin to work in the factories, swelling the population to over 400,000 by 1847 and bringing the city's infrastructure close to collapse. A year later, due to social volatility and restricted freedoms, Berlin joined with other German cities in a bourgeois democratic revolution. On 18 March two shots rang out during a demonstration, which then escalated into a full-fledged revolution. Barricades went up and a bloody fight ensued, leaving 183 revolutionaries and 18 soldiers dead by the time the king ordered his troops back. The dead revolutionaries are commemorated on Platz des 18 März immediately west of the Brandenburg Gate. In a complete turnabout, the king now put himself at the head of the movement and ostensibly professed support for liberalism and nationalism. On 21 March, while riding to the funeral of the revolutionaries in the Volkspark Friedrichshain (p153), he donned

1640	1685	1701
One of Brandenburg's greatest rulers, Friedrich Wilhelm, the aptly named Great Elector, comes to power and restores a semblance of normality by building major fortifications against marauding invaders and concentrating on rebuilding Berlin's infrastructure.	Friedrich Wilhelm issues the Edict of Potsdam, allowing French Huguenot religious refugees to settle in Berlin, exempting them from paying taxes for 10 years and granting them the right to hold services.	Brandenburg becomes a kingdom with the crowning of Elector Friedrich, who unites the five cities of Berlin, Cölln, Friedrichswerder, Dorotheenstadt and Friedrichstadt into a royal residence and capital with 55,000 inhabitants.

the red, black and gold tricolour of German unity. An elected Prussian national assembly met on 5 May.

However, disagreements between delegates from the different factions kept parliament weak and ineffective, making restoration of the monarchy child's play for General von Wrangel, who led 13,000 Prussian soldiers who had remained faithful to the king into the city in November 1848. Ever the opportunist, the king quickly switched sides again, dissolved the parliament and proposed his own constitution while insisting on maintaining supreme power. The revolution was dead. Many of its participants fled into exile.

BISMARCK & THE BIRTH OF AN EMPIRE

When Friedrich Wilhelm IV suffered a stroke in 1857, his brother Wilhelm became first regent and then, in 1861, King Wilhelm I (ruled 1861–88). Unlike his brother, Wilhelm had his finger on the pulse of the times and was less averse to progress. One of his key moves was to appoint Otto von Bismarck as Prussian prime minister in 1862.

Bismarck's glorious ambition was the creation of a unified Germany with Prussia at the helm. An old-guard militarist, he used intricate diplomacy and a series of wars with neighbouring Denmark and Austria to achieve his aims. By 1871 Berlin stood as the proud capital of the German Reich (empire), a bicameral, constitutional monarchy. On 18 January the Prussian king was crowned Kaiser at Versailles, with Bismarck as his 'Iron Chancellor'.

The early years of the German empire – a period called *Gründerzeit* (foundation years) – were marked by major economic growth, fuelled in part by a steady flow of French reparation payments. Hundreds of thousands of people poured into Berlin in search of work in the factories. Housing shortages were solved by building labyrinthine tenements (*Mietskasernen*, literally 'rental barracks'), where entire families subsisted in tiny and poorly ventilated flats without indoor plumbing.

New political parties gave a voice to the proletariat, foremost the Socialist Workers' Party (SAP), the forerunner of the Sozialdemokratische Partei Deutschlands (SPD; Social Democratic Party of Germany). Founded in 1875, the SAP captured 40% of the Berlin vote only two years later. Bismarck tried to make the party illegal but eventually, under pressure from the growing and increasingly antagonistic socialist movement, he enacted Germany's first modern social reforms, though this was not his true nature. When Wilhelm II (ruled 1888–1918) came to power, he wanted to extend social reform while Bismarck wanted stricter antisocialist laws. Finally, in March 1890, the Kaiser's scalpel excised his renegade chancellor from the political scene. After that, the legacy of Bismarck's diplomacy unravelled and a wealthy, unified and industrially powerful Germany paddled into the new century with incompetent leaders at the top.

WWI & REVOLUTION (AGAIN)

The assassination of Archduke Franz Ferdinand, the heir to the Austrian throne, on 28 June 1914, triggered a series of diplomatic decisions that led to WWI, the bloodiest European conflict since the Thirty Years' War. In Berlin and elsewhere, initial euphoria and faith in a quick victory soon gave way to despair as casualties piled up in the battlefield trenches and stomachs grumbled on the home front. When peace came with defeat in 1918, it also ended domestic stability, ushering in a period of turmoil and violence.

1740	1806	1810
Frederick the Great, the philosopher king, turns Berlin into 'Athens on the Spree', a centre of the Enlightenment and an architectural showcase; French is the main language spoken at court and among the ruling elite.	After his defeat of Prussia, Napoleon leads his troops on a triumphant march through the Brandenburg Gate, marking the start of a two-year occupation of Berlin.	After the Napoleonic occupation from 1806–08, Berlin embarks on a period of reconstruction and reform that includes the creation of the Universität zu Berlin by Wilhelm von Humboldt; in 1949 it is renamed for its founder.

On 9 November 1918, Kaiser Wilhelm II abdicated, bringing an inglorious end to the monarchy and 500 years of Hohenzollern rule. Power was transferred to the SPD, the largest party in the Reichstag, and its leader, Friedrich Ebert. This would not go unchallenged. Shortly after the Kaiser's exit, prominent SPD member Philipp Scheidemann stepped to a window of the Reichstag to announce the birth of the German Republic. Two hours later, Karl Liebknecht of the Spartakusbund (Spartacist League) proclaimed a socialist republic from a balcony of the royal palace on Unter den Linden. The struggle for power was on.

Founded by Liebknecht and Rosa Luxemburg, the Spartacist League sought to establish a left-wing, Marxist-style government; by year's end it had merged with other radical groups into the German Communist Party. The SPD's goal, meanwhile, was to establish a parliamentary democracy.

Supporters of the SPD and Spartacist League took their rivalry to the streets, culminating in the Spartacist Revolt in early January. On the orders of Ebert, government forces quickly quashed the uprising. Liebknecht and Luxemburg were arrested and murdered en route to prison by Freikorps soldiers (right-leaning war volunteers); their bodies were dumped in the Landwehrkanal.

THE WEIMAR REPUBLIC

In July 1919 the federalist constitution of the fledgling republic – Germany's first serious experiment with democracy – was adopted in the town of Weimar, where the constituent assembly had sought refuge from the chaos of Berlin. It gave women the vote and established basic human rights, but it also gave the chancellor the right to rule by decree – a concession that would later prove critical in Hitler's rise to power.

The so-called Weimar Republic (1920–33) was governed by a coalition of left and centre parties, headed by Friedrich Ebert and later Paul von Hindenburg – both of the SPD, which remained Germany's largest party until 1932. The republic, however, pleased neither communists nor monarchists. Trouble erupted as early as March 1920 when right-wing militants led by Wolfgang Kapp forcibly occupied the government quarter in Berlin. The government fled to Dresden, but in Berlin a general strike soon brought the 'Kapp Putsch' to a collapse.

THE 'GOLDEN' TWENTIES

The giant metropolis of Berlin as we know it today was forged in 1920 from the region's many independent towns and villages (Charlottenburg, Schöneberg, Spandau etc), making Berlin one of the world's largest cities, with around 3.8 million inhabitants.

Otherwise, the 1920s began as anything but golden, marked by the humiliation of a lost war, social and political instability, hyperinflation, hunger and disease. Around 235,000 Berliners were unemployed, and strikes, demonstrations and riots became nearly everyday occurrences. Economic stability gradually returned after a new currency, the Rentenmark, was introduced in 1923 and with the Dawes Plan in 1924, which limited the crippling reparation payments imposed on Germany after WWI.

Berliners responded like there was no tomorrow and made their city as much a den of decadence as a cauldron of creativity (not unlike today…). Cabaret, Dada and jazz flourished. Pleasure pits popped up everywhere, turning the city into a 'sextropolis' of Dionysian dimensions. Bursting with energy, it became a laboratory for anything new and modern, drawing giants of architecture (Bruno Taut, Martin Wagner, Hans Scharoun and Walter Gropius), fine

1838	1848	1862
Berlin's first train embarks on its maiden voyage from Berlin to Potsdam, making the city the centre of an expanding rail network throughout Prussia.	Berlin is swept up in the popular revolutions for democratic reform and a united Germany but after a few months the Prussian army restores the old order.	Chief city planner James Hobrecht solves the ever-growing housing shortage by constructing working-class ghettos where people are housed under claustrophobic conditions with poor hygiene in tenement blocks wrapped around multiple inner courtyards.

arts (George Grosz, Max Beckmann and Lovis Corinth) and literature (Bertolt Brecht, Kurt Tucholsky, WH Auden and Christopher Isherwood).

The fun came to an instant end when the US stock market crashed in 1929, plunging the world into economic depression. Within weeks, half a million Berliners were jobless, and riots and demonstrations again ruled the streets. The volatile, increasingly polarised political climate led to clashes between communists and members of a party that had been patiently waiting in the wings – the Nationalsozialistische Deutsche Arbeiterpartei (National Socialist German Workers' Party, NSDAP, or Nazi Party), led by a failed Austrian artist and WWI corporal named Adolf Hitler. Soon jack boots, brown shirts, oppression and fear would dominate daily life in Germany.

HITLER'S RISE TO POWER

The Weimar government's inability to improve conditions during the Depression spurred the popularity of Hitler's NSDAP, which gained 18% of the national vote in the 1930 elections. In the 1932 presidential election, Hitler challenged Hindenburg and won 37% of the second-round vote. A year later, on 30 January 1933, faced with failed economic reforms and persuasive right-wing advisors, Hindenburg appointed Hitler chancellor. That evening, NSDAP celebrated its rise to power with a torchlit procession through the Brandenburg Gate. Not everyone cheered. Observing the scene from his Pariser Platz home, artist Max Liebermann famously commented: 'I couldn't possibly eat as much as I would like to puke'.

As chancellor, Hitler moved quickly to consolidate absolute power and to turn the nation's democracy into a one-party dictatorship. The Reichstag fire in March 1933 gave him the opportunity to request temporary emergency powers to arrest communists and liberal opponents and push through his proposed Enabling Law, allowing him to decree laws and change the constitution without consulting parliament. When Hindenburg died a year later, Hitler fused the offices of president and chancellor to become Führer of the Third Reich.

NAZI BERLIN

The rise of the Nazis had instant, far-reaching consequences for the entire population. Within three months of Hitler's power grab, all non-Nazi parties, organisations and labour unions ceased to exist. Political opponents, intellectuals and artists were rounded up and detained without trial; many went underground or into exile. There was a burgeoning culture of terror and denunciation, and the terrorisation of the Jewish started to escalate.

Hitler's brown-shirted Nazi state police, the Sturmabteilung (SA), pursued opponents, arresting, torturing and murdering people in improvised concentration camps, such as the one in the Wasserturm in Prenzlauer Berg (p160). North of Berlin, construction began on Konzentrationslager Sachsenhausen (Sachsenhausen concentration camp; p287). During the so-called Köpenicker Blutwoche (Bloody Week) in June 1933, around 90 people were murdered (see p170). On 10 May, right-wing students burned 'un-German' books on Bebelplatz (p85), prompting countless intellectuals and artists to rush into exile.

JEWISH PERSECUTION

Jews were a Nazi target from the start. In April 1933, Joseph Goebbels, *Gauleiter* (district leader) of Berlin and head of the well-oiled Ministry of Propaganda, announced a boycott of Jewish

1871	1891	1902
Employing an effective strategy of war and diplomacy, Prussian chancellor Otto von Bismarck forges a unified Germany with Prussia at its helm and Berlin as its capital.	Aviation pioneer and Berlin engineer Otto Lilienthal, known as the 'Glider King', makes the world's first successful flight aboard a glider, staying in the air for 25m. Five years later he dies in an air accident.	After two decades of debate and eight years of construction, the first segment of the Berlin U-Bahn network is inaugurated, ferrying passengers between Warschauer Strasse and Ernst-Reuter-Platz.

THE NIGHT OF THE LONG KNIVES

Hitler demanded absolute loyalty and turned against anyone even remotely perceived as wanting to challenge his authority. That included the leaders of the Sturmabteilung (SA).

Conceived to police public meetings and enforce law, the SA had become a troublesome bunch by 1934. On the night of 30 June 1934, Hitler ordered the black-shirted Schutzstaffel (SS) storm troopers (whose dashing uniforms, incidentally, were made by Hugo Boss) to round up and kill high-ranking SA officers. Their leader, Ernst Röhm, was shot and 76 others were knifed to death.

Hitler hushed up what came to be known as the 'Night of the Long Knives' until 13 July, when he announced to the Reichstag that, from now on, the SA (which had 2 million members, easily outnumbering the army) would serve under the command of the army which, in turn, would swear an oath of allegiance to Hitler. Justice would be executed by the SS under the leadership of former chicken farmer Heinrich Himmler, effectively giving the SS unchallenged power and making it Nazi Germany's most powerful – and feared – force.

businesses. Soon after, Jews were expelled from public service and banned from many professions, trades and industries. The Nuremberg Laws of 1935 deprived 'non-Aryans' of German citizenship and forbade them to marry or have sexual relations with Aryans.

The international community, meanwhile, turned a blind eye to the situation in Germany, perhaps because many leaders were keen to see some order restored to the country after decades of political upheaval. Hitler's success at stabilising the shaky economy – largely by pumping public money into employment programmes, many involving re-armament and heavy industry – was widely admired. The 1936 Olympic summer games (see the boxed text, p30) in Berlin were a PR triumph, as Hitler launched a charm offensive, but terror and persecution resumed soon after the closing ceremony.

For Jews, the horror escalated on 9 November 1938, with the *Reichspogromnacht* (often called *Kristallnacht*, or Night of Broken Glass). Using the assassination of a German consular official by a Polish Jew in Paris as a pretext, Nazi thugs desecrated, burned and demolished synagogues, Jewish cemeteries, property and businesses across the country. Jews had begun to emigrate after 1933, but this event set off a stampede.

BACKGROUND HISTORY

THE FINAL SOLUTION

The fate of those Jews who stayed behind deteriorated after the outbreak of WWII in 1939. At Hitler's request, a conference in January 1942 in Berlin's Wannsee (p165) came up with the *Endlösung* (Final Solution): the systematic, bureaucratic and meticulously documented annihilation of European Jews, carried out by around 100,000 Germans. Sinti and Roma (gypsies), political opponents, priests, gays and habitual criminals were targeted as well. Of the roughly 7 million people who were sent to concentration camps, only 500,000 survived. In Berlin, the Holocaust Memorial (p82) is one of many commemorating this grim period in history.

For more on Jewish history, see the boxed text on p38.

RESISTANCE

Resistance to Hitler was quashed early by the powerful Nazi machinery of terror, but it never vanished entirely, as is thoroughly documented in the excellent exhibit called Topographie

1918	1919	1920
WWI ends on 11 November with Germany's capitulation, following the resignation of Kaiser Wilhelm II and his escape to Holland two days earlier. The Prussian monarchy is dead.	The Spartacist Revolt led by Karl Liebknecht, Rosa Luxemburg and later GDR leader Wilhelm Pieck is violently suppressed and ends with the murder of Liebknecht and Luxemburg by right-wing Freikorps troops.	On 1 October Berlin becomes Germany's largest city after seven independent towns, 59 villages and 27 estates are amalgamated into a single administrative unit. The population reaches 3.8 million.

OLYMPICS UNDER THE SWASTIKA

When the International Olympics Committee awarded the 1936 Games to Germany in 1931, the gesture was supposed to welcome the country back into the world community after its defeat in WWI and the tumultuous 1920s. No one could have known that only two years later, the fledgling democracy would be helmed by a dictator with an agenda to take over the world.

As Hitler opened the Games on 1 August in Berlin's Olympic Stadium, prisoners were putting the finishing touches on the first large-scale Nazi concentration camp at Sachsenhausen just north of town. As famous composer Richard Strauss conducted the Olympic hymn during the opening ceremony, fighter squadrons were headed to Spain in support of Franco's dictatorship. Only while the Olympic flame was flickering were political and racial persecution suspended and anti-Semitic signs taken down.

The Olympics were truly a perfect opportunity for the Nazi propaganda machine, which excelled at staging grand public spectacles and rallies, as was so powerfully captured by Leni Riefenstahl in her epic movie *Olympia*. Participants and spectators were impressed by the choreographed pageantry and warm German hospitality. The fact that these were the first Games to be broadcast internationally on radio did not fail to impress either.

From an athletic point of view, the Games were also a big success, with around 4000 participants from 49 countries competing in 129 events and setting numerous records. The biggest star was African-American track-and-fieldster Jesse Owens, who was awarded four gold medals in the 100m, 200m, 4 x 100m relay and the long jump, winning the hearts of the German public and putting paid to Nazi beliefs in the physical superiority of the Aryan race. German Jews, meanwhile, were excluded from participating with the one token exception being half-Jewish fencer Helene Mayer. She took home a silver medal.

des Terrors (Topography of Terror, p114). One of the best known acts of defiance was the 20 July 1944 assassination attempt on the Führer that was led by senior army officer Claus Graf Schenk von Stauffenberg. On that fateful day, Stauffenberg brought a briefcase packed with explosives to a meeting of the high command at the Wolfschanze (wolf's lair), Hitler's eastern-front military headquarters. He placed the briefcase under the conference table near Hitler's seat, then excused himself and heard the bomb detonate from a distance. What he didn't know was that Hitler had escaped with minor injuries thanks to the solid oak table which shielded him from the blast.

Stauffenberg and his co-conspirators were quickly identified and shot by firing squad at the army headquarters in the Bendlerblock in Berlin. The rooms where they hatched their plot now house the Gedenkstätte Deutscher Widerstand (p118), an exhibit about the efforts of the German Nazi resistance.

THE BATTLE OF BERLIN

With the Normandy invasion of June 1944, Allied troops arrived in formidable force on the European mainland, supported by unrelenting air raids on Berlin and most other German cities. The final Battle of Berlin began in mid-April 1945. More than 1.5 million Soviet soldiers barrelled towards the capital from the east, reaching Berlin on 21 April and encircling it on 25 April. Two days later they were in the city centre, fighting running street battles with the remaining troops, many of them boys and elderly men. On 30 April the fighting reached the government quarter where Hitler was ensconced in his bunker behind the chancellery, with his long-time mistress Eva

1923	1933	1936
The Golden Twenties show their dark side when inflation reaches its peak and a loaf of bread costs 3.5 million marks – an entire wheelbarrow's worth.	Hitler is appointed chancellor in January; the Reichstag burns; construction starts on Sachsenhausen concentration camp; books are burned on Bebelplatz; by June the NSDAP has eliminated all opposition and it rules as the only political party in Germany.	The 11th modern Olympic Games held in Berlin in August are a PR triumph for Hitler and a showcase of Nazi power as anti-Jewish propaganda is suspended.

Braun, whom he'd married just a day earlier. Finally accepting the inevitability of defeat, Hitler shot himself that afternoon; his wife swallowed a cyanide pill. As their bodies were burned in the chancellery courtyard, Red Army soldiers raised the Soviet flag above the Reichstag.

DEFEAT & AFTERMATH

The Battle of Berlin ended on 2 May with the unconditional surrender by Helmuth Weidling, the commander of the Berlin Defence Area, to General Vasily Chuikov of the Soviet army. Peace was signed at the US military headquarters in Reims (France) and at the Soviet military headquarters in Berlin-Karlshorst, now a German-Soviet history museum (Deutsch-Russisches Museum Berlin-Karlshorst; p173). On 8 May 1945, WWII in Europe officially came to an end.

The fighting had taken an enormous toll on Berlin and its people. Entire neighbourhoods lay in smouldering rubble and at least 125,000 Berliners had lost their lives. With around one million women and children evacuated, only 2.8 million people were left in the city in May 1945 (compared to 4.3 million in 1939), two-thirds of them women. It fell to them to start clearing up the 25 million tonnes of rubble, earning them the name *Trümmerfrauen* (rubble women). In fact, many of Berlin's modest hills are actually *Trümmerberge* (rubble mountains), piled up from wartime debris and then reborn as parks and recreational areas. The best known are the Teufelsberg (p131) in the Grunewald and Mont Klamott in the Volkspark Friedrichshain (p153).

Some small triumphs came quickly: U-Bahn service resumed on 14 May 1945, newspaper printing presses began rolling again on 15 May, and the Berliner Philharmonie gave its first postwar concert on 26 May.

OCCUPATION

At the Yalta Conference in February 1945, Winston Churchill, Franklin D Roosevelt and Joseph Stalin had agreed to carve up Germany and Berlin into four zones of occupation controlled by Britain, the USA, the USSR and France. By July 1945, Stalin, Clement Attlee (who replaced Churchill after a surprise election loss) and Roosevelt's successor Harry S Truman were at the table in Schloss Cecilienhof (p286) in Potsdam to hammer out the details.

Berlin was sliced up into 20 administrative areas. The British sector encompassed Charlottenburg, Tiergarten and Spandau; the French got Wedding and Reinickendorf; and the US was in charge of Zehlendorf, Steglitz, Wilmersdorf, Tempelhof, Kreuzberg and Neukölln – all these areas later formed West Berlin. The Soviets, meanwhile, held on to eight districts in the east, including Mitte, Prenzlauer Berg, Friedrichshain, Treptow and Köpenick, which would become the future East Berlin. The Soviets also occupied the zone surrounding Berlin, leaving West Berlin completely encircled by territories under Soviet control.

THE BIG CHILL

Friction between the Western Allies and the Soviets quickly emerged. For the Western Allies, a main priority was to help Germany get back on its feet by kick-starting the devastated economy. The Soviets, though, insisted on massive reparations and began brutalising and exploiting their own zone of occupation. Tens of thousands of able-bodied men and POWs ended up in labour camps deep in the Soviet Union. In the Allied zones, meanwhile, democracy was beginning to take root as Germany elected state parliaments in 1946–47.

1938	1944	1945
On 9 November Nazi henchmen set fire to nine of Berlin's 12 synagogues, vandalise Jewish businesses and terrorise Jewish citizens during a night of pogroms called *Kristallnacht*.	On 20 July, senior army officers led by Claus Graf Schenk von Stauffenberg stage an assassination attempt on Hitler. Their failure costs their own and countless other lives.	Soviet troops advance on Berlin in the final days of the war, devastating the city; Hitler commits suicide on 30 April, fighting stops on 2 May and the armistice is signed on 8 May; the Yalta Conference divides Berlin between the Allies.

THE BERLIN AIRLIFT

The Berlin Airlift was a triumph of determination and a glorious chapter in Berlin's post-WWII history. On 24 June 1948, the Soviets cut off all rail and road traffic into the city to force the Western Allies to give up their sectors and bring the entire city under their control.

Faced with such provocation, many in the Allied camp urged responses that would have been the opening barrages of WWIII. In the end wiser heads prevailed, and a mere day after the blockade began the US Air Force launched 'Operation Vittles'. The British followed suit on 28 June with 'Operation Plane Fare'. (France did not participate because its planes were tied up with less humanitarian missions in Indochina.)

For the next 11 months Allied planes flew in food, coal, machinery and other supplies to now-closed Tempelhof airport in the western city, 24/7. By the time the Soviets backed down, they had made 278,000 flights, logged a distance equivalent to 250 round trips to the moon and delivered 2.5 million tonnes of cargo. The Luftbrückendenkmal (Airlift Memorial; p145) outside the airport honours the effort and those who died carrying it out.

It was a monumental achievement that profoundly changed the relationship between Germany and the Western Allies, who were no longer regarded merely as occupational forces but as *Schutzmächte* (protective powers).

The showdown came in June 1948 when the Allies introduced the Deutschmark in their zones. The USSR regarded this as a breach of the Potsdam Agreement, whereby the powers had agreed to treat Germany as one economic zone. The Soviets issued their own currency, the Ostmark, and promptly announced a full-scale economic blockade of West Berlin. The Allies responded with the remarkable Berlin Airlift (see the boxed text, above).

THE TWO GERMAN STATES

In 1949 the division of Germany – and Berlin – was formalised. The western zones evolved into the Bundesrepublik Deutschland (BRD, Federal Republic of Germany or FRG) with Konrad Adenauer as its first chancellor and Bonn, on the Rhine River, as its capital. An economic aid package dubbed the Marshall Plan created the basis for West Germany's *Wirtschaftswunder* (economic miracle), which saw the economy grow at an average 8% per year between 1951 and 1961. The recovery was largely engineered by economics minister Ludwig Erhard, who dealt with an acute labour shortage by inviting about 2.3 million foreign workers, mainly from Turkey, Yugoslavia and Italy, to Germany, thereby laying the foundation for today's multicultural society.

The Soviet zone, meanwhile, grew into the Deutsche Demokratische Republik (German Democratic Republic or GDR), making East Berlin its capital and Wilhelm Pieck its president. From the outset, though, the Sozialistische Einheitspartei Deutschlands (SED, Socialist Unity Party of Germany), led by party boss Walter Ulbricht, dominated economic, judicial and security policy. In order to oppress any dissent, the Ministry for State Security, or Stasi, was established in 1950 and based its headquarters in Lichtenberg (p172). Regime opponents were incarcerated at the super-secret Gedenkstätte Hohenschönhausen (Stasi Prison; p173) nearby.

Economically, East Germany stagnated, in large part because of the Soviets' continued policy of asset stripping and reparation payments. Stalin's death in 1953 raised hopes for reform but only spurred the GDR government to raise production goals even higher. Smouldering discontent erupted in violence on 17 June 1953 when 10% of GDR workers took to the streets. Soviet troops quashed the uprising, with scores of deaths and the arrest of about 1200 people.

1948	1949	1953
After the Western Allies introduce their own currency, the Deutschmark, the Soviets blockade West Berlin; in response the US and Britain launch the Berlin Airlift, ferrying food, coal and machinery to the isolated city.	Two countries are born – the Bundesrepublik Deutschland (West Germany), and the Deutsche Demokratische Republik (East Germany, known as the German Democratic Republic or GDR); Berlin remains under Allied supervision, a status it keeps until 1990.	The uprising of construction workers on the Stalinallee (today's Karl-Marx-Allee) spreads across the entire GDR before being crushed by Soviet tanks, leaving several hundred dead and over 1000 injured.

THE WALL – WHAT GOES UP...

Through the 1950s the economic gulf between the two Germanys widened, prompting hundreds of thousands of East Berliners to seek a future in the west. At that time it was still pretty easy to travel between the two halves of the city and many people simply commuted to work in the western sectors. Many others, though, chose to permanently settle in the west. Eventually, the exodus of mostly young and well-educated East Germans strained the troubled GDR economy so much that – with Soviet consent – the government built a wall to keep them in. Construction of the Berlin Wall, the Cold War's most potent symbol, began on the night of 13 August 1961. Read more about it in the boxed text on p82.

This stealthy act left Berliners stunned. Formal protests from the Western Allies, as well as massive demonstrations in West Berlin,

were ignored. The building of the Wall marked a new low in East-West relations, and tense times were to follow. In October 1961, US and Soviet tanks faced off at Checkpoint Charlie (p144), pushing the world to the brink of WWIII. In 1963 US president John F Kennedy made a visit to West Berlin, praising locals for their pro-freedom stance in his famous 'Ich bin ein Berliner' speech at the Rathaus Schöneberg (p135), and putting the city firmly on the front line of the Cold War.

STUDENT UNREST & TERRORISM

In West Germany the two major parties, the Christliche Demokratische Union (Christian Democratic Union or CDU) and the SPD, formed a so-called grand coalition in 1966. In the coming years, the lack of parliamentary opposition provided fodder for a left-wing student movement that spawned the Ausserparlamentarische Opposition (APO, or extra-parliamentary opposition) dedicated to promoting opposition to the government from outside the parliament. In West Berlin the movement was centred on the Freie Universität (Free University or FU; p164). At sit-ins and protests, students demanded a reform of Germany's old-fashioned and hierarchical university system, criticised their parents' generation for their materialist lifestyle and unwillingness to confront the ghosts of the country's Nazi past, and condemned US policy in Vietnam, Latin America and the Middle East. These demonstrations were a thorn in the side of the government and crackdowns sometimes turned violent.

On 2 June 1967 police shot and killed an unarmed student named Benno Ohnesorg during a protest against a visit of the Shah of Persia to West Berlin. A year later, on 11 April 1968, Rudi Dutschke – the movement's charismatic leader at the FU – was shot in the head by a young worker outside his organisation's office on Kurfürstendamm. By 1970 the movement had fizzled, but not without ushering in a number of changes, including university reforms, politicisation

1961	1963	1967
Tragedy strikes just 11 days after the first stone of the Berlin Wall is laid. On 24 August, 24-year-old Günter Litfin is gunned down by border guards while attempting to swim across Humboldt Harbour.	US president John F Kennedy professes his solidarity with the people of Berlin when giving his famous 'Ich bin ein Berliner' speech at the town hall in Schöneberg on 26 June.	The death of Benno Ohnesorg, an unarmed student who is shot by a policeman while demonstrating against the visit to Berlin of the Shah of Persia, draws attention to the student movement.

of the student body and, eventually, the formation of the Green Party (Dutschke, who survived the attack, was a founding member).

Some of the most radical students, though, felt their goal had not yet been achieved and went underground. Berlin became the germ cell of the terrorist group Rote Armee Fraktion (Red Army Faction or RAF), led by Ulrike Meinhof, Andreas Baader and Gudrun Ensslin. Throughout the 1970s the RAF abducted and assassinated prominent business and political figures throughout Germany. By 1976, however, Meinhof and Baader had committed suicide (both in prison) and remaining members found themselves in jail, in hiding, or seeking refuge in the GDR. Eventually that country's demise would expose them to West German attempts to bring them to justice.

The story of the RAF and its impact on German society was grippingly depicted in the Oscar-nominated movie *Der Baader-Meinhof Komplex* (The Baader-Meinhof Complex, 2008).

RAPPROCHEMENT

It wasn't until the early 1970s that the frosty relations between the two Germanys began to thaw. In the GDR, Erich Honecker had succeeded Walter Ulbricht as general SED secretary, while former Berlin mayor Willy Brandt was now chancellor of West Germany. Brandt's goal was to normalise relations with East Germany, a policy that found support from the Western Allies and the USSR. In September 1971 all of them signed a new Four Power Accord in the Kammergericht (courthouse) in Schöneberg (p137). It guaranteed access to West Berlin from West Germany and eased travel restrictions between East and West Berlin. The accord paved the way for the Basic Treaty, signed a year later, in which the two countries recognised each other's sovereignty and borders and committed to setting up 'permanent missions' in Bonn and East Berlin, respectively.

REUNIFICATION

Hearts and minds in Eastern Europe had long been restless for change, but German reunification came as a surprise to the world and ushered in a new and exciting era. The so-called *Wende* (turning point, ie the fall of communism) came about as a gradual development that ended in a big bang – the collapse of the Berlin Wall on 9 November 1989 (for a more detailed account of events, see the boxed text on p82).

The unified Germany of today, with 16 unified states, was hammered out after a volatile political debate and a series of treaties to end post-WWII occupation zones. The newly united city of Berlin became a separate city-state. Economic union took force in mid-1990, and in August 1990 the Unification Treaty was signed in the Kronprinzenpalais (p92) on Unter den Linden. A common currency and economic union became realities in July 1990. Also in July, Pink Floyd replayed the original music of their 1980s album *The Wall* to a crowd of 200,000 (and a TV audience of millions worldwide) on Potsdamer Platz.

In September 1990, representatives of East and West Germany, the USSR, France, the UK and the US met in Moscow to sign the Two-Plus-Four Treaty, ending postwar occupation zones and paving the way for formal German reunification. One month later the East German state was dissolved; in December Germany held its first unified post-WWII elections.

In 1991 a small majority (338 to 320) of members in the Bundestag (German parliament) voted in favour of moving the government to Berlin and of making Berlin the German capital

1971	1976	1987
The four Allies sign the Four Power Accord, which confirms Berlin's independent status and eases traffic between the city and West Germany. East and West Germany recognise each other's sovereignty in the Basic Treaty.	The Palace of the Republic, which houses the GDR parliament and an entertainment centre, opens on 23 April on the site where the royal Hohenzollern palace stood for 500 years.	East and West Berlin celebrate the city's 750th birthday separately. On 12 June Ronald Reagan visits the city, proclaiming 'Mr Gorbachev, tear down this Wall!' while standing in front of the Brandenburg Gate.

WHAT'S IN A DATE?

The Berlin Wall fell on 9 November 1989, so when it came time to pick a date for a public holiday to mark German reunification it seemed only natural that would be it. Unfortunately, the same date had also played key roles in the fate of German history on two prior, less joyful, occasions. In 1923 Hitler launched his ill-fated Munich coup that landed him in jail where he penned *Mein Kampf*. And in 1938 Nazi thugs vandalised Jewish businesses and synagogues during the infamous *Kristallnacht* (see p29). On a positive note, 9 November was also the day in 1918 when Kaiser Wilhelm II abdicated, ending German monarchical rule and establishing the first German republic. Still, in the end, Germany's national holiday was set on the less evocative, but much more tactful, date of 3 October – the anniversary of administrative reunification in 1990.

once again. On 8 September 1994 the last Allied troops stationed in Berlin left the city after a festive ceremony.

THE POST-UNIFICATION YEARS

With reunification, Berlin once again became the German capital in 1990 and the seat of government in 1999. A brand new *Regierungsviertel* (government quarter), with the historic Reichstag as its anchor, sprang up, with new offices for parliamentarians, sleek embassies and, most notably, the striking chancellery.

Elsewhere, too, the face of Berlin changed enormously as the city embarked on an unprecedented building boom that saw the creation of an entirely new city quarter around Potsdamer Platz and the construction of new landmarks such as the Jewish Museum by Daniel Libeskind and the Holocaust Memorial by Peter Eisenman.

The cultural vibrancy of the 1920s also returned with a vengeance, transforming Berlin from a political curiosity to a vital presence among European capitals, with unbridled nightlife, an explosive art scene and a resurgence of theatre and cabaret. The summer of 1989 saw the inaugural Love Parade, a techno party that began with just 150 ravers and grew to 1.5 million at its peak in 1999. Interest ebbed in the early 2000s, though, and after a two-year hiatus in 2004 and 2005, the last Berlin parade was held in 2006.

As the country's most multicultural city, Berlin is heavily influenced by its minorities, with an amazing patchwork of people from 185 foreign nations making up almost 14% of the total population. The largest groups are those of Turkish descent and Eastern Europeans from Poland, the former states of Yugoslavia and the old Soviet republics. The steady growth in foreign nationals since reunification has, however, been offset by a decline in the indigenous population, due in part to the exodus of young families from the capital to the surrounding countryside, and the overall population of the city has actually fallen since 1993.

BERLIN TODAY

Berlin is whole once more, but rejoining the two city halves has proven to be painful and costly. Mismanagement, excessive spending and corruption led to the collapse of the centre-right city government under Eberhard Diepgen and the election of a 'red-red' coalition of the centre-left SPD and the far left Die Linke in 2001. Led by the charismatic Klaus Wowereit

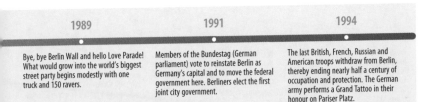

1989	1991	1994
Bye, bye Berlin Wall and hello Love Parade! What would grow into the world's biggest street party begins modestly with one truck and 150 ravers.	Members of the Bundestag (German parliament) vote to reinstate Berlin as Germany's capital and to move the federal government here. Berliners elect the first joint city government.	The last British, French, Russian and American troops withdraw from Berlin, thereby ending nearly half a century of occupation and protection. The German army performs a Grand Tattoo in their honour on Pariser Platz.

LIFE AS A BERLINER

Compared to other world capitals, daily life in Berlin moves to a less frantic rhythm. You rarely have to shoehorn your way inside buses or trains, street traffic tends to be light and moves quite smoothly, scoring a dinner reservation usually means calling the restaurant the same day and getting into a club doesn't require hustling your way onto the VIP list.

Berliners are refreshingly attitude-free and egalitarian, less impressed by Armani suits and Gucci bags than personal, individualistic style. Striving for material wealth and social status takes a back seat to living well, spending time with friends and enjoying the city's myriad cultural and natural offerings.

Many Berliners embrace life to the fullest, drinking a lot, smoking too much, partying late (and often) and having a laissez-faire attitude towards sex and sexual orientation. No wonder the lesbigay, SM and fetish scenes here are among the biggest in Europe.

Daily life is defined by activity, though not necessarily work. The average working week is 38 hours and Berliners always seem to be heading to or from somewhere, be it the office, gym, shops, bar, cinema, theatre or all of the above.

Perhaps because of their on-the-go lifestyle, family life is less of a priority. In fact, the singles' scene is intense here, with more than 50% of all people now living alone. There's also an increasing trend towards single parenthood, and as many children now live with one parent as with two.

Overall, locals are accommodating and fairly helpful towards visitors, and many will volunteer assistance if you look lost. This politeness does not necessarily extend to friendliness, however, and in public, people usually maintain a degree of reserve towards strangers – you won't find many conversations striking up on the U-Bahn or in the supermarket checkout line.

On the other hand, in younger company it's easy to chat with just about anyone, particularly around the many student hangouts (remember German students are generally older than elsewhere, often graduating at 28 rather than 21), and if you start frequenting a place you'll quickly get to know staff and regulars. You'll also probably find people very open after a relatively short time, discussing sex, politics, religion and life with equal candour.

In fact many locals are relatively new to the scene too, having moved here either from some other part of Germany or from another country. With people from 185 nations making up 14% of the population, Berlin is Germany's most multi-cultural city. Most immigrants hail from Turkey, Poland, the former states of Yugoslavia and the old Soviet republics.

(SPD) as governing mayor, the new government inherited a fiscal storm that had been brewing since 1990. Following reunification, Berlin lost the hefty federal subsidies it had received during the years of division. Also gone were 100,000 manufacturing jobs, most of them through closures of unprofitable factories in East Berlin. The result: a whopping debt of €60 billion.

Wowereit responded by making painful, across-the-board spending cuts, but with a tax base eroded by high unemployment and ever-growing welfare payments, these have done little towards getting Berlin out of the poorhouse. But Wowereit, who was re-elected in 2006 and reportedly aspires to national office, seems to remain undaunted. With his characteristic mix of substance and glamour, the openly gay mayor never tires of touting Berlin as a capital of cool. And with some success. Universal Music moved its German headquarters from Hamburg to Berlin in 2002, MTV followed in 2004, the same year the music trade show Popkomm moved here from Cologne. In 2007, Berlin's first fashion week was inaugurated. As more and more young creatives flock to town to share in Berlin's infectious spirit, visitor numbers have shot through the roof.

Meanwhile, social woes continue to bedevil Berlin. Poorly performing schools, violent racial attacks by right-wing groups and a spate of 'honour killings' of young Muslim women wishing to live a western lifestyle have all captured the headlines in recent years.

1999	2001	2006
On 19 April the German parliament holds its first session in the historic Reichstag building, after complete restoration by Lord Norman Foster following its draping by the artist couple Christo and Jeane-Claude in 1995.	At a party convention Klaus Wowereit of the Social Democratic Party comes out of the closet by declaring 'I am gay and that's OK'. In autumn that year he is elected governing mayor of Berlin.	Berlin's first central train station, the Hauptbahnhof, opens on 26 May, just two weeks before Germany kicks off the 2006 FIFA World Cup. In the final match on 9 July, Italy defeats France in a penalty shootout.

Two decades after the rejoining of the city halves, Berlin is reaching a watershed moment. Districts like Mitte and Prenzlauer Berg, once pioneers of progressiveness, are now firmly in the grip of gentrification and the boho-bourgeois class. Global developers are building up the banks of the Spree River, investors from Denmark to Ireland to America are snapping up bargain-priced apartments, and international chains are replacing homespun businesses.

All this begs the question: Can Berlin remain the homeland of social freedom and experimentation while increasingly becoming a more corporate-driven, 'normal' metropolis? Governing mayor Klaus Wowereit famously called Berlin 'poor but sexy'. In 10 years it may no longer be poor. But will it still be sexy?

ARTS

The arts are fundamental to everything Berlin holds dear, and the sheer scope of creative activity in the city is astounding. Half the reason Berliners are always so busy is because of the efforts required to keep up with the ever-changing cultural kaleidoscope of trends, events and publications. And with a history of international excellence in most fields, expectations and standards are always set high. The city itself provides an iconic setting for any number of books, films, paintings and songs, its unmistakeable presence influencing artists and residents just as it does those canny visitors who take the time to dive in.

LITERATURE

Since its beginnings, Berlin's literary scene has reflected a peculiar blend of provincialism and worldliness. As with the other arts, Berlin didn't emerge as a centre of literature until relatively late, reaching its zenith during the dynamic 1920s. Overall, the city was less a place that generated influential writers than one where they came to meet each other, exchange ideas and be intellectually stimulated.

Today there are several literary organisations and author forums serving the same purpose, including the Literaturforum im Brechthaus (Map pp102-3; ☎ 282 2003; www.lfbrecht.de, in German; Chausseestrasse 125, Mitte), which awards bursaries and prizes such as the Alfred-Döblin-Preis for unpublished work; the Literarisches Colloquium Berlin (off Map pp72-3; ☎ 816 9960; www.lcb.de, in German; Am Sandwerder 5, Zehlendorf); and literaturWERKstatt (Map pp156-7; ☎ 485 2450; www.literaturwerkstatt.org, in German; Kulturbrauerei, Knaackstrasse 97, Prenzlauer Berg), which organises regular large events. The major literary event in the city is the Internationales Literaturfestival (p19) in September.

First Words

Berlin's literary history began during the Enlightenment in the late 18th century, an epoch dominated by humanistic ideals. A major author was Gotthold Ephraim Lessing (1729–81), noted for his critical works, fables and tragedies, who wrote the play *Minna von Barnhelm* (1763) in Berlin.

The Romantic period, which grew out of the Enlightenment, was marked by a proliferation of literary salons, where men and women from all walks of life came together to discuss philosophy, politics, art and other subjects. Literary greats working in Berlin during this era included Friedrich and August Wilhelm von Schlegel, and the Romantic poets Achim von Arnim, Clemens Brentano and Heinrich von Kleist.

During the realist movement in the mid-19th century, novels and novellas gained in popularity, thanks to increased interest from the newly established middle class. Historical novels and works critical of society also caught on, such as those by Wilhelm Raabe (1831–1910), who examines various aspects of Berlin life in *Chronik der Sperlingsgasse* (Chronicle of Sperling Lane; 1857). The Berlin society novel was raised to an art form under the pen of Theodor Fontane (1819–98). Most of his works are set around Brandenburg and Berlin, and show both the nobility and the middle class mired in their societal confinements. His 1894 novel *Effi Briest* presents a sympathetic depiction of a woman's unhappy marriage, and was an influence on Thomas Mann.

Naturalism, a spin-off of realism, took things a step further after 1880, painstakingly recreating the milieu of entire social classes, right down to the local dialect. In Berlin, Gerhart Hauptmann

JEWISH BERLIN: MENDELSSOHN TO LIBESKIND

It's no longer an unusual sight: at sunset on Friday nights, dozens of Jewish men clad in traditional Shabbat garb with black hats and long coats strut past coffee shops, art galleries and fancy boutiques to attend services at Synagoge Rykestrasse (p160) in Prenzlauer Berg. Across town, in Wilmersdorf, another throng is heading for services at the synagogue in Münsterstrasse.

Since reunification, Berlin has had the fastest-growing Jewish community in the world. Their background is diverse; most are Russian Jewish immigrants but there are also Jews of German heritage, Israelis wishing to escape their war-torn homeland and American expats lured by Berlin's low-cost living and limitless creativity. Today there are about 13,000 active members of the Jewish community, including 1000 belonging to the Orthodox congregation Adass Yisroel. However, since not all Jews choose to be affiliated with a synagogue, the actual population is estimated to be at least twice as high.

The community supports 10 synagogues, two *mikve* ritual baths, several schools, numerous cultural institutions and a handful of kosher restaurants and shops. The golden-domed Neue Synagoge (New Synagogue; p102) on Oranienburger Strasse is the most visible beacon of Jewish revival, even though today it's not primarily a house of worship but a community and exhibition space. In Kreuzberg, the Jüdisches Museum (Jewish Museum; p142), a spectacular structure by Daniel Libeskind, tracks the ups and downs of Jewish life in Germany for almost 2000 years.

Records show that Jews first settled in Berlin in 1295, but their position hinged on a religious technicality that allowed them to be moneylenders, a practice forbidden to Christians. Throughout the Middle Ages they had to contend with being blamed for any kind of societal or economic woe. When the plague struck (1348–49), rumours that Jews had poisoned the wells led to the first major pogrom. In 1510, 38 Jews were publicly tortured and burned for allegedly stealing the host from a church because a confession by the actual (Christian) perpetrator was deemed too straightforward to be true.

Financial interests, not humanitarian ones, motivated the Great Elector Friedrich Wilhelm to invite 50 Jewish families expelled from Vienna to settle in Berlin in 1671. To his credit, he later extended the offer to Jews in general and also allowed them to practise their faith – which then was by no means common practice anywhere in Europe. Berlin's oldest Jewish cemetery, the Alter Jüdischer Friedhof (p109) on Grosse Hamburger Strasse, was founded during this time.

Among the people buried here was the great philosopher Moses Mendelssohn, who arrived in Berlin in 1743. His progressive thinking and lobbying paved the way for the Emancipation Edict of 1812, which made Jews full citizens of Prussia with equal rights and duties. The Mendelssohn family includes many other prominent citizens, as you will learn in the Mendelssohn Exhibit (p87) near Gendarmenmarkt.

By the end of the 19th century, many of Berlin's Jews, numbering about 5% of the population, had become thoroughly German in speech and identity. When a wave of Hasidic Jews escaping the pogroms of Eastern Europe arrived around the same time, they found their way to today's Scheunenviertel, which at that time was an immigrant slum with cheap housing. By 1933 Berlin's Jewish population had grown to around 160,000 and constituted one third of all Jews living in Germany. The well-known horrors of the Nazi years sent most into exile and left 55,000 dead. Only about 1000 to 2000 Jews are believed to have survived the war years in Berlin, often with the help of their non-Jewish neighbours. Many memorials throughout the city commemorate the Nazi victims. The most prominent is, of course, the Holocaust Memorial (p82) near the Brandenburg Gate. For an overview of several others, see the boxed text on p106.

(1862–1946) was a key practitioner of the genre, and many of his plays and novels focus on social injustice and the harsh life of workers – subjects so provocative that several of his premieres ended in riots. An 1892 production of his *Die Weber* (The Weavers), depicting the misery of Silesian weavers, even prompted the Kaiser to cancel his subscription at the Deutsches Theater. In 1912 Hauptmann won the Nobel Prize for Literature.

Modernism & Modernity

In the 1920s, which was renowned as a period of experimentation and innovation, Berlin became a magnet for writers from around the world. *Berlin Alexanderplatz,* by Alfred Döblin (1878–1957), provided a dose of big-city lights and the underworld during the Weimar Republic, and other notables from this era include the political satirists Kurt Tucholsky (1890–1935) and Erich Kästner (1899–1974). However, many such artists left Germany after the Nazis came to power, and those who stayed often went into 'inner emigration', keeping their mouths shut and working underground, if at all.

In West Berlin, the postwar literary scene didn't revive until the arrival of Günter Grass in the late 1950s. His famous *Die Blechtrommel* (The Tin Drum; 1958) traces recent German history through the eyes of a child who refuses to grow up; written in a variety of styles, the book is an enjoyable and significant retrospective of the Nazi years and the postwar period, and quickly made Grass a household name. He has followed up with an impressive body of novels, plays and poetry, becoming the ninth German to win the Nobel Prize for Literature in 1999. Together with Hans-Magnus Enzensberger, Ingeborg Bachmann and the Swiss writer Max Frisch, Grass paved the way for the political and critical literature that has been dominant since the 1960s. The post-1968 student movement led to a realistic literary style that often resembled reportage, as seen in the works of Berlin-based Peter Schneider.

In the mid-1970s, a segment of the East Berlin literary scene began to detach itself slowly from the SED party grip. Authors such as Christa Wolf (1929–) and Heiner Müller (1929–95) belonged to loose literary circles that regularly met in private houses. Wolf is one of the best and most controversial East German writers, while Müller had the distinction of being unpalatable in both Germanys; his dense, difficult works include *Der Lohndrücker* (The Man Who Kept Down Wages) and the *Germania* trilogy of plays.

Literary achievement stagnated at first after the *Wende,* as writers from the East and West began a process of self-examination. Only Heiner Müller and Botho Strauss stood out amid the creative void. In the late 1990s Berlin's literary scene finally picked up steam. Newer books dealing with the past are characterised not by analytical introspection but by emotionally distanced, nearly grotesque, imagery. Examples here include Thomas Brussig's *Helden wie wir* (Heroes Like Us; 1995) and Ingo Schulze's *Simple Stories* (1998). Bernhard Schlink, a former Berliner now living in the USA, caused perhaps the biggest furore with his novel *Der Vorleser* (The Reader; 1995), which approaches issues of collective and individual responsibility through an unusual relationship between a teenage boy and a woman accused of war crimes. A film adaptation (by David Hare) of the novel was released in late 2008, starring Kate Winslet and Ralph Fiennes.

Current Trends

History (especially the Wall) is still the focus of much writing about Berlin, fact and fiction, especially in works by outsiders (see boxed text, p41. Interesting recent volumes include Helga Schneider's *The Bonfire of Berlin: A Lost Childhood in Wartime Germany* (2005), one of many wartime memoirs, and Bernd Cailloux's *Das Geschäftsjahr 1968/69* (The Financial Year 1968/69; 2005), an insightful examination of youth revolt and culture during this turbulent period. A more recent release is *The Forger* (2009), the gripping memoir of Cioma Schönhaus, who saved countless fellow Jews by forging IDs for them. Re-released in English in 2005 (it was originally published in German in 1959), *Eine Frau in Berlin* (A Woman in Berlin) is an anonymous, intimate account of the harsh reality of the months after the Soviet victory in Berlin in 1945. Also re-released, in 2010, was *Alone in Berlin,* a 1947 classic by Hans Fallada, the tale of an extraordinary act of resistance against the Nazis and the suspenseful cat-and-mouse game that ensues. It became an instant bestseller around the world.

For a fantastic introduction to Berlin, get a hold of *City-Lit Berlin* (2009), an anthology of excerpts from texts about Berlin by classic writers like Theodor Fontane and Alfred Döblin, cult writers like Christopher Isherwood and Thomas Brussig and even bloggers like Simon Cole. Not exclusively about Berlin but still an excellent read is *Stalin's Nose* (2008) by Rory MacLean, a surreal and darkly comic tale based on the author's journey from Berlin to Moscow after the fall of the Berlin Wall.

top picks

BERLIN CULT READS

- Berlin Alexanderplatz (Alfred Döblin; 1929) This stylised meander through the seamy 1920s is still a definitive Berlin text.
- Berlin Blues (Herr Lehmann; 2001) It's hard to imagine a Berlin novel where the fall of the Wall is almost incidental to the plot, but this cult story of Kreuzberg nights pulls it off nicely.
- Goodbye to Berlin (Christopher Isherwood; 1939) A brilliant, semi-autobiographical perspective on Berlin's 'golden age', seen through the eyes of gay Anglo-American journalist Isherwood.
- The Wall Jumper (Der Mauerspringer; Peter Schneider; 1983) A taut, reportage-like depiction of Berliners from both sides of the Wall, which raises the issue of the *Mauer im Kopf,* or 'wall in the head', the much-quoted phrase first coined by Schneider.
- Russendisko (Russian Disco; Wladimir Kaminer; 2000) This collection of texts from Berlin's favourite Russian immigrant presents a whole host of unusual characters and some hilarious scenarios.

Since 2000, a whole new clutch of authors have come to the forefront of the literary scene with novels about Berlin itself, several of which have been translated into English. Thomas Brussig's tongue-in-cheek *Helden wie Wir* (Heroes Like Us; 1998) was one of the first reunification novels and offers poignant and humorous insights into the society of a now-extinct GDR. Brussig continued his engagement with the GDR era in *Wie es leuchtet* (How It Shines; 2004), depicting the fall of the Wall (and the German triumph at the 1990 World Cup).

Jana Hensel's *Zonenkinder* (2002) – cumbersomely translated to After the Wall: Confessions from an East German Childhood and the Life that Came Next – delivers an insightful memoir in which Hensel, who was 13 when the Wall fell, reflects upon the loss of identity and the challenge of adapting to a new culture.

Element of Crime frontman Sven Regener's million-selling *Herr Lehmann* (2001; translated into English as *Berlin Blues* in 2003), a boozy trawl through the *Wende*, was made into a film (Regener also wrote the screenplay). In 2008, Regener published the prequel *Der Kleine Bruder* (The Little Brother), which depicts life in Berlin during the 1980s.

On the comedy front, there's Horst Evers' *Wedding* (2003), an entertaining and slightly surreal collection of humorous texts centred on domestic life in Berlin's least popular residential district. Uli Hannemann does something similar for Neukölln with his witty vignettes in *Neulich in Neukölln* (Recently in Neukölln; 2008).

Turkish writer Yadé Kara addresses the crucial questions of multiculturalism and identity in *Selam Berlin* (2003), while Raul Zelik's *Berliner Verhältnisse* (2005) quickly became a cult classic. *Boxhagener Platz* (2005), by Torsten Schulz, is an unusual comedy-whodunnit set in 1968 Friedrichshain, with an 80-year-old protagonist sniffing out a murder. It too was turned into a film and released in 2010.

The runaway success story, however, has been the rise of Russian-born author Wladimir Kaminer, whose amusing, stranger-than-fiction collections *Russendisko* (Russian Disco; 2000) and *Schönhauser Allee* (2003) established both the author and his Russian disco parties as a firm part of the Berlin scenescape. He continues to crank out books like *Ich bin kein Berliner* (literally 'I Am No Berliner'; 2007) and his latest *Es gab keinen Sex im Sozialismus* (There was No Sex under Socialism; 2009), but so far no English translations are available.

Berlin's underground literary scene is as lively as in any other medium. To catch up-and-coming authors, look out for readings by individuals and groups such as the Surfpoeten (Surf Poets; www.surfpoeten.de, in German; ☺ 9pm Wed), a collective of young Berlin writers who read at Klub der Republik (p227) in Prenzlauer Berg; Reformbühne (www.reformbuehne.de, in German; ☺ 8.15pm Sun) at Kaffee Burger (p233), Chaussee der Enthusiasten at RAW Tempel (Map pp150-1; www.enthusiasten.de, in German; Stenzerhalle, Revaler Strasse 99; ☺ 9pm Thu) and Liebe Statt Drogen (Map pp102-3; www.liebestattdrogen.de, in German; Ackerstrasse 169, Mitte; ☺ 9.30pm Tue), currently performing at Schokoladen which was, however, threatened with closure at press time. Check the website for updates.

PAINTING & SCULPTURE
Art & History

Fine art only really began to flourish in Berlin in the late 17th century, when self-crowned King Friedrich I founded the Academy of Arts in 1696 at the instigation of court sculptor Andreas Schlüter (1660–1714). Schlüter repaid the favour with several outstanding sculptures, including the *Great Elector on Horseback* (1699), now in front of Schloss Charlottenburg (p122), and the haunting *Masks of Dying Warriors* in the courtyard of the Zeughaus (p84) on Unter den Linden.

The arts languished again under Friedrich's successor, Soldier King Friedrich Wilhelm I, but took a turn towards greatness when his son, Friedrich II (Frederick the Great), ascended the throne in 1740. Friedrich drew heavily on the artistic, architectural and decorative expertise of Georg Wenzeslaus von Knobelsdorff (1699–1753), a student of Frenchman Antoine Pesne, Prussia's official painter. Knobelsdorff is most famous for designing the Staatsoper Unter den Linden (p92) and Schloss Sanssouci (p285) in Potsdam.

In many ways, 19th-century styles reflected the new political and economic ideas coming from England and France, which resonated especially with the educated middle classes and found expression in neoclassicism. One major artist of the period was Johann Gottfried Schadow

THRILL CITY: CRIME & SPY NOVELS SET IN BERLIN

Berlin has often served as inspiration in the setting of crime and spy novels written by outsiders. The city's bullet-scarred history, divided loyalties and political intrigues make for some clever twists and turns. Here are some of the best:

- **Berlin Game, Mexico Set, London Match** (Len Deighton; 1983, 1984, 1985) There are more unexpected twists and turns than on a rollercoaster ride in this classic spy trilogy set in '80s Berlin.
- **Berlin Noir Trilogy** (Phillip Kerr; 1994) Kerr's compelling depictions of Berlin in the murky days before, during and after WWII follow private investigator Bernie Gunther through the city's seamy side.
- **Pavel & I** (Dan Vyleta; 2008) Beautifully written, this novel explores the friendship between a US soldier and a German orphan in the aftermath of WWII, during the bitterly cold winter of 1946–47.
- **Rift Zone** (Raelynn Hillhouse; 2004) A female smuggler between the East and the West in 1989 becomes a pawn in a KGB agent's game.
- **The Spy Who Came in from the Cold** (John le Carré; 1963) Graham Green called the tale of British spook Alex Leamas in early Cold War Berlin the finest spy story every written.

(1764–1850), whose most famous work is the *Quadriga* – the horse-drawn chariot that crowns the Brandenburger Tor (Brandenburg Gate; p81).

Another important neoclassical sculptor was Christian Daniel Rauch (1777–1857), a student of Schadow. Rauch had a talent for representing idealised, classical beauty in a realistic fashion. His most famous work is the 1851 monument of Frederick the Great on horseback (p93) on Unter den Linden.

A student of Rauch, the sculptor Reinhold Begas (1831–1911) developed a neo-baroque, theatrical style that was so ostentatiously counter-neoclassical that he met with a fair amount of controversy in his lifetime and was even given the dubious honour of being known as 'the worst sculptor in the world' by Berliners. The Neptune fountain (1891; p100) outside the Marienkirche is a Begas work, as is the Schiller monument (p86) on Gendarmenmarkt.

In painting, Romanticism gradually overtook neoclassicism in popularity. One reason for this was the awakening of a nationalist spirit in Germany – spurred by the Napoleonic Wars – during the reign of Friedrich Wilhelm III (1797–1840). Romanticism was the perfect form of expression for the idealism and emotion that characterised the period. The genre's leading light was Caspar David Friedrich (1774–1840), whose evocative works are a highlight of the Alte Nationalgalerie (p89). Paintings by Karl Friedrich Schinkel, Berlin's dominant neoclassical architect, are also here, and at the Neuer Pavillon of Schloss Charlottenburg (p123), which is closed for renovation until at least 2012; for more on Schinkel see the boxed text, p54. A parallel development during the period from 1815 to 1848 was the so-called Berliner Biedermeier, a more conservative and painstakingly detailed style that appealed to the Prussian middle class. The name itself is derived from the German word for conventional ('bieder') and the common surname of Meier. There was also an early interest in paintings that chronicled Berlin's constantly evolving cityscape, which sold especially well among the middle classes. One of the best-known exponents of this style was Eduard Gärtner (1801–1877), whose Berlin dioramas from Friedrichswerder Church provide fascinating insight into the city's 19th-century skyline. You can find works by Gärtner in the Alte Nationalgalerie (p89).

Into the 20th Century

The Berlin Secession was founded in 1892 by a group of artists who had come together to protest against the forced closure of an exhibition displaying pictures by Edvard Munch. Led by Max Liebermann (1847–1935) and Walter Leistikow (1865–1908), member artists were not linked by a common artistic style but by a rejection of reactionary attitudes towards the arts that stifled new forms of expression. They preferred scenes from daily life to historical and religious themes, shunned studios in favour of natural outdoor light and were hugely influential in inspiring new styles.

Liebermann himself evolved from a painter of gloomy naturalist scenes to an important representative of 'Berlin impressionism'. In the early 1900s Lovis Corinth (1858–1925) and Max Slevogt (1868–1932) joined the group, as did Käthe Kollwitz (1867–1945), who lived in Prenzlauer Berg and is still regarded as Germany's finest female artist. Her keen social and political awareness lent a tortured power to her work.

ZILLE SEASON

Born in Dresden in 1858, Heinrich Zille moved to Berlin with his family when he was a child. A lithographer by trade, he became the first prominent artist to evoke the social development of the city as the tendrils of modernity reached Berlin, creating an instantly recognisable style in his drawings of everyday life and real people, often featuring the bleak *Hinterhöfe* (inner courtyards) around which so much of their lives revolved. Even during his lifetime Zille was acknowledged as one of the definitive documenters of his time, and since his death in 1929 his prolific photographic work has also come to be seen as a valuable historical record.

In 1903 Zille was accepted into the Berlin Secession, although he didn't really regard himself as an 'artist' as such, more as a hard-working illustrator. When he died, thousands of Berliners turned out to pay their respects to the man whose pictures chronicled their daily lives with sharp humour and unsentimental honesty. In 2008 Berlin celebrated the 150-year anniversary of Heinrich Zille's birth with various exhibitions, and there's a Zille Museum (p98) dedicated to his life and work.

After the horror of WWI, this liberal tradition allowed Berlin to evolve into the centre of contemporary German and international art. Radical movements proliferated, and Dadaism, cofounded by George Grosz (1893–1959), emerged as a prevalent form. Dadaists rejected traditional art in favour of collage and montage, and considered chance and spontaneity to be determining artistic elements. The first Dada evening, in 1917, was by all accounts a chaotic affair, with Grosz urinating on the pictures, Richard Huelsenbeck declaring that too few people had been killed for art, and the police trying to close the whole thing down.

Parallel movements had Expressionist artists like Max Beckmann (1884–1950) and Otto Dix (1891–1969), who examined the threats of urbanisation, while Russian émigré Wassily Kandinsky, German-Swiss Paul Klee, German-American Lyonel Feininger and Russian-born Alexej Jawlensky formed 'The Blue Four' in 1924 and went on to work and teach at the Bauhaus art school.

The Bauhaus style was based on practical anti-elitist principles bringing form and function together, and had a profound effect on all modern design – visit the Bauhaus Archiv (p118) for ample examples. The movement itself was founded in Weimar and then based in Dessau, about 130km southwest of Berlin. Many of its most influential figures, however, worked in Berlin, and in 1932 the renowned art school moved wholesale to the capital to escape Nazi pressure.

As it turned out this was just a short reprieve as the Nazi takeover in 1933 proved devastating for the entire Berlin arts scene. Many artists left the country (indeed, Max Beckmann fled the day after the opening in Munich in 1937 of the 'Degenerate Art' exhibition), others ended up in prison or concentration camps, their works confiscated or destroyed. The art promoted instead was often terrible, favouring straightforward 'Aryan' forms and epic styles. Propaganda artist Mjölnir defined the typical look of the time with block Gothic scripts and idealised figures.

After WWII, Berlin's art scene was as fragmented as the city itself. In the east, artists were forced to toe the 'socialist-realist' line, which Otto Nagel and Max Lingner frequently managed to hurdle by feigning conformity while maintaining aesthetic and experimental aspects in their work. In the late '60s East Berlin established itself as an arts centre in the GDR with the formation of the Berliner Schule (Berlin School). Members such as Manfred Böttcher and Harald Metzkes succeeded in freeing themselves from the confines of officially sanctioned socialist art in order to embrace a more multifaceted realism. In the '70s, when conflicts of the individual in society became a prominent theme, underground galleries flourished in Prenzlauer Berg and art became a collective endeavour.

In postwar West Berlin, artists eagerly absorbed abstract influences from France and the USA, with some theorists positing that this was an avoidance of the reality of Germany's postwar destruction and turmoil. Pioneers included Zone 5, which revolved around Hans Thiemann, and surrealists Heinz Trökes and Mac Zimmermann. In the 1960s politics was a primary concern and a new style called 'critical realism' emerged, propagated by artists like Ulrich Baehr, Hans-Jürgen Diehl and Wolfgang Petrick. The 1973 movement, Schule der Neuen Prächtigkeit (School of New Magnificence), had a similar approach. In the late 1970s and early 1980s, expressionism found its way back onto the canvasses of painters like Salomé, Helmut Middendorf, Rainer Fetting and Peter Keil (a protégé of Otto Nagel), a group known as the Junge Wilde (Young Wild Ones). One of the best known of Germany's neo-expressionist painters is Georg Baselitz, who lives in Berlin and whose signature style is his upside-down works.

These days, all eyes are on Berlin when it comes to art. With some 10,000 artists from around the world and 600 galleries (more than in New York), the city is a key player on the contemporary art scene. Major leaguers like Olafur Eliasson, Thomas Demand, Jonathan Meese, Via Lewandowsky, Isa Genzken, Tino Seghal, Esra Ersen, John Bock and the artist duo Ingar Dragset and Michael Elmgreen all live and work in Berlin, or at least have a second residence here. To keep a tab on the scene, check out the latest shows at the city's many high-calibre galleries (see p190 for a select round-up) and visit the collections at Hamburger Bahnhof (p75) and the Sammlung Boros (p79). A good time to visit is during the Berlin Biennale, which brings art-world honchos to town every two years. Art Forum Berlin (p19), meanwhile, has become an important trade show. Another highlight is the Gallery Weekend (www.gallery-weekend-berlin.de), when you can hopscotch around 40 galleries for three days.

For more about art in Berlin, see the Berlin Art Attack section on p241.

MUSIC

Germany's contemporary music scene has many centres, but Berlin is still the big one for most of today's multifarious styles and genres. It boasts at least 2000 active bands, countless DJs and the country's leading orchestras, not to mention the three great state-funded opera houses. Like the city itself, music here is constantly evolving, changing shape and redefining itself, and Berlin continues to be a fertile breeding ground for new musical trends.

The Classics

For centuries Berlin was largely eclipsed by Vienna, Leipzig and other European cities when it came to music. In 1882, however, the Berliner Philharmoniker (p250) was established, gaining international stature under Hans von Bülow and Arthur Nikisch. In 1923 Wilhelm Furtwängler became artistic director, a post he held (with interruptions during and shortly after the Nazi years) until 1954. His successor, the legendary Herbert von Karajan, was an autocratic figure who established a position of real dominance on the world stage and remained director until 1989. He was followed by Claudio Abbado and, in 2002, flamboyant British conductor Sir Simon Rattle, who won a Grammy with the orchestra before he had even officially started in the post.

The pulsating 1920s drew numerous musicians to Berlin, including Arnold Schönberg and Paul Hindemith, who taught at the Akademie der Künste and the Berliner Hochschule, respectively. Schönberg's atonal compositions found a following here, as did his experimentation with noise and sound effects. Hindemith explored the new medium of radio and taught a seminar on film music. After the war, a key player in the GDR was Hanns Eisler, a lifelong communist, who became a professor at the state conservatory in East Berlin upon returning from exile in California in 1950. His most famous composition is the GDR's national anthem. After reunification, the conservatory was renamed for him and is now the Hochschule für Musik Hanns Eisler (p251).

Today the classical scene is considerably less high profile, but look out for composer Wolfgang Rihm, tenor Peter Schreier's oratorio performances and director Andreas Homoki's fresh productions at the Komische Oper (p253).

Popular Music Before WWII

Jazz and popular music came into their own in Berlin in the 1920s, providing the staple diet of the city's clubs, cabarets and drinking dens. Modern jazz is very much alive in the city; in particular, local lad Till Brönner is known as one of Germany's best contemporary jazz trumpeters. If you want to plug into the city's jazz scene, click to www.jazzinitiative-berlin.de (in German) and www.jazz-guide-berlin.de (in German). Major jazz venues like A-Trane, B-flat and Yorckschlösschen are covered in the Nightlife chapter (p235). Clärchens Ballhaus (p232) has regular swing parties on Wednesday and lindy hoppers take over Horst Krzberg (p233) on occasion. The Jazzfest Berlin (p20) brightens grey November days, while the newly founded Jazzinstitut Berlin produces the next generation of jazzmeisters.

Aside from jazz, another 1920s style entertaining the crowds in cabarets, dance halls and variety theatres was the Berlin *Schlager* – silly but entertaining songs with titles like 'Mein Papagei frisst keine harten Eier' ('My parakeet doesn't eat hard-boiled eggs') and 'Ich hab das

Fräulein Helen baden sehen' ('I've seen Miss Helen in the bathtub') that were an almost surreal reaction to the hyperinflation and corruption of the era.

The most successful singing group before WWII was the Comedian Harmonists, a 'boy band' founded in Berlin in 1927 by Harry Frommermann in the vein of the American group The Revelers. With a baritone, a bass, three tenors and a piano player, they performed perfect harmonies with their voices sounding like musical instruments. The group disbanded in 1934 because three of its members were Jewish; they subsequently fled Germany. The 1997 movie *The Harmonists* charts the course of their origin and success.

Another runaway hit was *The Threepenny Opera,* written by Bertolt Brecht with music by Kurt Weill. It premiered in 1928 with such famous songs as 'Mack the Knife' and combined classical music with cabaret and pop songs to create a new form of political theatre.

Friedrich Holländer was also a key composer in the cabaret scene, noted for his wit, improvisational talent and clever lyrics. Among his most famous songs is 'Falling in Love Again', sung by Marlene Dietrich in *The Blue Angel* (1930), where he cameos as a pianist. Like so many other talents (including Weill and Brecht), Holländer left Germany when the Nazis came to power and continued his career in Hollywood.

Popular Music since WWII

Since the end of WWII, Berlin has spearheaded most of Germany's popular music revolutions. In the late '60s Tangerine Dream helped to propagate the psychedelic sound. Meanwhile, on the other side of the Iron Curtain, Nina Hagen got an early taste of fame in the GDR as a *Schlager* singer with the band Automobil only to become the diva of punk after following her actress mother and stepfather Wolf Biermann, an outspoken singer-songwriter who'd been kicked out of the GDR, to West Germany. In 1977 she founded the Nina Hagen Band in Kreuzberg and soon delighted teens (and shocked their parents) with her provocative lyrics, shrieking voice and theatrical performances. One of her famous early songs is *'Auf'm Bahnhof Zoo',* which is about Zoo Station, then an infamous drug hangout and teenage prostitution strip. Hagen also helped pave the way for the major musical movement of the early '80s, NDW or Neue Deutsche Welle (German new wave), which gave the stage to Berlin bands like the Neonbabies, Ideal and UKW and, in East Berlin, Rockhaus.

The '80s saw the birth of Die Ärzte, who have been on and off again multiple times but in 2007 released their 15th album, *Jazz ist anders.* Another seminal band founded around that time is Einstürzende Neubauten, whose lead singer Blixa Bargeld also moonlighted as the guitarist in Nick Cave's band, The Bad Seeds, from 1984 to 2003. The Neubauten pioneered an experimental, proto-industrial sound that turns oil drums, electric drills and chainsaws into musical instruments. Also on the scene, since 1985, is the indie rock band Element of Crime, with singer-turned-author Sven Regener at the helm.

MARLENE DIETRICH Anthony Haywood

Marlene Dietrich (1901–92), born into a good middle-class family in Berlin by the name of Marie Magdalena von Losch, was the daughter of a Prussian officer. After acting school, she worked in the silent-film industry in the 1920s, stereotyped as a hard-living, libertine flapper. But she soon carved a niche in the film fantasies of lower-middle-class men as the dangerously seductive femme fatale, best typified by her 1930 talkie *Der Blaue Engel* (The Blue Angel), which turned her into a Hollywood star.

The film was the start of a five-year collaboration with director Josef von Sternberg, during which time she built on her image of erotic opulence – dominant and severe, but always with a touch of self-irony. Dressed in men's suits for *Morocco* in 1930, she lent her 'sexuality is power' attitude bisexual tones, winning a new audience overnight.

Dietrich stayed in Hollywood after the Nazi rise to power, though Hitler, not immune to her charms, reportedly promised perks and the red-carpet treatment if she moved back to Germany. She responded with an empty offer to return if she could bring Sternberg – a Jew and no Nazi favourite. She took US citizenship in 1937 and sang on the front to Allied GIs.

After the war, Dietrich retreated slowly from the public eye, making occasional appearances in films, but mostly cutting records and performing live. Her final years were spent in Paris, bedridden and accepting few visitors, immortal in spirit as mortality caught up with her.

In the GDR, access to Western rock and other popular music was restricted, but a slew of home-grown Ostrock (eastern rock) bands emerged. Major ones, like Die Puhdys, Karat, City and Silly, were allowed to perform in the West and built up huge followings on both sides of the Wall. The small but vital East Berlin underground scene was led by the punk band Feeling B; three of its members went on to form Rammstein in 1994, the industrial metal band that is perhaps the most visible member of the NDH (Neue Deutsche Härte, 'new German hardness') scene. Although its dark and provocative songs are almost entirely performed in German, it is one of the country's most successful musical exports, with fans around the world. Band members have their office behind the Knaack club (p236) and can often be spotted around Prenzlauer Berg.

West Berlin attracted a slew of international talent, most famously David Bowie, who bunked with buddy Iggy Pop in a flat at Hauptstrasse 155 in Schöneberg in the late '70s. Trying to kick drug addiction and greatly inspired by the city's brooding quality, Bowie partly wrote and recorded his Berlin Trilogy (*Low, Heroes, Lodger*) at the famous Hansa Studios (see p248), while Iggy came up with *The Idiot* and *Lust for Life*. Check out Thomas Jerome's *Bowie in Berlin: A New Career in a New Town* (2008) for cool insight into these heady days.

The following decade, Depeche Mode made its own pilgrimage to Hansa and produced *Some Great Reward, Black Celebration* and *Construction Time Again*. Irish rockers U2 popped by the same hallowed hall in 1991 to record large sections of *Achtung Baby*. International artists who've also let their creative juices flow in Berlin include Rufus Wainwright, Snow Patrol and Kele Okereke, the lead singer of British indie rockers Bloc Party. Singer-songwriter Joe Jackson also recently traded his cramped London pad for a giant one in Kreuzberg, while Fran Healy, frontman of the Scottish band Travis, has decamped to Prenzlauer Berg. Australian electro/rock band Dukes of Windsor (their main album is *It's a War*) has been based in Berlin since 2009.

Since reunification, hundreds of indie, punk, alternative and gothic bands have gigged to appreciative audiences. The still (or once again) active Die Ärzte, Element of Crime and Einstürzende Neubauten are joined by top exports such as the alt-rock band Beatsteaks, which had its breakthrough in 2004 as Best German Act at the MTV Europe Music Awards. On the scene for a while have been Wir sind Helden, a Kreuzberg band that was one of the first bands to field a female lead singer, the charismatic Judith Holofernes.

Another group that has enjoyed considerable commercial success is the duo Rosenstolz, whose radio-friendly rock ballads seem to be particularly popular with gays and 'desperate housewives'. Attracting a similar fan base is another pop duo called Ich + Ich, composed of Annette Humpe (who back in 1980 founded the NDW band Ideal) and Adel Tawil. Annette's sister Inga (formerly of Neonbabies), meanwhile, has teamed up with Tommi Eckart as 2raumwohnung, whose bittersweet but catchy dance melodies have nudged them swiftly into the big time. Another chart favourite is 'German soul queen' Joy Denalane, who infuses traditional R&B with jazz, Afrobeat and South African folk music. Others to watch include Berlin band The Bosshoss, known for its country-style cover versions of famous songs by such performers as Britney Spears and Beastie Boys. Their latest album, *Low Voltage*, was released in April 2010. Genre-hoppers Super700, who draw from trip hop, jazz, synthie pop and indie rock, also had a new album out in early 2010, called *Lovebites*.

Techno & Beyond

Techno may have its roots in Detroit-based house music, but it was from Berlin that it conquered the world. Dr Motte and DJ Westbam, who also had commercial success with house and electro sounds, are considered two of the 'godfathers' of the Berlin techno sound. In 1987–88, the two played their first DJ gigs at the UFO – which was the city's first (and illegal) techno club – and cofounded the Love Parade, which had its last gasp in Berlin in 2006. It was briefly revived in Essen and other Ruhr-district cities (near Cologne) but a mass panic during the 2010 event in Duisburg, which left over 20 people dead, brought the festival to a sudden and final end.

When the second UFO club closed in 1991, the techno sonic brotherhood moved on to megavenues E-Werk and the recently reopened Tresor (p235), which also launched camouflage-wearing Berlin superstar DJ Tanith along with trance pioneer Paul van Dyk. The Tresor label has since become an international brand with a full range of merchandising. Other early artists include Marusha, whose 1994 mega-hit 'Somewhere over the Rainbow' ushered in the commercialisation of dance music. Other DJanes kept it more real, most famously Ellen Allien, star act of the BPitch Control record label (along with Sascha Funke), and Monika Kruse, who's also moved into producing. An excellent movie about Germany's early techno scene and culture is *We Call it Techno!*, released by Sense Music & Media (www.sensemusic.de).

These days, pure techno has essentially been sidelined, as more and more splinter genres of electronic music percolate in the club scene. House is not as ubiquitous in Berlin as it is in the rest of Europe and the USA, but it does dominate über-hip spaces like the Panorama Bar (p232), where Cassy and André Galluzzi have residencies. Phonique is another sonically adventurous house and electro DJ.

Another offshoot is breakbeat, which has travelled east from the UK. The local label currently leading the pack is the charmingly named Shitkatapult (founded by Marco Haas, aka T.Raumschmiere in 1997). The main artist to watch is Apparat (aka Sasha Ring), whose experiments with sound and vocals result in vivid, melodic techno and rich electropop. His 2007 release, *Walls,* was one of the top electro albums that year, followed in 2008 by the remix compilation *Things to Be Frickled.* A new album was scheduled for release some time in 2010. Places to catch him include Berghain (p232) and Watergate (p235).

Apparat has also been involved in various collaborations, for instance with his former main squeeze Ellen Allien, but also with the duo Modeselektor, aka Gernot Bronsert and Sebastian Szary. All are with the BPitch Control label and churn out IDM (intelligent dance music) influenced by electro and hip hop. In 2009, Apparat and Modeselektor released the album *Moderat.*

Another key BPitch player with an international following is Paul Kalkbrenner, who starred in his first semi-autobiographical flick, *Berlin Calling,* released in 2008. Kalkbrenner's brother Fritz is also becoming increasingly well known.

Then there's heavyweight label Get Physical, a collective of almost 20 artists, including the dynamic DJ duo M.A.N.D.Y., who are known for infusing house and electro with minimal and funk. Another key member is label cofounder Thomas Koch (aka DJ T), who also started the magazine *Groove* (www.groove.de) in 1989; if you read German, it's an essential source for staying up with the electronic music and club scene. Other major mags are the monthly *de:bug* (www.de-bug.de, in German), published locally by Sascha Kösch, aka DJ Bleed, and *Spex* (www.spex.de, in German), which relocated to Berlin from Cologne in 2008. Another unmissable source is the English-language webzine *Resident Advisor* (www.residentadvisor.net).

Unsurprisingly, given Berliners' love of blazing beats, drum and bass also commands a dedicated following. Apollo, MC Santana and Xplorer are artists behind hard:edged records, Berlin's most important drum and bass label and the original founders of the Watergate club.

Some of the finest Berlin exports come from a jazz/breaks angle (electrojazz and breakbeats, favouring lush grooves, obscure samples and chilled rhythms). Remix masters Jazzanova, whose members met DJing at Delicious Doughnuts (p233) in 1995, now run the Sonar Kollektiv label and are the undisputed champions of the downtempo scene that blends dub, hip hop, house, African music, techno and jazz into highly individual soundscapes. Other artists represented by Sonar Kollektiv include Micatone, Daniel Paul, Georg Levin and Forss.

As elsewhere, soul, R&B and black music of all shades are very much in vogue, though few other European cities offer such a thriving reggae-dancehall scene. Such a Sound is among the longest-running of the many sound systems, while Seeed is the biggest reggae group in Germany. Seeed frontman Peter Fox's solo album *Stattaffe* (2008) was one of the best-selling albums in Germany in recent years, with over one million copies sold. Also commercially successful is Culcha Candela, who have essentially pop-ified the Seeed sound. Then there's Ohrbooten, who are coming up fast with their injection of *Berliner Schnauze* (wit) into the Rasta vibe.

Home-grown rap and hip hop has a huge following, even if its own local label Aggro Berlin went bust in 2009. Key players are Sido, Fler and Bushido, whose hardcore, gangsta-rap-style lyrics have often been criticised as anti-Semitic, misogynist, racist, nationalist and homophobic. After a long-time feud, Fler and Bushido, have buried their battle axe and are now touring and releasing albums together. Bushido continues to be the most successful German rapper, even though he's been busy changing his bad-boy image, partly through his own label ersguterjunge and his autobiographical movie *Zeiten ändern dich* (Times Change You), shot by Uli Edel and Bernd Eichinger and released in 2010; reviews, however, were scathing and it pretty much bombed at the box office.

Then there's K.I.Z., who see themselves as a parody of gangsta rappers by exaggerating the image and making fun of the genre and other social and political topics. Prinz Pi, a bespectacled fellow who used to go by the less wholesome name of Prinz Porno, has mellowed recently and, in his spare time, helps street kids in Tanzania. For a thorough survey of the scene, check out the DVDs *Rap City Berlin* and *Rap City Berlin II*.

Foreign artists continue to flock to Berlin in droves. Recent residents have included UK/Canadian techno innovator and DJ and producer legend Richie Hawtin (aka Plastikman) and Chilean minimalist master Ricardo Villalobos. Germans have also developed a taste for Peaches and Chili, ie the provocative Canadian songstress and her countryman Jason Beck, who created the alter ego Chili Gonzales, a self-proclaimed 'one-eyed Jewish rapper', after moving to Berlin (never mind he's only half-Jewish and has both eyes…). Both have since moved on but return to Berlin quite frequently.

Thanks to this ever-fluid mix of talents and visions, constant experimentation ensures that genres are invented, deconstructed, reinvented and combined in Berlin quicker than anyone can even define them.

CINEMA

In 1895 Germany's first commercial film projection took place at the Wintergarten in Berlin. The city soon became synonymous with movies in Germany, at least until the outbreak of WWII. When filming resumed in Potsdam in 1992, Berlin became the second-most important film centre in Germany (behind Munich), with a prolific experimental scene lurking in the shadows of the big names.

Berlin also plays host to most German premieres of international movies, and stages the single most important event on Germany's film calendar, the International Film Festival (p17). Better known as the Berlinale, it was founded in 1951 on the initiative of the Western Allies, and features screenings of around 400 films each year as part of the public programme, with some of them competing for the prestigious Golden and Silver Bear trophies. There are dozens of other film festivals taking place during the year, including Achtung Berlin featuring movies made in Berlin, and the Porn Film Festival. For the entire schedule, see http://berliner-filmfestivals.de (in German).

Berlin's pioneering role in movie history is undeniable. America had Edison, France the Lumière brothers, and Berlin had Max Skladanowsky, a former fairground showman whose 1895 'bioscope' – a prototype film projector – paved the way for the first era of film-making in Germany. By 1910, Berlin had 139 *Kinematographentheater* (which gives us the German word for cinema, *Kino*) showing mostly slapstick, melodramas and short documentaries. The city now has more cinemas than ever (over 250), from multiplexes to tiny single-screen venues; see p251 for a selection. For an entertaining introduction to movie-making in Germany, swing by the Museum für Film & Fernsehen (p111) in Potsdamer Platz.

German Movies Through the Ages

German movies can be divided into four distinct periods: early films from before WWII; *Trümmerfilme* (rubble films) made in the

top picks

BERLIN FILMS

Berlin itself has 'starred' in many films, providing an iconic and evocative backdrop for everything from historical dramas to modern thrillers (and, of course, *Cabaret*).

- Berlin: Die Sinfonie der Grosstadt (Berlin: Symphony of a City; Walter Ruttmann; 1927) Ambitious for its time, this fascinating silent documentary captures a day in the life of Berlin in the '20s.
- Der Himmel über Berlin (Wings of Desire; Wim Wenders; 1987) An angelic love story swooping around the old, bare no-man's-land of Potsdamer Platz.
- Lola rennt (Run Lola Run; Tom Tykwer; 1997) The geography's largely fictional, but parts of Berlin (especially the Oberbaumbrücke) are unmistakable in this inventive, energetic MTV-generation movie.
- Good Bye, Lenin! (Wolfgang Becker; 2003) This hugely successful comedy tells the story of a young East Berliner who replicates the GDR for his mother after the fall of the Wall.
- Das Leben der Anderen (The Lives of Others; Florian Henckel von Donnersmarck; 2006) A thought-provoking depiction of the underhanded techniques of the GDR and their effects on a husband and wife from East Berlin's theatre scene, and the Stasi agent who spies on them in the 1980s.

DOCUMENTING EVIL

'I filmed the truth as it was then. Nothing more.'
Leni Riefenstahl

Films made during the Nazi period bring their own historical dilemma, none more so than the works of brilliant Berlin director Leni Riefenstahl (1902–2003).

A former actress, Riefenstahl (who was born in working-class Wedding) caught the regime's attention with her first feature as director, *Das Blaue Licht* (The Blue Light; 1932), and was recruited to make 'informational' films. Considered a vital part of the Third Reich propaganda machine, Riefenstahl's epics depicted Nazi events such as the 1936 Olympics. Her visually stunning *Triumph des Willens* (Triumph of the Will; 1934), a documentary about Hitler that centres on the Nuremberg rallies, is one of the most controversial pieces in cinematic history.

After the war, Riefenstahl maintained that she had held no fascist sympathies, protesting both her right as a film-maker to record such events and her lack of choice in the matter under the Nazis. Demonised by the Allies and the industry, she spent four years in a French prison. In 1954, in an attempt to clear her reputation, she completed *Tiefland*, an allegorical, supposedly antifascist fairy tale she had started work on in 1944; with no distributor willing to touch it, however, her cinematic career was effectively over.

From then on Riefenstahl concentrated mainly on photography, producing several books about the Sudanese people, which went some way towards refuting accusations of racism. In 1992 she published her autobiography, and subsequently found herself the subject of a number of documentaries, including *Leni Riefenstahl: Die Macht der Bilder* (Leni Riefenstahl: The Power of the Image; 1993) and *The Wonderful Horrible Life of Leni Riefenstahl* (2003). Despite a consistently high public profile, she made only one more film, the nature documentary *Impressionen unter Wasser* (Impressions under Water; 2002).

In September 2003 Leni Riefenstahl died in Germany, aged 101, leaving no real answers in the debate over art and complicity.

immediate aftermath of the war; Cold War–era movies born from the tense climate after 1961, the year the Berlin Wall was built; and New Berlin films, a period roughly beginning in the mid-1990s.

The 1920s and early '30s were a boom time for Berlin cinema, with Marlene Dietrich's bone structure and distinctive voice seducing the world, and the mighty UFA studio producing virtually all of Germany's celluloid output. The two dominant directors of the time were Georg Wilhelm Pabst, whose use of montage and characterisation defined the Neue Sachlichkeit (new objectivity) movement, and Fritz Lang, whose seminal works *Metropolis* (1926) and *M* (1931) brought him international fame. After 1933, however, film-makers found their artistic freedom, not to mention funding, increasingly curtailed, and by 1939 practically the entire industry had fled abroad.

Like most of the arts, the film industry has generally been well funded in Berlin since 1945. In the 1970s in particular, large subsidies lured film-makers back to the city, including the leading lights of the Junge Deutsche Film (Young German Film) – directors such as Rainer Werner Fassbinder, Volker Schlöndorf, Wim Wenders and Werner Herzog.

Fassbinder, perhaps the most talented and challenging of the group, died in an accident in 1982, but the other three have remained at the forefront of German cinema. Herzog, best known for his work with volatile actor Klaus Kinski, is still an active documentary director and producer. Wenders has been highly acclaimed for his seminal 1987 work *Der Himmel über Berlin* (Wings of Desire) as well as USA-based films such as *Paris, Texas* (1984), *Buena Vista Social Club* (1999) and *Don't Come Knocking* (2005). Schlöndorf, with consistent foreign and domestic successes under his belt, has also served at Potsdam's Babelsberg complex, once the domain of the great UFA studios. Even cinematographer Michael Ballhaus, a former Fassbinder collaborator, has carved out a distinguished international career, working regularly with Martin Scorsese (eg on *The Departed*; 2006).

As befits a city with such a chequered past, recent history has always been an issue for Berlin film-makers, from early postwar *Trümmerfilme* (rubble films) to the post-*Wende Ostalgie* (GDR nostalgia). Some of the best films about the Nazi era include East Germany's first postwar film, *Die Mörder sind unter uns* (The Murderers are Among Us; 1946); Fassbinder's *Die Ehe der Maria Braun* (The Marriage of Maria Braun; 1979); Margarethe von Trotta's *Rosenstrasse*

(2003), about a group of women fighting for the release of their Jewish husbands (see the boxed text, p107); and the extraordinary *Der Untergang* (The Downfall; 2004), directed by Oliver Hirschbiegel and critically acclaimed for Bruno Ganz's stunning performance as Hitler in his final days. By contrast, Dani Levy's 2007 satire *Mein Führer*, which ridicules a depressed Hitler at the end of the war, met with enormous controversy and showed that German audiences were not ready for a comedic treatment of the Third Reich era.

In the post-reunification era, most feature films about the GDR have been light-hearted comedy dramas, perhaps because of the proximity of the events and a reluctance among audiences to engage with their implications. Director Leander Haussmann contributed two *Ostalgie* films with *Sonnenallee* (Sun Alley; 1999) and *NVA* (2005), but was outdone at his own game by the smash hit *Good Bye, Lenin!* (2003), Wolfgang Becker's witty and heart-warming tale of a son trying to recreate the minutiae of GDR life to reassure his sick mother. This very German film garnered nominations at both the Golden Globes and the Academy Awards, although it did not win either. In the end it was a movie that did shine the spotlight on the darker side of GDR life that garnered the Academy Award for Best Foreign Film in 2007: Florian Henckel von Donnersmarck's astonishing movie debut, *Das Leben der Anderen* (The Lives of Others; 2006; also see p47).

top picks

FILM LOCATIONS

- **Around the World in 80 Days** (2004) The Konzerthaus and Deutscher Dom (Map p76-7) on Gendarmenmarkt stood in for 19th-century London in this Jackie Chan action flick.
- **Bourne Supremacy** (2004) The epic car chase where Bourne (Matt Damon) forces Russian assassin Kirill (Karl Urban) to crash his car into a concrete divider in a tunnel was filmed in the Tiergartentunnel (Map p112), a year and a half before its official opening in 2006.
- **Good Bye, Lenin!** (2003) The flat where Alexander Kerner recreates the GDR for his ailing mother is in a modern high-rise at Berolinastrasse 21 (Map pp156-7).
- **One, Two, Three** (1961) In this Billy Wilder mad-cap caper, flaming communist Otto Ludwig Piffl (played by Horst Buchholz) careens through the border post at the Brandenburger Tor (Brandenburg Gate; Map pp76-7) on a BMW250 motorcycle with side car. The scene was filmed days before the Wall went up on 13 August.
- **The Lives of Others** (2006) The apartment where two of the main characters, the playwright Georg Dreymann (Sebastian Koch) and his actress wife Christa-Maria Sieland (Martina Gedeck), make their home is at Wedekindstrasse 21 in Friedrichshain (Map p150-1).

Source: Alexander Vogel, Videobustour (www.videobustour.de; p312).

THEATRE
Theatre Today

Since reunification, major artistic, structural and personnel changes have swept Berlin's theatrical landscape on a regular basis. Today, Berlin has no fewer than 47 dedicated theatres, offering a wide variety of settings for the 9600-odd productions staged every year. The major stages have traditionally been very well subsidised, and hence often play it disappointingly safe with their schedules, leading to some colourful rows over cultural policy and official appointments. However, the current directors of the city's leading venues are, for the most part, presiding over a boom period, with a lively fringe scene flourishing around them.

Enfant terrible Frank Castorf is the man behind much of this new wave, igniting a creative firestorm at the Volksbühne (p255). Meanwhile, Claus Peymann has restored pomp and authority to the Berliner Ensemble (p254). The Deutsches Theater, which reached its first peak before WWII under Max Reinhardt, has been reeling in the awards lately under director Bernd Wilms, who also made the Maxim Gorki Theater (p255) Berlin's cultural fund; his job has been taken over by Ulrich Khuon, who last shepherded Hamburg's Thalia Theatre to great success. Meanwhile, Armin Petras took over the Gorki in 2006; he's also a playwright writing under the *nom de plume* of Fritz Kater and made a name for himself with a stage adaptation of Fatih Akin's screenplay *Gegen die Wand* (Head On). Also part of the new generation are Thomas Ostermeier and Jens Hillje, codirectors of the Schaubühne am Lehniner Platz (p255).

BABELSBERG & THE HOLLYWOOD CONNECTION

On the outskirts of Berlin, technically in the town of Potsdam, the Studio Babelsberg is the modern successor of the legendary UFA, founded in 1911 and thus the world's oldest major movie studio. By the 1920s, it was churning out such blockbusters as Fritz Lang's *Metropolis* and *The Blue Angel* with Marlene Dietrich. After WWII, it became the base of the East German production company DEFA. Today it produces or coproduces about 80% of all German feature films, as well as TV.

But not only that: of late, the hallowed studio has also become a Hollywood darling. A highly qualified crew base, modern studio facilities, a huge collection of props, and government subsidies that lower production costs by as much as 20% have attracted such key players as Quentin Tarantino, who filmed *Inglorious Basterds* (2009) here; Stephen Daldry (*The Reader*, 2008) and Brian Singer (*Valkyrie*, 2008). A watershed year was 2007, when three major flicks – *Valkyrie*, *The International* and *Speed Racer* – were all in production simultaneously. Roman Polanski, who had recreated the Warsaw ghetto at the studios for Academy winner *The Pianist*, returned in 2009 for *The Ghost Writer*, starring Pierce Brosnan. And there's no end in sight. Movies filmed in 2010 include *Unknown White Male* with Liam Neeson and the horror flick *The Apparition*, both produced by Joel Silver, as well as Roland Emmerich's *Anonymous* and *Hanne* with Cate Blanchett and Eric Bana in the lead roles.

Another asset that lures Hollywood to Berlin is the versatile look of the city itself. It can stand in as London and Paris, as it did in Jackie Chan's *Around the World in 80 Days* (2004), or as Moscow, as in the *Bourne Ultimatum* (2007) starring Matt Damon.

Dramatic History

Surprisingly, Berlin's theatre scene had rather modest beginnings. The first quality productions weren't staged until the arrival of such stellar dramatists as Gotthold Ephraim Lessing and Johann Wolfgang von Goethe in the middle of the 18th century. One of the first impresarios was August Wilhelm Iffland (1759–1814), who took over the helm of the Royal National Theatre in 1796 and was noted for his natural yet sophisticated productions.

Iffland's act proved hard to follow: when he died in 1814, Berlin theatre languished until Otto Brahm became director of the Deutsches Theater in 1894. Dedicated to the naturalistic style, Brahm coaxed psychological dimensions out of characters and sought to make their language and situations mirror real life. The critical works of Gerhart Hauptmann and Henrik Ibsen were staples on his stage throughout the 1890s.

In 1894 Brahm hired a young actor named Max Reinhardt (1873–1943), who became one of the most famous and influential directors in German theatre. Born in Vienna, Reinhardt began producing, and eventually inherited the reins of the Deutsches Theater from Brahm. Stylistically, Reinhardt completely broke the naturalist mould and became known for his lavish productions, using light effects, music and other devices. In 1919 he opened the Grosse Schauspielhaus, now the Friedrichstadtpalast (p238).

Reinhardt's path later crossed that of another seminal theatre figure, Bertolt Brecht (1898–1956), who moved to Berlin in 1924. The two worked together briefly at the Deutsches Theater, until Brecht developed his own unique style of so-called epic theatre, which, unlike 'dramatic theatre', forces its audience to detach themselves emotionally from the play and its characters and to reason critically and intellectually.

Over the next decade Brecht developed this theory and its 'alienation techniques' in plays like *Die Ausnahme und die Regel* (The Exception and the Rule; 1930) and *Die Mutter* (The Mother; 1932). A staunch Marxist, he went into exile during the Nazi years, surfaced in Hollywood as a scriptwriter, then left the USA in the late 1940s during the communist witch-hunts of the McCarthy era. Many of his key plays were written in exile: *Mutter Courage und ihre Kinder* (Mother Courage and Her Children; 1941), *Leben des Galilei* (The Life of Galileo; 1943), *Der gute Mensch von Sezuan* (The Good Woman of Setzuan; 1943) and *Der kaukasische Kreidekreis* (The Caucasian Chalk Circle; 1948) are considered among the finest examples of his extraordinary style.

Brecht returned to East Berlin in 1949 and founded the Berliner Ensemble with his wife, Helene Weigel, who directed it until her death in 1971. *Mutter Courage und ihre Kinder* premiered successfully in 1949 at the Deutsches Theater, but for much of the rest of his lifetime the great playwright was both suspected in the East for his unorthodox aesthetic theories and scorned in the West for his communist principles.

At the same time as Brecht was experimenting in prewar Berlin, new expressionistic approaches to musical theatre came from classically trained composers, including Hanns Eisler and Kurt Weill, who collaborated with Brecht on *Die Dreigroschenoper* (The Threepenny Opera) and *Aufstieg und Fall der Stadt Mahagony* (Rise and Fall of the City of Mahagony). On the more mainstream variety circuit, champagne, cancan and long-legged showgirls were all the rage, and Mischa Spoliansky was among the leading lights of the cabaret stages.

After WWII, artistic stagnation spread across German theatre for more than two decades. In West Berlin the first breath of recovery came in 1970 with the opening of the Schaubühne am Halleschen Ufer under Peter Stein. The theatre, which later moved to the Ku'damm and became the Schaubühne am Lehniner Platz, rapidly developed into one of West Germany's leading stages. In East Berlin, the Volksbühne grew to be a highly innovative venue, along with the Deutsches Theater. Taking advantage of relative political and artistic freedoms granted by the government, they provided platforms for political exchange and contributed to the peaceful revolution of 1989.

DANCE
Dance Today

While today Berlin's ballet troupes (there are three state-sponsored ones, attached to Berlin's three opera houses) often concentrate on audience-pleasing classical repertoires, the Staatsballet Berlin's current director and first male soloist, the extraordinary Ukrainian Vladimir Malakhov, has done much to raise the profile of classical dance in the city. More experimental and cutting-edge fare is produced by the company's most talented and ambitious dancers every two years as part of the project 'Shut up and Dance!'.

Contemporary dance took some hard knocks in the new millennium, with government funding cuts affecting the Berlin scene. However, the city's appetite for innovative works still thrives and Berlin's dancers and choreographers continue to kick up their heels. Performances are often staged in unconventional settings, geared to the creation of site-specific works and multimedia engagement. Important venues are the Sophiensaele (p251) and Hebbel am Ufer (HAU; p255).

Sascha Waltz remains the leading lady of contemporary dance in Berlin. In 2005 she returned to lead her own unconventional dance company (Sasha Waltz & Guests) after sharing the high-profile directorship of the Schaubühne with theatre director Thomas Ostermeier, though she still collaborates regularly with her former colleague. Waltz originally founded the company in 1993 together with Jochen Sandig and counts 16 major internationally acclaimed choreographies within its repertoire. Sandig is also the cofounder and artistic director of Radialsystem V (p251), where Waltz has a residency. All in all, she's probably done more than anyone else to shake up the contemporary dance scene in Berlin, and any performance with her involvement is worth catching.

TOLLER & PISCATOR

The names of playwright Ernst Toller (1893–1939) and producer Erwin Piscator (1893–1966) no longer mean much to the average theatregoer, but they were key figures of their time, and their single collaboration, the Berlin premiere of Toller's play *Hoppla, wir leben!* (Whoops, We're Alive!), was arguably the biggest theatrical event of the 1920s.

From the start the two men clashed. Toller was a committed socialist with humanist leanings, traumatised by WWI and the years he spent in prison after the short-lived 1919 Munich revolution, and his play was based on his experience of postwar society and the problems of political activism. Piscator, on the other hand, was a radical communist aiming to establish 'total theatre' as an extreme, agitating form of political engagement – the premiere was carefully timed to coincide with the 10th anniversary of the Russian Revolution.

Piscator's revolutionary production methods, using elaborate multisectioned sets, revolving stages, music and film clips, were actually ideally suited to Toller's vision of a world swamped in new technology, and had a profound influence on modern documentary theatre. However, the play's indeterminate ending was not the radical statement Piscator wanted to make; he rewrote it to have the lead character commit suicide, a crass stroke that undermined Toller's thoughtful attempt to examine the issues of political commitment and progress. The two never spoke again, and Toller reinstated his original ending for every subsequent run of the play.

BACK TO THE TWENTIES – GLAM CAB

Cabaret may have been born in 1880s Paris, but it became a wild and libidinous grown-up in 1920s Berlin. In those giddy Weimar years, creativity and decadence blossomed despite – or perhaps because of – raging inflation and political instability. Cabarets provided a titillating fantasy of play and display, where transvestites, singers, magicians, dancers and other entertainers made audiences forget about the harsh realities of daily life. It's a world vividly portrayed in the 1930 movie *The Blue Angel*, starring Marlene Dietrich, and of course in Bob Fosse's acclaimed film musical *Cabaret* (1972) with Liza Minnelli.

Over the last decade, cabaret has made a big comeback in Berlin, thanks in large part to post-reunification euphoria and a renewed unleashing of creativity. More mainstream and less lurid than in the Roaring Twenties, today's shows consist mostly of a series of snazzily choreographed variety acts. The edgiest venue is the Bar Jeder Vernunft (p238), whose reprise of *Cabaret* plays to sell-out audiences. Across town, the Friedrichstadtpalast (p238) is Europe's largest revue theatre, where leggy, feather-clad dancers kick and strut their stuff. If you like smaller, more intimate venues, try Chamäleon Variété (p238).

Elsewhere, US choreographer Meg Stuart has been working since 2003 with the Volksbühne, bringing movement and music to the city's most provocative stage. Other local choreographers to look out for include Christina Ciupke, Jo Fabian, Jochen Roller and Isabelle Schad. Those who wish to see a uniquely Berlin combination of contemporary dance as an exploration of bondage and 'ritual sexuality' may want to check out the Schwelle7 (www.schwelle7.de) company's performance space in Wedding.

Past Productions

Historically, ballet arrived under Friedrich II, who brought Italian star La Barberina to the city in 1744. The first royal company was formed in 1811, and eccentric American dancer Isadora Duncan opened her own school here in 1904. It was in the 1920s, however, that dance really took off. Berlin even gave birth to a new form, so-called grotesque dance. Influenced by Dadaism, it was characterised by excessive, often comical expressiveness. One of its prime practitioners was Valeska Gert, the film star and founder of Kohlkopp cabaret. Even more influential was Mary Wigman, who regarded body and movement as tools to express the universal experience of life. Her style inspired some of today's leading German choreographers, including Pina Bausch and Reinhild Hoffmann. Another famous Berlin hoofer from the 1920s was the notorious 'sex dancer' Anita Berber (1899–1928), immortalised in a famous portrait by Otto Dix in 1925.

Ballet also experienced a postwar renaissance under the Russian immigrant Tatjana Gsovsky, though it came and went quicker than the theatre revival. Initially working without a permanent stage, Gsovsky choreographed a number of memorable productions, including *Hamlet* (1953) and *The Idiot* (1954), at the Theater des Westens, before becoming ballet director at the Deutsche Oper.

ARCHITECTURE

The definition of a great city is different for each of us. For some it's about the many ways it entertains us with its neighbourhoods, restaurants, shops, bars, theatres and clubs. Others detect urban greatness in a city's impact on the senses – the velocity, the smells, the beauty and the noise all being parts in the grand vision of how it sees itself, and how it wants to be seen. But it's through a careful appraisal of architecture – the buildings, public spaces and streets themselves – that a city speaks with its most intimate voice of the secrets it holds. How a city is built reveals much of its soul.

After visiting Berlin in 1891, Mark Twain remarked, 'Berlin is the newest city I've ever seen.' What was new to Twain then was an energetic colossus, thrust into greatness by the madness of construction following the founding of the German empire in 1871. While still preserving the grandeur of the palaces and regal estates wrought by centuries of Prussian rulers, this new Berlin was built to foment revolutions in technology and learning, and to exploit the successes of its middle-class merchants and manufacturers. From a hotchpotch of loosely affiliated villages, Berlin became, almost overnight in terms of its history, *the* powerhouse of European endeavour and expression.

Then came WWII, near obliteration and the bifurcation into East and West. What was so quickly laid to waste in the 'counter-blitzkrieg' of the victorious powers was (not quite as quickly) rebuilt from the rubble, with little else in mind than to restore the hopes of Berliners and once again to provide them with a sense of civility. This massive reconstruction, naturally, took on decidedly different forms of expression in the Allied zones and in the 'worker's paradise' being touted in the socialist East. The contrast between Western European sensibilities and Moscow's penchant for bombast could not have been made more evident.

Then, following reunification, Berlin again hurled its prodigious energies into a veritable orgy of new construction to signal to the world that it was poised to reposition itself at the centre of European commerce, thought and creativity. The removal of the Berlin Wall quite literally opened up vast areas of empty space that hadn't been touched since WWII. Large sections of the historic centre were a blank canvas awaiting the visions of architects, urban planners and futurists.

And so Berlin became a virtual laboratory of architectural possibilities, as evidenced by the enormity of the Potsdamer Platz and Government Quarter undertakings, and the return of diplomatic courtiers and corporate headquarters. Berlin has indeed become an overnight showcase for the world's elite architects – IM Pei, Frank Gehry and Renzo Piano among them. Their corporate palaces and governmental centres arose to signal that Berlin was once again the heart, soul and primary engine of the nation and its people.

MODEST BEGINNINGS

Berlin is essentially a creation of modern times. Only a few Gothic churches bear silent witness to the days when today's metropolis was just a small trading town. The rebuilt Nikolaikirche (Church of St Nicholas, 1230; p96), Berlin's oldest church, offers a good introduction to medieval building techniques. Excavations revealed that it has Romanesque origins, but when the Gothic style became all the rage it was converted to a three-nave hall church, topped by a pair of slender spires.

Not far behind in age are the Marienkirche (Church of St Mary's; p95), first mentioned in 1294, and the Franziskaner Klosterkirche (Franciscan Abbey Church; p98), although the latter only survives as a picturesque ruin. All three churches were built in a style called *Backsteingotik* (Brick Gothic) in reference to the red bricks used in their construction. A hint of residential medieval architecture survives in Spandau, in the Gotisches Haus (p167) and the pint-sized Kolk (p167) quarter, with its half-timbered houses and a section of town wall.

Not many traces remain from the Renaissance, which reached Berlin in the early 16th century. The single most important structure from that period, the Berliner Stadtschloss (Berlin City Palace; 1540), was demolished by the GDR government in 1951. Its replacement, the brutalist Palast der Republik (Palace of the Republic), completed in 1975, was recently dismantled to make room for a modern version of the royal palace to be called Humboldtforum (p91).

Renaissance survivors include the Jagdschloss Grunewald (p163), the Zitadelle Spandau (p166) and the ornately gabled Ribbeckhaus (p91), which is the oldest extant residential building in Berlin from this period.

GOING FOR BAROQUE

As the city grew, so did the representational needs of its rulers, especially in the 17th and 18th centuries. This was the age of baroque, a style merging architecture, sculpture, ornamentation and painting into a single *Gesamtkunstwerk* (complete work of art). In northern Germany it retained a formal and precise bent, never quite reaching the exuberance achieved further south.

The emergence of baroque architecture is linked to the period of absolutism following the Thirty Years' War (1618–48), when central European feudal rulers asserted their power by building grand residences. In Berlin this role fell to Great Elector Friedrich Wilhelm, who brought in an army of architects, engineers and artists to systematically expand the city. When they were done, Berlin had grown three new quarters (Dorotheenstadt, Friedrichstadt and Friedrichswerder), a fortified town wall and a grand tree-lined boulevard known as Unter den Linden (p84).

His father may have laid the groundwork, but Berlin didn't truly acquire the stature of an exalted residence until Friedrich III came to power in 1688. His appetite for grand structures only grew bolder after he had himself crowned *King* Friedrich I in 1701, and during his reign

Berlin gained two major baroque buildings. In 1695, shortly before his death, Johann Arnold Nering began work on the Zeughaus (armoury) and Schloss Lietzenburg, a summer palace for Friedrich's wife, Sophie-Charlotte; it was renamed Schloss Charlottenburg (p122) after her death in 1705. Johann Friedrich Eosander then expanded the latter structure into a three-wing palace inspired by Versailles, topping it with a domed central tower.

Across town, construction of the Zeughaus proved to be fraught with obstacles. After Nering's death, Martin Grünberg took over but he had to resign in 1699 and pass the baton to Andreas Schlüter, who added the celebrated masks of dying warriors to the central courtyard with remarkable effect. Schlüter, however, turned out to be more skilled as a sculptor than as an architect, for part of his structure collapsed and the whole project subsequently passed over to Jean de Bodt. The square, two-storey structure was finally completed in 1706. After a recent renovation, the Zeughaus, which now houses the Deutsches Historisches Museum (German Historical Museum; p84), has gained a glass-and-steel roof above its courtyard and a modern annex named the IM Pei Bau (IM Pei Building) after its architect. Fronted by a transparent, spiralling staircase shaped like a snail shell, it is a harmonious interplay of glass, natural stone and light, and is an excellent example of Pei's muted postmodernist approach.

Meanwhile, back in the early 18th century, two formidable churches were taking shape south of the Zeughaus on Gendarmenmarkt, the central square of Friedrichstadt and the home of immigrant Huguenots. These were the Deutscher Dom (German Cathedral; p86) by Martin Grünberg, and the Französischer Dom (French Cathedral; p86) by Louis Cayart – the latter was modelled on the Huguenots' destroyed mother church in Charenton. Both churches received their splendid domes in 1785, courtesy of Carl von Gontard.

Friedrich I's son, Friedrich Wilhelm I, wasn't much into fiddling with Berlin's skyline. He was a pragmatic fellow who loved soldiers more than art and architecture, and thus saw nothing wrong with converting sections of Tiergarten (p117) and Lustgarten (Pleasure Garden; p92) into military exercise grounds. His most lasting architectural legacy, though, was a new city wall, which hemmed in Berlin until 1860.

The king with the greatest impact on central Berlin's layout was Frederick the Great. Together with his childhood friend, the architect Georg Wenzeslaus von Knobelsdorff, he masterminded the Forum Fridericianum, a cultural quarter centred on today's Bebelplatz, in a style called 'Frederician Rococo' that blended baroque and neoclassical elements. Not all structures were built, because the king's many war exploits had emptied his coffers. But those added to the cityscape were truly stunning and included the neoclassical Staatsoper Unter den Linden (State Opera House; p92); Sankt-Hedwigs-Kathedrale (St Hedwig Cathedral; p85), inspired by Rome's Pantheon; the playful Alte Königliche Bibliothek (Old Royal Library; p92); and the Humboldt Universität (Humboldt University; p92), originally a palace for the king's brother Heinrich. Knobelsdorff also added the Neuer Flügel (New Wing; p122) to Schloss Charlottenburg. His crowning achievement, though, was Schloss Sanssouci (Sanssouci Palace; p285) in Potsdam.

After Knobelsdorff's death in 1753, two architects continued in his tradition: Philipp Daniel

PRUSSIA'S BUILDING MASTER: KARL FRIEDRICH SCHINKEL

No single architect stamped his imprimatur on the face of Berlin more than Karl Friedrich Schinkel (1781–1841). The most prominent and mature architect of German neoclassicism, Schinkel was born in Neuruppin in Prussia and studied architecture under Friedrich Gilly and his father David at the Building Academy in Berlin. He continued his education with a two-year trip to Italy (1803–05) to study the classics up close, but returned to a Prussia hamstrung by Napoleonic occupation. Unable to practise his art, he scraped by as a romantic painter, and furniture and set designer.

Schinkel's career took off as soon as the French left Berlin. He steadily rose through the ranks of the Prussian civil service, starting as surveyor to the Prussian Building Commission and ending as chief building director for the entire state. He travelled tirelessly through the land, designing buildings, supervising construction and even developing principles for the protection of historic monuments.

His travels in Italy notwithstanding, Schinkel actually drew greater inspiration from classic Greek architecture. From 1810 to 1840 his vision very much defined Prussian architecture and Berlin even came to be known as 'Athens on the Spree'. In his buildings he strove for the perfect balance between functionality and beauty, achieved through clear lines, symmetry and an impeccable sense for aesthetics. Driven to the end, Schinkel fell into a coma in 1840 and died one year later in Berlin.

Boumann – who designed Schloss Bellevue (Bellevue Palace; p118) for Frederick's youngest brother, August Ferdinand – and Carl von Gontard, who added the domed towers to the Deutscher Dom and Französischer Dom on Gendarmenmarkt.

THE SCHINKEL TOUCH

The architectural style that most shaped Berlin's cityscape was neoclassicism, thanks in large part to one man: Karl Friedrich Schinkel, arguably Prussia's greatest architect (see the boxed text, opposite). A reaction against baroque flamboyance, it brought a return to classical design elements such as columns, pediments, domes and restrained ornamentation that had been popular throughout antiquity.

Schinkel's first commission was the Mausoleum (p123), built for Queen Luise in Schloss Charlottenburg's park, although he didn't really make his mark until 1818, with the Neue Wache (New Guardhouse; p85), originally an army guardhouse and now a war memorial.

Nearby, the Altes Museum (Old Museum; p89), with its colonnaded front, is considered Schinkel's most masterwork. Other neoclassical masterpieces include the magnificent Schauspielhaus (now the Konzerthaus; p86) on Gendarmenmarkt, and the small Neuer Pavillon (New Pavilion; p123) in the palace garden of Schloss Charlottenburg. Schinkel's most significant departure from neoclassicism is the Friedrichswerdersche Kirche (p85), which was inspired by a Gothic Revival in early-19th-century England.

After Schinkel's death, several of his disciples kept his legacy alive, notably Friedrich August Stüler, who built the Neues Museum (New Museum; p90), the Alte Nationalgalerie (Old National Gallery; p89) and the Matthäuskirche (Church of St Matthew; p117).

THE HOBRECHT PLAN

The onset of industrialisation in the middle of the 19th century saw Berlin's population explode, as hundreds of thousands flocked to the capital city in hope of improving their lot in the factories. Between 1850 and 1900 the number of inhabitants surged from 511,000 to 2.7 million.

Berlin quickly began bursting at the seams. To combat the acute housing shortage and improve canals and other infrastructure, an 1862 commission, helmed by chief city planner James Hobrecht, drew up plans for an expanded city layout. It called for two circular ring roads, bisected by diagonal roads radiating in all directions from the centre – much like the spokes of a wheel. The land in between was divided into large lots and sold to speculators and developers. In a move uncharacteristic of Prussian bureaucracy, there were practically no building codes except for a maximum building height of 22m and a minimum courtyard size of 5.34 sq metres to make enough room for fire-fighting equipment to be used.

Driven by short-term profitability, ruthless private developers pounced on such lax regulations, which led to the uncontrolled spread of *Mietskasernen* (literally, rental barracks). These sprawling tenements, four or five storeys high, wrapped around as many as five inner courtyards and crammed the largest possible number of people into the smallest possible space. Yes, they put a roof over the heads of incoming masses, but only in tiny, dark and depressing flats that sometimes even doubled as workshops or sewing studios. The plan's principal legacy was the ring of working-class districts with high-density housing (such as Prenzlauer Berg, Kreuzberg, Wedding and Friedrichshain) that almost encircled central Berlin by 1900.

THE GRÜNDERZEIT

The founding of the German empire in 1871 under Kaiser Wilhelm I ushered in the so-called *Gründerzeit* (Foundation Years), which architecturally went hand in hand with Historicism. This retro approach to architecture merely recycled earlier styles, sometimes even blending several together in an aesthetic hotchpotch called Eclecticism. Public buildings from this period reflect the confidence of the united Germany and tend towards the ostentatious. The most prominent examples of Historicism are the Reichstag (p75) by Paul Wallot, and the Berliner Dom (Berlin Cathedral; p90) by Julius Raschdorff, both in neo-Renaissance style; Franz Schwechten's Anhalter Bahnhof (p147), now ruined, and the Kaiser-Wilhelm-Gedächtniskirche

(Memorial Church; p127), also ruined, both examples of neo-Romanesque; and the neo-baroque Staatsbibliothek zu Berlin (State Library; p93) and Bodemuseum (p89) by Ernst von Ihne. The Theater des Westens (p254), meanwhile, takes even Eclecticism to new heights.

It was Otto von Bismarck who turned his attention to the residential development of the western city, and Charlottenburg in particular. He widened the Kurfürstendamm (p126), lining it and its side streets with attractive townhouses for the middle classes. Like the *Mietskasernen*, they were four or five storeys high and wrapped around a central courtyard, but there the similarities ended. Courtyards were large, allowing light to enter the roomy flats, some of which had as many as 10 rooms. These days, some harbour charming old-Berlin-style B&Bs, such as the Hotel-Pension Funk (p275) or Hotel Askanischer Hof (p273).

Berlin's upper crust sought refuge in the fashionable villa colonies of Grunewald and Dahlem, far away from the claustrophobic centre. Bankers, academics, scientists, entrepreneurs and plenty of famous folk – including writers Gerhart Hauptmann and Lion Feuchtwanger – were among those attracted to Berlin's own 'Beverly Hills'.

THE BIRTH OF MODERNISM

The *Gründerzeit* was not a time of experimentation, but a few progressive architects still managed to make their mark, mostly in industrial and commercial design. The main trailblazer was Peter Behrens (1868–1940), who is sometimes called the 'father of modern architecture'. Later modernist luminaries such as Le Corbusier, Walter Gropius and Ludwig Mies van der Rohe were all students of Behrens.

Elements characterising Modernism include a simplification of forms, the almost complete lack of ornamentation and the extensive use of glass, concrete and steel. Behrens designed the 1930 Berolinahaus on Alexanderplatz (now a C&A clothing store), but his most accomplished structure is outside the centre: the 1909 AEG Turbinenhalle (Map pp124-5; AEG Turbine Factory; Huttenstrasse 12-16, Tiergarten; Beusselstrasse), an airy, functional and light-flooded 'industrial cathedral' with exposed structural beams. It is essentially a frill-free reinterpretation of Schinkel's classical lines, replacing stone columns with steel trusses, and an ornamented triangular gable with an unadorned polygonal one. The building is considered an icon of early industrial architecture.

THE WEIMAR YEARS

WWI put creativity on hold, but it flourished all the more during the years of the Weimar Republic, ie the 1920s. The spirit of innovation lured some of the finest avant-garde architects to Berlin, including Bruno and Max Taut, Le Corbusier, Ludwig Mies van der Rohe, Erich Mendelsohn, Hans Poelzig and Hans Scharoun. In 1923 they formed an architectural association called Der Ring (The Ring), which later evolved into the Bauhaus. Members were united not by a single architectural vision, but by the desire to break with traditional aesthetics (especially the derivative Historicism, p55) and to create a modern, healthier and affordable – yet human-scale – approach to building.

Their theories were put into practice as Berlin entered another housing shortage. In cahoots with chief city planner, Martin Wagner, Ring members devised a new form of social housing called *Siedlungen* (housing estates), which ditched the claustrophobic *Mietskasernen* and instead opened up the living space and incorporated gardens, schools, shops and other communal areas that promoted social interaction. Together with Bruno Taut, Wagner himself designed the Hufeisensiedlung (Horseshoe Colony; p168) in southern Neukölln, an eye-catching horseshoe-shaped structure wrapped around a central garden. In 2008 it was one of six 1920s housing estates in Berlin entered on Unesco's list of World Heritage sites (see the boxed text, p58, for more).

In non-residential architecture, expressionism flourished with Erich Mendelsohn as its leading exponent. In architecture, expressionism takes an organic, sculptural approach, as nicely exemplified by the Universum Kino (Universum Cinema; 1926), today's Schaubühne am Lehniner Platz (p255), which greatly influenced the Streamline Moderne movie palace designs of the 1930s. Emil Fahrenkamp's 1931 Shell-Haus (Map p112; Reichspietschufer 60; Mendelsohn-Bartholdy-Park) follows similar design principles. Reminiscent of a giant upright staircase, it was one of Berlin's earliest steel-frame structures concealed beneath a skin of travertine. Its extravagant silhouette is best appreciated from the southern bank of the Landwehrkanal.

NAZI MONUMENTALISM

Modernist architecture had its legs cut out from under itself as soon as Hitler came to power in 1933. The new regime immediately shut down the Bauhaus School, one of the most influential forces in 20th-century architecture. Founded by Walter Gropius in 1919, it had moved to Berlin from Dessau only in 1932. Many of its visionary teachers, including Gropius, Mies van der Rohe, Wagner and Mendelsohn, went into exile in the USA, where they found a more welcoming climate for their visions.

Back in Berlin, Hitler, who was a big fan of architectural monumentalism, put Albert Speer in charge of turning Berlin into the 'Welthauptstadt Germania', the future capital of the Reich (see the boxed text, below). Today, only a few surviving Nazi-era buildings offer a hint of what Berlin might have looked like had history taken a different turn. A key relic is the coliseum-like Olympiastadion (p131), designed by Walter and Werner March. The legacy of another major Third Reich architect, Ernst Sagebiel, survives in the massive Reichsluftfahrtsministerium (Reich Aviation Ministry; p114), now the Federal Ministry of Finance, and the Flughafen Tempelhof (Tempelhof airport; p145). Heinrich Wolff designed the Reichsbank (cnr Kurstrasse & Jägerstrasse; ◉ Hausvogteiplatz), which, along with a modern annex by Thomas Müller and Ivan Reimann, now houses the Federal Foreign Office. In the Diplomatenviertel (Diplomatic Quarter; p118) south of Tiergarten – another Speer idea – the giant embassies of Nazi allies Italy and Japan also reflect the pompous grandeur in vogue at the time (see the Walking Tour, p119).

THE DIVIDED CITY

Long before the Wall turned Berlin into a tale of two cities, the clash of ideologies and economic systems between East and West also found expression in the architectural arena. East Germans looked to Moscow, where Stalin favoured a style that was essentially a socialist reinterpretation of good old-fashioned neoclassicism. This was in stark contrast to the modernist aspirations of the democratic West.

East Berlin

The most prominent architect in the GDR was Hermann Henselmann, the mastermind of the Karl-Marx-Allee (called Stalinallee until 1961; p152) in Friedrichshain. Built between 1952 and 1965, it was East Berlin's first 'socialist boulevard' and the epitome of Stalinist pomposity. It culminates at Alexanderplatz, where East Berlin city planners finally began embracing modern architectural principles after Stalin's death in 1953, although not necessarily in an aesthetically appealing fashion. Based on a carefully crafted 'socialist master plan', the square was enlarged, turned into a pedestrian zone and developed into East Berlin's commercial hub and architectural showcase. The only prewar buildings restored rather than demolished were

---

GERMANIA MANIA

Part of Hitler's Third Reich vision was to transform Berlin into Germania, a utopian world capital for the new Nazi empire. The man Hitler hired for the job was Albert Speer (1905–81), a brilliant architect who worked closely with Hitler and eventually became his armaments minister in 1942, in charge of – among many other things – bringing in forced labourers from the concentration camps.

At the core of Germania would be two major intersecting roads, the north-south axis stretching from the Reichstag to Tempelhof, and the east-west axis (today's Strasse des 17 Juni) linking the Brandenburg Gate with Theodor-Heuss-Platz (then Adolf-Hitler-Platz) in Charlottenburg. At the top of the north-south axis, near today's Reichstag, would rise the Grosse Halle des Volkes (Great Hall of the People), big enough for up to 180,000 people and topped by a 250m-wide dome.

Entire neighbourhoods north and east of Tiergarten were bulldozed to make room for these ambitious architectural projects. Fortunately, Speer only got as far as the huge Reichskanzlei (Hitler's office) before the realities of WWII put paid to his efforts.

Having survived to see his dreams bombed to bits, Speer served 20 years in Spandau prison. On his release, he wrote *Inside the Third Reich* (1970), a detailed account of the day-to-day operations of Hitler's inner circle. Read it alongside Gitta Sereny's biography *Albert Speer: His Battle with Truth* (1996) for an insight into the complicated life of this controversial Nazi figure.

Peter Behrens' sober and functional Berolinahaus (1930) and the Alexanderhaus (1932) just north of the railway tracks.

Buildings orbiting Alexanderplatz include Henselmann's Haus des Lehrers (House of the Teacher), decorated with a colourful frieze showing scenes from daily life in East Germany. The massive building on the north side of the square is the 1970 Haus der Elektroindustrie (House of Electrical Industry; Map p96; Ⓢ Alexanderplatz), which now houses Germany's federal environmental ministry. The letters on its facade spell out a quote from the 1929 novel *Berlin Alexanderplatz* by Alfred Döblin. The two tallest structures here are the Park Inn Hotel (formerly the Interhotel Stadt Berlin), which locals have nicknamed 'Bed Tower' and, of course, the Fernsehturm (TV Tower; p95), whose design was based on an idea of Henselmann's.

West Berlin

In West Berlin, by contrast, urban planners sought to eradicate any hint of monumentalism and to rebuild the city in a modern, rhythmic and organic manner with wide-open spaces as a metaphor for a free society. Case in point: the Hansaviertel (Hansa Quarter; Map pp72-3; Ⓢ Hansaplatz), built from 1954 to 1957, northwest of Tiergarten, is a loosely structured leafy area blending high-rises and single-family homes. It grew from an architectural exposition, the Internationale Bauausstellung, or 'Interbau', held in 1957, and represents the pinnacle of architectural vision in the 1950s. More than 50 architects from 13 countries – including Gropius, Luciano Baldessari,

UNCOMMON ENVIRONS FOR THE COMMON MAN

Architecturally speaking, Museumsinsel (p87), Schloss Sanssouci (p285) and the Hufeisensiedlung in Neukölln (p168) could not be more different. Yet they all have one thing in common: they are Unesco World Heritage sites. Along with five other working-class housing estates throughout Berlin, the Hufeisensiedlung was inducted onto this illustrious list in July 2008.

Created between 1910 and 1934 by such leading architects of the day as Bruno Taut and Martin Wagner, these icons of modernism are the earliest examples of innovative, streamlined and functional – yet human-scale – mass housing. They reflect the spirit of the Weimar Republic, a period of unbridled experimentation and social reform, and stand in stark contrast to the slum-like, crowded tenements of the late 19th century. The flats, though modest, were functionally laid out and had kitchens, private baths and balconies that let in light and fresh air. Today we take these features for granted, but back then the approach was nothing but revolutionary. Here's a roll call of the honoured colonies.

Gartenstadt Falkenberg (off Map pp72-3; Akazienhof, Am Falkenberg & Gartenstadtweg; Köpenick; Ⓡ Grünau) Built by Bruno Taut between 1910 and 1913, the oldest of the six Unesco-honoured estates is a cheerful jumble of colourfully painted cottages. From the S-Bahn, approach from Am Falkenberg.

Grossiedlung Siemensstadt (Map pp72-3; Geisslerpfad, Goebelstrasse, Heckerdamm, Jungfernheideweg, Mäckeritzstrasse, Charlottenburg; Charlottenburg/Spandau; Ⓢ Siemensdamm) This huge development (1929–31) combines the visions of several architects, including Walter Gropius' minimalism, Hugo Häring's organic approach and Hans Scharoun's ship-inspired designs. Best approach is via Jungfernheideweg.

Schillerpark Siedlung (Map pp72-3; Barfussstrasse, Bristolstrasse, Corker Strasse, Dubliner Strasse, Oxforder Strasse, Windsorer Strasse; Wedding; Ⓢ Rehberge) Taut's first large-scale building project was inspired by Dutch architecture and sports a dynamic red-and-white-brick facade. Best approach from the U-Bahn stop is via Barfussstrasse.

Weisse Stadt (off Map pp72-3; Aroser Allee, Baseler Strasse, Bieler Strasse, Emmentaler Strasse, Genfer Strasse, Gotthardstrasse, Romanshorner Weg, Schillerring, Sankt-Galler-Strasse; Reinickendorf; Ⓢ Paracelusbad, Residenzstrasse) Martin Wagner designed this dominantly white colony between 1929 and 1931; it includes shops, a kindergarten, a cafe, a central laundry and other communal facilities. Because most of its streets are named for Swiss towns, it's also known as 'Swiss Quarter'. Best approach is via Aroser Allee.

Wohnstadt Carl Legien (Map p156-7; Erich-Weinert-Strasse, Georg-Blank-Strasse, Gubitzstrasse, Küselstrasse, Lindenhoekweg, Sodtkestrasse, Sültstrasse, Trachtenbrodtstrasse; Prenzlauer Berg; Ⓡ Prenzlauer Allee) For this development, the one closest to the city centre, Taut arranged rows of four-to-five-storey-high houses and garden areas in a semi-open space. It was built between 1928 and 1930 and is named for a union leader. Best approach is via Erich-Weinert-Strasse.

Alvar Aalto and Le Corbusier – participated in its design. Interbau also produced Hugh A Stubbins' Haus der Kulturen der Welt (House of World Cultures; p78) and the Corbusierhaus (p132), a giant apartment complex of unflinching angularity.

Meanwhile, another daring construction project was taking shape in the wartime wasteland southeast of Tiergarten: the Kulturforum (p114), a museum and concert hall complex just west of Potsdamer Platz that was part of Hans Scharoun's vision of a cultural belt stretching from Museumsinsel to Schloss Charlottenburg. The Berlin Wall put an end to such ambitions. Instead of being a central link between the eastern and western city halves, the Kulturforum found itself rubbing up against the concrete barrier.

Construction proceeded nevertheless. First to be completed in 1963, and considered a masterpiece of sculptural modernism, was Scharoun's Philharmonie (p116). Scharoun also drew up the plans for the Staatsbibliothek zu Berlin (State Library; p93) on Potsdamer Strasse, and the Kammermusiksaal (Chamber Music Hall; p116), but didn't live to see their completion.

Mies van der Rohe's Neue Nationalgalerie (New National Gallery; p115) also has a commanding presence within the Kulturforum. This temple-like art museum takes the shape of a 50m-long, glass-and-steel cube perching on a raised granite podium. Its coffered, rib-steel roof seems to defy gravity with the help of eight steel pillars and a floor-to-ceiling glass front.

Parallel Developments

Alexanderplatz and the Kulturforum may have been celebrated prestige projects, but both Berlins also had to deal with more pragmatic issues, such as the need for inexpensive, modern housing to accommodate growing populations. This led to several urban planning mistakes on both sides of the Wall in the 1970s and '80s, most notably in the birth of soulless, monotonous satellite cities for tens of thousands of people.

In West Berlin, Walter Gropius drew up the plans for the Grosssiedlung Berlin-Buckow in southern Neukölln (renamed Gropiusstadt after his death). The Märkisches Viertel in Reinickendorf, northwest Berlin, is another such development. On the other side of the Wall, Marzahn, Hohenschönhausen and Hellersdorf became three new city districts consisting almost entirely of high-rise *Plattenbauten* made from precast concrete slabs. Although equipped with modern conveniences such as private baths and lifts, these giant developments had little open space, green areas or leisure facilities.

CRITICAL RECONSTRUCTION

While mass housing mushroomed on the peripheries, the inner city suffered from decay and neglect, especially in the shadow of the Berlin Wall and nowhere more so than in Kreuzberg. To kick-start the district's revitalisation, another Interbau was held in 1978. It would blend two architectural principles: 'careful urban renewal', which would focus on preserving, renovating and reusing existing buildings; and 'critical reconstruction', which meant filling vacant lots with new buildings that reflected the layout or design of surrounding structures. The goal was to re-knit the urban fabric that had been torn apart by Speer's megalomania, wartime bombing and hasty postwar planning.

Under the leadership of Josef Paul Kleihues, the royalty of international architecture descended upon Berlin to take up the challenges of Interbau. Their ranks included Rob Krier, James Stirling, Rem Koolhaas, Charles Moore, Aldo Rossi and Arata Isozaki, as well as Germans such as the late OM Ungers, Gottfried Böhm, Axel Schultes and Hans Kollhoff. Collectively, they introduced a new aesthetic to Berlin, moving away from the harsh modernist look and replacing it with a more diverse and decorative approach. *Time* magazine called it 'the most ambitious showcase of world architecture in this generation'.

One area that got particular attention was the Fraenkelufer in Kreuzberg, where Hinrich and Inken Baller created innovative apartment buildings inspired by Art Nouveau and expressionism. Elsewhere, a more austere, neo-rationalist approach ruled, especially in Aldo Rossi's residential buildings at Wilhelmstrasse 36, and on Rauchstrasse south of Tiergarten.

THE NEW BERLIN

Reunification presented Berlin with both the challenge and the opportunity to redefine itself architecturally. With the Wall gone, huge gashes of empty space opened up where the two city halves were to be physically rejoined. Critical reconstruction again became the guiding principle. City planning director Hans Stimmann looked back to the Prussian tradition and drew up a catalogue of parameters (building height, facade material etc) that placed tight restrictions on architects.

top picks

BUILDINGS WE LOVE

- Berliner Dom (p90)
- Jüdisches Museum (p142)
- Neues Museum (p90)
- Philharmonie (p116)
- Fernsehturm (p95)

Potsdamer Platz

The biggest and grandest of the post-1990 Berlin developments is Potsdamer Platz (p110), a complete reinterpretation of the famous historic square that was the bustling heart of the city until WWII. From the Cold War-era death strip has sprung a dynamic urban quarter swarming with shoppers, revellers, travellers, cineastes, diners, suits and residents. Renzo Piano's master plan is based on a dense, irregular street grid typical of a 'European city'. Structures are of medium height, except for three high-rises overlooking the intersection of Potsdamer Strasse and Ebertstrasse, which form a kind of visual gateway.

An international roster of renowned architects collaborated on Potsdamer Platz, which is divided into DaimlerCity, the Sony Center and the Beisheim Center. Helmut Jahn's Sony Center, with its dramatic tented plaza and svelte glass skin, emphasises transparency, lightness and layering and is the most visually striking complex. The Kollhoff Haus, across Potsdamer Strasse, has a more elegant outline but with its mantle of reddish-brown clinker bricks, it comes across as more traditional and somewhat dull. Other architects involved in redeveloping Potsdamer Platz included Arata Isozaki, who created the waffle-patterned, coffee-coloured Berliner Volksbank; Rafael Moneo, who conceived the sleek, minimalist Grand Hyatt Hotel (p272); and Richard Rogers (best known for the Centre Pompidou in Paris), who planned the Potsdamer Platz Arkaden (p187), a three-storey shopping mall. Engulfed by all these modern structures stands the sole survivor from the original Potsdamer Platz, the Weinhaus Huth (Map p112).

Pariser Platz

Pariser Platz was also reconstructed from the ground up. It's a formal, introspective square framed by banks and embassies that, in keeping with critical reconstruction, had to be clad in sober yellow, white or grey stone. Even California-based deconstructivist architect Frank Gehry, known for his outrageously warped designs, had to cool his creative jets for the DZ Bank (2000; p81), but only on the outside. Enter the foyer and you can glimpse a sci-fi-esque atrium with an enormous free-form, stainless-steel sculpture – a fish? a horse's head? It's actually a conference room. Daylight streams in through the curving glass roof, with its steel girders as intricate as a spider's web.

Next to the DZ Bank, the last gap on Pariser Platz was filled in 2008 by the US Embassy to the right of the DZ Bank. The design, by the Los Angeles firm of Moore, Ruble and Yudell, stays closely within the trajectory of critical reconstruction with its blunt and plain stone facade facing the square.

In the far southeast corner is the Akademie der Künste (Academy of Arts; 2005; p81) by Günter Behnisch, the only Pariser Platz building with a glass front. Behnisch had to fight tooth and nail for this facade, arguing that the square's only public building should feel open, inviting and transparent.

Flanking the Brandenburg Gate, the Haus Liebermann and Haus Sommer by Kleihues closely resemble Stüler's original 19th-century structures, while the Adlon Hotel is practically an exact copy of the 1907 original.

Diplomatenviertel

Some of Berlin's most exciting new architecture is clustered in the revitalised Diplomatenviertel (Diplomatic Quarter; p118) on the southern edge of Tiergarten, where many countries rebuilt their embassies on their historic pre-WWII sites. For an introduction to the most interesting ones, follow the Walking Tour on p119.

Regierungsviertel

More cutting-edge architecture awaits in the government quarter. Arranged in linear east-west fashion are the Bundeskanzleramt (Federal Chancellery; p78), the Paul-Löbe-Haus (p79) and the Marie-Elisabeth-Lüders-Haus (p79). Together with the Kanzlergarten (chancellor's garden), the Kanzlerpark (chancellor's park) and the Spreebogenpark, they form the *Band des Bundes* (Band of Federal Buildings), which represents a symbolic linking of the formerly divided city halves across the Spree River.

Overlooking all these shiny new structures is the Reichstag (p75), whose total makeover under Lord Norman Foster was completed in 1999. Its crowning glory is, quite literally, a high-tech glass cupola, with a ramp spiralling up around a central mirrored cone. With this dazzling addition, Foster managed to inject levity into this mammoth building burdened with a rather weighty history. It is now one of Berlin's most beloved landmarks and tourist magnets.

The glass-and-steel spaceship north of here is Berlin's first-ever central railway station, the sparkling Hauptbahnhof (Map pp76-7). Designed by the Hamburg firm of Gerkan, Marg und Partner and completed in 2006, the five-level terminal is one of the largest railway stations in Europe and a great place to watch daily life unfold.

More Architectural Trophies

In Kreuzberg, the deconstructivist Jüdisches Museum (142), by Daniel Libeskind, is among the most daring and provocative structures in the new Berlin. With its irregular, zigzagging floor plan and shiny zinc skin pierced by gash-like windows, it is not merely a museum but a powerful metaphor for the troubled history of the Jewish people.

One of the less successful developments was the Friedrichstadtpassagen (p87), a trio of luxurious shopping complexes, including the glamorous Galeries Lafayette. Intended to restore bustling street life to Friedrichstrasse, they fail in their mission by hiding their jewel-like interiors behind bland, postmodern facades.

Other remarkable new buildings include the Dutch Embassy (p98), at Klosterstrasse 50, a starkly geometric glass cube by Rem Koolhaas, intended to embody 'Dutch openness', with a large terrace offering good views of the Spree River. Another standout is the energy-efficient extension of the GSW Headquarters (Map pp140-1; Charlottenstrasse 4; ⊙ Kochstrasse) by Louisa Hutton and Matthias Sauerbruch, which sports a double-layer convection facade with blinds that automatically change colour depending on the temperature.

BERLIN LIVING

The typical Berlin dwelling is a spacious rented 1½-bedroom flat on at least the first floor of a large postwar house (no-one wants to live at street level), probably facing onto a *Hinterhof* (courtyard) full of coloured recycling bins. The apartment itself has very high ceilings, large windows and, as often as not, stripped wood floors. The kitchen will almost invariably be the smallest room in the house and used mainly for stacking crates of beer and mineral water. A few flats still have the traditional tiled heating stoves in place, though no-one actually uses them.

Berlin flats are usually nicely turned-out, whatever the style favoured by the occupant, and a lot of attention is paid to design, though comfort is also considered. At least one item of furniture will come from IKEA; depending on income, the rest may come from the Stilwerk centre, Polish craftsmen, a flea market or eBay – or any combination thereof.

Rent is calculated according to space, starting at around €400 a month for 50 sq metres (depending on the district). Any conversation about costs with a Berlin tenant will inevitably lead to them asking you how many square metres your place is – do some sums before you leave home!

For a sneak peek into some of the city's more stylish flats, look for the *Berlin Apartments* book (teNeues, 2002) by Anja Jaworsky.

Across town, in Charlottenburg, several new structures have added some spice to the rather drab postwar architecture in the Ku'damm area. The Ludwig-Erhard-Haus (p134), home of the Berlin stock market, is a great example of the organic architecture of British architect Nicholas Grimshaw. Nearby, Kleihues' Kantdreieck (p134) establishes a visual accent on Kantstrasse by virtue of its rooftop metal 'sail'.

Other noteworthy buildings include Helmut Jahn's Neues Kranzler Eck (p133) and the 2001 Ku'damm Eck (Map p128; cnr Kurfürstendamm & Joachimsthaler Strasse; ◎ Kurfürstendamm), a corner building with a gradated and rounded facade festooned with sculptures by Markus Lüppertz.

In 2009, the building that captured worldwide headlines was David Chipperfield's reconstruction of the Neues Museum (p90) on Museumsinsel. Like a giant jigsaw puzzle, it beautifully blends fragments from the original structure, which was destroyed in WWII, with modern elements. The end result is so harmonious and impressive it immediately racked up the accolades, including the prestigious award from the Royal Institute of British Architects (RIBA) in 2010.

THE FUTURE

You'd think there'd be hardly any room left to build in Berlin, but that is not the case. North of the Scheunenviertel, the cranes are dancing above the new headquarters of the Bundesnachrichtendienst (BND; Map pp102–3; Chausseestrasse 85; ◎ Zinnowitzer Strasse), the German equivalent of the CIA. Designed by Kleihues + Kleihues, the enormous complex is being built on a lot formerly occupied by the GDR-era Stadium of the World Youth and is expected to provide 4000 jobs when it opens in 2013.

The biggest project on the drawing board, though, is the rebuilding of the Berliner Stadtschloss (Royal City Palace) on Schlossplatz, right where the historic palace once stood and where the GDR had built its recently demolished Palast der Republik. Construction was supposed to begin in 2010 but had to be postponed until at least 2014 because of empty federal and state coffers. Read more about it in the boxed text, p91.

Completion of the vast Berlin Brandenburg International (BBI) airport, next to the existing Schönefeld airport in southeast Berlin, was also postponed by six months; the first flights are expected to start in mid-2012. Back in town, an entire new city quarter is being master-planned for the empty land north of the Hauptbahnhof (central train station). Other projects include the redesign of Gendarmenmarkt as well as the gradual construction of the Mediaspree, a mix of hotels, residential and office buildings on the Spree River banks along a 3.6km stretch south of Jannowitzbrücke.

ENVIRONMENT
THE LAND

In 1920 seven towns and countless distinct communities were amalgamated into Gross-Berlin (Greater Berlin), making it one of the largest cities in the world, with an area of 870 sq km and a population of nearly four million. Today the numbers are similar: 892 sq km, 3.4 million people. Most visitors never stray outside the central districts, but just try walking from Friedrichshain to Charlottenburg and you'll realise Berlin's a lot bigger than the transport system makes it feel.

Berlin is cradled by the vast North German Plains and largely built on sandy glacial soil. It is surrounded by a belt of lakes hemmed in by mixed pine and birch forests. Two rivers, the Havel and the Spree, flow through the city, and the Teltowkanal and the Landwehrkanal are the major canals. Water covers 6.6% of the city's territory, almost 18% is forestland, another 11.5% is devoted to recreation areas and more than 5% is used for farming.

Apart from rivers and lakes, Berlin lacks distinctive geographical features. The highest natural elevation is the Müggelberge hills in Köpenick, which rise to a modest 115m. Several other 'bumps', including the Teufelsberg (p131), are actually *Trümmerberge* (rubble mountains) piled up from WWII debris.

GREEN BERLIN

Berlin may be vast and urban, but with parks, forests, lakes and rivers taking up about one-third of its area, it's surprisingly easy to leave the concrete jungle and commune with nature.

All in all, there are some 2500 green oases, from the rambling Tiergarten, which takes up a huge chunk of valuable real estate right in the city centre, to the Grunewald and other vast woods hemming in the outer suburbs. Every *Kiez* (neighbourhood) has its own park (eg Volkspark Friedrichshain, p153) and, thanks to a successful tree-planting campaign, more than 400,000 linden (lime), maple, oak, plane and chestnut trees cast their shade on city streets.

The local fauna, however, has not fared nearly so well. Loss of habitat, low groundwater levels and dry biotopes have caused more than half of all animal and plant species to limp onto the endangered species list.

Larkspur, early purple orchid and wild carnations are among the species that are practically extinct, while the survival of otters, partridges, lapwings and natterjack toads is severely threatened. Only about 33 fish species still inhabit the city's rivers and lakes, the most common being perch, pike, roach and bream. But there are also some success stories – beavers, grey bunting and quails have been spotted in increasing numbers and certain mammals are also thriving in the outlying forests. Keep your peepers open and you may well encounter wild rabbits, red foxes, martens and especially wild boar, which have all thrived in recent years (see the boxed text, below). Berlin is also popular with bats, thousands of which choose to hibernate in the dark vaults of the Zitadelle Spandau (p166), a grand old fortress in the suburb of Spandau. You can take bat tours and observe the animals as they forage for food around the castle grounds.

Aware that it has some of the highest air-pollution levels in Germany, Berlin joined the International Climate Convention in 1991. Between 1990 and 2006 (the last year for which numbers were available), CO_2 emission dropped from 27 million tonnes to 19.9 million.

Since the city's 1.2 million vehicles are the single major pollution culprit, Berlin stepped up its efforts on 1 January 2008 and now keeps vehicles with excessive emissions out of the so-called *Umweltzone* (Environmental Zone), which covers the inner city within the ring formed by the S-Bahn tracks. Vehicles that meet the standard must display a windscreen sticker; driving without one incurs a fine of €40 (for details on how to get a sticker, see p304).

Other steps towards improving Berlin's ecological balance sheet have included covering the vast roof of the new Hauptbahnhof with solar panels that generate 160,000 kwh per year. Owners of older buildings with poor insulation receive public subsidies to make them more energy efficient. The number of coal stoves, too, has been reduced from 400,000 in 1990 to 60,000 today.

Awareness also happens at a personal level. Bicycle lanes abound, there are solar-powered parking-voucher dispensers and recycling is the norm – even U-Bahn and S-Bahn stations have colour-coded *Trennmüll* (sorted rubbish) bins. The city has a comprehensive and efficient public transport system, which the majority of people use regularly. Car-sharing programmes are popular as well.

Greenpeace (www.greenpeace-berlin.de, in German) is very active in Germany, and another important and similarly outspoken environmental group is the Grüne Liga (Green League; www.grueneliga-berlin.de, in German), which is particularly concerned with sustainable future development, education and renewable energy sources. The local chapter of the latter publishes an excellent, multilingual sustainable city guide (www.berlingoesgreen.de) that's available for free online. The Green Party has also

PIG IGNORANCE

Berlin is hardly truffle country, but the city's leafy outer suburbs have become a paradise for wild boar in recent years. The districts most affected are Grunewald, Zehlendorf, Wilmersdorf, Reinickendorf and Spandau, where many a resident has woken up to find their garden trashed by porcine marauders.

The pig population explosion is said to have been caused by mild winters and an abundance of acorns and other foods, with many of the porcine baby boomers then having developed a taste for lawns, flower beds and scraps scavenged from compost heaps and garbage bins. According to a report in the *Berliner Morgenpost,* wild pigs even wait regularly on the steps of one school to beg for food at break times.

Reactions to the problem are mixed; even the most green-minded Berliners start screaming 'cull' the moment they see their lovingly tended geraniums massacred by careless trotters. In response, the senate has published an information pamphlet on city boars, giving advice about their diet and habits, and encouraging people to be more tolerant of their piggy visitors. Still, failing that, the pigs are fair game outside populated areas, and licensed hunters bag around 1000 hapless porkers a year.

traditionally been strong in Berlin, winning 13.1% of the vote in the 2006 municipal elections (the next ones are in 2011).

GOVERNMENT & POLITICS

Along with Hamburg and Bremen, Berlin is a German city-state with a government made up of the *Abgeordenetenhaus* (parliament, or legislative body) and the *Senat* (senate, or executive body). Members of parliament are voted in directly by the electorate for a five-year term. Their primary function is to pass legislation and to elect and supervise the senate, which consists of the *Regierender Bürgermeister* (governing mayor) and eight senators. The mayor sets policy and represents Berlin internationally and nationally; senators have similar roles to cabinet ministers, with each in charge of a particular portfolio. The mayor and senators are based at the Rotes Rathaus (Berlin Town Hall; p100), while the *Abgeordenetenhaus* meets in the former Prussian parliament at Niederkirchnerstrasse 5. Since 2001 Berlin has been governed by a coalition of the centre-left Sozialdemokratische Partei Deutschlands (SPD) and the far-left Die Linke, with Klaus Wowereit of the SPD as governing mayor. Wowereit was re-elected in 2006. The next elections are in 2011.

Since 1999 Berlin has also been the seat of the national government. The *Bundestag* (federal parliament) moved into the remodelled Reichstag, while the *Bundesrat* (upper house) set up shop in the former Preussisches Herrenhaus building. Ministries and embassies followed in their wake.

MEDIA
PRINT

Media coverage in liberal, politicised Berlin is typically broad for a European capital. The newspaper with the largest circulation is the tabloid *BZ*, while its rival *Berliner Kurier* is also popular. National über-rag *Bild* is the pride of media tycoon Axel Springer's publishing empire

KING OF THE SPRINGERS

Hamburg-born publisher Axel Springer (1912–85) was essentially the German answer to Rupert Murdoch, a colourful and often controversial figure who did much to shape the current state of the German media. Having taken over the family firm from his father after WWII, Springer created *Bild* in 1952, based on the model of British tabloid newspapers, and went on to build a huge portfolio of magazines and papers including *Die Welt,* the *Berliner Morgenpost* and pioneering teen mag *Bravo*.

The first wave of controversy came in 1967, when students and the Gruppe 47 forum of liberal authors protested that Springer's virtual monopoly was a threat to press freedom. *Bild*, too, became notorious for its vocal criticism of student demonstrations and for supposedly aggressive investigative tactics on the part of reporters. In 1977 journalist Günter Wallraff went undercover at the *Bild* offices and later published a book alleging serious breaches of ethics among its staff (tapping subjects' phones, for example). The following year the paper was sued for erroneously labelling student Eleonore Poensgen a terrorist.

Amid all this attention, Springer maintained a dual existence, often reviled in public, but highly respected for his commitment to German-Jewish reconciliation, a personal project that he pursued for most of his life. By the time he died in 1985 he had received countless awards, citations and honorary doctorates from Jewish institutions in Germany and Israel, as well as the American Friendship Medal.

Springer also considered himself a German patriot and was a staunch proponent of reunification – in 1958 he even visited Moscow to outline his plans to Khrushchev in person. When this somehow failed to work, he made support for reunification editorial policy in all his titles and refused to recognise the legitimacy of the East German state; to hammer home the point, any mention of the GDR was put in inverted commas. Sadly for Springer, he died just four years before his vision was realised, missing out on what would doubtless have been publishing's biggest ever 'I told you so'.

Even after his death, Springer managed to make his presence felt: his will left Axel Springer Ltd to his fifth wife and his two children, stipulating that they couldn't sell any of it for 30 years. In 2005 the firm even managed to stir up controversy again by bidding to acquire the ProSieben and Sat1 TV channels, a move currently under the scrutiny of the monopolies watchdog. The man may have gone, but his name clearly lives on – at least until 2015.

(see the boxed text, opposite). *BZ* should not be confused with the respected *Berliner Zeitung,* a left-leaning daily newspaper that is most widely read in the eastern districts.

Of the other broadsheets, the *Berliner Morgenpost* is especially noted for its vast classified section, while *Der Tagesspiegel* has a centre-right political orientation, a solid news and foreign section, and decent cultural coverage. At the left end of the spectrum is the *tageszeitung* or *taz,* which appeals to an intellectual crowd with its news analysis and thorough reporting. Early editions of many dailies are available after 9pm.

Die Zeit is a highbrow national weekly newspaper, with in-depth reporting on everything from politics to fashion. Germany's most widely read weekly news magazines are *Der Spiegel* and the much lighter *Focus* – both offer hard-hitting investigative journalism and a certain degree of government criticism. *Stern* bites harder on the popular nerve, and *Neon* pushes for the hipster market. *Zitty* and *Tip* are Berlin's best what's-on magazines (see p230 for more). You'll also inevitably encounter people selling *Motz* and *Der Strassenfeger,* the city's two homeless self-help publications.

English-language newspapers and magazines, mostly from the UK and the USA, are readily available in bookstores and at international newsagents. The *Ex-Berliner* is aimed primarily at the Anglophone expat community, providing a very readable perspective on the city.

TELEVISION

Germany has two national public TV channels, the ARD (Allgemeiner Rundfunk Deutschlands) and the ZDF (Zweites Deutsches Fernsehen). RBB (Rundfunk Berlin Brandenburg) is the regional public station; local cable stations include TVB, FAB and the non-commercial Offener Kanal Berlin. Generally, programming is relatively highbrow, featuring political coverage, discussion forums, foreign films and restricted advertising.

Private cable TV provides a familiar array of sitcoms, soap operas, chat shows, feature films and drama, overwhelmingly dominated by dubbed US imports. ProSieben, Sat1 and Vox generally have the best selection; Kabel Eins shows popular sitcoms (*Two and a Half Men*), classic series (*Star Trek*) and US drama hits (*Cold Case, Medium*). RTL and RTL II have more home-grown series, sitcoms and the hugely popular German version of *Pop Idol.* RTL shows the long-running cult teen soap *Gute Zeiten, Schlechte Zeiten* (GZSZ; Good Times, Bad Times), which is filmed at Studio Babelsberg in nearby Potsdam (p287).

For high-brow programming, there's Arte, a French/German coproduction. Among their specialities are 'theme nights' that mix documentaries, features and talk shows dealing with the same subject.

The channel n-tv is Germany's all-news, all-the-time channel, while DSF and EuroSport are dedicated sports channels. MTV (in German), whose German HQ is in Berlin, also owns its former German rival VIVA. Several Turkish-language channels cater for Germany's large population with roots in Turkey. Commercial breaks are frequent on all these stations. After 11pm, roughly twice a week, a handful of the private cable channels switch entirely to erotic content. English-language stations available on cable or satellite include CNN, BBC World, CNBC and MSNBC.

RADIO

Berlin has a bewildering choice of radio stations, many modelled on the US format of chart pop and oldies interspersed with inane banter and adverts. One of the most popular stations is Radio Eins (FM 95.8), which has high-quality topical programming. Jazz fiends should check out Jazzradio at 101.9, while classical music rules Klassik-Radio at 101.3. For cool indie tunes, often by unsigned bands from around Europe, dial in to Motor FM at 100.6. InfoRadio at 93.1 has an all-news format, including live interviews. The BBC broadcasts on 90.2.

WEB

As you'd expect from a city with such a strong alternative scene, independent media has a considerable presence here, and all kinds of small-scale publications hit the streets and the web every week, covering themes from the political to the cultural and the very marginal. Internet blogging has also taken off as a logical continuation of this trend. See our Top Picks for the best blogs from the city, right.

LANGUAGE

Only a small number of Berliners speak the pure Berlinisch dialect, but the strong regional accent is also very distinctive. Listen out for *ge* pronounced as a soft *je*, the soft *ch* as a hard *ck*, or *das* as *det*; reading the phonetic spelling in Berlin cartoons will give you an idea of how it works. Slang words abound for just about anything (*Olle* is a woman, *Molle* or *Pulle* a beer, *Stampe* a pub) and almost all of the public buildings in the city have nicknames – only a true Berliner would think to call the Haus der Kulturen der Welt (p78) the 'Pregnant Oyster', for example.

top picks

BLOGS

- Berlin Reified (http://reified.typepad.com) – food, design and life in the city
- Berlin Unlike (www.berlin.unlike.net) – hip, up-to-the-minute, essential
- Expat Blog (www.expat-blog.com) – gateway to Berlin bloggers
- I Heart Berlin (www.iheartberlin.de) – a love story
- Modekultur (www.modekultur.info) – anything you ever wanted to know about Berlin fashion

In 1998 Berlin, along with the rest of Germany, had to adapt to a thorough spelling reform, standardising some of the quirks and inconsistencies in the German language. Surprisingly for such an opinionated bunch, most Berliners took the changes in their stride, but many other states organised citizens' petitions in protest. In the end, though, the reform prevailed, and from 2005 the new orthography became the official standard, with barely a peep of complaint to be heard. For more information about the spelling changes visit www.neue-rechtschreibung.de, in German.

See the Language chapter (p318) for useful phrases in German. For a free, basic online course in German, go to www.deutsch-lernen.com.

NEIGHBOURHOODS

top picks

- **East Side Gallery** (p149) Open-air gallery on the longest surviving stretch of the Berlin Wall.
- **Gendarmenmarkt** (p86) Architecture in harmony on Berlin's most beautiful square.
- **Holocaust Memorial** (p82) Accessible yet disorienting football-field-sized labyrinth of grey concrete stelae.
- **Jüdisches Museum** (p142) A chronicle of trials and triumphs in German Jewish history.
- **Pergamonmuseum** (p88) Pirate's chest of treasure from ancient civilisations.
- **Reichstag Dome** (p75) Bird's-eye Berlin from atop Norman Foster's masterpiece.
- **Schloss Charlottenburg** (p122) Prussian palace dripping with precious art and artefacts.
- **Sony Center** (p111) Eye-popping 'tented' complex on the site of the former Berlin Wall.
- **Unter den Linden** (p84) Phalanx of blockbuster sights peels away the many layers of Berlin history.

What's your recommendation? www.lonelyplanet.com/berlin

NEIGHBOURHOODS

Built upon the ashes of WWII, Berlin is a modern, sprawling and well-structured mosaic of distinctive neighbourhoods that locals affectionately call *Kieze*. Fortunately, the areas of greatest visitor interest are fairly well defined and the flat terrain and superb public transport make it easy to cover a lot of ground quickly.

'To truly experience Berlin you need to venture off the tourist grid'

The central district is Mitte, a high-octane cocktail of culture, architecture and commerce and home to such blockbuster attractions as the Brandenburger Tor (Brandenburg Gate), the Holocaust Memorial, the Reichstag, Gendarmenmarkt and Museumsinsel (Museum Island). The grand boulevard Unter den Linden recalls the glory days of royal Prussia, while Friedrichstrasse is a swanky artery of shops, hotels, restaurants and theatres. At first, Alexanderplatz further east comes across as a showcase of socialist architecture, with the Fernsehturm (TV Tower) as its most prominent feature. But dig a little deeper and you'll find evidence of the city's modest 13th-century beginnings in the maze of quiet streets southwest of the square. To the north is the Scheunenviertel, the old Jewish quarter, anchored by the Hackesche Höfe (courtyards) and jammed with bars and restaurants, leading galleries and urban designer boutiques. Oranienburger Strasse is the most tourist-intensive strip here, but the side streets yield plenty of authentic experiences.

To truly experience Berlin, though, you need to venture off the tourist grid. North of Mitte, largely residential Prenzlauer Berg may have surrendered completely to gentrification but is a joy to explore thanks to a vibrant cafe culture, 19th-century townhouses lining leafy avenues, a bevy of owner-run boutiques and bars ranging from saucy to sedate.

South of Mitte, Kreuzberg is one of Berlin's most diverse and vibrant neighbourhoods. The eastern section is the hub of the city's vast Turkish population and the place to get low-down and dirty in the bars and clubs along Schlesische Strasse, Oranienstrasse and around Kottbusser Tor. By contrast, western Kreuzberg around Bergmannstrasse gives off more of a boho-chic vibe. Checkpoint Charlie and the Jüdisches Museum (Jewish Museum) are the district's must-do attractions.

Across the river, Friedrichshain is an eccentric cauldron of Stalinist architecture, gritty squat-style bars and clubs, polished cocktail culture and chilly beach bars. The main sight here is East Side Gallery, the longest surviving stretch of the Berlin Wall. In coming years, though, the face of Friedrichshain will likely change forever with the construction of mostly office buildings along the river bank in what's been dubbed Mediaspree.

East of the Brandenburger Tor, Mitte segues into Tiergarten, a huge park and fantastic urban playground, which rubs up against the Potsdamer Platz quarter, the city's most ambitious post-reunification building project. Across Potsdamer Strasse you spot the oddly shaped Philharmonie concert hall, a cornerstone of the Kulturforum museum complex with world-class art by all major players since the 13th century.

Tiergarten links Mitte with Charlottenburg, the heart of Western Berlin, with great shopping along Kurfürstendamm and the royal splendour of Schloss Charlottenburg. Much of Charlottenburg is upmarket residential, as is nearby Schöneberg, which also has Berlin's oldest gay and lesbian quarter around Nollendorfplatz.

Berlin's outer areas are grouped together by compass direction. The Northern Suburbs (Pankow and Wedding) have a largely working-class flavour and are thin on sights. Spandau in the West is worth visiting for its amazing 16th-century fortress and historic old town, while Dahlem and Zehlendorf are upscale residential areas hemmed by large swathes of forest and dappled with palaces and museums.

The Southern Suburbs include gritty Neukölln and Treptow and green and historic Köpenick. Vast forests, royal palaces, swimming lakes, historic buildings and fancy villas are the main draws. The Eastern Suburbs of Lichtenberg-Hohenschönhausen and Marzahn-Hellersdorf clearly bear the stamp of socialism and, save for a few historical German Democratic Republic (GDR) sites, are fairly devoid of visitor appeal.

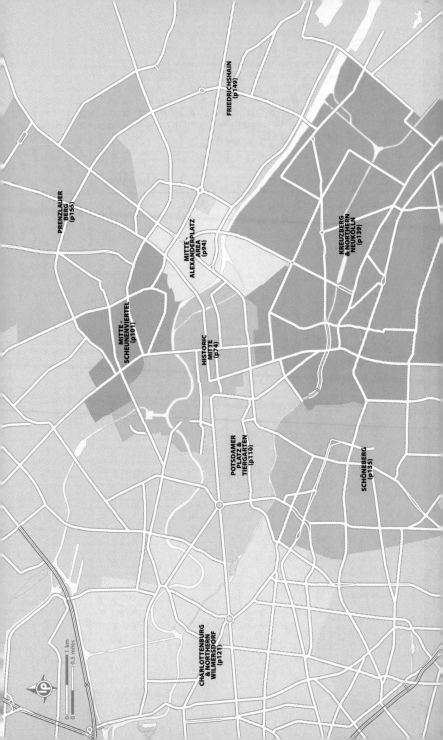

FRIEDRICHSHAIN (p149)

PRENZLAUER
BERG (p155)

MITTE-
ALEXANDERPLATZ
AREA
(p94)

MITTE-
SCHEUNENVIERTEL
(p101)

HISTORIC
MITTE
(p74)

KREUZBERG
& NORTHERN
NEUKÖLLN
(p139)

POTSDAMER
PLATZ &
TIERGARTEN
(p110)

SCHÖNEBERG
(p135)

CHARLOTTENBURG
& NORTHERN
WILMERSDORF
(p121)

0   1 km
0   0.5 miles

ITINERARY BUILDER

Berlin is your oyster and you won't have any trouble filling your days with fun things to do. To help you plan your adventure, this handy Itinerary Builder lists our picks of recommended sights, shops, restaurants and night-time venues in seven of the city's key neighbourhoods. For the purposes of this table, Schöneberg is included in Charlottenburg & Northern Wilmersdorf or Potsdamer Platz & Tiergarten and the outer suburbs are not included. And for good measure, we've also thrown in a few ideas for exploring Berlin's 'underbelly'. Happy trails!

AREA	ACTIVITIES	Sights	Shopping
	Historic Mitte	Reichstag (p75)	Dussmann – Das Kulturkaufhaus (p183)
		Neues Museum (p90)	Galeries Lafayette (p184)
		Sammlung Boros (p79)	Contemporary Fine Arts (p190)
	Mitte – Scheunenviertel	Neue Synagoge (p102)	Bonbonmacherei (p186)
		Museum für Naturkunde (p103)	Neugerriemschneider (p190)
		Gedenkstätte Berliner Mauer (p106)	Lala Berlin (p185)
	Potsdamer Platz & Tiergarten	Gemäldegalerie (p115)	Potsdamer Platz Arkaden (p187)
		Sony Center (p111)	
		Topographie des Terrors (p114)	
	Charlottenburg & Northern Wilmersdorf	Schloss Charlottenburg (p122)	KaDeWe (p189)
		Kaiser-Wilhelm-Gedächtniskirche (p127)	Winterfeldtmarkt (p189)
		Museum Berggruen (p123)	Türkenmarkt (p192)
	Kreuzberg	Jüdisches Museum (p142)	Space Hall (p193)
		Checkpoint Charlie (p144)	Marheineke Markthalle (p192)
		Bergmannstrasse (p144)	Berlinomat (p194)
	Friedrichshain	East Side Gallery (p149)	Flohmarkt am Boxhagener Platz (p194)
		Café Sybille (p152)	Grosser Antikmarkt am Ostbahnhof (p193)
		Karl-Marx-Allee (p152)	
	Prenzlauer Berg	Kollwitzplatz (p158)	Flohmarkt am Mauerpark (p196)
		Kulturbrauerei (p158)	VEB Orange (p196)
		Jüdischer Friedhof (p158)	Flagshipstore (p195)

HOW TO USE THIS TABLE

The table below allows you to plan a day's worth of activities in any area of the city. Simply select which area you wish to explore, and then mix and match from the corresponding listings to build your day. The first item in each cell represents a well-known highlight of the area, while the other items are more off-the-beaten-track gems.

Eating	Drinking/ Nightlife/Arts	Offbeat & Off the Beaten Path
Cookies Cream (p201) Fischers Fritz (p200) Ishin (p202)	Cookies (p233) Konzerthaus Berlin (p251) Tausend (p221)	Berliner Medizinhistorisches Museum (p80) Tadschikische Teestube (p221) Automobil Forum Unter den Linden (p93)
Schwarzwaldstuben (p203) Reinstoff (p203) Chi Sing (p203)	Babylon Berlin (p252) Clärchens Ballhaus (p232) Chamäleon Variété (p238)	Bonbonmacherei (p186) Volksbühne am Rosa-Luxemburg-Platz (p255) Ramones Museum (p105)
Edd's (p208) Facil (p205) Balikci Ergün (p205)	Berliner Philharmonie (p250) Arsenal (p252) Café am Neuen See (p223)	Kumpelnest 3000 (p225) GDR border watchtower (p179) Panoramapunkt (p113)
Good Friends (p206) Moon Thai (p206) Duke (p206)	Deutsche Oper (p253) Schleusenkrug (p207) Bar Jeder Vernunft (p238)	Käthe-Kollwitz-Museum (p129) Rogacki (p208) Hautnah (p188)
Café Jacques (p210) Lavanderia Vecchia (p210) Henne (p212)	Watergate (p235) Möbel Olfe (p226) Schlesische Strasse (p232)	Badeschiff (p147) Madame Claude (p225) Gruselkabinett Berlin (p146)
Schneeweiss (p214) Vineria del Este (p215) Schwarzer Hahn (p214)	Berghain/Panorama Bar (p232) Suicide Circus (p235) CSA (p226)	Salon zur Wilden Renate (p234) Märchenbrunnen (p153) Monster Ronson's Ichiban Karaoke (p227)
W-Imbiss (p217) Oderquelle (p216) Si An (p217)	Prater (p228) White Trash Fast Food (p238) Klub der Republik (p227)	Mauerpark (p159) Zum Schmutzigen Hobby (p260) Deck 5 (p224)

CENTRAL BERLIN

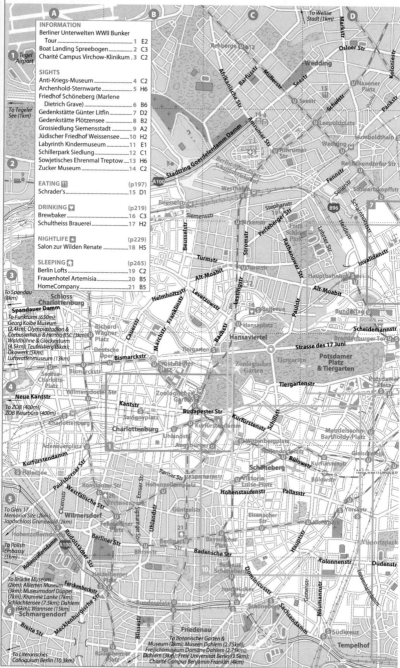

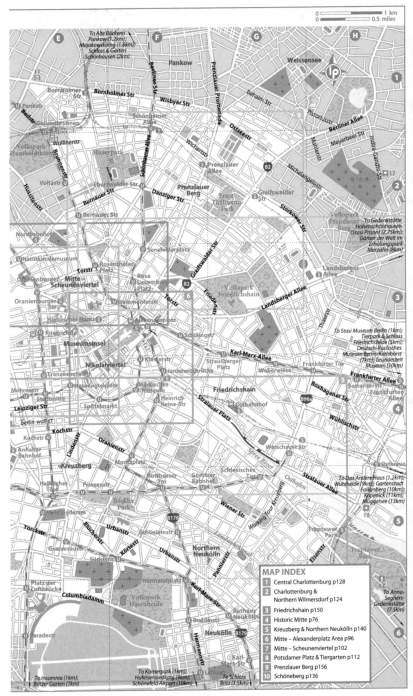

MAP INDEX

Drinking p220; Eating p200; Shopping p182; Sleeping p268

Even cynics can't deny it: Historic Mitte has magnetism. Once trapped behind the Berlin Wall, the city centre – literally called Mitte or 'Middle' – is the glamorous heart of Berlin, a cocktail of culture, commerce and history. This is where you'll likely concentrate your sight-seeing time, where you come to play and learn, to admire and marvel, and to be astounded and bewildered.

Berlin's most famous and beloved landmarks are here, lined up like Prussian soldiers for inspection along the elegant boulevard called Unter den Linden. This ribbon of mostly baroque beauties and haughty neoclassical edifices stretches from the Brandenburger Tor to the giant treasure chest of the Museumsinsel. Granted, souvenir shops, coffee chains and car showrooms add an element of tackiness, but keep your gaze up and it's not hard to recognise the boulevard as an architectural *Gesamtkunstwerk* (total work of art).

Alas, it's pretty dead after dark, but fortunately there is at least some action along Friedrich-strasse, which bisects it. Once dead-ending at Checkpoint Charlie, this strip has, since reuni-fication, reclaimed its role as a trendy dining and imbibing hub, especially the theatre district north of Unter den Linden, dubbed SoTo (south of Torstrasse) by the local press.

Until 1989 the Berlin Wall used to sully the view of the Brandenburger Tor from the western side. Several memorials recall this period of the city's division and honour its many victims. Northwest of here, Berlin's new government quarter, created in the '90s, unfolds along a bend in the Spree River. It's presided over by the city's first central train station, the Hauptbahnhof, which is a dominant gleaming presence on the river's north bank. Since it opened in 2006, the surrounding area has seen a lot of construction, mostly in the form of hotels. In the coming years, an entire new quarter will spring up in the wasteland along Heidestrasse north of the station. Google 'Masterplan Heidestrasse' and you'll see what's in the pipeline.

Changes have been afoot on Unter den Linden, too. The dust has finally settled near Pariser Platz where the new Brandenburger Tor U-Bahn station went online in 2009. At Friedrich-strasse, a bland office-residential-retail behemoth pretentiously named Upper Eastside Berlin has replaced the GDR-era Hotel Unter den Linden, where comrades used to camp out. On Museumsinsel, the David Chipperfield–designed Neues Museum (New Museum) has been raking in the accolades and awards since its opening in late 2009. And across the street, the Humboldt-Box provides a preview of the controversial construction of a replica of the Hohenzollern palace that stood on Schlossplatz for 500 years. The GDR demolished it in 1951 and replaced it with the Palast der Republik, which in turn was demolished a few years ago. Construction of the doppelgänger Schloss is expected to begin in 2014. Historic Mitte is still making history.

top picks

HISTORIC MITTE

- Holocaust Memorial (p82)
- Gendarmenmarkt (p86)
- Neues Museum (p90)
- Pergamonmuseum (p88)
- Reichstag (p75)
- Sammlung Boros (p79)

REICHSTAG & GOVERNMENT QUARTER

Berlin's government quarter snuggles neatly into the Spreebogen, a horseshoe-shaped bend in the Spree River. Its historic anchor is the Reichstag (parliament building), which once rubbed against the western side of the Berlin Wall and is now part of the Band des Bundes (Band of Federal Buildings), a series of glass-and-concrete buildings symbolically linking the former West and East Berlins across the Spree. North of the river looms the solar-panel-clad Hauptbahnhof (main train station).

Not a single structure had to be torn down to make room for the new power district. That job had already been done by the Nazis, who demolished an entire high-end residential quarter to make room for a massive – though thankfully never realised – domed Great Hall capable of holding up to 180,000 people (see the boxed text, p57).

Bus 100, 200 and the Tegel airport–bound express bus, TXL, run along Unter den Linden to Alexanderplatz.

S-Bahn S1 and S2/25 stop at Brandenburger Tor and at Friedrichstrasse.

Tram Museumsinsel is served by the M1 coming from Prenzlauer Berg via Hackescher Markt.

U-Bahn Stadtmitte (U2, U6), Französische Strasse (U6) or Hausvogteiplatz (U2) are all convenient for Gendarmenmarkt. For Unter den Linden, get off at Brandenburger Tor (U55) or Französische Strasse (U6).

REICHSTAG Map pp76-7

☎ 2273 2152; www.bundestag.de; Platz der Republik 1; admission free; ⏱ lift to dome 8am-midnight, last entry 10pm; Ⓤ Bundestag, 🚌 100

The Reichstag will likely give you more flashbacks to high-school history than any other Berlin landmark. This grand old building by Paul Wallot (1894) is where the German parliament, the Bundestag, has been hammering out its policies since 1999. This followed a total makeover by architectural top dog Lord Norman Foster, who preserved only the building's historic shell while adding the striking glass dome which is accessible by lift. There's almost always a long queue waiting to catch it, though, so budget some extra time – it's worth it, especially in good weather. Once at the top, take in the 360-degree views from the terrace, then pick up a free audioguide and follow the spiralling rampway inside the dome while listening to commentary about the building, parliament and famous Berlin sights.

Queues are shortest early in the day or at night. You can skip 'em altogether if you're disabled, happen to have a kid in a stroller, are on an organised tour or make reservations at the Dachgartenrestaurant (☎ 226 2990) on top. In that case, proceed straight to the left entrance. Other areas of the Reichstag, including the Plenary Hall, may only be seen on guided tours or during lectures, which are usually in German and must be booked ahead of time, in writing – the website has details.

HAMBURGER BAHNHOF – MUSEUM OF CONTEMPORARY ART Map pp76-7

☎ 3978 3411; www.hamburgerbahnhof.de; Invalidenstrasse 50-51; adult/concession/child

under 18 €8/4/free; ⏱ 10am-6pm Tue-Fri, 11am-8pm Sat, 11am-6pm Sun; Ⓤ Naturkundemuseum, Ⓤ 🚉 Hauptbahnhof, 🚌 147, 245

The collection here at Berlin's premier contemporary art museum picks up where Neue Nationalgalerie (p115) leaves off, ie roughly around 1950. There are key works by Nam June Paik, Wolf Vostell and other Fluxus artists as well as plenty of American pop art, including Andy Warhol's famous portraits of Marilyn Monroe and Mao Zedong. Anselm Kiefer and Cy Twombly get quite a bit of play but not as much as the ultimate artistic boundary-pusher Joseph Beuys, whose works fill the entire ground floor of the western wing. Pride of place goes to the sculpture *The End of the Twentieth Century*.

Just as eye-catching as the art is the exhibit space itself, converted from a 19th-century train station. Architect Josef Paul Kleihues kept the elegant historic facade, which at night is bathed in the mystical blues and greens of a Dan Flavin light installation. The interior, though, was gutted and turned into modern minimalist galleries that orbit the lofty central hall, with its exposed iron girders, like chapels in a cathedral.

In 2004 the museum expanded into the adjacent Rieckhallen, a 300m-long warehouse where it shows changing exhibits from the collection of German industrialist Friedrich Christian Flick, who has a penchant for Bruce Naumann, Paul McCarthy, Rodney Graham and Jason Rhoades. There are also works by those who pushed the artistic envelope earlier in the 20th century – among them Sol Lewitt, Marcel Duchamp, Nam June Paik and Sigmar Polke.

Wrap up with a browse through the well-stocked bookshop or a coffee in

top picks

KEY CANVASSES AT HAMBURGER BAHNHOF

- Andy Warhol *Chairman Mao* (1975)
- Anselm Kiefer *Volkszählung* (Census, 1991)
- Joseph Beuys *Strassenbahnhaltestelle* (Streetcar Stop, 1989)
- Robert Rauschenberg *Pink Door* (1954)
- Roy Lichtenstein *Reflections on the Artist's Studio* (1989)

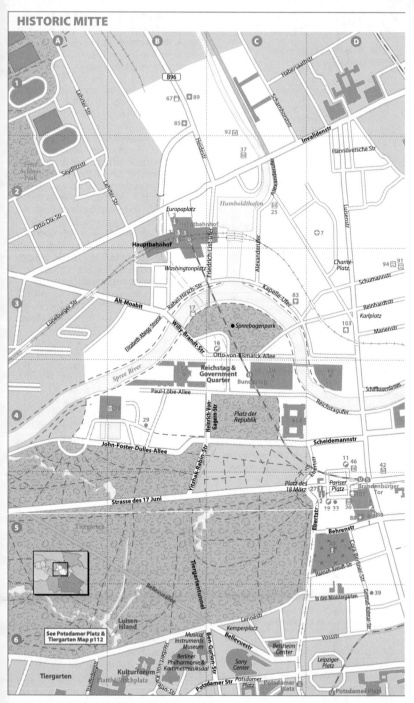

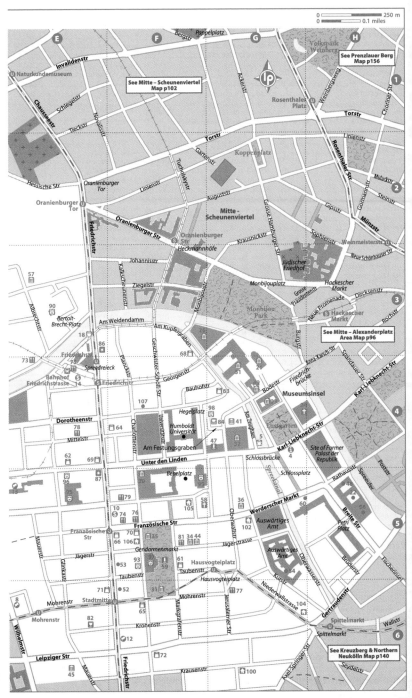

See Mitte – Scheunenviertel Map p102

See Prenzlauer Berg Map p156

See Mitte – Alexanderplatz Area Map p96

See Kreuzberg & Northern Neukölln Map p140

HISTORIC MITTE

Berlin's smartest museum cafe, Sarah Wiener
im Hamburger Bahnhof (p201).

BUNDESKANZLERAMT Map pp76-7
Willy-Brandt-Strasse 1; ☽ **closed to public;**
🚇 **Reichstag,** 🚌 **100**
Germany's 'White House', the Federal
Chancellery is a sparkling, modern design
by Axel Schultes and Charlotte Frank.
The 'H'-shaped compound consists of
two long office blocks flanking a central
white cube where current Chancellor

Angela Merkel keeps her desk. Eduardo
Chillida's rusted-steel Berlin sculpture
graces the eastern forecourt. The best
views of the entire building are from the
Moltkebrücke (bridge) or the northern
river promenade.

HAUS DER KULTUREN DER WELT
Map pp76-7
☎ 397 870; www.hkw.de; John-Foster-Dulles-Allee
10; admission varies; ☽ 11am-7pm Wed-Mon;
Ⓤ Bundestag, 🚌 100

IN AWE OF HISTORY

Home of the German parliament from 1894 to 1933 and again since 1999, the hulking Reichstag has witnessed many milestones in German history. On 9 November 1918, after the end of WWI and the abdication of the Prussian Kaiser, parliament member Philipp Scheidemann proclaimed the German republic from one of its windows. When fire mysteriously broke out in 1933, the Nazis used the event as a pretext to seize dictatorial powers. A dozen years later, victorious Red Army troops raised the Soviet flag on the bombed-out building, which stood damaged and empty on the western side of the Berlin Wall throughout the Cold War. In the '80s, megastars including David Bowie, Pink Floyd and Michael Jackson performed concerts on the lawn in front of the building. When word got out that fans from East Berlin had gathered on the other side, the stars turned some of the loudspeakers around, thus provoking an international incident!

Fortunately, the Wall collapsed soon after, paving the way to German reunification, which was enacted here in 1990. Five years later the Reichstag made headlines once again when the artist couple Christo and Jeanne-Claude wrapped the massive structure in 100,000 sq metres of silvery fabric. It had taken an act of the German parliament to approve the project in 1994 and it was intended to mark the end of the Cold War and the beginning of another era. For two weeks starting in late June, visitors from around the world flocked to Berlin to admire this unique sight. Shortly after the fabric came down, Lord Norman Foster set to work. Now the dome has become a symbol of the New Berlin.

Originally a congress hall, the House of World Cultures is now an exhibit space and cultural forum that presents performances, readings, lectures, concerts and other artistic endeavours from around the world, especially from non-European cultures. It was designed by Hugh Stubbins and was the American contribution to the 1957 architectural exhibition Interbau. The extravagant building is topped by a gravity-defying parabolic roof that inspired Berliners to give it the nickname 'pregnant oyster'. Alas, the architect's vision outdistanced the technology of the time, causing the roof to partly collapse in 1980. The curvaceous reflecting pool features Henry Moore's sculpture *Large Divided Oval: Butterfly*, whose outline echoes the building's.

Computerised chime concerts ring out at noon and 6pm daily from the 68-bell, black-marble and bronze carillon (Map pp76-7; www.carillon-berlin.de) – the largest in Europe – outside the hall. On Sundays at 3pm from May to September (2pm in December), a carillonneur gives live concerts.

PAUL-LÖBE-HAUS Map pp76-7

☎ 2270; www.bundestag.de; Konrad-Adenauer-Strasse; ⊗ closed to public; ⊕ Bundestag, ⊕ ⊛ Hauptbahnhof

Part of the Band des Bundes, the glass-and-concrete Paul-Löbe-Haus houses offices for the Bundestag's parliamentary committees. From above it looks like a double-sided comb and on the inside there's an atrium long enough to be a bowling alley for giants. It's linked by a double footbridge to the Marie-Elisabeth-Lüders-Haus (below) across the Spree in a visual symbol of reunification.

MARIE-ELISABETH-LÜDERS-HAUS
Map pp76-7

☎ 2270; www.bundestag.de; Schiffbauerdamm; ⊗ closed to public; ⊕ Bundestag, ⊕ ⊛ Hauptbahnhof

Across the river, on the former East Berlin side, the Marie-Elisabeth-Lüders-Haus houses the parliamentary library. Its most eye-catching design elements are the massive tapered stairway, a flat roofline jutting out like a springboard over a plaza, and a cube with giant circular windows containing the library reading room. The library itself is not open to the public but two art spaces are: the *Wall Installation* by Ben Wagin (see the Berlin Wall Cycling Tour, p178) and the Kunst-Raum (☎ 2273 2027; admission free; ⊗ 11am-5pm Tue-Sun), below the staircase, which presents contemporary art infused with a political slant.

SAMMLUNG BOROS Map pp76-7

☎ 2759 4065; www.sammlung-boros.de; Reinhardtstrasse 20; adult/concession €10/6; ⊗ 10am-5.30pm Sat & Sun; ⊕ Oranienburger Tor, ⊕ ⊛ Friedrichstrasse

The vibe of war, vegetables and whips still hangs over the 80 rooms of this monstrous Nazi bunker-turned-shining beacon of art thanks to advertising guru Christian Boros. Boros collects bold artists that are currently writing art history – Olafur Eliasson, Elmgreen & Dragset, Damien Hirst, Sarah Lucas, Wolfgang Tilmanns, and so on. Since June 2008 he has shared a selection of his treasures with the public in a war-scarred civilian air-raid shelter that preserves the original fittings, pipes, steel doors and vents. A completely new exhibit is mounted every two years (next in 2012). Make online reservations as early as possible to join the excellent 90-minute tours; alternatively show up spontaneously and hope for no-shows. Tours starting at 11.30am, 1.30pm and 3.30pm are in English.

During the tour you'll also pick up fascinating nuggets about the structure itself. Built to shelter 2000, its dank rooms crammed in twice as many people during the heaviest air raids towards the end of the war. The Soviets briefly used it as a POW prison before it assumed a more benign use as a fruit and vegetable storeroom in GDR times (hence the nickname 'Banana Bunker'). In the 1990s, the claustrophobic warren saw some of Berlin's naughtiest techno raves and fetish parties; Boros finally snapped it up in 2003.

BERLINER MEDIZINHISTORISCHES MUSEUM Map pp76-7

☎ 450 536 156; www.bmm.charite.de; Charité Hospital Mitte, Charitéplatz 1; adult/concession/ family €5/2.50/10; ⏱ 10am-5pm Tue, Thu, Fri & Sun, 10am-7pm Wed & Sat; ◉ ◉ Hauptbahnhof Rudolf Virchow (1821–1902) was a famous doctor, researcher and professor whose pathology collection forms the basis of the Berlin Medical History Museum. Think of it as a 3-D medical textbook on human disease and deformities. Monstrous tumours, inflamed organs and a colon the size of an elephant's trunk are all pickled in formalin and neatly displayed in glass jars. If you think this is bad, skip the last row, which features two-headed babies and deformed foetuses not even the makers of *Alien* could imagine. Definitely not for the squeamish. In fact, anyone under 16 must be accompanied by an adult.

Exhibits on the 4th floor are a lot less grisly and basically focus on medical conditions and milestones in dealing with or treating them, from the birthing chair of the 19th century to the iron lung of the 1950s, to organ transplants of today. Changing exhibits are shown on the 2nd floor. Also have a quick look at Virchow's lecture hall – a preserved ruin – that is used for special events.

PRIVATE ART GOES PUBLIC

Until the 19th century, art used to be collected and viewed only by royalty and aristocrats and so it was no small sensation when King Friedrich Wilhelm III ordered the construction of Berlin's first public museum, the Altes Museum (p89), which opened on Museumsinsel in 1830. These days, a new trend has emerged that sees private collectors sharing their precious collections with the public. In Berlin, the most famous of these is the Sammlung Boros (p79) but there are actually a few more worth checking out:

Sammlung Hoffmann (Map pp102-3; ☎ 2849 9120; www.sammlung-hoffmann.de; Sophienstrasse 21; tours €8; ⏱ 11am-4pm Sat by appointment only; ◉ Weinmeisterstrasse) In 1997, long before it became fashionable, Erika and Rolf Hoffmann opened up their two-storey apartment/gallery in the Sophie-Gips-Höfe (p105) for guided 90-minute tours of their contemporary art collection. Displays change every July, so you never know what you're going to see, but most likely it'll include works by Frank Stella, Michael Basquiat, AR Penck and other latter-day art luminaries.

Sammlung Haubrok (Map pp150-1; ☎ 0172-210 9525; Strausberger Platz 19; admission free; ⏱ noon-6pm Sat & by appointment; ◉ Strausberger Platz) His first purchase was a painting by Raoul de Keyser in 1988. Since then, investment consultant Axel Haubrok has amassed some 500 works, many by such leading conceptual artists as Jonathan Monk, Christopher Williams and Martin Boyce. Other key works are Gregor Schneider's *Das Schlafzimmer* (The Bedroom) and *This is Propaganda* by Tino Sehgal. Selections from the collection are showcased in four shows per year on the 2nd floor of the GDR-era Henselmann-Tower, the former Haus des Kindes (p154) on monumental Karl-Marx-Allee.

Me Collectors Room (Map pp102-3; ☎ 8600 8510; www.me-berlin.com; Auguststrasse 68; adult/concession €6/4; ⏱ noon-6pm Tue-Sun; ◉ Oranienburger Strasse) Thomas Olbricht, a doctor of endocrinology, collects works that reflect the existential themes of death, transience and sexuality, often in a slightly provocative and irreverent fashion. There are big names like Cindy Sherman and Gerhard Richter but also lesser known artists such as Rachel Goodyear and Jonas Burgert. Upstairs is Olbricht's own *Wunderkammer* (Cabinet of Curiosities), a type of exhibit popular in the Renaissance and baroque periods.

BRANDENBURGER TOR & AROUND

Here's a trivia question for you: who said 'Mr Gorbachev – tear down this wall!'? Answer: former US president Ronald Reagan, during a speech in 1987, with the Brandenburger Tor trapped behind the Berlin Wall as a backdrop. Two years later, the Wall was history and the famous gate went from symbol of division to symbol of a reunited Germany. Since then, Pariser Platz, the former wasteland east of the gate, has resumed its historic role as the capital's 'reception room' and is framed by embassies, banks and hotels.

BRANDENBURGER TOR Map pp76-7

Pariser Platz; admission free; ⊙ 24hr;
ⓢ ⓡ Brandenburger Tor, ⓐ 100, TXL
Where were you when the Berlin Wall fell? For tens of thousands the answer is 'at the Brandenburg Gate'. Who can forget the images of the happy throngs sitting atop the hated barrier, sharing champagne and shaking hands with border guards? Amid cheers and champagne, the Cold War was over and a new era of hope and freedom began. Since that day – 9 November 1989 – the symbol of division has epitomised German reunification.

Carl Gotthard Langhans looked to the Acropolis in Athens for inspiration for this elegant triumphal arch, which came online in 1791 as the royal city gate. If you look closely, you'll see that the columns are not evenly spaced. Only the royal family was allowed to enter through the extra-wide centre section. Its entourage used the adjacent walkways, while common folk had to make do with the narrow outer ones.

The gate is topped by the Quadriga, Johann Gottfried Schadow's sculpture of the winged Goddess of Victory piloting a chariot drawn by four horses. After trouncing Prussia in 1806, Napoleon kidnapped the lady and held her hostage in Paris until she was freed by a gallant Prussian general in 1815.

The neatly restored gate is now the backdrop for raucous New Year's Eve parties, concerts, festivals and mega-events. Platz des 18 März, the little square just west of the gate, commemorates the victims of the failed bourgeois revolution staged on 18 March 1848 (p25).

There's a nondenominational meditation room, the Raum der Stille, in the north wing and a tourist office (p316) in the south wing.

PARISER PLATZ Map pp76-7

ⓢ ⓡ Brandenburger Tor, ⓐ 100, TXL
The Brandenburger Tor stands sentinel over this elegant square, which was completely flattened in WWII, then spent the Cold War trapped just east of the Berlin Wall. Look around now: embassies, banks and a luxury hotel have snapped up the city's priciest real estate and hired top architects to rebuild in style and from the ground up.

California-based deconstructivist Frank Gehry, for instance, masterminded the DZ Bank (Map pp76-7; admission free; www.axica.de; ⊙ 8am-7pm Mon-Fri) at No 3, which packs a visual punch past those bland doors. You'll only get as far as the foyer but that's enough for a glimpse at the atrium, with its bizarre free-form sculpture vaguely reminiscent of a fish but actually a conference room! Next door is the final addition to Pariser Platz, the US Embassy (Map pp76-7) by Gehry's LA colleagues at Moore, Ruble and Yudell, which opened in 2008.

The only building on Pariser Platz with a glass facade is the Akademie der Künste (Map pp76-7; ☎ 200 570; www.adk.de, in German) at No 4, designed by Günter Behnisch. The Academy of Arts is one of Berlin's oldest cultural institutions, founded by King Friedrich I in 1696 as the Prussian Academy of Arts. Come here for readings, lectures, workshops and exhibits.

THE TRACKS OF DEATH

The Holocaust Memorial may be big, central and artistic, but it's another commemorative site that is at least as poignant in its simplicity. Gleis 17 (platform 17; off Map pp72-3) is in the S-Bahn station Grunewald, a mere 20-minute train ride away on the S7. It was from these tracks in this leafy, villa-studded suburb that 186 trains left for Theresienstadt, Riga, Lodz and Auschwitz, carrying their Jewish cargo like cattle to the slaughter. More than 50,000 Jewish Berliners were deported between 1941 and 1945; nearly every day hundreds of them stood on this very platform waiting for the last train they would ever take. In their honour, iron plaques recording the departure dates, numbers of people and destinations of the trains have been fastened to the edge of the platform paralleling some 100m of the rusting tracks. It's quiet here, with only the trees rustling in the breeze, but the silence speaks loudly.

The Academy rubs up against the venerable Hotel Adlon, Berlin's poshest caravanserai. In 1932 the movie *Grand Hotel* was filmed here, starring Greta 'I vont to be alone' Garbo as a washed-up ballerina. Now called the Adlon Kempinski (see p268 for the review), the building is a near-replica of the 1907 original and is once again a favourite haunt of politicians, diplomats and celebrities. Remember Michael Jackson dangling his baby out of the window? It happened at the Adlon.

MUSEUM THE KENNEDYS Map pp76-7
☎ 2065 3570; www.thekennedys.de; Pariser Platz 4a; adult/concession €7/3.50; ☯ 10am-6pm; ⊕ ⊛ Brandenburger Tor, ⬛ 100, TXL

Next to the French Embassy, this small museum is an intimate, non-political exhibit set up like a walk-through family photo album. The spotlight, of course, is on John F Kennedy, who has held a special place in German hearts since his 'Ich bin ein Berliner' speech at the height of the Cold War (there's a video of the speech playing in the back). Besides pictures there are various relics, including scribbled notes, JKF's crocodile-leather briefcase, Jackie's Persian lamb pillbox hat and a hilarious *Superman* comic-book edition starring the president.

HOLOCAUST MEMORIAL Map pp76-7
Denkmal für die Ermordeten Juden Europas, Memorial to the Murdered Jews of Europe; ☎ 200 7660; www.holocaust-mahnmal.de; Cora-Berliner-Strasse 1; admission free; ☯ memorial 24hr, Ort der Information 10am-8pm Tue-Sun Apr-Sep, to 7pm Oct-Mar; ⊕ ⊛ Brandenburger Tor, ⬛ 100, 200, M41, TXL

THE BERLIN WALL

It's more than a tad ironic that Berlin's most popular tourist attraction is one that no longer exists. For 28 years the Berlin Wall, the most potent symbol of the Cold War, divided not only a city but the world.

The Beginning

Construction began shortly after midnight on 13 August 1961, when thousands of East German soldiers and police rolled out miles of barbed wire that would soon be replaced with prefab concrete slabs. All of a sudden, streets were cut in two, vehicle and U-Bahn traffic between the city's halves was halted and East Germans, including commuters, were no longer allowed to travel to West Berlin.

The Wall was a desperate measure launched by the German Democratic Republic (GDR) government to stop the sustained brain and brawn drain the GDR had experienced since its founding in 1949. Some 3.6 million people had already headed west, putting the country on the brink of economic and political collapse. The building of the wall was a shock to many. In fact, only a couple of months before that fateful August day, GDR head of state Walter Ulbricht had declared at a press conference: 'No one has the intention of constructing a wall'.

The Physical Border

Euphemistically called the 'Anti-Fascist Protection Barrier', the Wall was a 155km-long symbol of oppression that turned West Berlin into an island of democracy within a sea of socialism. Continually reinforced and refined over time, it eventually grew into a complex border-security system that included a 'death strip' riddled with trenches, floodlights, patrol roads, attack dogs, electrified alarm fences and watchtowers staffed with trigger-happy guards. A second wall, the so-called Hinterlandmauer (inner wall), hemmed in the death strip on the other side. From the West, artists tried to humanise the grey concrete scar by covering it in colourful street art. The West Berlin government erected viewing platforms, which people could climb up on and peek across into East Berlin.

Escapes

Nearly 100,000 GDR citizens tried to escape, many using spectacular contraptions like homemade balloons or U-boats. There are no exact numbers, but it is believed that hundreds died in the process of escaping by drowning, suffering fatal accidents or killing themselves when caught. More than 100 were shot and killed by border guards – the first only a few days after 13 August 1961. Guards who managed to bag a fugitive were rewarded with commendations, promotions and bonuses. The full extent of the system's cruelty became crystal clear on 17 August 1962 when 18-year-old would-be escapee Peter Fechtner was shot and wounded and then left to bleed to death as East German guards looked on.

The End

The demise of the Wall came as unexpectedly as its creation. Once again the GDR was losing its people in droves, this time via Hungary, which had opened its borders with Austria. East Germans took to the streets by the hundreds

It took 17 years of discussion, planning and construction, but on 10 May 2005 the memorial to the Jewish victims of the Nazi-planned genocide of WWII was finally dedicated. Colloquially known as the Holocaust Memorial, it was designed by New York architect Peter Eisenmann and consists of 2711 sarcophagi-like columns rising up in sombre silence from undulating ground. You're free to access this maze at any point and make your individual journey through it. For a guided tour (adult/concession €3/1.50) in English show up at 4pm on Sunday. German tours take place at 11am and 2pm on Saturday and Sunday.

For context, visit the subterranean Ort der Information (information centre; enter from Cora-Berliner-Strasse), whose exhibits will leave no one untouched. A graphic time-line of Jewish persecution during the Third Reich is followed by exhibits documenting the fates of individuals and entire families. In one darkened room, the names of the victims and the years of their birth and death are projected onto all four walls while a solemn voice reads their short biographies. It takes almost seven years to commemorate all known victims in this fashion. Audioguides are available (adult/concession €3/1.50). Last admission to the information centre is 45 minutes before closing.

HITLER'S BUNKER Map pp76-7
cnr In den Ministergärten & Gertrud-Kolmar-Strasse; ⊕ ⓡ Brandenburger Tor

Berlin was burning and Soviet tanks advancing relentlessly when Adolf Hitler holed up in his bunker in the final days of

of thousands demanding improved human rights and an end to the Sozialistische Einheitspartei Deutschlands (SED) monopoly. On 4 November 1989 at least 500,000 gathered on Alexanderplatz demanding political reform. Something had to give.

On 9 November SED spokesperson Günter Schabowski made a surprise announcement on GDR TV: all travel restrictions to the West would be lifted. Immediately. Amid scenes of wild partying and mile-long parades of GDR-made Trabant cars, the two Berlins came together again. The dismantling of the hated barrier began almost immediately.

Today
Only 1.5km of the Berlin Wall still stands as a symbol of the triumph of freedom over oppression. By now the two city halves have visually merged so perfectly that it takes a keen eye to tell East from West. Fortunately, there's help in the form of a double row of cobblestones that guides you along 5.7km of the Wall's course.

Fat Tire Bike Tours (p311) and Berlin on Bike (p311) offer guided bike trips along the course of the Wall. If you're feeling ambitious, follow all or part of the 160km-long Berliner Mauerweg (Berlin Wall Trail; www.berlin.de/mauer), a signposted walking and cycling path that follows the former border fortifications with 40 multilingual information stations posted along the way.

A high-tech way to walk the Wall is with the Mauerguide (www.mauerguide.de; adult/concession per 4hr €8/5, per 24hr €15/10), a handheld GPS-guided minicomputer that provides intelligent commentary and historic audio and video. Rental stations are at Checkpoint Charlie, Brandenburger Tor, Bernauer Strasse, East Side Gallery and on Niederkirchner Strasse.

Wall Remnants
- East Side Gallery (p149)
- Mauerpark (p159)
- Niederkirchner Strasse at Topographie Des Terrors (p114)
- Potsdamer Platz (p110)
- Watchtower Erna-Berger-Strasse (p179)

Memorials
- Checkpoint Charlie (p144)
- Gedenkstätte Weisse Kreuze (White Crosses Memorial) Installation inside the Marie-Elisabeth-Lüders-Haus (p178)
- Parlament der Bäume (Parliament of Trees; p178)

Exhibits & Museums
- Gedenkstätte Berliner Mauer (Berlin Wall Memorial; p106)
- Gedenkstätte Günter Litfin (Günter Litfin Memorial; p177)
- Mauermuseum (Wall Museum; p144)

Websites for Further Reading
www.berlin.de/mauer
www.chronik-der-mauer.de
www.stadtentwicklung.berlin.de/denkmal (go to Berliner Mauer, then click English)

IF YOU HAVE...

One Day

Get up early to beat the crowds to the dome of the Reichstag (p75), then snap a picture of the Brandenburger Tor (Brandenburg Gate; p81) and get lost in the maze of the Holocaust Memorial (p82), followed by a stroll around Potsdamer Platz (p110). Catch the U2 to Stadtmitte and ponder Cold War history at Checkpoint Charlie (p144), then double back for a dose of retail therapy in the Friedrichstadtpassagen (p87). Saunter over to Gendarmenmarkt (p86), then follow Unter den Linden (below) east towards Museumsinsel (Museum Island; p87). Postpone your date with Nefertiti until another time and instead forage for home-grown art and fashion in the Scheunenviertel (p101), then wind down the day with dinner, perhaps at Schwarzwaldstuben (p203) or Weinbar Rutz (p203). Wrap up the day hitting the planks at Clärchens Ballhaus (p232) retro ballroom.

Two Days

Follow Day One, then devote the morning to ancient treasure at the Pergamonmuseum (p88) and Queen Nefertiti at the Neues Museum (p90). Take tram M1 north to Eberswalder Strasse and launch a leisurely saunter around boho-chic Prenzlauer Berg. Swing by the Kulturbrauerei (p158), then stroll over to leafy Kollwitzplatz (p158) before resting your legs over coffee and cake at Anna Blume (p228) or a cold one at the Prater (p228) beer garden. Fuel up on naan pizza at W-Imbiss (p217) and get down to the Hackesche Höfe in time to catch the latest show at Chamäleon Variété (p238).

Three Days

On Day Three, go royal at Schloss Charlottenburg (p122), where you should miss neither the Neuer Flügel (New Wing) nor a spin around the park. In nice weather, you could follow up your visit with a boat ride (p311) back to Mitte or take the U2 to the KaDeWe (p189) to satisfy your shopping cravings. For extended retail therapy, follow Tauentzienstrasse to Kurfürstendamm, which has all the international chains. Or, if your tastes run more in the boho vein, take the M19 bus from Wittenbergplatz to Mehringdamm in Kreuzberg. Gobble a sausage at Curry 36 (p214), then poke around the little stores along Bergmannstrasse. For dinner, you could go haute at Hartmanns (p210) or local at Henne (p212) or Hasir (p211). Finish up with drinks at Freischwimmer (p225) or Club der Visionäre (p233).

WWII along with his closest aides and long-time female companion, Eva Braun. The two got married on 29 April 1945, then committed joint suicide 40 hours after the ceremony, she by popping a cyanide pill, he by putting a gun to his head. After the war, the 'suicide' bunker was blown up, flooded and filled in. Today, there's just a parking lot and an information panel (in German and English) with a diagram of the vast bunker network, technical data on how it was constructed and what happened to it after WWII.

ALONG UNTER DEN LINDEN

Unter den Linden is Berlin's most splendid boulevard, a 1.5km-long ribbon running east from Brandenburger Tor through the city's historic heart. Originally a riding path to the hunting grounds in Tiergarten, it was developed into a showpiece road in the 18th century. Grand old buildings line up here,

offering a handy introduction to Berlin's royal past.

DEUTSCHES HISTORISCHES MUSEUM & IM PEI BAU Map pp76-7

☎ 203 040; www.dhm.de; Unter den Linden 2; adult/child under 18 €6/free; ⊙ 10am-6pm; ᗺ 100, 200, TXL

If you're wondering what the Germans have been up to for the past 2000 years, take a spin around this engaging museum in the baroque Zeughaus, formerly the Prussian arsenal. Upstairs, exhibits hopscotch from the Roman occupation to the early Middle Ages to the Reformation, imperial Germany and finally WWI. The history of Nazi Germany and the Cold War era is tracked on the ground floor.

Exhibits range from the sublime to the trivial. There's splendid medieval body armour for horse and rider and a felt hat once worn by Napoleon I, but also a packing crate used by ex-Chancellor Gerhard Schröder in 1999. A startling highlight is a big globe that originally stood in the Nazi Foreign Office with bullet holes where Germany should be. In the glass-covered courtyard, Andreas Schlüter's heart-wrenching mask sculptures of dying soldiers make a strong case against war. Panelling throughout is in German and English, but the audioguide (€3) is a worthwhile investment.

High-calibre temporary exhibits take up a modern annexe designed by IM Pei and hence called IM Pei Bau (Hinter dem Giesshaus 3). Fronted by a glass spiral, it's a strikingly geometrical space, made entirely from triangles, rectangles and circles, yet imbued with a sense of lightness achieved through an airy atrium and generous use of glass.

NEUE WACHE Map pp76-7

Unter den Linden 4; admission free; ☺ 10am-6pm; 🚌 100, 200, TXL

Now an antiwar memorial, this royal guardhouse was Karl Friedrich Schinkel's first major Berlin commission, built in 1818 in the style of a Roman temple. In 1931 the inner courtyard was covered up, leaving only a circular skylight, which now spotlights Käthe Kollwitz' moving sculpture of a mother cradling her dead soldier son. Buried beneath the austere floor are the remains of an unknown soldier and a resistance fighter, as well as soil from nine European battlefields and concentration camps.

BEBELPLATZ Map pp76-7

Ⓤ Hausvogteiplatz, Französische Strasse, 🚌 100, 200, TXL

Named for August Bebel, the cofounder of the Social Democratic Party (SPD), Bebelplatz is the square where members of the Nazi German Student League held the first full-blown public book burning on 10 May 1933. Books by Bertolt Brecht, Thomas Mann, Karl Marx and other 'subversives' went up in smoke and with it the cultural greatness Germany had achieved in previous centuries. Micha Ullmann's installation Empty Library, beneath a glass pane at the square's centre, commemorates the barbaric event.

The buildings framing Bebelplatz were part of the Forum Fridericianum, a cultural extension of the city palace envisioned by Frederick the Great. Money woes meant that only some of the structures were built, including the Alte Königliche Bibliothek (p92), a palace for Fritz' brother Heinrich (now the Humboldt Universität, p92), the Staatsoper Unter den Linden (p92) and the copper-domed Sankt-Hedwigs-Kathedrale (below).

SANKT-HEDWIGS-KATHEDRALE
Map pp76-7

☎ 203 4810; www.hedwigs-kathedrale.de; Behrenstrasse 39; admission free; ☺ 10am-5pm Mon-Sat, 1-5pm Sun; Ⓤ Französische Strasse, 🚌 100, 200, TXL

Looming above Bebelplatz, this copper-domed church (1773) was designed by Knobelsdorff, inspired by the Pantheon in Rome and named for the patron saint of Silesia (a region in Poland that Frederick the Great had just conquered). It was Berlin's only Catholic house of worship until 1854. During WWII St Hedwig was a centre of Catholic resistance led by Bernard Lichtenberg, who died en route to Dachau in 1943 and is buried in the crypt. Blown to bits during WWII, the church now has a circular, modern interior, lidded by a ribbed dome and accented with Gothic sculpture and a copy of Michelangelo's Pietà.

FRIEDRICHSWERDERSCHE KIRCHE
Map pp76-7

☎ 2090 5577; www.smb.spk-berlin.de; Werderscher Markt; admission free; ☺ 10am-6pm; Ⓤ Hausvogteiplatz, Französische Strasse

This perkily turreted church is a rare neo-Gothic design by Schinkel (1830) and cuts a commanding presence on the Werderscher Markt. It's now a museum of 19th-century sculpture; works by all of the period's heavyweights, including Johann Gottfried Schadow, Christian Daniel Rauch and Christian Friedrich Tieck, fill the softly lit nave. Upstairs is an exhibit on Schinkel's life and accomplishments.

The postmodern hulk next to the church, by the way, is the German Foreign Office.

DEUTSCHE GUGGENHEIM BERLIN
Map pp76-7

☎ 202 0930; www.deutsche-guggenheim-berlin .de; Unter den Linden 13-15; adult/concession/child under 12/family €4/3/free/8, Mon free; ☺ 10am-8pm; Ⓤ Französische Strasse, 🚌 100, 200, TXL

A joint venture between the Guggenheim Foundation and Deutsche Bank (hence the name), this small gallery is a treasure-box showcase for big-name contemporary artists. Works by Eduardo Chillida, Georg Baselitz and Gerhard Richter have all graced the minimalist space. There are daily tours at 6pm and all day Monday. Nice shop and cafe, too.

MADAME TUSSAUDS Map pp76-7

☎ 01805-545 800; www.madametussauds.com /berlin; Unter den Linden 74; adult/concession/ child 3-14 Mon-Fri €19/18/14, Sat & Sun €20/19/15; ☾ 10am-7pm; ◐ ⊞ Brandenburger Tor, ⊟ 100, TXL

No celebrity in town to snare your stare? Don't fret: at this legendary wax museum Brangelina, Leo and Elvis stand still – very still – for you to snap their picture. Sure, it's an expensive haven of kitsch and camp but where else can you cuddle with Robbie Williams or hug the Pope? Best of all, you're free to touch and prod all the 75 figures, look under their skirts, give them a kiss or whatever other silliness you can dream up. There are dozens of German and international stars from politics (Obama, Dalai Lama), culture (Marlene Dietrich), sports (Muhammad Ali, Cristiano Ronaldo), music (Beatles, Bono) and Hollywood (George Clooney, Nicole Kidman). The most controversial figure is the waxen likeness of Adolf Hitler, depicted as a beaten man hunkered in the bunker during his final days. On opening day, the 'Führer' lost his head when a local unemployed man tore it off, not in protest it turned out, but to fulfil a beer bet. It was quickly reattached. You can learn how – in the section detailing the process of making these figures. Last admission is at 6pm; combination tickets with SeaLife (p95) or Legoland Discovery Centre (p111) cost €5 extra each.

GENDARMENMARKT & AROUND

The Gendarmenmarkt area is Berlin at its ritziest, dappled with luxury hotels, fancy restaurants and bars. The graceful square was named after the Gens d'Armes, an 18th-century Prussian regiment consisting of French Huguenots who settled here after being expelled from France in 1685. Their main house of worship was the Französischer

Dom, a domed church that closely mirrors the design of the Deutscher Dom opposite. Schinkel's Konzerthaus (concert hall), fronted by the 'Schiller Denkmal', a statue of Germany's most revered 18th-century poet and playwright Friedrich Schiller, completes the well-proportioned ensemble.

FRANZÖSISCHER DOM Map pp76-7

☎ 2064 9922; www.franzoesischer-dom.de, in German; Gendarmenmarkt; church free, museum adult/ concession/family €2/1/3.50; ☾ church & museum noon-5pm Tue-Sun; ◐ Französische Strasse
Virtually identical to the Deutscher Dom (below), the 1705 Französischer Dom in turn is more or less a carbon copy of the Huguenots' mother church in Charenton, France. A great time to visit is for the free 20-minute organ recitals held at 12.30pm Tuesday to Friday or during one of the frequent concerts. To learn more about the Huguenots, pop by the small Hugenotten Museum on the tower's ground floor. For a great view of Gendarmenmarkt and historic Berlin, you can once again climb up the tower (adult/child €2.50/1; ☾ 10am-7pm).

DEUTSCHER DOM Map pp76-7

☎ 2273 0431; Gendarmenmarkt 1; admission & tours free; ☾ 10am-7pm Tue-Sun May-Sep, to 6pm Oct-Apr; ◐ Französische Strasse, Stadtmitte
This 1708 church wasn't much of a looker until getting its dazzling galleried dome courtesy of Carl von Gontard in, like Französischer Dom, 1785. It's now home to a hopelessly academic exhibit called Milestones-Setbacks-Sidetracks that charts the path to parliamentary democracy in Germany and regularly bores field-tripping school kids to tears. Borrow a free audioguide or join a guided one-hour tour (also in English by prior arrangement) to make better sense of it all.

KONZERTHAUS BERLIN Map pp76-7

☎ 203 090; www.konzerthaus.de; Gendarmenmarkt 2; ◐ Französische Strasse, Stadtmitte
One of Schinkel's finest buildings, the Konzerthaus (1821; originally the Schauspielhaus) rose up from the ashes of Carl Gotthard Langhans' National Theatre. Schinkel kept the surviving walls and columns and added a grand staircase leading to a raised columned portico. Today, the Konzerthaus is a shining beacon of Berlin culture and a fabulous building,

both inside and out. Catch a concert or take a free, 30-minute, volunteer-led spin offered once daily. Thorough 90-minute tours (€3, in German) usually run at 1pm on Saturdays but do confirm ahead. Also see p251).

FRIEDRICHSTADTPASSAGEN Map pp76-7
Friedrichstrasse btwn Französische Strasse & Mohrenstrasse; ⓜ Französische Strasse, Stadtmitte
Even if you're not part of the Gucci and Prada brigade, the wow factor of this trio of shopping complexes (called Quartiere) linked by a subterranean passageway is undeniable. Start at OM Ungers' Quartier 205, whose lofty atrium is dominated by a three-storey tower by John Chamberlain, an American artist known for his bold metal sculptures created from crushed automobile parts. Next up is the Art Deco Quartier 206, a visual home run with dazzlingly patterned black-and-white marble floors and thick leather chairs for resting. The biggest stunner, though, is Jean Nouvel's Quartier 207, where the exclusive French department store Galeries Lafayette (p184) centres on a giant plexiglass funnel reflecting light like some mutated hologram.

EMIL NOLDE MUSEUM Map pp76-7
☎ 4000 4690; www.nolde-stiftung.de; Jägerstrasse 55; adult/student €8/3, audioguide €4; ⓧ 10am-7pm; ⓜ Französische Strasse, Hausvogteiplatz
Bright flowers, stormy seas and red-lipped women with jaunty hats – the paintings and watercolours of Emil Nolde (1867–1956) are intense, sometimes melancholic and lyrically captivating. Admire a rotating selection of works by this key figure of German expressionism in a brightly converted 19th-century bank building. A member of the artist group Die Brücke (The Bridge), Nolde was closely connected with Berlin and spent many winters here with his wife Ada, starting in 1905. Although somewhat sympathetic to the Nazis, the regime deemed him a 'degenerate artist' and forbade him from painting. In defiance, he nevertheless secretly produced some 1300 'unpainted pictures' at his main home in Seebüll in the northern German countryside.

MENDELSSOHN EXHIBIT Map pp76-7
☎ 8170 4726; www.jaegerstrasse.de; Jägerstrasse 51; admission free; ⓧ noon-6pm; ⓜ Hausvogteiplatz

The Mendelssohns are one of the great German family dynasties, starting with the *pater familias*, the philosopher Moses Mendelssohn (1729–86), the founder of the Jewish Enlightenment. In 1815 his sons Joseph and Abraham (father of composer Felix Mendelssohn-Bartholdy) founded a private banking house in Jägerstrasse 51, Berlin's historical banking quarter. The Nazis forced the bank into bankruptcy, prompting many family members to flee the country. An exhibit in the resurrected bank headquarters traces the fate and history of this influential family. Other personalities associated with Jägerstrasse include Alexander von Humboldt, who was born at No 22, and the painter Georg Grosz, who lived at No 63. Rahel Varnhagen held her intellectual salons at No 54, now the restaurant Vau (p201).

MUSEUM FÜR KOMMUNIKATION BERLIN Map pp76-7
☎ 202 940; www.mfk-berlin.de, in German; Leipziger Strasse 16; adult/concession/child under 15 €3/1.50/free; ⓧ 9am-8pm Tue, to 5pm Wed-Fri & 10am-6pm Sat & Sun; ⓜ Mohrenstrasse, Stadtmitte
Three cheeky robots welcome you to this smart museum, which takes you on an entertaining romp through the evolution of communication technology. If you're old enough, expect flashbacks when seeing all those rotary phones, cassette recorders and black-and-white TVs. Other galleries explore such heady questions as how the media has changed our perception of space and time or examine the role of mass media in modern society. To see the most precious items, report to the 'treasure chamber', where you can marvel at ultra-rare Blue and Red Mauritius stamps and the world's first telephone, built by German inventor Philipp Reis in 1863.

MUSEUMSINSEL

The sculpture-studded Schlossbrücke (Palace Bridge) leads to the little Spree island where Berlin's settlement began in the 13th century. Its northern half, Museumsinsel (Museum Island), is a fabulous treasure trove of art, sculpture and objects spread across five grand museums. Construction began in the early 19th century, when it had become fashionable among European royalty to open up their private collections to the public. The Louvre in Paris, the British Museum in London, the Prado in Madrid and the Glyptothek in Munich all date back to this period. Back in Berlin, not to be outdone, Friedrich Wilhelm III and his successors followed suit, thereby creating one of the world's great museum-going experiences.

In 1999 the Museumsinsel repositories collectively became a Unesco World Heritage site. The distinction was at least partly achieved because of a master plan that will unite four of the five buildings by a subterranean passageway decorated with archaeological objects. Masterminded by British architect David Chipperfield, the complex will eventually be entered through a colonnaded modern foyer named for early-20th-century German-Jewish philanthropist James Simon. Projected completion is in 2025. Learn more at www .museumsinsel-berlin.de.

PERGAMONMUSEUM Map pp76-7

☎ 2090 5577; www.smb.spk-berlin.de; Am Kupfergraben 5; adult/concession €10/5; ⏰ 10am-6pm, to 10pm Thu; 🚇 Hackescher Markt, 🚌 100, 200, TXL, 🚋 M1, 12

An Aladdin's cave of treasures, the Pergamon opens a fascinating window onto the ancient world and is the one museum in Berlin that should not be missed. Inside the vast complex – custom-built on Museumsinsel in 1930 – awaits a veritable feast of sculpture and monumental architecture from Greece, Rome, Babylon and the Middle East. Most of it was excavated and shipped to Berlin by German archaeologists at the turn of the 20th century. Budget at least two hours for this amazing place and be sure to pick up the free and excellent audioguide. Also note that some sections may be closed while the museum is being renovated and a fourth wing added, all part of Chipperfield's master plan.

The Pergamon unites three major collections, each with their own signature sights. The undisputed highlight of the Antikensammlung (Collection of Classical Antiquities) is the museum's namesake, the Pergamon Altar (165 BC), which cuts a commanding presence in the first hall. This massive marble shrine hails from the Greek metropolis of Pergamon (now Bergama in Turkey) and centres on a steep and wide staircase. Climbing up the stairs you arrive in a colonnaded courtyard adorned with a vivid frieze featuring episodes from the life of Telephos, the mythical founder of Pergamon.

But it's another frieze – reconstructed along the walls of the hall – that deservedly hogs most visitor attention. About 113m long, it shows the gods locked in an epic battle with the giants; it was originally a painted and gilded band wrapped around the entire altar. The anatomical detail, the emotional intensity and the dramatic composition of the figures show Hellenic art at its finest.

A small door to the right of the altar opens to another key exhibit: the giant Market Gate of Miletus (2nd century AD). Merchants and customers once flooded through here onto the market square of this Roman trading town (also in today's Turkey) that functioned as a link between Asia and Europe.

Step through the gate and travel back 800 years to yet another culture and civilisation: Babylon during the reign of King Nebuchadnezzar II. You're now in the Vorderasiatisches Museum (Museum of Near Eastern Antiquities), where it's impossible not to be awed by the reconstructed Ishtar Gate, the Processional Way leading up to it and the facade of the king's throne hall. All are sheathed in glazed bricks glistening in radiant blue and ochre. The strutting lions, horses and dragons, which represent major Babylonian gods, are so striking that you can almost hear the roaring and fanfare.

Upstairs is the Pergamon's third collection, the Museum für Islamische Kunst (Museum of Islamic Art). Standouts here include the fortress-like, 8th-century caliph's palace from Mshatta in the desert of what today is Jordan, and the 17th-century Aleppo Room from the house of a Christian merchant in Syria, with its richly painted, wood-panelled walls. If you look closely, you can make out The Last Supper and Mary and Child amid all the ornamentation (straight ahead, to the right of the door).

ALTES MUSEUM Map pp76-7

☎ 2090 5577; www.smb.spk-berlin.de; Am Lustgarten; adult/concession €8/4; ⏰ 10am-6pm Fri-Wed, to 10pm Thu; 🚇 Hackescher Markt, Friedrichstrasse, 🚌 100, 200, TXL, 🚊 M1, 12

Schinkel pulled out all the stops for the grand neoclassical Old Museum, the first exhibition space to open on Museumsinsel in 1830. A curtain of fluted columns gives way to a Pantheon-inspired rotunda that's the focal point of the prized Antiquities Collection of Greek, Roman and Etruscan art and sculpture. The museum has been revamped and reorganised as part of the Museumsinsel master plan, so if you haven't visited in a while, you're in for lots of surprises.

The Etruscan collection, for instance, gets airplay for the first time since 1939 in the new upstairs exhibit. Admire a circular shield from the grave of a warrior and amphora, vessels, jewellery, coins and other items from daily life dating back as far as the 8th century BC. Ensuing rooms are dedicated to the Romans. There's fantastic sculpture (lots of naked men with missing body parts), a stylised replica of a Roman country villa with an original mosaic, and busts of Roman leaders, including Caesar and Caracalla. There's even an 'erotic cabinet' (behind a closed door, no less) with not-so-subtle depictions of satyrs, hermaphrodites and giant phalli.

The ground floor was under wraps at press time but was expected to reopen with the museum's famous Greek collection in early 2011. A standout among the Hellenic figurines, friezes, vases and jewellery is the 'Praying Boy' sculpture from around 300 BC Rhodes. For more classical works, head to the nearby Pergamonmuseum (opposite).

BODEMUSEUM Map pp76-7

☎ 2090 5577; www.smb.spk-berlin.de; Am Kupfergraben/Monbijoubrücke; adult/concession €8/4; ⏰ 10am-6pm Fri-Wed, to 10pm Thu; 🚇 Hackescher Markt, Friedrichstrasse, 🚌 100, 200 & TXL, 🚊 M1, 12

Mighty and majestic, the Bodemuseum has pushed against the northern wedge of Museumsinsel like a proud ship's bow since 1904. The gloriously restored neobaroque beauty presents several collections in largely naturally lit galleries with marble floors and wood-panelled ceilings.

Prime billing goes to the sculpture collection, hailed as 'the most comprehensive display

top picks

HISTORIC BUILDINGS

- Bodemuseum (opposite)
- Brandenburger Tor (Brandenburg Gate; p81)
- Reichstag (p75)
- Schloss Charlottenburg (p122)
- Zitadelle Spandau (p166)

of European sculpture anywhere' by none other than British Museum director Neil MacGregor. There are works here from the early Middle Ages to the late 18th century, including serious masterpieces like Donatello's early Renaissance *Pazzi Madonna,* Giovanni Pisano's *Man of Sorrows* relief and the portrait busts of Desiderio da Settignano. From the Italians cruise on over to the Germans, perhaps to compare the emotiveness of Tilman Riemenschneider's carvings to those by his contemporaries Hans Multscher or Nicolaus Gerhaert van Leyden.

Before breaking for coffee at the museum's elegant cafe, pop down to the Museum of Byzantine Art, which takes up just a few rooms off the grand domed foyer. Roman sarcophagi, ivory carvings and mosaic icons are among the items revealing the level of artistry in the early days of Christianity. Coin collectors should also get a kick out of the Numismatic Collection on the 2nd floor, where the oldest farthing is from the 7th century BC. Kids, meanwhile, can learn how to make mosaics in the interactive Kindergalerie (Children's Gallery) in the basement.

ALTE NATIONALGALERIE Map pp76-7

☎ 2090 5577; www.smb.spk-berlin.de; Bodestrasse 1-3; adult/concession €8/4; ⏰ 10am-6pm Tue-Sun, to 10pm Thu; 🚇 Hackescher Markt, Friedrichstrasse, 🚌 100, 200, TXL, 🚊 M1, 12

The Greek temple–style Old National Gallery, open since 1876, is a three-storey showcase of top-notch, 19th-century European art. To get a sense of the virtuosity of the period, study the canvasses glorifying Prussia – epics by Franz Krüger and Adolf Menzel and the moody landscapes by Romantic heartthrob, Caspar David Friedrich. There's also a sprinkling of French impressionists in case you're keen on seeing yet another version of Monet's *Waterlilies* and plenty of sculpture by Rauch and Schadow, possibly to tease you into visiting the much larger collection in the nearby Friedrichswerdersche Kirche (p85).

NEUES MUSEUM Map pp76-7

☎ 266 424 242; www.neues-museum.de; Bodestraβe 1; adult/concession/child under 18 €10/5/free; ☻ 10am-6pm Sun-Wed, to 8pm Thu-Sat; ☒ Hackescher Markt, Friedrichstrasse, ☒ 100, 200 & TXL, ☒ M1, 12

Open since October 2009, the New Museum is a shining beacon on Museumsinsel thanks in equal part to its stellar exhibits and to David Chipperfield's glorious reconstruction. Just like the original museum, a Friedrich August Stüler design of 1859, the building harbours the Egyptian Museum and Papyrus Collection as well as the Museum of Pre- and Early History. This is where you come for an audience with Berlin's most beautiful woman, the 3330-year-old Queen Nefertiti, she of the long, graceful neck and timeless good looks. The bust was part of the treasure trove unearthed by a Berlin expedition of archaeologists around 1912 while sifting through the sands of Armana. This royal city was built by Nefertiti's husband, Akhenaten (r 1353–1336 BC), the renegade pharaoh who raised the previously obscure sun god Aten to the status of supreme deity. Other items on display include statues of the king and the royal family along with objects from everyday life. A key item from the Late Egyptian Period, which shows Greek influence, is the so-called Berlin 'Green Head' (around 400 BC), the head of a priest carved from smooth green stone.

At the Museum of Pre- and Early History, meanwhile, pride of place goes to the Trojan antiquities (some original, some replicas) unearthed by Heinrich Schliemann in 1870. Other highlights include a preserved Neanderthal skull and the 3000-year-old Berliner Goldhut, a gilded conical ceremonial hat that doubles as a lunisolar calendar.

Competing with the exhibits is the building itself, which was destroyed in the war and languished as a ruin behind the Iron Curtain. Like a giant jigsaw puzzle, Chipperfield incorporated every original shard, scrap and brick he could find into the new building. This brilliant blend of historic and modern has resulted in a dynamic space that juxtaposes massive stairwells, intimate domed rooms, muralled halls and airy, high-ceilinged spaces.

Because of demand, admission is by timed ticket only. Avoid queuing by getting advance tickets online at no extra charge.

BERLINER DOM Map pp76-7

☎ 2026 9110; www.berlinerdom.de; Am Lustgarten; adult/concession/child under 14 €5/3/free, audioguide €3; ☻ 9am-8pm Mon-Sat, noon-8pm Sun Apr-Sep, to 7pm Oct-Mar; ☒ Hackescher Markt, Alexanderplatz, ☒ 100, 200, ☒ M4, M5, M6

Pompous yet majestic, the Italian Renaissance–style former court church of the Prussian royals was completed in 1905 and now does triple duty as house of worship, museum and concert hall. It's extravagant inside and out. At first, all eyes are on the main altar, made of marble and onyx by Friedrich August Stüler, but nose around and you'll find all sorts of artistic treasures. Andreas Schlüter's elaborate sarcophagi sculpted for Friedrich I and Sophie Charlotte, for instance, in the right side niche, deserve a closer look. For more dead royals, albeit in less extravagant coffins, drop down below to the crypt.

BERLIN ON A RAINY DAY

With more museums than rainy days, there's no shortage of quality things to do in Berlin when the weather gods are in a foul mood. The classic way to start the day is with a leisurely breakfast, served until well into the afternoon at such places as Anna Blume (p228), Jules Verne (p207) and Tomasa (p211). Afterwards, lug your gut to one of the 175 museums, which range from mega-hits like the Neues Museum (above) to such speciality gems as the Deutsches Technikmuseum Berlin (p143). Shopaholics won't have a problem giving their credit cards a workout during a couple of dry hours spent at the KaDeWe (p189) or the Friedrichstadtpassagen (p87). Or head to the Liquidrom (p314), an ethereal pool, sauna and bar, where a dreary winter afternoon is quickly forgotten. Celebrity-watchers can scan the crowd over coffee or cocktails in the lobby lounge of the legendary Adlon Kempinski (p268). Also check *Tip* and *Zitty* (p311) for what's playing at the all-English cinema Cinestar Original (p252) or the Arsenal (p252) art-house cinema, both at the Sony Center.

PRUSSIAN POMP, 21ST-CENTURY STYLE

Nothing of today's Schlossplatz evokes memories of the grand palace where the Prussian royal family made its home for 500 years. Despite international protests, the GDR government razed the barely war-damaged structure in 1951 and replaced it with a multipurpose hall called Palast der Republik (Palace of the Republic). Behind its orange-tinted mirrored facade, the GDR parliament hammered out policy and common folk came to hear Harry Belafonte sing or to party on New Year's Eve. By all accounts, the interior was both a study in ostentation and tastelessness, exemplified by the foyer with its hundreds of dangling lamps, which gave rise to the nicknames Erich's Lampenladen (Erich's Lamp Shop) and Palazzo Prozzo (roughly, 'Braggers' Palace').

After the fall of the Wall, the Palast closed instantly because of asbestos contamination. Years of debate resulted in the demolition of the behemoth. Then came the plan to build a replica of the Prussian palace shell – but with a modern interior. To be called Humboldtforum (www.humboldt-forum.de, in German), it would shelter art and artefacts from Africa, Asia, Oceania and the Americas currently on display at the Museen Dahlem (p162) as well as a library and research facility. Alas, it all comes with a price tag of €700 million, no small change in times of fiscal belt-tightening.

And so, in June 2010, the Federal Government announced that construction of the Humboldtforum would be delayed until 2014 because of empty coffers. With the federal budget requiring cuts to social services and infrastructure, it seemed frivolous to go ahead with a mega-project that could only be financed with public funding to the tune of half a billion euros. As some opinion polls taken after the decision show, Berliners on the whole were not displeased. In fact, the lawn that replaced the Palace of the Republic has become a popular gathering point for sun-seeking locals and foot-weary tourists.

In the meantime, though, construction of the Humboldt-Box (www.sbs-humboldtforum.de, www.humboldt-box.info, both in German), a temporary information centre and viewing platform, is going full speed ahead. Starting in spring 2011, the five-storey building will present exhibits on the architectural concept of the Humboldtforum as well as teasers from the ethnological collections that will eventually take up residence in the rebuilt palace. And so that people can keep tabs on how their money is spent, there'll also be a viewing platform on the rooftop. A tourist office (p316) opened up for business in 2010.

Skip the cathedral museum unless you're interested in the building's construction and instead climb up the 267 steps to the gallery just below the central copper dome for glorious views over the city. The sanctuary has great acoustics and is often used for concerts. If possible catch one played on the famous Sauer organ, which, with 7200 pipes, is one of the largest in Germany. Admission to the Dom is free during the short prayer services at noon Monday to Saturday and 6pm Monday to Friday. The service at 6pm on Thursday is in English. Last paid admission is one hour before closing.

NEUER MARSTALL Map pp76-7
Breite Strasse; ⊕ Spittelmarkt, Hausvogteiplatz, 🚌 148

Southeast of Schlossplatz, the 1901 neo-baroque Neuer Marstall (New Stables) by Ernst von Ihne once sheltered royal horses and carriages. In 1918, revolutionaries hatched their plans to bring about the end of the Hohenzollern monarchy here. A bronze relief on the northern facade shows Karl Liebknecht proclaiming (unsuccessfully) the German socialist republic from the balcony of the Berlin City Palace. In recent years the building has found new use as the second home of the Hochschule für Musik Hanns Eisler (p251), a prestigious music academy.

The Neuer Marstall is an extension of the 1670 Alter Marstall (Old Stables; Map pp76-7), which is Berlin's oldest baroque building. It rubs shoulders with the Ribbeckhaus (Map pp76-7), the city's only surviving Renaissance structure. Both are now home to public libraries.

STAATSRATSGEBÄUDE Map pp76-7
Schlossplatz 1; ⊕ Spittelmarkt, Hausvogteiplatz, 🚌 100, 200

With the Palast der Republik dismantled, Erich Honecker's former HQ, the State Council Building, is the only remaining GDR structure on Schlossplatz. It's now a business school and of interest only for its arched portal from the demolished Prussian city palace. The GDR honchos decided to spare it because it was from its balcony in 1918 that their ideological godfather Karl Liebknecht proclaimed a Socialist republic.

A MILE OF HISTORICAL MILESTONES IN MITTE
Walking Tour

1 Lustgarten Fronting the Altes Museum, this patch of green has seen more makeovers than Madonna. It started as a royal kitchen garden, became a military exercise ground before being turned into a pleasure garden by Schinkel. The Nazis held mass rallies here, the East Germans ignored it. Restored to its Schinkel-era appearance, it's now a favourite resting spot for foot-weary tourists.

2 Schlossbrücke This would be just any old bridge were it not for the eight marble sculptures depicting the life and death of a warrior. Designed by Schinkel in the 1820s, empty royal coffers kept them from being chiselled until the 1840s, after the master's death.

3 Kronprinzenpalais The froufrou baroque Crown Prince's Palace was young Frederick's residence before he became 'the Great'. In the 1920s the National Gallery showcased top contemporary artists here until the Nazis deemed them 'degenerate' and closed down the exhibit. In 1990 the formal German re-unification agreement was signed here on 31 August.

4 Prinzessinnenpalais Looking for digs for his three daughters, Friedrich Wilhelm III took a liking to this smaller baroque palace built in 1733 for the Prussian treasurer. It briefly housed a Schinkel Museum in the

WALK FACTS
Start **Lustgarten**
End **Pariser Platz**
Distance **1.4km**
Time **One hour**
Exertion **Easy**
Fuel stop **Deutsche Guggenheim Berlin cafe** (p85)

1930s but is now known as the Opernpalais, with a plush restaurant-cafe famous for its cake selection.

5 Staatsoper Unter den Linden The opulent Staatsoper Unter den Linden (National Opera House, p253), designed by Knobelsdorff, has graced Bebelplatz since 1743 and has risen from the ashes three times. Again in need of an overhaul, the famous song palace will remain closed until at least 2013.

6 Alte Königliche Bibliothek Thanks to its curvaceous facade, this handsome baroque building is nicknamed *Kommode* (chest of drawers). Built to shelter the royal book collection, it has been part of the university since 1914. Lenin used to hit the books in the Reading Room behind the central columns. It now houses the Humboldt University law school.

7 Humboldt Universität Marx and Engels studied and the Brothers Grimm and Albert Einstein taught at Berlin's oldest university (1810), a former royal palace. It has produced enough Nobel Prize winners (29 at last count) to keep the Swedish Academy busy. These

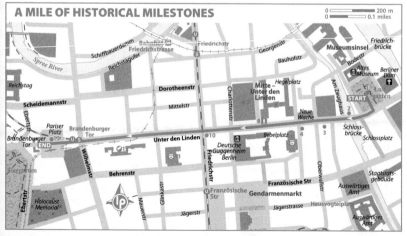

A MILE OF HISTORICAL MILESTONES

days, some 35,000 students strive to uphold this illustrious legacy.

8 Reiterdenkmal Friedrich des Grossen
Seemingly surveying his domain, Frederick the Great cuts a commanding figure on horseback in this famous 1850 monument, which kept Christian Daniel Rauch busy for a dozen years. The plinth features a parade of famous German military men, scientists, artists and thinkers.

9 Staatsbibliothek zu Berlin
The original sheet music of Beethoven's ninth symphony, a Gutenberg Bible and a third-century book of proverbs are among the treasures of the hulking Berlin State Library. You need a library card to get inside, but not to join a free tour (10.30am on the first Saturday of the month).

10 Automobil Forum Unter den Linden
It's shiny cars galore in this commercial ode to the auto where VW, Bugatti, Bentley and other makers showcase their latest wheels. To entice even non-car-freaks, free art shows – often surprisingly good – are periodically mounted in the basement.

11 Komische Oper
The Komische Oper (Light Opera, p253) is one of Berlin's three opera houses. A theatre has stood in this spot since 1764, but the core of the current structure dates only to 1892. After WWII the richly festooned baroque interior was largely restored, clashing with the decidedly functional '60s facade.

12 Russian Embassy
This hulking behemoth is a fine example of Stalinist *Zuckerbäckerstil* (wedding-cake style), although a tall wall allows only glimpses of the compound. If you're interested in this type of monumental architecture, you can gorge on it along Karl-Marx-Allee (p152) in Friedrichshain.

13 Pariser Platz
Wind back the clock to 1989 and this elegant square was an empty lot bisected by the Berlin Wall and punctuated with GDR guard towers. Since then, embassies, banks and a luxury hotel have returned to their historic spots, once again making Pariser Platz (p81) Berlin's 'reception room'.

MITTE – ALEXANDERPLATZ AREA

Eating p202; Shopping p184; Sleeping p269

Noisy, hectic and chaotic, Alexanderplatz (Alex for short) is not the kind of square that invites lingering. Despite post-reunification attempts to temper the socialist look created during the 1960s, Alexanderplatz remains an oddly cluttered, soulless square that's all concrete, no trees. The main plaza is anchored by the tacky GDR-era Brunnen der Internationalen Freundschaft (Fountain of International Friendship; Map p96), where pierced anarcho types and their pit bulls linger next to chipper school kids on a field trip and foot-weary tourists hunched over their city maps. The rest of Alex is confusingly bifurcated by roads, train and tram tracks and littered with a hodgepodge of architectural styles. Sure, there are some solitary gems like Peter Behrens 1929 Alexanderhaus (now the C&A clothing store) or J Paul Kleihues redesigned Galleria Kaufhof, but it's all far from being a harmonious ensemble. The recent addition of the pink behemoth Alexa and the bunker-like Neue Mitte, both shopping malls, have done little to improve the square's aesthetics or vitality.

Yet, there's usually no escaping Alex. It's a major traffic and shopping hub, so you'll likely be passing through here at some point during your stay. At least it's easy to locate. No matter where you are in the city, simply look up and chances are pretty good that you will see the square's most prominent landmark – the Fernsehturm (TV Tower) – sticking out from the city skyline like the tall kid in your school photograph.

top picks

MITTE – ALEXANDERPLATZ AREA

- DDR Museum (opposite)
- Fernsehturm (opposite)
- Nikolaikirche (p96)

The tower was the crowning glory in Alex's 1960s conversion into a poster child of socialist architecture, an effort that also birthed the 123m-high Interhotel Stadt Berlin (now Park Inn), the World Time Clock, the Haus des Lehrers (House of the Teacher), the House of Travel (now with the Weekend club on three upper floors) and the Haus der Elektroindustrie (House of Electrical Industry, now the Federal Ministry of the Environment). In other words, it's light years away from the stinking, filthy low-life district Alfred Döblin called 'the quivering heart of a cosmopolitan city' in his 1929 novel Berlin Alexanderplatz. The letters on the facade of the Haus der Elektroindustrie, incidentally, spell out a passage from the book.

To find some open space, wander west and south of the Fernsehturm. This is the germ cell of the medieval city, where traders first settled along the Spree River in the twin towns of Berlin (on the northeast bank) and Cölln (on an island in the Spree). Much of Old Berlin survived until bombed to bits in WWII. In the aftermath, East German city planners tore down whatever was left, retaining only a few token historic sites such as the 13th-century Marienkirche (church) and the Rotes Rathaus (town hall).

Then, only a few years later, GDR cultural honchos got together to figure out how to properly celebrate Berlin's 750th anniversary. Eureka – we shall recreate the city's medieval birthplace! And so the twee Nikolaiviertel (Nicholas Quarter) was born, a faux maze of cutesy, cobbled lanes. A few original buildings were moved here but most are replicas, some even made with the prefab concrete block so favoured in GDR construction. Granted, the quintessential surrealism of this quarter can be a hoot, but don't expect to see too many Berliners patronising the pricey cafes, restaurants and shops.

South of the Nikolaiviertel, the Molkenmarkt was Berlin's oldest square and, engulfed in roaring traffic, is now a contender for its most hideous. Originally called Old Market, it got its current name in 1685 when a nearby dairy started selling its products here. Alas, only four years later, Elector Friedrich III turned it into a military parade ground. Still, the Molkenmarkt more or less kept its medieval look until the 1960s demolition campaign left only the Stadthaus and the Palais Schwerin standing.

For some relief from such brutalist city planning, wander along the Spree River, past locks and the Dutch Embassy, to the quiet streets around Klosterstrasse U-Bahn station, where you'll find a piece of medieval town wall and the delightful Old Berlin restaurant Zur Letzten Instanz (p202). For a full primer on city history, pop across the river to the Märkisches Museum.

FERNSEHTURM Map p96

www.tv-turm.de; Panoramastrasse 1a; adult/
child under 16 €11/7, VIP €19.50/11.50; ☉ 9am-
midnight Mar-Oct, 10am-midnight Nov-Feb;
⊕ ⓧ Alexanderplatz

As iconic to Berlin as the Eiffel Tower is to
Paris, the TV Tower is Germany's tallest
structure and has been soaring 368m high
since 1969. Come early to beat the queue
for the lift to the panorama platform at
203m, where views are unbeatable on clear
days. Pinpoint city landmarks from here or
the upstairs retro-style cafe, which makes
one revolution in 30 minutes. If you want to
skip the line, buy a VIP ticket.

The tower was supposed to demonstrate the GDR's technological prowess but
became a bit of a laughing stock when it
turned out that, when hit by the sun, the
steel sphere below the antenna produces
the reflection of a giant cross. And this
coming from a country where crosses
had been removed from churches! West
Berliners gleefully dubbed the phenomenon
'the Pope's revenge'.

Fat Tire Bike Tours (p311) on the north side of
the tower base sells discounted tickets for
€9.50 if you book a tour with them.

DDR MUSEUM Map p96

☎ 847 123 731; www.ddr-museum.de; Karl-
Liebknecht-Strasse 1; adult/concession €5.50/3.50;
☉ 10am-8pm Sun-Fri, to 10pm Sat; 🚌 100,
200, TXL

In East Germany kids were put through
collective potty training, engineers earned
little more than farmers and everyone, it
seems, went on nudist holidays. Such are the
fascinating nuggets you'll learn at the small,
interactive DDR (Deutsche Demokratische
Republik) Museum dedicated to teaching
the rest of us about daily life behind the Iron
Curtain. Small and delightfully interactive,
this is where you can turn the ignition key
of an authentic Trabant car or learn how to
dance the Lipsi, the GDR's answer to rock 'n'
roll. A must for *Good Bye Lenin!* fans. Lest you
get the impression that life in the GDR was
cute and wholesome, though, you might
want to follow up a visit here with a trip
out to the Gedenkstätte Hohenschönhausen (Stasi
Prison; p173).

MARIENKIRCHE Map p96

☎ 242 4467; www.marienkirche-berlin.de; Karl-
Liebknecht-Strasse 8; admission free; ☉ 10am-

6pm; ⓧ Hackescher Markt, Alexanderplatz,
🚌 100, 200, TXL, 🚋 M4, M5, M6

This Gothic brick gem has welcomed
worshippers since the 13th century and,
alongside the Nikolaikirche (p96), is one
of Berlin's oldest surviving churches. A
vestibule gruesomely decorated with
a (badly faded) *Dance of Death* fresco
created after the plague of 1486 leads
to a relatively plain interior enlivened by
elaborate epitaphs and a baroque alabaster
pulpit by German sculptor and architect
Andreas Schlüter (1703).

AQUADOM & SEALIFE BERLIN Map p96

☎ 01805-6669 0101; www.sealifeeurope.com;
Spandauer Strasse 3; adult/concession/child under
14 €17/16/12; ☉ 10am-7pm; ⓧ Hackescher
Markt, Alexanderplatz, 🚌 100, 200, TXL, 🚋 M4,
M5, M6

Pricey but entertaining, this aquarium
follows the Spree River to the North
Atlantic, introducing you to aquatic
denizens living in the rivers, lakes and seas
along the way. There are some 30 tanks,
including a 360-degree aquarium where a
school of mackerel makes its head-spinning
rounds. Other crowd favourites include
smile-inducing seahorses, ethereal jellyfish
and a big ocean tank patrolled by manta
rays and small sharks. New since 2010 is the
enchanting sea dragon exhibit, although
we're not sure how these camouflage kings
from the Pacific fit into the overall concept.
Visits conclude with a slow lift ride through
the Aquadom, a 16m-tall cylindrical tank,
where 1500 tropical marine beasties flit
and dart amid luminous coral. Catch a free
preview from the lobby of the adjacent
Radisson Blu Hotel (p269).

TRANSPORT: MITTE –
ALEXANDERPLATZ AREA

Bus M48 links Alexanderplatz with Potsdamer
Platz; No 248 goes to the Märkisches Museum via
Nikolaiviertel.

S-Bahn S5, S7/75 and S9 all converge at Alexanderplatz.

Tram M4, M5 and M6 connect Alexanderplatz with
Marienkirche.

U-Bahn U2, U5 and U8 stop at Alexanderplatz.
Other main stops are Klosterstrasse and Märkisches
Museum (U2) and Jannowitzbrücke (U8).

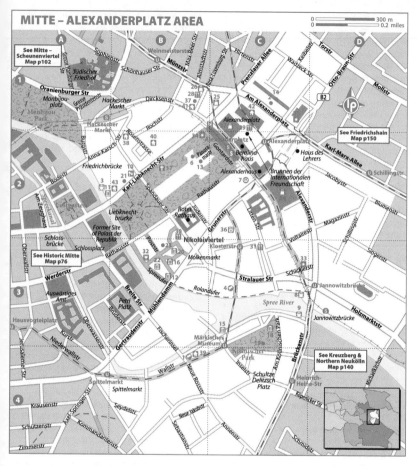

MITTE – ALEXANDERPLATZ AREA

All labelling is in English and German. The website has an online booking function and the occasional ticket deal; combination tickets with ~~Madame Tussauds (p86)~~ and ~~Legoland Discovery Centre (p111)~~ are €29/28/24. Last admission is at 6pm.

MÄRKISCHES MUSEUM Map p96

☎ 2400 2162; www.stadtmuseum.de, in German; Am Köllnischen Park 5; adult/concession/child under 18 €5/3/free; ☺ 10am-6pm Tue & Thu-Sun, noon-8pm Wed; ⊙ Märkisches Museum

Berlin's main history museum is a bit of a musty, old-fashioned jumble, but still gives you a grasp of how the tiny trading village of Berlin-Cölln evolved into today's metropolis. The exhibit called 'Here is Berlin!' takes you into such neighbourhoods as Mitte and

Tiergarten and uses both artistic objects and those from everyday life to bring out their distinct character. There are some gloriously restored rooms, such as the Gothic chapel with its medieval sculpture, the Great Hall and the Arms Hall. A 19th-century highlight is the Kaiserpanorama, basically a 3-D slide show that was a form of mass entertainment back then. A good time to visit is around 3pm on Sundays when the historic automatophones (mechanical musical instruments) are launched on their cacophonous journey (adult/concession €2/1).

NIKOLAIKIRCHE Map p96

☎ 2400 2162; www.stadtmuseum.de, in German; Nikolaikirchplatz; adult/concession/child under 18 €5/3/free; ☺ 10am-6pm; ⊙ Alexanderplatz

MITTE – ALEXANDERPLATZ AREA

Lording it over the Nikolaiviertel are the twin spires of the late-Gothic Nikolaikirche, first mentioned in 1230 and thus Berlin's oldest surviving building. No longer a church, it's now a museum with exhibits smoothly integrated into the harmonious, lofty space. Grab the free audioguide for the scoop on the octagonal baptismal font and the life-size Virtues from the baroque altarpiece or find out why the building is nicknamed 'pantheon of prominent Berliners'. Getting buried here, by the way, cost a nobleman 80 thalers, an 'old person' 50 thalers. Also head upstairs for close-ups of the organ, a sweeping view of the building and a few meditative minutes treating your ears to church hymns at interactive listening stations.

EPHRAIM-PALAIS Map p96

☎ 2400 2162; www.stadtmuseum.de, in German; Poststrasse 16; adult/concession/child under 18 €5/3/free; ⊙ 10am-6pm Tue & Thu-Sun, noon-8pm Wed; ⊙ Klosterstrasse, ⊜ M48

The handsome 1762 Ephraim-Palais was once the home of the court jeweller and coin minter Veitel Heine Ephraim. These days, the pint-sized palace presents changing exhibits focusing on aspects of art and the cultural history of Berlin as well as the graphics collection of the Stadtmuseum (City Museum). Architectural highlights include the oval staircase and

the Schlüterdecke, an ornate ceiling, on the 1st floor.

KNOBLAUCHHAUS Map p96

☎ 2400 2162; www.stadtmuseum.de, in German; Poststrasse 23; admission free; ⊙ 10am-6pm Tue & Thu-Sun, noon-8pm Wed; ⊙ Klosterstrasse, ⊜ M48

The 1761 Knoblauchhaus is the oldest residential building in the Nikolaiviertel and the one-time home of the prominent Knoblauch family, which included politicians, architects and patrons of

BEARMANIA

No longer eclipsed by polar bear Knut of Berlin Zoo fame (see p126), the city's true 'official mascots' are back in the limelight. Schnute and her daughter Maxi romp around in an open-air pit and enclosure in the Köllnischer Park behind the Märkisches Museum. The girls theoretically receive visitors from 7.30am, although there's no guarantee they'll actually show up, especially in winter when they seem to prefer hanging out in their enclosure. Brown bears have made their home here since 1939, when four of them were donated to the city in celebration of the fact that bears have graced the Berlin flag since 1280. Berlin even celebrates the 'Day of the Berlin Bear' on 22 March. For more information, see the website of the Friends of the Berlin Bears (www .berliner-baerenfreunde.de, in German).

the arts, who enjoyed tea and talk with Schinkel, Schadow and Begas. Rooms have been neatly furnished in period style, giving you a sense of how the well-to-do lived, dressed and made their money during the 18th-century Biedermeier period.

HISTORISCHER HAFEN BERLIN Map p96

☎ 2147 3257; www.historischer-hafen-berlin.de; Märkisches Ufer; ◷ 11am-5pm Thu-Sun; admission €2; ◉ Märkisches Museum

Laced by rivers, canals and lakes, it's not surprising that Berlin has a long history in inland navigation and even had the busiest river port in Germany until WWII. The Historischer Hafen (Historical Harbour) is an outdoor museum with over 20 vessels, barges and tugboats, many still operational. One boat doubles as a cafe in summer while another contains a small exhibit documenting 250 years of river shipping on the Spree and Havel.

ZILLE MUSEUM Map p96

☎ 2463 2500; www.heinrich-zille-museum.de, in German; Propststrasse 11; adult/concession €5/4; ◷ 11am-7pm Apr-Oct, to 6pm Nov-Mar; ◉ Klosterstrasse, Alexanderplatz

Like no other artist of his time, Heinrich Zille (1859–1929) managed to capture the hardships of working-class life in the age of industrialisation with empathy and humour. This three-room private museum in the Nikolaiviertel preserves his legacy with a selection of drawings, photographs and graphic art. The video on his life, though, is in German only. Afterwards, you can channel Zille's ghost over a beer at Zum Nussbaum (Am Nussbaum 3), his rather authentically re-created favourite watering hole. For more about the man, flick to the boxed text on p42.

LOXX MINIATUR WELTEN BERLIN
Map p96

☎ 4472 3022; www.loxx-berlin.de; 3rd fl, Alexa shopping mall, Grunerstrasse 20; adult/concession/ child €12/11/7; ◷ 10am-7pm year-round, last admission 6pm Apr–mid-Oct; ◉ ⬜ Alexanderplatz

If you want to see dad turn into a little kid, take him to this huge model railway where digitally controlled trains zip around central Berlin en miniature. Landmarks from the Brandenburger Tor to the Fernsehturm have been recreated on a scale of 1:87; more are added all the time: the Government Quarter was 'under construction' when we visited. Note the charming details: the fire engine careening towards a building on fire and the airport where tiny aeroplanes noisily land and take off.

BACK TO THE ROOTS
Walking Tour

1 Justizgebäude Littenstrasse The very sight of this monumental 1912 courthouse should be enough to make even the most hardened criminals shake in their boots. All the more surprising is the graceful Art Nouveau foyer, where floating staircases hemmed in by white filigree balustrades swirl towards a cathedral-like star-vaulted ceiling in a fashion that would make MC Escher proud.

2 Stadtmauer May we introduce to you? The Berlin wall. No, not *that* Berlin Wall, but the original one from 1250, built to protect the city's first settlers from jealous marauders. Only an 8m-long fragment, crudely built from boulders and bricks, survives.

3 Franziskaner Klosterkirche The roofless torso of its Gothic church is all that war and time have left of this Franciscan abbey. After secularisation in 1534, it became a prestigious school that launched Schinkel, Bismarck and other luminaries on their exalted career paths. From May to October the romantic ruin hosts art exhibits and concerts.

4 Dutch Embassy Architect Rem Koolhaas was tasked with creating a building that would be both secure and reflect 'Dutch openness'. He came up with this critically acclaimed freestanding, glass-and-concrete cube with a rooftop terrace, projecting conference room and cantilevered facade. It looks most dramatic when lit up at night. Peeking inside is possible as part of a guided tour; register on www.dutchembassy.com (in German) at least four business days before your visit.

5 Cafeteria of Berliner Wasserbetriebe
The food's only so-so, but for scenic location this cafeteria (Neue Jüdenstrasse 1) is hard to beat – and it's open to all! On a sunny day, lug your tray to a sunny waterfront table and watch the tourist boats being heaved through the historic Mühlendamm lock.

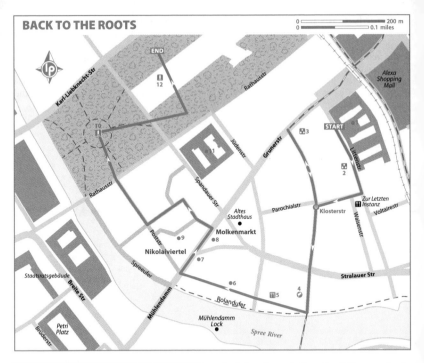

BACK TO THE ROOTS

END
12
TO
11
3 START
2
Alexa Shopping Mall
Zur Letzten Instanz
Altes Stadthaus
Molkenmarkt
8
9
Nikolaiviertel
7
6
5
Staatsratsgebäude
Petri Platz
Mühlendamm Lock
Spree River

Karl-Liebknecht-Str
Rathausstr
Jüdenstr
Grunerstr
Littenstr
Parochialstr
Klosterstr
Waisenstr
Voltairestr
Spandauer Str
Poststr
Spreeufer
Mühlendamm
Breite Str
Rolandufer
Stralauer Str
Brüderstr

0   200 m
0   0.1 miles

WALK FACTS

Start Justizgebäude Littenstrasse
End Neptunbrunnen
Distance 2.7km
Time One hour
Exertion Easy
Fuel stop Zur Letzten Instanz (p202) or Cafeteria of Berliner Wasserbetriebe (tour stop 5)

6 Direktorenhaus The opening of the Direktorenhaus in 2010 injected a dose of artsy spirit into this rather stodgy part of town. Housed in the director's office of the former state mint (hence the name), it's a postmodern art space where exhibits blur the boundaries between art, design, craft and performance. For more see www.direktorenhaus.com (in German).

7 Münze Berlin Until it moved to the suburbs in 2006, Berlin's money factory, the old mint, occupied the building at Molkenmarkt 2. Reichsmark, GDR Mark, Deutsche Mark and even Euro coins were all produced here, as many as seven million per day. It's now an event location. Note the decorative frieze depicting the evolution of metallurgy and coin minting.

8 Molkenmarkt Berlin's oldest square started out as a thriving marketplace where folk came to stock up on capons and cabbage and exchange gossip. Today it's hard to hear yourself talk amid the roaring traffic. The goddess Fortuna frowns upon the scene from atop the Altes Stadthaus, home of government pencil-pushers since 1911.

9 Nikolaiviertel With its cobbled lanes and twee buildings, the Nikolai Quarter may look medieval, but don't be fooled: like legwarmers and leotards it's a product of the 1980s, built by the GDR government to celebrate Berlin's 750th birthday. The 1230 Nikolaikirche (p96) and a handful of small museums are worth a quick look.

10 Marx-Engels-Forum Even die-hard capitalists can't resist having their picture snapped with the godfathers of communism, Karl Marx (seated) and Friedrich Engels. Put up in 1977, the giant sculpture looks out towards the Fernsehturm and is one of the few relics of the defunct GDR.

11 Rotes Rathaus Berlin's hulking town hall is called 'red' because of the colour of the bricks used in its construction, not because of the political leaning of its occupants. The terracotta frieze along its facade illustrates Berlin's history until 1871, while the two bronze figures near the entrance symbolise the men and women who helped rebuild the city after WWII.

12 Neptunbrunnen This fountain outside the Marienkirche (p95) was designed by Reinhold Begas in 1891 and depicts Neptune holding court over a quartet of buxom beauties symbolising the rivers Rhine, Elbe, Oder and Vistula. Kids gets a kick out of the water-squirting turtle, seal, crocodile and snake.

Drinking p222; Eating p203; Shopping p184; Sleeping p270

Fanning out northwest of Alexanderplatz, the Scheunenviertel (literally 'Barn Quarter') is Berlin's old Jewish Quarter that's been rebooted as a charismatic shopping, eating and partying zone. It's hard to imagine that, until reunification, this dapper area was a neglected, down-at-heel barrio with tumbledown buildings and dirty streets. Since then it's catapulted from drab to fab, teems with enticing restaurants, bars, clubs and owner-run boutiques and counts a fair number of celebrities among its residents. The area's other major draw is its legacy as Berlin's main Jewish quarter, a role it has been gradually reprising since reunification.

The Scheunenviertel's most visible anchor is the Hackescher Markt area, where the tangle of beautifully restored courtyards called Hackesche Höfe is a major tourist magnet. The bars and cafes beneath the ornately decorated red-brick arches of the Hackescher Markt S-Bahn station are also a favourite spot for cooling one's heels. In summer, tables spill out onto the car-free Neue Promenade, creating light-hearted Italian piazza flair, complete with flickering torches illuminating breezy palm trees. North of here, Oranienburger Strasse is a main drag that in the daytime lures punters to its amazing Moorish-domed Neue Synagoge and the post-atomic artists' squat house Kunsthaus Tacheles, whose survival was threatened at press time. In true Jekyll and Hyde fashion, the street shows a different side at night when it seems to be largely in the hands of long-legged, corseted sex workers and rowdy 20-year-olds on an organised pub crawl.

The Scheunenviertel reveals its greatest charms in the village-like labyrinth of lanes off Oranienburger Strasse. Embark on an aimless wander and you'll find surprises lurking around every corner: here an idyllic courtyard or intriguing public sculpture, there a bleeding-edge gallery, a cosy watering hole or 19th-century ballroom. Retail therapy too gets a unique Berlin twist here with edgy and stylish boutiques that are light years away from high-street conformity. Alte Schönhauser Strasse, Neue Schönhauser Strasse, Gipsstrasse and Rosa-Luxemburg-Strasse are particularly

top picks

MITTE – SCHEUNENVIERTEL

- Hackesche Höfe (p104)
- Heckmann Höfe (p104)
- Museum für Naturkunde (p103)
- Neue Synagoge (p102)

promising for fashion. Art-ficionados, meanwhile, still flock to the galleries on Auguststrasse and Linienstrasse, which have shepherded emerging artists to fame since the 1990s.

Torstrasse, though loud and busy, is also coming into its own and, in recent years, has seen a flurry of bar, restaurant and boutique openings. Chausseestrasse, north of U-Bahn station Oranienburger Tor, is more mellow and mainly the access route for the Brecht-Weigel Gedenkstätte (Brecht House) and the dino-heaven that is the Museum für Naturkunde (Museum of Natural History). South of Torstrasse ('SoTo' as pundits like to say), Friedrichstrasse has developed into an artsy hipster strip with chi-chi bars and restaurants; the city's main theatre district is also along here.

The Scheunenviertel's curious name ('Barn Quarter'), by the way, harks back to the 17th century, an age of wooden houses, frequent fires and poor fire-fighting techniques, which is why the Great Elector ordered all flammable crops to be stored outside the city walls. Just imagine, where all those ladies-for-sale, Starbucks and the Volksbühne theatre vie for patrons, there once used to be dozens of barns bursting with hay and straw.

The quarter wasn't settled until 1737, when the Great Elector's grandson, Friedrich Wilhelm I (aka the Soldier King), forced non-landowning Jews to live among the barns. In the early 20th century, the Scheunenviertel absorbed huge numbers of new Jewish immigrants from Eastern Europe, and its streets and shops soon rang with the sound of Yiddish. Most newcomers were Hasidic Jews who had trouble assimilating with the existing and more liberal Jewish community along Grosse Hamburger Strasse in the Spandauer Vorstadt quarter a few blocks west.

The Scheunenviertel quickly became a poor people's quarter. Prostitution, petty and not-so-petty crime, and revolutionary rumblings flourished here from the late 19th century until Hitler assumed power in 1933 and began the annihilation of the Jewish population. For more on Jewish history and the community's recent renaissance, turn to the boxed text on p38.

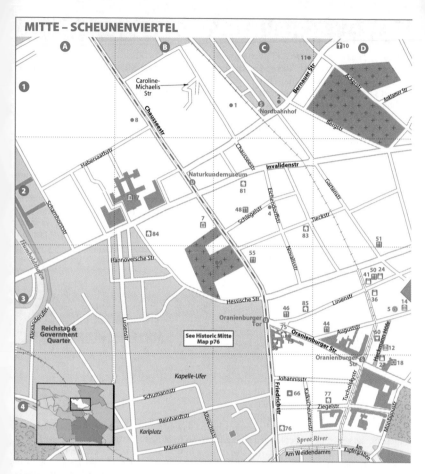

NEUE SYNAGOGE Map pp102-3

☎ 8802 8300; www.cjudaicum.de; Oranienburger Strasse 28-30; adult/concession €3/2, tours €1.50/1; ⌚ 10am-8pm Sun & Mon, to 6pm Tue-Thu, to 5pm Fri Mar-Oct, 10am-6pm Sun-Thu, to 2pm Fri Oct-Mar; Ⓡ Oranienburger Strasse

The gleaming gold dome of the Neue Synagoge is the most visible symbol of Berlin's revitalised Jewish community. Designed in Moorish-Byzantine style by Eduard Knoblauch, the 1866 original seated 3200 people and was Germany's largest synagogue. During the 1938 *Kristallnacht* pogroms, a local police chief prevented SA thugs from setting it on fire, an act of courage commemorated by a plaque. It was eventually desecrated anyway, but not destroyed until hit by bombs in 1943.

Largely reconstructed in the 1990s, today's Neue Synagoge is not so much a house of worship (although prayer services do take place) but a museum and cultural meeting point called Centrum Judaicum. Architectural fragments and objects unearthed during excavations, including a Torah scroll and an eternal lamp, help tell the history of the building and the lives of the people associated with it. A multilingual audioguide (€3) further helps bring the past to life. The dome (adult/concession €1.50/1) can be climbed.

Behind the reconstructed building a glass-and-steel mantle props up the remaining ruins of the sanctuary and a stone band in the ground traces the outline of the original synagogue. Note that this section is only accessible on a guided tour (2pm Sunday, in German).

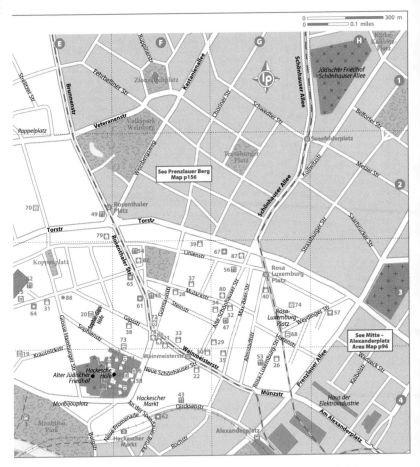

MUSEUM FÜR NATURKUNDE
Map pp102-3

☎ 2093 8591; www.naturkundemuseum-berlin
.de; Invalidenstrasse 43; adult/concession/family
€6/3.50/11; ☉ 9.30am-6pm Tue-Fri, 10am-6pm Sat
& Sun; ⊙ Naturkundemuseum

Fossils and minerals don't quicken your
pulse? Well, how about a 23m-long and
12m-high brachiosaurus? Do we have your
attention? The world's largest mounted dino
is the star of Berlin's famed natural history
museum. The gentle giant is joined by
about a dozen Jurassic buddies, including
the ferocious allosaurus and a spiny-backed
kentrosaurus. All are about 150 million years
old and hail from the Tendaguru in southeast
Tanzania. Clever 'Juraskopes' bring half a
dozen of them back to virtual flesh-and-bone

life. In the same hall, in the far left corner,
is the museum's rarest critter, a 25cm tall
archaeopteryx, which shows the evolutionary
link between dinosaurs and birds. Beyond
here is the mini-planetarium where you can
journey deep into space and learn what the
big bang was all about and how the planets
were formed. The narration is in German but
the visuals alone are stunning. The Evolution
in Action hall clears up such age-old mysteries
as why zebras are striped and why peacocks
have such beautiful feathers.

Other rooms are still old-school,
inadvertently offering insight into the
evolution of museum displays. The Mineral
hall, for instance, has changed little since
the 19th century and features specimens
collected by Alexander von Humboldt
in Russia. Some of the stuffed elephants,

gazelles and deer in the Hoofed Animal hall are over 80 years old but still oddly beautiful to see. A crowd favourite is Bobby the gorilla, who was born in Berlin and was the first such animal raised in captivity to adulthood. Want to know how to stuff a gorilla? Study the displays on preparation techniques in the same room.

HACKESCHE HÖFE Map pp102-3

☎ 2809 8010; www.hackesche-hoefe.com, in German; admission free; enter from Rosenthaler Strasse or Sophienstrasse; ☼ 24hr; Ⓡ Hackescher Markt

Thanks to its congenial mix of cafes, galleries, boutiques and entertainment venues, this attractively restored complex of eight interlinked courtyards is very popular with the tourist brigade. Court I, prettily festooned with patterned Art Nouveau tiles, is the liveliest, while Court VII leads off to the romantic Rosenhöfe, a single courtyard with a sunken rose garden and tendril-like balustrades.

HECKMANN HÖFE Map pp102-3

Oranienburger Strasse 32; Ⓡ Oranienburger Strasse

For a retreat from the urban frenzy, skip on over to this idyllic courtyard complex linking Oranienburger Strasse with Auguststrasse. Kick back with cake and cappuccino in the cafe or browse around some unique shops like the Bonbonmacherei (p186), an old-fashioned candy kitchen, and Sterling Gold, which specialises in retro ball gowns.

Bus No 142 runs from Rosenthaler Platz along Torstrasse to the Hauptbahnhof and east to Strausberger Platz and Ostbahnhof.

S-Bahn S5, S7 and S9 link Hauptbahnhof, Friedrichstrasse and Hackescher Markt with Zoologischer Garten station in the west and Alexanderplatz in the east.

Tram M4, M5 and M6 connect Hackescher Markt with Alexanderplatz; the M6 continues to the Museum für Naturkunde; M1 connects Museuminsel and Prenzlauer Berg with the Scheunenviertel.

U-Bahn Handy stations are Weinmeisterstrasse and Rosenthaler Platz (both U8), Rosa-Luxemburg-Platz (U2) and Oranienburger Tor (U6).

KW INSTITUTE FOR CONTEMPORARY ART Map pp102-3

☎ 243 4590; www.kw-berlin.de; Auguststrasse 69; adult/concession €6/4; ⏱ noon-7pm Tue-Sun, to 9pm Thu; ⒭ Oranienburger Strasse

In an old margarine factory, nonprofit KW helped chart the fate of the Scheunenviertel as Berlin's original post-Wall art district. Today, it still enjoys an international reputation as a laboratory and cooperative platform for radical new trends in contemporary art. Its founder, Klaus Biesenbach, was also the engine behind the Berlin Biennale (p18) art fair, inaugurated in 1990. He's since flown the coop for a curating gig at MOMA New York but remains closely associated with KW. The complex also harbours the stylish Café Bravo (p222) in the lovely courtyard.

SOPHIE-GIPS-HÖFE Map pp102-3

Sophienstrasse 21; ⒭ Weinmeisterstrasse

Blink and you'll miss the plain doorway leading to this artsy trio of 19th-century courtyard complexes linking Sophienstrasse with quiet Gipsstrasse. Originally a sewing-machine factory, it now harbours stores, offices, flats, the prestigious Sammlung Hoffmann (p80) art collection and the popular Barcomi's Deli (p222).

ANNE FRANK ZENTRUM Map pp102-3

☎ 288 865 610; www.annefrank.de; Rosenthaler Strasse 39; adult/concession/child under 10 €5/2.50/ free; ⏱ 10am-6pm Tue-Sun; ⒭ Hackescher Markt, ⒪ Weinmeisterstrasse

This small museum is about a girl that needs no introduction. Who hasn't read the diary of the German-Jewish girl penned while in hiding from the Nazis in Amsterdam? Anne Frank didn't even live to see her 16th birthday, perishing from typhus at Bergen-Belsen concentration camp just days earlier. This small but poignant museum uses artefacts and photographs to tell her extraordinary story, with an entire room devoted to her diary and its profound impact on postwar generations. Displays are in German and English. Museum staff also rent an 'i-guide' tour through the Scheunenviertel Jewish quarter (€5).

MUSEUM BLINDENWERKSTATT OTTO WEIDT Map pp102-3

☎ 2859 9407; www.blindes-vertrauen.de, in German; Rosenthaler Strasse 39; admission free; ⏱ 10am-8pm; ⒭ Hackescher Markt, ⒪ Weinmeisterstrasse

Small but poignant, this exhibit space tells the story of how 'Berlin's Oskar Schindler', Otto Weidt, a broom and brush maker, protected his blind and deaf Jewish workers from the Nazis. Weidt hid an entire family in a room behind a cabinet in his workshop, provided food and false papers, bribed Gestapo officials into releasing Jews scheduled for deportation and even went to Auschwitz to help his girlfriend escape from the camp. A highlight of the exhibit, set up in the original workshop, is an emotional video in which survivors recall Weidt's efforts to save their lives.

RAMONES MUSEUM Map pp102-3

☎ 7552 8890; www.ramonesmuseum.com; Krausnickstrasse 23; admission €3.50; ⏱ noon-8pm; ⒭ Oranienburger Strasse

One of their songs was 'Born to Die in Berlin'. But fact is that the legacy of the Ramones, one of the seminal US punk bands in the '70s and '80s, is kept very much alive in the German capital, thanks to super-fan Florian Hayler. His collection of memorabilia forms the basis of this little 'shrine' crammed with vintage T-shirts, signed album covers, Marky Ramone's sneakers and drumsticks, Johnny Ramone's jeans and other flotsam and jetsam along with posters, flyers, photographs and articles. Learn how to dress like your

For the past 20 years, punk politics and squat aesthetics have ruled at the Kunsthaus Tacheles (Map pp102-3; ☎ 282 6185; www.tacheles.de; Oranienburger Strasse 54-56; ◉ Oranienburger Tor, ⊕ Oranienburger Strasse), a graffiti-covered cultural centre that's been a lodestar of anti-mainstream cinema, dance, jazz, cabaret, readings, workshops, art and theatre, with a trashy-cool beer garden out back. Although it has lost much of its anarchic edge and no longer provides the creative impulses that it did in the heady '90s, it's still one of the few islands of alternative spirit in this heavily gentrified area, with some 30 resident artists. Like so many other spaces in Berlin, its survival, though, is threatened by development and, in fact, by the time you're reading this, the Tacheles may be relegated to the ash heap of history.

Originally part of a shopping arcade that linked Oranienburger Strasse with Friedrichstrasse, the building was later used by the Nazis before receiving a drubbing in WWII. The East German government targeted it for demolition but never fully followed through with it, so the partly ruined structure was still left standing when the Wall fell in 1989. A few months later, dozens of artists 'discovered' it and turned it into a giant art squat.

In 1998, an investors' group purchased the Tacheles and surrounding land from the government with plans to build a luxury hotel, offices and apartment buildings. When the project got delayed, the group agreed to allow the artists to use the space for 10 years, paying only a symbolic rent of 50 cents for the entire building. When the lease expired in 2008, the artists stayed. Meanwhile, the investor group had filed for bankruptcy which, in 2010, spurred the creditor bank to announce plans to auction off the plot, including the Tacheles. Initial attempts to evict the artists and clear the space in summer 2010 failed, in part because of the backing by the Berlin Senate. It wants to preserve the Tacheles, at least in part because it draws 400,000 visitors per year and has thus become a major tourist attraction. Stay tuned…

favourite Ramone, learn about the rise of punk and swap stories with other fans in the on-site cafe. Admission includes a Ramones button.

GEDENKSTÄTTE BERLINER MAUER
Map pp102-3

☎ 464 1030; www.berliner-mauer-dokumentationszentrum.de; Bernauer Strasse; admission free; ◷ Documentation Centre & Visitor Centre 9.30am-7pm Apr-Oct, to 6pm Nov-Mar, outdoor installations 24hr; ⊕ Nordbahnhof

There are some disgruntled Germans who say that they would like to have

top picks

BEYOND THE SCHEUNENVIERTEL: LESSER-KNOWN JEWISH SITES

The Holocaust Memorial, the Neue Synagoge and the Jüdisches Museum are Berlin's flagship Jewish sites, but there are numerous other important places of remembrance. Here's a roundup:

- Gleis 17 (p81)
- Haus der Wannsee Konferenz (p165)
- Jüdischer Friedhof Weissensee (p176)
- Jüdischer Friedhof Schönhauser Allee (p158)
- Mendelssohn Exhibit (p87)
- Block der Frauen (p109)
- Synagoge Rykestrasse (p160)

the Berlin Wall back. Well, at the Berlin Wall Memorial they get their wish – sort of. Stretching along Bernauer Strasse between Gartenstrasse and Ackerstrasse, this is where you can still see the longest surviving section of the outer Wall (the one that bordered the West) as well as the National Monument, which is essentially a reconstructed death strip complete with patrol paths and a guard tower. Start with a short introductory film in the new Visitors' Centre near Gartenstrasse, then pick up a map of the site and proceed to the outdoor exhibit. Its most moving element is the Window of Remembrance – a wall of portraits of many of the people who lost their lives at the Berlin Wall. The park-like area was once part of the adjacent cemetery; more than 1000 graves were relocated to make room for the Wall. The memory of the victims is also kept alive in 15-minute prayer services held at noon from Tuesday to Friday in the Kapelle der Versöhnung (Chapel of Reconciliation). The oval structure was built on the foundations of an 1894 brick church also blown up for being in the way of the Wall. For a great overview of the entire grounds, climb up the tower of the Documentation Centre near Ackerstrasse, which also has a small exhibit that chronicles the events leading up to that fateful day in August 1961 when the first spools of barbed wire were unrolled.

BRECHT-WEIGEL GEDENKSTÄTTE

Map pp102-3

☎ 200 571 844; www.adk.de/de/archiv
/gedenkstaetten, in German; Chausseestrasse 125;
tours adult/concession €5/2.50; ☺ tours half-
hourly 10-11.30am & 2-3.30pm Tue, 10-11.30am
Wed & Fri, 10-11.30am & 5-6.30pm Thu, 10am-
3.30pm Sat, hourly 11am-6pm Sun; ☺ Oranienburger
Tor, Naturkundemuseum

Bertolt Brecht, one of Germany's seminal
20th-century playwrights, lived in this
house not far from his theatre, the Berliner
Ensemble, from 1953 until his death in
1956. Guides take you inside Brecht's office,
with its multiple desks, his large library
where shelves are filled with classics to
crime stories, and the tiny bedroom where
he died. Decorated with Chinese artwork,
it's been left as though he'd briefly stepped
out, leaving his hat and woollen cap
hanging on the door.

Downstairs are the cluttered quarters
of his actress wife Helene Weigel, who
continued to live here until her death in
1971. The couple are buried at the adjacent
Dorotheenstädtischer Friedhof (below).

Call ahead to find out about English-
language tours. The cellar restaurant
Brechtkeller (mains €12-18) serves Austrian food
prepared from Weigel's recipes, amid
family pictures and original set models
from Brecht's productions.

DOROTHEENSTÄDTISCHER
FRIEDHOF Map pp102-3

Chausseestrasse 126; admission free; ☺ 8am-
dusk, 8pm latest; ☺ Oranienburger Tor,
Naturkundemuseum

Compact and leafy, this cemetery is the
place of perpetual slumber for a veritable
roll call of famous Germans departed since

STUMBLING UPON HISTORY

If you lower your gaze, you'll see them everywhere,
but especially in the Scheunenviertel: small brass paving stones engraved with names and placed in front
of house entrances. Called *Stolpersteine* (stumbling
blocks), they are part of a nationwide project by
Berlin-born artist Gunter Demnig and are essentially
mini-memorials honouring the people (usually Jews)
who lived in that house before being killed by the
Nazis. Dörte Frank's movie *Stolperstein*, released in
Germany in late 2008, documents Demnig's efforts
and the obstacles and controversies he encountered.
For more on Berlin's Jewish community, see p38.

the 18th century. Many tombstones here
are fine works of art, above all Schinkel's
– designed by himself – which features a
gilded portrait of the artist as a young man.
Also look for the 'six-feet-under' homes of
composers Paul Dessau and Hanns Eisler,
industrialist August Borsig and writers Anna
Seghers and Bertolt Brecht (along with
his wife Helene Weigel). Brecht lived in a
house just north of here, allegedly to be
close to his idols, the philosophers Hegel
and Fichte, who are interred here side by
side. More recent additions include German
president Johannes Rau and the dramatist
Heiner Müller; fans still leave cigars for him.
To locate particular graves, refer to the map
in a display case next to the administrative
building near the entrance.

JEWISH BERLIN
Walking Tour

1 Neue Synagoge The Scheunenviertel
synagogue was inaugurated in 1866 as
Germany's largest Jewish house of worship.

THE BRAVE WOMEN OF ROSENSTRASSE

Rosenstrasse is a small, quiet and nondescript street where, in 1943, one of the most courageous acts of civilian protest
against the Nazis took place. It was at Nos 2–4, outside a Jewish welfare office, where hundreds of local women gathered
in freezing rain in the middle of winter. They all had one thing in common: they were Christians whose Jewish husbands
had been rounded up and locked up inside to be processed for deportation to Auschwitz. Until that time, Jews married
to non-Jewish Germans had enjoyed a certain degree of protection – but no more. 'Give us our husbands back', the
women shouted – unarmed, unorganised and leaderless but with one voice. When the police threatened to shoot them,
they shouted even louder. It took several weeks, but eventually they were heard. Propaganda minister Joseph Goebbels
himself ordered the release of every single prisoner. Shooting down a bunch of unarmed German women just wasn't
good PR. Today a memorial called Block der Frauen (p109) stands in place of the building. The incident was movingly
recounted in the 2003 feature film *Rosenstrasse* by renowned film-maker Margarethe von Trotta.

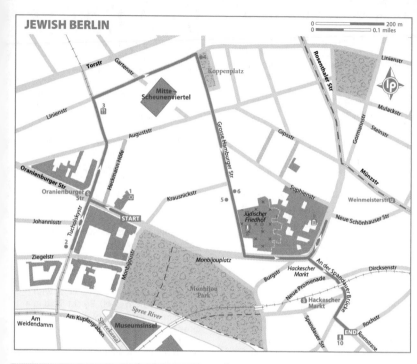

JEWISH BERLIN

0 — 200 m
0 — 0.1 miles

WALK FACTS
Start **Neue Synagoge**
End **Block der Frauen**
Distance **2.2km**
Time **One hour**
Exertion **Easy**
Fuel stop **Beth Café (tour stop 3)**

The GDR government blew up the wartime ruin in 1958 but 30 years later decided to rebuild it. The united German government adopted the plan and the Neue Synagoge (p102) opened in May 1995.

2 Leo Baeck Haus This building at Tucholskystrasse 9 started out in 1872 as a Higher Institute for Jewish Studies, where prominent Rabbi Leo Baeck was one of the professors. Today it houses the Central Council of Jews in Germany and the European Jewish Congress.

3 Beth Café This kosher cafe-bistro at Tucholskystrasse 40 is affiliated with the conservative Jewish congregation Adass Jisroel, whose synagogue is in the same building. The pretty inner courtyard is perfect for enjoying a leisurely lunch of lox on toast, various salads, gefilte fish or other staples of Jewish cuisine.

4 Der Verlassene Raum Karl Biedermann's 'Deserted Room' installation on quiet Koppenplatz consists of a table and two chairs, one knocked over. It commemorates Jewish residents forced to flee in panic from their homes. A band engraved with a poem by Jewish poet and playwright Nelly Sachs frames the 'room'.

5 Missing House The 'missing house' in question was a neo-baroque apartment building that stood at Grosse Hamburger Strasse 15/16 until a direct bomb hit in WWII. Christian Boltanski's 1990 memorial installation consists of signs bearing the names of former residents affixed to the facades of the adjacent buildings.

6 Jewish Boys School The building at Grosse Hamburger Strasse 27 housed a school founded in 1788 at the instigation of Moses Mendelssohn; he's honoured here with a plaque. The Nazis shut it down but it survived the war intact. Since 1993 both boys and girls – Jewish and not – have once again hit the books in its hallowed rooms.

7 Alter Jüdischer Friedhof What looks like a small park was in fact Berlin's first Jewish cemetery, destroyed by the Gestapo in 1943. Some 12,000 people were buried here between 1672 and 1827, including Enlightenment philosopher Moses Mendelssohn. His solitary tombstone (not the original) stands representative for all the six-feet-under residents.

8 Memorial to the Jewish Victims of Fascism Berlin's first Jewish seniors' home opened in 1844 in front of the cemetery and was turned into a deportation centre under the Nazis. Bombs flattened the building and it was never rebuilt. Since 1958 Will Lammert's haunting sculpture of 13 fatigued women has commemorated the site's history.

9 Museum Blindenwerkstatt Otto Weidt

The small Museum Blindenwerkstatt Otto Weidt (p105) is set up in the original workshop of Otto Weidt and tells the story of how this German broom and brush maker saved many of his blind and deaf Jewish workers from the Nazi death camps.

10 Block der Frauen Inge Hunzinger's 1994 sandstone sculpture called *Block of the Women* stands in Rosenstrasse on the site where non-Jewish German women peacefully but tenaciously protested the planned deportation of their Jewish husbands, in a rare and courageous act of defiance against the Nazi regime. Also see the boxed text on p107.

Drinking p223; Eating p205; Shopping p187; Sleeping p272

Despite the name, Potsdamer Platz is not just a square but Berlin's newest quarter and a show-case of urban renewal. It's built on terrain once bifurcated by the Wall, a short walk south of the Brandenburger Tor on the edge of Tiergarten. After 1989, big developers quickly swooped on the real estate of the former death strip (which was several hundred metres wide here) and pretty soon an international cast of 'starchitects', including Helmut Jahn, Renzo Piano and Rafael Moneo, got to work. Their goal: to create a modern reinterpretation of the historic Potsdamer Platz, which had all the verve and vibrancy of New York's Times Square until WWII sucked all life out of the area. Back in the 1920s, dapper doormen welcomed celebs and high society to fancy hotels like the Bellevue and the Esplanade. Weekends were spent dancing the charleston at Haus Vaterland, catching a Garbo flick at the UFA Filmpalast and raising a toast at Weinhaus Huth (p113). Five roads carrying 20,000 cars daily – as well as 26 tram and five bus lines – converged here, bringing tens of thousands to work and play. In 1924 Europe's first (hand-operated) traffic light in the shape of a pentagonal clock tower helped get the madness under control, instantly becoming a symbol of progressive Berlin. A replica now stands in the same spot near the corner of Potsdamer Strasse and Stresemannstrasse.

Stand next to it and you can see quite clearly that Potsdamer Platz 2.0 is divided into three slices. To the left (south) of Potsdamer Strasse is DaimlerCity, completed in 1998 and home to a large mall, plenty of public art and several high-profile entertainment venues. The Sony Center in the middle, which opened in 2000, is the flashiest of the three, with a central plaza canopied by a glass roof whose supporting beams emanate like bicycle spokes. Finally, there's the much more subdued Beisheim Center, whose design is homage to classic American skyscrapers. The Ritz-Carlton Hotel, for instance, is modelled on the Rockefeller Center in New York.

Potsdamer Platz is easily combined with the Kulturforum, a cluster of world-class fine arts museums and concert halls, including the famous Philharmonie. Black limousines are a common sight further west in the Diplo-matenviertel (Diplomatic Quarter), which is also distinguished by some fine contemporary architecture (see the Walking Tour, p119).

And if your head is spinning after all that cultural stimulus, the leafy paths of the vast Tiergarten, Berlin's response to New York's Central Park, will likely prove to be a restorative antidote.

top picks

POTSDAMER PLATZ & TIERGARTEN

- Gedenkstätte Deutscher Widerstand (p118)
- Gemäldegalerie (p115)
- Tiergarten (p117)
- Sony Center (opposite)
- Topografie des Terrors (p114)

POTSDAMER PLATZ

Although critics complain about Potsdamer Platz's commercialisation and its attractive but relatively unmemorable architecture, Ber-liners and visitors have by and large embraced the new quarter. Up to 100,000 people bar-rel through its streets and squares each day, heading to the 150 shops of the Potsdamer Platz Arkaden (p187) mall; the roulette tables of Europe's largest casino, the Spielbank Ber-lin (p239); the three state-of-the-art multiplex cinemas, including the all-English Cinestar at the Sony Center (opposite); or perhaps just to take advantage of the free wi-fi hot spot in the Sony Center. Every February, celebs sashay down the red carpet to the Theater am Potsdamer

Platz (p254), the main venue of the Berlin International Film Festival.

Another big attraction is the row of Berlin Wall segments outside the Potsdamer Platz train station entrance. Bilingual explanatory texts talk about other memorial sites and fu-ture Wall-related projects. An original GDR border watchtower (Map p112) is just a short walk away on Erna-Berger-Strasse (off Strese-mannstrasse).

In late 2010 Berlin went even more Hol-lywood with its own version of the Walk of Fame, here called Boulevard of the Stars (www .boulevard-der-stars-berlin.de, in German). This row of brass stars embedded in a red asphalt carpet along the centre strip of Potsdamer Strasse honours famous actors and directors from German film and TV, such as Marlene Dietrich, Werner Herzog and Romy Schneider. There will be 40 stars initially, with up to 10 more to be added every summer.

SONY CENTER Map p112

Designed by Helmut Jahn, the Sony Center is visually the most dramatic of the three Potsdamer Platz sections, fronted by a 26-floor, glass-and-steel tower that's the highest building on Potsdamer Platz. It integrates remnants of the prewar Hotel Esplanade, including a section of facade (visible from Bellevuestrasse) and the opulent Kaisersaal hall, which had to be moved 75m to its current location using some wizardly technology. The heart of the Sony Center, though, is a central plaza dramatically canopied by a tentlike glass roof with supporting beams emanating like spokes of a bicycle. After dark it erupts in a light show of changing colours. The plaza and its many cafes are great for hanging out and people-watching. Also integrated into the ensemble is the historic Kaisersaal, which is a rare relic from the prewar Potsdamer Platz days.

MUSEUM FÜR FILM & FERNSEHEN
Map p112

☎ 300 9030; www.filmmuseum-berlin.de; Potsdamer Strasse 2; adult/concession/family €6/4.50/12; ☉ 10am-6pm Tue-Sun, to 8pm Thu; ⊙ ⊛ Potsdamer Platz, ⊜ 200
A multimedia journey through German film history and a behind-the-scenes look at special effects are what await visitors to the Filmmuseum Berlin. Be sure to make use of the excellent free audioguide as you work your way through various themed galleries.

The tour kicks off with an appropriate sense of drama as it sends you through a dizzying mirrored walkway that conjures visions of *The Cabinet of Dr Caligari*. Major themes include pioneers and early divas, silent-era classics such as Fritz Lang's *Metropolis,* Leni Riefenstahl's ground-breaking Nazi-era documentary *Olympia* (see boxed text on p48), German exiles in Hollywood and post-WWII movies. Stealing the show as she did in real life, though, is *femme fatale* Marlene Dietrich, whose glamour lives on through her original costumes, personal finery, photographs and documents. Finally, there's the special-effects room where you learn such handy titbits as how Spiderman climbs up those walls.

Unless you're familiar with German TV, the Museum für Fernsehen will probably be of less interest. Its centrepiece is the Hall of Mirrors, where snippets from five decades of seminal TV shows in both Germanys are projected onto an 8m-high wall. Afterwards, head upstairs to access an archive of favourite shows at private viewing consoles. If you ever wondered what *Star Trek* sounds like in German, this is your chance.

The museum is part of the Filmhaus, which also harbours a film school, the Arsenal (p252) cinemas, a library, a museum shop and a bistro.

LEGOLAND DISCOVERY CENTRE
Map p112

☎ 301 0400; www.legolanddiscoverycentre.de /berlin; Potsdamer Strasse 4; adult/child 3-11 €15.95/12.95; ☉ 10am-7pm; ⊙ ⊛ Potsdamer Platz, ⊜ 200
The world's first indoor Legoland is a fantasy environment made entirely of those little coloured plastic building blocks that many of us grew up with. It's very cute but quite low-tech and best suited for kids aged three to eight. It's also pretty commercial, starting with an animated introductory film about the making of Lego bricks, a process also explained next door in the Lego Factory. In the next rooms, children can build their own structures, then test them for 'earthquake safety'.

The most enchanting feature is the Jungle Trail inspired by the Indiana Jones movies, where big Lego crocs lurk in the dark and tigers frolic around. 'Thrills' include the 4-D cinema (with tactile special effects), and

TRANSPORT: POTSDAMER PLATZ & TIERGARTEN

Bus The 100 goes through Tiergarten to the government quarter; M29 goes to Checkpoint Charlie and Görlitzer Bahnhof in Kreuzberg; 200 travels west along the southern park edge and east to Alexanderplatz; M41 connects Potsdamer Platz with the government quarter, Hauptbahnhof, Kreuzberg and Neukölln.

S-Bahn S1 and S2 link Potsdamer Platz with Kreuzberg to the south and the Scheunenviertel to the north.

U-Bahn U2 stops at Potsdamer Platz and Mendelssohn-Bartholdy-Park.

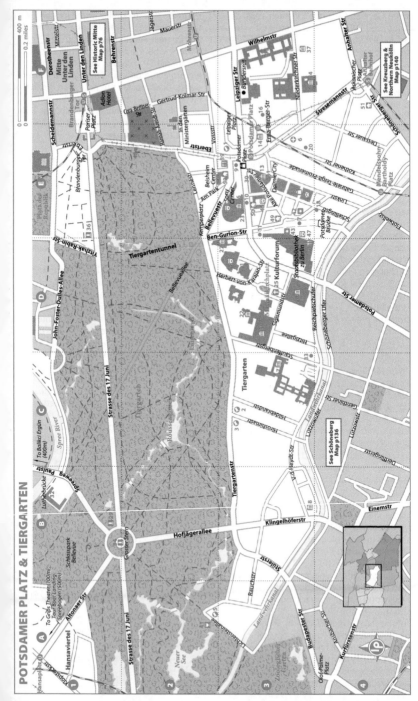

POTSDAMER PLATZ & TIERGARTEN

112

POTSDAMER PLATZ & TIERGARTEN

a ride through the Dragon's Castle (top speed: 10km/h), a medieval world inhabited by knights and dragons and outfitted with a 'torture-tickle chamber'.

Reconstruction of the Stadtschloss (Berlin City Palace; p91) may be delayed by a few years but a model replica of the imposing building will soon be part of Miniland, which also recreates other Berlin landmarks like the Reichstag, Unter den Linden and Potsdamer Platz (though, disturbingly, complete with marquees for Legoland's sister properties SeaLife and Madame Tussauds).

Last admission to Legoland is at 5pm. Check the website for ticket deals – a combination ticket with Madame Tussauds and SeaLife is €29.50/27.50 per adult/child.

PANORAMAPUNKT Map opposite

☎ 2529 4372; www.panoramapunkt.de; Potsdamer Platz 1; adult/concession/family €6.50/ 4.50/16.50; ☻ 10am-8pm; ◉ ⊛ Potsdamer Platz

For fantastic 360-degree views, take what's billed as Europe's fastest lift to the two top floors of the red-clinker-clad Kollhoff-Tower, designed by Renzo Piano and one of the most prominent buildings on Potsdamer Platz. From a lofty 100m, you can pinpoint the sights, make a java stop in the glass cafe, enjoy the sunset from the terrace and check out the outdoor exhibit that peels back the layers of the history of the quarter.

DAIMLER CONTEMPORARY Map opposite

☎ 2594 1420; www.sammlung.daimler.com; 4th fl, Weinhaus Huth, Alte Potsdamer Strasse 5; admission free; ☻ 11am-6pm; ◉ ⊛ Potsdamer Platz

Escape the city bustle at this quiet, loft-style gallery where the Daimler corporation shares selections from its considerable collection of international abstract, conceptual and minimalist art with the public. It's on the top floor of the historic Weinhaus Huth, the only surviving building from pre-WWII Potsdamer Platz. Ring the bell to be buzzed in. There's a different exhibit every three months.

Daimler also sponsored several sculptures dotted around DaimlerCity. These include Keith Haring's *The Boxers* on Eichhornstrasse, Jeff Koons' *Balloon Flower* on Marlene-Dietrich-Platz, Mark Di Suvero's *Galileo* within the pond, Auke de Vries' *Gelandet* (Landed) on Schellingstrasse and

Robert Rauschenberg's *The Riding Bikes* on Fontaneplatz.

DALÍ – DIE AUSSTELLUNG Map p112

☎ 01805-103 323; www.dali-ausstellung.de; Leipziger Platz 7; adult/concession €11/9; ☻ noon-8pm Mon-Sat, 10am-8pm Sun; ☻ ☻ Potsdamer Platz

If you only know Salvador Dalí as the painter of melting watches, burning giraffes and other surrealist imagery that plumbs the depths of the unconscious, this privately owned museum will likely offer new perspectives on the man. The more than 400 works focus primarily on his graphics, illustrations, sculptures, drawings and films. Highlights include the etchings on the theme of Tristan and Isolde, epic sculptures like *Surrealist Angel* and the Don Quixote lithographs. The museum does not receive public subsidies, thus admission is rather steep.

TOPOGRAPHIE DES TERRORS Map p112

☎ 2545 0950; www.topographie.de; Niederkirchner Strasse 8; admission free; ☻ 10am-8pm; ☻ ☻ Potsdamer Platz, ☻ Kochstrasse

Along Niederkirchner Strasse, next to a 200m stretch of the Berlin Wall, once stood the most feared institutions of Nazi Germany: the Gestapo headquarters, the SS central command, the SS security service and, after 1939, the Reich Security Head Office. From their desks, top honchos like Himmler and Heydrich hatched Holocaust plans and organised the systematic persecution of political opponents; many of them suffered torture and death in the Gestapo prison.

The excellent Topography of Terror exhibit, now in a permanent charcoal-grey cube, documents the anatomy of the Nazi state and encourages active confrontation of this dark chapter in German history. Exhibits trace the stages of terror and persecution, put a face on the perpetrators and detail the impact these brutal institutions had on all of Europe.

Displays are in English and German. You can also borrow an audioguide for a self-guided tour of the historic grounds, which leads you past the foundations of the original buildings, including the Gestapo prison.

MARTIN-GROPIUS-BAU Map p112

☎ 254 860; www.gropiusbau.de; Niederkirchner Strasse 7; admission varies, child under 16 free;

☻ usually 10am-8pm Wed-Mon; ☻ ☻ Potsdamer Platz

With its mosaics, terracotta reliefs and airy atrium, the Martin-Gropius-Bau is Berlin's treasure-box showcase for crème-de-la-crème travelling shows. Retrospectives of legendary artists (eg Man Ray and Frida Kahlo) are complemented by ethnological exhibits like 'Egypt's Sunken Treasures' or the 'Mysteries of Angkor Wat'.

The 1881 three-storey cube exudes the majesty of an Italian Renaissance palace, a design that sprang from the fevered brow of Martin Gropius (Walter's great-uncle). After WWII, the pretty building stood neglected just west of the Berlin Wall (there's still a short stretch of it running east along Niederkirchner Strasse), patiently awaiting its restoration.

The Berlin state parliament convenes in the stately neo-Renaissance structure across the street.

FORMER REICHSLUFTFAHRTSMINISTERIUM Map p112

Leipziger Strasse 5-7; ☻ Kochstrasse

Another design springing from the fevered brow of Tempelhof architect Ernst Sagebiel, the Reich Aviation Ministry was Hermann Göring's massive power centre. It's one of the few Nazi-era architectural relics that survived the epic Battle for Berlin. After the war it was used by several GDR ministries and in 1990, quite ironically, became the seat of the agency charged with privatising East German companies and property. It is now the home of the Federal Finance Ministry and not open to the public.

HANSA STUDIOS & MEISTERSAAL Map p112

☎ 325 999 710; www.meistersaal-berlin.de, in German; Köthener Strasse 38; ☻ ☻ Potsdamer Platz

David Bowie, Depeche Mode and U2 are among the megastars who have recorded albums in the acoustically supreme Meistersaal at Hansa Studios, Berlin's answer to London's Abbey Road. Fritz Music Tours (p312) offers guided tours. See p248 for the full scoop.

KULTURFORUM

It's easy to spend a day or more mingling with masters old and modern in the five top-notch museums that make up this enormous cultural complex just west of Potsdamer Platz. Also incorporating Berlin's premier classical music venue, the Philharmonie, it was master-planned by Hans Scharoun, one of the top post-WWII architects, in the 1960s. Intended to be at the centre of the divided city, the Kulturforum found itself on the outer edge of West Berlin after the Wall went up in 1961. Construction proceeded nevertheless but was not completed until the 1990s.

GEMÄLDEGALERIE Map p112

☎ 266 423 040; www.smb.spk-berlin.de; Matthäikirchplatz 8; adult/concession/child under 18 €8/4/free; ☻ 10am-6pm Tue-Sun, to 10pm Thu; ⊕ ⊛ Potsdamer Platz, ⊟ M29, M41, M48, 200
When the star-studded Gemäldegalerie (Picture Gallery) opened in its custom-built space in 1998, it marked the happy reunion of an outstanding collection of European paintings separated by the Cold War for half a century. Some had remained at the Bodemuseum in East Berlin, the rest went on display in the West Berlin suburb of Dahlem. Today about 1500 works span the arc of artistic vision in Europe between the 13th and 18th centuries. Be sure to make use of the excellent free audioguide to get the low-down on selected works by such key figures as Rembrandt, Dürer, Hals, Vermeer and Gainsborough. A tour of all 72 rooms covers almost 2km, with galleries radiating out from the lofty great hall. Budget at least a couple of hours.

NEUE NATIONALGALERIE Map p112

☎ 266 2951; www.neue-nationalgalerie.de; Potsdamer Strasse 50; adult/concession/child under 18 €10/5/free; ☻ 10am-6pm Tue, Wed & Fri, 10am-10pm Thu, 11-6pm Sat & Sun; ⊕ ⊛ Potsdamer Platz, ⊟ M29, M41, M48, 200
The first of the Kulturforum museums to open in 1968, the Neue Nationalgalerie

(New National Gallery) is also the most spectacular, architecturally speaking. All glass and steel squatting on a raised platform, this late masterpiece of Ludwig Mies van der Rohe resembles a postmodern Buddhist temple; it presents paintings and sculpture created by 20th-century European artists working until 1960.

All major genres are represented, including cubism (Pablo Picasso, Gris Leger), surrealism (Salvador Dalí, Joan Miró, Max Ernst), new objectivity (Otto Dix, George Grosz) and Bauhaus (Paul Klee, Wassily Kandinsky). Most impressive, though, is the German expressionist collection. The warped works of Otto Dix (eg *Old Couple*, 1923), the 'egghead' figures of George Grosz, and Ernst Ludwig Kirchner's chaotic *Potsdamer Platz* (1914) peopled by a demimonde of prostitutes and revellers are all stand-outs. Of special significance is the group of 11 Max Beckmann paintings, which trace the artist's development between 1906 and 1942.

Galleries on the ground floor often feature high-calibre travelling exhibitions. These occasionally also displace the permanent collection in the basement.

KUNSTGEWERBEMUSEUM Map p112

☎ 266 423 040; www.smb.spk-berlin.de; Matthäikirchplatz; adult/concession €8/4; ☻ 10am-6pm Tue-Fri, 11am-6pm Sat & Sun; ⊕ ⊛ Potsdamer Platz, ⊟ M29, M41, M48, 200
The cavernous Kunstgewerbemuseum (Museum of Decorative Arts) harbours a mind-boggling collection of precious objects created from gold, silver, ivory, wood, porcelain and other fine materials. From medieval gem-encrusted crosses to Art Deco ceramics and modern appliances, it's all here.

The curatorial concept is to explore the museum chronologically, starting with the Middle Ages on the ground floor. Pride of place goes to the so-called Guelph Treasure, which consists mostly of bones of various saints encased in precious reliquaries. It's a bit macabre but the artistry is supreme, especially considering some pieces are a thousand years old.

Next up is the Renaissance, where a key display is the municipal silver of Lüneberg, essentially a bunch of bowls, plates, goblets and other trinkets once used by the council members. The two rooms also feature delicate Venetian glass, colourful majolica

top picks

DON'T MISS: GEMÄLDEGALERIE

- **Last Judgement**, Petrus Christus, 1452 (Room IV) You'll think twice about sinning after seeing this sadistically grinning skeleton hovering above a truly terrifying hell.

- **Hieronymus Holzschuher**, Albrecht Dürer, 1529 (Room 2) Exceptional portrait of Dürer's friend, painted with utmost precision down to the furrows and wrinkles.

- **Leda with the Swan**, Antonio da Corregio, 1532 (Room XV) Hey, what's she smiling about? Naughty, naughty.

- **Fountain of Youth**, Lucas Cranach the Elder, 1546 (Room III) Old crones leaping into a pool and emerging as dashing hotties – this fountain would surely put plastic surgeons out of business.

- **Dutch Proverbs**, Pieter Bruegel, 1559 (Room 7) This moralistic yet humorous painting magically illustrates 119 proverbs in a single seaside village scene.

- **Malle Babbe**, Frans Hals, 1633 (Room 13) Fantastically lively portrait of the 'Witch of Haarlem'.

earthenware, rich tapestries, elegant furniture and other objects reflective of the exalted lifestyle at court or in patrician households.

Trooping up one floor catapults you centuries ahead to the baroque, neo-classical, Art Nouveau and Art Deco periods. It's an eclectic collection that includes historical board games, amazing baubles fashioned in ivory and exquisite porcelain. A particular eye-catcher is the exotic late-19th-century furniture by Carlo Bugatti, who found inspiration in Islamic and Japanese design.

The basement showcases international 20th- and 21st-century glass, ceramics, jewellery and utilitarian products, including furniture by Michael Thonet, Charles Eames, Philippe Starck, Frank Gehry and other top practitioners.

MUSIKINSTRUMENTEN-MUSEUM
Map p112

☎ 2548 1178; www.mim-berlin.de, in German; Tiergartenstrasse 1, enter from Ben-Gurion-Strasse; adult/concession/child under 18 €4/2/free; ☼ 9am-5pm Tue, Wed & Fri, to 10pm Thu, 10am-5pm Sat & Sun; ⊕ ⓡ Potsdamer Platz, ⊜ M29, M41, M48, 200

Packed with fun, precious and rare sound machines, the Musical Instruments Museum shares a building with the Philharmonie (below). There are plenty of old trumpets, bizarre bagpipes and even a talking walking stick as well as a handful of 'celebrity instruments': the glass harmonica invented by Ben Franklin, a flute played by Frederick the Great and Johann Sebastian Bach's cembalo. Stop at the listening stations to hear what some of the more obscure instruments sound like.

A crowd favourite is the Mighty Wurlitzer (1929), an organ with more buttons and keys than a troop of beefeater guards. It's cranked up at noon on Saturday. Classical concerts, many free, take place year-round (ask for a free schedule or check the website).

KUPFERSTICHKABINETT Map p112
☎ 266 423 040; www.smb.spk-berlin.de; Matthäikirchplatz; adult/concession €8/4; ☼ 10am-6pm Tue-Fri, 11am-6pm Sat & Sun; ⊕ ⓡ Potsdamer Platz, ⊜ M29, M41, M48, 200

Botticelli's original illustrations for Dante's *Divine Comedy* are among the prized possessions of art on paper held by the Museum of Prints and Drawings. This is one of the world's largest and finest collections of its kind, a bonanza of hand-illustrated books, illuminated manuscripts, drawings and prints produced mostly in Europe from the 14th century onward – Dürer to Botticelli, Rembrandt to Schinkel, Picasso to Giacometti to Warhol.

The works don't do well under light, which is why only a tiny fraction of the collection is shown on a rotating basis.

PHILHARMONIE & KAMMERMUSIKSAAL Map p112
☎ 254 880; www.berliner-philharmoniker.de; Herbert-von-Karajan-Strasse 1; ⊕ ⓡ Potsdamer Platz, ⊜ M29, M41, M48, 200

Hans Scharoun masterminded this iconic concert venue and home base of the Berliner Philharmoniker, one of the world's leading orchestras. From the outside, the 1963 building is shaped somewhat like a postmodern Chinese teahouse, clad in a honey-coloured facade. The auditorium feels like the inside of a finely crafted instrument and boasts supreme acoustics and excellent sightlines from every seat. It's an imposing yet intimate hall with terraced and angled 'vineyard' seating wrapped around a central orchestra stage. Try catching a concert (p250) here or join the daily guided tour (in German; ☎ 254 88156; adult/concession €3/2; ⊗ 1pm) which meets at the artist entrance across the parking lot facing Potsdamer Strasse.

The adjacent Kammermusiksaal (Chamber Music Hall), also based on a design by Scharoun, is essentially a more compact riff on the Philharmonie.

MATTHÄUSKIRCHE Map p112

☎ 262 1202; www.stiftung-stmatthaeus.de, in German; Matthäikirchplatz; admission free; ⊗ noon-6pm Tue-Sun; ⊕ ⊛ Potsdamer Platz, ⊒ M29, M41, M48, 200

Standing a bit lost and forlorn within the Kulturforum, the Stüler-designed Matthäuskirche (1846) is a beautiful neo-Romanesque confection with alternating bands of red and ochre brick and a light-flooded, modern sanctuary that doubles as a gallery. German resistance fighter Dietrich Bonhoeffer was ordained a Lutheran minister here in 1931. A few years later the church was scheduled to be transplanted to Spandau to make room for Albert Speer's Germania (see the boxed text, p57). Fortunately the war – and history – took a different turn. Bonhoeffer, however, was executed by the Nazis on 9 April 1945, a day after V-E Day. Climb the tower for good views of the Kulturforum and Potsdamer Platz. A nice time to visit is for the free 20-minute organs recitals at 12.30pm Tuesday to Sunday.

TIERGARTEN

Berlin's rulers used to hunt boar and pheasants in the rambling Tiergarten until master landscape architect Peter Lenné landscaped the grounds in the 18th century. Today one of the world's largest urban parks is a popular place for strolling, jogging, picnicking, Frisbee tossing, grill parties and, yes, nude tanning and gay cruising (especially around the Löwenbrücke). Walking across the entire park takes about an hour, but even a shorter stroll has its rewards.

One of the most idyllic spots is the Rousseauinsel, a little island in a placid pond that's a memorial to 18th-century French philosopher Jean-Jacques Rousseau. It was designed to resemble his burial site on an island near Paris. East of here is Luiseninsel, a tranquil enclosed garden with flower beds and a statue of Queen Luise. The largest lake is the Neuer See southwest of the Siegessäule, where you can rent boats to take your sweetie for a spin or quaff a cold one in the Café am Neuen See (p223).

SIEGESSÄULE Map p112

☎ 391 2961; www.monument-tales.de; Grosser Stern; adult/concession €2.20/1.50; ⊗ 9.30am-6.30pm Mon-Fri, to 7pm Sat & Sun Apr-Oct, 10am-5pm Mon-Fri, to 5.30pm Sat & Sun Nov-Mar; ⊒ 100

Like arms of a starfish, five roads merge into the roundabout called Grosser Stern at the heart of the Tiergarten. At its centre is the landmark Victory Column, built to celebrate 19th-century Prussian military triumphs over Denmark, Austria and France and now a symbol of Berlin's gay community. It stood in front of the Reichstag until the Nazis moved it here in 1938 to make room for their utopian Germania urban planning project (see the boxed text, p57). The pedestal was added at the time, so that today the column stands 67m high.

The gilded lady on top represents the Goddess of Victory, but locals irreverently call her Goldelse. Film buffs might remember her from a key scene in Wim Wenders' 1985 flick *Wings of Desire*. The so-so views from below her skirt mostly take in Tiergarten. Several other monuments were also moved here in the late 1930s, including Reinhold Begas' imposing depiction of Otto von Bismarck; it's in the park northeast of the column.

At the time of writing, the column was closed for restoration, which was expected to be completed by May 2011.

STRASSE DES 17 JUNI Map p112

⊕ ⊛ Brandenburger Tor, ⊛ Tiergarten, ⊒ 100

This broad boulevard bisecting the park was originally called Charlottenburger Chaussee and linked the City Palace on Unter den Linden with Schloss Charlottenburg. In 1937 Hitler doubled its width and turned it into a triumphal road called, rather mundanely, East-West Axis. Its present name commemorates the 1953 workers' uprising in East Berlin (p32), which brought the GDR to the brink of collapse.

The section of Strasse des 17 Juni between the Brandenburger Tor and the Siegessäule turns into a mega-party zone on New Year's Eve, for such festivals as

Christopher Street Day (p262) and during major events such as the FIFA World Cup. Also along here is the bombastic Sowjetisches Ehrenmal (Soviet War Memorial) flanked by two Russian tanks said to have been the first to enter the city in 1945.

SCHLOSS BELLEVUE Map p112
Spreeweg 1; ☺ closed to public; ▣ Bellevue, ▣ 100

The German president (currently Christian Wolff) makes his home in snowy white Schloss Bellevue. The neoclassical palace was built in 1785 by Philipp Daniel Boumann for the youngest brother of Frederick the Great, then became a school under Kaiser Wilhelm II and a museum of ethnology under the Nazis. It's closed to the public. The president and his staff have their offices in the oval Bundespräsidialamt just south of the residence.

DIPLOMATENVIERTEL

In the 19th century the quiet, villa-studded colony west of the Kulturforum and south of the Tiergarten was popular with members of Berlin's cultural elite, including the Brothers Grimm and the poet Hoffmann von Fallersleben, who composed the German national anthem. After WWI several embassies began moving into the neighbourhood, but it wasn't until Hitler's chief architect, Albert Speer, arranged for others to follow suit in the 1930s that the term Diplomatenviertel (Diplomatic Quarter) was coined. After WWII the obliterated area remained in a state of quiet decay while the embassies all set up in Bonn, the new West German capital. After reunification many countries rebuilt on their historic lots, which is why some of Berlin's boldest new architecture can be found on these quiet streets (see the Walking Tour, opposite).

BAUHAUS ARCHIV/MUSEUM FÜR GESTALTUNG Map p112
☎ 254 0020; www.bauhaus.de; Klingelhöferstrasse 14; adult/concession incl audioguide Wed-Fri €6/3, Sat-Mon €7/4; ☺ 10am-5pm Wed-Mon; ◉ Nollendorfplatz, ▣ 100, M29

The Bauhaus School, founded in 1919 by Walter Gropius, is regarded as the most influential architecture and design movement of the 20th century. Chances are you have a little Bauhaus in your house too: perhaps the chair you sit on or the table at

top picks
WWII SITES

- Berliner Unterwelten Bunker (p312)
- Gedenkstätte Deutscher Widerstand (p118)
- Haus der Wannsee Konferenz (p165)
- Holocaust Memorial (p82)
- Sowjetisches Ehrenmal Treptow (p169)

which you dine. 'Form follows function' was the main credo of its practitioners, which included Paul Klee, Lyonel Feininger and Wassily Kandinsky. In 1933 the Nazis forced the group to disband.

Walter Gropius himself designed the avant-garde building that now houses the Bauhaus archive and museum, whose gleaming white shed roofs look a bit like the smokestacks of an ocean liner. Using a combination of study notes, workshop pieces, photographs, blueprints, models and other objects and documents, curators mount changing exhibits that illustrate the Bauhaus theories. Highlights include Gropius' 1925 Bauhaus buildings in Dessau and Lázló Moholy-Nagy's clever kinetic sculpture called *Light-Space-Modulator*. There's a nice cafe in case you need a break, and a cool shop for stocking up on Bauhaus-inspired gewgaws.

GEDENKSTÄTTE DEUTSCHER WIDERSTAND Map p112
☎ 2699 5000; www.gdw-berlin.de; Stauffenbergstrasse 13-14; admission free; ☺ 9am-6pm Mon-Fri, to 8pm Thu, 10am-6pm Sat & Sun; ◉ ▣ Potsdamer Platz, ▣ M29, M48

If you've seen the 2008 film *Valkyrie*, starring Tom Cruise, you're well aware of Claus Schenk Graf von Stauffenberg, the poster boy of the German resistance against Hitler and the Third Reich. The very rooms where a group of senior army officers, led by Stauffenberg, plotted the bold but ill-fated assassination attempt on the Führer on 20 July 1944 (see p30) are now part of the German Resistance Memorial Centre. The building itself, the historic Bendlerblock, harboured the Wehrmacht high command from 1935 to 1945. Today the complex is the secondary seat of the German Ministry of Defense (the primary is still in Bonn, the former West German capital).

The centre's exhibit documents the efforts not just of Stauffenberg but of many other Germans who actively opposed the Third Reich for ideological, religious or military reasons. Most were just regular folks, such as the students Hans and Sophie Scholl or the craftsman Georg Elser; others were prominent citizens like the artist Käthe Kollwitz and the theologian Dietrich Bonhoeffer. All of them risked not only their own lives and livelihoods but also those of their friends and families. Labelling is in German, so be sure to make use of the excellent and free audioguide (available in English and other languages).

The entrance to the centre takes you through the yard where Stauffenberg and three of his co-conspirators were shot on 20 July 1944. A statue of a nude male and a plaque in the courtyard mark the very spot. More than 600 others were arrested in the post-coup aftermath, many of them completely unaffiliated; about 100 were tortured and executed, many at Plötzensee Prison, now the Gedenkstätte Plötzensee (p177) site.

AMBASSADORIAL AMBLE
Walking Tour

1 Egyptian Embassy There's no mistaking this elegant, polished, red granite building at Stauffenbergstrasse 6–7 as anything other than the base of Egypt's delegation, engraved as it is with hieroglyphs and Pharaonic encryptions. Cairo architect Samir Rabie juxtaposed traditional and modern elements to reflect both the country's 7000-year history and its aspirations as a modern industrial nation.

2 Austrian Embassy Vienna-based architect Hans Hollein designed one of the quarter's most extravagant representations at Stauffenbergstrasse 1. It houses embassy, consulate and residence in three colourful and linked, but visually very disparate, structural parts: an elliptical front building clad in patina-green copper; a terracotta-hued centre with a jutting roof; and a grey concrete cube.

3 Indian Embassy A cubic design clad in pinkish rough-cast Indian sandstone, this embassy at Tiergartenstrasse 16–17 cuts a formidable presence based on the interplay between mass and void. A narrow vertical

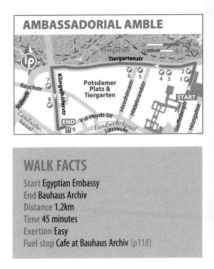

AMBASSADORIAL AMBLE

WALK FACTS
Start **Egyptian Embassy**
End **Bauhaus Archiv**
Distance **1.2km**
Time **45 minutes**
Exertion **Easy**
Fuel stop **Cafe at Bauhaus Archiv** (p118)

incision in the facade opens up the cylindrical atrium of the public entrance and provides a view deep into the structure.

4 South African Embassy Modest and modern by comparison, South Africa presents itself at Tiergartenstrasse 18 with a streamlined building that's clad in yellow sandstone – shipped from the motherland – atop a grey granite base. Two L-shaped wings form a rectangle linked by a central element made of glass, a design by Jo'burg-based MMA Architects.

5 Italian Embassy The Italian delegation has taken up offices at Hiroshimastrasse 1 in the restored 1942 digs that were drawn up by Friedrich Hetzelt, Hermann Göring's favourite architect. Inspired by the Palazzo della Consulta in Rome, the building is a reinterpretation of a Renaissance palace whose bombast is somewhat tempered by the girly-pink paint job.

6 Japanese Embassy Looking very much like a foreboding fortress, the 1940 Japanese Embassy at Hiroshimastrasse 6 is almost an exact replica of the Nazi-era original by Ludwig Moshamer. Only the elliptical structure along Hiroshimastrasse, which houses a conference room, is a nod to modernity. The golden sun above the main entrance symbolises imperial Japan.

7 Nordic Embassies This compact compound at Rauchstrasse 1 unites the representations of

Denmark, Sweden, Finland, Iceland and Norway behind one dramatic turquoise facade made of copper lamellas. It's entered through the only shared building, the Felleshus, and at night glows like a giant ice-blue crystal.

8 Mexican Embassy This avant-garde building by Teodoro Gonźalez de Léon and Francisco Serrano is fronted by two soaring, slanted curtains of slender concrete pillars that protect a glass front and the main entrance. It doubles as a cultural institute and sits at Klingelhöferstrasse 3.

9 Bauhaus Archiv Conclude your walk at the Bauhaus Archiv (p118), a museum celebrating the legendary architectural and design school founded by Walter Gropius in 1919. The neat cafe inside makes for a fine refuelling stop.

CHARLOTTENBURG & NORTHERN WILMERSDORF

Drinking p223; Eating p206; Shopping p188; Sleeping p272

During the Cold War, ritzy Charlottenburg and its largely residential neighbour Wilmersdorf were the glittering heart of West Berlin. This is where the jet set wallowed in the fruits of capitalism, gorging themselves on steak and lobster in chic restaurants, debating politics in smoke-filled cafes and disco-foxing at cocaine-addled parties in glamorous Kurfürstendamm (Ku'damm for short) haunts. Alas, after reunification, the western suburbs almost instantly lost their edge as the adventurous avant-garde moved on to the artists' squats and crumbling tenements formerly trapped behind the Wall. Mitte and Prenzlauer Berg have since mutated into posh enclaves of models, media professionals and trust-fund bohemians and not even Friedrichshain is immune to gentrification thanks to the impending Mediaspree development. Still, compared to the spunky rebel-child character of the 'Wild East', the city west gives off the self-satisfied air of middle-aged burghers happy with the status quo. Experimentation is elsewhere.

But Berlin demands that you keep up, or else. And so, in recent years, Charlottenburg has lost the Egyptian Museum with Nefertiti and her entourage to Museumsinsel and the Berlinale film festival to Potsdamer Platz. Even Zoo Station (Bahnhof Zoo or, officially, Zoologischer Garten) has been demoted to regional train station status since the shiny new Hauptbahnhof opened in 2006. For a while, an adorable polar bear named Knut born at the Berlin Zoo recaptured some of the spotlight for Charlottenburg. Right now, city boosters hope that the luxury hotel Waldorf-Astoria, which is under construction next to Zoo Station, will inject some spark when it opens in late 2011.

Charlottenburg grew up around its namesake palace, which continues to delight 'royal groupies' and garden fans. Still a village in the 18th century, it became a favourite getaway for the bourgeoisie, who began to settle here around 1850. After the founding of the German Empire in 1871, the still-independent town grew in leaps and bounds, getting its own university, opera house and grand boulevard, the Ku'damm. In the giddy Golden Twenties, it became a major nightlife hub with glamorous cinemas, theatres and restaurants. The Romanisches Café, which stood on the site of today's Europa-Center (p130) was practically the second living room for artists, actors, writers, photographers, film producers

top picks

CHARLOTTENBURG & NORTHERN WILMERSDORF

- Kaiser-Wilhelm-Gedächtniskirche (p127)
- Berlin Zoo (p126)
- Museum Berggruen (p123)
- Museum für Fotografie/Helmut Newton Stiftung (p129)
- Schloss Charlottenburg – Neuer Flügel (p122)

and other creative types. Some were famous, like Bertolt Brecht, Otto Dix and Billy Wilder. Most were not. German writer Erich Kästner even called it the 'waiting room of the talented'. In fact, the cafe was split into two areas: the 'small room' for the success stories and the 'large room' for the wannabes. After the city's division in 1961, Charlottenburg evolved into the commercial heart of West Berlin. There was lots of new construction (not always of the flattering kind) but as soon as the Wall came down, the true centre shifted back east.

Still, Charlottenburg's long-time draws are in no danger of disappearing. If you're more into high quality and high brow than experimentation and trashy locations, you'll feel quite Piccadilly here. Catch a cabaret at Bar Jeder Vernunft (p238), Anna Netrebko at the Deutsche Oper Berlin (p253) or international jazz greats at A-Trane (p236). Nightlife is liveliest around Savignyplatz, which is framed by chic cafes, restaurants and boutiques. It's hard to imagine now that as recently as the 1970s this square was the haunt of the local demi-monde, where prostitution and drug dealing were part of daily life.

Shopaholics can get their kicks on Ku'damm, Berlin's longest and busiest shopping strip, and its continuation Tauentzienstrasse. This is where you'll find big department stores, including the famous KaDeWe (p189), along with mainstream fashion stores like H&M and Mango. Further west on Ku'damm, shops get smaller and more exclusive; more Rodeo Drive than Oxford Street.

More big-label boutiques await in leafy side streets such as Fasanenstrasse and Bleibtreustrasse, while interior design shops cluster along Kantstrasse. Though existing far from the cutting edge, you'll find plenty to keep you busy in Charlottenburg.

South of Lietzenburger Strasse Charlottenburg segues into affluent, sedate and bourgeois Wilmersdorf, which is at its liveliest along Pariser Strasse and around Ludwigkirchplatz.

SCHLOSS CHARLOTTENBURG

Schloss Charlottenburg is an exquisite baroque palace and one of the few sites in Berlin that still reflects the one-time grandeur of the royal Hohenzollern clan. It's a wonderful place to visit, especially in summer when you can fold a stroll, sunbathing session or picnic in the lush palace park into a day of peeking at royal treasures.

The compound consists of the main palace and two smaller structures in the lovely Schlossgarten (park). Schloss Charlottenburg wasn't always so large and lavish but started out rather modestly as the petite summer retreat of Sophie-Charlotte, wife of Elector Friedrich III. Arnold Nering drew up the initial plans, which were expanded in the mode of Versailles by Johann Friedrich Eosander after the elector became King Friedrich I in 1701. Subsequent royals dabbled with the compound, most notably Frederick the Great, whose reign saw the addition of the spectacular Neuer Flügel (New Wing, 1746).

Schloss Charlottenburg is about 3km northwest of Bahnhof Zoo. The most scenic approach is from the south via Schlossstrasse (get off at U-Bahn stop Sophie-Charlotte-Platz), a leafy avenue flanked by dignified townhouses built for senior court officials.

A palace visit is easily combined with a spin around the trio of nearby museums, described below.

ALTES SCHLOSS Map pp124-5

☎ 320 911; www.spsg.de; Spandauer Damm; adult/concession incl guided tour or audioguide €10/7; ⏰ 10am-6pm Tue-Sun Apr-Oct, to 5pm Tue-Sun Nov-Mar; ⊙ Sophie-Charlotte-Platz, then 🚌 309, ⊙ Richard-Wagner-Platz, then 🚌 145

Also known as the Nering-Eosander Building after its two architects, this is the central, and oldest, section of the palace and fronted by Andreas Schlüter's grand equestrian statue of the Great Elector (1699). The baroque living quarters of Friedrich I and Sophie-Charlotte are an extravaganza in stucco, brocade and overall opulence. Highlights include the Oak Gallery, a wood-panelled festival hall draped in family portraits; the charming Oval Hall overlooking the park; Friedrich I's bedchamber, with the first-ever bathroom in a baroque palace; the fabulous Porcelain Chamber, smothered in Chinese and Japanese blueware; and the Eosander Chapel, with its trompe l'oeil arches.

Before or after the tour, skip upstairs to admire the paintings, vases, tapestries, weapons, porcelain, a 2600-piece silver table setting and other items essential to a royal lifestyle in the old apartments of Friedrich Wilhelm IV.

NEUER FLÜGEL Map pp124-5

☎ 320 911; www.spsg.de; Spandauer Damm; adult/concession incl audioguide €6/5; ⏰ 10am-6pm Wed-Mon Apr-Oct, to 5pm Wed-Mon Nov-Mar; ⊙ Sophie-Charlotte-Platz, then 🚌 309, ⊙ Richard-Wagner-Platz, then 🚌 145

The palace's most beautiful rooms are the flamboyant private chambers of Frederick

---

SCHLOSS CHARLOTTENBURG INSIDER TIPS

- Each Schloss building charges separate admission, but it's best to invest in the *Tageskarte* (adult/concession €14/10) for one-day admission to every open building. Do come between Wednesday and Sunday when all are open and do arrive early, especially on weekends and in summer, when queues can be long.
- From April to December, you can feel like royalty during the Berliner Residenz Konzerte (www.concerts-berlin .com), a series of classical concerts performed by candlelight with musicians dressed in powdered wigs and historical costumes.
- If you need sustenance, there's a pretty – if overpriced – cafe with tree-shaded outdoor seating in the Kleine Orangerie building near the entrance to the palace park. Or pack a picnic and find a nice spot in the park.
- A lovely way to travel to or from Schloss Charlottenburg is by boat cruise (p311) on the Spree River. The landing docks are just outside the northeast corner of the park.
- The Schloss is at its most photogenic from the front and when seen from the carp pond in the Schlosspark.

the Great, designed in 1746 by royal buddy and 'starchitect du jour' Georg Wenzeslaus von Knobelsdorff. The confection-like White Hall banquet room; the Golden Gallery, a rococo fantasy of mirrors and gilding; and the Concert Room filled with 18th-century paintings by French masters such as Watteau, Boucher and Pesne are especially impressive. The austere neoclassical ones of his successor, Friedrich Wilhelm II, in the same wing, pale in comparison.

You're free to explore on your own, but it's worth following the two audioguides included in the admission price.

SCHLOSSGARTEN CHARLOTTENBURG
Map pp124-5

Spandauer Damm; admission free; ⊕ Sophie-Charlotte-Platz, then ⊜ 309, ⊕ Richard-Wagner-Platz, then ⊜ 145
The expansive park behind Schloss Charlottenburg is part formal French, part unruly English and all idyllic playground. Hidden among the shady paths, flower beds, lawns, mature trees and carp pond are two smaller royal buildings, the sombre Mausoleum (p123) and the charming Belvedere (p123). It's a fantastic place for strolling, jogging or lazing on a sunny afternoon.

BELVEDERE Map pp124-5

☎ 3209 1445; www.spsg.de; Spandauer Damm; adult/concession €3/2.50; ☉ 10am-6pm Tue-Sun Apr-Oct, noon-4pm Tue-Sun Nov-Mar; ⊕ Sophie-Charlotte-Platz, then ⊜ 309, ⊕ Richard-Wagner-Platz, then ⊜ 145
This pint-size palace with the distinctive cupola got its start in 1788 as a teahouse for Friedrich Wilhelm II. Here he enjoyed reading, listening to chamber music and holding spiritual sessions with fellow members of the mystical Order of the Rosicrucians. These days, the late-rococo vision by Carl Gotthard Langhans makes an elegant backdrop for porcelain masterpieces by the royal manufacturer KPM.

MAUSOLEUM Map pp124-5

☎ 3209 1446; Spandauer Damm; www.spsg.de; adult/concession €2/1.50; ☉ 10am-6pm Tue-Sun Mar-Oct, noon-4pm Tue-Sun Nov-Apr; ⊕ Sophie-Charlotte-Platz, then ⊜ 309, ⊕ Richard-Wagner-Platz, then ⊜ 145
In the Schlosspark, west of the carp pond, the neoclassical Mausoleum (1810) was conceived as the final resting place of

Queen Luise but twice expanded to make room for other royals, including Luise's husband Friedrich Wilhelm III and Emperor William I and his wife Augusta. Their ornate marble sarcophagi are great works of art, but unfortunately it's impossible to get close enough to truly admire them. A few other royals are in the crypt but it's not open to the public.

NEUER PAVILLON Map pp124-5

Schinkel Pavillon; ☎ 3209 1443; www.spsg.de; Spandauer Damm; ☉ closed for renovation; ⊕ Sophie-Charlotte-Platz, then ⊜ 309, ⊕ Richard-Wagner-Platz, then ⊜ 145
This Schinkel-designed mini-palace was built for Friedrich Wilhelm III (r 1797–1848) as a summer retreat and modelled on the Villa Reale del Chiatamonte in Naples, where the king had stayed on a trip. It normally displays paintings from the Romantic and Biedermeier periods but an extensive renovation will keep it closed until at least 2012.

AROUND SCHLOSS CHARLOTTENBURG

A visit to Schloss Charlottenburg is easily combined with a spin around the museums in its immediate vicinity. All three are based on the donated collections of private individuals.

MUSEUM BERGGRUEN Map pp124-5

☎ 3435 7315; www.smb.museum/mb; Schlossstrasse 1; adult/concession/child under 18 €8/4/free; ☉ 10am-6pm Tue-Sun; ⊕ Sophie-Charlotte-Platz, then ⊜ 309, ⊕ Richard-Wagner-Platz, then ⊜ 145
This intimate museum is a delicacy for fans of classical modern art, especially of Picasso, Klee, Matisse and Giacometti. Picasso is especially well represented

BARGAIN BOX

Tickets to any one of the three national museums in Charlottenburg are also valid for same-day admission to the permanent collection of the other two. Participating venues are the Museum Berggruen, the Sammlung Scharf-Gerstenberg, both near Schloss Charlottenburg, and the Museum für Fotografie behind Zoo Station. Admission at any is free if you're under 18. Special exhibitions cost extra.

CHARLOTTENBURG & NORTHERN WILMERSDORF

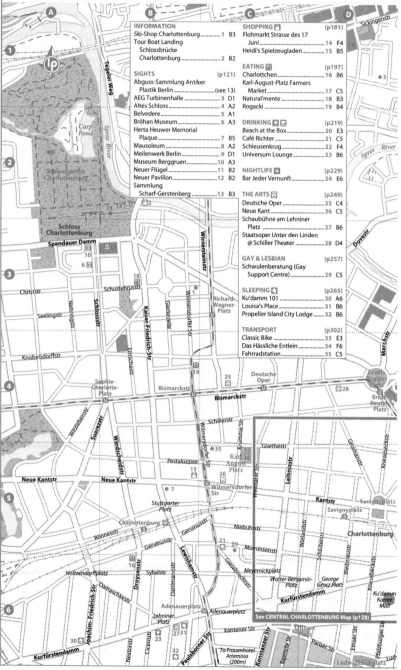

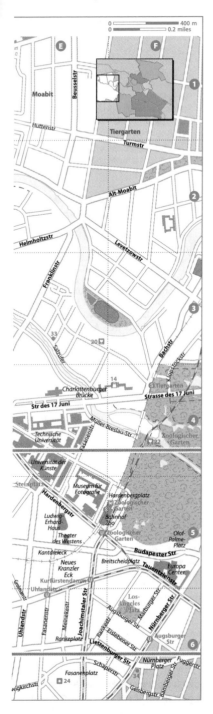

with more than 100 paintings, drawings and sculptures from all his major creative phases. The early blue and rose periods (eg *Seated Harlequin,* 1905) give way to his bold cubist canvases (eg the portrait of George Braque, 1910) and the mellow creations of his later years (eg *The Yellow Pullover,* 1939).

Elsewhere it's off to the delicate and emotional world of Paul Klee, with a selection of 60 works created between 1917 and 1940. There are also paper cut-outs by Matisse and Giacometti's famous sculptures alongside a sprinkling of African art that inspired both Klee and Picasso.

SAMMLUNG SCHARF-GERSTENBERG
Map opposite

☎ 3435 7315; www.smb.museum/ssg; Schlossstrasse 70; adult/concession/child under 18 €8/4/free; ☼ 10am-6pm Tue-Sun; ◎ Sophie-Charlotte-Platz, then ☐ 309, ◎ Richard-Wagner-Platz, then ☐ 145

Insurance founder Otto Gerstenberg was a man with a Midas touch and a passion for the arts who, in the early 20th century, parlayed his millions into a respectable collection of canvases. Although much of it was destroyed in WWII or disappeared to Russia as war booty, his grandsons used the remainder as a starting point for their own collection, mostly of surrealist nature. A sampling of these 'family jewels', 300 works in all, is now on display in the 19th-century former royal stables across from Schloss Charlottenburg. You'll be treated to a complete survey of the surrealist genre with large bodies of work by René Magritte and Max Ernst along with samplings of dreamscapes by Salvador Dalí and Jean Dubuffet. Among their 18th-century forerunners, Goya's spooky etchings and the creepy dungeon scenes by Italian engraver Giovanni Battista Piranesi stand out. Regularly screened films by Buñuel, Dalí and contemporary directors show how the surrealist aesthetic was interpreted on screen.

BRÖHAN MUSEUM Map opposite

☎ 3269 0600; www.broehan-museum.de; Schlossstrasse 1a; adult/concession/child under 18 €6/4/free; ☼ 10am-6pm Tue-Sun; ◎ Sophie-Charlotte-Platz, then ☐ 309, ◎ Richard-Wagner-Platz, then ☐ 145

Entrepreneur Karl Bröhan (1921–2000) had a knack for collecting furniture and furnishings from the Art Nouveau, Art Deco and functionalism periods. These decorative styles were very much in vogue from 1889 to 1939 and are considered the midwives of modern design. Bröhan was also an extremely generous man: on his 60th birthday he donated his entire prized collection to the city of Berlin.

On the ground floor you can wander past outstanding period rooms, each fully furnished and decorated with lamps, porcelain, glass, silver, carpets and other items by such famous designers as Hector Guimard, Émile Ruhlmann and Peter Behrens.

Upstairs, the museum's picture gallery has great works by Berlin Secession painters, including Hans Baluschek, Willy Jaeckel and Walter Leistikow. Henry van de Velde (1863–1957), the multitalented Belgian Art Nouveau artist, gets his own room on the top floor, which is also used for special exhibitions.

ABGUSS-SAMMLUNG ANTIKER PLASTIK BERLIN Map pp124–5

☎ 342 4054; www.abguss-sammlung-berlin.de, in German; Schlossstrasse 69b; admission free; ⓨ 2-5pm Thu-Sun; ⊕ Sophie-Charlotte-Platz, then 🚌 309, ⊕ Richard-Wagner-Platz, then 🚌 145

If you are a fan of classical sculpture or simply enjoy posing with naked guys with missing noses or other body protrusions, make this small collection a definite stopover. With works spanning 3500 years created by cultures as diverse as the Minoan, Roman or Byzantine, you will be able to trace the evolution of this ancient art form. The shop sells plaster-cast copies of popular sculptures.

MEILENWERK BERLIN Map pp124–5

☎ 364 0780; www.meilenwerk.de, in German; Wiebestrasse 36-37; admission free; ⓨ 8am-8pm Mon-Sat, 10am-8pm Sun; 🚊 Beusselstrasse

Tucked in among factories, industrial buildings and tenements across the Spree and about 1km east of Schloss Charlottenburg, Meilenwerk is a place of pilgrimage for those who worship at the altar of the auto. Lined up for inspection inside the vast, slickly converted 19th-century tram depot are limited-edition beauties by Alfa Romeo, logo-less mystery cars, sleek racing wheels like the Maserati Ghibli, lovable veterans like the old VW Beetle and rarities like a GDR-made EMW 327. There are hundreds of other old-timers,

TRANSPORT: CHARLOTTENBURG & NORTHERN WILMERSDORF

Bus Zoologischer Garten is the western terminal for sightseeing favourites 100 and 200 (see p312); M19, M29 and X10 travel along Kurfürstendamm; 109 does too but veers off to Tegel airport which is also served by X9; for Schloss Charlottenburg take M45.

S-Bahn S5, S7/75 and S9 link Wilmersdorfer Strasse, Savignyplatz and Zoologischer Garten with the Hauptbahnhof, Scheunenviertel, Alexanderplatz and Friedrichshain; S41, 42 and 46 bisect Wilmersdorf.

U-Bahn Zoologischer Garten is the main hub served by the U2 from Mitte, Tiergarten, Schöneberg and Olympic Stadium; Uhlandstrasse is the western terminus of the U1 to Schöneberg, Kreuzberg and Friedrichshain. U9 travels north–south between the suburbs of Wedding and Steglitz via Wilmersdorf.

classic and new cars, yet this is no museum: it's a 'Forum for Driving Culture' that also harbours repair shops, car clubs and dealerships. Best of all: anyone is welcome to nose around for free. A great time to come is during the Sunday jazz brunch (☎ 2061 3030; per person €11.90; ⓨ 10am-2pm).

KURFÜRSTENDAMM & AROUND

The 3.5km-long Kurfürstendamm is a ribbon of commerce that began as a bridle path to the royal hunting lodge in the Grunewald forest. In the early 1870s, Otto von Bismarck, the Iron Chancellor, decided that the capital of the newly founded German Reich needed its own representative boulevard, bigger and better even than the Champs-Élysée. The 1920s added the luxury hotels and shops, art galleries and restaurants as well as theatres and cinemas that turned Berlin into the equivalent of Broadway. The lavish Marmorhaus (now Zara clothing store) at Ku'damm 236 premiered the *Cabinet of Dr Caligari* in 1919. Across the street, the Gloria-Palast hosted the 1930 premiere of the *Blue Angel*, starring Marlene Dietrich; today, only the sign is left. There's also some interesting contemporary architecture, including Helmut Jahn's Neues Kranzler Eck (p133).

BERLIN ZOO Map p128

☎ 254 010; www.zoo-berlin.de; Hardenbergplatz 8 & Budapester Strasse 34; adult/child/student

€12/6/9, with aquarium €18/9/14; ⊙ 9am–7pm
mid-Mar–Sep, 9am–5pm Oct–mid-Mar;
⊙ ⓡ Zoologischer Garten
Germany's oldest animal park was founded
by King Friedrich Wilhelm IV in 1844
and was initially stocked with critters,
including bears and kangaroos, from
the royal family's private reserve on the
Pfaueninsel (see p165). These days, almost
16,000 international furry and feathered
friends representing 1500 species make
their home in this attractively landscaped
park, including, of course, Knut (pronounced
'knoot'), the polar bear born at the zoo in
2006. Rejected by his mum, a former GDR
circus diva, the cub was raised 24/7 by
a hunky zoo keeper and soon they both
started stealing hearts around the world.
Thomas Dörflein, the keeper, passed away
suddenly in 2008 but Knut has grown into
a strapping adolescent, even if he's no
longer quite so cute.

There's an entire menagerie of other
crowd-pleasers, of course, including cheeky
orang-utans, kuddly koalas, endangered
rhinos, playful penguins and Bao Bao, a rare
giant panda donated by China.

Three floors of exotic fish, amphibians and
reptiles await next door at the endearingly
old-fashioned Aquarium (www.aquarium-berlin.de;
enter at Budapester Strasse 32; adult/child/student €12/6/9;
⊙ 9am–6pm) with its darkened halls and
glowing tanks. Some of the specimens in
the famous Crocodile Hall are truly the stuff
of nightmares, but tamer diversions such
as communing with poison frogs, watching

ethereal jellyfish and encountering a real-life
'Nemo' should bring smiles to even the most
PlayStation-jaded youngster.

KAISER-WILHELM-GEDÄCHTNISKIRCHE Map p128
☎ 218 5023; www.gedaechtniskirche-berlin.de;
Breitscheidplatz; admission free; ⊙ 9am–7pm;
⊙ ⓡ Zoologischer Garten, ⓡ Kurfürstendamm
The bombed-out tower of this landmark
church serves as an antiwar memorial,
standing quiet and dignified among the
roaring traffic and commerce. Built in 1895
in honour of Kaiser Wilhelm I, it was once
a real beauty, as you'll be able to tell from
the before and after photographs in the
memorial hall at the foot of the tower and
the few surviving mosaics, marble reliefs
and liturgical objects also displayed here.
Alas, the tower ruin, nicknamed Hollow
Tooth, is suffering a major case of cavities
and will be under scaffolding until at least
2012. Church and memorial hall will remain
open. More than €1.2 million of the €4.2
million restoration budget came from
private donors.

In 1961 a modern octagonal hall of worship designed by Egon Eiermann was built
next to the ruin. Stepping inside feels a bit
like entering a giant crystal because of the
intensely midnight-blue glass walls which
were fashioned by an artist in Chartres,
France. The single most striking element
is the giant golden Jesus 'floating' above
the altar. In the back are the Stalingrad
Madonna (a charcoal drawing made by a

KÄTHE KOLLWITZ

Käthe Kollwitz (1867–1945) was the superstar among 20th-century female German artists, although she herself
would probably frown at such a label. Modest, selfless and empathetic, Kollwitz is best known for her deeply moving,
often heart-wrenching woodcuts, sculptures and lithographs that profoundly capture the depth of human hardship,
suffering and sorrow.

Kollwitz was born Käthe Schmidt in Königsberg (today's Kaliningrad, Russia) and attended art schools in Berlin,
Munich, Florence and Paris. In 1891 she married Karl Kollwitz, a physician with a practice on Weissenburger Strasse
(today's Kollwitzstrasse), right in the Prenzlauer Berg working-class ghetto. The despair and poverty she observed
all around her on a daily basis greatly shaped her pacifist and socialist outlook as well as her art. Such realities were
compounded by personal tragedies, especially the deaths of her son in the battlefields of WWI and of her grandson
in WWII. It's no coincidence that one of her most poignant works is Mother and Her Dead Son, on view at the Neue
Wache (p85) in Mitte.

A member of the Berlin Secession (p41), Kollwitz was the first female professor at the prestigious Prussian Academy
of Arts until the Nazis forced her to resign in 1933. During the war she remained in Berlin as long as she could, finally
evacuating in 1943, first to Nordhausen, then to Moritzburg, near Dresden, where she died of natural causes in 1945,
shortly before the end of the war. For an intimate look at this fascinating woman and her body of work, swing by the
excellent Käthe-Kollwitz-Museum (p129) in Charlottenburg.

CENTRAL CHARLOTTENBURG

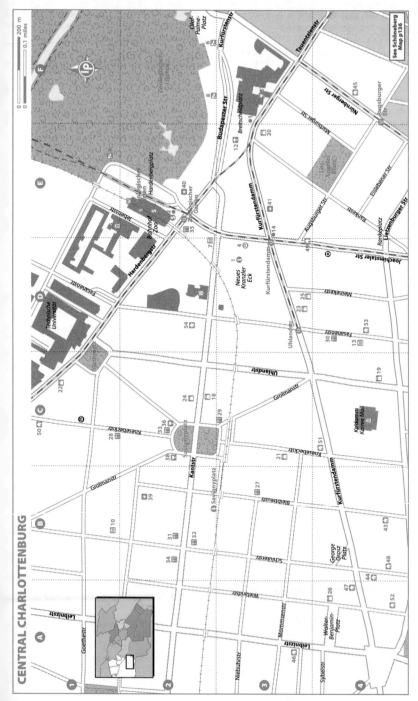

CENTRAL CHARLOTTENBURG

German soldier trapped in Russia during the winter of 1942), and a 13th-century crucifix from Spain that honours Nazi resistance fighters.

KÄTHE-KOLLWITZ-MUSEUM Map opposite

☎ 882 5210; www.kaethe-kollwitz.de; Fasanenstrasse 24; adult/concession €6/3; ⏰ 11am-6pm; ⊕ Uhlandstrasse

This exquisite museum is devoted to Käthe Kollwitz, one of the greatest German women artists (see boxed text p127), whose social and political awareness lent a tortured power to her lithographs, graphics, woodcuts, sculptures and drawings. Highlights include the anti-hunger lithography *Brot!* (Bread!, 1924) and the woodcut series *Krieg* (War, 1922–23). Recurring themes include motherhood and death; sometimes the two are strangely intertwined as in works that show death as a nurturing figure, cradling its victims. There's also a copy of Gustav Seitz' Kollwitz sculpture (p160) on Kollwitzplatz in Prenzlauer Berg. Special exhibits supplement the permanent collection twice annually. English-language audioguides cost an additional €3.

MUSEUM FÜR FOTOGRAFIE/HELMUT NEWTON STIFTUNG Map opposite

☎ 3186 4825; www.smb.museum/mf, www.helmut -newton.de; Jebensstrasse 2; adult/concession/

child under 18 €8/4/free; ⏰ 10am-6pm Tue-Sun, to 10pm Thu; ⊕ 🚉 Zoologischer Garten, 🚌 100

Shorty before his deadly car crash in 2004, Helmut Newton, the celebrated, if controversial, *enfant terrible* of fashion and lifestyle photography, donated 1500 images along with personal effects to his birth city. They form the core exhibit of the Museum of Photography, in a decommissioned Prussian officers' club behind Bahnhof Zoo. Born in Berlin in 1920, Newton studied photography here with famed fashion photographer Yva before fleeing Nazi Germany in 1938. His work reflects a lifelong obsession with the female body, which he often portrayed in controversial, quasi-pornographic poses. One famous image shows a crouched model wearing a horse's saddle, while his best-known work – the 'Big Nudes' series – stars a flock of stark-naked Amazons. Even his landscapes and still lifes are often charged with cold eroticism. The galleries on the 1st floor showcase his vision, while the ground floor is essentially a shrine to the man. Highlights include his partially recreated office in Monte Carlo, his first camera (an Agfa Box he bought aged 12) and his blue Jeep (dubbed the Newton-Mobile).

Also skip up to the 2nd floor where the building's most beautiful room, the recently restored Kaisersaal (Imperial Hall), presents selections from the photographic archive of the State Art Library. A retrospective of Magnum photographer Erich Hartmann and a survey of shots taken during India's colonial days were in the works at the time of writing.

BEATE UHSE EROTIKMUSEUM Map p128
☎ 886 0666; www.erotikmuseum.de; Joachim-staler Strasse 4; single/couple before noon €10/20, after noon €14/25; ☺ 9am-midnight Mon-Sat, 11am-midnight Sun; ◉ ᴙ Zoologischer Garten
Does size really matter? How hard should I spank her? Where is the male G-spot? If you're over 18, you can find the answers to these and other sexy questions in Berlin's Erotic Museum, the brainchild of Beate Uhse, Germany's late sex-toy queen. At this self-proclaimed 'Academy of Sex', right on a suitably seedy corner near Zoo Station, you can take lessons in bedroom antics, often in interactive fashion. Feel up the doll and be rewarded with a deep sigh if you find her (or his) G-spot. Elsewhere you can pick up flirt tips or learn all about erogenous zones. Upstairs, the exhibit is a bit more, shall we say, artistic. On display are items of erotica from around the world like Japanese *shunga* (with exaggerated genitalia), Chinese sex-ed 'wedding tiles' and hardcore watercolours by George Grosz. If that's not enough stimulus, drop by the affiliated garish sex shop with toys, books and video cabins on the ground floor.

STORY OF BERLIN Map pp128
☎ 8872 0100; www.story-of-berlin.de; Kurfürstendamm 207-208; adult/concession/child 6-13/family €10/8/5/23; ☺ 10am-8pm; ◉ Uhlandstrasse
This multimedia museum breaks down 800 years of Berlin history into bite-sized chunks that are easy to swallow but substantial enough to be satisfying. In other words, it's the kind of history museum that'll even entertain kids and teens. Each of the 23 exhibit rooms encapsulates a different epoch in the city's fascinating history, from its founding in 1237 to its days as the Prussian capital, the Golden Twenties, the dark days of the Third Reich and the fall of the Berlin Wall. Budget at least two hours, including a tour of a still fully functional 1970s atomic bunker beneath the building, which brings the Cold War era creepily to life. The museum

entrance is inside the Ku'damm Karree mall. The last admission and bunker tour is at 6pm.

DAS VERBORGENE MUSEUM Map p128
☎ 313 3656; www.dasverborgenemuseum.de; Schlüterstrasse 70; adult/concession €2/1; ☺ 3-7pm Thu & Fri, noon-4pm Sat & Sun; ◉ Ernst-Reuter-Platz, ᴙ Savignyplatz
Founded by a pair of feminist artists and art historians, the nonprofit Hidden Museum gets its name not from having an obscure location but from its artistic focus: the largely forgotten works by early-20th-century women artists, mostly from Germany. Past exhibits have highlighted the photography of Helmut Newton mentor Else Simon (aka Yva), and the works of Bauhaus artist Gertrud Arndt and the architect Lucy Hillebrand. Curators mount about two exhibits annually, which run for three or four months each. At other times, the museum is closed, so call or check the listings magazines for current shows.

EUROPA-CENTER Map p128
www.europa-center-berlin.de; Breitscheidplatz; ◉ Kurfürstendamm
Easily recognised by the giant Mercedes star that rotates on its rooftop, the Europa-Center was Berlin's first high-rise when it opened in 1965. Rising 103m tall, it stands on the spot of the Romanisches Café, the 'living room' of the city's literary elite before WWII. These days, the aging 20-storey temple of commerce exudes tacky retro flair tempered only slightly by such quirky sights as the Lotus Fountain and the psychedelic *Flow of Time Clock* by Bernard Gitton. You can also catch the lift to the 20th floor to enjoy the panorama or, at night, if you're feeling flush, get an eyeful of pretty people and Berlin from above at the swish Puro Skylounge (p223).

The complex flanks bustling Breit-scheidplatz, where everyone from footsore tourists to buskers, punks and souvenir hawkers gathers around the quirky *Weltbrunnen* (World Fountain, 1983) by local artist Joachim Schmettau. It's made from red granite and bronze and is festooned with sculptures of humans and animals. Naturally, Berliners have found a nickname for it: *Wasserklops* (water meatball).

top picks

FOR CHILDREN

Keeping the kids entertained is child's play in Berlin. For Berlin's best playgrounds see p153.

- **Berlin Zoo & Aquarium (p126)** Head here for an audience with Knut, the world's most famous polar bear, and other beloved critters.
- **Britzer Garten (p168)** Romp around the water playground, pat a sheep and get creative in a clay village while exploring this rambling, redolent park.
- **Freilichtmuseum Domäne Dahlem (p163)** Find out how food travels from farm to table at this charming outdoor museum of agrarian history.
- **Labyrinth Kindermuseum (p178)** Slip into a fantasy world while learning about tolerance, working together and just having fun.
- **Kinderbad Monbijou (p315)** Keep cool on hot days splashing about this family-friendly public pool.
- **Legoland Discovery Centre (p111)** A bit commercial but still lots of interactive fun for the milk-tooth set.
- **Museum für Naturkunde (p103)** Meet giant dinosaurs and travel through space back to the beginning of time.
- **Puppentheater-Museum Berlin (p146)** Be enthralled by adorable singing and dancing puppets and marionettes during live stage shows.
- **Science Centre Spectrum (p144)** Push buttons, pull knobs and engage in experiments at this interactive wing attached to the Deutsches Technikmuseum.

WESTERN CHARLOTTENBURG

The main attraction in far-flung western Charlottenburg is the Olympic Stadium, which hosted the 1936 Games. The Olympic grounds are just north of the vast Grunewald forest, home to the Teufelsberg, a hillock made from WWII rubble, and about 2km northwest of the Eiffel Tower-like Funkturm radio tower and the trade-fair grounds.

OLYMPIASTADION off Map pp72-3

☎ 2500 2322; www.olympiastadion-berlin.de; Olympischer Platz 3; self-guided tour adult/concession/family €4/3/8, guided general tour in German €8/7/16, Hertha BSC tour €10/8.50/24; ⏲ 9am-8pm Jun–mid-Sep, to 7pm mid-Mar–May & mid-Sep–Oct, to 4pm Nov–mid-Mar; ⬚ Olympiastadion
Even though it was put through a total modernisation for the 2006 FIFA World Cup,

it's hard not to remember the fact that this massive coliseum-like stadium was built by the Nazis for the 1936 Olympic Games (see the boxed text, p30). The bombastic bulk of the structure undoubtedly remains, although it's now softened by the addition of a spidery oval roof, snazzy VIP boxes and top-notch sound, lighting and projection systems. It seats up to 74,400 people for games played by the local Hertha BSC soccer team, concerts, the Pope or Madonna.

On non-event days, you can explore the stadium on your own, although renting an audioguide is recommended (€2.50). Several times daily, guided tours take you into the locker rooms, warm-up areas and VIP areas that are otherwise off-limits. Access the stadium from the Osttor (eastern gate). It's a long way out here, so call ahead to make sure the stadium is open for touring.

GLOCKENTURM off Map pp72-3

☎ 305 8123; www.glockenturm.de; Am Glockenturm; adult/child €3.50/1.50; ⏲ 9am-6pm Apr-Oct; ⬚ Pichelsberg
Call it impressive or preposterous, there's no denying that the Olympic Stadium is an imposing feat of architecture. To truly appreciate its dimensions, head to the outdoor viewing platform of the 77m-high Glockenturm (Bell Tower), also built for the 1936 Olympics west of the Maifeld parade grounds. On good days, you can see all the way into town and as far as Potsdam. Your way up takes you past a copy of the Olympic bell (the damaged original is displayed south of the stadium). Downstairs, an exhibit chronicles the infamous 1936 games with labelling in German and English and a compelling documentary featuring rare original footage.

TEUFELSBERG off Map pp72-3

Teufelsseechaussee; ⬚ Heerstrasse
It may have a terrifying name, but at 115m high, the Teufelsberg (Devil's Mountain), just south of the Olympic grounds, ain't no Matterhorn. It is, however, the tallest of Berlin's 20 'rubble mountains', built by citizens, initially most of them women, during the clean-up of their bomb-ravaged city after WWII. It took 20 years to pile up 25 million cubic metres of debris. The curious domed structure up on top used to be a listening post operated by the

American military to spy on East Germany during the Cold War.

The hill that was born from destruction is now a fun zone, especially in snowy winters when hordes of squealing kids toboggan or ski down its gentle slopes. At other times you can explore the terrain on mountain bikes or watch colourful kites flutter like swarms of butterflies. The little Teufelsee lake at the bottom of the hill is popular with nudists (especially the south shore).

On its eastern shore is the Ökowerk (☎ 300 0050; www.oekowerk.de, in German; admission free, exhibit adult/concession €2.50/1; ☺ 9am-6pm Tue-Fri, noon-6pm Sat & Sun Apr-Oct, 10am-4pm Tue-Fri, 11am-4pm Sat & Sun Nov-Mar), a nature conservation and education centre that's grown up around Berlin's oldest existing water works (1872). There's an exhibit about water and its role in our lives, but it's more fun to romp around the grounds and check out the beehives, learn how to grow herbs or watch bread being made.

FUNKTURM off Map pp72-3
☎ 3038 1905; Hammarskjöldplatz; ☺ 10am-8pm Mon, to 11pm Tue-Sun; adult/concession €4.50/2.50; ⊖ Kaiserdamm, ☒ Messe Nord/ICC
The Funkturm (radio tower), next to the trade-fair grounds, is by far the most visible structure in western Charlottenburg. Its filigree outline, which bears an uncanny resemblance to Paris' Eiffel Tower, soars 129m into the Berlin sky (146m with antenna) and has been transmitting signals since 1925. In 1935 the first regular TV programme in the world was broadcast from this tower, which looks especially pretty when lit up at night.

From the viewing platform at 126m or the restaurant at 55m you can enjoy sweeping views of the Grunewald forest and the western city, as well as the AVUS, Germany's first car-racing track, which opened in 1921; AVUS stands for Automobil-, Verkehrs- und Übungsstrasse (auto, traffic and practice track). The Nazis made it part of the autobahn system, which it still is today.

GEORG KOLBE MUSEUM off Map pp72-3
☎ 304 2144; Sensburger Allee 25; www.georg-kolbe-museum.de; ☺ 10am-6pm Tue-Sun; adult/concession €5/3; ☒ Heerstrasse
Georg Kolbe (1877–1947) was one of Germany's most influential sculptors in the first half of the 20th century. A member of the Berlin Secession, he distanced himself from traditional sculpture and became a chief exponent of the idealised nude. After his wife's death in 1927, Kolbe's figures took on a more solemn and emotional air, whereas his later works focus on the athletic male, an approach that found favour with the Nazis.

The attractive museum, in Kolbe's former studio, shows works from all phases of the artist's life alongside temporary exhibits often drawn from his rich private collection of 20th-century sculpture and paintings. The sculpture garden is an oasis of tranquillity and the cafe one of the nicest in a Berlin museum.

CORBUSIERHAUS off Map pp72-3
Flatowallee 16; ☒ Olympiastadion
This honeycomb-like housing estate just south of the Olympic Stadium was the contribution of French master architect Le Corbusier (1887–1965) to the 1957 International Building Exhibition (Interbau). It represents his attempt to address the post-WWII housing shortages all over Europe, but especially in bomb-ravaged Berlin. Some 575 flats are crammed into the 17-storey structure standing on stilts, its monotonous exterior brightened by colour accents. This was the third in a series of complexes he called *Unité d'Habitation* (Housing Unit); the others are located in Marseille and Nantes.

Le Corbusier's original plan called for the complex to be an autonomous vertical village, complete with a post office, shops, a school and other infrastructure. In Berlin, though, this vision never came to fruition because of lack of funding, and the architect later distanced himself from the project.

CHARLOTTENBURG LOOP
Walking Tour
1 Bahnhof Zoo Until 2006, if you arrived in Berlin by train, your first stop would most likely have been Bahnhof Zoo, the station that inspired the U2 song 'Zoo Station'. In the 1980s this was the haunt of drug pushers and child prostitutes, as bitterly portrayed in the 1978 autobiographical novel (and 1981 movie) *Christiane F.*

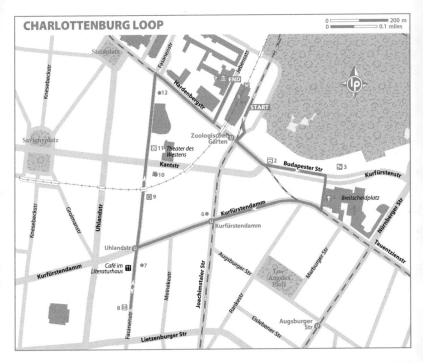

CHARLOTTENBURG LOOP

2 Zoo Palast This venerable, though thoroughly modernised, cinema at Hardenbergstrasse 29a opened in 1957 as a *bikino* (ie with two silver screens) and until 1999 hosted movie royalty as the main venue of the Berlin International Film festival. It's now a nine-screen multiplex.

3 Berlin Zoo Bahnhof Zoo and Zoo Palast take their names from the Berlin Zoo (p126), home of polar bear celebrity Knut. Check out the exotic 1899 'Elephant Gate' at Budapester Strasse 34 and the adjacent Aquarium (p127), whose facade depicts the fossil relatives of the species inside.

4 Kaiser-Wilhelm-Gedächtniskirche Architect Franz Schechten drew inspiration from a medieval fortress for the design of what must have been a most magnificent church, the Kaiser-Wilhelm-Gedächtniskirche (p127), until its WWII bombing. The ruined tower husk was paired with a modern house of worship built by Egon Eiermann in 1961.

5 Europa-Center A modern counterpoint to the church ruin, the soaring Europa-Center (p130) was Berlin's first high-rise when it opened in 1965. With its gleaming Mercedes star

WALK FACTS

Start Bahnhof Zoo
End Museum für Fotografie
Distance 3.2km
Time 90 minutes
Exertion Moderate
Fuel stop Café im Literaturhaus (p207)

rotating on the rooftop, it quickly became a symbol of West Berlin, but these days its narrow passageways feel cramped and uninviting.

6 Neues Kranzler Eck In recent years the Europa-Center has been eclipsed by bold modern buildings such as this glass monolith by Helmut Jahn at the corner of Ku'damm and Joachimstaler Strasse. A retail and office complex, it replaced the venerable Café Kranzler, one of the western city's most traditional coffee houses, of which only the rooftop rotunda remains.

7 Fasanenstrasse Nowhere does the aura of Charlottenburg's late-19th-century bourgeois grandeur survive as visibly as on this quiet, leafy avenue lined by palatial townhouses. Sneak a peek into some of their foyers to discover stucco ceilings, romantic murals, marble fireplaces and creaky wrought-iron or brass lifts resembling giant birdcages.

8 Käthe-Kollwitz-Museum The small Käthe-Kollwitz-Museum (p129) displays works by a key 20th-century woman artist. The Literaturhaus, at No 23, hosts readings and literary discussions and also houses a gallery, a book store and the sophisticated Café im Literaturhaus (p207).

9 Jewish Community Centre The majestic Moorish-style synagogue that stood at Fasanenstrasse 79–80 was destroyed by the Nazis during the 1938 *Kristallnacht* pogroms; only the portal survived. A broken Torah roll in the courtyard commemorates the event, while a memorial wall lists the names of concentration camps and Jewish ghettos.

10 Kantdreieck The award-winning 1994 'Kant Triangle' at Kantstrasse 155 was Josef Paul Kleihues' first Berlin commission. The attractive office building combines a five-storey glass-and-slate base with a 36m square

tower. At the top is the landmark triangular 'sail', which shifts in the wind like a giant metal weather vane.

11 Delphi Filmpalast The historic Delphi Filmpalast at Kantstrasse 12a, next to the Theater des Westens (p254), began life as a popular dance hall before getting a drubbing in WWII. In 1949 it was reborn as Germany's most modern cinema at the time. In the basement is a jazz club.

12 Ludwig-Erhard-Haus Structure, space, skin – this 1997 building at Fasanenstrasse 83–84 perfectly illustrates the philosophy of British architect Nicholas Grimshaw. The hi-tech design was inspired by an armadillo, with a 'rib cage' of steel girders clad in a glass 'skin'. Inside are the local stock exchange and chamber of commerce.

13 Museum für Fotografie Berlin-born photographer Helmut Newton built his reputation as a fashion photographer by often depicting women in controversial, erotic poses. His personal collection forms the core of the Museum für Fotografie (p129), in a Prussian-era art library right next to Bahnhof Zoo.

Drinking p224; Gay & Lesbian p259; Eating p208; Shopping p189; Sleeping p275

Residential Schöneberg has a radical pedigree rooted in the squatter days of the '80s but now flaunts a comfortable middle-class, though still relaxed, identity. There are no major conventional sights in this former West Berlin borough, but the KaDeWe department store – Berlin's equivalent of London's Harrods and New York's Bloomingdale's – is certainly one of the key attractions. Schöneberg's laid-back character best reveals itself on a stroll from Nollendorfplatz to Hauptstrasse, via Maassenstrasse, Goltzstrasse and Akazienstrasse, which are lined with well-edited indie boutiques, comfy cafes and laid-back bars. The route skirts Winterfeldtplatz square, which draws people from all over town for its bountiful farmers market every Wednesday and Saturday morning.

Near Nollendorfplatz, the gay crowd has partied on Motzstrasse and Fuggerstrasse since the 1920s, cheered on by the ghost of Anglo-American author Christopher Isherwood, who lived nearby in the 1920s. One local gal who liked to party with the 'boyz' was Marlene Dietrich. She's buried in southern Schöneberg (see p137) not far from Rathaus Schöneberg, the town hall where John F Kennedy declared his solidarity with the people with his morale-boosting 'Ich bin ein Berliner!' speech back in 1963. West of the Rathaus, the Volkspark Schöneberg is a long, narrow ribbon of green that links Schöneberg with Wilmersdorf and passes by the Cold War–era RIAS (Radio in the American Sector) broadcasting station, which was in operation until 1992.

Schöneberg shows its most multi-culti face along Hauptstrasse, northeast of the Rathaus, where David Bowie and Iggy Pop shared a flat at No 155 in the late '70s. At Kleistpark, Hauptstrasse blends into Potsdamer Strasse, which mixes seediness (lots of street prostitution) with an up-and-coming gallery district.

NOLLENDORFPLATZ Map p136

Ⓤ Nollendorfplatz

Paintings and photographs from the early 20th century show Nollendorfplatz as a bustling urban square filled with cafes, theatres and people on parade. It was just this kind of liberal and libertine flair that so enticed British author Christopher Isherwood.

To Isherwood, 'Berlin meant boyz' and boys he could find aplenty in such famous bars as the Eldorado, haunt of a demimonde that included Marlene Dietrich and chanteuse Claire Waldorff. The Nazis put

an end to the fun, but not for good. After WWII, the area south of Nollendorfplatz reprised its role as Berlin's gay mecca and continues to be a major gay nightlife hub today. A small memorial plaque near the south entrance of Nollendorfplatz U-Bahn station commemorates homosexual victims of the Nazi era.

Nollendorfplatz is dominated by the ornate Metropol Theater, with its rather erotic frieze. It started life in 1906 as the Neue Schauspielhaus (New Theatre) and now hosts the monthly Propaganda@Goya (p261) gay bash and other parties.

TRANSPORT: SCHÖNEBERG

Bus M19 and M29 travel along the Ku'damm to the KaDeWe; M19 continues via Nollendorfplatz to U-Bahn Mehringdamm in western Kreuzberg, M29 goes to eastern Kreuzberg via Potsdamer Platz, Checkpoint Charlie and Oranienstrasse.

S-Bahn S1 and S2 go to central Berlin via Yorckstrasse; S41, S42 and S45 stop at Schöneberg and Innsbrucker Platz.

U-Bahn Nollendorfplatz is the main hub served by U1 from Kurfürstendamm and Kreuzberg; U2 from Zoologischer Garten, Mitte and Prenzlauer Berg; U3 from Dahlem; and the short intra-Schöneberg U4.

RATHAUS SCHÖNEBERG Map p136

John-F-Kennedy-Platz; Ⓤ Rathaus Schöneberg

The Rathaus Schöneberg (Town Hall) was the seat of the West Berlin government from 1948 to 1990 but is really best remembered for a single day in 1963 when President John F Kennedy was in town. From the steps of the Rathaus, the silver-tongued orator flayed the forces of darkness to the east and applauded the powers of light in the west, concluding with the now famous words: 'All free men, wherever they live, are citizens of Berlin. And therefore, as a free man, I take pride in the words: Ich bin ein Berliner'. The adoring

135

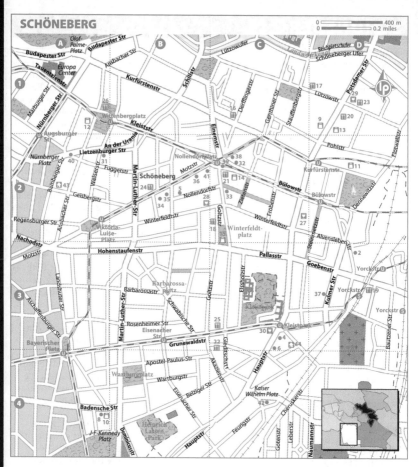

SCHÖNEBERG

0 — 400 m
0 — 0.2 miles

---

crowd of half a million cheered his words all the way into the history books.

The Rathaus clock tower holds a copy of the Liberty Bell, presented to the city in 1950 by the US army commander in Berlin, General Lucius D Clay. More than seven million Americans had donated money towards this replica of the Philadelphia original.

A popular flea market, the Flohmarkt Schöneberg (p189), takes place at weekends outside the town hall.

ALTER ST MATTHÄUS-KIRCHHOF
Map above

☎ 781 1850; www.zwoelf-apostel-berlin.de, in German; Grossgörschenstrasse 12-14; ☼ 8am-dusk; Ⓤ Ⓡ Yorckstrasse, Ⓤ Kleistpark

This pretty Alter St Matthäus-Kirchhof (Old St Matthew's Cemetery), created in 1856, was a favourite among Berlin's 19th-century bourgeoisie and brims with opulent gravestones and memorials. Celebrities buried here include the Brothers Grimm and physician Rudolf Virchow. A memorial tombstone honours Claus Schenk Graf von Stauffenberg and fellow conspirators in the July 1944 plot against Hitler. Their bodies were initially buried here, but SS members had them exhumed, cremated and their ashes scattered.

Pick up a map with grave locations of these and other famous Berliners at the cemetery office or download it from the website.

SCHÖNEBERG

KLEISTPARK & AROUND Map opposite

Potsdamer Strasse; ⊙ Kleistpark

This romantic little park is dominated by the richly ornamented sandstone Königskolonnaden (Royal Colonnades), designed in 1780 by Carl von Gontard (he of Gendarmenmarkt churches fame). They originally stood near the Rotes Rathaus in Mitte but were displaced by road construction in 1910.

West of Kleistpark, the imposing 1913 Kammergericht (Elssholzstrasse 30-33) was the courthouse that staged the notorious show trials of the Nazi Volksgericht (People's Court) against the participants – real and alleged – in the July 1944 assassination

FAMOUS SCHÖNEBERG RESIDENTS

Today's celebs may prefer Mitte or Zehlendorf as their place of residence, but throughout the 20th century Schöneberg was where 'it' was at. Here's a sampling of famous folks who once called the district home.

Marlene Dietrich

Germany's first actress to hit the big time in Hollywood, Marlene Dietrich was born Marie Magdalena von Losch at Leberstrasse 65 in 1901. She returned to Schöneberg after her death in 1992, and the 'Blue Angel' now makes her final home in a surprisingly unglamorous plot on Friedhof Schöneberg (Map p69; Stubenrauchstrasse 43-45; ⊙ 24hr; ⊙ ⑧ Bundesplatz). Her tombstone says simply 'Marlene' along with the inscription: 'Here I stand on the marker of my days'. Look for the map inside the cemetery entrance to locate the grave, which is near the Fehlerstrasse (north) side of the grounds. From the U- or S-Bahn station, walk southwest on Südwestkorso to Stubenrauchstrasse. In 2004 avant-garde fashion photographer Helmut Newton was buried four plots away from the grand dame.

Christopher Isherwood

In 1929 Isherwood moved to a pretty residential building (Map opposite; Nollendorfstrasse 17; ⊙ Nollendorfplatz) from London to escape the sexual oppression in England and to live out his homosexual fantasies. His experiences and impressions – as well as the looming threat of the Nazis – are vividly chronicled in *The Berlin Stories*, which was adapted into the play 'I am a Camera' and later became the basis of the musical *Cabaret* starring Liza Minnelli as Sally Bowles.

David Bowie & Iggy Pop

If you want to see where the 'White Duke' and his buddy bunked in the late '70s, make your pilgrimage to the doorstep of a ho-hum apartment building (Map opposite; Hauptstrasse 155; ⊙ Kleistpark). Bowie and Pop frequently hung out at the nearby Café Neues Ufer (Map opposite; Hauptstrasse 157), one of Berlin's oldest lesbian and gay joints, when it was still known as 'Anderes Ufer'.

attempt on Hitler. Led by the fanatical judge Roland Freisler, hundreds of people were handed their death sentences; many were executed at Plötzensee prison, now a memorial site called Gedenkstätte Plötzensee (p177). Freisler, alas, was crushed to death by a falling beam in the court building during an air raid in February 1945, thereby avoiding what would undoubtedly have been a starring role at the Nuremberg Trials.

When the war was over, the Allies used the building first as the seat of the Allied Control Council, and then, until 1990, as the headquarters of the Allied Air Control. On 3 September 1971 the Western Allies and the USSR, represented by their foreign ministers, signed the Four Power Agreement on Berlin (p34) in this building. Today it's again a courthouse.

Drinking p225; Gay & Lesbian p259; Eating p209; Shopping p190; Sleeping p275

Kreuzberg gets its street cred from being delightfully edgy, bipolar, wacky and, most of all, unpredictable. While the western half around Bergmannstrasse is solidly in the hands of the digital *bohéme*, eastern Kreuzberg (still nicknamed SO36, after its pre-reunification postal code) is a multicultural mosaic with the most dynamic nightlife in town. Between Kottbusser Tor and the Spree River *döner* shops rub up against Brazilian cafes, head-scarfed mamas push prams past punks with metal-penetrated faces, and black-haired goths draped in floor-length leather coats chill next to bright-faced students at an outdoor cinema.

SO36's alternative spirit has its roots in the Cold War years. Boxed in by the Wall on three sides, this was West Berlin's poorest district. Neglected, rundown and cheap, many of its residents were holed up in apartments still fuelled by coal-burning stoves and without private plumbing. Over time, this little existentialist corner evolved into a countercultural catch basin for students, punks, anarchists, draft dodgers and squatters, (in)famous for its violent May Day brawls with police. Although the fall of the Wall catapulted the area from the city's edge to its centre, hipper types bypassed it in favour of the equally derelict – but somehow more enticing – districts in the former East Berlin. More recently, though, the trend seems to be reversing, if rising rents and a steady influx of an unconventional creative class are any indication. For now, though, mainstream gentrification is – thankfully – a long way away.

Thanks to its large Turkish population, eastern Kreuzberg is also nicknamed 'Little Istanbul'. Though aesthetically unappealing (ie ugly), the area around Kottbusser Tor (Kotti, for short) brims with *shisha* cafes, little grocery stores, *döner* shops and giggling Turkish gals, their jet-black hair tucked under colourful scarves. It's also an evolving nightlife zone, as joints like Möbel Olfe (p226) and Monarch (p225) lure scenesters bored with slicker neighbourhoods.

A bit south of Kotti is the placid Landwehrkanal, whose idyllic, tree-lined banks lend themselves to strolling and picnicking. Every Tuesday and Friday afternoon, Berlin goes Bosporus along the south bank (Maybachufer) during the liveliest farmers market in town. The canal-zone in general has some fun boho cafes and restaurants, especially along Paul-Linke-Ufer opposite the market, and in the beautifully restored townhouses along Planufer west of Kottbusser Damm.

And then there is Northern Neukölln, currently Berlin's latest frontier of hipness and sometimes called Kreuzkölln for its proximity to Kreuzberg. In recent years, students, artists and creatives of all stripes have been flocking here, drawn by cheap rents and a longing for the improvisational spirit of the '90s, the kind that used to make Prenzlauer Berg and Mitte so exciting. Most of the newcomers may be asset-poor but they're rich in creativity, which often finds expression in exciting new ways. It's this DIY ethos and underground spirit that inspired the listing magazine *Tip* to compare northern Neukölln with New York's Lower East Side in the '70s and '80s. Trash-trendy bars, cafes, galleries and boutiques catering for the new residents are popping up all the time, especially around Friedelstrasse, Pannierstrasse, Reuterstrasse, Hobrechtstrasse and Weserstrasse. A neighbourhood that's definitely worth keeping an eye on and great for some DIY exploring.

If you follow the canal west, you'll eventually get to western Kreuzberg, which feels comparatively sedate and upmarket. Nudging against Mitte in the north and Schöneberg in the west, this is where you find such heavyweight attractions as Checkpoint Charlie and the Jüdisches Museum. Gentrification has arrived here with a vengeance, resulting in cleaner streets, prettier buildings, fancier restaurants and a more relaxed overall pace. The liveliest strips are cafe- and boutique-studded Mehringdamm and Bergmannstrasse. The nearby hill that gave Kreuzberg (literally 'cross hill') its name is now the rambling Viktoriapark, topped by a memorial celebrating Prussia's 1815 victory over Napoleon. Lawns for sunning, a beer garden and an artificial waterfall make this a great summer play zone.

top picks

KREUZBERG

- Bergmannstrasse (p144)
- Checkpoint Charlie (p144)
- Flughafen Tempelhof & Tempelhofer Park (p145)
- Jüdisches Museum (p142)

KREUZBERG & NORTHERN NEUKÖLLN

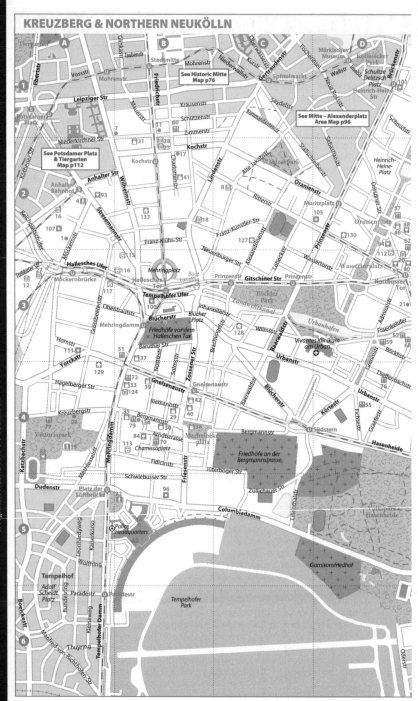

See Historic Mitte
Map p76

See Mitte – Alexanderplatz
Area Map p96

See Potsdamer Platz
& Tiergarten
Map p112

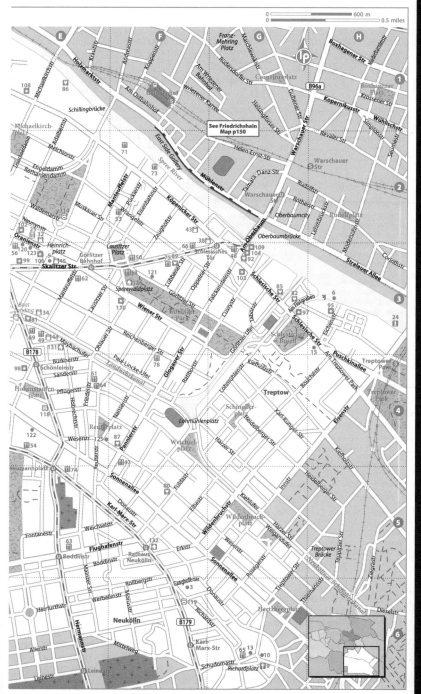

0 _____ 600 m
0 _____ 0.5 miles

See Friedrichshain
Map p150

141

JÜDISCHES MUSEUM Map pp140-1

☎ 2599 3300; www.juedisches-museum-berlin
.de; Lindenstrasse 9-14; adult/concession/family
€5/2.50/10; ☻ 10am-10pm Mon, to 8pm Tue-Sun;
ⓔ Hallesches Tor, Kochstrasse, ⓦ M29, M41, 248
Berlin's Jewish Museum is an eye-opening,
emotional and interactive romp through
2000 years of Jewish history in Germany.
Yup, 2000 and not just the 12 Nazi horror
years that such presentations often focus
on, although those are of course addressed
as well. This exhibit, though, navigates
through all major historic periods, from
the Roman days to the Middle Ages, the
Enlightenment to the community's current
renaissance. You'll learn about Jewish
cultural contributions, holiday traditions
and the difficult road to Emancipation.

TRANSPORT: KREUZBERG

Bus M29 travels from Potsdamer Platz to Checkpoint Charlie and Oranienstrasse; No 140 shuttles between western and eastern Kreuzberg via Tempelhof Airport, Gneisenaustrasse and Kottbusser Tor ending at Ostbahnhof.

S-Bahn S1 and S2/25 stop at Yorckstrasse.

U-Bahn Served by U1 from Charlottenburg, Schöneberg and Friedrichshain; U6 and U8 from Mitte; U7 from Schöneberg and Neukölln.

Elsewhere the spotlight is trained on outstanding individuals, such as the philosopher Moses Mendelssohn, jeans inventor Levi Strauss and the painter Felix Nussbaum. It's an engaging presentation with listening stations, videos, documents 'hidden' in drawers and other multimedia devices. For an even more in-depth experience, rent an audioguide (€2).

Long before the exhibits opened to the public, Daniel Libeskind's spectacular design for the museum building itself was generating a lot of interest. Essentially a 3-D metaphor for the tortured history of the Jewish people, its zigzag outline symbolises a broken Star of David – a great idea in theory, but one best appreciated from a helicopter. Still, the building's sharply angled zinc walls perforated only by small window gashes are definitely eye-catching. Best of all, the visual allegory continues on the inside.

There's no direct entrance to the museum, which instead is reached through an adjoining baroque building. A steep staircase descends to three intersecting walkways – called 'axes' – representing the fates of Jews during the Nazi years. The Axis of Exile leads to a disorienting 'garden' of tilted concrete columns. The Axis of the Holocaust ends in the tomblike 'void' that stands for the loss of humanity, culture and life. Only the Axis of Continuity leads to the actual exhibit, but it too is a cumbersome journey up a sloping walkway and several steep flights of stairs. Libeskind's architecture is a powerful language indeed. In 2010 it was announced that the architect would also be in charge of a museum expansion into a former flower market across the street.

Last admission is one hour before closing, but you should budget at least two to

do the exhibit justice, more if you drop by the on-site, kosher-style cafe-restaurant (no pork or shellfish). Security is airport-style, so expect to send your stuff through the X-ray machine.

BERLINISCHE GALERIE Map pp140-1

☎ 7890 2600; www.berlinischegalerie.de; Alte Jakobstrasse 124-128; adult/concession/child under 18 €6/3/free; ⏱ 10am-6pm Wed-Mon; Ⓜ Kochstrasse, Hallesches Tor

Berlin may be all hip and hot in today's art circles but fact is the city has long inspired creatives from around the world. The Berlin Gallery, in a converted glass warehouse around the corner from the Jüdisches Museum, is a superb spot for taking stock of what the local scene has been up to for, oh, the past century or so. The stark, whitewashed hall, anchored by two intersecting floating stairways, presents edgy works from major artistic periods – Berlin Secessionism (Lesser Ury, Max Liebermann) to New Objectivity (Otto Dix, George Grosz) and contemporary art by such 'Junge Wilde' (Young Wild Ones) members as Salomé and Rainer Fetting. Temporary exhibits inject additional impulses, as do the occasional lecture or movie screening. Jewish Museum ticket holders qualify for reduced admission on the same day and the following two, and vice versa.

DEUTSCHES TECHNIKMUSEUM BERLIN Map pp140-1

☎ 902 540; www.dtmb.de; Trebbiner Strasse 9; adult/concession €4.50/2.50, child under 18 free after 3pm, audioguide €2/1; ⏱ 9am-5.30pm Tue-Fri, 10am-6pm Sat & Sun; Ⓜ Möckernbrücke, Gleisdreieck

The first thing you see is a C-54 Skymaster plane, better known as a Rosinenbomber (candy bomber), the kind of plane that kept Berlin afloat during the 1948 Berlin Airlift (see p32). Spectacularly mounted to the roof, it's merely the overture to the huge German Museum of Technology, a fantastic place to spend a few hours, and not just on a rainy afternoon.

There's an entire hall of vintage locomotives and rooms crammed with historic printing presses, early film projectors, old TVs and telephones and lots more. A new permanent exhibit reveals the mysteries of pills and the pharmaceutical industry.

A major a highlight is the reconstruction of the world's first computer, the Z1 (1938) by Konrad Zuse. All throughout, there's plenty of opportunity to push buttons and pull knobs or to watch the museum staff explain and demonstrate bizarre machines.

A separate wing presents the museum's superb collections on aviation and navigation. Among the exhibits are several original naval vessels, including a WWII-era *Biber*, a one-man U-Boat used to attack anchoring ships, a nearly always fatal mission. The aviation section chronicles 200 years of German flight, from experimental hot-air balloons to the Cold War. Outside, in the sprawling Museumspark, you can explore working windmills, a waterwheel, an engine shed and a historic brewery.

In fact, it can all be pretty overwhelming after a while, so it's best to prioritise what you want to see, especially if you're here with attention-span-challenged kids. Little ones will probably have the most fun in the adjacent Science Center Spectrum (☎ 9025 4284; www.sdtb.de; Möckernstrasse 26; admission included; ⊗ 9am-5.30pm Tue-Fri, 10am-6pm Sat & Sun; ◉ Möckernbrücke, Gleisdreieck), where they can participate in about 250 entertaining experiments that playfully explain why the sky is blue, whether toilets flush anti-clockwise in Australia and other questions you always wanted to ask in science class.

CHECKPOINT CHARLIE Map pp140-1
cnr Friedrichstrasse & Zimmerstrasse; ◉ Kochstrasse
Checkpoint Charlie was the principal gateway for Allies, other non-Germans and diplomats between the two Berlins from 1961 to 1990. This was where US and Soviet tanks infamously faced off shortly after the Wall went up. Unfortunately, this potent symbol of the Cold War has become a tacky tourist trap where folks dressed in US, French and Russian (not even Soviet!) uniforms pose for cold cash in front of a replica guardhouse. Near the famous sign warning 'You are now leaving the American sector' souvenir shops hawk T-shirts and plastic Trabis (aka Trabants). The only museum around is the privately financed Mauermuseum (right), which is more a labour of love than a properly curated exhibit. The one redeeming aspect around Checkpoint Charlie is the free open-air exhibit set up along Friedrichstrasse, Zimmerstrasse and Schützenstrasse, which uses photos and

documents to illustrate milestones in Cold War history.

MAUERMUSEUM Map pp140-1
Haus am Checkpoint Charlie; ☎ 253 7250; www .mauermuseum.de; Friedrichstrasse 43-45; adult/ student/child under 11 €12.50/9.50/5.50; ⊗ 9am-10pm; ◉ Kochstrasse
The Cold War years, especially the history and horror of the Berlin Wall, are haphazardly, but well-meaningly, chronicled in this private tourist magnet. The best bits are about ingenious escapes to the West in hot-air balloons, tunnels, concealed compartments in cars and even a one-man submarine. Elsewhere the focus is on historic milestones: the Berlin Airlift, the 1953 workers' uprising, the Wall construction and reunification. Other rooms zero in on the stories of such human-rights heroes as Gandhi and Lech Walesa.

Displays are in various languages, including English, and a cafe and store selling great Wall-related paraphernalia are also on site.

STASI INFORMATIONS- UND DOKUMENTATIONSZENTRUM
Map pp140-1
☎ 2324 7951; www.bstu.bund.de; 1st fl, Zimmerstrasse 90/91; admission free; ⊗ 10am-6pm Mon-Sat; ◉ Kochstrasse
How were people spied on in the GDR? How did the surveillance apparatus function? What role did the Ministry for State Security (Stasi) play in the political process? How many escapes did the secret police prevent? If you've seen the Oscar-winning movie *The Lives of Others,* you already know about the all-out zeal of the GDR's Stasi when it came to controlling, manipulating and repressing its own people. Now in new digs near Checkpoint Charlie, the Stasi Information and Documentation Centre peels back the many layers of this sinister organisation. It's organised by the federal agency charged with documenting and providing information about the Stasi. A new permanent exhibit is expected to open in early 2011.

BERGMANNSTRASSE Map pp140-1
◉ Platz der Luftbrücke, Mehringdamm, Gneisenaustrasse
Bergmannstrasse, between Mehringdamm and Marheinekeplatz, is western

Kreuzberg's main drag for shopping (lots of second-hand stores), eating and bar-hopping and is great for soaking up the district's bohemian spirit. On Marheinekeplatz, the Marheineke Markthalle (p192) is one of Berlin's few surviving market halls, although it traded its grungy 19th-century charm for bright and airy modern digs thanks to a renovation a few years ago. The red-brick Passionskirche, also on the square, often hosts classical and jazz concerts.

FLUGHAFEN TEMPELHOF & TEMPELHOFER PARK Map pp140-1

☎ 01805-288 244; www.flughafen-berlin -tempelhof.com; Platz der Luftbrücke; tours adult/ concession/child under 14 €12/8/4; ❤ tours 4pm Mon-Fri, 1pm Fri, 11am & 4pm Sat & Sun (call ahead to confirm); ❻ Platz der Luftbrücke, Paradestrasse

In Berlin history, Tempelhof airport is a site of legend and mythology. Aviation pioneer Orville Wright put on flight shows over its grassy field as early as 1903, the first Zeppelin landed in 1909 and Lufthansa ran its first scheduled flights from here in 1926. The Nazis turned it into a massive compound that is still reportedly the world's second-largest building after the Pentagon. After the war, in 1948–49, the airport saw its finest hours during the Berlin Airlift (p32). British architect Lord Norman Foster once called it 'the mother of all airports'. Flight operations stopped in 2008 after much brouhaha and against the wishes of many Berliners. The massive compound is now open for touring and hosts special events like rave parties and trade fairs like the Bread & Butter street fashion show.

The airfield, meanwhile, reopened in 2010 as Tempelhofer Park (☎ 280 18 162; www .gruen-berlin.de; admission free, tours €4.50-5.90; ❤ sunrise-sunset) where you can ponder the past while cycling, blading or strolling along the former tarmacs. It's pretty windy here, though, making the space popular for kite-flying and even kite-blading. There's also a designated barbecue area, three dog parks for off-leash romping and a fenced-in bird refuge. Airfield tours on foot and by bike or bus are available. Call or check the website for the latest timings.

LUFTBRÜCKENDENKMAL Map pp140-1

Platz der Luftbrücke; ❻ Platz der Luftbrücke

The Luftbrückendenkmal (Airlift Memorial) right outside Tempelhof airport honours all those who participated in keeping the city fed and free during the Berlin Airlift. Berliners have nicknamed it *Hungerharke* (Hunger Rake), a moniker inspired by the trio of spikes representing the three air corridors used by the Western Allies. The names of 79 airmen and other personnel who died during this colossal effort are engraved in the plinth.

MUSEUM DER DINGE Map pp140-1

☎ 9210 6311; www.museumderdinge.de; Oranienstrasse 25; adult/concession/child under 16 €4/2/free; ❤ noon-7pm Fri-Mon; ❻ Kottbusser Tor

With its extensive assemblage of everyday items and objects, the Museum of Things ostensibly traces German design history from the early 20th century to today but actually feels more like a cross between a cabinet of curiosities and a cool flea market. Alongside detergent boxes and cigarette cases are plenty of bizarre items, like a spherical washing machine, inflation money from 1923 and a Swastika-adorned mug. The collection is based on the archive of the Deutscher Werkbund (German Work Federation), an association of artists, architects, designers and industrialists formed in 1907 to integrate traditional crafts and industrial mass-production techniques. It was an important precursor of the 1920s Bauhaus movement.

KREUZBERG MUSEUM Map pp140-1

☎ 5058 5233; www.kreuzbergmuseum.de, in German; Adalbertstrasse 95a; admission free; ❤ noon-6pm Wed-Sun; ❻ Kottbusser Tor

If you want to learn about the ups and downs of one of Berlin's most colourful districts, swing by this multi-floor museum in an old red-brick factory. The permanent exhibit is still a work in progress but zeros in on such themes as Kreuzberg's radical legacy or how immigrants have shaped the area over the past 300 years. The 1928 printing press on the mezzanine level still cranks into action, usually from noon to 4pm Wednesday to Friday.

KÜNSTLERHAUS BETHANIEN
Map pp140-1

☎ 616 9030; www.bethanien.de; Kottbusser Strasse 10; admission free; ❤ 2-7pm Tue-Sun; ❻ Kottbusser Tor

After 35 years in the former 19th-century Bethanien hospital on Marianneplatz, which its founders helped save from demolition back in the 1970s, this seminal Kreuzberg art space moved to new and bigger digs in 2010. Its mission, though, stayed the same: to be an artistic sanctuary and creative laboratory for emerging artists from around the globe. With 25 international artists in residence at any given time, it's one of the largest residency programmes in Germany. Exhibits showcase their work, as well as that of former residents and other artists, and are always well worth checking out.

VIKTORIAPARK Map pp140-1
Btwn Kreuzbergstrasse, Methfesselstrasse, Dudenstrasse & Katzbachstrasse; ⊙ **Platz der Luftbrücke**

This unruly, rambling park drapes over the Kreuzberg hill, Berlin's highest natural elevation, although at 66m it's not exactly the Matterhorn. Still, views are quite impressive from the top (especially in winter) where a pompous Schinkel-designed Kreuzberg memorial heralds Prussia's military triumph over Napoleon in 1815. On New Year's Eve thousands come up here to drink, dance and watch the fireworks.

In summer the park is a popular spot for tanning, taking the kids to the playground, strolling along steep, meandering trails or quaffing a cold one at the Golgatha (p226) beer garden. An artificial waterfall tumbles downhill into a pool where Neptune is frolicking with an ocean nymphet; another hillside is covered in what some claim is Germany's northernmost vineyard.

BERLIN HI-FLYER Map pp140-1
☎ 5321 5321; www.air-service-berlin.de; cnr Wilhelmstrasse & Zimmerstrasse; adult/concession/family €19/13/46; ☾ 10am-10pm Apr-Oct, 11am-6pm Nov–mid-Dec & Feb-Mar; ⊙ Kochstrasse

top picks

VIEWS

- Berlin Hi-Flyer (above)
- Fernsehturm (p95)
- Glockenturm (p131)
- Panoramapunkt (p113)
- Reichstag (p75)
- Solar (p225)
- Weekend (p235)

Views with a thrill. Drift up but not away aboard this helium-filled balloon that remains tethered to the ground as it lifts you noiselessly 150m into the air for panoramas of the historic city centre. Your pilot will help you pinpoint all the key sights, including nearby Checkpoint Charlie and the Holocaust Memorial. Confirm ahead (☎ 226 678 811) as there are no flights in windy conditions.

PUPPENTHEATER-MUSEUM BERLIN Map pp140-1
☎ 687 8132; www.puppentheater-museum.de, in German; rear bldg, Karl-Marx-Strasse 135; adult/child €3/2.50, shows €5; ☾ 9am-4pm Mon-Fri, 11am-4.30pm Sun; ⊙ Karl-Marx-Strasse

At the little Puppet Theatre Museum, you'll enter a fantasy world inhabited by adorable hand puppets, marionettes, shadow puppets, stick figures and all manner of dolls, dragons and devils from around the world. Many of them hit the stage singing and dancing during shows that enthral both the young and the young at heart.

GRUSELKABINETT BERLIN Map pp140-1
☎ 2655 5546; www.gruselkabinett-berlin.de; Schöneberger Strasse 23a; adult/youth/child under 14 €8.50/6.50/5.50; ☾ 10am-7pm Sun, Tue, Thu & Fri, 10am-3pm Mon, noon-8pm Sat; ☒ Anhalter Bahnhof

This 'horror cabinet' is housed within a WWII air-raid shelter, once part of a network of bunkers, including Hitler's, which extended for miles beneath the city. A small exhibit in the basement has displays on the bunker's history, along with wartime-era newspapers, recordings of Allied plane attacks and a smattering of actual belongings left behind by those once holed up here during the bombing raids.

Other exhibits are more hokey than historical, but seem to score well with teenaged school groups, thanks perhaps to the eccentric couple who run the place. On the ground floor, groaning dummies demonstrate the niceties of medieval surgery techniques, and upstairs you'll be spooked by creepy characters while exploring a dark and dank maze. Things can get pretty scary and perhaps too intense for tender souls or little kids.

PLAY IT COOL BY THE POOL

Viva Berlin! Take an old river barge, fill it with water, moor it in the Spree and – voila – an urban lifestyle pool is born. In summer the artist-designed Badeschiff (Map pp72-3; ☎ 533 2030; www.arena-berlin.de, in German; Eichenstrasse 4; adult/concession/child €4/3/1.50; ☒ from 8am), at the south end of the Schlesische Strasse party drag, is the preferred swim-and-sweat spot for Berlin kool kids. With music blaring, a sandy beach, wooden decks, lots of hot bods and a bar to fuel the fun, the vibe is distinctly 'Ibiza on the Spree'. On scorching days it's often filled to capacity by noon. Or come late in the day to watch the sun tinge the Oberbaumbrücke (p152) a sensuous pink; this is followed by some sort of after-dark action, be it chilling to DJs, dancing till sunrise or listening to visiting bands. In winter an eerily glowing plastic membrane covers up the pool and a deliciously toasty chill zone is set up, including a sauna and bar.

RIXDORF Map pp140-1
Richardplatz; ⊕ Karl-Marx-Strasse, Neukölln
The contrast between the cacophonic bustle of Karl-Marx-Strasse and the quiet streets of Rixdorf, a tiny historic village centred on Richardplatz, seems almost surreal given that they're only steps apart. Weavers from Bohemia first settled here in the early 18th century and some of the original buildings still survive, including a blacksmith (Map pp140-1; Richardplatz 24), now a women's centre, and a farmhaus (Map pp140-1; Richardplatz 3A). Even these structures are mere saplings, though, compared to the Bethlehemskirche (Map pp140-1; Richardplatz 22), which has origins in the 15th century.

GRENZWACHTURM SCHLESISCHER BUSCH Map pp140-1
Am Flutgraben 3; ⊕ Schlesisches Tor
East German guards, machine guns at the ready, used to keep an eye on the inner-city border and the infamous 'death strip' from the top of this grey concrete watch tower.

ANHALTER BAHNHOF Map pp140-1
Askanischer Platz; ⊕ Anhalter Bahnhof
Only a forlorn fragment of the entrance portal is left of the Anhalter Bahnhof, once Berlin's finest and busiest railway station, surrounded by luxury hotels and bustling cafes. Marlene Dietrich departed from here for Hollywood, and the king of Italy and the tsar of Russia were among the official visitors to Berlin arriving at this station. Although badly bombed in WWII, Anhalter Bahnhof remained operational for years but was eventually eclipsed by Ostbahnhof. Not even vociferous protests could halt its demolition in 1960.

RADICAL KREUZBERG
Walking Tour
1 Bethanien This twin-turreted 1847 building by three Schinkel students was originally a hospital where writer and poet Theodor Fontane briefly worked as a pharmacist in 1848–49. Closed in 1970, it was saved from demolition by a coalition of squatters and preservationists. From 1984 to 2010, it was the home of the artist community Künstlerhaus Bethanien (p145).

2 Rote Harfe & Zum Elefanten When the West Berlin Senate announced plans to tear down and gentrify large swathes of SO36 in the 1970s, antidevelopment protesters gathered at these pubs on Heinrichplatz to discuss a counterstrategy.

3 SO36 The legendary SO36 (p237) club at Oranienstrasse 187 originated in the early 1970s as an artist squat and soon evolved into Berlin's seminal punk venue, known for wild concerts by the Dead Kennedys and home-grown bands like Die Ärzte and Einstürzende Neubauten.

4 May Day Riot Supermarket On May Day 1987 an initially peaceful protest escalated into a full-fledged riot that saw a mob of radicals looting dozens of stores and burning down two, including a supermarket at the corner of Wiener Strasse and Skalitzer Strasse. Empty for nearly two decades, the site is now occupied by the Omar-Ibn-Al-Khattab Moschee (Mosque), which opened in 2010.

5 Görlitzer Park With its dog poop, unkempt grass and wacky ruins, chaotic Görli was forged from a former railway station and is really more of an 'antipark', though much beloved by locals. Attractions include a children's farm

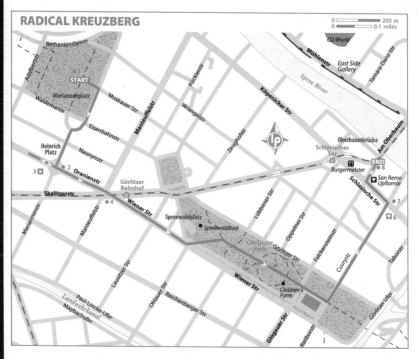

near Glogauer Strasse and Spreewaldbad, a public indoor pool on the western edge.

6 Barbie Deinhoff's This shrill bar at Schlesische Strasse 16 is absolutely, undeniably the last word in gender-fluid trash kitsch art – and that's saying something in Berlin. The name was inspired by the owner's fascination with both Barbie dolls and the Baader-Meinhof terrorist gang.

7 Blu Murals Two floating giants, one upside down, are a house-size piece of street art by Italian artist Blu in collaboration with French artist JR. in 2008, he added a second work, showing a tie-wearing man handcuffed to his watches. Both are at the corner of Cuvrystrasse and Schlesische Strasse. For a video of the process, go to www.youtube .com/watch?v=kdhhEbCXYmQ&feature =related.

WALK FACTS

Start Bethanien
End Backjump Mural
Distance 3km
Time 90 minutes
Exertion Moderate
Fuel stop San Remo Upflamör (p226), Burgermeister (p213)

8 Backjump Mural Another signature piece by Blu is at Falckensteinstrasse 48 (next to the Watergate club, p235). It took him five days to cover this entire fire wall with a huge pink body consisting of hundreds of smaller bodies writhing like worms. Check it out here: www.flickr.com/photos/16997404@ N07/2716703657.

FRIEDRICHSHAIN

Drinking p226; Gay & Lesbian p260; Eating p214; Shopping p193; Sleeping p276

Friedrichshain, in the former East Berlin, is a shape-shifter, a slippery creature, fluid in identity and defiant of all standard labels. In many ways, it's the 'anti-Mitte', still unsettled in its world view and offering a rambunctious stage for good times and DIY surprises. It celebrates its underground-punk-squatter roots in the derelict industrial outposts along Revaler Strasse and the graffiti-slathered funkytown around Ostkreuz. Mere steps away, Simon-Dach-Strasse is a bar-stumbling zone where the young and the restless drink, dance and flirt with all the mad exuberance of a stag party. In quieter side streets like Wühlischstrasse and Kopernikusstrasse, you can join the league of meticulous daydreamers in trendy coffee shops or blow your budget in sassy urban designer boutiques.

Over on post-socialist Karl-Marx-Allee, a post-college crowd gets liquefied on martinis – pinkie raised, and all – at swish GDR vintage bars before drifting off into the utopia of the Berghain/Panorama Bar and other high-energy techno temples. Right next door, the gleaming O2 World Arena signals that not even Friedrichshain will forever remain immune to gentrification.

top picks

FRIEDRICHSHAIN

- Karl-Marx-Allee (p152)
- East Side Gallery (below)

When the East German government decided to build a showpiece road in Berlin, they didn't pick historic Mitte but humble working-class Friedrichshain as its setting. It was along today's Karl-Marx-Allee that the Soviet Red Army had clawed its way into Berlin block by block in the last days of WWII. All they had to do was to clean up the heap of debris and start building anew. For many East Germans, grand Karl-Marx-Allee symbolised hope and faith in the future of a socialist state. Some 45,000 regular folks volunteered their time to help with the clean-up and the construction. Many of them were among the first residents who moved into modern and comfortable flats in January 1953.

While the residential neighbourhoods north of the boulevard are dominated by boxy, socialist-era housing developments, other streets teem with 19th-century tenements that are getting spruced up block by block. Rising rents mean that Friedrichshain too is a-changing but, for now, it's still the most affordable among Berlin's central districts, attracting a mellow meld of the young and free-spirited, wide-eyed students and artists, shower-phobic punks and squatters, eccentrics and white trash, not to mention a sizeable number of folk on the dole.

Friedrichshain's conventional tourist sights are limited to the East Side Gallery (the longest remaining stretch of the Berlin Wall) and the Karl-Marx-Allee, the epitome of Stalinist pomposity. Pockets of pleasantness include the Volkspark Friedrichshain (p153), a wonderland of tamed wilderness and perfect for sunning, grilling and picnicking. The beach bars along the East Side Gallery, meanwhile, lure night crawlers and people for whom the meaning of life seems to be in whiling the day away doing nothing in particular.

EAST SIDE GALLERY Map pp150-1

☎ 251 7159; www.eastsidegallery-berlin.de; Uhlandstrasse btwn Ostbahnhof & Oberbaumbrücke; admission free; ☯ 24hr; ◉ ⓡ Warschauer Strasse, ⓡ Ostbahnhof

The year was 1989. After 28 years, the Berlin Wall, that grim and grey divider of humanity, had finally met its maker. Most of the Wall was quickly dismantled, but along Mühlenstrasse, paralleling the Spree, a 1.3km stretch was spared. It became the East Side Gallery, the world's largest open-air gallery, drenched in over 100 murals.

Dozens of international artists translated the era's global euphoria and optimism into a mix of political statements, drug-induced musings and truly artistic visions. Birgit Kinder's *Test the Best,* showing a Trabi bursting through the Wall, *The Mortal Kiss* by Dimitri Vrubel, which has Erich Honecker and Leonid Brezhnev locking lips, and Thierry Noir's bright cartoon faces are all shutterbug favourites. Alas, time, taggers and tourists insisting on signing their favourite picture took their toll. In 2009, though, the entire thing got a total

See Mitte – Scheunenviertel Map p102

See Prenzlauer Berg Map p156

See Mitte – Alexanderplatz Area Map p96

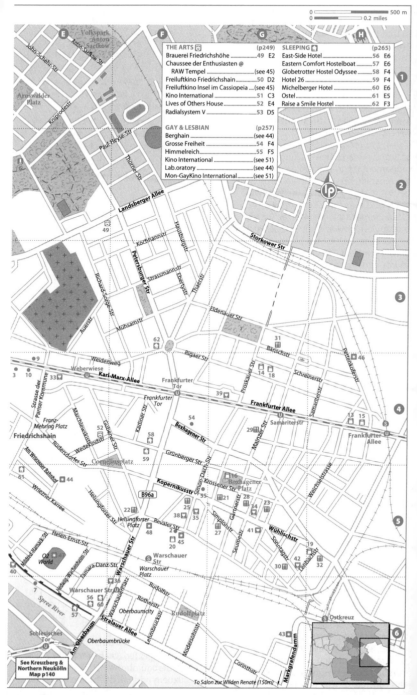

THE ARTS ☺   (p249)
Brauerei Friedrichshöhe 49 E2
Chaussee der Enthusiasten @
     RAW Tempel ....(see 45)
Freiluftkino Friedrichshain............50 D2
Freiluftkino Insel im Cassiopeia ....(see 45)
Kino International 51 C3
Lives of Others House......................52 E4
Radialsystem V 53 D5

GAY & LESBIAN   (p257)
Berghain...(see 44)
Grosse Freiheit...............................54 F4
Himmelreich....................................55 F5
Kino International ....(see 51)
Lab.oratory.....................................(see 44)
Mon-GayKino International...........(see 51)

SLEEPING 🛏   (p265)
East-Side Hotel...............................56 E6
Eastern Comfort Hostelboat 57 E6
Globetrotter Hostel Odyssee 58 F4
Hotel 26 ....59 F4
Michelberger Hotel 60 E6
Ostel...61 E5
Raise a Smile Hostel 62 F3

See Kreuzberg &
Northern Neukölln
Map p140

To Salon zur Wilden Renate (150m)

makeover and is looking better than ever, even though a short section was removed so that the O2 World Arena could have its own boat landing. In summer, fun beach bars like Strandgut (p224) and Oststrand (p224) set up shop on the waterfront.

KARL-MARX-ALLEE Map pp150-1

Btwn Alexanderplatz & Frankfurter Tor; ⊙ Alexanderplatz, Schillingstrasse, Strausberger Platz, Weberwiese, Frankfurter Tor

It's easy to feel like Gulliver in the Land of Brobdingnag when walking down monumental Karl-Marx-Allee (KMA), one of the most impressive GDR-era relics. Built between 1952 and 1960, the 90m-wide boulevard runs for 2.3km between Alexanderplatz and Frankfurter Tor and is a fabulous showcase of East German architecture. Despite the bloody workers' uprising in 1953, KMA was a considerable source of national pride. It's flanked with massive 'workers' palaces' honeycombed with modern flats featuring French windows, patterned parquet floors, tiled baths and built-in kitchens. Facades are swathed in nothing less than Meissen tiles. In fact, for the longest time, there was no better standard of living in the GDR, which is why many of the 'workers' living here were actually members of the country's elite: professors, diplomats, politicians, journalists and actors. KMA's chief architect, Hermann Henselmann, lived in a nine-room flat in one of the towers on Strausberger Platz.

Along with fellow architects Hartmann, Hopp, Leucht, Paulick and Souradny, Henselmann found inspiration in Moscow, where Stalin favoured a style that was essentially a socialist reinterpretation of good old-fashioned neoclassicism. In East Berlin, Prussian building master Karl Friedrich Schinkel would be the stylistic godfather, not Walter Gropius and the boxy Bauhaus aesthetic so fashionable in the West.

The result was undoubtedly impressive, but its lack of human-scale proportions never made it particularly lively. Sure, people flocked to fancy restaurants like the Café Moskau, to see movies in the glamorous Kino Kosmos or to shop at chic department stores, but the broad, treeless and windy pavements didn't exactly invite strolling.

They still don't. Nevertheless, KMA is undergoing a modest renaissance, with bars and businesses infusing some life into this concrete canyon and a slew of young

---

TRANSPORT: FRIEDRICHSHAIN

Bus 140 for Ostbahnhof from Kreuzberg; 200 for Volkspark Friedrichshain from Mitte; 240 from Ostbahnhof to Boxhagener Platz.

S-Bahn S3, S5, S7/75 and S9 stop at Ostbahnhof, Warschauer Strasse and Ostkreuz; S8, S41 and S42 stop at Frankfurter Allee and Ostkreuz.

Tram M10 from Nordbahnhof to Warschauer Strasse via Prenzlauer Berg; M13 from Warschauer Strasse for Boxhagener Platz and Frankfurter Allee.

U-Bahn U1 from Charlottenburg, Schöneberg and Kreuzberg terminates at Warschauer Strasse; U5 from Alexanderplatz along Karl-Marx-Allee/Frankfurter Allee.

---

galleries taking over vacant spaces ever since the private art collection Sammlung Haubrok (p80) moved into one of the towers on Strausberger Platz. On the ground floor of the same building is Im Namen des Raumes (Karl-Marx-Allee 19); others to check out include Capitain Petzel (Karl-Marx-Allee 45), Krome Gallery (Karl-Marx-Allee 82) and Galerie Wagner und Partner (Karl-Marx-Allee 87).

To learn more about KMA, check out the exhibit at Café Sybille (see below). The best way to explore this unique boulevard is on foot or by bicycle. Our Cycling Tour (opposite) pinpoints the key places for you.

CAFÉ SYBILLE Map pp150-1

☎ 2935 2203; www.karlmarxallee.eu, in German; Karl-Marx-Allee 72; ☉ 10am-8pm Mon-Fri, noon-8pm Sat & Sun; admission free; ⊙ Weberwiese, Strausberger Platz

One of the most popular cafes in East Berlin until the fall of the Wall, Café Sybille closed in 1997 but was taken over in 2001 by a nonprofit organisation. With its early '60s charm, it's a great spot for a coffee break and also has an excellent exhibit charting the milestones of KMA from inception to today. There are portraits and biographies of the architects, alongside posters, toys and other items from socialist times; even a piece of Stalin's moustache scavenged from the nearby statue that was torn down in 1961.

For a bird's-eye view of KMA, head up to the viewing platform (1-5 people €15, extra person €3).

OBERBAUMBRÜCKE Map pp150-1

⊙ Schlesisches Tor, ⊙ ⓡ Warschauer Strasse
The Oberbaumbrücke (1896), which links Kreuzberg and Friedrichshain across the

Spree, gets our nod for being Berlin's prettiest bridge. With its jaunty towers and turrets, crenellated walls and arched walkways, it has a fairytale quality and played a key scene in the movie *Run Lola Run*. There are great views of the Mitte skyline from here, although they used to be better before the electronic billboard of the O2 World Arena started competing with the TV Tower. Looking south you'll spot the Universal Music HQ, MTV Europe and the amazing NH Hotel with its gravity-defying cube jutting out over the water. On the Kreuzberg side you'll spot the Badeschiff (p147) and, in the distance, a giant aluminium sculpture called Molecule Man (Map pp140-1) by American artist Jonathan Borofsky. Right in the river, it shows three bodies embracing and is meant as a symbol of the joining together of the three districts of Kreuzberg, Friedrichshain and Treptow across the former border.

VOLKSPARK FRIEDRICHSHAIN
Map pp150-1

Am Friedrichshain & Friedenstrasse; 🚌 **200, tram M5, M6, M8 & M10**

Berlin's oldest public park has provided treasured relief from urbanity since 1840 but only gained its two hills after WWII, when wartime debris was piled up atop two demolished flak towers; the taller one (78m) is nicknamed Mont Klamott. Explore this splotch of green and you'll find expansive lawns for lazing alongside diversions for active types (tennis courts and a half-pipe for skaters) and a couple of handily placed beer gardens. In summer, cinephiles flock to the amphitheatre for an outdoor film series (see the boxed text, p252).

Travelling with kids? This is also one of the best park for them thanks to imaginatively themed playgrounds (see boxed text, right) and the enchanting 1913 Märchenbrunnen (Map pp150-1; Fairy-tale Fountain). At this sandstone marvel, turtles and frogs frolic in terraced water basins flanked by Cinderella, Snow White and other famous characters from Brothers Grimm tales. (Caveat: don't bring your little ones here at night, though, when the fountain turns into a gay cruising zone…)

If you have a soft spot for revolutionaries, visit the park's trio of memorial sites. Southeast of the fountain, along Friedenstrasse, the Denkmal der Spanienkämpfer (Memorial to the Fighters in Spain; Map pp150–1) pays respect to the German members (most of

top picks
CHILD'S PLAY

Berlin has plenty of fabulous playgrounds where kids can let off steam and make new friends in imaginative surrounds. These are our favourites:

- Arnimplatz (Map pp156-7) Little ones can fancy themselves knight and damsel while clambering around a medieval castle complete with treasure chest and resident dragon in this pint-sized Prenzlauer Berg park.
- Kollwitzplatz (p158) A Prenzlauer Berg favourite, kids romp around the jungle gym, play catch around the Käthe Kollwitz statue or build castles in the sandbox.
- Volkspark Friedrichshain (left) Play cowboys and Indians in the 'Indian Village' or gather your pirate mateys on the boat in the 'harbour', just two of the wonderful playgrounds in this sprawling neighbourhood park.

them communists) of the International Brigades who lost their lives fighting against fascism in the Spanish Civil War (1936–39). On the southern edge, off Landsberger Allee, is the Friedhof der Märzgefallenen (Map pp150-1), a cemetery for the 183 victims of the revolutionary riots in March 1848, a tumultuous time also commemorated at the Platz des 18 März (p81), west of Brandenburger Tor. Finally, in the northeastern corner, the Deutsch-Polnisches Ehrenmal (German-Polish Memorial; Map pp150-1) honours the joint fight of Polish soldiers and the German resistance against the Nazis during WWII.

A SOCIALIST RIDE ALONG KARL-MARX-ALLEE
Cycling Tour

1 Strausberger Platz Here, KMA widens into a vast traffic circle. The western end of the square is punctuated by two 13-storey high-rises, Haus Berlin and Haus des Kindes. Traffic roars around a central fountain called Schwebender Ring (floating ring) because of the circular copper plate contraption in the middle.

2 Haus Berlin On the square's north side, House Berlin was a hugely popular entertainment venue where East Berliners came for

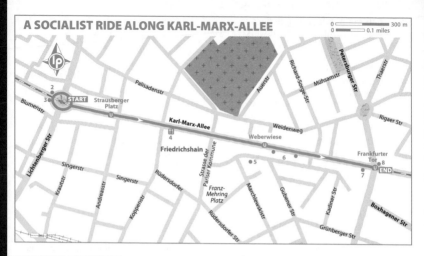

A SOCIALIST RIDE ALONG KARL-MARX-ALLEE

CYCLE FACTS

Start Strausberger Platz
End Haus des Sports
Distance 1.6km
Time 25 minutes
Exertion Easy
Fuel stop Café Sybille (p152)

dinner, dancing or a tête-à-tête in the rooftop wine tavern. Today only a lone restaurant on the ground floor tries to keep up the legacy.

3 Haus des Kindes Across the street, the House of the Child was where parents shopped for toys or T-shirts, kids could watch puppet shows or romp around the kindergarten. Afterwards, everyone had chocolate in the top-floor cafe where a sign said: 'Adults must be accompanied by children'. Now called Henselmann-Tower, it's home to the Sammlung Haubrok (p80) and the small project gallery Im Namen des Raumes.

4 Café Sybille The Café Sybille (p152) at No 72 was one of the most popular hang-outs in East Berlin, a place to take your sweetie for a milkshake or knock back vodka with your chums. Thankfully, even a renovation in the 1990s didn't erase the air of sober functionality. Today it's a cafe-cum-history exhibit.

5 Hochhaus an der Weberwiese This residential high-rise at Marchlewskistrasse

35, designed by Hermann Henselmann, set new standards for modern living in the East Berlin of 1952. Tenants enjoyed central heating, running hot water, a lift, garbage disposal, private telephones and a shared rooftop terrace. The architect called it the 'swan that has risen from the ruins of Berlin'.

6 Laubenganghäuser These boxy apartment buildings at Nos 102–104, with the vanilla, peach and cherry paint job, were designed by Hans Scharoun and are the only Bauhaus structures on KMA. More were planned, but upon their completion in 1949, East German leader Walter Ulbricht stopped the project because he considered them too 'primitive' for the East German capital.

7 Frankfurter Tor This buzzy square marks the eastern end of KMA. Its general layout closely mirrors that of Strausberger Platz, while the two striking towers were inspired by the French and German cathedrals on Gendarmenmarkt (p86). It features other neoclassical elements, most notably columns, French windows and external walkways.

8 Haus des Sports The House of Sports, on the northeast corner of Frankfurter Tor, is now a second-hand clothing store. Note Gabriele Mucci's bizarre mural of men chopping wood past the brass-and-glass door and check out the retro neon lamps in the room on your right.

Drinking p227; Gay & Lesbian p260; Eating p215; Shopping p194; Sleeping p278

Once a neglected backwater, Prenzlauer Berg went from rags to riches after reunification and is now one of Berlin's most attractive neighbourhoods. There are no major sights, which is just fine because its true charms reveal themselves in subtler, often unexpected ways. Look up at gorgeously ornamented facades that not long ago bore the scars of war. Push open a sturdy door to stumble upon quiet courtyards such as the artsy Hirschhof (p161) or the radical Tuntenhaus (Map pp156-7, Kastanienallee 86), a gay punk co-op. Browse for home-grown fashions and accessories in indie designer boutiques on boho-trendy Kastanienallee and Oderberger Strasse or carve out a spot in a cafe on yuppified Kollwitzplatz or in the nearby Wasserturm area. On Sundays, the Mauerpark draws tens of thousands to the city's best flea market, outdoor karaoke, pick-up basketball and other fun and games.

It helps that Prenzlauer Berg has always had great bone structure. Badly pummelled but not destroyed during WWII, it languished for decades with its grand 19th-century townhouses crumbling but largely intact. In GDR days, it was not at all a popular area in which to live. Quite the opposite. Comrades with enough money or connections happily exchanged their inner-city hovels for a pad in massive prefab housing estates on the city periphery that came with plumbing, lifts and other mod cons. Prenzlauer Berg was left to the artists, creatives, intellectuals, gays and political dissidents. It was this community that stood up when the government came within a whisker of tearing down the old buildings in the late '80s. And it was they who fuelled the fire of opposition that led to the Peaceful Revolution of 1989.

top picks

PRENZLAUER BERG

- Kollwitzplatz (p158)
- Kulturbrauerei (p158)
- Mauerpark (p159)

After the Wall collapsed, the district was among the first to show up in the crosshairs of West Germans and foreign developers. They snapped up the decrepit buildings for virtual pennies and peeled away decades of grime to reveal gorgeous facades and stucco-ornamented interiors. Now pretty as a polished penny, Prenzlauer Berg's townhouses sparkle in freshly applied pastels, their sleekly renovated flats and lofts the haunts of an increasingly boho-bourgeois, middle-aged middle class. Residents tend to be prosperous, well-educated and worldly; many speak several languages and have put in stints in New York, London or Barcelona. Many are expats, mostly from America, Britain and Spain. They keep alive the many restaurants and cafes, designer boutiques and 'bio' (organic) supermarkets.

Ironically, these relatively recent arrivals have displaced nearly 80% of the original residents, who could simply no longer afford the ever-rising rents or felt no cultural affinity for Italian cafes pouring a dozen types of coffee drinks. And the newcomers keep multiplying. Prenzlauer Berg is one of the most family-friendly districts in town: safe, quiet and with plenty of playgrounds, toy stores and children's cafes. Wherever you walk, you'll likely be dodging an astonishing number of prams, from vintage versions to high-tech strollers.

Not surprisingly, these demographic changes have significantly undermined the district's alt-flavoured, relaxed vibe that attracted people in the first place. Beloved party places such as the Magnet Club, Knaack Club and the gay bar Zum Schmutzigen Hobby, all of which have been around for years (Knaack since 1952), have all come under fire from noise-sensitive neighbours. Magnet finally capitulated and moved to Kreuzberg. The latest casualty (well, at press time) was Berlin's best drum 'n' bass club, Icon, whose licence was not renewed and which will have to close at the end of 2010.

To plug into the *Kiez* quickly, stop by the TIC tourist office (Map pp156-7; ☎ 4435 2170; Maschinenhalle; ⏰ noon-8pm Tue-Sat, to 6pm Sun & Mon; ⊕ Eberswalder Strasse) in the Kulturbrauerei, which specialises in Prenzlauer Berg and also sells tickets to events around town.

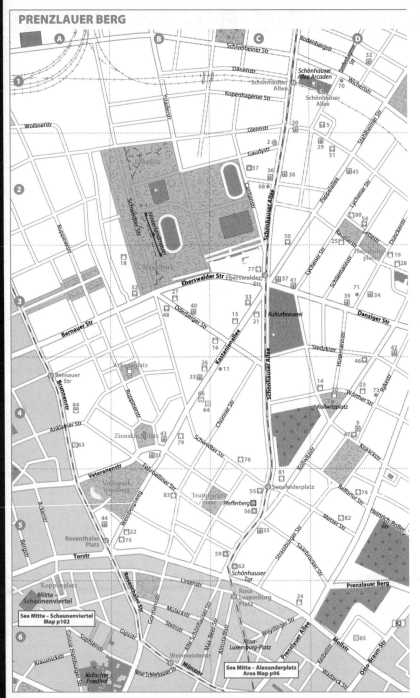

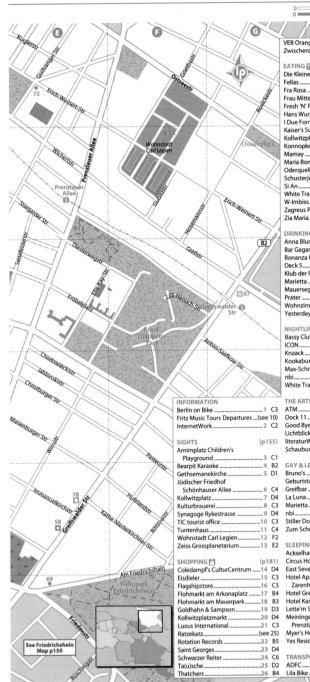

See Friedrichshain Map p150

TRANSPORT: PRENZLAUER BERG

S-Bahn S8, S9, S41 and S42 stop at Schönhauser Allee, Prenzlauer Allee, Greifswalder Strasse, Landsberger Allee and Storkower Strasse.

Tram M1 from Museumsinsel via Scheunenviertel, Kastanienallee and Schönhauser Allee; M4 from Hackescher Markt and Alexanderplatz along Greifswalder Strasse, M10 from Warschauer Strasse (Friedrichshain) to Nordbahnhof via Bernauer Strasse.

U-Bahn U2 from Charlottenburg, Schöneberg and Mitte stops at Senefelderplatz, Eberswalder Strasse and Schönhauser Allee.

KOLLWITZPLATZ Map pp156-7
Ⓤ Senefelderplatz

This pretty triangular square was ground zero of the district's gentrification and went posh with a vengeance. Nary a crumbling facade in sight! Grab a table in a cafe and watch the leagues of tattooed mamas, designer-jean hipsters and gawking tourists on parade. The park-like centre is a haven for the tot brigade with not one but three playgrounds as well as the bronze sculpture of the square's namesake, the artist Käthe Kollwitz (see p127), to clamber on. A great time to visit is during the Thursday or Saturday farmers markets (p207).

JÜDISCHER FRIEDHOF SCHÖNHAUSER ALLEE Map pp156-7
☎ 441 9824; Schönhauser Allee 23-25; admission free; ⏰ 8am-4pm Mon-Thu, to 1pm Fri; Ⓤ Senefelderplatz

Berlin's second Jewish cemetery opened in 1827 and, behind a thick wall, hosts such famous dearly departed as the artist Max Liebermann and the composer Giacomo Meyerbeer. The Nazis devastated the grounds, stealing decorative elements from the tombstones and even using some to build barricades against approaching Soviet tanks. It's a pretty place with dappled light filtering through big old trees, but there's also a deeply melancholic air emanating from the overgrown graves and toppled tombstones. The nicest and oldest have been moved to the Lapidarium (lapis is Latin for stone), a new hall by the main entrance. Liebermann's tomb is next to his family's crypt roughly in the centre along the back wall. Men must cover their heads; pick up a free skullcap by the entrance.

KULTURBRAUEREI Map pp156-7
☎ 4431 5152; www.kulturbrauerei-berlin.de; Schönhauser Allee 36; Ⓤ Eberswalder Strasse

Architect Franz Schwechten got his creative juices flowing back in 1889 to give the former Schultheiss brewery a fairy-tale look complete with towers, turrets, gables and arches. The result was a fanciful complex of 20 ornate red-and-yellow brick buildings framing a series of courtyards. The last bottle of beer was filled in 1967 and the place more or less lingered until 1991, when it was reborn as the Kulturbrauerei (literally 'cultural brewery'). Today, it's a cultural powerhouse where the roll-call of venues includes a multi-screen cinema, concert halls, clubs, galleries, a supermarket, theatres and the bike touring company Berlin on Bike (p311). In December, the old buildings make a lovely backdrop for a Swedish-style Lucia Christmas market (www .lucia-weihnachtsmarkt.de, in German).

German-language tours (adult/concession €7.50/6; ☎ registration 4435 2170) taking you into the vaulted cellars and other hidden spaces of the former brewery run at 3.30pm on Saturday and Sunday. Registration is

BERLIN ON A SUNDAY

Unlike other metropolises, Berlin doesn't sink into a pious stupor on Sundays and – except for the shops – is pretty much open for business. This goes for all the museums, sights, boat cruises, cinemas, theatre and concert stages, cabarets and other entertainment venues. Cafes are in full swing all day long, serving big brunch buffets until the last bleary-eyed night owls have had their fill, ie about 3pm or 4pm. In the afternoon, the time-honoured German tradition of coffee and cake brings out people of all generations and walks of life. If you're suffering from shopping withdrawal, get your fix at a flea market. Flohmarkt am Mauerpark (p196) and Flohmarkt am Arkonaplatz (p195) are among the city's best and conveniently located close to each other. In summer, the former has the added benefit of free entertainment – Bearpit Karaoke (opposite). For diehard dancers, there are plenty of after-parties; the waterfront Club der Visionäre (p233) has one of the best vibes in town. Queer folk should steer to Café Fatal (p261) at SO36 with dance lessons, a show and ballroom dancing or GMF at Weekend (p261). At the KitKatClub@Sage (p234) the party continues well into Monday.

BEARPIT KARAOKE

Every Sunday afternoon in good weather a phenomenon takes over the Mauerpark. Up to 2000 people pack into a small amphitheatre carved into the former death strip for a few hours of mobile karaoke, courtesy of an Irish lad who goes by the name of Joe Hatchiban. He calls it Bearpit Karaoke (www.bearpitkaraoke.de) and his concept is simple: bring a laptop full of songs, set up a couple of speakers on the concrete stage and then hand eager crooners the microphone.

From giggling 11-year-olds to grizzled karaoke vets, everyone is welcome. Some of them are regulars, like Detlef (Berlin's very own Paul Potts), an elderly, bearded man in a tweed jacket who gives everyone goose bumps with his rendition of 'My Heart Will Go On'. Or Gabriel, who owns a local pizza joint, who revs up the crowd with his vamping *Hello Dolly* song-and-dance routine. And seemingly every time someone does 'Billy Jean', a trio of teens beams in from nowhere to do a killer breakdance in support.

The entertainment is free (although Joe does occasionally clamber into the stands with a donation box), but over time an entire industry has sprung up around the amphitheatre. Roving vendors supply the crowd with cold drinks, while sustenance comes mostly from expats earning some pocket change with homemade cookies, empanadas and other exotic snacks.

It's a show, it's a party, it's laid-back and it's fun. Only in Berlin.

required, call ahead or stop by the tourist office in the Maschinenhalle.

GETHSEMANEKIRCHE Map pp156-7

☎ 445 7745; www.gethsemanekirche.de, in German; Stargarder Strasse 77; ❻ Schönhauser Allee
This statuesque red-brick church is an 1893 neo-Gothic pile by August Orth and was among the dozens commissioned by Emperor Wilhelm II to 'create a bulwark against socialism, communism and atheism' which, he feared, were fomenting in Prenzlauer Berg and other working-class districts. Ironically, rather than stifling such movements, the Gethsemane church encouraged them. Its congregation can look back on a proud tradition of dissent and as a haven for nonconformists and freethinkers. During GDR times it was a key player in the nonviolent movement that eventually brought down the regime. Such action, of course, placed it firmly in the crosshairs of the Stasi which, as late as October 1989, brutally quashed a peaceful gathering outside the church. Today the church is a small but active parish that hosts concerts and other events. Ernst Barlach's *Geistkämpfer* (Ghost Fighter, 1928) sculpture stands on the church's south side. It's usually closed except for concerts and services (11am Sunday).

MAUERPARK Map pp156-7

Btwn Bernauer Strasse, Schwedter Strasse, Gleimstrasse; admission free; ⏲ 24hr; ❻ Eberswalder Strasse
From anti-park to Berlin's most vibrant urban oasis, Mauerpark has become the go-to place in Prenzlauer Berg, and not just for the famous Flohmarkt am Mauerpark (Sunday flea market; p196) and Bearpit Karaoke (above). Pretty it ain't, with its scraggly bushes and anaemic lawn, but then you might forgive such aesthetics when realising that it was forged from the former death strip. Yup, the Wall used to run right through here where people now gather for barbecues, basketball, boules and other diversions. A 300m-long stretch of it still stands, but the one-time symbol of oppression is now a legal practice ground for budding graffiti artists. The floodlights behind this colourful strip belong to the Friedrich-Ludwig-Jahn-Sportpark, the stadium where Stasi chief Erich Mielke used to cheer on his beloved Dynamo Berlin football (soccer) team. Just north of here is the Max-Schmeling-Halle (p237) venue.

But the magic of Mauerpark isn't about its facilities, it's about the relaxed, almost neo-hippie vibe that attracts folks from all walks of life, many still unencumbered by the traps and trappings of adult life. It's a place to chill with friends amid summer wildflowers, watch the sunset – cold beer in hand – or catch an impromptu concert. Even the mommy-and-child brigade is happy here, where kids can romp around the playground, test their mettle on the climbing wall or meet barnyard animals in the children's farm.

The park itself is still a work in progress, as part of the land in and around it is privately owned. Plans to build a row of large residential buildings south of the Gleimstrasse tunnel were thwarted in 2010, even though the developer was granted permission to build a new residential quarter north of the tunnel in exchange for donating part of the land and thus expanding the park.

SYNAGOGE RYKESTRASSE Map pp156-7
☎ 8802 8316; www.synagoge-rykestrasse.de; Rykestrasse 53; ⓢ Senefelderplatz

A rambling red-brick, neo-Romanesque pile, Berlin's largest synagogue was built in 1904 and bears silent testimony to the size and importance of the city's pre-WWII Jewish community. It was one of the few Jewish houses of worship that didn't go up in flames during the 1938 *Kristallnacht* pogroms, probably to avoid torching the adjacent non-Jewish residential building. Nazi thugs still smashed the sanctuary and later used it as a munitions depot and horse stable. After the war the giant synagogue served East Berlin's tiny Jewish congregation. Now fully restored, it hosts services but tours had been suspended indefinitely at the time of writing. Call for updates.

ZEISS GROSSPLANETARIUM Map pp156-7
☎ 421 8450; www.sdtb.de; Prenzlauer Allee 80; adult/concession €5/4; ⓧ show times vary; ⓡ Prenzlauer Allee

The people of East Berlin were not allowed to see what was across the Wall, but at least they could gaze at the entire universe at this fine planetarium. It opened in 1987 as one of the largest star theatres in Europe, boasting a 'Cosmorama', back then the finest star projector ever built. Today, programming ranges from traditional narrated shows (in German) to 'music under the stars' and children's events.

PRENZLAUER BERG
Walking Tour
1 Senefelderplatz Trivia quiz: who's the inventor of lithography? Why, Aloys Senefelder (1771–1834), of course. That's him in marble on this little triangular splotch of green right by the U-Bahn station exit. Note that his name is chiselled into the pedestal in mirror-writing, just as it would be using his printing technique.

2 Pfefferberg The sprawling brick Pfefferberg across busy Schönhauser Allee is actually a brewery turned cultural centre with

a cross-cultural bent and a leafy beer garden for summertime chilling. Beer-making was actually Prenzlauer Berg's bread and butter all through the 19th century, though no breweries are left today.

3 Site of Kollwitz home The dark-blue postwar building at the corner of Kollwitzstrasse and Knaackstrasse replaced the war-damaged, late-19th-century structure where Kollwitz and her husband Karl lived for more than 40 years while tending to the destitute all around them. Note the memorial plaque above the entrance.

4 Käthe Kollwitz sculpture In the park at the centre of Kollwitzplatz square is this 1958 bronze sculpture by Gustav Seitz, which shows the artist as an elderly woman, tired but dignified. Children often leave the nearby playgrounds to clamber around this larger-than-life sculpture or sit in her maternal lap.

5 Wasserturm May we introduce to you – 'Fat Hermann'. That's what P'bergers have nicknamed this round water tower, a handsome 1877 structure with a dark past. Soon after Hitler's power grab, the Nazis turned the cellar into an improvised concentration camp. Now it's honeycombed with a dozen pie-shaped flats.

6 Rykestrasse 'Ryke' is old German for 'rich', which must have been a slap in the face to its 19th-century working-class residents who were penned up like cattle in tenements without proper heating or plumbing. GDR city planners came within an inch of tearing down the crumbling buildings but decided to give them a reprieve. At No 53 is the Synagoge Rykestrasse (left).

7 Husemannstrasse Back in the 1980s, East Berlin apparatchiks decided to restore Husemannstrasse to its 19th-century splendour in celebration of the city's 750th anniversary. In typical smoke-and-mirrors fashion, though, only the facades and street-level shops got spruced up, giving the street as much 'authenticity' as a Hollywood film set.

8 Oderberger Strasse If Husemannstrasse exudes artifice, Oderberger is the real deal. In the late '70s, neighbours banded together against socialist town planners who wanted to

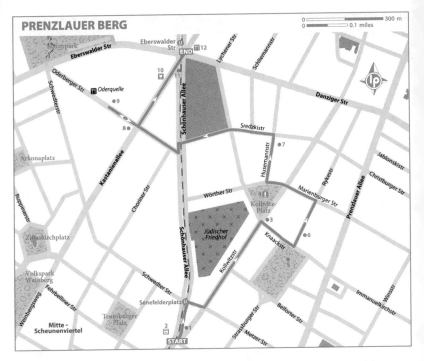

0 ——— 300 m
0 ——— 0.1 miles

Eberswalder Str
END 12
Ebersswalder Str
Oderberger Str
Oderquelle
10
11
9
8
Schönhauser Allee
Danziger Str
Sredzkistr
Arkonaplatz
Kastanienallee
Husemannstr
7
Jablonskistr
Christburger Str
Choriner Str
Wörther Str
4
Kollwitz-Platz
Marienburger Str
Rykestr
Prenzlauer Allee
Rupinstr
3
Zionskirchplatz
Jüdischer Friedhof
Knaackstr
6
Kollwitzstr
Schönhauser Allee
Volkspark Weinberg
Schwedter Str
Fehrbelliner Str
Weinbergsweg
Senefelderplatz
Belforter Str
Immanuelkirchstr
Winsstr
Mitte - Scheunenviertel
Teutoburger Platz
2
1
Strassburger Str
Metzer Str
START

WALK FACTS

Start **Senefelderplatz**
End **Konnopke's Imbiss**
Distance **2.5km**
Time **Two hours**
Exertion **Moderate**
Fuel stop **Konnopke's Imbiss** (p217), **Oderquelle** (p216), **Prater** (p228)

replace their historic townhouses with prefab structures. Since reunification, the drag has been heavily gentrified and is now a popular food, booze and cafe spot.

9 Hirschhof A giant sci-fi-esque stag made from recycled metal guards this hidden mini-park with a sandbox, a ping pong table and stone fragments scavenged from historic Berlin buildings. To get there, walk up the driveway between Oderberger Strasse Nos 18 and 19 and turn right past the car mechanic shop.

10 Prater The chestnut-shaded beer garden at Prater (p228) has been serving suds and entertainment since 1852, when it was a popular stopover for people heading out for a day in the countryside. After WWI August Bebel and Rosa Luxemburg were among those who fanned up the workers' movement with their fiery speeches here.

11 Skladanowsky mosaic Keep your nose to the ground at the corner of Kastanienallee and Schönhauser Allee. The line mosaic in the pavement commemorates Emil and Max Skladanowsky, brothers and cinematography pioneers who had their office in the corner building. Their earliest 'moving pictures' date back to 1892.

12 Konnopke's Imbiss Below the elevated U-Bahn tracks Konnopke's Imbiss (p217) has been serving the quintessential Berlin snack since 1930: the *Currywurst*, a spicy sausage, slivered, doused with tomato sauce and sprinkled with curry powder. Eat 'em while they're hot!

DAHLEM & AROUND

One of Berlin's most upper-crust residential zones, Dahlem is sprinkled with enough cultural and natural appeal to keep you busy and stimulated for at least an entire day. Southwest of the city centre, it is part of the administrative district of Zehlendorf and borders the vast Grunewald forest, a fresh-air refuge extending all the way west to the Havel River.

After WWII, with the division of Berlin, Zehlendorf became part of the American sector and thus a preferred neighbourhood for US forces. Such institutions as the international John F Kennedy School and the Allied Museum in a former military compound are a legacy from that period. There's also a major German university, the Freie Universität, but don't expect Latin Quarter flair: most students can't afford a pad in this villa-studded suburb.

MUSEEN DAHLEM off Map pp72-3

☎ 830 1438; www.smb.spk-berlin.de; enter at Lansstrasse 8; adult/concession/child under 18 €6/3/ free; ☷ 10am-6pm Tue-Fri, 11am-6pm Sat & Sun; ☉ Dahlem Dorf

Until some mad scientist invents a magic time-travel-teleporter machine, the Dahlem museums, which display non-European art and objects, are your best bet for exploring the world in a single afternoon. Exhibits combine the collections of the Museum of Ethnology and the Museum of Asian Art, which will eventually move into the planned Humboldtforum (p91) in Mitte, although that's probably a decade away. Until then, you won't regret making the trip out here: the depth and wealth of the exhibits is truly stunning and it's all beautifully and engagingly presented.

There are plenty of highlights in the Museum of Ethnology, including the newly revamped Africa exhibit, where artfully crafted masks, ornaments, vases, musical instruments and other objects from Benin and Cameroon provide insight into ceremonies and aspects of daily life. There's also contemporary art from Africa as well as art created by African artists living in Berlin, including a fantastic *Ijele* mask. In another hall you'll be transported to the far-away South Seas as you wander among outriggers and other handcrafted vessels, traditional

huts and exhibits on architecture, seafaring and pottery and other crafts.

The Asian Art Museum, meanwhile, tracks the evolution of art in such countries as India, Nepal, China, Thailand, Japan and Korea from the 4th millennium BC to today. It's considered one of the world's most important collections of its type. Highlights here include Japanese paintings and East Asian lacquer art as well Chinese ceramics from the Neolithic period up to the 15th century. Check out the Japanese tea room and a 16th-century Chinese imperial throne made of lacquered rosewood with mother-of-pearl inlay.

The museum complex also houses the Museum of European Cultures, whose rooms are undergoing a major overhaul and are closed until at least June 2011. The Junior-Museum in the basement was also closed during our visit in preparation for a brand new exhibit; it should be open by the time you're reading this.

BRÜCKE MUSEUM off Map pp72-3

☎ 831 2029; www.bruecke-museum.de, in German; Bussardsteig 9; adult/concession €5/3; ☷ 11am-5pm Wed-Mon; ☉ Oskar-Helene-Heim, then ☐ 115 to Pücklerstrasse

In 1905 Karl Schmidt-Rottluff, Erich Heckel and Ernst Ludwig Kirchner founded Die Brücke (The Bridge, 1905–13), one of the first modern artists' groups in Germany. Rejecting traditional techniques taught in the academies, they turned the art world on its head with ground-breaking visions that paved the way for German expressionism. Shapes and figures that teeter on the abstract – without ever quite getting there – drenched with bright, emotional colours characterise the style of Die Brücke.

top picks

GREEN ESCAPES

- Britzer Garten (p168)
- Gärten der Welt im Erholungspark Marzahn (p174)
- Liebermann-Villa am Wannsee (p165)
- Müggelsee (p171)
- Pfaueninsel (p165)

It was Schmidt-Rottluff's idea to bring the works of Brücke members together under a single roof. He got things going in the 1960s by donating his personal collection, which has since been steadily expanded. Housed in a Bauhaus-inspired building by Werner Düttmann, this is a small museum where quality matters more than quantity.

Combine your visit here with a stroll over to the Jagdschloss Grunewald (below) near the Grunewaldsee (swimming allowed), which is a paradise for joggers and doggies.

JAGDSCHLOSS GRUNEWALD
off Map pp72-3

☎ 813 3597; Hüttenweg 100; adult/concession Apr-Oct €4/3, Nov-Mar €5/4; ☷ 10am-6pm Tue-Sat Apr-Oct, visit by guided tour only 11am, 1pm & 3pm Sat & Sun Nov-Mar; ◉ Fehrbelliner Platz, then 🚌 115 to Finkenstrasse

Prussian rulers loved to hunt and the Grunewald forest was one of their favourite stomping grounds ever since Elector Joachim II first got the dogs running back in 1542. He also picked a scenic spot near a pretty lake, the Grunewaldsee, to build his hunting palace, which is the oldest existing royal palace in town and was used by the family until 1918. After a recent renovation, which is documented on the ground floor, its walls are once again decorated with paintings by Dutch and German masters from the 15th to the 18th centuries, including the famous portraits of the royal family by Lucas Cranach the Elder and his son. An architectural highlight is the Great Hall downstairs. There's also a small exhibit on the royal hunt and the building of the palace in the Jagdzeugmagazin (hunting storehouse; adult/concession €2/1.50), open the same hours as the palace, in the courtyard. The graphic hunting scenes and monstrous representations of animals are not for everybody.

The palace is about a 1km walk from the bus stop.

BOTANISCHER GARTEN & MUSEUM
off Map pp72-3

☎ 8385 0100; www.bgbm.org, in German; Königin-Luise-Strasse 6-8; adult/concession/family gardens & museum €6/3/12, museum only adult/concession €2.50/1.50; ☷ garden 9am-dusk, museum 10am-6pm; ◉ Botanischer Garten, ◉ Dahlem Dorf, 🚌 M48

If you're all shopped or museumed out, Berlin's botanical garden is an inspirational spot to reconnect with nature. One of the largest in Europe, it's a symphony of colour and scents with some 22,000 plant species from around the planet to enchant floweristas. A highlight is the massive Grosse Tropenhaus greenhouse, the muggy home of an entire bamboo forest; others shelter orchids, cacti, 'flesh-eating' plants, water lilies and other petalled beauties. Sight-impaired visitors can experience a special smell-and-touch garden. There are entrances on Unter den Eichen and on Königin-Luise-Platz. Near the latter is the rather turgid botanical museum. In summer, you can listen to everything from jazz to flamenco during a popular alfresco concert series (tickets with garden admission €15; ☷ 6pm Fri & Sat May-Aug).

FREILICHTMUSEUM DOMÄNE DAHLEM off Map pp72-3

☎ 666 3000; www.domaene-dahlem.de, in German; Königin-Luise-Strasse 49; adult/concession/child under 18 €3/1.50/free; ☷ 10am-6pm Wed-Mon; ◉ Dahlem-Dorf

TRANSPORT: WESTERN SUBURBS

Bus Bus 145 connects Schloss Charlottenburg with central Spandau. In Dahlem, X10 and 115 run along Clayallee. From ◉ Wannsee take 316 for Schloss Glienicke and the Glienicker Bridge and 218 for Pfaueninsel and north through Grunewald.

S-Bahn S1 from central Berlin to Dahlem and Wannsee, S7 from central Berlin to Wannsee via Grunewald, S9 and S75 from central Berlin to Spandau.

U-Bahn Spandau is served by U7 from Charlottenburg, Schöneberg and Kreuzberg; U3 goes to Dahlem from Schöneberg.

Pet a potbellied pig or clamber around a historical tractor at this open-air museum that's really a modern working farm attached to a rambling manor house. There are exhibits on the region's agricultural history, rural handicrafts and beekeeping, but kids will likely get more of a kick from watching daily farm life unfold. They can interact with the many barnyard animals, watch staff clean out the stables, collect eggs or tend to the vegetable gardens. All products are organic and sold in a little shop on site and during the farmers market (noon-5pm Wed, 8am-1pm Sat). On some days volunteers demonstrate spinning, weaving, pottery making, furniture painting and other retro-crafts.

FREIE UNIVERSITÄT BERLIN
off Map pp72-3
☎ 8381; www.fu-berlin.de; Habelschwerdter Allee 45; ⊕ Thielplatz

The Free University (FU) was founded in 1948 in reaction to the growing restrictions on academic freedoms at the Humboldt University, then in the Soviet sector. In the 1960s the FU played a leading role in the country's student movement, which sparked major nationwide academic and political reforms (p33). Today it's the largest of Berlin's three public universities, with nearly 40,000 students.

The latest addition (2005) is the Philology Library (☎ 8385 8888; admission free; 9am-10pm Mon-Fri, 10am-5pm Sat & Sun; ⊕ Thielplatz), a masterpiece of modern architecture by Lord Norman Foster. Nicknamed the 'Berlin Brain' because of its cranial shape, it has four floors sheltered within a naturally ventilated, bubble-like enclosure draped in aluminium and glazed panels.

ALLIIERTEN MUSEUM off Map pp72-3
☎ 818 1990; www.alliiertenmuseum.de; Clay-allee 135; admission free; 10am-6pm Thu-Tue; ⊕ Oskar-Helene-Heim

The Alliierten Museum (Allied Museum) documents the history and challenges faced by the Western Allies in Berlin after WWII and during the Cold War. Exhibits are presented chronologically starting in a former troop cinema, where the 1948 Berlin Airlift (see p32) is a major focus. Another building presents the confrontations of the Cold War years in all their drama. A highlight here is the partial reconstruction of the Spy

top picks

IT'S FREE

Berlin has lots of museums and venues that don't charge a single cent. Here's a sampling, but for the full list go to www.museumsportal-berlin.de and click through to Visitor Services/Free Entry.

- Alliierten Museum (Allied Museum; left)
- Anti-Kriegs-Museum (p177)
- Checkpoint Charlie (p144)
- East Side Gallery (p149)
- Kaiser-Wilhelm-Gedächtniskirche (p127)
- Gedenkstätte Berliner Mauer (p106)
- Holocaust Memorial (p82)
- Ort der Information at Holocaust Memorial (p83)
- Meilenwerk Car Museum (p126)
- Deutsch-Russisches Museum Berlin-Karlshorst (p173)
- Reichstag Dome (p75)
- Schlossgarten Charlottenburg (p123)
- Stasi Informations- Und Dokumentationszentrum (p144)
- Topographie des Terrors (p114)
- Unter den Linden (p84)

Tunnel, built in 1953–54 by US and British intelligence services to tap into the central Soviet telephone system. The original recorded half a million calls until a double agent blabbed to the Soviets. Finally there's a survey of events leading to the collapse of communism and the fall of the Berlin Wall.

The most memorable objects are in the yard: the original 1960s guard cabin from Checkpoint Charlie, a Hastings plane used during the Berlin Airlift, the restaurant car of a French military train, a small section of the Wall and a GDR guard tower.

All explanatory panelling is in German, English and French. To get here take the U-Bahn to Oskar-Helene-Heim, then catch any bus or walk 10 minutes north on Clayallee.

MUSEUMSDORF DÜPPEL off Map pp72-3
☎ 2400 2162; www.stadtmuseum.de, in German; Clauertstrasse 11; adult/concession/child under 18 €2/1/free; 3-7pm Thu, 10am-5pm Sun mid-Mar–early Oct; ⊕ Krumme Lanke, Zehlendorf, 115

This intriguing museum village is a window into the Middle Ages. Over a dozen reed-thatched buildings have been recreated on the grounds of a 12th-century settlement surrounded by fields and woods. Museum volunteers breed endangered sheep and pig species and grow historic strains of rye and, on Sunday only, stage tours, medieval games and craft demonstrations. Kids love it. Last admission is one hour before closing.

WANNSEE

Wannsee is the southernmost suburb of Zehlendorf and right on its namesake lake. It counts lush parks, a palace, a romantic royal island and key Nazi-era and Cold War sites among its attractions. It's about a 45-minute S-Bahn ride from the city centre to Wannsee station.

HAUS DER WANNSEE KONFERENZ

☎ 805 0010; www.ghwk.de; Am Grossen Wannsee 56-58; admission free; ☽ 10am-6pm; ☒ Wannsee, then ☐ 114

In January 1942 a group of elite Nazi officials under the leadership of Reinhard Heydrich met in a stately villa near Lake Wannsee to hammer out the details of the 'Final Solution', the systematic deportation – and murder – of the European Jews in Eastern Europe. Today the building houses a memorial exhibit and an education centre about this fateful gathering and its ramifications.

You can stand in the room where discussions took place, study the minutes of the conference (taken by Adolf Eichmann) and look at photographs of those involved, many of whom lived to a ripe old age. The other rooms chronicle, in a thorough and graphic fashion, the horrors leading up to and perpetrated during the Holocaust. English-language pamphlets may be borrowed from the desk, which also sells various publications on the subject.

LIEBERMANN-VILLA AM WANNSEE

☎ 8058 5900; www.max-liebermann.de; Colomierstrasse 3; adult/concession/family €6/4/14, audioguide €3; ☽ 10am-6pm Wed-Mon, to 8pm Thu; ☒ Wannsee, then ☐ 114 to Colomierstrasse

Influenced by French Impressionism, Berlin Secession founder Max Liebermann loved the lyricism of nature, and gardens in particular. From 1914 until his death in 1935, he spent his summers in this villa, which he nicknamed his 'lakeside palace'. The house has two gardens: a kitchen garden and a formal garden facing the Wannsee whose symmetry is charmingly interrupted by an unruly grove of birch trees. In summer there are few more placid spots than the cafe terrace overlooking this idyllic setting.

Both gardens inspired more than 200 of Liebermann's oil paintings, pastels and prints, some of which can now be seen upstairs in the restored house. A wooden easel sits in the same spot as it did when Liebermann painted in his barrel-vaulted studio. On the ground floor is a small description of the history of the villa, which was appropriated by the Nazis in 1940, five years after Liebermann's death. His wife Martha committed suicide in 1943, days before her scheduled deportation to Theresienstadt concentration camp.

PFAUENINSEL

☎ 805 867 513; www.spsg.de, www.pfaueninsel .info, in German; adult/concession ferry €2/1, palace €3/2.50, Meierei €2/1.50; ☽ ferry 8am-9pm May-Aug, 9am-7pm Apr & Sep, 9am-6pm Mar & Oct, 10am-4pm Nov-Feb, palace tours 10am-6pm Tue-Sun May-Sep, 10am-5pm Oct, Meierei 10am-5pm Mon-Fri, 10am-6pm Sat & Sun Jun-Sep, 10am-5pm daily Oct; ☒ Wannsee, then ☐ 218 to Pfaueninsel

Back to nature was the dictum in the 18th century, which is why King Friedrich Wilhelm II, a nephew and successor of Frederick the Great, had Peacock Island turned into an idyllic playground. The remoteness of the island and its lush park were perfect for retreating from state affairs and for frolicking with his mistress in a snowy-white fairy-tale palace whose exotic interior can only be seen on a guided tour.

Ambling beneath the ancient oaks of the lush park, you might – with some luck – run into one of the strutting peacocks that give the island its name. You'll also come across a smattering of other buildings, including the Kavaliershaus with its Gothic facade and the Meierei (dairy), part of a farming estate oddly embedded within a faux monastery ruin.

Since the island is a nature preserve, the *verboten* (forbidden) list is rather long and includes smoking, cycling, swimming, animals and radios. Picnicking, though, remains legal and this is a nice place to do it. There are no cafes or restaurants on the island, which is accessed by ferry.

HAUS AM WALDSEE

☎ 801 8935; www.hausamwaldsee.de;
Argentische Allee 30; adult/concession/family €5/
3/10; ⏰ 11am-6pm Tue-Sat, to 8pm Wed;
🚇 Krumme Lanke

The House on the Waldsee was one of
the first spaces in Germany to present
international contemporary art in Germany
after WWII. And it hasn't lost a step since.
Early shows were dedicated to Picasso
and Max Ernst but today it's primarily
international hotshots living and working in
Berlin (eg the Brit Jonathan Monk or Arturo
Herrera from Venezuela) that get to show
their works in this storied villa. Sculpture
takes centre stage in the huge park, where
you can also admire Werner Aisslinger's
futuristic Loftcube, a minimalist glass house
on stilts that the artist refers to as a 'living
container'. German-speaking architecture
fans can rent audioguides (€5) and a bicycle
(€5) for a 90-minute self-guided tour of
nearby villas built by such prominent
architects as Walter Gropius, Mies van der
Rohe and Hermann Muthesius.

SCHLOSS GLIENICKE

☎ 805 3041; www.spsg.de; Königstrasse 36; palace
tours adult/concession €5/4, casino €1; ⏰ 10am-
6pm Tue-Sun Apr-Oct, 10am-5pm Sat & Sun Nov-
Mar; 🚉 Wannsee, then 🚌 316

Glienicke Palace, at the far southwestern tip
of Berlin, is what happens when a rich royal
kid goes to Italy and falls in love with the
country. Prince Carl of Prussia (1801–83),
a son of Friedrich Wilhelm III, was only
21 when he returned to Berlin giddy with
dreams of building his own Italian villa.
He hired Schinkel to turn an existing
estate – surrounded by a rambling,
romantic garden designed by Peter Joseph
Lenné – into an elegant, antique-looking
compound.

When Schinkel was through, he had
indulged the prince's love of antiquities by expanding the existing mansion,
converting the former billiard house into
the Casino, an Italian villa with a double
pergola, and building two pavilions, the
Kleine Neugierde (literally 'Small Curiosity') and
Grosse Neugierde ('Big Curiosity'). The latter
sits in an especially scenic spot overlooking
the Havel River, Schloss Babelsberg and
the outskirts of Potsdam. A stroll through
the park is a true delight, as beautiful vistas
open up at every bend in the path.

The palace itself is richly decorated
with marble fireplaces, sparkling crystal
chandeliers, gold-framed paintings and fine
furniture. The turquoise bedroom of the
princess and the midnight-blue library are
especially memorable. Tour tickets are also
good for the HofgärtnerMuseum (Royal Court
Gardeners' Museum), where you can peek
into the lives and practices of landscape
artists like Lenné.

The restaurant with its lovely terrace is a
good place to relax.

SPANDAU

Spandau is a congenial mix of green expanses,
rivers, industry and almost rural residential areas wrapped around a medieval core
famous for its 16th-century fortress, the
Spandauer Zitadelle. Older than Berlin by a
few years, Spandau thrived as an independent city for nearly 800 years and only became
part of Berlin in 1920. Its people, though,
continue to feel as Spandauers first, Berliners
second. To this day, they talk about 'going
to Berlin' when heading to any other city
district.

Central Spandau is about 10km northwest
of Bahnhof Zoo. Nearly all its sights cluster in
the Altstadt, served by the U7. There's a tourist office in the Gotisches Haus (opposite).

ZITADELLE SPANDAU

☎ 354 9440; www.zitadelle-spandau.de, in
German; Strasse am Juliusturm; adult/concession/
family €4.50/2.50/10, audioguide €2; ⏰ 10am-
5pm; 🚇 Zitadelle

The 16th-century Spandau Citadel, on a little island in the Havel River, is one of the most important and best-preserved Renaissance fortresses in the world. With its moat, drawbridge and arrowhead-shaped bastions, it is also a veritable textbook in military architecture. Imagine yourself a guard keeping an eye out for enemies as you climb up the crenellated tower called Juliusturm. From 1874 to 1919, somewhere deep in the tower's bowels, Prussia's rulers hid the war booty wrestled from France after the war of 1870–71. If you want to fill any gaps in your historical knowledge, drop by the Stadtgeschichtliches Museum Spandau (Spandau City History Museum) in the former armoury. Artsy types should check out the latest exhibit in the Bastion Kronprinz. In winter, you can go 'batty' over thousands of bats spending the freezing months in the citadel's catacombs. You can see them from a viewing room (☉ noon-5pm) or join a guided tour (☎ 3675 0061; www.berliner-artenschutz .de, in German; adult/concession €10/7) offered sporadically in summer and early autumn (registration required). The entry fee to the citadel includes the museum, tower and galleries.

NIKOLAIKIRCHE

☎ 333 5639; www.nikolai-spandau.de, in German; Reformationsplatz 6; admission free, tower €1; ☉ noon-4pm Mon-Fri, 11am-3pm Sat, 2-4pm Sun, tower tours 12.30pm Sat, 2.30pm Sun Apr-Oct; ☉ Altstadt Spandau
Original Gothic churches are a rare sight in Berlin, so that's the first thing that makes St Nicholas special. The other is its key role during the Reformation. For it was behind these thick walls in 1539 that Elector Joachim II took the then-radical step of celebrating Brandenburg's first public Lutheran-style worship service. That's the elector in bronze outside the church. Inside, important treasures include a baptismal font (1398), a baroque pulpit (1714) and a late-Renaissance altar (1582) whose centre panel depicts the Last Supper. Church acoustics, by the way, are splendid, making this a great place to catch a concert. If you're here on a summer weekend, try to time your visit with a tour of the tower for great views.

GOTISCHES HAUS

☎ 333 9388; Breite Strasse 32; admission free; ☉ 10am-6pm Mon-Fri, to 5.30pm Sat; ☉ Altstadt Spandau
Whoever built this late-medieval Gothic House must not have been hurting for money, for it's made of stone not wood, as was customary in those times. The well-preserved Altstadt gem sports ornate net-ribbed vaulting on the ground floor, which houses the local tourist office. Check out the Biedermeier-era living room and late-19th-century kitchen upstairs.

KOLK

☉ Altstadt Spandau
Separated from the Altstadt by the busy Strasse am Juliusturm, the Kolk quarter exudes medieval village flair with its romantic narrow lanes, crooked, half-timbered houses and 78m-long section of town wall. Its key sight is the church of St Marien am Behnitz (☎ 353 9630; www.behnitz.de, in German; Behnitz 9; admission free; ☉ 2-5pm). A top-to-bottom makeover of the 1848 brick pile saw the return of the hand-painted murals, decorative stucco and stained-glass windows that had been destroyed during a botched 1960s restoration job. Try catching a concert here – the acoustics are tremendous.

LUFTWAFFENMUSEUM off Map pp72-3

☎ 811 0769; www.luftwaffenmuseum.de; Flugplatz Gatow, Gross Glienicker Weg; admission free; ☉ 10am-6pm Tue-Sun Apr-Oct, 9am-4pm Nov-Mar; ☉ ☒ Zoologischer Garten, then ☒ X34 to General-Steinhoff-Kaserne
About 9km south of Altstadt Spandau, the German Air Force Museum spreads its wings over the former military air field Berlin-Gatow. Built as a Nazi air-combat and technical-training academy, it fell to the British after WWII. After the Union Jack was taken down in 1994, the German armed forces set up exhibits about military aviation and aerial warfare in Germany in the old hangars. Plane buffs, though, come here to study the 100 historical aircraft, including WWI biplanes, a Russian MiG-21 and a GDR-era Antonov An-14 littering the runway. Last admission is one hour before closing. Bus X34 needs about 30 minutes for the trip from Zoo Bahnhof.

NEUKÖLLN

Neukölln is no stranger to headlines, though rarely of the positive kind. All too often, they're about drug-dealing 11 year olds, poorly performing schools, escalating gang violence and the problem of immigrant integration. But of late, there's been different news coming out of this former West Berlin district. It's about a hot gallery opening, a trashy-cool new bar, a daytime rave or a wicked underground party. With rising rents and tendrils of gentrification reaching Kreuzberg and Friedrichshain, an upwardly hopeful but penniless avant-garde of students, artists, musicians, DJs and designers is pushing the frontier to the northern reaches of 'bad-rap' Neukölln. Because of its proximity to Kreuzberg, northern Neukölln is also sometimes called Kreuzkölln, which is why we cover sights, bars and other points of interest in this area in the Kreuzberg & Northern Neukölln section (p139).

But as Berlin's largest district, Neukölln has many other faces and some surprising discoveries, including fantastic gardens, a palace and even a Unesco World Heritage site. A stroll down Karl-Marx-Strasse, with its penny stores and doner kebab shops, is great for catching a glimpse of the daily lives of Berlin's immigrant population. Often overlooked and definitely underrated, this up-and-coming *Kiez* is perfect for DIY types and adventurous urbanites willing to look beyond the headlines.

BRITZER GARTEN off Map pp72-3

☎ 700 9060; www.gruen-berlin.de; Sangerhauser Weg 1; adult/concession €2/1; ☺ park 9am-dusk; ⓞ Alt-Mariendorf, then 🚌 179

It's a bit off the beaten track, but on a sunny day one of Berlin's prettiest gardens is well worth the trip. It puts on a dazzling show from spring to autumn but especially so during 'Tulipan', when thousands of tulips in a rainbow of colours brighten early spring, and in late summer when the dahlias are at their redolent best. But actually any time is a fine time to spend an afternoon amid the greenery, spring-fed lake and flower fields of this fantastic, rambling park that originated as the 1985 Federal Garden Show. It's so big, there's even a miniature train to carry around the foot-weary. There are plenty of places for kids to let off steam, including

top picks

SOUTHERN SUBURBS

- Britzer Garten (left)
- Sowjetisches Ehrenmal (opposite)
- Schloss Köpenick (p171)

a water playground, a petting zoo and Makunaima, an entire village made of clay. The old windmill on the eastern park edge still produces flour (bread sold Friday to Sunday) and is open for guided tours (adult/child €3/1.50; tours 11am-4pm on the hour on Sunday from April to October). The garden is open till dusk but tickets are sold from 9am to 8pm April to September, to 6pm March and October and to 4pm November to February.

SCHLOSS BRITZ off Map pp72-3

☎ 6097 9230; www.schloss-britz.de, in German; Alt-Britz 73; historical rooms €1.50, park free, exhibits vary; ☺ 11am-6pm Tue-Sun, park 9am-dusk; ⓞ Parchimer Allee

More a large country estate than a palace, Schloss Britz has a pedigree going back to the 16th century but, having been toyed with repeatedly, now sports more of a French Renaissance look. In recent years it has emerged as a hub for highbrow culture and frequently hosts concerts and exhibits in its historical rooms, the former horse barn or the park. Tours of the interior offer a look at the lifestyle of a wealthy family in the late 19th century. In fine weather the pretty gardens invite strolling and picnicking. To get here from Parchimer Allee U-Bahn station walk west about 500m or take bus M46.

HUFEISENSIEDLUNG off Map pp72-3

Lowise-Reuter-Ring; ⓞ Parchimer Allee

Anyone interested in modern architecture should swing by the Hufeisensiedlung (Horseshoe Colony), a 1920s housing project by Bruno Taut and Martin Wagner and not far from Schloss Britz. It features about 1000 balconied flats in a three-storey-high, horseshoe-shaped building wrapped around a park and is considered one of the earliest attempts to humanise high-density housing. In 2008 it was one of several modernist colonies in Berlin inducted into Unesco's list of World Heritage sites (see the boxed text, p58). To get here from Parchimer Allee U-Bahn station, walk 250m north.

KÖRNERPARK off Map pp72-3

☎ 902 392 431; Schierker Strasse; admission free; ☉ park 24hr, gallery 10am-6pm Tue-Sun; ⊕ Neukölln, Hermannstrasse

This elegant sunken baroque-style garden comes with a clever secret: it's actually a reclaimed gravel pit! Ponder this as you stroll past the flower beds and the cascading fountain, sip a cuppa in the cafe or check out the latest exhibit in the adjacent gallery. From mid-June to August, join the locals for free classical, jazz and world-music concerts on Sundays.

TREPTOW

Treptow, a former East Berlin district along the western Spree bank, has been a popular getaway since the early 19th century, when urbanites would party in its riverside restaurants or take a spin on the Spree, a tradition continued by Stern & Kreisschiffahrt (p311) boats to this day. The district's dominant feature is Treptower Park, which stretches south for several kilometres, smoothly segueing into the Plänterwald forest. It's a lovely, unhurried sprawl of green with shady paths for strolling and jogging and expansive lawns for picnicking. The main sight is the impressive Sowjetisches Ehrenmal Treptow. Southern Treptow, meanwhile, has staked its future on the Adlershof, a science, media and

TRANSPORT: SOUTHERN SUBURBS

Bus 104 runs to Treptow and Neukölln from Tempelhof airport in western Kreuzberg, M41 goes from Neukölln to Hauptbahnhof.

S-Bahn S3 for Köpenick; S8, S9, S41, S42 for Treptower Park.

Tram From S-Bahn station Köpenick: 62 and 68 for Altstadt and Schloss; 60 and 61 for Müggelsee from Altstadt; 62 north goes to Mahlsdorf.

U-Bahn U7 and U8 for Neukölln.

technology centre built in the 1990s. Northern Treptow rubs up against Kreuzberg. In fact, Schlesische Strasse, the lively party drag, links the two districts.

SOWJETISCHES EHRENMAL TREPTOW Map pp72-3

Treptower Park; admission free; ☉ 24hr; ⊠ Treptower Park

At the heart of Treptower Park, the gargantuan Soviet War Memorial (1949) looms above the graves of 5000 Soviet soldiers killed in the Battle of Berlin, a bombastic and sobering testament to the immensity of the country's wartime losses.

For the full effect, approach from the north and walk past the statue of Mother Russia grieving for her dead children. Two mighty walls fronted by soldiers kneeling in sorrow flank the gateway; the red marble used here was supposedly scavenged from Hitler's ruined chancellery. Beyond lies a massive sunken lawn lined by sarcophagi representing the then 16 Soviet republics, each decorated with war scenes and Stalin quotes. This all culminates in a mausoleum, topped by a 13m statue of a Russian soldier clutching a child, his sword resting melodramatically on a shattered swastika. The socialist-realism mosaic inside the plinth shows grateful Soviets honouring the fallen.

To reach the memorial from the S-Bahn station, head southeast for 750m on Puschkinallee, then enter the park through the stone gate.

ARCHENHOLD-STERNWARTE Map pp72-3

☎ 536 063 719; www.sdtb.de; Alt-Treptow 1; exhibit adult/concession €2.50/2, tours €4/3; ☉ exhibit 2-4.30pm Wed-Sun, tours 8pm Thu, 3pm Sat & Sun; ⊠ Plänterwald

Germany's oldest astronomical observatory, in the southeastern corner of Treptower Park, is the place where Albert Einstein first introduced his theory of relativity in 1915. The main attraction, though, is a 21m-long refracting telescope, the longest in the world, built in 1896 by astronomer Friedrich Simon Archenhold. Demonstrations of the giant usually take place at 3pm on Sunday. Exhibits in the foyer are a bit ho-hum but still impart fascinating nuggets about the planetary system, astronomy in general and the history of the observatory. Kids love finding out how much they weigh on Mars and having their picture taken with a big meteorite chunk.

ANNA SEGHERS GEDENKSTÄTTE
off Map pp72-3

☎ 677 4725; www.anna-seghers.de/gedenk staette.php, in German; Anna-Seghers-Strasse 81; adult/concession €4/2; ☼ 10am-4pm Tue & Thu & by appointment; 🚇 Adlershof

Anna Seghers (1900–83) is best known for her chilling novel *The Seventh Cross* (1941), which was turned into a movie starring Spencer Tracy in 1944. A committed communist, she spent the Nazi years in exile in France and Mexico before moving into this small flat with her husband in 1955. It's a modest, functional 1950s-style place that practically drowns in books. A Remington typewriter sits silently on her desk surrounded by souvenirs Seghers brought back from her travels. A small exhibit traces her life and work.

KÖPENICK

A 20-minute S-Bahn ride away, Köpenick, deep in the former East Berlin, is a wonderful antidote to the urban velocity of central Berlin. The district is famous for its handsome baroque castle, an old town centre that has withstood the ravages of time, war and modernism, and such natural assets as Berlin's largest lake (Müggelsee), largest forest (Köpenicker Stadtforst) and highest natural elevation (Müggelberge, 115m). A leisurely ramble, relaxed boat ride or cooling dip in the water will quickly restore balance to an overstimulated brain.

Köpenick's pint-sized Altstadt squats at the convergence of the Spree and Dahme Rivers, about 1.5km south of S-Bahn station Köpenick along Bahnhofstrasse and Lindenstrasse, served by tram 62 or 68 (get off at Rathaus Köpenick). Schloss Köpenick is just south on a little island in the Dahme, with the Kietz fishing quarter visible across the water looking east. Friedrichshagen and the Müggelsee are about 3.5km further east of the Altstadt.

The local tourist office (☎ 655 7550; www.berlin -tourismus-online.de; Alt-Köpenick 31-33; ☼ 9am-6.30pm Mon-Fri year-round, 10am-4pm Sat May-Sep, 10am-1pm Sat Oct-Apr), near Schloss Köpenick, rents out self-guided audiotours of the Altstadt for €4.

ALTSTADT

Many of the cobblestone streets in Köpenick's Altstadt still follow their original, medieval layout. To walk there from the Köpenick S-Bahn station, follow Borgmannstrasse two blocks south to Mandrellaplatz, site of the imposing Amtsgericht (municipal court). It houses the Gedenkstätte Köpenicker Blutwoche Juni 1933 (☎ 902 975 671; enter from Puchanstrasse 12; admission free; ☼ 10am-6pm Thu & by appointment), a small memorial exhibit for the victims of a brutal Nazi crackdown against local communists between 21 and 26 June 1933. Around 90 people were killed, most of them in the court prison itself, during what went down in history as Köpenicker Blutwoche (Bloody Week). The entrance is via the courtyard at Puchanstrasse 12.

The victims were raised to martyr status in the GDR's day and given a monument on the Platz des 23 April, about 750m south of the courthouse (via Puchanstrasse). The square's name recalls the date in 1945 when the Red Army arrived in Köpenick.

From the square it's just a short walk south via Lindenstrasse to the Altstadt proper across the Dammbrücke. Lindenstrasse turns into Strasse Alt-Köpenick, a historic street lined with baroque beauties and the neo-Gothic 1904 town hall.

KÖPENICK RATHAUS

☎ 6172 3351; Alt-Köpenick 21; admission free; ☼ 8am-6pm Mon-Fri, 10am-6pm Sat; 🚇 62 or 68 to Rathaus Köpenick

With its frilly turrets, soaring tower and stepped gable, Köpenick's town hall exudes a fairy-tale quality but is actually more famous for an incident back in 1906. It involved an unemployed cobbler named Wilhelm Voigt, who managed to make a laughing stock of the Prussian authorities: costumed as an army captain, he marched upon the town hall, arrested the mayor, confiscated the city coffers and disappeared with the loot. And no one questioned his authority! At least for a while. Although quickly caught and convicted, Voigt became quite a celebrity for his chutzpah. Today a bronze statue of the Hauptmann of Köpenick guards the town hall entrance.

There's an entire exhibit about the man and his preposterous scheme in the nearby Heimatmuseum (Local History Museum; ☎ 902 973 351; Alter Markt 1; admission free; ☼ 10am-4pm Tue & Wed, to 6pm Thu, 2-6pm Sun), in a 17th-century half-timbered building. The story is also re-enacted every summer during a raucous festival.

SCHLOSS KÖPENICK

☎ 266 3666; www.smb.museum/kgm; Schlossinsel; adult/concession/child under 18 €4/2/ free; ⊗ 10am-6pm Tue-Sun; ⨀ Köpenick, then ⨀ 62, 68

On a little island just south of the Altstadt (via Alt-Köpenick), the baroque Köpenick Palace houses a branch of the Kunstgewerbemuseum (Museum of Decorative Arts, p115). Exhibits showcase a rich and eclectic collection of decorative furniture, tapestries, porcelain, silverware, glass and other items from the Renaissance, baroque and rococo periods. Highlights include four lavishly panelled rooms and the stunning Wappensaal (Coat of Arms Hall). It was in this very hall where, in 1730, a military court meted out questionable justice against two soldiers accused of attempted desertion. The verdicts? The guillotine for Captain Hans and the throne – eventually – for Captain Friedrich, the later Frederick the Great.

East of the Schloss, you can spot the former fishing village called Kietz across the little bay called Frauentog, where a solar-powered boat rental station has set up shop. A stroll along the cobbled lanes of Kietz, past the nicely restored but modest cottages of the fisherfolk, is a tranquil diversion.

FRIEDRICHSHAGEN & GROSSER MÜGGELSEE off Map pp72-3

⨀ Friedrichshagen, then ⨀ 60 or 61

Berlin 'muggles' love their Müggelsee, especially on hot summer days when scores of city slickers escape the urban cauldron by heading to the edge of town. At 4km long and 2.5km wide, it's a large and lovely lake with plenty of sandy beaches and boats puttering along on placid waters.

The easiest access is by taking the S-Bahn to Friedrichshagen, a village-like suburb first settled in 1753 by Bohemian cotton spinners who padded their income by growing mulberry trees to fatten up small armies of silkworms. From the station, head south on the main drag, Bölschestrasse, past a few of the original 18th-century cottages and some scraggly mulberry trees. On Sundays, between 60 and 100 flea market stalls next to the S-Bahn station invite rummaging for GDR memorabilia and other bric-a-brac.

Bölschestrasse dead-ends at the lake, near a big brewery, the Berliner Bürgerbräu, which has a beer garden and restaurant. From the nearby landing docks, Reederei Kutzker (☎ 03362-6251; www.reederei-kutzker.de; 1hr tour €6; ⊗ Apr-Oct) operates one-hour boat trips around the lake. Get off at the Rübezahl stop on the south shore to pick up an easy forest trail into the Müggelberge hills, past the tiny Teufelssee (Devil's Lake). Beyond here looms the GDR-era Müggelturm, which is sadly disintegrating and closed indefinitely.

If you prefer to walk to the south shore, duck through the underground tunnel near the brewery and pick up the lakeside trail for a couple of kilometres.

On the eastern shore, the canal-laced medieval fishing village of Rahnsdorf is worth a small detour. The prettiest section is about 1km south of the Wilhelmshagen S-Bahn station via Schönblicker Strasse. Kutzker boats make the trip here as well.

EASTERN SUBURBS

LICHTENBERG

East of Friedrichshain, Lichtenberg is a prime destination for East German history buffs. Both the former Stasi headquarters and the prison where real and imagined regime opponents were locked up offer chilling evidence of the machinations of the ultimate 'Big Brother' state.

These days, life's still tough in Lichtenberg. Its giant high-rise ghettos are veritable petri dishes of discontent that have spawned both neo-Nazi and neo-communist sympathisers. Pockets of delight include the sprawling animal park, which is bigger than the zoo in Charlottenburg but with fewer animals, and a tidy little baroque palace contained within the same grounds.

STASIMUSEUM BERLIN off Map pp72-3

☎ 553 6854; www.stasi-museum.de; Ruschestrasse 103, House 1; adult/concession €4/3.50; ☽ 11am-6pm Mon-Fri, 2-6pm Sat & Sun; ◎ Magdalenenstrasse

You may never have heard his name, but Erich Mielke was the GDR's own 'Wizard of Oz', the sinister man behind the curtain who pushed the buttons and levers to keep the East German regime operating. As head of the Ministry of State Security (MfS, aka Stasi) from 1957 to 1989, the beady-eyed and dour-faced apparatchik knew the dirt on just about anyone, including Honecker and other government honchos. His place of work – the Stasi HQ – now houses a research centre and the Stasimuseum.

top picks

EASTERN SUBURBS

▪ Gedenkstätte Hohenschönhausen (Stasi Prison; opposite)
▪ Stasimuseum Berlin (left)
▪ Gärten der Welt im Erholungspark Marzahn (p174)

A prisoner transport van with five teensy, lightless cells creates a creepy Cold War aura right in the functional foyer of this massive compound. Upstairs, rooms are filled with Stasi memorabilia, including clunky, if cunning, bugging devices (hidden in watering cans, rocks and even neckties), and exhibits explaining the extent of institutionalised surveillance and repression in the GDR as well as efforts of resistance against the regime. One floor up is the 'lion's den' itself, Mielke's obsessively neat offices and private quarters. At press time, the original museum digs had closed for renovation expected to last until early 2012. In the meantime, exhibits have been moved to House 22 (opposite House 1) in what used to be the Stasi leadership cafeteria, nicknamed 'General's Hill' by Stasi employees.

Panelling is in German only and exhibits are not always self-explanatory, so you may want to invest a few euros in the English-language booklet.

THE STASI – FEAR & LOATHING IN THE GDR

The walls had ears. Modelled after the Soviet KGB, the GDR's Ministerium für Staatssicherheit (MfS, or Ministry of State Security, 'Stasi' for short) was founded in 1950. It was secret police, central intelligence agency and bureau of criminal investigation, all rolled into one. Called the 'shield and sword' of the East German party, it put millions of GDR citizens under surveillance in order to suppress internal opposition. The Stasi grew steadily in power and size and, by the end, had 91,000 official full-time employees plus 173,000 IMs (*inoffizielle Mitarbeiter*, unofficial informants). The latter were recruited among regular folks to spy on their co-workers, friends, family and neighbours as well as on people in West Germany. When the Wall fell, the Stasi fell with it.

Although the MfS worked at shredding documents, files on millions of people were found in the aftermath. They reveal the efforts of the Stasi when it came to controlling, manipulating and repressing. Its members used wire-tapping and videotape observation, and opened private mail. Even more bizarre was the practice of collecting a suspected enemy's body odour. Samples taken during interrogations – usually by wiping the unfortunate victim's crotch with a cotton cloth – were stored in hermetically sealed glass jars. If a person needed to be identified, specially trained groin-sniffing canines – euphemistically known as 'smell differentiation dogs' – sprang into action.

GEDENKSTÄTTE HOHENSCHÖN-HAUSEN (STASI PRISON) off Map pp72-3

☎ 9860 8230; www.stiftung-hsh.de; Genslerstrasse 66; adult/concession tours €5/2.50; ✆ hourly 11am-3pm Mon-Fri & 10am-4pm Sat & Sun; ⓧ M5 from Alexanderplatz to Freienwalder Strasse

Victims of Stasi persecution often ended up in this grim prison complex, now a memorial site. Tours (in English at 2.30pm on Wednesday and Saturday), often led by former prisoners, reveal the full extent of the terror and cruelty perpetrated upon thousands of suspected regime opponents, many utterly innocent. If you've seen the Academy Award–winning film *The Lives of Others*, you'll recognise many of the original settings.

Old maps of East Berlin show only a blank spot where the facility was: officially, it did not exist. In reality, though, the compound actually had three incarnations. Right after WWII, the Soviets used it to process prisoners (mostly Nazis, or those suspected to be) destined for the Gulag. Over 3000 detainees died here because of the atrocious living conditions – usually by freezing to death in their unheated cells – until the Western Allies intervened in October 1946.

The Soviets then made it a regular prison, dreaded especially for its 'U-Boat', an underground tract of damp, windowless cells outfitted only with a wooden bench and a bucket. Prisoners were subjected to endless interrogations, beatings, sleep deprivation and water torture. *Everybody* signed a confession sooner or later.

In 1951 the Soviets handed over the prison to the East German Stasi, who ended up adopting their mentors' methods.

top picks

COLD WAR SITES

- Alliierten Museum (p164)
- DDR Museum (p95)
- East Side Gallery (p149)
- Gedenkstätte Berliner Mauer (p106)
- Mauermuseum (p144)
- Stasimuseum Berlin (opposite)
- Gedenkstätte Hohenschönhausen (Stasi Prison; above)

Prisoners were locked up in the U-Boat until a new, much bigger, cell block was built with prison labour, in the late '50s. Psycho-terror now replaced physical torture: inmates had no idea of their whereabouts and suffered total isolation and sensory deprivation. Only the collapse of the GDR in 1989 put an end to the horror.

To get here from the tram stop, walk east for 10 minutes along Freienwalder Strasse.

DEUTSCH-RUSSISCHES MUSEUM BERLIN-KARLSHORST off Map pp72-3

☎ 5015 0810; www.museum-karlshorst.de; Zwieseler Strasse 4; admission free; ✆ 10am-6pm Tue-Sun; ⓧ Karlshorst

WWII buffs will want to make the trip out to this historic site, where on 8 May 1945, Field Marshall Wilhelm Keitel signed the unconditional surrender of the German armed forces. With one stroke of the pen, WWII was officially over.

Since 1995 the German-Russian Museum has commemorated this fateful day and the events leading up to it. Documents, photographs, uniforms and memorabilia illustrate such topics as the Hitler-Stalin Pact, the daily grind of life as a WWII Soviet soldier and the fate of Soviet civilians during wartime. You can stand in the great hall where the surrender was signed and see the office of Marshal Zhukov, the first Soviet supreme commander after WWII, when he was building the headquarters of the Soviet Military Administration in Germany. Outside is a battery of Soviet weapons, including a Howitzer canon and the devastating *Katjuscha* multiple rocket-launcher, also known as the 'Stalin organ'.

The museum is a 10- to 15-minute walk from the S-Bahn station; take the Treskowallee exit, then turn right onto Rheinsteinstrasse.

TIERPARK BERLIN off Map pp72-3

☎ 515 310; www.tierpark-berlin.de; Am Tierpark 125; adult/child/student €11/5.50/8; ✆ 9am-5pm late Oct–mid-Mar, to 7pm mid-Mar–mid-Sep, to 6pm mid-Sep–late Oct; ⓞ Tierpark

With gorgeous landscaping and around 8000 critters in often generously sized enclosures, this huge animal park is one of Berlin's major attractions. Perennial crowd-pleasers include the tigers and lions in the Alfred-Brehm-Haus; the elephants (including adorable little ones born at the zoo) and rhinos that reside in the Dickhäuterhaus; and the Schlangenfarm, which has more slithering, poisonous snakes than even Harry Potter could handle. The zoo is particularly proud of its oryx antelopes and Vietnamese sika stags, which are extinct in the wild.

Before becoming an animal park in 1955, the grounds were the Peter Lenné–designed park of Schloss Friedrichsfelde (☎ 5153 1407; www.schloss-friedrichsfelde.de, in German; Am Tierpark 125; ⏰ 11am-5pm Tue, Thu, Sat & Sun), a small palace built in 1685 by a local nobleman in a combination baroque/neoclassical style. It was enlarged a few times, most notably under Prince August Ferdinand, the youngest brother of King Frederick the Great, who bought the place in 1762. Napoleon Bonaparte and Czar Alexander I were among the guests who once roamed the same halls you can visit today. Recently restored, the palace's most impressive room is the upstairs ballroom lidded by an impressive ceiling fresco. It's used for classical concerts and weddings. New exhibits on the history of Berlin's zoo as

well as on the palace itself were in the works at press time. Tickets for the zoo are also valid here; there is no separate admission.

MARZAHN

Marzahn, along with Hohenschönhausen and Hellersdorf, is a satellite suburb built quick and cheap in the 1970s and early '80s to combat an acute housing shortage in East Berlin. Row upon row of prefab housing developments – so-called *Plattenbauten* – rush skyward like concrete stalagmites. Since reunification, attempts have been made to beautify these *Arbeiterschliessfächer* (workers' lockers), which were actually in hot demand in GDR times – too great was the lure of private baths, central heating, lifts and parking aplenty. Such is no longer the case today. Although many have been painted with bright colours and retrofitted with balconies, welfare recipients, asylum seekers and impecunious migrants constitute a large portion of the residents. In other words, unless you have a fascination with socialist town planning, there aren't many reasons to make the trip out here except, that is, for the exotic gardens described below.

GÄRTEN DER WELT IM ERHOLUNG-SPARK MARZAHN off Map pp72–3

☎ 700 906 699; www.gruen-berlin.de; Eisenacher Strasse 99; adult/concession €3/1.50, Nov-Feb €2/1; ⏰ park 9am-dusk, ticket office 9am-8pm Apr-Sep, to 6pm Mar & Oct, to 4pm Nov-Feb; Ⓡ Marzahn, then Ⓑ 195 towards Mahlsdorf or Ⓢ Hellersdorf, then Ⓑ 195

THE WONDERFUL, HORRIBLE LIFE OF CHARLOTTE VON MAHLSDORF

Charlotte von Mahlsdorf, née Lothar Berfelde, was born in 1928 and, much to the consternation of her Nazi father, was much more into dresses and dolls than trains and automobiles. Papa Berfelde's efforts to whup his son into manhood ended abruptly when s/he bludgeoned him to death with daddy's revolver at the tender age of 15. After a short stint in prison, Charlotte turned into the ultimate pack rat with a particular passion for furnishings and bric-a-brac from the Gründerzeit, eventually collecting enough to open her own museum in an old farmhouse. It doubled as a gathering place for East Germany's gay scene, thus becoming a thorn in the side of the government. In 1974, the state tried to nationalise the collection. Rather than having her stuff confiscated, Charlotte ended up giving much of it away to friends and visitors until the famous GDR actress Annekathrin Bürger and the lawyer Friedrich Karl Kaul managed to put an end to the process (although there are rumours that Charlotte had to become an unofficial informant for the Stasi).

Charlotte continued to show people around her museum until 1995 but finally decamped to Sweden, scared away by a neo-Nazi attack and financial troubles. She died of a heart attack during a visit to Berlin in 2002, shortly after publishing her autobiography, *I Am My Own Woman*. Her life was adapted into the 1992 feature film *Ich Bin Meine Eigene Frau* by Rosa von Praunheim and a 2004 Broadway play, *I Am My Own Wife*, by Doug Wright that won Tony and Pulitzer awards.

For many the main (or even only) reason to visit Marzahn are the poetically named 'Gardens of the World', which offer an exotic escape into global garden architecture. Europe is represented with an Italian Renaissance garden, a German country garden and an English maze, but it's the five Asian gardens that steal the show.

Cream of the crop is the Chinese Garden, the largest of its kind in Europe and a collaborative effort between Berlin and its sister city Beijing. It takes up 2.7 hilly hectares in the southern park and is anchored by a large lake. At an authentic teahouse (10.30am-6pm daily Apr-Oct, weekends in good weather Nov-Mar) you can relax over a cuppa or make advance reservations for a traditional tea ceremony (☎ 0179 394 5564; per person €8).

Another favourite place to unwind in Zen-like tranquillity is the much smaller Japanese Garden, a spiritual gem designed by Yokohama-based priest and professor Shunmyo Masuno. A harmonious jumble of water, rocks and plants creates an oasis of serenity and spirituality. It's on the park's eastern edge, just south of the Korean Garden, where you can meditate in a pavilion and wander among authentic sculpture intended to ward off demons and bad spirits.

Keep going and you'll soon get to the Balinese Garden. Inside a greenhouse, it re-creates a traditional family home in a jungle setting and puts on a dazzling tropical show of lush ferns, perky orchids and fragrant frangipani trees. Great in winter! Finally there's the romantic Oriental Garden, tucked into a walled courtyard where a fountain feeds water into four beautifully tiled pools surrounded by roses, jasmine, oranges, oleander and other redolent beauties.

In 2010, the Gardens of the World became the first German park to receive the prestigious 'Green Flag Award', which recognises the best green spaces in the UK and beyond.

GRÜNDERZEIT MUSEUM off Map pp72-3
☎ 567 8329; www.gruenderzeitmuseum.de; Hultschiner Damm 333; adult/concession €4.50/ 3.50; 10am-6pm Wed & Sun; Mahlsdorf, then 62 to Alt-Mahlsdorf
Unless you're fan of Gründerzeit (ie late 19th-century) furniture, the idea of travelling to this far-flung museum in an old farmhouse in the suburb of Mahlsdorf might leave you cold. But what if we told you that its founder was the GDR's most famous transvestite and gay icon? And, boy, what a life s/he led! For a brief rundown, see the boxed text opposite.

Tours take in such period rooms as a kitchen, servants' quarters and living room. In the basement is the Mulackritze, a famous Scheunenviertel bar that counted Heinrich Zille and Marlene Dietrich but also whores and petty criminals among its patrons. After the bar closed in 1951, Charlotte rescued the entire interior from demolition and reassembled it in her museum. There's also a smattering of mechanical musical instruments such as an Edison phonograph and a mechanical piano.

PANKOW

Leafy Pankow, Berlin's northernmost district, was once the preferred residential area of the East German political and intellectual elite. These days, it preserves a pleasant, slow-paced atmosphere but is modest in terms of visitor attractions. Part of its appeal lies in the forests and parks that cover more than one-third of its area.

JÜDISCHER FRIEDHOF WEISSENSEE
Map pp72-3

☎ 925 3330; Herbert-Baum-Strasse 45; admission free; ⏰ 8am-5pm Sun-Thu Apr-Oct, to 4pm Sun-Thu Nov-Mar, to 3pm Fri year-round; ⛶ 200
First laid out in 1880, this enormous Jewish cemetery is the final resting place of more than 115,000 people, including such prominent players as the painter Lesser Ury and publisher Samuel Fisher. Bauhaus fans should check out the cubist tomb designed by Walter Gropius for Albert Mendel. For tomb locations consult a chart near the entrance. Also here is a grave containing 90 Torah scrolls that were damaged during the 1938 pogroms. There is also a monument honouring the victims of the Holocaust. The cemetery is near the terminus of bus 200.

SCHLOSS & GARTEN SCHÖNHAUSEN
off Map pp72-3

☎ 0331 969 4200; www.spsg.de; Tschaikowsk-istrasse 1; adult/concession €6/5; ⏰ 10am-6pm

TRANSPORT: NORTHERN SUBURBS

Bus 107 connects Pankow U-Bahn and S-Bahn station with central Pankow and the palace; 245 connects Zoologischer Garten with Moabit and Hauptbahnhof.

S-Bahn S2 connects Pankow with the Scheunenviertel and Potsdamer Platz; S8 goes from Pankow to Prenzlauer Berg and Friedrichshain.

Tram M1 connects Pankow with Hackescher Markt via Prenzlauer Berg; a main line through Wedding is M13 to Friedrichshain.

U-Bahn Pankow is the northern terminus of the U2; Wedding is served by the U8 and U9.

Tue-Sat Apr-Oct, to 5pm Nov-Mar; ⊙ Pankow, ⛶ M1 to Schillerstrasse
Hemmed in by lovely gardens, Schönhausen Palace packs a lot of German history into its pint-size frame. Originally a country estate of Prussian nobles, in 1740 it became the summer residence of Frederick the Great's estranged wife Elisabeth Christine who had it enlarged and rendered in playful rococo style. Taking a page from Sleeping Beauty, the palace fell into a long slumber after her death in 1797 until the Nazis used the dilapidated structure as a storeroom for 'degenerate' modern art. In 1949, the building was restored once more and became the seat of the GDR's first head of state, Wilhelm Pieck, and later East Germany's state guesthouse.

Closed for a mega-makeover for years, the palace now sparkles in renewed splendour. The downstairs rooms, where the queen had her private quarters, reflect the 18th-century style with partly original furniture and wallpaper. However, if you've been to Schloss Charlottenburg (p122) or Schloss Sanssouci (p285) you may find their comparative modesty underwhelming. More interesting – largely for their uniqueness – are the upstairs rooms where GDR fustiness is alive in the heavy furniture in Pieck's '50s office and in the baby-blue bedspread in the Gentlemen's Bedroom where Castro, Ceausescu, Gaddafi and other 'bad boys' slept.

MAJAKOWSKIRING off Map pp72-3
Admission free; ⏰ 24hr; ⛶ M1 to Tschaikowskistrasse
Until 1960, the senior GDR leadership lived along this oval road, named for an early 20th-century Russian poet. Wall builder Walter Ulbricht was at No 28, next to first GDR president Wilhelm Pieck. Erich Honecker later moved into No 58. Nicknamed the Städtchen (little town), the enclave was completely walled off from the public, lest anyone saw the lavish 1920s villas (seized from industrialists after WWII) in which the country's leaders lived. In 1960, however, fearing a populist uprising similar to the one in 1956 Hungary, the apparatchiks relocated to a gated community especially constructed for them

just outside Berlin. After the fall of the Wall, a TV documentary showing the overall luxury in which the leadership wallowed while denying basic amenities such as a car or telephone to their own people contributed greatly to the disillusionment even loyalists felt for the regime.

WEDDING

If you listen very closely, you'll hear faint murmurings about Wedding being the next 'hot' district. But for now very few signs lend substance to the rumour. Scarred by industry and devoid of grand historic buildings or happening nightlife, *der Wedding* (the article is proper use in German) is still a no-nonsense, roll-up-your-sleeves kind of place. Still, those with an interest in WWII and Cold War history will find a handful of intriguing sights.

GEDENKSTÄTTE GÜNTER LITFIN

Map pp72-3

☎ 2362 6183, 0163 379 7290; www.gedenkstaette guenterlitfin.de, in German; Kieler Strasse 2; admission free; ☺ noon-5pm Mar-Oct or by appointment; ⊕ Ⓡ Hauptbahnhof, then 🚌 120

The Berlin Wall had been in existence for 11 days and Günter Litfin was 24 years old when a hailstorm of bullets ripped through his body as he tried to swim to freedom across a 40m-wide canal. On 24 August 1961, a Sunday, the skilled tailor became the first victim of the GDR's shoot-to-kill policy. Jürgen Litfin learned about his older brother's death later that day – on TV. Since 2003 he has kept Günter's legacy alive with a modest but poignant exhibit in an authentic GDR watchtower. On some days, Jürgen himself is on hand to talk to visitors.

ANTI-KRIEGS-MUSEUM Map pp72-3

☎ 4549 0110; www.anti-kriegs-museum.de; Brüsseler Strasse 21; admission free; ☺ 4-8pm; ⊕ Amrumer Strasse, Seestrasse

It may be small, but the Antiwar Museum sends a big message about the importance of pacifism and the horror of war. Beneath a map pinpointing current areas of conflict, it displays an eclectic collection of rusty steel helmets, land mines, military toys, prosthetic limbs, horrifying pictures of wounded soldiers and an original air-raid shelter with a creepy gas-mask cot for babies.

Just as interesting as the exhibits is the story of the museum itself. It was founded

in 1925 by Erich Friedrich, an avowed peacenik who garnered international fame with his book *War against War* (1924), which is chockfull of shockingly graphic images of dead and disfigured soldiers, starving civilians and army executions. The museum served as a meeting place for pacifists until the Nazis trashed it in 1933, arresting Friedrich. Upon his release, he emigrated to Belgium and later joined the French resistance. His grandson, Tommy Spree, reopened the exhibit in 1982 and still runs it with the help of dedicated volunteers.

ZUCKER MUSEUM Map pp72-3

☎ 3142 7574; www.sdtb.de; Amrumer Strasse 32; admission free; ☺ 9am-4.30pm Mon-Thu, 11am-6pm Sun; ⊕ Amrumer Strasse

Got a sweet tooth? Check out the quirky Zucker Museum (Sugar Museum), a surprisingly entertaining exhibit where you'll learn all about the history of sugar making, including the revolutionary discovery – in 1747 – by a Berlin pharmacist that sugar could be extracted from beets. Find out about sugar's uses in the production of vinegar, pesticides and even interior car panelling and also discover its role in the slave trade. Descriptions are in German only, but a free English-language pamphlet is available.

GEDENKSTÄTTE PLÖTZENSEE

Map pp72-3

☎ 2699 5000; www.gedenkstaette-ploetzensee. de; Hüttigpfad; admission free; ☺ 9am-5pm Mar-Oct, to 4pm Nov-Feb; ⊕ Turmstrasse or Ⓡ Beusselstrasse, then 🚌 123

The Nazis executed nearly 3000 people at Plötzensee prison, about half of them German resistance fighters. The room where the beheadings and hangings took place is now a hauntingly simple memorial. Housed in a plain brick shed, only a steel bar with eight hooks pierces its emptiness. Explanatory panels document the Nazis' perverted justice system, which gleefully handed out death sentences like candy at a parade. The failed assassination attempt on Hitler on 20 July 1944 set off a veritable orgy of hangings of the conspirators and many of their (mostly uninvolved) relatives and friends, a process the Führer had allegedly captured on film.

For a translation of the information panels, pick up the free English brochure at the desk. Sections of the original prison are now a juvenile detention centre.

LABYRINTH KINDERMUSEUM Map pp72-3
☎ 800 931 150; www.kindermuseum-labyrinth.de, in German; Osloer Strasse 12; adult/child/family €4.50/4/12; 🕐 1-6pm Fri & Sat, 11am-6pm Sun, daily during German school holidays; Ⓢ Osloer Strasse, Pankstrasse

Don't be put off by the word 'museum' – this place inside an old factory is a fun and educational playground for the pre-teen set. Staff put on different themed exhibits every nine months to subtly teach cultural sensitivity, tolerance, community spirit and other good values. Expect lots of interactive games, puzzles, toys, crazy mirrors and other fun features. Bring some thick socks or slippers as shoes are a no-no inside.

MOABIT
Originally settled by French Huguenots, Moabit has become home to a multicultural mix of blue-collar Berliners, immigrants and government employees, but is slowly starting to appear on the radar of hipsters. Although devoid of sights, this is another neighbourhood worth keeping tabs on.

BERLIN WALL
Cycling Tour
1 Bornholmer Strasse Not the Brandenburg Gate but the Bornholmer Brücke steel bridge was the first border crossing to open on 9 November 1989. Masses of East Berliners headed here on that night, completely overwhelming the border guards who had no choice but to open the gates.

2 Mauerpark From the S-Bahn station head east on Bornholmer Strasse, turn right on Malmöer Strasse and right again on Behmstrasse. Near the hilltop, cross the street and take the Schwedter Steg footbridge over the railway tracks. Continuing straight takes you to Mauerpark, a hugely popular park built atop the former death strip. A roughly 300m-long section of the inner wall runs along the back of the Friedrich-Ludwig-Jahn-Stadion; it was higher here than usual to deter would-be escapees from among the spectators.

3 Bernauer Strasse Mauerpark adjoins Bernauer Strasse, where several notorious

escape attempts took place. Turn right (east) and look for the four multilingual information panels, which tell such stories as that of Ida Siekmann who became the first Wall victim when jumping to her death from a 3rd-floor window on 22 August 1961.

4 Gedenkstätte Berliner Mauer Follow Bernauer Strasse to the Berlin Wall Memorial (p106), the only place where you can see how all the elements of the Wall and the death strip fit together, including the sand strip patrolled by motorised guards, the lamps that bathed the strip in fierce light at night, and an original guard tower.

5 S-Bahn Station Nordbahnhof The Wall also divided the city's transportation system. Three lines with stations in West Berlin used tracks that ran through the eastern sector to return to stations back on the western side. Stations on East Berlin turf were closed and patrolled by GDR guards. Nordbahnhof, just west of the Berlin Wall Memorial, was one of these so-called 'ghost stations'; an interesting exhibit in the station has more details and photographs.

6 Friedrichstrasse/Tränenpalast From Nordbahnhof, go west on Invalidenstrasse, then south on Chausseestrasse and follow it to Friedrichstrasse train station, which was a border crossing for travellers from both parts of Berlin. The actual checkpoint was inside a pavilion nicknamed Tränenpalast (Palace of Tears) because of the many tearful goodbyes suffered here. You'll ride past it when turning right on Reichstagsufer.

7 Parlament der Bäume Follow the Spree via the Reichstagsufer, then turn right on Luisenstrasse and left on Adele-Schreiber-Krieger-Strasse. Just north of the Marie-Elisabeth-Lüders-Haus, the Parliament of Trees is a Wall memorial consisting of trees, memorial stones, pictures, text, an original section of the barrier and the names of 258 victims inscribed on slabs of granite.

8 Ben Wagin Wall Installation Carry your bike down the stairs to the Schiffbauerdamm river walk and pedal a short stretch to the Marie-Elisabeth-Lüders-Haus where, in the basement, you'll find an art installation featuring original Wall segments, each painted with a year and the number of people killed at the border in that year. It's open from 1pm to 7pm

BERLIN WALL

0 —————— 1 km
0 —————— 0.5 miles

CYCLE FACTS

Start **Bornholmer Strasse S-Bahn station**
End **Oberbaumbrücke**
Distance **15km**
Duration **2½ hours**
Exertion **Moderate**
Fuel stop **Mauersegler** (p228), **Oststrand** (p224),
Strandgut Berlin (p224)

Friday to Sunday but if the doors are closed, simply sneak a peek through the window.

9 Brandenburger Tor Continue on Schiffbauerdamm, turn right on Luisenbrücke and right again on Unter den Linden to get to the Brandenburger Tor (Brandenburg Gate; p81),

where construction of the Wall began on 13 August 1961. An exhibition in the new U-Bahn station Brandenburger Tor pinpoints milestones in the history of this landmark, which has become both a symbol of division and reunification.

10 Potsdamer Platz From the Brandenburger Tor follow Ebertstrasse south to Potsdamer Platz, which used to be a massive no man's land during the city's division. The death strip was several hundred metres wide here. Outside the S-Bahn station entrance are a few Berlin Wall segments.

11 Border Watchtower Continue south on Stresemannstrasse, then hook a left on Erna-Berger-Strasse to get to one of the few remaining GDR watchtowers. Guards had to climb up a slim round shaft via an iron ladder to reach the octagonal observation perch on top. Introduced in 1969, this cramped model was later replaced by larger, square towers.

12 Berlin Wall on Niederkirchner Strasse Backtrack and continue south on Stresemannstrasse, then turn left on Niederkirchner Strasse to get to a 200m-long section of the original outer border wall. Badly scarred by souvenir hunters, it's now protected by a fence. The border strip was very narrow here, with the inner wall abutting such buildings as the Abgeordnetenhaus and the Former Reichsluftfahrtsministerium (Nazi Air Force Ministry; p114).

13 Checkpoint Charlie Keep going east on Niederkirchner Strasse, which becomes Zimmerstrasse and takes you straight to this famous border crossing, which took its name from the NATO phonetic alphabet. Checkpoint Alpha was near Helmstedt at the border of West Germany and East Germany. Checkpoint Bravo was near Drewitz at the border of East Germany and West Berlin. Checkpoint Charlie thus marked the border between West and East Berlin.

14 Heinrich Heine Border Crossing Continue east on Zimmerstrasse, turn right on Axel-Springer-Strasse and left on Oranienstrasse, then left again (at Moritzplatz) onto Heinrich-Heine-Strasse. Just past Sebastianstrasse was one of the largest border crossings, used primarily for mail and merchandise but also as a civilian crossing for West Germans headed for East Berlin.

15 East Side Gallery Follow Heinrich-Heine-Strasse north, turn right on Köpenicker Strasse, left on Engeldamm, cross the Spree, turn right on Stralauer Strasse and you'll soon arrive at the East Side Gallery (p149), a 1.3km-long stretch of outer wall painted by artists in 1990. The river itself belonged to East Berlin and border guards patrolled the Spree in boats. An original boat shed is part of the Kiki Blofeld beach bar (p224).

16 Oberbaumbrücke The East Side Gallery terminates near this lovely 19th-century bridge, which links Kreuzberg and Friedrichshain and served as a pedestrian border checkpoint. A particularly nasty incident occurred here in 1975 when a five-year-old child fell into the water from the West Berlin side. Since the river was in GDR territory, West Germans would have been shot if they tried to rescue him, while East German border guards refused to do so. The child drowned.

SHOPPING

top picks

- Berlinomat (p194)
- Contemporary Fine Arts (p190)
- Flagshipstore (p195)
- Flohmarkt am Mauerpark (p196)
- Scratch Records (p193)
- Stilwerk (p189)
- KaDeWe (p189)

SHOPPING

Berlin is a great place to shop, and we're definitely not talking malls and chains. The city's appetite for the individual manifests in small, unique boutiques that are a pleasure to explore. Shopping here is a benign activity that's as much about visual stimulus as it is about actual purchasing power. Whether you're into frugality or you're a power-shopper, you'll find plenty of intriguingly put-together windows that turn your head and make you explore Berlin's multifaceted neighbourhoods (known as *Kieze*).

The closest the German capital comes to having a shopping boulevard is Kurfürstendamm (Ku'damm) and its extension, Tauentzienstrasse. It's largely the purview of the same mainstream retailers you probably know from back home, from Mango to H&M to Levi's and Esprit. You'll find more of the same in such malls as Alexa and Potsdamer Platz Arkaden.

Getting the most out of shopping in Berlin, though, means venturing off the high street and into the *Kieze*. This is where you'll discover a cosmopolitan cocktail of indie boutiques stirred by the city's zest for life, envelope-pushing energy and entrepreneurial spirit.

Each *Kiez* comes with its own flair, identity and mix of stores calibrated to the needs, tastes and bank accounts of local residents. Go to posh Charlottenburg for international couture and to Kreuzberg for vintage garb and progressive streetwear. In Mitte, bustling Friedrichstrasse has cosmopolitan flair and big-label boutiques, while the Scheunenviertel and Prenzlauer Berg are local designer hotbeds. Schöneberg has the fabulous KaDeWe department store, but its side streets are lined with niche shops.

Note that most stores, especially smaller ones, do not accept credit cards.

OPENING HOURS

In theory, Berlin's shopkeepers are allowed to decide their opening hours from Monday to Saturday. In practice, only department stores, supermarkets, shops in major commercial districts (such as the Kurfürstendamm), and those in malls take full advantage of this. These stores usually open around 9.30am and close at 8pm or even later. Boutiques and other smaller shops keep flexible hours, opening some time mid-morning and generally closing at 7pm or 8pm, sometimes an hour or two earlier on Saturday. Stores are closed on Sunday, except for some bakeries, flower shops and souvenir shops. Shops are allowed to open from 1pm to 8pm on two December Sundays before Christmas and on a further six Sundays throughout the year.

For the low-down on late-night and Sunday grocery shopping, see the boxed text on p214.

HISTORIC MITTE

Mitte's historic area makes for a pleasant day's wander, with a popular market close to Museumsinsel (Museum Island) and some good options for souvenir hunting among the tourist attractions. For heavy-hitting international retail names, make a beeline to Friedrichstrasse, especially the elegant Friedrichstadtpassagen, anchored by the visually dazzling Galeries Lafayette.

KUNST- & NOSTALGIEMARKT
Map pp76-7   Antiques & Collectibles
Am Kupfergraben; ☺ **10am-4pm Sat & Sun;**
Ⓢ Ⓡ **Friedrichstrasse**
Just west of Museumsinsel, this art and collectible market gets high marks for scenic location, but you're more likely to

top picks

SHOPPING STRIPS

- Alte & Neue Schönhauser Strasse & Münzstrasse (Map pp102-3) Up-to-the-minute fashions hot off the catwalk or sewing machine
- Friedrichstrasse (Map pp76-7) The place for big-name hunters to stake out their turf
- Kastanienallee (Map pp156-7) Neat knick-knacks and buzzing boutiques
- Kurfürstendamm & Tauentzienstrasse (Map p128) From household-name chains to high-end spends
- Oranienstrasse (Map pp140-1) Fashion-forward streetwear, local stalwarts and a laid-back spirit

be fighting over that antique coaster set with Maggie from Brighton than Mimi from Berlin. Antique book collectors have plenty of boxes to sift through and there's also a good sampling of furniture, bric-a-brac and small-scale Eastern Bloc detritus.

TASCHEN Map pp76-7
Books

☎ 2532 5991; www.taschen.com; Friedrichstrasse 180-184; ⓨ 10am-8pm Mon-Sat; ⓞ Stadtmitte, Französische Strasse

Low-brow to high art, nothing is off-limits for Benedikt Taschen, the cheeky German publisher who finally opened a flagship store in Berlin in 2009. In the stylish ambience of the Philippe Starck–designed space, you find coffee-table tomes on Picasso and Frank Lloyd Wright snuggling up to *The Big Butt Book* and a hardcover/DVD combo on porn legend Vanessa del Rio. Never a boring browse, for sure.

BERLIN STORY Map pp76-7
Books & Music

☎ 2045 3842; www.berlinstory.de; Unter den Linden 26; ⓨ 10am-7pm; ⓞ ⓡ Friedrichstrasse

Berlin in a nutshell – this is the ultimate one-stop shop for Berlin-related books, maps, DVDs, CDs and magazines, in English and a dozen other languages, many published inhouse. Also check out the free historical movie about Berlin and the basement exhibit with its GDR-era Trabi car and Berlin city model from 1930.

DUSSMANN – DAS KULTURKAUFHAUS
Map pp76-7
Books & Music

☎ 2025 1111; www.kulturkaufhaus.de, in German; Friedrichstrasse 90; ⓨ 10am-midnight Mon-Sat; ⓞ ⓡ Friedrichstrasse

It's easy to lose track of time as you browse through Dussmann's four floors of wall-to-wall books, DVDs and an astonishing selection of music CDs that leaves no genre unaccounted for. Unique services such as rentals of reading glasses are a definite bonus, as are the reading nooks, a cafe and a performance space used for concerts, political discussions and high-profile book readings and signing.

FASSBENDER & RAUSCH
Map pp76-7
Chocolates

☎ 2045 8443; www.fassbender-rausch.de; Charlottenstrasse 60; ⓨ 10am-8pm Mon-Sat, 11am-8pm Sun; ⓞ Stadtmitte

If the Aztecs thought of chocolate as the elixir of the gods, then this emporium of quality truffles and pralines must be heaven. Bonus: the chocolate volcano and detailed replicas of Berlin landmarks. The cafe serves sinful drinking chocolates and cakes that are little works of art.

RITTER SPORT BUNTE SCHOKOWELT
Map pp76-7
Chocolates

☎ 2009 5080; www.ritter-sport.de, in German; Französische Strasse 24; ⓨ 10am-8pm Mon-Fri, to 6pm Sat; ⓞ Französische Strasse

Fans of the colourful square chocolate bars can pick up limited edition, organic and diet varieties in addition to all the classics at Ritter Sport's new flagship store. Upstairs, a ho-hum free exhibit explains the journey from cocoa bean to finished product, but the biggest hit is the *Schokolateria* where you can mix and match dozens of ingredients to make your own personalised bar.

CLOTHING SIZES

Women's clothing

Aus/UK	8	10	12	14	16	18
Europe	36	38	40	42	44	46
Japan	5	7	9	11	13	15
USA	6	8	10	12	14	16

Women's shoes

Aus/USA	5	6	7	8	9	10
Europe	35	36	37	38	39	40
France only	35	36	38	39	40	42
Japan	22	23	24	25	26	27
UK	3½	4½	5½	6½	7½	8½

Men's clothing

Aus	92	96	100	104	108	112
Europe	46	48	50	52	54	56
Japan	S		M	M		L
UK/USA	35	36	37	38	39	40

Men's shirts (collar sizes)

Aus/Japan	38	39	40	41	42	43
Europe	38	39	40	41	42	43
UK/USA	15	15½	16	16½	17	17½

Men's shoes

Aus/UK	7	8	9	10	11	12
Europe	41	42	43	44½	46	47
Japan	26	27	27½	28	29	30
USA	7½	8½	9½	10½	11½	12½

Measurements approximate only; try before you buy

top picks

BOOKSHOPS

- Berlin Story (p183)
- Dussmann – Das Kulturkaufhaus (p183)
- Marga Schoeller Bücherstube (p188)
- Pro QM (opposite)
- Taschen (p183)

NIVEA HAUS Map pp76-7   Cosmetics
www.nivea.de/haus; Unter den Linden 28;
☽ 10am-8pm Mon-Sat; ⊕ ⓡ Friedrichstrasse,
Brandenburger Tor
Nivea is Latin for Snow White whose 'castle' sits right on prestigious Unter den Linden. At the flagship store of this German beauty purveyor you can peruse the entire product palette, sign up for a consultation or get a quick pick-me-up facial or massage (no reservation; €12-45).

GALERIES LAFAYETTE
Map pp76-7   Department Store
☎ 209 480; www.galerieslafayette.de;
Friedrichstrasse 76; ☽ 10am-8pm Mon-Sat;
⊕ Französische Strasse
Part of the Friedrichstadtpassagen, the Berlin branch of the exquisite French emporium is centred on a glass cone shimmering with kaleidoscopic intensity. From here, three floors of concentric circles rise up. Aside from racks packed with Prada & Co, you can get your mitts on sexy Agent Provocateur lingerie, edgy Berlin fashions and gourmet treats in the food hall.

MITTE – ALEXANDERPLATZ AREA

Alexanderplatz is the hub of mainstream shopping in the eastern centre with department stores on the square itself and the massive Alexa shopping mall making sure that you can pick up a rainbow of goods in one location.

BUBBLE.KID Map p96   Berlin Fashion
☎ 9440 4252; www.bubblekid.de; Rosa-Luxemburg-Strasse 7; ☽ 11.30-7pm Mon-Sat; ⊕ Alexanderplatz
Helmed by Berlin moms, this local label keeps kids looking good in cotton-based

outfits that are functional not frilly. Much attention is paid to colour, detail and durability – those zippers are made to last! Lena König and her team put out two collections twice annually: one for babies (0-12 months) and another for pre-school kids. Halle Berry and Björk are reportedly fans.

GALERIA KAUFHOF
Map p96   Department Store
☎ 247 430; www.galeria-kaufhof.de, in German;
Alexanderplatz 9; ☽ 9.30am-8pm Mon-Wed, to 10pm Thu-Sat; ⊕ ⓡ Alexanderplatz
A few years ago, a total renovation by John P Kleihues turned this former GDR-era department store into a retail cube fit for the 21st century, complete with a glass-domed light court and a sleek travertine skin that glows green at night. A large in-house supermarket makes for a handy place to stock up on groceries.

AUSBERLIN Map p96   Gifts & Souvenirs
☎ 4199 7896; www.ausberlin.de, in German;
Karl-Liebknecht-Strasse 17; ☽ 11am-7pm Mon-Sat;
⊕ ⓡ Alexanderplatz
This unpretentious store has made it its mission to discover, promote and sell only articles made in Berlin. We're not talking trashy souvenirs but wallet-friendly stuff you might actually want or need, including T-shirts, accessories, toys, chocolates, music, lingerie and jewellery by hundreds of local designers.

ALEXA Map p96   Shopping Mall
☎ 269 3400; www.alexacentre.com, in German;
Grunerstrasse 20; ☽ 10am-9pm; ⊕
ⓡ Alexanderplatz
Power shoppers love this XXL-sized mega-mall that cuts a rose-hued presence near Alexanderplatz. Besides the usual mainstream retailers, there's also a store by German rapper Bushido, and Loxx, the world's largest model railway. Good food court for a bite on the run.

MITTE – SCHEUNENVIERTEL

Simply window-shopping in Mitte's Scheunenviertel could take a day and involve a lot of fun, with merchants catering for all manner of tastes and budgets. If it's Berlin-made fashions and accessories you're after, concentrate your browsing along and around Alte Schönhauser Strasse, Neue Schönhauser Strasse, Münzstrasse and inside the Hackesche Höfe (p104). A string of cutting-edge galleries filled with thought-provoking contemporary art holds court on Linienstrasse and Auguststrasse and their side streets.

IC! BERLIN Map pp102-3 — Accessories
☎ 2472 7200; www.ic-berlin.de; Max-Beer-Strasse 17; ☽ 11am-8pm Mon-Sat; ◉ Weinmeisterstrasse
What looks like a bachelor pad, with worn sofas, wacky art and turntables, is the flagship store of this internationally famous eyewear maker. The feather-light frames with their klutz-proof, screwless hinges are stored in retro airline serving trolleys and have added 'spec appeal' to celebs from Madonna to the king of Morocco.

BERLINERKLAMOTTEN
Map pp102-3 — Berlin Fashion
www.berlinerklamotten.de; Court III, Hackesche Höfe; ☽ 11am-8pm Mon-Sat; ⊠ Hackescher Markt
Keen on keeping tabs on what's humming on the sewing machines of Berlin's indie designers? Flip through the racks of this arbiter of fashion cool to dig up outfits – casual to couture – with that urban, cheeky and fresh capital twist. On weekends, a DJ pumps out high-energy sounds to get you into a party mood.

C'EST TOUT Map pp102-3 — Berlin Fashion
☎ 2759 5532; www.cesttout.de; Mulackstrasse 26; ☽ noon-7pm; ◉ Weinmeisterstrasse
Katja Fuhrmann is the creative head behind this up-and-coming Berlin label for women. Her signature piece is the unfussy yet elegant and form-flattering dress. Made from soft fabrics like silk and jersey, it transitions well from office to opera. Of late, fur vests, cashmere cardigans, blazers and leggings have also been seen hanging on the racks in her minimalist store.

CLAUDIA SKODA Map pp102-3 — Berlin Fashion
☎ 280 7211; www.claudiaskoda.com; Alte Schönhauser Strasse 35; ☽ noon-7pm Mon-Sat; ◉ Weinmeisterstrasse
Berlin-born Claudia Skoda has been a local design icon since the 1970s, when she used to party with David Bowie and Iggy Pop. Fashionistas from around town make regular visits to this gorgeous boutique to

check out her latest figure-hugging knitted couture, from bold, but classy, dresses to colour-happy wrist warmers and snug sweaters, all made from top quality yarns.

EAST BERLIN Map pp102-3 — Berlin Fashion
☎ 2472 4189; www.eastberlinonline.de, in German; Alte Schönhauser Strasse 33/34; ☽ 11-8pm Mon-Sat, 1-6pm Sun; ◉ Weinmeisterstrasse
An outgrowth of the techno scene, East Berlin has kept girls and boys looking good in their signature TV Tower–emblazoned tees and hoodies since the early 1990s. These days, their expanded label selection includes the latest streetwear by Adelheid, Minikum, Nikita and about a dozen other style makers. Cute jewellery, too.

LALA BERLIN Map pp102-3 — Berlin Fashion
☎ 6579 5466; www.lalaberlin.com; Mulackstrasse 7; ☽ noon-8pm Mon-Sat; ◉ Rosa-Luxemburg-Platz
Former MTV editor Leyla Piedayesh makes top-flight women's fashion that flatters both the twig-thin and the well-upholstered. Check out the elegant knitwear in jewel-like hues or her witty takes on logo obsession. Leyla's celebrity fan base includes Claudia Schiffer.

PRO QM Map pp102-3 — Books
☎ 2472 8520; www.pro-qm.de, in German; Almstadtstrasse 48; ☽ 11-8pm Mon-Sat; ◉ Rosa-Luxemburg-Platz
Don't come here looking for the latest John Grisham novel: at this treasure trove of the printed word the focus is squarely on design, art and architecture with a sprinkling of political and philosophical tomes (many in English) thrown in for good measure. Also a good source for obscure and unlikely mags, such as the Israeli fashion culture quarterly 360 Maalot.

GROBER UNFUG Map pp102-3 — Comics
☎ 281 7331; www.groberunfug.de, in German; Weinmeisterstrasse 9; ☽ 11am-7pm Mon-Wed, to 8pm Thu & Fri, to 6pm Sat; ◉ Weinmeisterstrasse
Fans of international comics and graphic novels can easily lose a few hours in this very cool repository of books, DVDs, soundtracks and knick-knacks. There's a mega-selection of indie and mainstream imports from the US, Japan and elsewhere. Exhibits, auctions, signings and performances take over the adjacent gallery space. There's

a smaller branch in Kreuzberg (Map pp140-1; ☎ 6940 7331; Zossener Strasse 3; ⏰ 11am-7pm Mon-Fri, to 6pm Sat; ◉ Gneisenaustrasse).

AM1, AM2, AM3 Map pp102-3 — Fashion

☎ 3088 1945; www.andreasmurkudis.net; Münzstrasse 21 & 23; ⏰ noon-8pm Mon-Sat; ◉ Weinmeisterstrasse

Andreas Murkudis' trio of minimalist-chic shops offers a wealth of sartorial temptations from designers such as his Berlin-based brother Kostas, internationals Sophia Kokosalaki and Martin Margiela, sturdy Ludwig Reiter footwear and Schiesser underwear (given a special Kostas twist). There's also accessories and jewellery, plus helpful, refreshingly honest service. AM1 (menswear) and AM2 (women) are tucked into the second courtyard past Acne, AM3 (underwear and accessories) is right on Münzstrasse itself.

HERR VON EDEN Map pp102-3 — Fashion

☎ 2404 8682; www.herrvoneden.com; Alte Schönhauser Strasse 14; ⏰ 10.30am-8pm Mon-Sat; ◉ Weinmeisterstrasse

Over a decade of ensuring that Berlin's dandies look the part has made this store a must-visit for chaps looking to make an impression. Fabrics, cuts, colours, details – all are designed to release the inner peacock and help you strut your stuff in style. Prices are high, but so are the standards.

NO 74 BERLIN Map pp102-3 — Fashion

☎ 5306 2513; www.no74-berlin.com; Torstrasse 74; ⏰ noon-8pm Mon-Sat; ◉ Rosenthaler Platz

Get your kicks at this slammin' sneaker (trainer) shop, which is a collaboration between Adidas and London's No 6 store. This is the place to come for limited editions and hard-to-source lines created by such red-hot designers as Stella McCartney, Jeremy Scott and Kazuki. A must for sneaker fetishists.

SOMMERLADEN Map pp102-3 — Fashion

☎ 2404 9988; Linienstrasse 153; ⏰ 2-8pm Mon-Fri, noon-5pm Sat; ◉ Oranienburger Strasse

If you have diva tastes without the matching bank account, Johanna Mattner's little basement store is a godsend. Racks and shelves here bulge with well-edited, barely-worn clothing and accessories from designers big and small, local and international. The stock is always changing,

which is dangerous because it means you could find something new that you love every time.

BONBONMACHEREI Map pp102-3 — Food

☎ 4405 5243; www.bonbonmacherei.de, in German; Oranienburger Strasse 32, Heckmann Höfe; ⏰ noon-8pm Wed-Sat; ◉ Oranienburger Strasse

The old-fashioned art of handmade sweets has been lovingly revived in this basement-store-cum-show-kitchen. Watch candy masters Katja and Hjalmar using their antique equipment to churn out such tasty treats as their signature leaf-shaped *Berliner Maiblätter* right before your eyes. Note that the kitchen is closed in July and August and from Christmas to mid-January.

1. ABSINTH DEPOT BERLIN
Map pp102-3 — Food & Drink

☎ 281 6789; www.erstesabsinthdepotberlin.de, in German; Weinmeisterstrasse 4; ⏰ 2pm-midnight Mon-Sat; ◉ Weinmeisterstrasse

Van Gogh, Toulouse-Lautrec and Oscar Wilde were among the *fin-de-siècle* artists who drew inspiration from the 'green fairy', as absinthe is also known. This quaint little shop has over 60 varieties of the potent stuff and an expert owner who'll happily help you pick out the perfect bottle for your own mind-altering rendezvous.

AMPELMANN GALERIE SHOP
Map pp102-3 — Gifts & Souvenirs

☎ 4472 6438; www.ampelmannshop.com; Court V, Hackesche Höfe; ⏰ 9.30am-11pm Mon-Sat, 10am-7pm Sun; ◉ Hackescher Markt

It took a vociferous grassroots campaign to save the little Ampelmann, the endearing fellow on the pedestrian traffic lights who helped generations of East Germans safely

top picks

GASTRO DELIGHTS

- Bonbonmacherei (above)
- Fassbender & Rausch (p183)
- Goldhahn & Sampson (p196)
- KaDeWe food hall (p189)
- Kollwitzplatzmarkt (p195)

across the street. Now a beloved cult figure, his likeness fills an entire store's worth of T-shirts, fridge magnets, pasta, onesies, umbrellas and other knick-knacks. Other branches: DomAquarée (Map p96; ☎ 2758 3238; Karl-Liebknecht-Strasse 5; ⏰ 9.30am-9pm; Ⓜ Alexanderplatz) and in the Potsdamer Platz Arkaden (Map p112; ☎ 2592 5691; Alte Potsdamer Strasse 7; ⏰ 10am-9pm Mon-Sat, 1-7pm Sun; Ⓜ Ⓡ Potsdamer Platz) and Gendarmenmarkt (Map pp76-7; ☎ 4003 9095; Markgrafenstrasse 37; ⏰ 9.30am-8pm daily; Ⓜ Hausvogteiplatz).

MICHAELA BINDER Map pp102-3 — Jewellery
☎ 2838 4869; www.michaelabinder.de, in German; Gipsstrasse 13; ⏰ noon-7pm Tue-Fri, to 4pm Sat; Ⓜ Weinmeisterstrasse
This talented jeweller makes stylish rings, ear studs and necklaces in clean, basic shapes from brushed silver and gold. The twist? Each piece is accented with felt inlays that can easily be exchanged to match your mood or outfit from a palette of 12 colours. Aside from her own creations, Binder also showcases jewellery from other artists in her workshop/showroom.

SCHMUCKWERK Map pp102-3 — Jewellery
☎ 281 3114; Court IV, Hackescher Höfe; ⏰ noon-6.30pm Mon-Sat; Ⓡ Hackescher Markt
Sabine Dubbers' modern, organic take on traditional jewellery will have you wanting to bedeck your fingers, earlobes, neck, shirt cuffs and wrists with her beautifully made baubles. Working with a variety of precious metals and rounded, polished stones, pieces can be adjusted to suit individual requirements.

BLUSH DESSOUS Map pp102-3 — Lingerie
☎ 2809 3580; www.blush-berlin.com, in German; Rosa-Luxemburg-Strasse 22; ⏰ noon-8pm Mon-Fri, to 7pm Sat; Ⓜ Rosa-Luxemburg-Platz
There's nothing sleazy about the selection at Blush – it's all five-star sex appeal at this little boudoir, which stocks some of the finest of women's scanties in town. Dress up (or down) in ensembles by Princess Tam Tam and Cosabella, add some Falke socks in winter and top off the night with sweet little silk-satin eye covers.

FRAU TONIS PARFUM Map pp102-3 — Perfume
☎ 2021 5310; www.frau-tonis-parfum.com; Alte Schönhauser Strasse 50; ⏰ noon-8pm Mon-Fri,

11am-7pm Sat; Ⓜ Weinmeisterstrasse, Rosa-Luxemburg-Platz
Follow your nose to this little perfume boutique that only sells scents made in Berlin. Lining up for olfactory inspection in the minimalist white space are 20 pure liquids shimmering in shades from gold to grass. Try Marlene Dietrich's favourite: a bold and eccentric violet or request a customised perfume composed just for you. Prices start at €12 for a 7ml bottle.

TRIPPEN Map pp102-3 — Shoes
☎ 2839 1337; www.trippen.com; Courts IV & VI, Hackesche Höfe, Rosenthaler Strasse 40/41; ⏰ 11am-8pm Mon-Fri, 10am-8pm Sat; Ⓡ Hackescher Markt
Forget about 10cm heels! Berlin-based Trippen's shoes are designed with the human anatomy in mind, yet light years ahead in style compared to the loafers grandma used to buy in the orthopaedic store. The brand prides itself on its 'socially responsible' manufacturing and love of unusual shapes. For relative bargains, check out their outlet store in Kreuzberg (Map pp140-1; ☎ 280 7517; Köpenicker Strasse 187-88; ⏰ 10am-6pm Mon-Sat; Ⓜ Schlesisches Tor).

POTSDAMER PLATZ & TIERGARTEN

Taken up mostly by its giant namesake park, and the government and embassy quarters, the Tiergarten area has few spending temptations, although it compensates by having a handily situated shopping mall on bustling Potsdamer Platz.

POTSDAMER PLATZ ARKADEN
Map p112 — Shopping Mall
☎ 255 9270; www.potsdamer-platz-arkaden.de; Alte Potsdamer Strasse 7; ⏰ 10am-9pm Mon-Sat; Ⓜ Ⓡ Potsdamer Platz
This airy indoor mall brims with mainstream chains such as H&M, Mango and Zara for clothing, Hugendubel for books and Saturn for electronics. In between are smaller stores selling everything from eyewear to stationery. The basement has Kaiser's and Aldi supermarkets, and lots of fast-food outlets. There's a post office at street level and decadent ice cream upstairs at Caffé e Gelato (p216).

CHARLOTTENBURG & NORTHERN WILMERSDORF

Charlottenburg's shopping spine is Kurfürstendamm, and its eastern extension, Tauentzienstrasse. The area around the Gedächtniskirche is chock-a-block with multiple outlets of international chains flogging fashion and accessories. To satisfy exclusive label cravings, head to Ku'damm between Schlüterstrasse and Leibnizstrasse, where consumer temples such as Hermès, Cartier and Bulgari attend to the needs of the cashed-up. Kantstrasse is good for homewares and has the impressive Stilwerk serving as the mother lode. Wander along the side streets connecting Ku'damm and Kantstrasse, which are lined with numerous individualistic boutiques, bookshops and galleries.

YOSHIHARU ITO Map p128   Berlin Fashion
☎ 4404 4490; www.yoshiharu-ito.de; Wielandstrasse 31; ◐ 10am-6pm Mon-Sat; ◉ Savignyplatz
This Tokyo-trained couturier has built his considerable reputation on putting an inventive, personal spin on classic cuts, which are perfectly tailored and made of high-quality, sober-coloured fabric. Men's clothing is his main strength, but his women's line turns heads as well.

HUGENDUBEL Map p128   Books
☎ 01801 484 484; www.hugendubel.de, in German; Tauentzienstrasse 13; ◐ 9.30am-8pm Mon-Sat; ◉ Kurfürstendamm
This excellent all-purpose chain has a sweeping selection of books, including Lonely Planet titles and novels in English. You can browse as long as you like, or preview your purchase while perched on a comfy sofa, or even while recaffeinating at the in-store cafe. There are several smaller branches around town, including one in the Potsdamer Platz Arkaden (p187).

MARGA SCHOELLER BÜCHERSTUBE
Map p128   Books
☎ 881 1112; www.margaschoeller.de, in German; Knesebeckstrasse 33; ◐ 9.30am-7pm Mon-Wed, to 8pm Thu & Fri, to 6pm Sat; ◉ Uhlandstrasse, ◉ Savignyplatz
Founded in 1929, this well-regarded warren-like bookstore has counted literary lions

like Bertolt Brecht and Elias Canetti among its customers. Its sophisticated assortment is especially focused on English titles and includes classics and new lit, biographies and children's books. The staff, headed by the late Marga's son, is bend-over-backwards helpful and only too happy to source the perfect read for you.

SCHROPP p128   Books & Maps
☎ 2355 7320; www.landkartenschropp.de, in German; Hardenbergstrasse 9a; ◐ 10am-8pm Mon-Fri, to 6pm Sat; ◉ Ernst-Reuter-Platz
No other shop in Berlin is better placed than Schropp to tell you where to go. It's been in business for more than 250 years, and you'll find the entire world beneath its roof with every conceivable map, travel guide, dictionary and globe. Come here for some quality armchair travelling or to plan your next trip.

HAUTNAH Map p128   Erotica
☎ 882 3434; www.hautnahberlin.de, in German; Uhlandstrasse 170; ◐ noon-8pm Mon-Fri, 11am-4pm Sat; ◉ Uhlandstrasse
Berlin being the sort of city it is, sooner or later you may just need to update your fetish wardrobe, and Hautnah's three floors of erotic costuming should do the job naughtily. Expect a vast range of latex bodices, leather goods, themed get-ups, sex toys and vertiginous footwear, plus an interesting wine selection (Marquis de Sade champagne anyone?).

TITUS ZOOPREME Map p128   Fashion
☎ 3259 3239; www.titus.de, in German; Meinekestrasse 2; ◐ 10am-8pm Mon-Sat; ◉ Kurfüstendamm
Perhaps not what you were expecting in this quiet street off Ku'damm, but definitely the place to come for streetwear and skatewear (for both men and women) plus an impressive selection of skate decks. It's part of a Germany-wide chain and the clued-up staff can also provide information about the local skating scene.

FLOHMARKT STRASSE DES 17 JUNI
Map pp124-5   Flea Market
www.berliner-troedelmarkt.de, in German; Strasse des 17 Juni; ◐ 10am-5pm Sat & Sun; ◉ Tiergarten
Some vintage junkies think Berlin's oldest flea market west of the Tiergarten S-Bahn station is the cat's pyjamas, but we're not

impressed by the fact that bargains here are as rare as hen's teeth. Hundreds of vendors vie for your euros with Berlin collectibles, stuff from granny's attic, jewellery and plenty of surprising stuff. It spills over into an arts- and crafts-market selling mostly new stuff.

STILWERK Map p128   Homewares

☎ 315 150; www.stilwerk.de, in German; Kantstrasse 17; ☿ 10am-7pm Mon-Sat; 🚇 Savignyplatz

This four-storey temple of good taste will have devotees of the finer things itching to redecorate (perhaps even to their own Stilwerk CD!). Everything you could possibly want – from tactile key rings to glossy grand pianos and quality vintage design – is here, plus all the top names (Bang & Olufsen, Ligne Roset, Niessing et al). There's also a restaurant, a jazz club and the occasional piano recital.

HEIDI'S SPIELZEUGLADEN

Map pp124-5   Toys

☎ 323 7556; Kantstrasse 61; ☿ 9.30am-6.30pm Mon-Fri, to 2pm Sat; 🚇 Wilmersdorfer Strasse

Since the 1970s Heidi Mallmann's charming toy store has specialised in low-tech, quality toys, from wooden trains to sturdy stuffed animals and 'edutaining' children's books, all holding the fort despite the digital age's noisy onslaught. A great selection of doll's houses and play kitchens help spur kids' social skills but also provoke many an adult to get down on the floor and mix it with the little ones.

STEIFF IN BERLIN Map p128   Toys

☎ 8862 5185; www.steiff.de; Kurfürstendamm 220; ☿ 10am-8pm Mon-Sat; 🚇 Uhlandstrasse

The cuddly creations of this famous stuffed-animal company, founded in 1880 by Margarete Steiff (who in 1902 invented the teddy bear – named for US president Teddy Roosevelt, whom she admired), are tailor-made for snuggles. The fluffy menagerie at this central store will have all ages feeling warm and fuzzy.

SCHÖNEBERG

Schöneberg's big draw is undeniably the KaDeWe, one of Europe's grandest department stores. Don't neglect the *Kiez* itself, though. Strolling from Nollendorfplatz to Hauptstrasse, via Maassenstrasse, Goltzstrasse and Akazienstrasse, takes you past lots of small, independent shops selling everything from clothing to books to gifts. On Saturday the farmers market on Winterfeldtplatz brings in fans from throughout the city.

KADEWE Map p136   Department Store

☎ 212 10; www.kadewe.de; Tauentzienstrasse 21-24; ☿ 10am-8pm Mon-Thu, 10am-9pm Fri, 9.30am-8pm Sat; 🚇 Wittenbergplatz

This century-old department store has an assortment so vast that a pirate-style campaign is the best way to plunder its bounty. If pushed for time, at least hurry up to the legendary 6th-floor food hall, a culinary treasure trove of artfully arranged chocolates, banks of decadent cheese and an entire wing of sausages. The name, by the way, stands for *Kaufhaus des Westens* (department store of the West).

WINTERFELDTMARKT

Map p136   Farmers Market

Winterfeldtplatz; ☿ 8am-2pm Wed, to 4pm Sat; 🚇 Nollendorfplatz

A Berlin institution, this market is ideal for stocking up on fruit and vegetables, eggs, meat and other comestibles that will fatten your Berlin goose in style. The much larger Saturday edition features numerous stalls selling candles, jewellery, scarves and artsy-crafty stuff. Do as the locals do and cap off a spree with lunch from one of the many markets kitchens or with coffee in a nearby cafe.

FLOHMARKT SCHÖNEBERG

Map p136   Flea Market

John-F-Kennedy-Platz; ☿ 9am-4pm Sat & Sun; 🚇 Rathaus Schöneberg

Pro and amateur vendors mix it up at this neighbourhood market, where bargaining skills are easily honed. It's not the trendiest of markets, but it's fun to ricochet between here and the food market on Winterfeldtplatz (above) on Saturdays.

AVE MARIA Map p136   Gifts & Souvenirs

☎ 265 2284; www.avemaria.de, in German; Potsdamer Strasse 75; ☿ noon-6pm Mon-Fri, to 3pm Sat; 🚇 Kurfürstenstrasse

The devil would drop dead at the doorstep of this shrine to all things Mary and Jesus. Wedged between Turkish grocers and sex and *döner* shops, Ave Maria is the go-to place for frankincense, myrrh, smiling

LONELY PLANET GALLERY GUIDE

Berlin is a great place for contemporary art with 10,000 artists and over 600 galleries, more than in New York City. Many collectors have moved here and the entire art world gets together for key events like the Berlin Biennale. The scene is changing constantly, but here's a round-up of spaces to watch.

Mitte

Auguststrasse and Linienstrasse in the Scheunenviertel were the birthplaces of Berlin's post-Wall contemporary art scene. Some pioneers have since moved on to bigger digs but key players remain.

Barbara Wien (Map pp102-3; ☎ 2838 5352; www.barbarawien.de; Linienstrasse 158; ⏱ 1-6pm Tue-Fri, noon-6pm Sat; ⊙ Oranienburger Tor, ⓡ Oranienburger Strasse) Tucked away in a courtyard off one of Mitte's artiest streets, Barbara Wien's relaxed gallery-cum-bookstore specialises in works on paper (drawings, watercolours and such) and features regular exhibitions by such artists as Nina Canell, Haegue Yang and Dieter Roth. Head downstairs to get lost amid a fantastic selection of art books and magazines.

Contemporary Fine Arts (Map pp76-7; ☎ 288 7870; www.cfa-berlin.com; Am Kupfergraben 10; ⏱ 10am-1pm & 2-6pm Tue-Fri, 11am-4pm Sat; ⊙ ⓡ Friedrichstrasse) With an international reputation for showing some of the city's best contemporary art, this gallery (with a prime location opposite Museumsinsel in a building designed by David Chipperfield) is a must for any art buff who wants to take the city's aesthetic pulse. Artists represented include Georg Baselitz, Sarah Lucas, Jonathan Meese and Daniel Richter.

Eigen+Art (Map pp102-3; ☎ 280 6605; www.eigen-art.com; Auguststrasse 26; ⏱ 11am-6pm Tue-Sat; ⓡ Oranienburger Strasse) A pioneer of the post-reunification Berlin gallery scene, this heavy hitter represents some of Germany's leading living artists, such as Neo Rauch, Martin Eder, and gardener-turned-artist Carsten Nicolai, who creates installations based on both music and art.

Haunch of Venison (Map pp76-7; ☎ 3974 3963; www.haunchofvenison.com; Heidestrasse 46; ⏱ 11am-6pm Tue-Sat; ⊙ ⓡ Hauptbahnhof) With other branches in New York, London and Zurich, this is the most prestigious among several exciting galleries that have set up shop along gritty Heidestrasse north of the Hauptbahnhof. Owned by the auction house Christie's, it only represents international hot shots such as Bill Viola, Ed and Nancy Kienholz and Dan Flavin.

Kicken (Map pp102-3; ☎ 2887 7882; www.kicken-gallery.com; Linienstrasse 155; ⏱ 2-6pm Tue-Sat; ⊙ Oranienburger Tor, ⓡ Oranienburger Strasse) In business for over 30 years, Kicken is one of Germany's most respected galleries for high-end photography from all phases of the medium. One major focus in on the German and Czech avant-garde from the 1920s and '30s, especially by such masters as Man Ray, Moholy-Nagy and Rodschenko. The gallery space, featuring an amazing moveable wall, is a work of art in itself.

Kunstagenten (Map pp156-7; ☎ 6950 4142; www.kunstagenten.de; Linienstrasse 155; ⏱ 2-7pm Wed-Sat; ⓡ Oranienburger Strasse, ⓡ Rosenthaler Platz, Oranienburger Tor) Since 2005, this dynamic gallery has championed young, international artists who push the creative envelope with their highly individualistic, idiosyncratic style. Look for exciting shows featuring such artists as Thorsten Brinkmann, Anna Lehmann-Brauns and Felix Wunderlich.

Neugerriemschneider (Map pp102-3; ☎ 2887 7277; www.neugerriemschneider.com; Linienstrasse 155; ⏱ 11am-6pm Tue-Sat; ⊙ Oranienburger Tor, Rosenthaler Platz ⓡ Oranienburger Strasse) Expect to see some of

Madonnas, Jesus T-shirts, pope candles and all manner of rosaries and crucifixes. Gregorian chants enhance the browsing experience, not just for the faithful but also for pagans in search of kitsch-cool knick-knacks.

MR DEAD & MRS FREE Map p136   Music
☎ 215 1449; www.deadandfree.com, in German; Bülowstrasse 5; ⏱ noon-7pm Mon-Fri, 11am-4pm Sat; ⊙ Nollendorfplatz
With a pedigree going back to 1983, this little place is a veritable institution on Berlin's music scene. Techno types should look elsewhere,

though, for here the focus is clearly on rock, pop, country, indie, alternative, even jazz, soul and blues – much of it on import from the UK and US. Both vinyl and CDs are available.

KREUZBERG & NORTHERN NEUKÖLLN

Kreuzberg has a predictably eclectic shopping scene. Bergmannstrasse in the western district and Oranienstrasse both offer a fun cocktail of vintage frocks, and hot-label streetwear and the city's most intriguing exhibitions at this cutting-edge gallery representing such hot shots as Olafur Eliasson, Franz Ackermann and Jorge Pardo.

Thomas Schulte (Map pp76-7; ☎ 2060 8990; www.galeriethomasschulte.de; Charlottenstrasse 24; ⊙ noon-6pm Tue-Sat; ⊕ Stadtmitte) Contemporary art since the 1960s, with a special focus on conceptual art, is the name of the game at this excellent stalwart of the New Berlin. Artists represented include Robert Mapplethorpe, Katharina Sieverding, Gordon Matta-Clark and Richard Deacon.

Charlottenburg

Camera work (Map p128; ☎ 310 0773; www.camerawork.de; Kantstrasse 149; ⊙ 11am-6pm Tue-Sat; ⊕ Savignyplatz) The big names of photography are displayed to good effect in this light and airy space. Among those represented are Lee Miller, Ansel Adams, Man Ray, Irving Penn, Helmut Newton, Herb Ritts, Richard Avedon and Leni Riefenstahl. All the photos are for sale, but be prepared to spend big.

Schöneberg

Since 2007–08, the slightly seedy area around Potsdamer Strasse and Kurfürstenstrasse has emerged as one of Berlin's most exciting art quarters with a great mix of established galleries and newcomers.

Arndt (Map p136; ☎ 2061 3870; www.arndtberlin.com; Potsdamer Strasse 96; ⊙ 11am-6pm Tue-Sat; ⊕ Kurfürstenstrasse) Thomas Hirschhorn, Sophie Calle and Keith Tyson are among the artists Matthias Arndt has taken under his wing. Another post-reunification pioneer, he's now sitting pretty in a cool apartment-style exhibition space, complete with ballroom, above the Wintergarten Variété.

Giti Nourbahksch (Map p136; ☎ 4404 6781; www.nourbahksch.de; Kurfürstenstrasse 12; ⊙ 11am-6pm Wed-Sat; ⊕ Kurfürstenstrasse) Giti Nourbahksch's was the first gallery to make the leap from Mitte to this gritty part of Schöneberg, setting up shop in huge industrial halls whose lofty ceilings lend themselves to the daring, large-scale installations and conceptual works she represents. Her stable of international artists includes Vlassis Canaris, Matias Faldbakken and Cathy Wilkes.

Klosterfelde (Map p136; ☎ 283 5305; www.klosterfelde.de; Potsdamer Strasse 93; ⊕ Kurfürstenstrasse) One of the seminal Berlin galleries since the 1990s, Klosterfelde has just moved to glam 19th-century digs on grungy Potsdamer Strasse. In brightly lit rooms lidded by ornate stucco-ornamented ceilings, it presents such makers and shakers of the international art scene as Michael Snow, Jorinde Voigt, Armin Linke and Kay Rosen. Call ahead for opening hours.

Kreuzberg

There's long been a cluster of important galleries on Zimmerstrasse and Rudi-Dutschke-Strasse, but of late interesting new turf has opened up in an ugly flat-roofed '60s building near Markgrafenstrasse and Charlottenstrasse.

September (Map pp140-1; ☎ 2593 0684; www.september-berlin.com; Charlottenstrasse 1; ⊙ noon-6pm Tue-Sat; ⊕ Kochstrasse) Gallery owners Oliver Koerner von Gustorf and Frank Müller like it bold, which is why they primarily ferret out artists who draw inspiration from film, art, design and architecture and translate them into themes concerning gender, cultural identity and alternative living concepts. Names to keep an eye out for include Sandra Meisel, Henry Kleine and Discoteca Flaming Star.

clubwear alongside music and accessories. Nearby Kottbusser Damm is almost completely in Turkish hands, with vendors selling everything from billowing bridal gowns to water pipes and exotic teas and spices. On Tuesday and Friday the Türkenmarkt (Turkish market) lures crowds from outside the district with inexpensive fresh produce and other goods.

This little store is stacked floor to ceiling with all the latest designs by local and international bag labels such as Crumpler, Leonca and Kultbag. Materials of choice include recycled rubber, air mattresses and even GDR-era postal sacks, which are turned into innovative designs, capturing the city's individualistic spirit nicely.

BAGAGE Map pp140-1   Bags
☎ 693 8916; www.bag-age.de, in German; Bergmannstrasse 13; ⊙ 11am-8pm Mon-Fri, 10am-5pm Sat; ⊕ Mehringdamm

MOLOTOW Map pp140-1   Berlin Fashion
☎ 693 0818; www.molotowberlin.de, in German; Gneisenaustrasse 112; ⊙ 2-8pm Mon-Fri, noon-4pm Sat; ⊕ Mehringdamm

When he opened Molotow in 1986, Arno Karge became one of the first entrepreneurs to champion fashion made by Berlin designers, even smuggling collections from East Berlin across the Berlin Wall. The boutique is still a good spot to stay ahead of the fashion curve with beautifully crafted clothing by Ute Henschel or Ibrahim Lopez and accessories by d:KS.

SAMEHEADS Map pp140-1 — Berlin Fashion
☎ 6950 9684; www.myspace.com/sameheads; Nostitzstrasse 11; ⊙ noon-8pm Mon-Sat; ◉ Gneisenaustrasse
Sameheads, that's Nathan, Leo and Harry, three 20-something brothers from Britain keen on carving out a spot for true subculture through their fashion and music network. Their basement shop is a portal for dozens of up-and-coming local designers. While there, probe them for details on their next underground party.

ANOTHER COUNTRY Map pp140-1 — Books
☎ 6940 1160; www.anothercountry.de; Riemannstrasse 7; ⊙ 11am-8pm Mon-Fri, to 4pm Sat; ◉ Gneisenaustrasse
Presided over by eccentric owner Alan Raphaeline, this comfortably worn-round-the-edges 'culture club' overflows with around 20,000 used English-language books, from classic lit to a vast science fiction collection. Best of all, you can sell back any book you've purchased, minus a €1.50 borrowing fee. Also hosts an English Filmclub (8pm Tuesday), TV Night (8pm Thursday) and dinners (9pm Friday).

TÜRKENMARKT Map pp140-1 — Farmers Market
Maybachufer; ⊙ noon-6.30pm Tue & Fri; ◉ Schönleinstrasse
Berlin goes Bosporus during the lively canal-side Turkish farmers market where headscarf-wearers mix it up with impecunious students and hobby cooks. Stock up on olives, feta spreads, loaves of fresh bread and mountains of fruit and vegetables, all at bargain prices. Grab your loot and head west along the canal and hang with the locals on the pretty little iron Admiralsbrücke (bridge) or carve out your picnic spot in the little park at the Urbanhafen.

FASTER, PUSSYCAT! Map pp140-1 — Fashion
☎ 6950 6600; Mehringdamm 57; ⊙ 11am-8pm Mon-Fri, to 7pm Sat; ◉ Mehringdamm

Russ Meyer's 1965 camp classic about go-go dancers gone bad inspired the store's name, and many fashions here also teeter towards the outlandish. But there's also plenty of smart streetwear and accessories by Skunkfunk, Gsus, Pussy Deluxe, Stoffrausch and other favourites of label-bunnies.

OVERKILL Map pp140-1 — Fashion
☎ 6107 6633; www.overkill.de, in German; Köpenicker Strasse 195a; ⊙ 11am-8pm Mon-Sat; ◉ Schlesisches Tor
What started as a graffiti magazine back in 1992 has evolved into one of Germany's top spots for streetwear. Now with four times the space, there's a mindboggling selection of limited-edition sneakers by Onitsuka Tiger, Converse and Asics alongside import threads by cult labels Stüssy, Carhartt and Rocksmith.

UKO FASHION Map pp140-1 — Fashion
☎ 693 8116; www.uko-fashion.de, in German; Oranienstrasse 201; ⊙ 11am-8pm Mon-Fri, to 4pm Sat; ◉ Görlitzer Bahnhof
High quality at low prices is the magic formula that has garnered this uncluttered clothing store a loyal clientele. It's a veritable gold mine for the latest girl threads by Pussy Deluxe and Muchacha, second-hand items from Esprit to Zappa and hot-label samples by Vero Moda, only and boyco.

UVR CONNECTED Map pp140-1 — Fashion
☎ 6981 4350; www.uvr-connected.de, in German; Oranienstrasse 36; ⊙ 11am-8pm Mon-Sat; ◉ Kottbusser Tor, Görlitzer Bahnhof
This deceptively large space holds what seems to be 1001 local and international streetwear labels by and for bright young things. Kit yourself out from top to bottom – the range includes hats, hoodies, T-shirts, dresses, jeans, shoes and jewellery – and much of it with an edge or a twist.

MARHEINEKE MARKTHALLE
Map pp140-1 — Food
☎ 398 9610; www.meine-markthalle.de, in German; Marheinekeplatz; ⊙ 8am-8pm Mon-Fri, to 6pm Sat; ◉ Gneisenaustrasse
The historic market hall has been updated for the 21st century and now brims with gourmet vendors selling regional and organic produce. Despite its somewhat sterile new look, sweet touches abound

(such as being asked if you want your apples polished). There's also a decent selection of food stalls for snacking, and spotless loos in the basement.

BOXOFFBERLIN Map pp140-1   Gifts & Souvenirs
☎ 4470 1555; www.boxoffberlin.de; Zimmerstrasse 11; ◷ 11am-8pm Mon-Sat; ◉ Kochstrasse
If the TV Tower fridge magnets or Reichstag snow globes in the stores around Checkpoint Charlie don't appeal, head a few steps west to Boxoffberlin, or Bob for short. Owners Torsten and Stephan ('the Bobs') have put together an assortment of quality Berlin souvenirs that ranges from hand-crocheted Berlin bears to Brandenburger Tor cookie cutters. Cap off a browse with a peek inside the gallery or a cuppa of fair-trade coffee in the cafe.

DIE IMAGINÄRE MANUFAKTUR
Map pp140-1   Gifts & Souvenirs
☎ 2850 3012; Oranienstrasse 26; ◷ 10am-7pm Mon-Fri, 11am-4pm Sat; ◉ Kottbusser Tor, Görlitzer Bahnhof
Blind and sight-impaired artisans have been hand-making traditional brooms and brushes in this mini factory-cum-store for over a century. More recently, the product palette has been expanded to include beautifully designed ceramics, wicker goods, wooden toys and all sorts of quirky souvenirs, such as brushes shaped like the Berlin bear or the Brandenburger Tor. Prices are very affordable and the store alone is worth a visit for the original 1920s interior.

HERRLICH Map pp140-1   Gifts & Souvenirs
☎ 6784 5395; www.herrlich-online.de in German; Bergmannstrasse 2; ◷ 10am-8pm Mon-Sat; ◉ Gneisenaustrasse
Next time you're looking for a gift for 'Him', peruse the racks of this fun store stocked with carefully culled men's delights. From retro alarm clocks to futuristic espresso machines – even a walking stick with hidden whisky flask – it's all here without a single sock or tie in sight.

HARDWAX Map pp140-1   Music
☎ 6113 0111; http://hardwax.com; 3rd fl, door A, 2nd courtyard, Paul-Lincke-Ufer 44a; ◷ noon-8pm Mon-Sat; ◉ Kottbusser Tor
In the epicentre of the electronic music scene, this well-hidden indie music store has been on the cutting edge for about

20 years. A must-stop for fans of techno, house, minimal, dubstep and whatever sound permutation comes along next.

SCRATCH RECORDS Map pp140-1   Music
☎ 6981 7591; www.scratchrecords.de; Zossener Strasse 31; ◷ 11am-7pm Mon-Wed, to 8pm Thu & Fri, to 4pm Sat; ◉ Gneisenaustrasse
A small but choice selection of soul, funk, electro, R&B, jazz and soundtracks on vinyl and CD – much of it hard-to-find imports and re-issues – forms the core of Scratch Records. The in-the-know staff will be only too happy to help you source a new favourite. Even the discount bin holds the occasional treasure.

SPACE HALL Map pp140-1   Music
☎ 694 7664; www.space-hall.de; Zossener Strasse 33; ◷ 11am-8pm Mon-Wed, to 10pm Thu & Fri, to 8pm Sat; ◉ Gneisenaustrasse
This galaxy for electronic music gurus has four floors filled with everything from acid to techno by way of drum and bass, neotrance, dubstep and whatever other genres take your fancy. Alas, it's not terribly well organised and staff – while extremely knowledgeable – can be tad snooty, so pack patience and you'll be fine.

FRIEDRICHSHAIN

As in other areas, Friedrichshain is coming up in the shopping department, with clothing boutiques and specialty stores sprinkled throughout the area around Boxhagener Platz and Sonntagstrasse and its side streets near Ostkreuz. Retail activity along Karl-Marx-Allee concentrates on Frankfurter Allee U-Bahn station, which is where you find an all-purpose mall (the Ring-Center) but also a couple of terrific Berlin designer stores, Berlinomat and F95. There's also a fun Sunday flea market on Boxhagener Platz and an antique market at Ostbahnhof.

GROSSER ANTIKMARKT AM
OSTBAHNHOF Map pp150-1   Antiques
Erich-Steinfurth-Strasse, Ostbahnhof; ◷ 9am-5pm Sun; ◉ Ostbahnhof
Exit the station's northern side and you're immediately greeted by a cheerful line of antiques and collectibles (such as old coins and banknotes, Iron Curtain–era relics, gramophone records, books, stamps and jewellery). There's also a good assortment of snack vendors to assuage hunger pangs.

top picks

MADE IN BERLIN

- Berlinomat (below)
- Berlinerklamotten (p185)
- Bonbonmacherei (p186)
- Die Imaginäre Manufaktur (p193)
- Flagshipstore (opposite)
- Lala Berlin (p185)
- Ta(u)sche (opposite)

BERLINOMAT off Map pp150-1   Berlin Fashion
☎ 4208 1445; www.berlinomat.com; Frankfurter Allee 89; ⏰ 11am-8pm Mon-Sat; ⓔ ⓡ Frankfurter Allee

This mini-department store presents the latest visions from a pool of around 150 Berlin creatives working in fashion, accessories, furniture and jewellery. Products are innovative and Zeitgeist-savvy, like a peppermill made from Berlin trees by Sawadee, kidney warmers by Kidney Karen and Volksmarke T Shirts. A selection of Berlinomat designs can also be found on the top floor of the Galeries Lafayette (p184) department store in Mitte and in a vending machine at the Hauptbahnhof (central train station).

EAST OF EDEN Map pp150-1   Books
☎ 423 9362; www.east-of-eden.de; Schreinerstrasse 10; ⏰ noon-7pm Mon-Fri, to 4pm Sat; ⓔ Samariterstrasse

This charismatic living room–type bookstore is crammed with used novels, nonfiction, cookbooks and other printed matter, mostly in English but with a few German and French works as well. On Tuesdays, it opens its stage for concerts, readings and performances, starting around 9.30pm.

F95 Map pp150-1   Fashion
☎ 4208 3358; Frankfurter Allee 95-97; ⏰ noon-8pm Mon-Fri, 11am-6pm Sat; ⓔ ⓡ Frankfurter Allee

The concept store of the Premium fashion fair, F95 is an outpost of icily smooth style. The taut collection of international and local labels attracts the pretty types to Friedrichshain to slap down credit cards for high-end denim brands, right-this-moment Maqua dresses, Filippa K separates, Veja trainers, and assorted fripperies such as tea, chocolate and perfume – all too cool for school.

FLOHMARKT AM BOXHAGENER PLATZ Map pp150-1   Flea Market
Boxhagener Platz; ⏰ 9am-4pm Sun; ⓔ ⓡ Warschauer Strasse, ⓔ Frankfurter Tor

Wrapping around leafy Boxhagener Platz, this is still one of the best flea markets in town. It's easy to sniff out the pros from the regular folks here to unload their spring-cleaning detritus for pennies. Best of all, it's just a java whiff away from cafes serving up big Sunday brunches.

RAW FLOHMARKT Map pp150-1   Flea Market
Revaler Strasse 99; http://raw-flohmarkt.de; ⏰ 8am-8pm Sun; ⓔ Warschauer Strasse

New since summer 2010, this smallish flea market is not yet as overrun as the established one on Boxhagener Platz, meaning there are still bargains galore. It sprawls among the derelict grounds of the former 19th-century train repair shop that's also home to Cassiopeia (p232) and the Skatehalle Berlin (p314).

MONDOS ARTS Map pp150-1   Gifts & Souvenirs
☎ 4201 0778; www.mondosarts.de, in German; Schreinerstrasse 6; ⏰ 10am-7pm Mon-Fri, 11am-4pm Sat; ⓔ Samariterstrasse

Cult and kitsch seem to be the GDR's strongest survivors at this funky little shop, named after a GDR-era brand of condoms. It's fun to browse even if you didn't grow up drinking Red October beer, falling asleep to the Sandmännchen (Little Sandman) TV show or listening to rock by the Puhdys.

PERLEREI Map pp150-1   Jewellery
☎ 9788 2028; www.perlerei.de; Lenbachstrasse 7; ⏰ noon-8pm Tue-Fri, to 6pm Sat; ⓡ Ostkreuz

Looking for a unique souvenir to bring back from Berlin? Simply make your own. Piece of jewellery, that is. Don't worry if you don't know how. At Meike Köster's bead boutique, you select your baubles and then turn them into beautiful necklaces, earrings, brooches or bracelets, with her help if you want it, at no extra charge, right there in the in-store workshop.

PRENZLAUER BERG

Kastanienallee and Oderberger Strasse are popular for Berlin-made fashions, with several designer stores just south of the U-Bahn station Eberswalder Strasse. More indie stores hold forth along Stargarder Strasse and in the streets around Helmholtzplatz, especially lower Dunckerstrasse. Cool-hunters should also steer to the Mauerpark and Arkonaplatz to forage for treasure at what are widely considered the best flea markets in town. For everyday needs stop by the Schönhauser Allee Arcaden mall right by the eponymous U-/S-Bahn station.

TA(U)SCHE Map pp156-7 Bags
☎ 4030 1770; www.tausche-berlin.de; Raumerstrasse 8; ⏱ 11am-8pm Mon-Fri, to 6pm Sat; Ⓔ Eberswalder Strasse
Heike Braun and Antje Strubels, both landscape architects by training, are the creative minds behind these ingenious messenger-style bags kitted out with exchangeable flaps that zip off and on in seconds. Bags come in seven sizes and start at €45, two flaps included. Additional ones can be purchased individually as can various inserts, depending on whether you need to carry a laptop, a camera, workout clothes or baby supplies. How handy is that?

EISDIELER Map pp156-7 Berlin Fashion
☎ 2839 1291; www.eisdieler.de; Kastanienallee 12; ⏱ noon-8pm Mon-Sat; Ⓔ Eberswalder Strasse
Cool as ice cream, the urban streetwear designed by this co-op is as tasty as the *gelati* that were once sold in the store before it was reincarnated as a clothes shop. Find T-shirts, jeans and other clothes created under the Eisdieler label, plus fashion and shoes by Onitsuka Tiger, Springcourt, Schmoove and Veja.

FLAGSHIPSTORE Map pp156-7 Berlin Fashion
☎ 4373 5327; www.flagshipstore-berlin.de; Oderberger Strasse 53; ⏱ noon-8pm Mon-Sat; Ⓔ Eberswalder Strasse
Beata and Johanna are geniuses when it comes to ferreting out the finest, limited-edition duds created by several dozen young Berlin labels (Hazelnut, Betty Bund or Slowmo, etc), plus a few imports, mostly from Scandinavia (eg Froks, Stylein). There's fashion for him and her, plus plenty of stylish accessories.

THATCHERS Map pp156-7 Berlin Fashion
☎ 2462 7751; www.thatchers.de; Kastanienallee 21; ⏱ noon-8pm Tue-Fri, to 6pm Sat; Ⓔ Eberswalder Strasse
Berlin fashion veterans Ralf Hensellek and Thomas Mrozek specialise in well-tailored

clothing that's feminine and versatile. Their smart dresses, skirts and shirts look almost plain on the rack but are transformed when worn into the sort of stylish garments that go from office to dinner to nightclub – and not hurriedly out of fashion. Also located at Court IV of the Hackesche Höfe (Map pp102-3; ☎ 2758 2210; Rosenthaler Strasse 40-41; ⏱ 11am-8pm Mon-Fri, to 6pm Sat; Ⓡ Hackescher Markt).

SAINT GEORGES Map pp156-7 Books
☎ 8179 8333; www.saintgeorgesbookshop.com; Wörther Strasse 27; ⏱ 11am-8pm Mon-Fri, to 7pm Sat; Ⓔ Senefelderplatz
Laid-back and low-key, Saint Georges' bookshop is a sterling spot to track down new and used Berlin-themed fiction and nonfiction, thanks to the helpful staff. The history section makes for some great time wasting (as do the Chesterfield couches).

SCHWARZER REITER Map pp156-7 Erotica
☎ 4503 4438; www.schwarzer-reiter.de; Torstrasse 3; ⏱ noon-8pm Mon-Sat; Ⓔ Rosa-Luxemburg Strasse
If you worship at the altar of hedonism, you'll find a wide range of accessories in this classy store decked out in sensuous black and purple. From rubber duckie vibrators, feather teasers and furry blindfolds to Edin DeSosa's sexy outfits and entire toy kits for curious beginners, there's plenty of cool stuff girls and boys with imagination might need for a night of naughtiness.

KOLLWITZPLATZMARKT
Map pp156-7 Farmers Market
Around Kollwitzplatz; ⏱ noon-7pm Thu, 9am-4pm Sat; Ⓔ Senefelderplatz
Berlin's poshest market has everything you need to put together a gourmet picnic or meal. Velvety gorgonzolas, juniper-berry smoked ham, crusty sourdough bread and homemade pesto are among the exquisite morsels scooped up by well-heeled locals. Lines can be long, so pack some patience. The Thursday edition has an organic focus, while the one that is held on Saturday also features handicrafts.

FLOHMARKT AM ARKONAPLATZ
Map pp156-7 Flea Market
Arkonaplatz; ⏱ 10am-5pm Sun; Ⓔ Bernauer Strasse
This smallish and moderately priced flea market feeds the retro frenzy with plenty

of groovy furniture, accessories, clothing, vinyl and books from the 1960s and '70s, much of it GDR-made. Fuel up in a nearby cafe then join the throngs of Berlin hipsters searching for half-buried treasure. This market is easily combined with a visit to the Flohmarkt am Mauerpark (below).

FLOHMARKT AM MAUERPARK
Map pp156-7   Flea Market

www.mauerparkmarkt.de, in German; Bernauer Strasse 63-64, Mauerpark, Wedding; ☽ 10am-5pm Sun; ◉ Eberswalder Strasse

This flea market, right on the one-time border, is something to behold on warm days when the sun is out (and so, it seems, is most of Berlin). There are all sorts of vendors, from T-shirt designers and students who've cleaned out their closets to down-at-heelers hawking trash. Follow up with a drink at the outdoor Mauersegler (p228) or a nap in the Mauerpark.

GOLDHAHN & SAMPSON   Map pp156-7 Food
☎ 4119 8366; www.goldhahnundsampson.de, in German; Dunckerstrasse 9; ☽ 8am-8pm Mon-Fri, 10am-8pm Sat; ◉ Eberswalder Strasse

Pink Himalaya salt, a gallery of fine oils and vinegars, handcrafted cheeses and crusty German breads are among the temptingly displayed delicacies at this posh food shop. Owners Sasha and Andreas personally source all items, most of them rare, organic and from small suppliers. For inspiration, nose around the cookbook library or book a class at the onsite cooking school.

LUXUS INTERNATIONAL
Map pp156-7   Gifts & Souvenirs

☎ 4432 4877; www.luxus-international.de, in German; Kastanienallee 101; ☽ 11am-8pm Mon-Fri, 1-7pm Sat; ◉ Eberswalder Strasse

There's no shortage of creative spirits in Berlin, but not many of them able to afford their own store. In comes Lexus International, a unique concept store that rents them a shelf or two to display their original designs: T-shirts, tote bags, ashtrays, lamps, candles, mugs. You never know what you'll find, but you can bet it's a Berlin original.

VEB ORANGE   Map pp156-7   Gifts & Souvenirs
☎ 9788 6886; www.veborange.de, in German; Oderberger Strasse 29; ☽ 10am-8pm Mon-Sat; ◉ Eberswalder Strasse

Viva retro! With its selection of the most beautiful things from the '60s and the '70s,

this place will remind you of how colourful, plastic and fun home decor once used to be. All kinds of orange kit, furnishings, accessories, lamps and fashions, much of it reflecting that irresistibly campy GDR spirit.

ZWISCHENZEIT   Map pp156-7   Gifts & Souvenirs
☎ 4467 3371; www.zwischenzeit.org, in German; Raumerstrasse 35; ☽ 2-7pm Mon-Fri, 11am-5pm Sat; ◉ Eberswalder Strasse

Berlin's retro-rage finds its perfect expression at this small but scintillating store where you can rummage through a rainbow assortment of crockery, furniture, board games, Krautrock vinyl and other vintage treats – all in better than good condition and sold at reasonable prices.

COLEDAMPF'S CULTURCENTRUM
Map pp156-7   Homewares

☎ 4373 5225; www.coledampfs.de, in German; Wörther Strasse 39; ☽ 10am-8pm Mon-Fri, to 6pm Sat; ◉ Senefelderplatz

The ultimate chef's playground, this store is stuffed with everything from the functional to the frivolous. From shiny copper pans to ravioli cutters, iced-tea glasses to espresso pots – you're sure to find something you can't live without among the 8000 or so items stocked here.

ROTATION RECORDS   Map pp156-7   Music
☎ 2532 9116; www.rotation-records.de; Weinbergsweg 3; ☽ noon-8pm Mon-Fri, 2-10pm Fri, 2-8pm Sat; ◉ Rosenthaler Platz

Click, click, click… is the sound of electroheads flipping through the in-the-know selection of what many consider Berlin's best store for techno, house, minimal and other electronic dance music, both new and used. Definitely a de rigueur stop for local and visiting DJs.

RATZEKATZ   Map pp156-7   Toys
☎ 681 9564; www.ratzekatz.de, in German; Raumerstrasse 7; ☽ 10am-7pm Mon-Sat; ◉ Eberswalder Strasse

This adorable store made headlines a few years ago when Angelina Jolie and son Maddox popped by to buy a Jurassic Park's worth of dinosaurs. Even without the celeb glow, it's a fine place to seek out quality playthings for kids from Siku cars and trucks to Ravensburger jigsaws, Lego and piles of plush toys.

top picks

- **Café Jacques** (p210)
- **Defne** (p211)
- **Cookies Cream** (p201)
- **Edd's** (p208)
- **Fischers Fritz** (p200)
- **Lavanderia Vecchia** (p210)
- **Reinstoff** (p203)
- **Schneeweiss** (p214)

What's your recommendation? www.lonelyplanet.com/berlin

EATING

If you crave traditional German comfort food, you'll find plenty of places to indulge in pork knuckles, smoked pork chops and calves' livers in Berlin. These days, though, 'typical' local fare is lighter, healthier, creative and more likely to come from gourmet kitchens, organic eateries and a UN worth of ethnic restaurants.

Even those finicky Michelin testers have confirmed that Berlin is ripe for the culinary big league by awarding coveted stars to no fewer than 12 chefs, including those helming the stoves at Facil (p205) and Weinbar Rutz (p203). Fortunately, you don't need deep pockets to put your tummy into a state of contentment. In fact, some of the best eating is usually done in neighbourhood restaurants like Café Jacques (p210) and Frau Mittenmang (p217) that feel as snug and comfortable as a warm mitten.

Meanwhile, Berlin's multicultural tapestry has brought the world's foods to town, from Austrian schnitzel to Zambian zebra steaks. Even finding decent sushi has become quite easy, despite Berlin being a landlocked city, and there's also a new crop of authentic Mexican eateries. Vegetarian (even vegan) restaurants, meanwhile, are sprouting as fast as alfalfa, as are bio eateries where dishes are prepared from organic and locally sourced ingredients.

Two more trends have emerged in recent times. First, Asian (especially Vietnamese) lifestyle eateries. The concept – steaming soups plus a few daily changing specials served in designer ambience – was pioneered a few years back by Monsieur Vuong (p204) and has since been copied ad nauseam. Among other Asian cuisines Thai and Indian are also popular, and even Korean restaurants are popping up increasingly. The other trend is 'guerrilla dining'. These are secret supper parties held in private homes for just a few weeks or at irregular intervals and often accessible by invitation only. See p213 for a roundup.

Berliners are big on breakfast and many cafes serve them until well into the afternoon. All-you-can-eat Sunday brunch buffets are a social institution in their own right, easily lasting a couple of hours, and provide an ideal excuse to recap Saturday night's shenanigans at leisure.

SPECIALITIES

Berlin Cuisine

If you want to try classic Berlin food, you better not be squeamish, a vegetarian, a health nut or a waist-watcher. Traditional dishes are hearty, rib-sticking and only give a passing nod to the vegetable kingdom. Pork is a staple, prepared in umpteen ways, including *Kasseler Rippchen* (smoked pork chops) and *Eisbein* (boiled pork hock), which is typically paired with sauerkraut, pureed peas and boiled potatoes. Other regulars are roast chicken, schnitzel and *Sauerbraten* (beef marinated in vinegar and spices), usually with sauerkraut and potatoes on the side. Minced meat tends to come in the form of a *Boulette*, a cross between a meatball and a hamburger, which is eaten with a little mustard and perhaps a dry roll. If local fish is on the menu, it'll most likely be *Zander* (pike-perch) or *Forelle* (trout).

Seasonal Specialities

What's white, hard and about 20cm long? Hey, not what you think, though dirty thoughts shall be forgiven in view of the unapologetically phallic shape of chlorophyll-deprived *Spargel* (white asparagus) that starts dominating menus in late April. Locavores will be pleased to hear that some of Germany's most celebrated erotic stalks hail from the sandy soils of Beelitz, just outside Berlin. The classic way to eat them is steamed alongside ham, hollandaise sauce and boiled potatoes, but chefs also whip up asparagus soup, quiches, salads and even ice cream.

Fresh fruit, especially all sorts of berries (strawberries, blueberries, raspberries, gooseberries, red currants) and cherries, brighten up the market stalls in summer. In late summer and early autumn, handpicked mushrooms such as *Steinpilze* (porcini) and loamy *Pfifferlinge* (chanterelles) show up in dishes everywhere. A typical winter meal is cooked *Grünkohl* (kale) with smoked sausage, which is a lot better than it sounds and often served at Christmas markets. *Gans* (stuffed goose) is a Martinmas tradition (November 11) and also popular at Christmas time.

GETTING VERSED IN WURST

Its aroma catches your nose like a crisp left hook. It's been ravenously gobbled up by chancellors, Madonna and George W, and has even been celebrated in popular song. 'It', of course, is the humble *Currywurst*, the iconic treat that's as much a part of Berlin's cultural tapestry as the Brandenburger Tor (Brandenburg Gate).

To the uncouth or uninitiated, we're talking about a smallish fried or grilled wiener sliced into bite-sized ringlets, swimming in a spicy tomato sauce and served on a flimsy paper plate with a plastic toothpick for stabbing. The wurst itself is subtly spiced and served with or without its crunchy epidermis.

The people of Hamburg might disagree, but Berliners know that their city is the true birthplace of this beloved calorie bomb. The first sausage started its triumphant course to snack stands across the nation from the steaming *Imbiss* (snack bar) of Herta Heuwer on 4 September 1949.

What exactly went into Herta's sauce will never be known, as in 1999 she took the secret to her grave. Her contribution to culinary history has garnered her a memorial plaque (Map pp124–5; Kantstrasse 101) where her *Imbiss* once stood.

There's always a healthy debate about where to find the best dog in town, but we're going to stick our necks out and share our very own favourite top three: Curry 36 (p214) in Kreuzberg, Konnopke's Imbiss (p217) in Prenzlauer Berg and Witty's (p209) organic wieners in Schöneberg. Pair 'em with *pommes rot-weiss* (fries with ketchup and mayo).

For more, check out *Best of the Wurst* (2004), a hilarious short film made by a Korean-American woman about her quest to get to know Berlin and its people one sausage at a time. See it for free at www.bestofthewurst.com.

Fast Food

International fast-food chains are ubiquitous, of course, but there's plenty of home-grown fast food as well. If there ever was a snack food with cult status, Berlin's humble *Currywurst* is it. A slivered, subtly spiced pork sausage swimming in tomato sauce and dusted with curry powder, it is as iconic to the German capital as the Fernsehturm (TV Tower). So what's the best 'wurst' place? See the boxed text, above, for our favourites.

The *Currywurst* competes with the *Döner* (doner kebab) for title of best hangover cure or prevention. The ultimate 'Turkish delight' is a lightly toasted bread pocket stuffed with thinly shaved veal or chicken, salad and doused with garlicky yoghurt sauce. In fact, the snack was invented in Berlin more than 25 years ago and there are now 1500 *Dönerias* in town.

Berlin polyglot society has also introduced Lebanese felafel, Californian burrito and Vietnamese pho. Global burger chains are getting some stiff competition from local joints popping up all over town.

WHERE TO EAT

Restaurants are often formal places with full menus, crisp white linen and high prices. Some restaurants are open for lunch and dinner only but more casual places tend to be open all day. Same goes for cafes, which usually serve both coffee and alcohol, as well as light meals, although ordering food is not obligatory. Fast-food joints are called *Imbiss* or *Schnellimbiss*. Sausage kiosks and *Dönerias* are ubiquitous and many bakeries serve sandwiches alongside pastries. Restaurant-clubs, where you can go straight from dining table to dance floor, have also been popping up in recent years.

VEGETARIANS & VEGANS

While Berlin could hardly be called a vegetarian paradise, animal-free cuisine is no longer an afterthought on most restaurant menus. Meat substitutes like tofu, tempeh and *seitan* (wheat gluten) have entered chefs' repertory and meals made with organic, local produce are plentiful. Gone are the days when joining your meathead friends for dinner meant filling up on uninspired salads or suspicious vegetable lasagne. In fact, these days they may well be joining *you* at that hot new veg-temple for veggie burgers with avocado-gorgonzola topping or Ayurvedic vegetable soup with sprouts and fresh herbs. Aside from dedicated vegetarian restaurants, Asian places generally have the best selection of meat-free dishes. We can only make a few suggestions on these pages (see p201), but you'll find more pointers, in German, at at http://veganleben.info /gastrolist.htm.

PRACTICALITIES
Opening Hours

One thing's for sure, you'll never go hungry in Berlin. Most restaurants and cafes are open daily, roughly from 11am to 11pm. Actual hours vary widely, though, depending on the location, time of year, the weather and even the mood of the proprietor. Practically all but the top nosh spots serve food throughout the day, although tables are predictably most crowded from 12.30pm to 2pm for lunch, and from 7.30pm to 10.30pm for dinner. If you get the midnight (or 3am) munchies, you'll usually find some *Döner*, falafel or sausage shops still doing brisk business, especially at weekends.

Hotels usually stop serving breakfast at 10am, although trendier joints will keep the buffet open until a more hangover-friendly 11am or even noon. But don't worry too much if you've overslept: most self-respecting Berlin cafes serve breakfast until well into the afternoon.

How Much?

Berlin offers fantastic value for money when it comes to food, and in this chapter we've given you a scrumptious spread of options to match all tastes and budgets. Even when you eat cheaply, you're spoiled for choice. For €3 or less, you can easily fill up on a grilled sausage, plump *Döner*, crispy falafel or a fresh sandwich. Cafes and many restaurants, including upmarket ones, offer weekday 'business lunches' under €10 that usually include an appetiser, main course and drink. For dinner at midpriced restaurants you should budget about €25 per person for a full meal, including beverage. At gourmet temples, though, the tab for à la carte dining or tasting menus can run €100 or higher.

Booking Tables

Reservations are essential at the top eateries and recommended for midrange restaurants – especially at dinnertime and at weekends. Berliners are big fans of eating out and tend to linger at the table, so if a place is full at 8pm it's likely that it will stay that way for a couple of hours.

Tipping

Though tipping is not compulsory, most people add about 10% to the bill for good service. It's customary to tip as you're handing over the money, rather than leaving change on the table. For example, say '30, *bitte*' if your bill comes to €28 and you want to give a €2 tip. If you have the exact amount – including

PRICE GUIDE

The following breakdown is a rough guide. A meal is defined as an appetiser, a main course and one drink at dinnertime.

€€€	over €25
€€	€10-25
€	under €10

the tip you wish to give – just say '*Stimmt so*' (that's fine).

If you're eating out as a group, it's perfectly fine for each party to pay separately (*getrennt*). Usually the server will go from person to person and calculate the amount each owes – to which you then add a tip at your own discretion.

Self-Catering

Several supermarket chains compete for shoppers throughout Berlin. Kaiser's and especially Reichelt have fresh meat, cheese and deli counters, and usually an attached bakery. Discount chains include Aldi, Lidl, Netto and Penny Markt, which all offer decent quality and selection, albeit in a rather helter-skelter, warehouse-style setting. For the ultimate selection, the food hall of the KaDeWe (p189) department store is simply unbeatable, but the prices reflect this. Farmers markets and small Turkish corner stores are also good food sources. 'Bio stores' that specialise in natural, organic, hormone-free and sustainable food are now fairly widespread in most of the central neighbourhoods.

HISTORIC MITTE

Mitte is awash with swanky restaurants where the decor is fabulous, the crowds cosmopolitan and menus stylish. Sure, some places may be more sizzle than substance, but the see-and-be-seen punters don't seem to mind. Genuine gourmets should focus on the Gendarmenmarkt area, where several innovative chefs have been crowned by the Michelin crew.

FISCHERS FRITZ Map pp76-7   International €€€
☎ 2033 6363; www.fischersfritzberlin.com;
Charlottenstrasse 49; 4-/5-/6-course dinner
€110/130/150; ☻ noon-2pm & 6.30-10.30pm;
🚇 Französische Strasse
At Berlin's only two-Michelin-star restaurant, Christian Lohse jazzes up fish and seafood

into a carnival of surprising flavour compositions. The dining room at the ultra-posh Regent Hotel is formal and fussy, so pack your manners along with your platinum card. The three-course lunch, though, is practically a steal at €47.

VAU Map pp76-7 International €€€
☎ 202 9730; www.vau-berlin.de; Jägerstrasse 54; mains lunch €18, dinner €38, 5-course menu €110; ⏰ noon-2.30pm & 7-10.30pm Mon-Sat; Ⓗ Hausvogteiplatz

In the same locale where Rahel Varnhagen held her literary salons a couple of centuries ago, Michelin-starred chef Kolja Kleeberg now pampers a Rolls Royce crowd of diners with his fanciful gourmet creations using regionally grown ingredients. In fine weather the courtyard tables beckon, although the interior – a cocktail of glass, steel, slate and wood by Meinhard von Gerkan – is well worth savouring along with the food.

UMA Map pp76-7 Japanese €€€
☎ 301 117 324; www.uma-restaurant.de; mains €15-38; ⏰ 6pm-midnight Mon-Sat; Ⓡ Brandenburger Tor, Ⓑ 100, 200, TXL

Uma is Berlin's guiding light when it comes to progressive Japanese cuisine. Aside from expertly cut sushi and sashimi, there are such classics as bison *shabu shabu* and lobster with pepper-mango relish, complemented by meaty mains from the *robata* (charcoal) grill. The airy dining room, accented with Asian artwork, also provides plenty of eye candy.

BORCHARDT Map pp76-7 French-German €€€
☎ 8188 6262; Französische Strasse 47; mains €18-28; ⏰ 11.30am-1am; Ⓗ Französische Strasse

They make one of the best wiener schnitzel in town, but many patrons come to this high-ceilinged brasserie to scan the crowd for power players, A-list babes and pasty-faced politicians – ever so discreetly, of course. The neo-baroque setting oozes tradition going back to 1853 when the place was founded by the chief caterer to the Prussian imperial court. Downsides: snooty servers and a steep bill.

BACKROOM CANTINA Map pp76-7 Fusion €€€
☎ 2758 2070; www.tausendberlin.com, in German; Schiffbauerdamm 11; mains €10-25; ⏰ from 7.30pm Tue-Sat; Ⓗ Ⓡ Friedrichstrasse

top picks
HERBIVOROUS HAVENS

- brennNessel (p295)
- Cookies Cream (below)
- Natural'mente (p207)
- Seerose (p212)
- Vöner (p215)

Magic is happening in the backroom of the stylish bar Tausend (p221), and foodies are all over it. Head chef The Duc Ngo creates culinary alchemy by effortlessly blending Japanese, Mediterranean and South American flavours. Seared tuna gets paired with foie gras and risotto, while raw fish is available both as sashimi and ceviche. Even the crème brûlée is cleverly infused with sweetened Asian azuki beans. Yum!

COOKIES CREAM Map pp76-7 Vegetarian €€€
☎ 2749 2940; www.cookiescream.com; Behrenstrasse 55; 3-course menu €32; ⏰ from 7pm Tue-Sat; Ⓗ Ⓡ Friedrichstrasse; Ⓥ

Combining coolness with substance, this is one of Berlin's favourite hidden restaurants, reached via the smelly service alley of the Westin Grand Hotel. Ring the bell to enter this elegantly industrial haven of flesh-free but flavour-packed dishes. It's all so good and gorgeous, even diehard meatheads should have no complaints. George Clooney and Robbie Williams certainly didn't.

SARAH WIENER IM HAMBURGER BAHNHOF Map pp76-7 Austrian €€
☎ 7071 3650; www.sarahwieners.de, in German; Invalidenstrasse 50-51; mains €13-20; ⏰ 10am-6pm Tue-Fri, 11am-8pm Sat, 11am-6pm Sun; Ⓗ Ⓡ Hauptbahnhof

Berlin's smartest museum cafe is the domain of culinary star Sarah Wiener, famous as much for her classic veal schnitzel as for her tasty Sachertorte and other classic Austrian cakes. The huge, high-ceilinged room gets texture from a long bar, patterned stone floor, dimmed lights and various conversation corners where artsy types discuss the latest exhibit.

GOOD TIME Map pp76-7 · Thai €€

☎ 2007 4870; www.goodtime-berlin.de; Hausvogteiplatz 11a; mains €10-19; ◷ noon-midnight; ◉ Hausvogteiplatz

It's good vibes all around at this gorgeous spot with a romantic garden courtyard and a Thai and Indonesian menu deeply inflected by the flavours of ginger, peanut and chilli. Satays, curries or an entire *rijstafel* spread (an elaborate buffet-style meal of Indonesian dishes served with steamed rice) – everything tastes genuine and fresh. Leave room for the honey-fried banana with vanilla ice cream.

SAGRANTINO Map pp76-7 · Italian €€

☎ 2064 6895; www.sagrantino-winebar.de; Behrenstrasse 47; mains €7.50-12.50; ◷ 7.30am-midnight Mon-Fri, 9am-noon & 5pm-midnight Sat; ◉ Französische Strasse

The ambience here is so classically Italian you'd half expect to see a sprawling vineyard out the window. That would be a vineyard in Umbria, for that's the region showcased at this fantastic little spot that usually gets mobbed at lunchtime for its good-value pasta salad (or soup) combos for a mere €5.90.

ISHIN Map pp76-7 · Japanese €€

☎ 2067 4829; www.ishin.de, in German; Mittelstrasse 24; platters €7-18; ◷ 11am-8pm Mon-Sat; ◉ ⊞ Friedrichstrasse

This bustling sushi parlour scores two for looks and 10 for value, especially when you order a combination platter where chefs often sneak in an extra piece or two. Prices drop even lower during happy hour (all day Wednesday and Saturday and 11am to 4pm on other days). Not in the mood for raw fish? Get one of the steaming rice bowls. Nice touch: the unlimited free green tea. Other branches include a handy one near Checkpoint Charlie in Kreuzberg (Map pp140-1; ☎ 6050 0172; Charlottenstrasse 16, enter on Zimmerstrasse; ◉ Kochstrasse).

MITTE – ALEXANDERPLATZ AREA

Trust us, we've tried, but we simply cannot find a restaurant right on Alexanderplatz that's worth precious ink, so if you do, we're all ears. Your best bets (for traditional German and, surprise, sushi) are in the Nikolaiviertel.

For an informal self-service lunch, you could also steer towards the cafeteria of the Berliner Wasserbetriebe (Berlin Water Works; p98).

ZUR LETZTEN INSTANZ

Map p96 · German €€

☎ 242 5528; www.zurletzteninstanz.de; Waisenstrasse 14-16; mains €9-18; ◷ noon-1am Mon-Sat; ◉ Klosterstrasse

Oozing folksy, Old Berlin charm, this rustic eatery has been an enduring hit since 1621 and has fed everyone from Napoleon to Beethoven to Angela Merkel. It's still one of the best places in town for classic Berlin rib-stickers such as *Eisbein* and *Bouletten* (meat patties).

STEEL SHARK Map p96 · Japanese €€

☎ 2576 2461; www.steelshark.de; Propststrasse 1; *nigiri* €2.10-3.70, *maki* €2.20-5.30; ◷ 11.30am-10pm Mon-Sat, 3-10pm Sun; ◉ ⊞ Alexanderplatz

We're usually leery of cheap sushi, but we'll make an exception for this hole-in-the-wall tucked into a hidden corner in the Nikolaiviertel. All morsels are carefully assembled and feature thick cuts of fresh fish and perfectly cooked rice. Best of all: they deliver. Order by phone or online. Also in northern Neukölln (Map pp140-1; ☎ 6298 3503; Karl-Marx-Strasse 13; ◉ Hermannplatz).

DOLORES Map p96 · American €

☎ 2809 9597; www.dolores-online.de, in German; Rosa-Luxemburg-Strasse 7; burrito €4-6; ◷ 11.30am-10pm Mon-Fri, 1-10pm Sat & Sun; ◉ ⊞ Alexanderplatz; ♥

A lunchtime favourite, Dolores wins hearts and tummies with the best burritos this side of San Francisco's Mission district. Select your preferred combo of meats (the lime cilantro chicken is yummy) or tofu, rice, beans, veggies, cheese and salsa and the cheerful staff will build it for you on the spot. Great homemade lemonade, too.

MITTE – SCHEUNENVIERTEL

Berlin's only genuine 'old town', the Scheunenviertel is wonderfully chain-free and packed with so much culinary variety you could eat your way around the world in a day. Practically all tastes, budgets and food neuroses are catered for in eateries ranging from fast-food institutions to healthnut havens, ho-hum tourist joints to Michelin-starred gourmet haunts.

WEINBAR RUTZ Map pp102-3 German €€€
☎ 2462 8760; www.rutz-weinbar.de; Chausseestrasse 8; bar mains €10.50-23.50, 4-/5-/6-course bar menu €62/76/90; ☒ 4-11pm Tue-Sat; ◉ Oranienburger Tor
With one Michelin star decorating his toque, Marco Müller cooks up high-concept cuisine in his upstairs gourmet temple but we actually prefer the downstairs bar, where prices and grub are considerably more down-to-earth. The menu features artisanal Iberian hams and robust German dishes such as the signature Saumagen burger (kind of a German haggis) or granny-style beef rouladen. Grape geeks go ga-ga over the huge wine cellar; many vintages are available by the glass. Great rieslings!

REINSTOFF Map pp102-3 Gourmet €€€
☎ 3088 1214; www.reinstoff.eu; Schlegelstrasse 26c; mains €38-98, 4-/5-/6-/8-course dinner €59/74/89/119; ☒ 7-11pm Tue-Sat; ◉ Nordbahnhof

top picks

BERLIN'S BEST FOR...

- Celebrity spotting Grill Royal (right)
- Museum cafe Sarah Wiener im Hamburger Bahnhof (p201)
- Newcomer Reinstoff (above)
- Old Berlin Zur Letzten Instanz (opposite)
- Pizza Il Casolare (p211)
- Tapas Mar y Sol (p206)
- Vegetarian Cookies Cream (p201)
- With kids Charlottchen (p207)

It took culinary wunderkind Daniel Achilles only six months to snap up a Michelin star and the accolades keep rolling in. The young chef cooks up cuisine 'for the senses' by creating a sort of molecular regional menu. Sample compositions: duck liver with cocoa and mango or Norwegian lobster poached in vanilla milk with cauliflower and almond cream. Out there? Perhaps, but your tastebuds will do summersaults.

GRILL ROYAL Map pp102-3 International €€€
☎ 2887 9288; www.grillroyal.com, in German; Friedrichstrasse 105b; mains €12-39, steaks €16-55; ☒ from 6pm; ◉ ◉ Friedrichstrasse
A platinum card is a handy accessory at this 'look-at-me' temple where power politicians, A-listers, Russian oligarchs, pouty models and 'trust-afarians' can be seen slurping oysters and tucking into their Wagyu steak. No complaints about the quality of the food or the sensibly sensuous decor, even if the service doesn't always measure up. The entrance is on the canal side below the hotel.

SCHWARZWALDSTUBEN
Map pp102-3 German €€
☎ 2809 8084; Tucholskystrasse 48; dishes €6-14; ☒ 9am-midnight; ◉ Oranienburger Strasse
The ironic olde-worlde decor is as delicious as the authentic southern German food served in gut-busting portions at this hipster hunting lodge. We can't get enough of the *geschmelzte Maultaschen* (sautéed ravioli-like pasta) and the schnitzel (ask for extra lemon!), but we hear the pizza-like *Flammekuche* is a winner too. Everything goes down well with a glass of Rothaus Tannenzäpfle beer, straight from the Black Forest. Reservations advised at dinnertime.

CHI SING Map pp102-3 Asian €€
☎ 2008 9284; www.chising-berlin.de; Rosenthaler Strasse 62; mains €13-16; ☒ noon-1am; ◉ Rosenthaler Platz; Ⓥ
A fleet of white silk origami blossoms sway below the ceiling of this mod Viet house, as delicate and pretty as the dishes streaming from the busy kitchen. From noodle soups to grilled meats, all is fresh, light and brimming with complex aromas. Tip: on weekdays from noon to 6pm a special 'business lunch' menu features six dishes costing just €4, but you do have to ask for it. Order

one for a mid-shopping snack or combine several for a full meal.

SUSURU Map pp102-3 — Asian €€

☎ 211 1182; www.susuru.de, in German; Rosa-Luxemburg-Strasse 17; mains €6.50-9; ⏰ 11.30am-11.30pm; ⊚ Rosa-Luxemburg-Platz; Ⓥ
Go ye forth and slurp! *Susuru* is Japanese for slurping and, quite frankly, that's the best way to deal with the big bowls of steaming *udon* at this noodle bar that's as neat and stylish as a bento box. We also love the rock shrimp appetizer and the chocolate-mint 'spring roll' dessert.

YAM YAM Map pp102-3 — Modern Korean €€

☎ 2463 2485; www.yamyam-berlin.de; Alte Schönhauser Strasse 6; mains €5.50-8; ⏰ noon-11pm Mon-Sat, noon-10pm Sun; ⊚ Rosa-Luxemburg-Platz
In a dashing move of career derring-do, Sumi Ha has morphed her fancy fashion boutique into a stylish Korean bijou with all-white decor and piles of international magazines. International too is the crowd that chows down on *bibimbap* (a spicy rice dish), mung-bean pancakes, seaweed rolls and other exotic offerings. Grazers should bring a friend and order the Banzan Set for two, composed of nine dishes.

STRANDBAD MITTE Map pp102-3 — Cafe €€

☎ 2462 8963; www.strandbad-mitte.de, in German; Kleine Hamburger Strasse 16; breakfast €5-12, mains €4.50-13.50; ⏰ 9am-2am; ⓡ Oranienburger Strasse;
In a quiet cul-de-sac, this is a popular breakfast joint (served until 4pm), especially with families who appreciate the playground just opposite. Also a good spot for a quick lunch or supper composed of organic ingredients whenever possible.

ATAME Map pp102-3 — Spanish €€

☎ 2804 2560; www.atame-tapasbar.de; Dircksenstrasse 40; tapas & dishes €2-12; ⏰ from 10am Mon-Fri, 11am Sat & Sun; ⊚ Weinmeisterstrasse
The Spanish tapas tradition translates well to the easy-going Berlin lifestyle but oddly there aren't many good bars around. Atame, although right in tourist central, does a better job than most with its a colourfully tiled bar, smiling Spanish staff and delicious nibbles served in satisfying portions. The *boquerones fritos* (fried

sardines) and the *mojama con almendras* (dried tuna with almonds) are recommended.

SPAGHETTI WESTERN Map pp102-3 Italian €€

☎ 2033 9011; www.spaghettiwestern.de, in German; Torstrasse 179; mains €5.50-11; ⏰ noon-midnight Mon-Fri, 6pm-midnight Sat & Sun; ⊚ Rosenthaler Platz, Oranienburger Tor
On restaurant row along Torstrasse you'll find the good, the bad and the ugly. Fortunately, Spaghetti Western fits in the first category and you won't have to spend a fistful of dollars to eat well here. The menu is as its says: pasta in all its glorious variations, paired with shrimp, *salsiccia* (spicy sausage) or veal, stuffed with ricotta and spinach or served classic Bolognese- or carbonara-style.

MONSIEUR VUONG

Map pp102-3 — Vietnamese €€
☎ 9929 6924; www.monsieurvuong.de; Alte Schönhauser Strasse 46; mains €7.40; ⏰ noon-midnight; ⊚ Weinmeisterstrasse, Rosa-Luxemburg-Platz
Berlin's 'godfather' of upbeat Indochina nosh-stops, Monsieur has been copied many times – his concept is just that good. Pick from a compact menu of flavour-packed soups and two or three oft-changing mains, then sit back and enjoy your leftover money. Amazingly, the quality hasn't come down despite the tourist invasion and never-ending queue. Come in the afternoon to avoid the frenzy.

CAFÉ NORD-SUD Map pp102-3 — French €

☎ 9700 5928; Auguststrasse 87; 3-course menu €7.50; ⏰ noon-3pm & 6-11pm Mon-Sat; ⓡ Oranienburger Strasse, ⊚ Oranienburger Tor
Truth be told, this place we'd rather keep secret. It's just one of those little gems, you know, always packed to the rafters thanks to Jean-Claude's Gallic charm, the kitchen's considerable skills and, let's face it, the rock-bottom prices. A mere €7.50 for three courses, even at dinnertime – how do they do it? Don't ask: score a table and find out.

DADA FALAFEL Map pp102-3 Middle Eastern €

☎ 0179-510 5435; www.dadafalafel.de, in German; Linienstrasse 132; dishes €3-7; ⏰ 10am-2am; ⊚ Oranienburger Tor
Famished tourists mix with local loyalists at this teensy pit stop with jazzy decor

for freshly prepared falafel doused with a tangy homemade sauce. Skip the shwarma; it can be on the greasy side.

SCHLEMMERBUFFET
Map pp102-3   Middle Eastern €
☎ 283 2153; Torstrasse 125; dishes €2.50-7; ❧ 24hr; ◉ Rosenthaler Platz
One of the best *Döners* in town. Enough said.

POTSDAMER PLATZ & TIERGARTEN

Most of Tiergarten's eating options are as exalted as you'd expect from a neighbourhood populated by diplomats, politicians and business execs. For a quick nibble, head to the basement food court in the Potsdamer Platz Arkaden (p187) mall.

FACIL Map p112   French €€€
☎ 590 051 234; www.facil-berlin.de; Mandala Hotel, Potsdamer Strasse 3; 1-/2-/3-course lunch €18/28/39, dinner mains €16-55, 4-/8-course dinner €85/140; ❧ noon-3pm & 7-11pm Mon-Fri; ◉ ⊛ Potsdamer Platz
This glass palace inside the Mandala Hotel (p272) is one of the city's most breathtaking dining rooms with its clean lines, sleek Donghia chairs and honey-hued natural stone. Top toque Michael Kempf constantly finds new ways to keep foodies happy. Dishes such as vanilla-braised bison with pea and pancetta puree or Charolais beef fillet with Swiss-chard ravioli are inspired flavour combos without excessive flights of fancy. Budget gourmets should come for lunch.

top picks

TOT-FRIENDLY EATERIES

Don't even think twice about bringing kids to cafes and casual restaurants, where highchairs are standard. Taking them to upmarket ones, though, might raise eyebrows, especially at dinnertime. The following places go the extra mile to make little ones comfortable.

- Charlottchen (p207)
- Desbrosses (right)
- Krokodil (p218)
- Tomasa (p211)
- Trattoria Venezia (p211)

DESBROSSES Map p112   French €€€
☎ 337 776 340; www.desbrosses.de; Ritz-Carlton Berlin, Potsdamer Platz 3; mains €15-32; ❧ 6.30-10.30am & 11.30am-11.30pm; ◉ ⊛ Potsdamer Platz
At the heart of this French brasserie is an open kitchen with a classic, race-car red enamel oven and toqued chefs turning out upmarket French country classics – bouillabaisse to foie gras *fruit de mer* (seafood). Be sure not to OD on the crusty breads made in the onsite *boulangerie*. Also look for special promotions like the all-you-can-eat oyster feast (€29) or the Sunday champagne brunch (€78) with unlimited supplies of bubbly.

BALIKCI ERGÜN off Map p112   Turkish €€
☎ 397 5737; S-Bahn arch at Lüneburger Strasse 382; mains €7-12; ❧ 3pm-midnight; ⊛ Bellevue
If it weren't for the occasional humming of the S-Bahn running above, you'd think you were in seaside Turkey in this funky fish parlour that's been packing 'em in since 1992. No gimmicks here, just fresh fish, fried or grilled and served with nothing but lemon and warm fluffy bread. Pair it with a side of crunchy salad and a glass of Doluca and you may understand the profusion of compliments scribbled on note cards and forming a mobile.

VAPIANO Map p112   Italian €€
☎ 2300 5005; www.vapiano.de; Potsdamer Platz 5; mains €5.50-8.50; ❧ 11am-midnight Mon-Sat, to 11pm Sun; ◉ ⊛ Potsdamer Platz
Matteo Thun's jazzy decor is a great foil for the tasty Italian fare at the Potsdamer Platz outpost of this quickly proliferating German chain. Mix-and-match pastas, creative salads and crusty pizzas are all prepared à la minute before your eyes. Nice touch: a condiment basket with fresh basil. Your order is recorded on a chip card and paid for upon leaving. There are other branches in town, including one in Charlottenburg (Map p128; ☎ 8871 4195; Augsburger Strasse 43; ❧ 10am-midnight Mon-Sat, 11am-11pm Sun; ◉ Kurfürstendamm).

WEILANDS WELLFOOD
Map p112   International €€
☎ 2589 9717; www.weilands-wellfood.de, in German; meals €4-9; Marlene-Dietrich-Platz 1; ❧ 9.30am-midnight daily Apr-Oct, 10am-9.30pm Mon-Sat Nov-Mar; ◉ ⊛ Potsdamer Platz; 🛜 Ⓥ

The whole-wheat pastas, vitamin-packed salads and fragrant wok dishes at this upbeat self-service bistro are perfect for health- and waist-watchers but don't sacrifice a lick to the taste gods. Sit outside by a little pond, ideally outside the office-jockey lunch rush. There's another branch in Kreuzberg (Map pp140-1; ☎ 5015 4632; Bergmannstrasse 5-7; ⏰ 9.30am-midnight daily Apr-Sep, 11.30am-9.30pm Tue-Fri, 9.30am-6pm Sat & Sun Oct-Mar), which serves brunch on weekends (€8).

CHARLOTTENBURG & NORTHERN WILMERSDORF

The crowd may be packing bulging billfolds, driving BMWs and on familiar terms with Botox, but all in all, dining in subdued Charlottenburg is dependable and quality is rather high. Life pulsates around Savignyplatz, which exudes the relaxed and bustling vibe of an Italian piazza on balmy summer nights. Along Kantstrasse is a gaggle of more casual but excellent Asian and Spanish eateries. The residential streets south of Schloss Charlottenburg and off Ku'damm yield some great off-the-beaten-track finds.

DUKE Map p128   International €€€
☎ 683 154 000; www.duke-restaurant.com; Ellington Hotel, Nürnberger Strasse 50-55; 2-/3-course lunch €13/18.50, 5-course dinner €60, dinner mains €12.50-29; ⏰ 11.30am-midnight; Ⓢ Augsburger Strasse
If the words 'hotel restaurant' induce involuntary shudders, rest assured that Duke at the Ellington Hotel (p273) is a happy exception. Chef Carsten Obermayr pairs punctilious craftsmanship with local farm-fresh ingredients resulting in such dishes as Barbary duck with orange chicory or monkfish with saffron tomatoes. Budget gourmets should come for the weekday lunch specials with free mineral water and coffee.

BOND Map p128   International €€€
☎ 5096 8844; www.bond-berlin.de; Knesebeckstrasse 16; mains €13-27; ⏰ 6pm-midnight Tue-Sat, 10am-3pm Sun; Ⓢ Savignyplatz
If you're in Berlin On Her Majesty's Secret Service, you'll impress The Living Daylights out of your date at this chill designer den drenched in glamorous purple, ebony and

gold with a graffiti-style mural by local artists M:M tossed in for Berlin street cred. The standard menu is heavy on, well, standards, like grilled meats, club sandwiches and quality burgers, but to test the chef's true talents order one of the biweekly specials. Cheap it ain't but remember, You Only Live Twice.

MAR Y SOL Map p128   Spanish €€
☎ 313 2593; www.marysol-berlin.de; Savignyplatz 5; tapas €3-7, mains €14-20; ⏰ 11am-1am; Ⓢ Savignyplatz
This top tapas spot beautifully captures the sultry mood of Andalusia. On balmy nights, tables on the fountain-studded, tiled patio are a hot commodity, while in winter the dark-wood dining room lends a homey feel. The astonishing array of palate ticklers includes bacon-wrapped dates, spicy sardines and honey-and-pine-nut-coated chicken, while the New Zealand lamb chops make a winning main course.

CAFÉ BREL Map p128   European €€
☎ 3180 0020; www.cafebrel.de, in German; Savignyplatz 1; 3-course lunch €9, mains €11-18; ⏰ 9am-1am; Ⓢ Savignyplatz
Named for cult crooner Jacques Brel, this corner bistro in a former bordello now draws bleary-eyed bohos for coffee and croissants, suits and tourists for €9 lunches and stylish Francophile couples for frog legs, steaks and snails at dinnertime. Belgian expats invade for the superb moules frites during mussel season (September to February).

MOON THAI Map p128   Thai €€
☎ 3180 9743; www.moonthai-restaurant.com, in German; Kantstrasse 32; mains €8.50-14.50; ⏰ noon-midnight Mon-Fri, 1pm-midnight Sat & Sun; Ⓢ Savignyplatz; Ⓥ
Orange walls accented with exotic art create a feel-good ambience at this family affair serving classic Thai dishes with more than a modicum of authenticity. Anything revolving around duck or squid is excellent and even the seitan dishes strut their stuff when paired with fresh vegetables and bold spices.

GOOD FRIENDS Map p128   Chinese €€
☎ 313 2659; Kantstrasse 30; mains €8-16; ⏰ noon-2am; Ⓢ Savignyplatz

Sinophiles tired of the Kung Pao school of Chinese cooking know this Cantonese stalwart serves the real thing. The ducks dangling in the window are merely the overture to a menu long enough to confuse Confucius. If jellyfish with eggs or fried fish-head soup sound too much like a *Survivor* challenge, you can always fall back on, well, Kung Pao chicken.

CAFÉ IM LITERATURHAUS
Map pp124-5   Cafe €€
☎ 882 5414; www.literaturhaus-berlin.de, in German; Fasanenstrasse 23; mains €8-16; ⊙ 9.30am-1am; ⊖ Uhlandstrasse
The hustle and bustle of Ku'damm is only a block away from this genteel oasis in an Art Nouveau villa. Get a dose of Old Berlin flair in the gracefully stucco-ornamented rooms or, in fine weather, repair to the idyllic garden for breakfast (until 2pm), coffee, a glass of wine paired with excellent cheeses or a weekly changing menu of bistro delights.

CHARLOTTCHEN Map pp124-5   International €€
☎ 324 4717; www.charlottchen-berlin.de, in German; Droysenstrasse 1; mains €5-12.50; ⊙ 3-10pm Mon-Fri, 10am-10pm Sat & Sun; ⊖ Charlottenburg
Kids get their kicks at this adorable cafe-cum-indoor-playground-cum-theatre designed with them in mind. While they chow down on spaghetti, pizza or fish sticks, grown-ups can treat their palate to meat-free casseroles, classic German dishes

(roast pork in beer sauce) or crunchy salads. Organic and locally sourced ingredients are used whenever possible, but breakfast is served on weekends only.

JULES VERNE Map p128   International €€
☎ 3180 9410; www.jules-verne-berlin.de, in German; Schlüterstrasse 61; breakfast €4-9, 2-course lunch €5.50-7.50, dinner mains €7-17.50; ⊙ 9am-1am; ⊖ Savignyplatz
Jules Verne was a well-travelled man, so it's only fitting that a cafe bearing his name would feature a globetrotting menu. French *flammekuche*, Austrian schnitzel and North African couscous are all perennial bestsellers. It's also a great 'greet-the-day' spot with substantial breakfasts named after Verne's books served until 3pm. Bonus: the pile of international periodicals.

NATURAL'MENTE Map pp124-5   Vegetarian €€
☎ 341 4166; www.naturalmente.de, in German; Schustehrusstrasse 26; mains €8-12; ⊙ noon-3.30pm Mon-Fri; ⊖ Richard-Wagner-Platz; Ⓥ
This Macrobiotic Society-run resto has been supplying herbivores with reliable, healthy and organic lunches long before vegetarianism became sexy. It's got a bit of an institutional feel but is a nicely untouristed spot to break up a day of sightseeing in nearby Schloss Charlottenburg.

SCHLEUSENKRUG Map pp124-5   German €€
☎ 313 9909; www.schleusenkrug.de, in German; Tiergarten locks, Müller-Breslau-Strasse; breakfast

---

NOW EAT THIS: BERLIN'S FARMERS MARKETS

Practically every Berlin *Kiez* (neighbourhood) has its own weekly or biweekly farmers market, but these are our favourites:

Karl-August-Platz Farmers Market (Map pp124-5; Karl-August-Platz, Charlottenburg; ⊙ 8am-1pm Wed, to 2pm Sat; ⊖ Wilmersdorfer Strasse) Fresh fruit and veg plus artisanal cheeses, pesto etc, on a beautiful square around a neo-Gothic church.

Kollwitzplatzmarkt (Map pp156-7; Kollwitzplatz, Prenzlauer Berg; ⊙ noon-7pm Thu, 9am-4pm Sat; ⊖ Senefelderplatz) Posh player with velvety gorgonzola, juniper-berry smoked ham, homemade pesto and other exquisite morsels. The Thursday market is smaller and all organic. Kids' playground nearby. See also p195.

Ökomarkt Chamissoplatz (Map pp140-1; www.oekomarkt-chamissoplatz.de, in German; Chamissoplatz, Kreuzberg; ⊙ 8am-2pm Sat; ⊖ Mehringdamm, Gneisenaustrasse) One of the oldest and largest organic farmers markets in Berlin (operating since 1994) on a pretty square in the Bergmannkiez with adjacent playground.

Türkenmarkt (Map pp140-1; Maybachufer, Kreuzberg; ⊙ noon-6.30pm Tue & Fri; ⊖ Schönleinstrasse) Bazaar-like canalside market with bargain-priced produce and a bonanza of Mediterranean deli fare (olives, feta, etc). Also see p192.

Winterfeldtmarkt (Map p136; Winterfeldtplatz, Schöneberg; ⊙ 8am-2pm Wed, to 4pm Sat; ⊖ Nollendorfplatz) Local institution with quality produce alongside artsy-crafty stuff and global snack stands. Also see p189.

& mains €6.50-12; ⊗ from 10am May-Sep or Oct, 11am-7pm Mon-Fri, 10am-7pm Sat & Sun Oct-Apr; ⊙ ⊛ Zoologischer Garten

Sitting pretty on the edge of the Tiergarten, next to a Landwehr canal lock, Schleusenkrug truly comes into its own in summer when the beer garden kicks into full swing. Finding a weathered table can be a tall order in fine weather when people from all walks of life hunker at weathered tables over mugs of foamy beer and satisfying comfort food, from grilled sausages to Flammkuche (Alsatian pizza) and seasonal offerings. Breakfast is served until 3pm.

ROGACKI pp124-5 — German €€

☎ 343 8250; www.rogacki.de, Wilmersdorfer Strasse 145; meals €4-15; ⊗ 9am-6pm Mon-Wed, 9am-7pm Thu, 8am-7pm Fri, 8am-4pm Sat; ⊙ Bismarckstrasse

Family-run since 1928, it's chiefly a deli that's a foodie's daydream with separate counters stocked with cheeses, cold cuts, bread, game, salads, smoked fish (done inhouse) and whatever else demanding palates desire. Put together a picnic-to-go, or stay put and join the locals crowded around the stand-up tables for oysters and wine, a feisty stew or a plate of pasta.

ALI BABA Map p128 — Italian €

☎ 881 1350; www.alibaba-berlin.de, in German; Bleibtreustrasse 45; dishes €3-9; ⊗ 11am-2am Sun-Thu, to 3am Fri & Sat; ⊛ Savignyplatz

Everybody feels like family at this been-here-forever port of call where the pizza is cheap, the pasta piping hot and even the most expensive meat dish (pork filet in gorgonzola sauce) costs only €9. Popular with party people and posh Charlottenburgers in the mood to go slumming.

SCHÖNEBERG

If you're not sure what you're hungry for, take the U-Bahn to Nollendorfplatz and start pacing south. Chances are you'll find some favourite among the two dozen or so eclectic nosherias between the station and Haupt-strasse. Expect affordable food from Tur-key, India, Nepal, Thailand, Greece, Canada and so on, but no serious culinary flights of fancy. If you want those, head to the 6th floor food hall of the KaDeWe (p189) department store. There's also a bustling

top picks

GOING GOURMET

- Edd's (below)
- Facil (p205)
- Hartmanns (p210)
- Reinstoff (p203)
- Vau (p201)
- Weinbar Rutz (p203)

farmers market, the Winterfeldtmarkt (p189) on Saturdays.

EDD'S Map p136 — Thai €€€

☎ 215 5294; www.edds-thairestaurant.de, in German; Lützowstrasse 81; mains €15-25; ⊗ 11.30am-3pm & 6pm-midnight Tue-Fri, 5pm-midnight Sat, 2pm-midnight Sun; ⊙ Kurfürstenstrasse

Edd's grandma used to cook for Thai royals and the man himself has regaled Berlin foodies for over three decades with such palate-pleasers as twice-roasted duck and banana-blossom salad with shrimp. Budget gourmets invade for the €7.50 lunch menu. Dinner reservations essential.

CAFÉ EINSTEIN STAMMHAUS

Map p136 — Austrian €€€

☎ 261 5096; www.cafeeinstein.com, in German; Kurfürstenstrasse 58; breakfast €6-15, mains €15-21; ⊗ 8am-1am; ⊙ Nollendorfplatz

In a gorgeous villa that was once the home of silent movie star (and Goebbels mistress) Henny Porten, Berlin's finest Viennese coffeehouse is the living room of mon-eyed, genteel types indulging in oysters with champagne or tucking into succulent schnitzel or perky goulash. Marble table-tops, jumbo-sized mirrors and high stucco-trimmed ceilings create a stylish setting, although we wouldn't mind if the staff laid off the snootiness. The upstairs bar opens at 7pm.

MORE Map p136 — International €€

☎ 2363 5702; www.more-berlin.de; Motzstrasse 28; mains lunch €4.50-16.50, dinner €9.50-24.50; ⊗ 9am-midnight; ⊙ Nollendorfplatz

In the heart of queer Schöneberg, More's a designer den with substance. Sip a cab driver cocktail while casually scanning the crowd for pretty boyz and anticipating big inspired salads, succulent rump steak or lamb drizzled with Rioja jus. Busy from 'morn to night, and for good reason.

LA COCOTTE Map p136 French €€

☎ 7895 7658; www.lacocotte.de, in German; Vorbergstrasse 10; mains €10-20; ⏰ 6pm-1am; ⊖ Eisenacher Strasse

This place is so fantastically French you half expect to see the Eiffel Tower around the corner. The menu plays it more country than *haute* with boeuf bourguignon, bouillabaisse and *escargots* (snails) all making appearances. The signatures dishes, though, are the gutsy stews where you can choose from a selection of herbs – anything from rosemary to tarragon – to customise the flavour.

OUSIES Map p136 Mediteranean €€

☎ 216 7957; www.taverna-ousies.de; Grune-waldstrasse 16; small plates €3-9; mains €10-18; ⏰ from 7pm; ⊖ Eisenacher Strasse

You'll be as exuberant as Zorba himself at this hugely popular *ouzeria,* the Greek equivalent of a tapas bar. Assemble a posse of friends and sample all sorts of tantalising dishes, from *stifado* (beef stew) to *spetsofai* (homemade farmers' sausage) to spinach-stuffed sardines. We hear the meaty mains are great too, but we've never made it that far. Reservations advised.

MAULTASCHEN MANUFAKTUR
Map p136 German €€

☎ 0178-564 7645; www.maultaschen-manufaktur.de, in German; Lützowstrasse 22; dishes €7-10; ⏰ 5-10.30pm Mon-Sat; ⊖ Kurfürstenstrasse

If ravioli and dumplings had kids, they would look something like *Maultaschen,* a traditional dish from southern Germany. At this unfussy joint they're made fresh daily and served in soup, fried or paired with potato salad. The classic version is stuffed with meat but here they also have herbivore versions bulging with spinach and mozzarella or tomato and feta.

HISAR Map p136 Middle Eastern €€

☎ 216 5125; www.hisar-restaurant.de, in German; Yorckstrasse 49; takeaway €2-5, restaurant €9-18; ⏰ 10am-midnight; ⏹ Yorckstrasse

Hisar has kept the Turkish red-and-white flag flying next to the Yorckstrasse S-Bahn station since 1986. There's almost always a

queue of folks salivating for their fantastic doner kebabs, but for the full gamut of Anatolian cuisine, report to the attached two-storey restaurant. Grilled meats are a house speciality.

JOSEPH ROTH DIELE Map p136 German €

☎ 2636 9884; www.joseph-roth-diele.de, in German; Potsdamer Strasse 75; dishes €4-9; ⏰ 10am-midnight Mon-Fri; ⊖ Kurfürstenstrasse

Named for an Austrian Jewish writer forced into exile by the Nazis, this quirky retreat time-warps you back to the 1920s, when Roth used to live next door (now the Ave Maria store, p189). Walls decorated with bookshelves and quotes from his works draw a literary, intellectual crowd). Come here for coffee and cake or choose from two hearty dishes at lunchtime and dinner.

WITTY'S Map p136 Sausages €

☎ 211 9494; www.wittys-berlin.de; Wittenbergplatz 5, cnr Ansbacher Strasse; snacks €3-6; ⏰ 11am-1am; ⊖ Wittenbergplatz

This 'doggeria', close to KaDeWe (p189) department store, has certified organic sausages, although adding a helping of its crispy French fries topped with homemade mayo, peanut or garlic sauce will quickly ruin the illusion that this is anything like a guilt-free meal.

HABIBI Map p136 Middle Eastern €

☎ 215 3332; Goltzstrasse 24; snacks €2.50-5; ⏰ 11am-3am Sun-Thu, to 5pm Fri & Sat; ⊖ Nollendorfplatz

Habibi means 'my beloved' and the object of obsession in this popular snack place is soul-sustaining felafel best paired with a freshly pressed carrot juice. Great for restoring brain balance after a night on the razzle.

KREUZBERG & NORTHERN NEUKÖLLN

Kreuzberg has definitely come up in the culinary world of late and is the most exciting foodie district right now. Some of the best eating is done in comfy neighbourhood restos and in ethnic eateries. All throughout, this multicultural cauldron brims with bohemian cafes, Old Berlin pubs, buzzy *Dönerias* and the exuberant canalside Türkenmarkt (Turkish Market; p192). Aside from Paul-Lincke-Ufer, there are no proper restaurant rows and the best finds are in often nondescript side streets. Northern Neukölln is still more of a drinking and partying zone but even here we've found a few quality restos worthy of your attention.

HARTMANNS Map pp140-1   International €€€

☎ 6120 1003; www.hartmanns-restaurant.de, in German; mains lunch/dinner €14/28, 3-course lunch menu €21, dinner menu 3-7 courses €45-74; Fichtestrasse 31; ⊗ noon-2pm Mon-Fri, 6pm-midnight Mon-Sat; ◎ Südstern

Stefan Hartmann studied with star chefs in Hollywood and Berlin before lassoing the city's Chef of the Year title in 2008. Amid the vaulted ceilings, original art and lustily roaring fireplace of his romantic basement restaurant, he now regales demanding diners with boundary-pushing Franco-German cuisine. *Loup de mer* with tarragon risotto or dove with duck liver confit are typical menu items.

LAVANDERIA VECCHIA

Map pp140-1   Italian €€€

☎ 6272 2152; www.lavanderiavecchia.de, in German; Flughafenstrasse 46; lunch from €4.50; 13-course dinner menu €39.50; ⊗ noon-3pm & from 7.30pm Tue-Sat; ◎ Boddinstrasse

From the crusty bread to the limoncello digestif, the country-style dinners at the Old Laundry are truly on a culinary first-class journey. Starched linens separate tables in the rustic-industrial space where tastebuds are spoiled by no fewer than 10 antipasti (the *vitello tonnato* is tops!), followed by pasta or risotto and a fishy or meaty main, plus dessert. Best of all, the price includes all the delicious white and red wine from the Sabine hills north of Rome that you can drink.

SPINDLER & KLATT Map pp140-1   Fusion €€€

☎ 319 881 860; www.spindlerklatt.com, in German; Köpenicker Strasse 16-17; mains €13.50-29; ⊗ 8pm-1am; ◎ Schlesisches Tor

Summer on the riverside terrace are magical in this Prussian bread factory turned trendy nosh and party spot. Sit at a long table or lounge on a platform bed while sipping a Watermelon Man or tucking into Asian fusion fare. The tuna with Thai basil vegetables is a dependable choice. The interior is just as spectacular and morphs into a dance club after 11pm on Friday and Saturday.

SAGE RESTAURANT CLUB

Map pp140-1   European €€€

☎ 755 494 071; www.sage-restaurant.de; Köpenicker Strasse 18-20; mains €6-24; ⊗ from 11am May-Sep, 6pm Oct-Apr; ◎ Ostbahnhof

In a feat worthy of Rumplestilzken, the owners of Sage have spun an old silk factory into a scene-savvy urban hangout. The menu is casual enough not to intimidate (pizza, tapas) but also has plenty of highfalutin grub to keep more demanding foodies happy. In summer, when there's a lunch menu, the sunny terrace tables and Spree-side beach beckon.

KIMCHI PRINCESS Map pp140-1   Korean €€

☎ 0163-458 0203; www.kimchiprincess.com; Skalitzer Strasse 36; mains €7.50-19.50; ⊗ 6-11pm Tue-Sat; ◎ Görlitzer Bahnhof

If you're a Korean food virgin, this hip hangout is a fine place to lose your innocence. Barbecue is why you're here, grilled by you at your table and paired with several *panchan* (side dishes). The *so bulgogi* (beef slices) and *galbi gui* (beef ribs), both marinated in a tangy soy-based sauce, are tops as are *haemul pajean* (seafood crêpes) and *bibimbap* (rice and veg melding in a hot stone pot). Wash it down with *soju* (Korean sake), a cold Hite beer or a pot of fresh tea.

CAFÉ JACQUES Map pp140-1   Mediterranean €€

☎ 694 1048; Maybachufer 8; mains €10-16; ⊗ 6pm-midnight; ◎ Schönleinstrasse

A favourite with off-duty chefs and foodies from around town, Jacques infallibly charms with flattering candlelight, cosy decor and fantastic wine. It's the perfect date spot but, quite frankly, you only have to be in love with good food to appreciate the French- and North African–inspired supper choices splashed across the blackboard menu. We've never had a bad meal here but if undecided just ask charismatic owner Ahmad for advice. And do remember to make reservations, or forget about snagging a table.

LIBERDA Map pp140-1   Mediterranean €€

☎ 290 3367; Pflügerstrasse 67; mains €6-11.50; ⊗ 10am-midnight; ◎ Hermannplatz, Schönleinstrasse

Trade is justifiably roaring at this neighbourhood fave where you can fill up on delicious food from around the Med without breaking the bank. Dripping candles cast a cosy light over the woodsy room as you tuck into a plate of plump antipasti and contemplate your menu choices, which range from spinach-artichoke casserole to thyme-infused lamb chops. Portions are ample, service only so-so.

DEFNE Map pp140-1 Turkish €€

☎ 8179 7111; www.defne-restaurant.de, in German; Planufer 92c; mains €10-16; ⏰ 4pm-1am Apr-Sep, 5pm-1am Oct-Mar; ⓪ Kottbusser Tor, Schönleinstrasse

If you thought Turkish cuisine stopped at the doner kebab, Defne will teach you otherwise, and quick. The appetiser platter is a divine mix of hummus, garlicky carrot, walnut-chilli paste and other treats, nicely followed up with *ali nacik* ('elegant Ali') – sliced lamb on a bed of pureed eggplant drizzled with yoghurt. The canal-side location is idyllic, the decor warmly exotic and the service top notch.

HASIR Map pp140-1 Turkish €€

☎ 614 2373; www.hasir.de; Adalbertstrasse 12; mains €8-14; ⏰ 24hr; ⓪ Kottbusser Tor

This is the mother ship of the small local chain whose owner, Mehmed Aygün, invented the Berlin-style *Döner* back in 1971 by taking it off the plate and wrapping it into toasted bread. But there's more to Turkish cuisine, which is why tables at his sunset-coloured and tiled restaurant are packed at all hours with punters lusting for feisty soups, tangy appetizers, grilled meats and syrupy desserts.

TRATTORIA VENEZIA Map pp140-1 Italian €€

☎ 6981 4605; Liegnitz Strasse 28; pizza €12-20; ⏰ 6pm-midnight Tue-Sun; ⓪ Görlitzer Bahnhof

This no-nonsense pizza joint will make you feel like Gulliver in the Land of Brobdingnag. Why? The pies here are simply colossal – easily the size of a truck wheel – and perfect for feeding your posse or a gaggle of hungry teenage kids. The setting is simple and you have to get your own cutlery, but that just adds to the boho charm of the place.

IL CASOLARE Map pp140-1 Italian €€

☎ 6950 6610; Grimmstrasse 30; pizza €5.50-8.50; ⏰ noon-midnight; ⓪ Kottbusser Tor

This place has a longstanding reputation for rude servers but on our last few visits

it seemed as though they'd gotten a serious talking to. So we'd like to encourage them to keep it that way. The pizzas here are truly dynamite – thin, crispy, cheap and wagon-wheel-sized – and the canal-side beer garden is both frantic and idyllic.

MUSASHI Map pp140-1 Japanese €€

☎ 693 2042; Kottbusser Damm; mains €10-20; ⏰ noon-10.30pm Mon-Sat, 7-10pm Sun; ⓪ Schönleinstrasse

Sushi purists rejoice: you won't find any truffle-infused wasabi nonsense at this tiny parlour with a massive following. From dark red tuna to marbled salmon, it's all fresh, expertly cut by Nippon natives and affordably priced to boot. Come at off-hours to snag a table or get it to go and source a picnic spot by the canal.

ECKSTÜCK pp140-1 International €€

☎ 6162 5413; www.eckstueck.de; Wrangelstrasse 20; mains €6-16.50; ⏰ 11am-11pm; ⓪ Görlitzer Bahnhof

What do Bimer, Pabo und M:M have in common? They're all local street artists who've immortalised themselves, quite legally, on the walls and ceiling of this corner cafeteria where the menu hits on all comfort-food cylinders. Star of the show is the wood-fired pizza, but the spaghetti with scampi and salmon in chilli-cream sauce is also a perennial favourite.

TOMASA Map pp140-1 International €€

☎ 8100 9885; www.tomasa.de, in German; Kreuzbergstrasse 62; lunch specials €5, mains €5-17; ⏰ 9am-1am Sun-Thu, to 2am Fri & Sat; ⓪ Mehringdamm

Breakfast is a joy at this lovingly renovated late-19th-century villa, but the latest outpost of this popular local mini-chain also puts creative spins on seasonal dishes forged from farm-fresh ingredients. Bring the kids: there's a menu just for them, plus a playroom and crayons for entertainment.

LOUIS Map pp140-1 Austrian €€

☎ 681 0210; Richardplatz 5; mains €8-15; ⏰ 11am-midnight; ⓪ Karl-Marx-Strasse

If you thought a schnitzel is a schnitzel is a schnitzel, you'll think again when you see Louis' elephant-ear-sized contenders. With an average diameter of 50cm, this may well be the largest pounded patty in the city, breaded just so and perfectly paired with a sudsy Austrian brew. If that doesn't make you want to trek out to Neukölln's village-like historic Rixdorf quarter (p147), we don't know what will.

CHAI YO Map pp140-1   Thai €€

☎ 6951 5260; Skalitzer Strasse 95a; mains €7-13; ⏰ noon-11.30pm Tue-Sun; ⊕ Görlitzer Bahnhof
No prefab curry pastes at this Thai parlour run by a congenial German–Thai couple. Although most dishes are familiar, they're prepared with great integrity and from scratch using authentic recipes that have stood the test of time. Even simple curries become culinary poetry here, but it's dishes such as the whole fried fish that turn first-timers into regulars. Don't be deterred by the ho-hum decor.

TANG'S KANTINE Map pp140-1   Chinese €€

☎ 6981 4658; Dieffenbachstrasse 18; mains €6-12.50; ⏰ 11.30am-11pm; ⊕ Schönleinstrasse
Black tables and red acrylic chairs, Tang's oozes Sino-Berlin chic but doesn't sacrifice a lick to the Chinese taste gods. From the subtly spiced *xia mai* (dumplings) to the flavour-drenched red chicken curry and the ample grill platter, it's all tasty and as authentically prepared as possible this side of the Wall of China. With advance reservations, you can also indulge in the Chinese fondue, perfect on a wintry evening.

MARIA PELIGRO Map pp140-1   Mexican €€

☎ 0176 7017 9461; www.maria-peligro.com, in German; Skalitzer Strasse 81; mains €6-12; ⏰ 2-11pm Tue-Thu, to midnight Fri & Sat, bar open late; ⊕ Schlesisches Tor
Some initial growing pains notwithstanding (slow service, watery salsas), there's no denying that Maria's food is a long way from bland Tex-Mex. The cooks wield the spice dispensers with confidence, the bar staff get the margaritas right and the cheerful decor puts you in the mood for fiesta.

HENNE Map pp140-1   German €€

☎ 614 7730; www.henne-berlin.de, in German; Leuschnerdamm 25; half chicken €7.50; ⏰ from 7pm Tue-Sat, 5pm Sun; ⊕ Moritzplatz
Don't like mile-long menus? Well, you won't have that problem at this Old Berlin institution, whose name *is* the menu: Chicken is it, take it or leave it. But these ain't your usual birds: they've been mild-fed and roasted to moist yet crispy perfection.

top picks

FAST FOOD FAVOURITES

- Burger Burgermeister (opposite)
- *Currywurst* Curry 36 (p214)
- Deli Rogacki (p208)
- *Döner* Schlemmerbuffet (p205)
- Falafel Dada Falafel (p204)
- Mexican Ta'Cabrón Taquería (opposite)
- Pizza Zia Maria (p217)
- Sushi Ishin (p202)
- Vegetarian Vöner (p215)
- Vietnamese Hamy (opposite)

The golden Landbier from Bavaria is the perfect complement. Eat in the garden or the woodsy, original interior from 1907. Reservations essential.

JIMMY WOO Map pp140-1   Asian €€

☎ 0176 2535 6205; www.jimmy-woo.de, in German; Friedelstrasse 24; mains €7.50-10; ⏰ noon-midnight; ⊕ Schönleinstrasse
Named for a Marvel Comics secret agent, this artsy Reuterkiez crib hopscotches around Asia with touchdowns in Vietnam, Laos and Thailand. Chinese movie posters, chill electro beats and candlelit tables set the mood for the curries, noodle dishes and specials like the curried duck with Thai beans, ginger and lemon leaves.

SEEROSE Map pp140-1   Vegetarian €€

☎ 6981 5927; www.seerose-berlin.de, in German; Mehringdamm 47; mains €7.50; ⏰ 8am-midnight Mon-Sat, noon-10pm Sun; ⊕ Mehringdamm; Ⓥ
Vegetarians in the know flock to this little cafe which tempts tastebuds with fresh, creative and animal-free pastas, casseroles, soups, salads and other creations. Order at the buffet-style counter, then start salivating at a pavement table or inside in the cosy cafe with its antique furnishings.

MAROUSH Map pp140-1   Lebanese €

☎ 6953 6171; www.maroush-berlin.de, in German; Adalbertstrasse 93; sandwiches €2.50, mains €5-8; ⏰ 11am-2am; ⊕ Kottbusser Tor
The staff is welcoming and warm at this always-busy hole-in-the-wall that serves possibly the best falafel in town: crunchy on the outside, moist on the inside and

drenched with tangy tahini and crunchy salad. If you want to try something new, go for the *shish tawok* (grilled marinated chicken) or *makanek* (fried sausage).

HAMY Map pp140-1 Vietnamese €

☎ 6162 5959; www.hamycafe.com; Hasenheide 10; mains €4.90; ⏰ from 5pm Wed-Sun; ◉ Hermannplatz

If you're in the mood for a quick pho (soup), glass noodle salad or fragrant curry, follow the locals to this low-key landmark. Clever spicing and mountains of fresh herbs give dishes a special kick, and even during busy times you can be in and out in half an hour or less.

TA'CABRÓN TAQUERÍA

Map pp140-1 Mexican €

☎ 3266 2439; Skalitzer Strasse 60; dishes €3-7; ⏰ 1-11pm; ◉ Schlesisches Tor

A standout among the recent flurry of new authentic Mexican eateries, Joaquín Robredo's tiny outpost feeds fans with the kind of homemade food his mom used to make back home in Culiacán. Tacos, burritos and quesadillas bulge with such finger-lickin' fillings as *cochinita pibil* (spicy pulled pork) and chicken *mole* (chicken in chocolate-based sauce), while the salsa packs a respectable punch and the guacamole is silky smooth. *Ay caramba*!

BERLIN BURGER INTERNATIONAL

Map pp140-1 American €

☎ 01577 388 7979; www.berlinburger international.com; Pannierstrasse 5; burger €3.70-4.90; ⏰ 1-11pm; ◉ Hermannplatz

The guys at BBI know that size matters. At least when it comes to burgers, which here are two-fisted, bulging and sloppy contenders. Delve beneath the bun and you'll find a patty ground from 90% beef and 10% lamb and cradled by fresh salads and three different sauces, all homemade and delicious. Unlimited kitchen roll is free. You'll need it.

BURGERMEISTER Map pp140-1 American €

☎ 2243 6493; Oberbaumstrasse 8; burger €3-4; ⏰ 11am-2am or later; ◉ Schlesisches Tor

You have to admire the gumption it takes to open a burger joint inside a century-old public toilet – neatly lacquered green – on a traffic island below the elevated U-bahn tracks. Don't fret, don't shudder, these are among the best burgers in town: big, juicy and eaten standing up.

MO'S KLEINER IMBISS Map pp140-1 Arabic €

☎ 7407 4666; Graefestrasse 9; dishes €2.50-6; ⏰ 11am-11pm; ◉ Schönleinstrasse

Completely unfazed by the queue forming outside their hole-in-the-wall, Mo and his wife may well operate the slowest fast-food

DINING UNDER THE RADAR

They're secretive, hard-to-find and only semi-legal, but in foodie culture private supper clubs are proliferating faster than rabbits on Viagra. In Berlin, too, a growing number of locals, many of them global transplants, organise underground dinner parties, usually in the intimate setting of their own flats. While some hosts are professionally trained chefs, most are amateurs, so the food can be hit-or-miss. But never mind: as flows the wine so does the conversation, making this a great way to make friends out of perfect strangers in a relaxed environment.

The best way to find out about upcoming dates (and to make reservations) is through the operation's website or blog. Once you've signed up, you'll usually be sent the address by email a few days before the dinner party.

Here are a few of our favourite guerrilla restaurants, but keep in mind that, because of their status, clubs may vanish without warning. To keep your finger on the pulse of the scene, check in with www.theghet.com.

- **b.alive** (www.balive.org) The vegan raw food fad has not yet reached Berlin, but Boris Lauser is working on it. The gourmet chef feeds up to 15 curious souls in his stylish studio loft with such delicious concoctions as walnut saffron pate, nut burgers and even pizza, all uncooked, unprocessed and organic. Three courses go for €30 to €35.
- **Fisk & Gröönsaken** (http://groonsaken.wordpress.com) A recent dish at this monthly supper club in Prenzlauer Berg featured seared tuna in raspberry molasses with gingered leeks. Pretty fancy, no? All the more surprising that the donation is only €20 and you can even bring your own wine.
- **Lotería Supper Club** (http://loteriasupperclub.blogspot.com) Let your tastebuds travel to California and Mexico at this monthly get-together for 10 people in a Friedrichshain flat near Boxhagener Platz. Five courses cost €50 with and €35 without wine.
- **Shy Chef** (http://theshychef.wordpress.com) At the best-known among Berlin's hidden restaurants, Maria from Sweden puts on secret food fests (sample dish: cod filet with rhubarb salsa and walnut vinaigrette) several times a month in her Kreuzberg apartment. Aperitif, five courses, wine, coffee and digestif cost €62.

joint in the world. But they sure know how to make a killer falafel! Secret spices give their garbanzo patties a special kick as does the homemade pomegranate-nut sauce. A true *Kiez* institution.

CURRY 36 Map pp140-1 Sausages €
☎ 251 7368; Mehringdamm 36; snacks €2-6; ⏲ 9am-4am Mon-Sat, 11am-3am Sun; ⊕ Mehringdamm
One of the top *Currywurst* purveyors in town, with all-day queues to prove it.

HÜHNERHAUS Map pp140-1 Chicken €
☎ 612 2532; Görlitzer Strasse 1; half chicken €2; ⏲ 9am-2am; ⊕ Görlitzer Bahnhof
Chicken life is cheap. Two euros to be exact. That's what buys you half a juicy bird sent through the rotisserie for just that perfect tan. There are a few tables outside this chicken shack or drag your kill to Görlitzer Park for an impromptu picnic.

FRIEDRICHSHAIN
Friedrichshain still does bars best (see p226), but times are a-changing. To be sure, you'll still find plenty of down-to-earth eateries sprinkled around Boxhagener Platz and its side streets and along Sonntagstrasse near Ostkreuz. However, as rising rents increasingly translate into changing demographics, you'll also find a growing crop of restaurants catering to folks with deeper pockets and more sophisticated palates.

MISERIA & NOBILTÀ Map pp150-1 Italian €€
☎ 2904 9249; Kopernikusstrasse 16; mains €12-22; ⏲ 5.30pm-midnight Tue-Sun; ⊕ ⓡ Warschauer Strasse
When Eduardo Scarpetti penned the comedy *Poverty and Nobility* in 1888, he had no idea that it would inspire the name of this intensely popular family-run trattoria. Thanks to the gracious owners, you'll definitely feel more king than pauper when digging into their deftly prepared – and daily changing – southern Italian seasonal compositions.

SCHNEEWEISS Map pp150-1 German €€
☎ 2904 9704; www.schneeweiss-berlin.de, in German; Simplonstrasse 16; mains €10-20; ⏲ 6-11pm daily, also 10am-4pm Sat & Sun; ⊕ ⓡ Warschauer Strasse
Friedrichshain goes New York glam at the aptly named 'Snow White' whose chilly-chic decor – awesome 'ice' chandelier – was inspired by the Alps. Same goes for the menu, which is big on southern German and Austrian classics (Wiener Schnitzel and the like) executed with a fresh postmodern twist.

SCHWARZER HAHN Map pp150-1 German €€
☎ 2197 0371; Seumestrasse 23; mains lunch €6.50-10, dinner €9-18; ⏲ noon-3pm & 6-10pm Mon-Sat; ⓡ Ostkreuz, ⊕ ⓡ Warschauer Strasse
Kitchen chef Jan Uecker loves home cooking, which is why the small menu at this delightful slow-food bistro is heavy on comfort food like roast chicken and risotto.

LATE-NIGHT & SUNDAY SHOPPING
Out of baby formula at 9pm? Got a last-minute party invite but don't want to show up empty-handed? Don't fret. With Germany's newly liberalised shopping hours, there's bound to be some place open nearby. Of late, Kaiser's Supermarket (Schöneberg Map p136; Nollendorfplatz, Schöneberg; Friedrichshain Map pp150-1; Revaler Strasse 2, Friedrichshain; Prenzlauer Berg Map pp156-7; Schönhauser Allee 130, Prenzlauer Berg) keeps some of its busiest branches open until midnight from Monday to Saturday. Prenzlauer Berg also has Fresh 'N' Friends (Map pp156-7; 4171 7250; www.freshnfriends.com, in German; Kastanienallee 26), an organic food store/deli combo that's open 24/7 but charges premium prices.

Also keep an eye out for *Spätkauf* (*Späti* in the local vernacular), which are small neighbourhood stores stocked with the basics and open from early evening to 2am or later; they're usually found in areas with busy streetlife or nightlife. Petrol stations are minimally stocked, overpriced and should only be a last resort.

Another good bet for late-night purchases are the supermarkets in major train stations. The following are even open on Sundays.

- Edeka (Map pp76-7; Friedrichstrasse train station; ⏲ 6am-10pm Mon-Sat, 8am-10pm Sun)
- Lidl (Map pp150-1; basement, Ostbahnhof train station; ⏲ 8am-10pm)
- Rewe (Map pp150-1; basement, Ostbahnhof train station; ⏲ 8am-10pm)
- Ullrich (Map p128; Hardenbergstrasse 25; ⏲ 9am-10pm Mon-Sat, 11am-10pm Sun; ⊕ ⓡ Zoologischer Garten)

Service is impeccable and so are the wines (bottles from €12). At dinnertime, reserve ahead for a coveted seat at the conversation-friendly, long wooden table.

KASPAR + HAUSER

Map pp150-1   International €€

☎ 787 232; www.kasparundhauser.de; Knorrpromenade 2; mains €8-14.50, 3-course menu €21.50-23.50; ☯ 4-11pm; 🚇 Ostkreuz, Warschauer Strasse

Tucked away on Friedrichshain's most gorgeous (and entirely protected) street, this is a neighbourhood restaurant with ambition. In summer, the terrace is the perfect spot for indulging in truffle tortellini in lemon-almond butter or pork medallions topped with chantrelles. In winter, the cosy, candlelit interior, with its cool chairs draped in newspaper fabric, offers a welcome refuge from the elements.

PAVILLON IM VOLKSPARK
FRIEDRICHSHAIN Map pp150-1 International €€

☎ 4208 0990; www.pavillon-berlin.de, in German; Friedenstrasse 101; mains €6-12; ☯ 11am-midnight; Ⓢ Schillingstrasse, then 🚋 M5; 📶

An all-ages institution since GDR days, Pavillon is especially great for steering towards on sunny days when you can dig into schnitzel, pasta or pancakes in the sprawling beer garden. On colder days, tables beckon inside the cosy restaurant lidded by a huge thatched roof. Free wi-fi and breakfast until 4pm.

VINERIA DEL ESTE Map pp150-1   Spanish €€

☎ 4202 4943; www.vineriaytapas.de; Bänschstrasse 41; tapas €2.40-7.50, mains €7.50-16; ☯ 3pm-midnight; Ⓢ Samariterstrasse

Far off the tourist track, this low-key Iberian jumps with local foodies hungry for tapas that deliver a *piñata* of flavours. Go classic with the tortilla or bacon-wrapped dates or try the octopus salad with cilantro and sesame-soy or any of the other more adventurous compositions. Service tends to be slow, so go with the flow and just order another glass of the excellent Spanish or Uruguayan wine.

IL RITROVO Map pp150-1   Italian €€

☎ 2936 4130; Gabriel-Max-Strasse 2; pizza €5-8; ☯ noon-midnight; Ⓢ 🚇 Warschauer Strasse

Delicious thin-crust pizza with a side of attitude, just as at cousins Il Casolare (p211) in

Kreuzberg and the infamous I Due Forni (p217) in Prenzlauer Berg.

VÖNER Map pp150-1   Vegan €

☎ 9926 5423; www.voener.de, in German; Boxhagener Strasse 56; dishes €2.50-3.50; ☯ noon-11pm Mon-Fri, 1.30-11pm Sat & Sun; 🚇 Ostkreuz; Ⓥ

Owner Holger used to live in a so-called *Wagenburg,* a counterculture commune made up of old vans, buses and caravans. A number of these 'wagon forts' are still around, but Holger now sells his juicy vegan 'Wagenburger' in this funky joint where wall posters advertise the next antifascist demonstration. The eponymous 'vöner', an anti-*döner* made from seitan and vegetables, is the other bestseller. It's all paired with delicious homemade sauces (the garlic tahini rocks).

TRANSIT Map pp150-1   Asian €

☎ 2694 8415; Sonntagstrasse 28; dishes €3; ☯ noon-midnight; 🚇 Ostkreuz; Ⓥ

The concept at this always-packed Asian tapas joint is simple: sit down in the blood-red dining room beneath the colourful birdcages and order by ticking dishes on a tear-off menu pad. There's great variety – papaya salad to spicy salmon soup – but quality can be hit or miss. Expect to order three or four dishes to get fed. Great for waist-watchers and grazers keen on sampling a rainbow of flavours. Also in Mitte (Map pp102-3; ☎ 2478 1645; Rosenthaler Strasse 68; ☯ 11am-1am).

PRENZLAUER BERG

Being largely residential, Prenzlauer Berg has an exceptionally high density of neighbourhood restaurants to cater for on-the-go locals with more money than time. Most are convivial, elbows-on-the-table kind of places where nobody bats an eye if you're still in your sightseeing outfit or are toting the kids along. There are no Michelin-star shrines here, but that is not to say that standards aren't high. Major gastro clusters are around Kollwitzplatz, the Wasserturm and Helmholtzplatz, although the streets connecting them, such as Lychener Strasse, Schliemannstrasse or Rykestrasse, also yield lots of promise. Oderberger Strasse and Kastanienallee are also notable culinary strips lined with many enticing options.

top picks

I SCREAM ICE CREAM

- **Caffe e Gelato** (Map p112; Potsdamer Strasse 7; ☺ 10am-11pm Mon-Thu, to midnight Fri & Sat, 10.30am-11pm Sun; ⊖ ⓡ Potsdamer Platz) Traditional Italian-style ice cream gets a 21st-century twist at this huge space on the upper floor of the Potsdamer Platz Arkaden mall. Aside from creamy concoctions, there are also organic, lactose and sugar-free varieties, all of them delicious.

- **Die Kleine Eiszeit** (Map pp156-7; Stargarder Strasse 7, Prenzlauer Berg; ☺ noon-10pm; ⊖ ⓡ Schönhauser Allee) Brave the inevitable line to choose from a couple of dozen homemade flavours made only with fresh ingredients.

- **The Milkabilly** (Map pp150-1; Mainzer Strasse 5, Friedrichshain; ☺ 11am-9pm Mon-Thu, to 10pm Fri & Sat, to 8pm Sun; ⊖ Samariterstrasse) Go creative and personalise basic flavours like vanilla or strawberry with extras like chocolate sprinkles, mint, cinnamon or gummi bears.

ZAGREUS PROJEKT

Map pp156-7 International €€

☎ 2809 5640; www.zagreus.net; back courtyard, Brunnenstrasse 9a; dinner €30; ⊖ Rosenthaler Platz

An art gallery where a multi-course dinner is part of the exhibition concept – now there's a tasty idea. Every two months, chef-artist-gallery owner Ulrich Krauss invites a different artist to create an exhibition for his basement space. Together they compose a multi-course dinner inspired by the artwork, which is served several times weekly to a small group of diners right in the gallery. Reservations required – check the website or call for seating times.

FRA ROSA Map pp156-7 International €€

☎ 6570 6756; www.weinerei.com; Zionskirchstrasse 40; ☺ noon-midnight; ⊖ Rosenthaler Platz; ☜

This living-room-style restaurant is one of three outposts of the Weinerei cafe/wine bar/restaurant collective around Zionskirchplatz where you 'rent' a wine glass for €2, then help yourself to as much vino as you like and in the end decide what you want to pay. Fra Rosa works much the same way except that it also serves lunch and dinner. This is no simple gruel, though, so please be fair and do not take advantage of this fantastic concept. Dinner reservations are advised.

FELLAS Map pp156-7 German €€

☎ 4679 6314; www.fellas-berlin.de, in German; Stargarder Strasse 3; mains €9-19; ☺ 10am-1am; ⊖ ⓡ Schönhauser Allee; ☜

This unhurried neighbourhood resto employs a kitchen staff surely destined for fancier places. The huge salads are the best thing on the regular menu but most of the creativity goes into the big-flavoured specials that change with the seasons. Or come just for a snack and wine. Free wi-fi.

ODERQUELLE Map pp156-7 German €€

☎ 4400 8080; Oderberger Strasse 27; mains €9-19; ☺ 6pm-1am; ⊖ Eberswalder Strasse

Oderquelle has gone a bit more haute lately but still serves good-value fare, especially in light of the quality and freshness of the ingredients and the expertise that goes into the preparation. In addition to such standbys as thin-crust *Flammkuche* (French pizza), there's a daily calibrated menu featuring six meaty, fishy and veggie mains. In summer try scoring an outside table for keeping an eye on the buzzy action along this pretty street.

SCHUSTERJUNGE Map pp156-7 German €€

☎ 442 7654; Danziger Strasse 9; mains €5-12; ☺ 11am-midnight; ⊖ Eberswalder Strasse

Many German restaurants in this town are either of the rip-off tourist variety or exude an odd 'strangers not welcome' vibe. Not so this rustic corner pub where authentic charm is doled out with as much abandon as the delish home cooking. Big platters of goulash, roast pork and *Sauerbraten* feed both tummy and soul, and so do the locally brewed and highly regarded Bürgerbräu and Bernauer Schwarzbier.

WHITE TRASH FAST FOOD

Map pp156-7 American €€

☎ 5034 8668; www.whitetrashfastfood.com; Schönhauser Allee 6-7; mains €7-21; ☺ from noon Mon-Fri, 6pm Sat & Sun; ⊖ Rosa-Luxemburg-Platz

Wally Potts – city cowboy, California import and Berlin's coolest bar owner – presides over this ex-Irish pub turned culinary punk-hole that's always slammed with wide-eyed tourists, tattooed scenesters and even the occasional celebrity (Amy Winehouse and Mischa Barton apparently stopped by). DJs and bands of all sorts of musical persuasions (as long as they're loud) make conversation a challenge, thus helping you concentrate on the mouth-watering burgers and manly steaks flown in straight from the US of A. See also p238.

FRAU MITTENMANG

Map pp156-7   Modern German €€

☎ 444 5654; www.fraumittenmang.de, in German; Rodenbergstrasse 37; mains €9-17; ⏰ 5pm-midnight; ⊕ ⚇ Schönhauser Allee

Unhurried and unfussy, Frau Mittenmang is your classic neighbourhood restaurant with sidewalk seating for those balmy nights. Locals hunker at polished wooden tables for a pint of the house brew, hand-picked wines and a daily changing menu that folds international influences into classic German dishes. Service, alas, can be uneven.

I DUE FORNI Map pp156-7   Italian €€

☎ 4401 7373; Schönhauser Allee 12; pizzas €6-12; ⏰ noon-midnight; ⊕ Senefelderplatz

In this hectic hall run by a crew of Italian punks, the pizza is king, not you. Service can be slow and rude, but tattooed scenesters, fresh-faced students and boho families are not deterred: the pizzas are just that good. With its scribbled walls and pseudo-revolutionary decor, this place is quintessential Berlin. Make reservations if you hope to get fed after 8pm.

MAMAY Map pp156-7   Vietnamese €

☎ 444 7270; www.mamay-berlin.de; Schönhauser Allee 61; mains lunch €5, dinner €7-10; ⏰ noon-midnight; ⊕ Eberswalder Strasse, Schönhauser Allee

For some of the sharpest Vietnamese food in town, grab a stool at Pham Phuong's purist outpost accented merely with fresh flowers and the telling philosophical statement *Essen ist Frieden* (Eating is Peace). Low-fat, light and fresh noodle soups and grilled fish, duck and chicken dishes all hit the spot without weighing you down.

SI AN Map pp156-7   Vietnamese €

☎ 4050 5775; www.sian-berlin.de; Rykestrasse 36; mains €7-10; ⏰ noon-midnight; ⊕ Eberswalder Strasse

Sian Truong used to manage Monsieur Vuong (p204) in Mitte, the place that started the Vietnamese food craze in Berlin. His own stylish nosh spot is considerably less hectic and welcomes a steady stream of tousled hipsters, yoga mamas and even

the occasional celeb. Everything's prepared freshly, seasonally, healthily and using traditional recipes from the ancient monasteries of Vietnam. Afterwards wind down in the adjacent teahouse.

W-IMBISS Map pp156-7   International €

☎ 4302 0678; www.w-derimbiss.de; Kastanienallee 49; dishes €2-10; ⏰ noon-midnight; ⊕ Rosenthaler Platz, 🚋 M1, M12; Ⓥ

Popular with post-workers and pre-clubbers, the recently expanded W is the home of the naan pizza, freshly baked in the tandoor oven and mouth-wateringly topped with everything from goat cheese to rucola pesto. The wok curries and tasty tortillas are delicious too, and the spirulina-laced apple juice is a great hangover cure.

MARIA BONITA Map pp156-7   Mexican €

☎ 0176 7017 9461; Danziger Strasse 35; mains €4.50-6.50; ⏰ noon-11pm; ⊕ Eberswalder Strasse

Good Mexican food is still a rarity in Berlin, which is why we raise a cold Corona to this no-frills canteen. Finally a place where the tortillas are homemade, the salsas pack a pleasant punch and everything's prepared from scratch using seasonal produce. Menu highlights: the fish tacos and the chicken chipotle burritos.

ZIA MARIA Map pp156-7   Italian €

☎ 691 2841; www.zia-maria.de/website, in German; Pappelallee 32a; slices €1.50-3.50; ⏰ noon-midnight; ⊕ ⚇ Schönhauser Allee

This shoebox-sized pizza kitchen fills up with patrons lusting after habit-forming crispy-crust pies tastily decorated with all sorts of top-notch toppings: plump cherry tomatoes and nutmeg-laced artichokes to pungent Italian sausage. Sit outside at red beer tables or in the tiny dining room creatively clad in irregular strips of laminate.

KONNOPKE'S IMBISS

Map pp156-7   Sausages €

☎ 442 7765; Schönhauser Allee 44a; Currywurst €2; ⏰ 5.30am-8pm Mon-Fri, noon-6.30pm Sat; ⊕ Eberswalder Strasse

Brave the inevitable queue for great *Currywurst* from one of the city's cult sausage kitchens, now in shiny new glass digs but in the same historic spot since 1930.

OTHER SUBURBS

SPANDAU

SPANDOWER ZOLLHAUS — German €€
☎ 333 4841; www.spandauer-zollhaus.de, in German; Möllentordamm 1, Spandau; mains €5.50-14.50; ☺ 3pm-midnight Mon-Sat, 11am-midnight Sun; ◉ Altstadt Spandau

If you're in the market for German comfort food, make a beeline to this friendly and unpretentious restaurant in historic Spandau. The *Zollhaus Ente* (duck) is a perennial favourite, served moist off the bone with a tan as perfect as George Hamilton's. Or go the whole German hog with a belt-loosening portion of *Eisbein* (boiled pork knuckle).

KÖPENICK

RATSKELLER KÖPENICK — German €€
☎ 655 5178; www.ratskellerkoepenick.de, in German; Alt-Köpenick 21; mains €7-19; ☺ 11am-11pm; ☒ Köpenick, then ☒ 68

Restaurants with the word 'Ratskeller' in their name usually turn out to be overpriced tourist traps. The Köpenick contender, though, is a happy exception. If you're lusting after rib-sticking German food, descend into this vaulted, olde-worlde cellar below the historic town hall where a certain 'Hauptmann' once pulled a masterful stunt on the local authorities (see p170). Reservations advised for the Friday and Saturday live jazz nights.

KROKODIL — International €€
☎ 6588 0094; www.der-coepenicker.de, in German; Gartenstrasse 46-48; mains €7-15; ☺ 5pm-midnight Mon-Sat, 11am-11pm Sun; ☒ Köpenick, then ☒ 167

Close to the Köpenick Altstadt, in an idyllic riverside spot with its own beach and boat rental, Krokodil is tailor-made for kicking back, cold beer in hand. Capacity crowds invade for Sunday brunch and weekend live music (reservations key!). The pasta, salads, casseroles and fish dishes can be quite inspired but the main reason to come is the ambience. If you like it here, spend the night at the attached hostel (dorm/single/double €17/46/66).

PANKOW

MAJAKOWSKI GASTHAUS — German €€
☎ 4991 8250; Majakowskiring 63; ☺ noon-midnight Tue-Sat, 11am-midnight Sun; mains €9-25; ☒ M1 Pankow Kirche, Tschaikowskistrasse

In a half-timbered villa on the street where the East German political elite once lived, Majakowski is one of the foodie addresses in northern Berlin. On a balmy night, sit beneath the linden trees in the idyllic garden and dig into upscale German fare made with regionally sourced, organic ingredients whenever possible. Excellent cakes, too. Combine it with a visit to nearby Schloss Schönhausen (p176).

WEDDING

SCHRADER'S — Map pp72-3 — International €€
☎ 4508 2663; www.schraders-berlin.de; Malplaquetstrasse 16b; mains €6-18; ☺ from 3pm Mon-Fri, 10am Sat & Sun; ◉ Seestrasse; ☎

Gentrification has been slow to arrive in this part of town, but Schrader's add a sparkle to blandness. The decor is as globally eclectic as the menu in this thriving cafe-lounge-restaurant where Buddha meets Arabic brass tables meets grandma's plush sofa. The kitchen churns out pizzas, pasta, salads and tapas in a lot more exciting ways than it sounds. On Sundays clued-in locals worship at the brunch altar until 3pm.

DRINKING

top picks

What's your recommendation? www.lonelyplanet.com/berlin

DRINKING

Berlin is a great place for boozers. Cosy pubs, riverside beach bars, beer gardens, underground dives, DJ bars, snazzy hotel lounges, designer cocktail temples – with such variety, finding a party pen to match your mood is not exactly a tall order. The edgier, more underground venues are on the east side, with places out west being posher and more suited for date nights than dedicated drinking. Generally, the emphasis is on style and atmosphere, and some proprietors have gone to extraordinary lengths to come up with unique design concepts. That said, there's now such a glut of spacey Stanley Kubrick–inspired bars that someone should invent a vaccine. Enough already.

The line between cafe and bar is often blurred, with many places changing stripes as the hands move around the clock. Alcohol is served pretty much all day if you're keen to get a head-start. Dedicated bars open between 6pm and 8pm and usually keep pouring until the last tippler leaves, often until sunrise. Some have happy hours, especially in tourist-thick Mitte and student-flavoured Friedrichshain.

ETIQUETTE

Table service is common in German bars and pubs and you shouldn't go and order at the bar unless you intend to stay there, or if there's a sign saying *Selbstbedienung* (self-service). It's customary to keep a tab instead of paying for each round separately. Fortunately, the practice of bottle service has not yet caught on in Berlin, except at some fancy clubs and lounges in Charlottenburg, where tables are reserved for groups willing to shell out top euros for bottles of mediocre champagne or vodka.

Note that in bars with live DJs €1 is usually added to the cost of your first drink. Tip bartenders about 5%.

Drinking in public is legal and widely practised, but be civilised about it. No puking on the U-Bahn, please!

SPECIALITIES

Beer continues to be a beloved (and cheap) libation and most places pour a variety of local, national and imported brews. *Fassbier* (draught beer) is generally limited to one or two brands of local lager or Pils, usually served in 300mL or 500mL glasses.

All places stock at least one variety of *Weizenbier* (wheat beer), in 500mL bottles with a choice of *Hefe* (yeasty) and *Kristall* (filtered). Other options are *Schwarzbier* (black beer, like porter), *Dunkelbier* (dark ale) and *Bock* (strong, seasonal beer). In recent years, flavoured beers such as Becks Green Lemon or Schöfferhofer Grapefruit have made inroads. Nonalcoholic Clausthaler and Becks are common, and you can drink your lager as

an *Alster, Radler* or *Diesel* (mixed with Fanta, Sprite or Coke, respectively). If you're bored with beer, there are lots of alternatives, such as German *Sekt* or Italian *prosecco* (sparkling wines, sometimes served on the rocks), vodka or absinthe concoctions.

Cocktails have undergone a major renaissance, with caipirinhas and mojitos being common standbys; the vodka-based 'Watermelon Man' also has its share of fans. For the best taste sensations sample the house creations at one of the serious specialist places.

The quality of wine in bars and cafes ranges from drinkable to abysmal, which is probably why so many Germans drink it with fizzy water, called a *Weinschorle*. If you're not boozing, a *Saftschorle* (fizzy water and juice) is a refreshing alternative. Carbonated sodas also have their takers, with most preferring German-made organic Bionade to Coke and other imports.

HISTORIC MITTE

ADMIRALS ABSINTH BAR Map pp76-7   Bar
Friedrichstrasse 101; ⏰ **6pm-2am Sun-Thu, to 3am Fri & Sat;** Ⓢ Ⓡ **Friedrichstrasse**
Tucked speakeasy-style at the bottom of a dark staircase behind heavy doors is this Golden Twenties–style glamour pit where patrons pray at the altar of the Green Fairy. If you're an absinth novice, ask the expert bartender for a recommendation. And remember: sip don't gulp, or risk being catapulted into oblivion in no time. The entrance is from the courtyard of the Admiralspalast (p238).

CAPITAL SUDS

Beer has been brewed in Berlin since the Middle Ages, and the city even has its own home-grown type, the Berliner Weisse. A cloudy, slightly sour wheat beer, it's sweetened with a shot of woodruff or raspberry syrup and is low in alcohol (about 3%) and thus quite refreshing on a hot summer day. There used to be hundreds of breweries throughout Berlin, especially in Prenzlauer Berg. In fact, the Kulturbrauerei (p158) and Pfefferberg (p160) are both cultural centres wrought from former breweries. Today, only two big breweries are left. The biggest is Schultheiss, which produces the Berliner Pilsner, Schultheiss and Berliner Kindl brands. Berliner Bürgerbräu in Köpenick is the city's last large indie brewery alongside 36 microbreweries. Collectively, they produce about 3 million hectolitres per year.

If you're keen on a behind-the-scenes look, join a tour offered by the Schultheiss Brauerei (Mapp72-3; www.schultheiss.de, in German; Indira-Gandhi-Strasse 66-69, Hohenschönhausen; Ⓜ M13 to Betriebshof Indira-Gandhi-Strasse). The 90-minute tours (in German) run Monday to Thursday and cost €4 (€8 with a beer tasting, €12 with a beer tasting and hearty snack). Call for hours.

Hardcore beer fans might also want to time their Berlin visit with the Berliner Bierfestival (p18), when around 300 breweries set up the world's longest beer garden along Karl-Marx-Allee.

Here are our top three Berlin microbreweries:

- Brewbaker (Mapp72-3; ☎ 3930 5156; www.brewbaker.de, in German; S-Bahn Arch 415, nr Flensburger Strasse, Tiergarten; mains lunch €4.50-6.50, dinner €8-17; Ⓨ noon-11pm Mon-Fri, 4-11pm Sat & Sun; Ⓡ Bellevue) Tucked beneath the S-Bahn arches, this microbrewery-cum-restaurant is perfect for civilised imbibing instead of brainless guzzling. The trademark Bellevue Pils is always on tap alongside a changing roster of seasonal beers. Order the sampler for €2 to find your favourite. If the tummy grumbles, order from the small seasonal and regional menu.
- Hops & Barley (Mapp150-1; ☎ 2936 7534; www.hopsandbarley-berlin.de; Wühlischstrasse 22/23, Friedrichshain; Ⓨ from 5pm Sun-Fri, 3pm Sat; Ⓞ Ⓡ Warschauer Strasse) Conversation flows as freely as the mild and malty pilsner, dunkel and wheat beer (and cider) produced right at this congenial microbrewery inside a former butchers shop. Share a table with low-key locals swilling post-work pints among ceramic-tiled walls and shiny copper vats. Half a litre is €2.80.
- Brauhaus Georgbräu (Mapp96; ☎ 242 4244; www.georgbraeu.de; Spreeufer 4, Mitte; mains €6-13; Ⓨ noon-11pm Mon-Fri, 10am-11pm Sat & Sun; Ⓞ Ⓡ Alexanderplatz) Tourist-geared but cosy and rich in ambience, the brewpub is the only place where you can guzzle St Georg pilsner, which brewmeister Oliver Kassan has been making since 1992. In winter the woodsy beer hall is perfect for tucking into goulash and pork knuckle, while in summer the large riverside beer garden beckons.

ARTBAR 71 Map pp76-7   Bar
☎ 2087 9998; Kronenstrasse 71; Ⓨ from 7pm; Ⓞ Stadtmitte
At this chic gallery-cum-bar reached via a spiralling staircase you can drink in art while practising the art of drinking. The sleek design is very New York (lots of glass, metal and wood and a cool egg-shaped bar) and a perfect foil for the attractive crowd of arty intellectuals here for quiet conversation and quality cocktails.

BEBEL BAR Map pp76-7   Bar
☎ 460 6090; www.hotelderome.com; Behrenstrasse 37; Ⓨ 9am-1am; Ⓞ Französische Strasse
Channel your inner George Clooney and belly up to the super-long bar at this elegant, mood-lit thirst parlour at the Hotel de Rome (p268). Don't bother if you're the caipi type – you'd be wasting the barman's considerable talents. Made only with top labels, cocktails here have a progressive, sexy edge that even

translates to virgin drinks. La Bomba, a mix of strawberries, grapefruit, basil and Créme de Coco, is as smooth as a silk glove.

TAUSEND Map pp76-7   Bar
☎ 4171 5396; www.tausendberlin.com; Schiffbauerdamm 11; Ⓨ from 9pm Tue-Sat; Ⓞ Ⓡ Friedrichstrasse
The unofficial clubhouse of the see-and-be-seen scene. No sign, no light, no bell, just a heavy steel gate beneath a railway bridge with a small window through which you shall be assessed. Once inside the black and metal tunnel, though, there's expert cocktails (try the berry mojito) and fellow sippers provide the eye candy.

TADSCHIKISCHE TEESTUBE
Map pp76-7   Cafe
☎ 204 1112; www.restaurant-trofeo.de, in German; Am Festungsgraben 1; Ⓨ 5pm-midnight Mon-Fri, from 3pm Sat & Sun; 🚌 100, 200, TXL

This authentic Tajik tearoom inside an 18th-century town palace feels like a fairy-tale retreat. Students, old hippies and curious tourists loll on thick oriental carpets sipping teas poured from silvery samovars. The exotic room was originally displayed at the 1974 Leipzig fair and then given as a gift to the Society for German-Soviet Friendship, which had its seat in the building. Skip the food, though.

MITTE – SCHEUNENVIERTEL

BAR 3 Map pp102-3 Bar
☎ 2804 6973; Weydinger Strasse 20; ☽ from 9pm Tue-Sat; ☻ Rosa-Luxemburg-Strasse
With its wrap-around glass windows, black decor and dim lighting, this stylish, minimalist bar seems to be jostling for *Wallpaper* coverage but is actually a laid-back lair for local lovelies, artists and actors from the nearby Volksbühne theatre. Scope out the action huddled around the U-shaped bar and guzzling cold Kölsch beer imported from the owner's hometown of Cologne.

ESCHLORAQUE Map pp102-3 Bar
☎ 0172 311 1013; www.eschschloraque.de, in German; Rosenthaler Strasse 39; ☽ from 2pm; ☒ Hackescher Markt
This trashy-chic bar is a rare bulwark against Mitte's creeping yuppification. Find it past the trash cans at the end of the courtyard of Haus Schwarzenberg, one of the few unrenovated houses left around here. We love the surreal monster decor by the Dead Chickens art collective, the comfy sofas, the strong cocktails and wacky parties. If only the staff would give the snootiness a rest.

KING SIZE BAR Map pp102-3 Bar
Friedrichstrasse 112b; ☽ from 7pm; ☻ Oranienburger Tor
With the same owners as the nearby Grill Royal (p203), it was a foregone conclusion that this tiny (thus ironically named) joint would quickly become a favourite watering hole for Mitte's artsy boho-bourgeois elite. Prices too are 'royal', and it's a tight squeeze after midnight, so come early, sip a Moscow Mule and look coolly down from your perch on a silk-draped bar stool.

BARCOMI'S DELI Map pp102-3 Cafe
☎ 2859 8363; www.barcomis.de, in German; 2nd courtyard, Sophie-Gips-Höfe, Sophienstrasse 21; ☽ 9am-9pm Mon-Sat, 10am-9pm Sun; ☻ Weinmeisterstrasse
Train your java radar onto this New York–meets-Berlin deli where latte-rati, families and expats meet for coffee, bagels with lox (smoked salmon) and possibly some of the best brownies and cheesecake this side of the Hudson River. Another plus: the hidden setting in a classic Scheunenviertel courtyard.

CAFÉ BRAVO Map pp102-3 Cafe
☎ 2345 7777; Auguststrasse 69; ☽ 9am-8pm Mon, 9am-1am Tue-Thu, 9am-2am Fri & Sat, 10am-8pm Sun; ☒ Oranienburger Strasse
Is it art? Is it a cafe? Answer: it's both. The glass-and-chrome cube in the quiet and pretty courtyard of the KW Institute for Contemporary Art (p105) was dreamed up by US artist Dan Graham and is a suitably edgy refuelling stop on any Scheunenviertel saunter. The food's quality is uneven, so stick with liquids.

CHÉN CHÈ Map pp102-3 Cafe
☎ 2888 4282; www.chenche-berlin.de; Rosenthaler Strasse 13; ☽ noon-midnight; ☻ Rosenthaler Platz

CREEPY CRAWLERS
It's no secret that Berlin's a great place for drinking, but some people can't seem to find a bar on their own. In comes the organised pub crawl, a phenomenon that's been taking over the Scheunenviertel every night for the past few years. For about €12 each, 100 or so global nomads descend like locusts on a handful of touristy bars and pubs, getting wasted on free shots and cheap drinks along the way. Insider Tour (p313) and New Berlin Tours (p313) were among the first companies to offer these guide-led drinkathons that seem to be especially popular with the 'triple-A crowd' (Anglo-Saxons, Americans and Australians). Other operators have jumped on the bandwagon, some with a slightly different concept. Alternative Berlin (see p313), for instance, runs the '666 Anti-Pub Crawl', which takes smallish groups (about 10 to 20 folks) to more off-beat, less-touristy bars, from flower-power joints to Goth dungeons to transvestite bars. In the end, though, the objective seems to be the same: to be wasted, but not alone.

When it's time for tea, follow the smouldering joss sticks to this postmodern Vietnamese tea house tucked into the back of a Scheunenviertel courtyard. Feel your stress evaporate in the little Zen garden or beneath the huge hexagonal chandelier, sipping ginger tea spiked with lime juice and lemon grass or the exotic butterfly-blueflower tea made with organic rice milk. There's also a small menu of dishes, many of them meat-free.

ZOSCH Map pp102-3 — Pub

☎ 280 7664; www.zosch-berlin.de, in German; Tucholskystrasse 30; ⏰ from 4pm; 🚇 Oranienburger Strasse

Bask in the vintage vibe of this low-key booze parlour that's managed to maintain its funky-skunky '90s vibe while seeing its neighbours go all snazzy and glam. Live jazz steams up the cellar on Wednesday and Thursday; Friday and Saturday cater more to indie, punk and folk tastes.

POTSDAMER PLATZ & TIERGARTEN

CAFÉ AM NEUEN SEE Map p112 — Beer Garden

☎ 254 4930; Lichtensteinallee 2; ⏰ from 10am daily Mar-Oct, Sat & Sun Nov-Feb; 🚇 Zoologischer Garten

This lakeside, Bavarian-style beer garden feels like a micro-vacation from the city bustle. Cold beers go well with the (pricey) bratwurst, pizza and pretzels. Romantics can even rent a boat and take their sweetie for a spin.

CHARLOTTENBURG & NORTHERN WILMERSDORF

GAINSBOURG Map p128 — Bar

☎ 313 7464; www.gainsbourg.de, in German; Savignyplatz 5; ⏰ from 5pm; 🚇 Savignyplatz

An American bar with a Paris vibe right in the middle of Berlin – it doesn't get more international. Cramped and casual, this warmly lit den speaks to a crowd probably old enough to have made out to *Je t'aime,* Serge's steamy duet with Jane Birkin, when it was first released. Awesome cocktails, Gauloises optional.

PURO SKYLOUNGE Map p128 — Bar

☎ 2636 7875; www.puro-berlin.de, in German; Tauentzienstrasse 11; ⏰ from 8pm Tue-Sat; 🚇 Kurfürstendamm

Puro has quite literally raised the bar in Charlottenburg, by moving it to the top of the Europa Center, that is, with predictably fabulous views through floor-to-ceiling windows. It's a great place if you want to trade Berlin funky-trash for high heels, swish surrounds and a young but moneyed crowd whose mind erasers of choice are Moët, martinis and cosmos. Dress up, or forget about it.

UNIVERSUM LOUNGE Map pp124-5 — Bar

☎ 8906 4995; www.universumlounge.com, in German; Kurfürstendamm 153; ⏰ 6pm-3am; 🚇 Adenauerplatz

The curvaceous teak bar and white leather banquettes of this spacey, retro-glam libation station fill up quickly after the curtain falls at the Schaubühne theatre, which is located in the same building, a 1920s Bauhaus gem by the esteemed Erich Mendelsohn.

SCHLEUSENKRUG Map p128 — Beer Garden

☎ 313 9909; www.schleusenkrug.de, in German; Müller-Breslau-Strasse; ⏰ 10am-2am May-Sep, 11am-7pm Mon-Fri & 10am-7pm Sat & Sun Oct-Apr; 🚇 🚌 Zoologischer Garten, Tiergarten

Watch the boats slip into the lock that gives this canal-side beer garden its name. From morn to night, punters from all walks of life partake in pints of Pils and simple, filling treats beneath the shady beech trees. Nice spot for breakfast or afternoon cakes, too.

CAFÉ RICHTER Map pp124-5 — Cafe

☎ 324 3722; Giesebrechtstrasse 22; ⏰ 8am-7pm Mon-Sat, 9am-7pm Sun; 🚇 Adenauerplatz

It's a bit of a detour, but trust us, the homemade cakes (yummy apricot-almond tart!) are worth the trip. Richter's may look like your grandma's cafe, but a quick scan of the crowd sitting below the big picture of Neuschwanstein Castle reveals its cross-generational appeal. Truly an authentic throwback to the West Berlin of yesteryear. Perhaps combine it with shopping along Wilmersdorfer Strasse or a spin around the Karl-August-Platz Farmers Market (p207).

ZWIEBELFISCH Map p128 — Pub

☎ 312 7363; www.zwiebelfisch-berlin.de, in German; Savignyplatz 5; ☽ noon-6am; ⓜ Savignyplatz

With its clientele of grizzled and aspiring artists, actors and writers, this cosy pub is Charlottenburg at its boho best, and it has been so since the patchouli-perfumed late 1960s. Everyone's a little older these days, but it's still a great place for guzzling that final drink while the iBook crowd is gearing up for another day at the office.

SCHÖNEBERG

GREEN DOOR Map p136 — Bar

☎ 215 2515; www.greendoor.de; Winterfeldtstrasse 50; ☽ from 6pm; ⓜ Nollendorfplatz

This been-here-forever place is one of Berlin's finest cocktail bars, tended by a long line of renowned mixologists. For that added feeling of exclusivity, you have to ring the bell to get in. It's tiny and usually

packed, so dress nicely, flash a winning smile and hope for the best.

ZOULOU BAR Map p136 — Bar

☎ 784 6894; www.zouloubar.de, in German; Hauptstrasse 4; ☽ 8pm-6am; ⓜ Kleistpark

Nothing to do with Michael Caine or bloody spears – the theme at this cocktail-bar institution is more American than African, which is probably just as well if you've ever seen a Soweto speakeasy. Expert bartenders and drink specials most nights.

EX'N'POP Map p136 — Pub

☎ 2199 7470; Potsdamer Strasse 157; ☽ from 10pm; ⓜ Kleistpark

The ghosts of Einstürzende Neubauten, Element of Crime and other seminal Berlin bands still may be partying at this rough-house with a pedigree going back to the pre-Wende punk era. Ex has moved to a new location, but it's still a good place to pop the last bottle of the night. A techno,

---

LIFE'S A BEACH

Paris may claim to have invented the beach bar, and other landlocked cities have jumped on the 'sandwagon', but with more than 30 outdoor playgrounds Berlin has definitely got the edge. Daytime chilling is often followed by alfresco parties that go till sunrise and beyond. Most are open from May to September, although exact timings depend on the weather. Also see Badeschiff (p147).

▪ Kiki Blofeld (Map pp140-1; www.kikiblofeld.de, in German; Köpenicker Strasse 48/49, Mitte; ☽ from 2pm Mon-Fri, from noon Sat & Sun; ⓜ Heinrich-Heine-Strasse) A Spree-side rendezvous with Kiki will have you swinging in a hammock, lounging on natural grassy benches, chilling on the riverside beach, waving to passing boats from the wooden deck or shaking it in an East German army boat patrol bunker. Plus pizza and grilled foods for sustenance. To find it, look for the sign DAZ 48/49, go past the car dealer, look for the gap in the construction fence and you're there.

▪ Oststrand (Map pp150-1; www.oststrand.de, in German; Mühlenstrasse, Rummelsburger Platz, Friedrichshain; ☽ from 10am; ⓡ Ostbahnhof) A beach paradise along the East Side Gallery. Drink a toast to Berlin as you wiggle your toes in the sand. Tanning and chilling in the daytime, partying at night.

▪ Deck 5 (Map pp156-7; www.freiluftrebellen.de, in German; Schönhauser Allee 80; ☽ 10am-midnight Mon-Sat, noon-midnight Sun; ⓜ ⓡ Schönhauser Allee) Soak up the city lights along with your beer at this beach bar in the sky, while sinking your toes into sand lugged to the top parking deck of the Schönhauser Allee Arcaden mall. Take the lift (elevator) from within the mall or enter via a heart-pumping flight of stairs on Greifenhagener Strasse.

▪ Strandgut Berlin (Map pp150-1; ☎ 7008 5566; www.strandgut-berlin.com, in German; Mühlenstrasse 61-63, Friedrichshain; ☽ from 10am; ⓡ Ostbahnhof) Next to Oststrand, this is the most chic of the East Side Gallery sandpits, where the beer is cold, the cocktails strong, the crowd more grown-up and the DJs tops.

▪ Beach at the Box (Map pp124-5; ☎ 2504 1515; www.beachberlin.com; Englische Strasse 21; ☽ noon-11pm Mon-Fri, noon-midnight Sat & Sun; ⓜ Ernst-Reuter-Platz) Polo shirts and micro-dresses sip mojitos in the sand amid awnings sporting corporate advertising at this beach bar hidden behind the local Mercedes dealership. When it's time to wrap up outside, continue beneath the disco ball in the adjacent Box.

▪ BundesPresseStrand (Map pp76-7; ☎ 809 9119; www.derbundespressestrand.de; Kapelle-Ufer 1; ☽ from 10am; ⓜ ⓡ Hauptbahnhof, ⓜ Bundestag) Watch the sun set over the government district from this beachy perch outside the federal press office (hence the name). Boogie nights, salsa lessons, VIP parties, beach volleyball and a kids' zone bring together everyone from families to desk jockeys to suburban day trippers.

rap and hip hop–free zone, it also hosts the occasional radical reading or concert.

KUMPELNEST 3000 Map p136 Pub
☎ 261 6918; Lützowstrasse 23; ☽ 7pm-5am;
ⓤ Kurfürstenstrasse
A former brothel, this lurid bat cave would be sensuous, kooky and kitschy enough to feature in a 1940s Shanghai noir thriller. A classic dive, famous for its wild, debauched all-nighters, it attracts a hugely varied public, although there can be a preponderance of butch boys. Watch out for pickpockets.

KREUZBERG & NORTHERN NEUKÖLLN

FREISCHWIMMER Map pp140-1 Bar
☎ 6107 4309; www.freischwimmer-berlin.de, in German; Vor dem Schlesischen Tor 2a; ☽ from 2pm Mon-Fri, from 11am Sat & Sun; ⓤ Schlesisches Tor
In summertime, few places are more idyllic than this rustic ex-boathouse turned all-day, canal-side chill zone. Come for chit-chat or postcard writing in the afternoon or a pre-clubbing warm-up. Snacks and light meals are served, but they're more of an afterthought. The entrance is to the right of Berlin's oldest petrol station. It's sometimes open in winter, but it's not the same – call ahead for hours.

HAIFISCHBAR Map pp140-1 Bar
☎ 691 1352; www.haifischbar-berlin.de, in German; Arndtstrasse 25; ☽ from 7pm; ⓤ Platz der Luftbrücke, Mehringdamm
With two sharks beckoning you in above the entrance portal, this unassuming thirst parlour plays it cool for cocktail lovers. The bartender wields the shaker with confidence, there's tapas on the menu in the back room, and the toilets get a 10 on the kitsch-o-meter.

KUSCHLOWSKI Map pp140-1 Bar
☎ 0176-2438 9701; www.kuschlowski.de, in German; Weserstrasse 202; ☽ from 8pm; ⓤ Hermannplatz
Winter, when fierce winds blow in from Russia, is the perfect time to hole up by the crackling fireplace in this cosy bar. Loll with local hipsters on hand-picked retro furniture and stave off the chills with a couple of vodkas.

LUZIA Map pp140-1 Bar
☎ 6110 7469; www.luzia.tc, in German; Oranienstrasse 34; ☽ from 9am; ⓤ Kottbusser Tor
Tarted up nicely with vintage furniture, baroque wallpaper and whimsical wall art by Chin Chin, Luzia draws its crowd from SO36's more sophisticated urban dwellers. Some punters have derided it as Mitte-goes-Kreuzberg, but it's still a comfy spot for imbibing, flirting and chilling while getting doused with electro beats.

MADAME CLAUDE Map pp140-1 Bar
☎ 8411 0859; Lübbener Strasse 19; ☽ from 7pm; ⓤ Schlesisches Tor, Görlitzer Bahnhof
Nope, it's not a David Lynch movie set, it's Madame's. Gravity is literally upended at this living-room-style booze burrow where tables, chairs and teapots dangle from the ceiling. Don't worry, there are still comfy sofas for slouching and entertaining your posse, plus music quiz night on Wednesday and the occasional live band and open-mike session. The name honours a famous French prostitute – très apropos given the place's bordello past.

MONARCH BAR Map pp140-1 Bar
Skalitzer Strasse 134; ☽ from 9pm Tue-Sat; ⓤ Kottbusser Tor
Bonus points if you can find this upstairs bar right away. Tip: the unmarked entrance is next to the doner kebab shop east of the Kaiser's supermarket. Behind a long steamed-up window front overlooking Kottbusser Tor awaits an ingenious blend of trashy sophistication, strong drinks and a relaxed vibe popular with chatty internationals. A popular weekend pit stop on a Kreuzberg bar crawl.

SOLAR Map pp140-1 Bar
☎ 0163 765 2700; www.solar-berlin.de; Stresemannstrasse 76; ☽ from 6pm Mon-Sat, from 10am Sun; ⓡ Anhalter Bahnhof
The door's tight (on weekends, at least), service is slow and the cocktails are only so-so, but the views – oh, the views – really are worth the vertigo-inducing trip aboard an exterior glass lift to this 17th-floor Manhattan wannabe. The entrance is off-street in an ugly high-rise behind the Pit Stop auto shop. There's also a restaurant, but it can hit or miss (though the tables still have that same gorgeous view).

WÜRGEENGEL Map pp140-1 — Bar

☎ 615 5560; www.wuergeengel.de, in German; Dresdner Strasse 122; ☼ from 7pm; ◎ Kottbusser Tor

For a swanky night out, point the compass to this '50s-style cocktail cave complete with glass ceiling, chandeliers and shiny black tables. It's always busy, but especially so after the final credits roll at the adjacent Babylon (p252). The name, by the way, pays homage to the surreal 1962 Buñuel movie *Exterminating Angel*.

GOLGATHA Map pp140-1 — Beer Garden

☎ 785 2453; www.golgatha-berlin.de, in German; Dudenstrasse 48-64; ☼ from 10am Apr-Sep; ◎ ☒ Yorckstrasse

A Kreuzberg classic right in the heart of Viktoriapark, with a changing cast of characters throughout the day. Families invade in the daytime, lured by the adjacent adventure playground. Laid-back locals catch the day's final rays, cold beer in hand, on the rooftop terrace. And after 10pm a DJ hits the decks. The easiest access is from Katzbachstrasse near Monumentenstrasse.

HEINZ MINKI Map pp140-1 — Beer Garden

☎ 6953 3766; www.heinzminki.de; Vor dem Schlesischen Tor 3; ☼ from noon; ◎ Schlesisches Tor

This rambling beer garden with its old fruit trees and coloured twinkle lights is an enchanting spot for wrapping up a day of turf-pounding. It's behind an old customs house whose red-brick walls also enclose a teensy bar that's open year-round. Pizza and grilled sausage provide much-needed sustenance.

Ä Map pp140-1 — Pub

☎ 0177 406 3837; www.ae-neukoelln.de, in German; Weserstrasse 40; ☼ from 5pm; ◎ Rathaus Neukölln

This *Kiez* (neighbourhood) pioneer is a fine place to feed your party animal an appetiser or wrap up a long night on the razzle. Or maybe just claim one of the colourful chairs and camp out for the night. There are DJs and concerts, but once a month it's wall-to-wall with people here for the live *Schmusetiersoap*, a soap opera starring numerous cast-off stuffed animals.

ANKERKLAUSE Map pp140-1 — Pub

☎ 693 5649; www.ankerklause.de, in German; Kottbusser Damm 104; ☼ from 4pm Mon, from 10am Tue-Sun; ◎ Kottbusser Tor

Ahoy there! This nautical-kitsch tavern in an old harbour-master's shack is a great place for quaffing, waving to the tourist boats puttering along the Landwehrkanal and feeding the eclectic jukebox. On Thursdays it's party time with an anything-goes alchemy of beats raining down on attitude-free clubbers.

MÖBEL OLFE Map pp140-1 — Pub

www.moebel-olfe.de, in German; Reichenberger Strasse 177; ☼ from 6pm Tue-Sun; ◎ Kottbusser Tor

An old furniture store has been recast as an always-busy drinking den with cheap libations and a friendly crowd that's mixed in every respect (although gays definitely dominate on Thursdays). Watch out: the skeletons above the bar get downright trippy after a few Polish beers or high-octane vodkas. The entrance is on Dresdner Strasse.

SAN REMO UPFLAMÖR Map pp140-1 — Pub

☎ 7407 3088; Falckensteinstrasse 46; ☼ from 10am; ◎ Schlesisches Tor

Gather your posse at this laid-back hangout before heading next door to a concert at Magnet or a night of clubbing at Watergate. If chilled clientele, nice waiters, DJ sessions and cold beers won't get you in the party mood, what will? The odd name, by the way, ironically combines the two 'glamour towns' of San Remo, Italy, and tiny Upflamör in southern Germany. Coffee and cake in the daytime.

FRIEDRICHSHAIN

CSA Map pp150-1 — Bar

☎ 2904 4741; www.csa-bar.de; Karl-Marx-Allee 96; ☼ from 8pm; ◎ Weberwiese

Friedrichshain's fanciest bar has been carved out of the Cold War–era Czech Airline offices and sports clean lines and a wonderfully self-ironic, Soviet vintage vibe. Dim lights and strong cocktails make this a favourite of the grown-up set, keeping the white leather bar stools and comfy sofas nice and warm.

PLACE CLICHY Map pp150-1   Bar

☎ 2313 8703; Simon-Dach-Strasse 22; ◷ 7pm-
2am Tue-Sat; ◉ ⓡ Warschauer Strasse
Clichy brings a whiff of the *Quartier Latin*
to the lower end of this stag-party drag.
Candle-lit, artist-designed and cosy, the
postage stamp–sized *boîte* exudes an
almost existentialist vibe, so don your black
turtleneck and join the chatty crowd for
Bordeaux and sweaty cheeses.

SANATORIUM 23 Map pp150-1   Bar

☎ 4202 1193; www.sanatorium23.de, in German;
Frankfurter Allee 23; ◷ from 2pm; ◉ Frankfurter
Tor; ◈
This 'sanatorium' is likely to cure whatever
ails you. The look is Zen-meets-pop-art-
in-hospital, the vibe is relaxed, the vodka
drinks creative and the leather lounge beds
and wispy curtains sensual. On weekends
DJs turn the place into an electro party zone
and if you're too trashed (or whatever) to go
home, you can crash upstairs (double €55,
apartment for three to eight €85 to €130).

SÜSS WAR GESTERN Map pp150-1   Bar

☎ 0176-2441 2940; Wühlischstrasse 43; ◷ from
8pm; ◉ ⓡ Warschauer Strasse, M10, M13
One of our favourite Friedrichshain bars,
where chilled electro and well-mixed
cocktails put you in a good mood and
the low light makes everyone look good.
Only problem: once you're swallowed by
the plush sofa, it's hard to get up to order
that next drink. Try the eponymous house
cocktail made with real root ginger, ginger
ale and whisky.

ZEBRANO Map pp150-1   Cafe-Bar

☎ 2936 5874; www.zebranobar.de, in German;
Sonntagstrasse 8; ◷ from 10am; ⓡ Ostkreuz
Named for the African striped wood, Zebrano is a relaxed am-to-am lounge that
gets a stylish look from onyx tables, leather
chairs and swirly gold and green wallpaper. Breakfast is served until 4pm, with
selections inspired by famous people: the
Brigitte Bardot comes with a croissant, the
Jacques Cousteau with seafood salad… For
a cheap early buzz, drop by between 7pm
and 9pm when cocktails cost just €3.80.

KPTN A MÜLLER Map pp150-1   Pub

www.kptn.de, in German; Simon-Dach-Strasse 32;
◷ from 6pm; ◉ ⓡ Warschauer Strasse; ◈

Glory hallelujah, the captain's in town,
bringing much-needed relief from Simon-
Dach-Strasse's cookie-cutter cocktail
lounge circuit. Pretentions are left at the
door at this self-service bar where the
drinks are cheap (0.5L beer or 0.2L glass of
wine for €2) and there's no charge for table
football or wi-fi. The unique Matterhorn
photo wallpaper in the DJ room out back
makes for an easy conversation starter.

MONSTER RONSON'S ICHIBAN
KARAOKE Map pp150-1   Pub

☎ 8975 1327; www.karaokemonster.com, in
German; Warschauer Strasse 34; ◷ from 7pm;
◉ Warschauer Strasse
Knock back a couple of brewskis if you
need to loosen your nerves before belting
out your best J Lo or Justin at this mad,
great karaoke joint. *Pop Idol* wannabes can
pick from thousands of songs and hit the
stage; shy types may prefer a private room
(per hour €12). Queers invade on Monday
for Fag Bar with flat-rate box hopping,
vintage porn and sweaty dancing.

PRENZLAUER BERG

KLUB DER REPUBLIK Map pp156-7   Bar

Pappelallee 81; ◷ from 10pm; ◉ Eberswalder
Strasse
There's no sign for this ballroom-turned-
bar, so look for the illuminated glasshouse
upstairs, head down the driveway and
teeter up the wobbly staircase. Inside it's
GDR retro flair: well-worn armchairs,
semi-psychedelic wallpaper and giant ball

lamps. Join hormone-happy hipsters for electronic music, wall projections and fuelling up cheaply for the night ahead.

YESTERDAY BAR Map pp156-7 Bar
☎ 2313 9274; www.musikbaryesterday.de, in German; Schönhauser Allee 173; ⏰ 8am-5am; ⊖ Senefelder Strasse

Dark, dim and drowning in tunes from the '60s to the '80s, this is the kind of psychedelic dive bar where Charles Bukowski might have ruined his liver. Popular with an international crowd, it's a universe of the bizarre where the two shady ladies at the bar turn out to be plastic mannequins, shots are served from test tubes and tables double as game boards. If you can't have fun here, check your pulse.

MAUERSEGLER Map pp156-7 Beer Garden
☎ 9788 0904; www.mauersegler-berlin.de, in German; Bernauer Strasse 63; ⏰ from 10am Apr-Oct; ⊖ Eberswalder Strasse; ☏

Pram-pushing mummies, laptop-toting workaholics and laid-back students all congregate at this funky-romantic beer garden for cold beers, cakes and barbecue. Right next to the Mauerpark, it's busiest on Sunday when the flea market is in full swing. Check the website for parties, live concerts and sports screenings.

PRATER Map pp156-7 Beer Garden
☎ 448 5688; www.pratergarten.de; Kastanienallee 7-9; ⏰ beer garden from noon mid-Apr–Sep in good weather, restaurant 6pm-1am Mon-Sat, noon-midnight Sun; ⊖ Eberswalder Strasse

Berlin's oldest beer garden (since 1837) has kept much of its traditional charm and is a fantastic place to hang and guzzle a cold one beneath the ancient chestnut trees (self-service). Kids can romp around the small play area. In foul weather or winter, the adjacent woodsy restaurant is a fine place to sample classic Berlin dishes (mains €7 to €17).

ANNA BLUME Map pp156-7 Cafe
☎ 4404 8749; www.cafe-anna-blume.de; Kollwitzstrasse 83; ⏰ 8am-2am; ⊖ Eberswalder Strasse

Named for a lyrical poem, this corner cafe is like a living room for the Prenzlauer Berg digital bohemians and the stroller mafia.

Potent java, homemade cakes and flowers from the attached shop perfume the Art Nouveau interior, but in fine weather the sidewalk tables are the best people-watching perch. Great for breakfast (the tiered tray for two is tops).

BONANZA COFFEE HEROES
Map pp156-7 Cafe
☎ 0178 144 1123; Oderberger Strasse 35; ⏰ 8.30am-7pm Mon, Tue & Fri, 10am-7pm Sat & Sun; ⊖ Eberswalder Strasse

If Synesso Cyncra and 'third wave coffee' are not mere gobbledygook to you, you speak the language of Kiduk and Yumi, owners of this pocket-sized shrine for javaholics. It's daytime only and packed to the rafters on Sunday when the Mauerpark flea market is in session.

BAR GAGARIN Map pp156-7 Cafe-Bar
☎ 442 8807; Knaackstrasse 22-24; ⏰ 10am-2am; ⊖ Senefelderplatz

Prepare for lift-off with vodka, Moskwa beer and borscht at this retro homage to Soviet cosmonaut Yuri Gagarin, the first man in space. Good breakfast and Sunday brunch. Ladies, if your make-up or hair needs a touch-up, check out the free toiletries in the loo.

MARIETTA Map pp156-7 Cafe-Bar
☎ 4372 0646; www.marietta-bar.de, in German; Stargarder Strasse 13; ⏰ 10am-2am Mon-Fri, to 4am Sat & Sun; ⊖ 🚉 Schönhauser Allee

Retro is now at this neighbourly self-service retreat where you can check out passing eye candy through the big window or lug your beverage to the dimly lit back room for quiet bantering. On Wednesday nights it's a launch pad for the local gay party circuit (see p261).

WOHNZIMMER Map pp156-7 Cafe-Bar
☎ 445 5458; www.wohnzimmer-bar.de, in German; Lettestrasse 6; ⏰ from 10am; ⊖ 🚉 Schönhauser Allee, Eberswalder Strasse

Bask in the vintage vibe of this cult 'living room', where talkative types hang out for vegetarian breakfast, cakes and beer on mismatched flea-market sofas and armchairs. It's buzzy at night, but daytime can be slow.

NIGHTLIFE

top picks

Berliners sure know how to party, and you'd better pack some stamina if you want to join them. With no curfew, this is a notoriously late city where bars stay packed from dusk to dawn and beyond and some clubs don't hit their stride until 4am.

Like most things in Berlin, crowd and vibe vary from district to district. These days, the most hot-steppin' night-time action is in alt-flavoured Kreuzberg and Friedrichshain across the Spree River. The latter's boho-anarcho spirit survives in the grungy party pits along Revaler Strasse and around the Ostkreuz S-Bahn station, a discreet distance away from the mainstream pub-crawl zone along Simon-Dach-Strasse and around Boxhagener Platz. In summer, there are few finer places to chill than the beach bars along the Spree River south of Ostbahnhof, while dedicated party people steer towards Berghain/Panorama Bar or Watergate in the wee hours.

Kreuzberg is happening in all sorts of ways and places. For the most part, the district defiantly retains the punky-funky alt feel that made it famous before reunification. For the greatest density of party spots, head to Schlesische Strasse, Oranienstrasse and Kottbusser Tor. Over the past couple of years, the party has spilled over into adjacent northern Neukölln (east of U-Bahn station Schönleinstrasse).

Further north, Potsdamer Platz teems with suits and tourists, but also has a few chic bars frequented by Berliners. Mitte is an eclectic beast, delivering grittiness in converted factories along Köpenicker Strasse, cosmopolitan sophistication around Gendarmenmarkt, tourist-geared haunts at Hackescher Markt and along Oranienburger Strasse, and hidden jewels just off the latter. Further north, Torstrasse and Kastanienallee boast non-elitist but fashionable haunts, as well as a few venues extending up into Prenzlauer Berg. The latter's ongoing gentrification, though, has resulted in the demise of a couple of well-established music clubs (Magnet and Icon), which have had to seek greener pasture in more party-friendly districts.

Charlottenburg, Wilmersdorf and Schöneberg in the western city, meanwhile, have been essentially cooling their heels since reunification and are largely the stomping ground of an older clientele alongside hormone-crazed teens with money to burn. These areas are best known for their chic but sedate bars, jazz clubs and theatres and a couple of velvet-rope discos, some with bottle service. Schöneberg is a bit different because of the well-established 'gay ghetto' along Motzstrasse and Fuggerstrasse, but even this is largely in the hands of more 'mature' types (see p258 for full coverage).

Listings

Berlin has its own English-language listings and cultural magazine called *ExBerliner* (www.exberliner.de). It's full of insider tips and colourful articles that peel away the city's layers. For German readers *Zitty* (www.zitty.de) and *Tip* (www.tip-berlin.de), published biweekly on alternate Thursdays, are the best sources; they also produce annual shopping and dining guides. *Tip* tends to be trendier but more mainstream, while *Zitty* feels a bit younger and edgier. Monthly *Prinz* (www.prinz.de, in German) is the glossiest of the three and can be too try-hard trendy. All are sold at kiosks anywhere. The best of the free 'zines is *030*, with clued-in reporting about offbeat, nonmainstream events and parties. For highbrow events, *Berlin Programm* (www.berlin-programm.de, in German) is another decent source. All publications have excellent websites where you can look up listings information for free.

Tickets

Credit-card bookings by telephone or online through a venue's box office are becoming more commonplace, but most only take reservations over the phone and then make you show up in person to pay for and pick up your tickets. Agencies, which are commonly found in shopping malls and department stores such as KaDeWe (p189) or Karstadt (Map pp124–5; Kurfürstendamm 231), usually add a steep service charge (up to 15%). Other outlets include:

Berlin Tourist Info (☎ 250 025; www.berlin-tourist -information.de) All Berlin tourist offices (see p316) sell tickets to events in person, by phone and online. Discounts of up to 50% are available for select same-day performances.

Hekticket (www.hekticket.de) Alexanderplatz (Map p96; ☎ 2431 2431; Karl-Liebknecht-Strasse 12; ☽ noon-8pm)

Mon-Sat; ⊖ ⓡ Alexanderplatz); Bahnhof Zoo (Map p128; ☎ 2309 9333; Hardenbergstrasse 29d; ⏰ 10am-8pm Mon-Sat, 2-6pm Sun; ⊖ ⓡ Zoologischer Garten) The Alexanderplatz branch is opposite Berlin Carrée, while the Bahnhof Zoo branch is in the foyer of Deutsche Bank.

Hekticket Last Minute (☎ 230 9930) Discounted tickets after 2pm for select performances that night are available in person at Hekticket outlets, by phone or online.

Koka 36 (Map pp140-1; ☎ 230 9930; www.koka36.de; Oranienstrasse 29, Kreuzberg; ⏰ 9am-7pm Mon-Fri, 10am-4pm Sat; ⊖ Kottbusser Tor) Indie ticket agency, especially good for nonmainstream concerts and events, with great service and best-seat guarantee. Takes orders from out-of-country.

CLUBBING

The sun may not be shining, the weather may not be sweet, but if you just want to move those dancing feet, Berlin is all you could ever want or need. Taste is no barrier to enjoyment either – whether you're into hardcore techno, high-speed drum and bass, kick-ass punk, sweet Britpop, fist-pumping hip hop, beat-free ambient or even swing and tango, you can find a place to party any night of the week. For the latest scoop, scan the listings magazines (opposite), sift through flyers in shops, cafes and bars and check internet platforms such as Resident Advisor (www.resident advisor.net).

Doors can be tough on busy nights at top clubs such as Berghain/Panorama Bar (p232), Watergate (p235) and Cookies (p233), but overall making it past the bouncer is still easier in Berlin than in other European cities. Individual style beats high heels and Armani in most cases, and there's no need to worry about those little wrinkles either – if your attitude is right, age rarely matters. If you have to queue, be respectful and don't talk too loudly. Don't arrive wasted, especially if you're a guy. If you do get turned away, don't argue. And don't worry, there's always another party somewhere…

Whatever club or party you're heading for, don't bother showing up before 1am unless you want to have a deep conversation with a bored bartender. And don't worry about closing times – Berlin's notoriously late nights have got even later lately and, thanks to a growing number of after parties and daytime clubs, not going home at all is definitely an option at weekends. In fact, many folks put in a good night's sleep, then hit the dance floor when other people head for Sunday church.

Since the definition of club, bar, DJ lounge and so on can get a bit hazy, you might also want to peruse the Live Music section (p235) and the Drinking (p219) and Gay & Lesbian Berlin (p257) chapters to figure out where to find your kind of dance-floor action.

For a look at the evolution of Berlin's music and party scene and its key players, flick to the special Berlin Art Attack section on p241 and the Music section of the Background chapter on p45.

2BE Map pp76-7
www.2be-club.de, in German; Heidestrasse 73, Mitte; cover €10; ⏰ Fri & Sat; ⊖ ⓡ Hauptbahnhof
At the 'place to be' for friends of Black Music, resident DJs B.Side, Beathoavenz and Rybixx, and visiting royalty such as Grandmaster Flash and Kanye West spin a bootylicious mix of hip hop, R&B and dancehall, largely for wrinkle-free hotties. Dress sharp, especially in summer when you can live it up Caribbean-style amid the palm trees on the sandy outdoor floor.

://ABOUT BLANK Map pp150-1
http://aboutparty.net, in German; Markgrafendamm 24c, Friedrichshain; ⏰ Fri & Sat; ⓡ Ostkreuz
Much more than a party spot, this club, sequestered in the no-man's land near Ostkreuz, is an open space that organises cultural and political events, usually with a left-leaning, nonmainstream bent. These often segue seamlessly into long, intense club nights when talented spinmeisters feed a diverse bunch of revellers with dance-worthy electronic gruel. Drinks are moderately priced and if you get the spirit of openness and tolerance you'll have a grand old time here.

BASSY CLUB Map pp156-7
☎ 281 8323; www.bassy-club.de, in German; Schönhauser Allee 176a, Prenzlauer Berg; ⏰ from 8pm Mon-Sat; ⊖ Senefelderplatz
Most punters have a post-Woodstock birth date but happily ride the retro wave at this trashy-charming den of darkness, which plays only pre-1969 surf, powerpop, wildstyle rock, country and other tunes. On Friday and Saturday bands are followed by wild dance parties, while weekdays are theme nights – rockabilly to burlesque to the infamous Chantals House of Shame (p261) tranny parties on Thursdays.

BERGHAIN/PANORAMA BAR Map pp150-1

www.berghain.de, in German; Am Wriezener Bahnhof, Friedrichshain; cover €12-15; ☽ from midnight Fri to late Sun; 🚉 Ostbahnhof

It may have lost DJ Mag's accolade as 'best club in the world' to Manchester's Club Sankey's in 2010, but among global clubbers getting into Berghain is still akin to capturing the Holy Grail. Only top vinyl masters heat up this hedonistic bass junkie hellhole inside a labyrinthine ex-power plant. The big factory floor (Berghain) is gay-leaning and pounds with minimal techno beats. Upstairs, Panorama Bar is smaller, more mixed and pulsating with house and electro. The huge close-up of a vagina by artist Wolfgang Tillmanns above the U-shaped bar more than hints at the club's sexually libertine nature with its dark-rooms and alcoves for, ahem, cuddling. The fantastic sound system feels as though god himself is barking orders. Strict door and no cameras. In summer, there's a beer garden for daytime chilling.

BOHANNON CLUB Map pp102-3

☎ 6950 5287; www.bohannon.de, in German; Dircksenstrasse 40, Mitte; cover €6-8; ☽ from 11pm Mon, Fri & Sat; 🚉 Hackescher Markt

If soul's your thang, drag your posse to this unpretentious and low-key basement club

where top Berlin groovemeisters and visiting stars (eg Gilles Peterson) spin a wicked genre-hopping mix of funk, hip hop, reggae and dancehall with as much emphasis on tunes as beats. It's linked to the Sonar Kollektiv record label owned by downtempo legends Jazzanova. Barney Millah's Monday residency Escobar is cult among reggae fans.

CASSIOPEIA Map pp150-1

☎ 2936 2966; www.cassiopeia-berlin.de; Revaler Strasse 99, Friedrichshain; cover €4-6; ☽ Tue & Thu-Sat; 🚇 🚉 Warschauer Strasse

An old-time train repair shop has been turned into a grungy playground that includes a skate hall, a beer garden, a climbing wall and this attitude-free, two-floor party den. The college-age crowd defines the word eclectic and so does the music, which covers the spectrum from vintage hip hop to hard funk, reggae and punk to the full spectrum of electronic beats.

CLÄRCHENS BALLHAUS Map pp102-3

☎ 282 9295; www.ballhaus.de, in German; Auguststrasse 24, Mitte; Fri & Sat cover €3; ☽ from 10pm Mon, 9pm Tue-Thu, 8pm Fri & Sat, 3pm Sun; 🚉 Oranienburger Strasse

Yesteryear is now at this late, great 19th-century dance hall where hipsters to

---

PARTY MILES

- Köpenicker Strasse (Map pp140-1; Mitte) Industrial riverside strip where nights might start with chic supper at Spindler & Klatt (p210), continue with a caipirinha at Kiki Blofeld (p224) and finish with steaming up the dance floor at Tresor (p235) or, if you're in the mood (and dressed right), the libidinous KitKatClub@Sage (p234).
- Kottbusser Tor/Oranienstrasse (Map pp140-1; Kreuzberg) Grungetastic area best suited to dedicated drink-a-thons at Möbel Olfe (p226), Würgeengel (p226) and Monarch Bar (p225). For live music and dancing, check out what's on at SO36 (p237).
- Mühlenstrasse (Map pp150-1; Friedrichshain) Paralleling the Spree, this strip is perfect for an extended beach-bar hop with stops at Oststrand (p224) and Strandgut Berlin (p224) as a warm-up for hardcore partying at Berghain/Panorama Bar (p232).
- Oranienburger Strasse (Map pp102-3; Mitte) Major tourist zone where you have to hopscotch around sex work-ers and pub crawlers to drown your sorrows in overpriced bars.
- Ostkreuz (Map pp150-1; Friedrichshain) Draw a bead on Berlin's best underground party zone by staggering through the dark trying to find the entrance to Salon zur Wilden Renate (p234) or ://about blank (p231).
- Revaler Strasse (Map pp150-1; Friedrichshain) Rare surviving (post)-squatter-punk-grunge bastion with recent arrivals such as Suicide Circus (p235) and Astra Kulturhaus (p236) nicely fitting in with classic haunts such as Cassiopeia (p232).
- Schlesische Strasse & Schlesisches Tor (Map pp140-1; Kreuzberg) Freestyle street where you could get liquid-ated at Heinz Minki (p226) or Freischwimmer (p225), catch a band at Lido (p236) or Magnet (p237), dance till sunrise at Watergate (p235), then wrap up with chilling at Club der Visionäre (p233) or Badeschiff (p147).
- Simon-Dach-Strasse (Map pp150-1; Friedrichshain) If you need a cheap buzz, head to this well-trodden party strip. Kptn A Müller (p227) and Place Clichy (p227) are best for escaping the cookie-cutter booze parlours along here.

grannies hoof it across the wooden floor to tango (Tuesday), swing (Wednesday) and ballroom (Thursday to Sunday). On Saturday it turns into a regular disco after the live band stops playing. Dance classes and Sunday concerts are held upstairs in the lavish *Spiegelsaal* (Mirror Hall). Pizza and German soul food are available from 12.30pm, and also in the lovely garden in summer months.

CLUB DER VISIONÄRE Map pp140-1

☎ 6951 8942; www.clubdervisionaere.com, in German; Am Flutgraben 1, Kreuzberg; cover free–€10; ☺ from 2pm Mon-Fri, from noon Sat & Sun; ④ Schlesisches Tor

This summertime chill and party playground in an old canal-side boatshed is great for a drink or two at any time of day or night. Hang out beneath the weeping willows or claim a spot on the planks above the water. On weekends it practically never closes, making it one of the buzziest after-party spots in town.

COOKIES Map pp76-7

www.cookies-berlin.de; Friedrichstrasse, Mitte; cover €12; ☺ 10.30pm-6am Tue & Thu; ④ Französische Strasse

This legendary party palace is now in its seventh incarnation in a retro-glam GDR-era cinema in the Westin Grand Hotel building. True to impresario Heinz Gindullis' style, there's no sign, a tough door, great cocktails (try the Watermelon Man) and a grown-up ambience. Celeb sightings possible. The entrance is next to the KPM store. Aside from the regular midweek parties, it also hosts the occasional special Saturday event, such as SpyClub (p261) or label parties.

DELICIOUS DOUGHNUTS Map pp102-3

☎ 2809 9279; www.delicious-doughnuts.de, in German; Rosenthaler Strasse 9, Mitte; Sun-Tue free, Wed-Sat cover €3; ☺ from 10pm; ④ Weinmeisterstrasse

A sweet Mitte staple since the '90s and a favourite with off-duty barkeeps, this living room-sized club is tailor-made for random partying with inebriated strangers when things are winding up everywhere else. In fact, its legendary 'Good Morning Vietnam' parties start when the garbage trucks start making their rounds. The vibe's welcoming and low-key, the door is easy and the drinks menu is endless.

FELIX CLUBRESTAURANT Map pp76-7

☎ 301 117 152; www.felix-clubrestaurant.de, in German; Behrenstrasse 72, Mitte; cover €5-15; ☺ from 7pm Thu-Sat; ④ Unter den Linden

Once past the rope of this exclusive supper club at the Hotel Adlon, you too can shake your booty to 'international club sounds', sip champagne cocktails pinkie raised and – who knows? – maybe even meet your very own Carrie or 'Mr Big'. The flirt factor is through the roof at Thursday's after-business parties hosted by chart radio station RTL.

GOLDEN GATE Map p96

www.goldengate-berlin.de; Dircksenstrasse 77-78, Mitte; ☺ from midnight Thu-Sat; cover €4-8; ④ Jannowitzbrücke

If you yearn for the rough sound and aesthetics of '90s Berlin, you'll break into a sweaty flashback at this grimy club in a graffiti-slathered crumbler beneath the Jannowitzbrücke train tracks. Dedicated hedonists, dressed down for business, slam the dance floor for 24-hour technofests. Cool crowd, great music, scary toilets. Best time: Thursday in the am.

HORST KRZBRG Map pp140-1

www.myspace.com/horstkrzbrg, in German; Tempelhofer Ufer 1, Kreuzberg; ☺ from midnight Fri & Sat; ④ Hallesches Tor

A former post office has taken on a new lease on life as a small electro club with a big sound, cool lighting system and hipster crowd that keeps it casual and attitude free. The bar is great for socialising and the free mints and deodorant come in handy in case of hook-ups.

K17 Map pp150-1

☎ 4208 9300; www.k17.de, in German; Pettenkoferstrasse 17a, Friedrichshain; cover €6; ☺ from 10pm; ④ ④ Frankfurter Allee

If you worship at the altar of darkness, you need to know about K17, Berlin's top club for all things Goth, industrial, metal etc. Kasi, as some say, has live concerts as well as a rotating roster of parties with colourful names (Volt Control, Hellsinki Vampires), some of them taking over all four dance floors.

KAFFEE BURGER Map pp102-3

☎ 2804 6495; www.kaffeeburger.de, in German; Torstrasse 60, Mitte; cover €1-5, concerts €5-7; ☺ nightly; ④ Rosa-Luxemburg-Platz

Nothing to do with either coffee or meat patties, this sweaty cult club with lovingly faded East German decor is the home of Wladimir Kaminer's twice-monthly Russendisko, where even Madonna once mixed it up with wrinkle-free hipsters. But even without a celebrity in sight, it's always a fun-for-all party pen (indie, punk, rock, Balkanbeats) with cheap drinks, nightly dancing, the occasional concert and Sunday literature readings.

NBI Map pp156-7

☎ 6730 4457; www.neueberlinerinitiative.de, in German; Kulturbrauerei, Schönhauser Allee 36, Prenzlauer Berg; cover €3-8; ☾ from 8pm; ⊕ Eberswalder Strasse

This dark and sweaty burrow in the Kulturbrauerei is a gay fave for Shade Inc (p261) electro parties on Wednesdays. On other nights the young and the restless of all persuasions invade for a pot-pourri of disco parties, live gigs, label nights, ping pong competitions and other smooth and fun(ky) events.

RITTER BUTZKE Map pp140-1

www.myspace.com/ritterbutzke; Ritterstrasse 24, Kreuzberg; ☾ Wed, Fri & Sat; ⊕ Moritzplatz

For the longest time, parties at Ritter Butzke were word-of-mouth, whispered between cognoscenti keen on keeping the riff-raff out. No more. Now officially licensed and with a decent sound system, Kreuzberg's best known 'underground' club keeps punters dancing to house and electro on two floors most weekends. Still without the riff-raff…

SALON ZUR WILDEN RENATE
off Map pp150-1

www.renate.cc; Alt Stralau 70, Friedrichshain; ☾ usually Fri & Sat; ☒ Ostkreuz

Getting inside Renate feels like entering a party organised by your best squatter friends. Literally spread over several flats in an abandoned and isolated residential building, it's stuffy, stuffed and stifling, but never mind: the gussied-up dive flair is why you're here and if not, you probably won't make it past the door anyway.

SEX & THE CITY

A steep flight of stairs spills into a hall-like room bathed in red and gold and bordered by a long bar. Thumping house music keeps the dance floor throbbing. The ambience is relaxed, friendly and uninhibited. This could be just your average Berlin nightclub were it not for the patrons clad in rubber suits, cupless corsets, kilts, capes and other sexy-kinky outfits. Many are busy with foreplay, turned on by large-screen porn, live shows and their own imaginations. Others have retreated upstairs to open lounge beds or to back rooms outfitted with toys, tubs and even a gynaecological chair.

Welcome to Insomnia, an erotic nightclub presided over by the statuesque Dominique (opposite). Yup, the decadence of the Weimar years is alive and kicking in this city long known for its libertine leanings. While full-on sex clubs are most common in the gay scene (eg Lab.Oratory, p261), places such as Insomnia and the KitKatClub allow straights, gays, lesbians, the bi-curious and polysexuals to live out their fantasies in a safe if public setting. Surprisingly, there's nothing seedy about this, but you do need to check your inhibitions – and much of your clothing – at the door. If fetish gear doesn't do it for you, wear something sexy or glamorous; men can usually get away with tight pants and an open (or no) shirt. No normal street clothes, no tidy whities. As elsewhere, couples and girl groups get in more easily than all-guy crews. And don't forget: always practice safe sex.

Insomnia (off Map pp72-3; ☎ 0178-233 3878; www.insomnia-berlin.de; Alt-Tempelhof 17-19; ☾ Tue-Sun; ⊕ Alt-Tempelhof) This late-19th-century ballroom has been reincarnated as a classy playground of passion. Besides the dance floor and big-screen Andrew Blake porn, there are performances and various pleasure pits, including a whirlpool, a gynaecological chair and a bondage room. Saturday's Circus Bizarre is good for first-timers (cover couples/men/women €22/17/12); most of the special-themed sex parties on other nights during the week are for more advanced players; some require preregistration. Check the website for full details.

KitKatClub@Sage (Map pp140-1; www.kitkatclub.org; Köpenicker Strasse 76, enter via Brückenstrasse; cover €6-12; ☾ from 11pm Fri & Sat, 8am Sun; ⊕ Heinrich-Heine-Strasse) This 'kitty' is naughty and sexy, raucous and decadent, listens to techno and house, and fancies leather and lace, vinyl and whips. It hides out at Sage with its four dance floors, shimmering pools and fire-breathing dragon. On weekends, the party never stops, starting with the classic Carneball Bizarre on Saturday and continuing through to midmorning Monday. The dress code varies; usually a combination of fetish, leather, uniforms, latex, costumes, Goth, evening dresses, glamour, or an extravagant outfit of any type. No dress code on Sunday.

DOMINIQUE – THE SOVEREIGN OF SEX

How did you get started in the erotic business? I've always been interested in sex. My mother was a dominatrix and I opened my own SM studio just before turning 18. Later I ran SM seminars, parties at the KitKatClub and erotic performances with Double Trouble (www.doubletrouble-berlin.de, in German).

What makes Insomnia special? It's a stylish and safe place that brings together night owls, clubbers, swingers and fetish and SM people.

Any tips for first-timers? Be open, friendly and communicative. Watching is ok but clumsily grabbing strangers is not.

What's so great about your job? I love it when people tell me that I've made a positive difference in their lives.

What do you do to relax? Definitely no partying! I take my son cycling in the forest, get together with friends or read a good book.

An interview with Dominique, dominatrix, performer and owner of Insomnia erotic nightclub, opposite.

SUICIDE CIRCUS Map pp150-1

www.suicide-berlin.com; Revaler Strasse 99, Friedrichshain; ⏰ from 8pm Thu, midnight Fri & Sat, 6pm Sun; ⓔ Ⓡ Warschauer Strasse

The permanent home of the vaunted Suicide Club draws tousled hipsters hungry for an eclectic electro shower to this funky-town dive that at times feels like a (non-mainstream) mini-Berghain – sweaty, edgy, industrial. In summer, watch the stars fade on the outdoor floor with chillier sounds and a Bratwurst man.

TAPE CLUB Map pp76-7

www.tapeberlin.de; Heidestrasse 14, Mitte; ⏰ midnight Fri & Sat; ⓔ Ⓡ Hauptbahnhof

In an obscure location in an industrial area north of the Hauptbahnhof, top local and visiting DJs get clued-in clubbers going with Chicago- and Detroit-influenced house on a dance floor anchored by a giant 'tree sculpture' that must be seen to be believed. Watch out for the 'Tape Modern' party series, a fusion of club and art expo and, if you're gay, the bimonthly Horse Meat Disco (p261). Major kudos for the Funktion One sound system.

TRESOR Map pp140-1

www.tresorberlin.de; Köpenicker Strasse 70, Mitte; cover €10-15; ⏰ from 11pm Wed, Fri & Sat; ⓔ Heinrich-Heine-Strasse

The rebirth of the quintessential '90s techno club, Tresor has all the right ingredients for success: the industrial maze of a derelict power station, awesome sound and a pretty consistent house and techno DJ line-up. Even the namesake vault has found a new home in the basement, reached via a

long tunnel. Compared with Berghain, the door is pretty loose, making this a popular destination for suburban weekend warriors.

WATERGATE Map pp140-1

www.water-gate.de; Falckensteinstrasse 49a, Kreuzberg; cover €10-12; ⏰ Wed, Fri & Sat; ⓔ Schlesisches Tor

It's a short night's journey into day at one of Berlin's best-established high-octane dance temples with a fantastic location overlooking the Spree opposite the colour-changing logo of Universal Music's German HQ. A killer DJ line-up keeps the clued-in crowd hot and sweaty with whipping techno, electro, house and minimal, both on the main floor upstairs and the 'water floor' below. In summer, the terrace floating in the Spree is for sunrise chilling. Long queues, tight door, especially on weekends.

WEEKEND Map p96

www.week-end-berlin.de; Alexanderplatz 5, Mitte; cover €12; ⏰ Thu-Sat; ⓔ Ⓡ Alexanderplatz

This hot 'n' heavy club in a high-rise GDR-era office building is a stunner, with awesome views, sleek minimalist design and high-profile spinners such as Tiefschwarz, Phonique and Monika Kruse whipping house and minimalist techno into a froth. There are three levels: the 12th floor with its panoramic windows, the inky-black 15th and, as the icing on the top, the rooftop lounge (summer only).

LIVE MUSIC

Berlin's live music scene is as diverse as the city itself. There's no Berlin sound as such, but many eclectic developments at once,

from punk rock by the Beatsteaks to Seeeds'
upbeat reggae and the sugar-sweet melodies
of 2raumwohnung, from Jazzanova's downtempo easy-listening to Bushido's aggressive
rap and the fun punk rock of Die Ärzte.

Harking back to the louche heyday of
the 1920s, Berlin's jazz scene just keeps
on jumpin', with several fancy places in
Charlottenburg balanced out by some
pleasingly insalubrious joints further east.
Wherever you go, you're guaranteed a good
mix of local and international performers pre-
senting some very diverse interpretations of
the core genre.

Famous international acts appear at the
city's big halls; see the boxed text, opposite, for
the roundup.

A-TRANE Map p128
☎ 313 2550; www.a-trane.de, in German;
Bleibtreustrasse 1, Charlottenburg; cover €5-
20; ☾ 9pm-2am Sun-Thu, 9pm-late Fri & Sat;
⊛ Savignyplatz
Herbie Hancock and Diana Krall have
anointed the stage of this intimate jazz
club, but mostly it's emerging talent
bringing their A-game to the A-Trane. Entry
is free on Monday, when local Andreas
Schmidt shows off his dexterous skills, and
after 12.30am on Saturday for the louche
late-night jam session.

ASTRA KULTURHAUS Map pp150-1
☎ 2005 6767; www.astra-berlin.de, in German;
Revaler Strasse 99, Friedrichshain; ticket prices vary;
☾ concert 8pm or 9pm; ⊙ ⊛ Warschauer Strasse
Brought to you by the folks of Lido (right)
across the river, Astra has been a kick-ass
addition to Berlin's live music scene. With
space for 1500, it's one of the biggest indie
spaces in town yet often fills up easily,
and not just for such headliners as Melissa
Etheridge, Kasabian and the Eels. Bonus:

top picks

BEST BOOKERS

- Astra Kulturhaus (above)
- b-flat (right)
- Lido (right)
- Magnet (opposite)
- Wild at Heart (p238)
- S036 (opposite)

the supersweet '50s GDR decor. There's a
beer garden in summer.

B-FLAT Map pp102-3
☎ 283 3123; www.b-flat-berlin.de, in German;
Rosenthaler Strasse 13, Mitte; most tickets €10;
☾ from 8pm; ⊙ Weinmeisterstrasse
Cool cats of all ages come out to this intimate venue, where the audience sits quite
literally within spitting distance of the
performers. The emphasis is on acoustic
music; mostly jazz, world beats, Afro-Brazilian
and other soundscapes. Wednesday's free
jam session often brings down the house.

FESTSAAL KREUZBERG Map pp140-1
☎ 6165 6003; www.festsaal-kreuzberg.de, in
German; Skalitzer Strasse 130, Kreuzberg;
⊙ Kottbusser Tor
Owned by the same folks as the nearby
Monarch Bar (p225), this former Turkish
wedding ballroom is increasingly becoming
an essential space to watch for up-and-
coming indie bands. The sound's good, the
crowd's cool and there's not a bad seat in
the house. If you can, though, score a spot
on the balcony for birds-eye views of the
action. Parties, readings and performances
pad the music schedule.

KNAACK Map pp156-7
☎ 442 7060; www.knaack-berlin.de, in German;
Greifswalder Strasse 224, Prenzlauer Berg; most
concerts €1, bigger names up to €20, parties free-€5;
☾ from 7pm; ⊛ M4
This 1952-vintage warren has done its part
in giving an early platform to megabands
such as Rammstein, Die Toten Hosen and
the Beatsteaks. Still going strong with the
youngster set, who come for indie concerts
and dance parties, the club's survival was
under threat at the time of writing because
of noise restrictions imposed after neighbours in adjacent condominiums had sued
in court. Knaack's owners were looking for
a new location in Kreuzberg, following the
move Magnet has made.

LIDO Map pp140-1
☎ 6956 6840, tickets 6110 1313; www.lido-berlin
.de, in German; Cuvrystrasse 7, Kreuzberg; cover
varies; ⊙ Schlesisches Tor
A 1950s cinema has been recycled into a
rock-indie-electropop mecca with moshpit
electricity and a crowd that cares more
about the music than about looking good.

Global DJs and talented upwardly mobile live noisemakers pull in the indie crowd with full force.

MAGNET Map pp140-1

☎ 4400 8140; www.magnet-club.de, in German; Falckensteinstrasse 48, Kreuzberg; concerts €5-20, parties €2-6; ◉ Schlesisches Tor

After being forced from its long-time Prenzlauer Berg location, this indie and alt-sound bastion is now in new digs next to Watergate. It's known for bookers with an astronomer's ability to detect stars in the making, which is why LCD Soundsystem and the Presets had early shows here. After the last riff, the mostly student-aged crowd hits the dance floor to Britpop, emo, indietronics, house or dub-step.

SO36 Map pp140-1

☎ 6140 1306; www.so36.de, in German; Oranienstrasse 190, Kreuzberg; cover €3-8; ◷ most nights; ◉ Kottbusser Tor, ☒ 129

Check your attitude at the door of scruffy 'Esso', the seminal club collective that's still the epicentre of Kreuzberg's alternative scene. The Dead Kennedys and Die Toten Hosen played early gigs here when many of today's patrons were still in nappies (diapers). Who goes depends on what's on that night: a concert, a gay party, a night flea market – anything goes at SO36. It's scary that this legend's survival was also recently threatened with closure after neighbours sued for noise. After much back and forth, the club finally won a reprieve until 2020, with the proviso that a costly sound protection wall be installed.

STAR ARENAS

From Shakira to Tina Turner to Coldplay, whenever big international acts and megastars roll into town, chances are they'll be heating up one of these venues. Tickets are either sold through the venue (via hotline or online) or through agencies such as Koka 36 (p231).

Arena (Map pp140-1; ☎ tickets 533 2030; www.arena-berlin.de, in German; Eichenstrasse 4, Treptow; ◉ Schlesisches Tor, ☒ Treptower Park) The midsized Arena easily holds its own against larger venues, particularly when the open riverside area is being used. The adjacent Glashaus hosts smaller gigs and some theatre; the Badeschiff (p147) and Hoppetosse restaurant club (with free wi-fi) are also part of the complex.

C-Halle (Map pp140-1; www.c-halle.com; Columbiadamm 13-21, Tempelhof; ◉ Platz der Luftbrücke) Renamed from Columbiahalle in 2010, C-Halle started out as a US air force gym and now hosts up to 3500 fans, primarily for hardcore rock concerts (eg Limp Bizkit, Apocalyptica).

Kindl-Bühne Wuhlheide (☎ tickets 6110 1313; www.kindl-buehne-wuhlheide.de; An der Wuhlheide 187, Köpenick; ◷ May-Sep; ☒ Wuhlheide) The eastern pendant to the Waldbühne, this 17,000-seat outdoor amphitheatre was built in the early 1950s from war debris and is much beloved for its vibe and variety. It has hosted such bandwidth bigwigs as Rammstein and Radiohead.

Max-Schmeling-Halle (Map pp156-7; ☎ tickets 4430 4430; www.max-schmeling-halle.de, in German; Falkplatz 1, Prenzlauer Berg; ◉ Eberswalder Strasse) This 8500-seat hall is home base for Berlin's German-league handball team Die Füchse (Foxes), and also hosts boxing matches, ballroom-dancing contests and alt-rock veterans such as Deep Purple and Alice Cooper.

O2 World (Map pp150-1; ☎ tickets 01803 206 070; www.o2-world.de; Mühlenstrasse 12-30, Friedrichshain; ☒ Ostbahnhof) The jewel among Berlin's multiuse venues, this 17,000-seat arena has welcomed entertainment royalty (Tina Turner, Linkin Park, Sting) since September 2008 and is also home turf for the city's professional ice hockey team, the Eisbären Berlin (p315), and basketball team Alba Berlin (p315).

Olympiastadion (off Map p72-3 www.olympiastadion-berlin.de; Olympischer Platz 3, Charlottenburg; ☒ Olympiastadion) Not even Madonna managed to fill the 74,400 seats of the historic Olympic stadium that's also home to Berlin soccer team Hertha BSC (p131).

Tempodrom (Map pp140-1; ☎ tickets 01805 54 111; www.tempodrom.de; Möckernstrasse 10, Kreuzberg; ☒ Anhalter Bahnhof) The white, tent-shaped Tempodrom has super-eclectic programming that may feature a salsa congress, a Steve Winwood concert and the German snooker masters all in the same month.

Waldbühne (off Map pp72-3; ☎ 01805 969 000 555; www.concert-concept.de, in German; Am Glockenturm, Charlottenburg; ◷ May-Sep; ☒ Pichelsberg) Summers in Berlin just wouldn't be the same without this chill spot for symphonies under the stars, big-name rock, jazz and comedy acts and film presentations. The Nazi-built, open-air amphitheatre in the woods has been around since 1936, and has exceptional acoustics and space for 22,000 people.

WHITE TRASH FAST FOOD Map pp156-7

☎ 5034 8668; www.whitetrashfastfood.com;
Schönhauser Allee 6-7, Mitte; cover €1-12; ⊙ from
6pm; ⊙ Rosa-Luxemburg-Platz
Edgy and borderline insane, this ex-Irish
pub with Chinese flourishes attracts a rock-
and-roll crowd with tasty burgers and live
punk, rock or country in the bar-restaurant
(p216) or in the cavernous downstairs
Diamond Lounge.

WILD AT HEART Map pp140-1

☎ 611 9231; www.wildatheartberlin.de; Wiener
Strasse 20, Kreuzberg; cover varies, usually €5-10;
⊙ from 8pm; ⊙ Görlitzer Bahnhof
Named after a David Lynch road movie,
this kitsch-cool dive with its blood-red
walls, tiki gods and Elvis paraphernalia
hammers home punk, ska, surf-rock and
rockabilly. Touring bands, including top
acts such as Girlschool and Dick Dale,
bring in the tattooed set nightly. It's really,
REALLY loud, so if your ears need a break,
head to the tiki-themed restaurant-bar
next door.

YORCKSCHLÖSSCHEN Map pp140-1

☎ 215 8070; www.yorckschloesschen.de;
Yorckstrasse 15, Kreuzberg; concerts €4-6;
⊙ 10pm-3am mid-Apr–mid-Oct, 5pm-3am
Mon-Sat, 10am-3am Sun mid-Oct–mid-Apr;
⊙ ⊛ Yorckstrasse; ⊚
The name means 'small Yorck castle', but
this Kreuzberg institution is no snazzy
palace. Instead, it's a knickknack-laden
watering hole that has plied an all-ages,
all-comers crowd of jazz and blues lovers
with tunes and booze for more than a
century. There's live music on Wednesday
and weekends in summer (also Thursday
and Friday in winter), food till 1am (dishes
€3 to €10), a pool table in the back and a
garden for chilling.

CABARET & VARIETY

The light, lively and lavish variety shows of
the Golden Twenties have been undergoing
a sweeping revival in Berlin. Get ready
for an evening of dancing and singing,
jugglers, acrobats and other entertainers.
These 'cabarets' should not be confused with
Kabarett, which are political and satirical
shows with monologues and short skits.
For the full retro flash you can often dine at
your table.

ADMIRALSPALAST Map pp76-7

☎ 4799 7499; www.admiralspalast.de, in German;
Friedrichstrasse 101-102, Mitte; ⊙
⊛ Friedrichstrasse
This beautifully restored 1920s party palace
stages crowd-pleasing plays, concerts and
musicals in its elegant, historic hall, and
more intimate shows – including comedy,
readings, dance, concerts and theatre –
on two smaller stages. Programming is
international and usually of high calibre.

BAR JEDER VERNUNFT Map pp124-5

☎ 883 1582; www.bar-jeder-vernunft.de, in
German; Schaperstrasse 24, Charlottenburg/
Wilmersdorf; ⊙ Spichernstrasse
Life's still a cabaret at this intimate 1912
Art Nouveau mirrored tent, which puts on
song-and-dance shows, comedy and
chanson evenings plus, intermittently, the
famous *Cabaret* cult musical itself. If you
just want to see the place, have a post-
show drink in the bar. Enter via the
parking lot.

BLUE MAN GROUP Map p112

☎ 01805-4444; www.bluemangroup.de;
Marlene-Dietrich-Platz 4, Tiergarten; tickets €60;
⊙ ⊛ Potsdamer Platz
This musical and visual extravaganza,
starring slightly nutty and energetic guys
dipped in Smurf-blue latex suits, performs
at its own permanent theatre, a converted
IMAX now called Bluemax.

CHAMÄLEON VARIÉTÉ Map pp102-3

☎ 400 0590; www.chamaeleonberlin.de;
Rosenthaler Strasse 40-41, Mitte; tickets €34-45;
⊛ Hackescher Markt
An alchemy of Art Nouveau charms and
high-tech theatre trappings, this intimate
former ballroom presents classy variety
shows – comedy, juggling, singing, dancing,
acrobatics – often in sassy, sexy and
unconventional fashion.

FRIEDRICHSTADTPALAST Map pp102-3

☎ 2326 2326; www.friedrichstadtpalast.de;
Friedrichstrasse 107, Mitte; tickets €17-105;
⊙ Oranienburger Tor
Europe's largest revue theatre is famous for
glitzy-glam Vegas-style productions with
leggy showgirls in skimpy costumes and
feather boas. After hovering on the brink
of bankruptcy in 2008, new impresario

Bernard Schmidt has brought the famous 1920s palace back to life with increasingly creative shows that not only impress provincial coach tourists.

COMEDY CLUBS

From stand-up to sketch and musical comedy, there are many ways to have your funny bones tickled in Berlin. Refreshingly, for all of us non-German speakers, there are even a couple of venues offering English-language shows.

COMEDY IN SIN Map pp140-1

☎ 6920 5103; http://sin-berlin.de; Schönleinstrasse 6, Kreuzberg; admission €3; ⏰ 9pm 1st Thu of month; ⊖ Schönleinstrasse

Once a month local ex-pat stand-up comedians unload their offbeat and equal-opportunity-offensive material on loyal fans and unsuspecting newcomers in a classic Kreuzberg pub called SIN (aka Stranded in Neverland). In case it changes venue, check host Paul Salamone's website (www.paulsalamone.com) for the latest news on the scene.

KOOKABURRA Map pp156-7

☎ 4862 3186; www.comedyclub.de; Schönhauser Allee 184, Prenzlauer Berg; tickets €3-10; ⊖ Rosa-Luxemburg-Platz

Berlin's first stand-up comedy club delivers an assembly line of laughs every night of the week in the living-room-vibe digs of a former bank building. On Tuesday nights and late on Saturdays (from 11.45pm), funny folk from English-speaking countries spin everyday material into comedy gold. Think you've got talent? Swing by open mike night, every first and third Saturday, hosted by the inimitable Summer Banks.

QUATSCH COMEDY CLUB Map pp102-3

☎ 2326 2326; www.quatschcomedyclub.de; Friedrichstrasse 107, Mitte; tickets €21-27; ⏰ Thu-Sun; ⊖ ⑤ Friedrichstrasse

The stars of German comedy (Ingo Appelt, Cindy von Marzahn) regularly pave the boards of this top-rated club in a side wing of the Friedrichstadtpalast (opposite). German TV host Thomas Hermanns is the man behind the curtain of what many consider the top club in the country. All shows are in German.

CASINOS

CASINO BERLIN Map p96

☎ 2063 099 102; www.casino-berlin.de, in German; Park Inn Berlin, Alexanderplatz, Mitte; cover €5; ⏰ 3pm-3am; ⊖ ⑤ Alexanderplatz

Craps with a view: Berlin's highest den of vice is on the 37th floor, offering all the usual card and random-chance games. Minimum age 18, tie and jacket required (may be borrowed). If you like it more casual – or are prone to vertigo – steer towards the slot machines on the ground floor of the Fernsehturm (TV Tower; Map p96; ☎ 2063 0990; Panoramastrasse 1a; cover €1; ⏰ 11am-3am).

SPIELBANK BERLIN Map p112

☎ 255 990; www.spielbank-berlin.de; Marlene-Dietrich-Platz 1, Tiergarten; admission €5; ⏰ slots 11am-3am, table games 3pm-3am; ⊖ ⑤ Potsdamer Platz

Parked next to the glass-fronted Potsdamer Platz Theater, the Spielbank claims to be Germany's largest casino, with tables and machines spread over three floors. The gaming areas are split into Classic Play (roulette, black jack and poker), a poker-only floor and slot machines. Admission throughout is for those over 18 only.

BERLIN ART ATTACK

Hamburger Bahnhof – Museum of Contemporary Art (p75)

DAVID PEEVER

Neue Nationalgalerie (p115)

Forget about New York and London: Berlin's the city to watch on the world's artistic circuit. Unemployment and the municipal debt may remain high, but when it comes to fashion, art, design and music, the German capital is firing on all cylinders. A steady influx of international creatives, bristling with imagination and optimism, has turned Berlin into a cauldron of cultural cool on par with New York in the '80s. What draws them is an adolescent energy, restlessness and an experimental climate infused with an undercurrent of grit and roughness that give this 'eternally unfinished' city its street cred. Go now! There's a vibrancy about Berlin that's simply irresistible.

GETTING VISUAL

Art aficionados will find their compass on perpetual spin in Berlin, which has developed the most exciting and dynamic arts scene in Europe. Galleries are opening, folding and moving at breathtaking speed but quality is only getting better. With an active community of as many as 10,000 artists, there have been

top picks

CONTEMPORARY MUSEUMS & GALLERIES

Sammlung Boros (p79) Cutting-edge works in a WWII bunker.

Hamburger Bahnhof (p75) All aboard the art express at this former train station.

KW Institute for Contemporary Art (p105) Edgy, alternative, out-there contemporary works.

Akademie der Künste (p81) Keeping an eye out for the best in big-name art du jour.

Sammlung Hoffmann (p80) See top-notch art in the intimate setting of a stylish private apartment.

Sidle up to a Warhol at Hamburger Bahnhof (p75)

VARIO IMAGES GMBH & CO.KG/ALAMY

some notable breakthroughs, most famously perhaps Danish-Icelandic artist Olafur Eliasson. Other major contemporary artists living and working in Berlin include Thomas Demand, Jonathan Meese, Via Lewandowsky, Isa Genzken, Tino Seghal, Esra Ersen, John Bock and the artist duo Ingar Dragset und Michael Elmgreen.

Gallery Quarters

Besides the main museums, Berlin has several gallery quarters. Established galleries are prevalent in the Scheunenviertel, especially along Linienstrasse and Auguststrasse and in Charlottenburg along Fasanenstrasse, Mommsenstrasse and Ku'damm. The Checkpoint Charlie area mixes old hands on Zimmerstrasse and newcomers, mostly on Markgrafenstrasse, while contenders on Brunnenstrasse tend to be more experimental and low-brow. A few galleries have also sprung up north

of Hauptbahnhof, especially on Heidestrasse and in the Halle am Wasser (Map pp76-7; Hall on the Water; Invalidenstrasse 50-51), a row of canal-side warehouse-style spaces located north of the Hamburger Bahnhof museum. Over the past couple of years, Potsdamer Strasse has also emerged as new hot spot, with some major galleries decamping to this gritty part of Schöneberg. In the east, meanwhile, the area to watch is Karl-Marx-Allee, especially around Strausberger Platz.

Art Forum Berlin (p19) and the Berlin Biennale (p18) are the highpoints of the art calendar.

Berlin's abundant art scene and relatively low cost of living have made it a haven for international emerging artists, many of whom can afford to base themselves in two cities. Other artists, like Australian art duo Sleep Club (Adam Cruickshank and Dell Stewart), participate in residency programmes at places like Takt Kunstprojektraum (www.taktberlin.org) in Friedrichshain. 'There's a real sense of opportunity in Berlin. There are loads of openings and it seems like there's a new gallery every week', reports Cruickshank, adding that the city allows artists to focus on producing art without having to resort to outside work.

Get inspired by local art at Berlinische Galerie (p143)
DAVID PEEVERS

Graffiti rules at Kunsthaus Tacheles (p106)
MARTIN MOOS

Street Art

Stencils, paste-ups, throw-ups, burners, bombings, pieces, murals, installations and 3-D graffiti are the magic words in street art, describing styles and techniques that have little to do with vandalism, tagging and illegal scrawls. With no shortage of vacant buildings, weedy lots and artists of all stripes, sometimes it seems as though all of Berlin has become a canvas. Some of the hottest names in international street art have left their mark on local walls, including Banksy, Os Gemeos, Romero, Swoon, Flix, Pure Evil, Miss Van and Italian artist Blu (also see p148). But there's plenty of home-grown talent as well. The portrait of Jack Nicholson behind bird wire is an iconic work by Bonk, while Bimer's signature subject is an angry-looking Berlin bear and Kripoe is known for his yellow hands. Other big names are Alias, El Bocho, XooooX and Emess. Some of them have also helped turn the Kreuzberg restaurant Eckstück (p211) into a 'Sistine Chapel' of street art.

Check out the colourful street art in neighbourhoods such as Prenzlauer Berg (p155)

DAVID PEEVERS

top picks

GO HERE FOR...

Berlin Fashions Berlinomat (p194)

Dessous Blush Dessous (p187)

Second-Hand Sommerladen (p186)

Streetwear Flagshipstore (p195)

Shoes Trippen (p187)

There's street art everywhere but the area around U-Bahn station Schlesisches Tor in Kreuzberg and around Boxhagener Platz in Friedrichshain are hubs. Another hot spot is Brauerei Friedrichshöhe (Map p150-1; Landsberger Allee 54; 🚉 Landsberger Allee), which hosts the Urban Affairs festival in summer. There's also some good work around Mitte and Prenzlauer Berg. The latter has Mauerpark (p159), where budding artists legally polish their skills along a 300m-long stretch of the Berlin Wall. A quick way to see plenty of urban art is by riding the S-Bahn lines S41 or S42, especially between Alexanderplatz and Treptow. The U1 line through Kreuzberg is another good one and ideal for seeing the famous, wall-sized *Astronaut* by Irish artist Ash (on the north side, between Kottbusser Tor and Görlitzer Bahnhof stations).

Shop for Skunkfunk wear at Faster, Pussycat! (p192)

Popping by the gallery ATM (Map pp156-7; ☎ 0176-6255 5810; Brunnenstrasse 24; 🕑 1-7pm Tue-Sat) also helps you keep the finger on the pulse of the scene. Alternative Berlin (p313) runs a 2½-hour street-art walking tour for €15 where you even get to meet local artists and pick up tips and techniques. To read up on the subject, pick up *Urban Illustration Berlin: Street Art City Guide* by Benjamin Wolbergs.

Modern designs in Mitte – Scheunenviertel (p184)

FASHION

In a city where individualism trumps conformity and experimentation is encouraged, it's only natural that the creative climate spawns a design culture that is an expression of Berlin's idiosyncratic spirit. Don't expect stuffy, snob-value couture for fashion clones: the Berlin look is down-to-earth, often practical (even when painstakingly crafted), slightly irreverent and with a fresh edge.

On a day-to-day basis most people aren't overly concerned about what they wear

Menswear store on Alte Schönhauser Strasse (p182)

JOERG BUNTENBACH

Joerg Buntenbach is a fashion expert and publisher of the online magazine Modekultur (www.modekultur.info) that reports on trends and events, new designers and stores around Berlin. He also organises fashion tours (public and by arrangement, from €20) where you gain an insider view of the local scene, meet designers right in their studios and get sneak previews of upcoming collections.

What defines the Berlin style? It's a highly individual style. People don't follow any particular trends but express their personality by combining pieces in unconventional ways. The ultra-casual look is no longer as prevalent. Jeans and T-shirt used to be okay for brunch and the opera. Now people tend to vary their style depending on the occasion.

What draws designers to Berlin? It's still inexpensive, doors are wide open and there are lots of opportunities that don't exist elsewhere. But it's also not a rich city, so designers focus on the international market. Berlin fashions may not be so well known within Germany but they're hugely popular in Asia, especially in Japan, China and South Korea, and also in North America.

What role does Berlin fashion play internationally? Over the past few years Berlin has succeeded in establishing itself as a fashion metropolis. The breakthrough was essentially the Mercedes Benz first Fashion Week in 2007. Since then international designers also show in Berlin and important critics like Suzy Menkes (of the *International Herald Tribune*) are paying attention. Berlin is finally being taken seriously and has become a key player on the international scene.

(despite the city being home to roughly 700 fashion designers and nine design schools), and with the ongoing retro craze many Berliners actually buy their duds by the kilo in second-hand stores. Different scenes have their own look, but there's never a single 'uniform' to follow. Accessories are important, and just about anything can be used to put the finishing touches on an outfit.

Fashion-forward local designers and labels such as the sister-act Talkingmeanstrouble, Claudia Skoda, Kostas Murkudis, Esther Perbrandt, C'est Tout, Kaviar Gauche, Nanna Kuckuck, Lala Berlin and Presque fini walk the line between originality and contemporary trends in a way that more mainstream labels do not. Often, these local labels are more insistent on fair-trade practices and ethical manufacturing than other fashion brands.

As in other arts, experimentation is the order of the day in Berlin, and with the recent streetwear boom (key local labels include Irie Daily, Hasipop and Butterfly Soulfire), Berlin has become a fertile zone for innovative young talent.

The twice-annual Berlin Fashion Week (p16 and p18), held in January and July, is great for keeping a tab on the scene.

THE BERLIN SOUND

Just like the city itself, Berlin's music scene is a shape-shifter, a dynamic and restlessly inventive creature fed by the city's appetite for diversity and change. With at least 2000 active bands and dozens of indie labels, including Bpitch Control, Shitkatapult, !K7 and Get Physical, the city is Germany's undisputed music capital. About 60% of the country's music revenue is generated here, up from a paltry 8% in 1998. In 2002 Universal Music moved its European headquarters here from Hamburg, followed by MTV in 2004. Popkomm, one of the world's top music trade shows, also relocated to Berlin and, in 2010, became part of the inaugural Berlin Music Week (p19), which brings together labels, agents, performers, DJs, club owners and fans for seven days of musical immersion.

top picks

BERLIN TRACKS

Berlin (Lou Reed, *Berlin*, 1973) In Berlin, by the Wall...Lou falls in love.

Dickes B (Seeed, *Dickes B*, 2000) Reggae ode to the 'Big B'.

Heroes (David Bowie, *Heroes*, 1977) Two lovers in the shadow of the 'wall of shame'.

Kreuzberg (Bloc Party, *A Weekend in the City*, 2007) Looking for true love...

Schwarz zu Blau (Peter Fox, *Stadtaffe*, 2008) Perfect portrait of Kottbusser Tor grit and grunge...

Clubbers enjoying the vibe at Watergate (p235)

EVERYNIGHT IMAGES/ALAMY

Berlin is the city where techno came of age, the living heart of the European electronic scene and the spiritual home of the lost weekend. From here, hard-edged techno conquered the world, using the impetus of reunification to tap into the simultaneous explosion of the UK rave scene and the popularity of ecstasy. These days, though, there are no longer any dominant currents but many parallel and crossover developments. Basically, anything goes. Whether you're into house, techno, drum and bass, punk, Britpop, dancehall, hip hop, reggae or ballroom, you'll find a place to party any night of the week.

Although the club scene in Berlin is gentrifying, some of the most vital venues here are still in abandoned postal offices, power stations, GDR buildings, bunkers and factories as well as various dark, dank and derelict locations.

THILO SCHMIED

Thilo Schmied is the owner of Fritz Music Tours (p312).

What makes Berlin special? First of all the so-called *Berliner Herz & Schnauze* (Berlin heart and wit). Then the mix of old and new, architecturally speaking, and the mix of people and cultures from all over the world.

What's your favourite Kiez? Mitte. I grew up when Berlin was still divided by the Wall and after spending some time in other cities I've now been back in my old neighbourhood for years.

What are essential Berlin experiences? Going up the TV Tower (Fernsehturm; p95), eating *Currywurst* at Curry 36 (p214), shopping in the Scheunenviertel (p184) and having a beer at Café am Neuen See (p223), followed by a relaxed walk through the Tiergarten (p117).

What would be your perfect day off? A late breakfast at Strandbad Mitte (p204), then with sunny weather a round of beach volleyball with friends. With bad weather: some shopping around Torstrasse or Alte and Neue Schönhauser Strasse in Mitte. In the evening a concert or a fun dance party somewhere in Kreuzberg or Prenzlauer Berg.

What are your favourite clubs? Lido (p236) for punk, Magnet (p237) for rock and Berghain (p232) for techno.

Venues range from small DJ bars like Delicious Doughnuts (p233) to trash dives such as Cassiopeia (p232), designer dens like Cookies (p233) and world-famous haunts like Berghain/Panorama Bar (p232) and Watergate (p235).

Nostalgia for the improvisational '90s, resentment of picky bouncers and high prices at established clubs – and a desire to keep out brawling suburbanites and tipsy hen parties – is also causing a resurgence of illegal and underground parties. These are impromptu dance-a-thons in S-Bahn stations and trains, tunnels, abandoned buildings, ATM foyers and other unlikely venues – at least until the police show up.

Since these parties rely on email lists or word of mouth, your best bet is to make friends with potentially clued-in locals (eg in places like music shops, cafes, bars and clubs). Facebook and MySpace are also good sources as is the blog http://restrealitaet.de, although you need a sponsor in order to obtain an access code.

top picks

GO HERE FOR...

Afterparty Club der Visionäre (p233)

Big-time DJs Watergate (p235)

Celebrity sightings Cookies (p233)

Hedonism Berghain/Panorama Bar (p232)

Indie sounds Magnet (p237)

Off-beat parties Salon zur Wilden Renate (p234)

Relaxed door Delicious Doughnuts (p233)

Sound system Berghain/Panorama Bar (p232)

Views Weekend (p235)

With so many major DJs living in Berlin – and others happy to visit – Berlin is a veritable musical testing laboratory. Line-ups are often amazing. Names to watch out for include Apparat, Ellen Allien, André Galluzzi, Ricardo Villalobos, Modeselektor, T.Raumschmiere, M.A.N.D.Y. and Sascha Funke, many of whom are both DJs and producers. Even pioneers like Marusha, Dr Motte, Tanith and Paul van Dyk still hit the decks at top clubs around town.

For the full lowdown on major players in Berlin's music and club scene, flick to p45 of the Background chapter.

HAVIN' A BALL IN THE 'HALL BY THE WALL'

Complete this analogy: London is to Abbey Road what Berlin is to...

Well…well? Hansa Studios, of course, that seminal recording studio that has exerted a veritable gravitational pull on international top artists since the murky and fearful Cold War days. The 'Big Hall by the Wall' was how David Bowie fittingly dubbed its glorious Studio 2, better known as the Meistersaal (Masters' Hall), through whose arched windows one could look across the concrete barrier and wave at the gun-toting guards in their watchtowers. In the late '70s, in this acoustically perfect hall, the 'White Duke' recorded his tortured visions in the seminal album *Heroes* and also worked on *Low* and *Lodger*, which together form the Berlin Trilogy. Bowie buddy Iggy Pop, meanwhile, cranked out *Idiot* and *Lust for Life* around the same time. More than two decades later, the lush room, with its coffered ceiling, gilded chandeliers and parquet floors, featured prominently in U2's original video for 'One' (watch it on YouTube).

The Meistersaal is part of the 1913 headquarters of the Greater Berlin construction trade guild. It was heavily damaged during WWII and for decades languished in the shadow of the Berlin Wall until being bought by the Meisel Musikverlag (Meisel Music Publishers) in 1976. In addition to Bowie, Pop and U2, a long list of music legends have taken advantage of Studio 2's special sound quality, including Nina Hagen, Nick Cave, Nena, Marillion, David Byrne, Einstürzende Neubauten, Lou Reed, Die Toten Hosen, Die Ärzte and, more recently, Irish alt-rockers Snow Patrol, Green Day, REM and The Hives. Another key band associated with Hansa is Depeche Mode – the band produced four albums at Hansa (*Construction Time Again*, 1983; *Some Great Reward*, 1984; *The Singles 81–85*, 1985; and *Black Celebration*, 1986). During their time here, they practically invented the art of 'sound sampling', with odd auditory bits they collected with cheap recorders from around the city.

The only way to learn such fascinating tidbits and get inside Hansa is by taking a guided tour with Thilo Schmied, owner of Fritz Music Tours (see our interview with Thilo on p247). The former sound engineer, music promoter and talent scout takes you inside the Meistersaal as well as Studio 1 on the 4th floor, an electronic wonder whose 64-channel mixing board looks like a star-ship command centre. He'll shower you with historical vignettes, technical know-how and cool anecdotes like the time Depeche Mode's Martin Gore stripped down naked for the recording of a love song; see p312.

top picks

- **Babylon Berlin** (p252)
- **Berliner Philharmonie** (p250)
- **Radialsystem V** (p251)
- **Staatsoper Unter den Linden** (p253)
- **Sonntagskonzerte im Spiegelsaal** (p250)

THE ARTS

Open the listings magazine *Tip* and *Zitty* at random and no matter what day you pick, there's no shortage of theatre, music and dance performances happening all over town. Berliners are enthusiastic supporters of the arts and venues are often filled to capacity. The city supports no fewer than three opera houses and seven classical orchestras, including the world-famous Berliner Symphoniker. Theatre has a long tradition also, and there are dozens of small and large venues, several in unusual spaces like abandoned churches or post offices. Key contenders like the Deutsches Theater and the Brecht's Berliner Ensemble cluster in the Mitte theatre district along northern Friedrichstrasse. Cinemas, too, are plentiful, from art houses showing obscure flicks to multiplexes screening the latest blockbusters. Because of Berlin's international nature, many flicks are presented in their original language.

CLASSICAL MUSIC

There's no need to go a day without music in Berlin, and classical music fans are truly spoilt – not only is there a phenomenal range of concerts throughout the year, but almost all the major concert halls are architectural (and acoustic) gems of the highest order. A trip to the Philharmonie or the Konzerthaus is a particular treat, and regular concerts are also organised in Berlin's palaces (☎ 4360 5390; www.berliner-schlosskonzerte.de, in German), including Schloss Köpenick (p171) and Schloss Glienicke (p166). Aficionados under 30 should look into the Classic Card (www.classiccard.de, in German). Note that most venues take a summer hiatus (usually July and August).

BERLINER PHILHARMONIE Map p112
☎ 254 880; www.berliner-philharmoniker.de; Herbert-von-Karajan-Strasse 1, Tiergarten; tickets €15-150; ⊙ ⓡ Potsdamer Platz

This world-famous concert hall has supreme acoustics and, thanks to Hans Scharoun's clever terraced vineyard design, not a bad seat in the house. It's the home base of the Berliner Philharmoniker, currently led by Sir Simon Rattle. Smaller concerts are held at the adjacent Kammermusiksaal (tickets €8–35). Also popular: the free Tuesday lunchtime concerts (⊙ 1pm Tue Sep-Jun) in the foyer of the Philharmonie. For more on the buildings, see p116.

BERLINER SYMPHONIKER
☎ 325 5562; www.berliner-symphoniker.de; tickets €13-35
Founded in 1966, the Berlin Symphony Orchestra performs Sunday concerts featuring wide-ranging classical and popular works in the Berliner Philharmonie (left). Israeli conductor Lior Shambadal has been the man in charge since 1997.

SUNDAY SOUNDS

Wind down the weekend with a classical Sonntagskonzerte (Sunday concert; ☎ 5268 0256; www.sonntagskonzerte .de, in German) held in one of the most unique spaces in Berlin: the Spiegelsaal (Mirror Hall) upstairs at Clärchens Ballhaus (p232), a 19th-century ballroom right in the heart of the Scheunenviertel. On Sundays at 7pm, a small crowd of clued-in fans gathers amid the faded elegance of this historic room to listen to piano concerts, opera recitals, string quartets and other musical offerings. Best of all: it's free (though donations are much appreciated).

Damaged during WWII, the Spiegelsaal was only provisionally restored and then sunk into a long slumber of disuse until being reawakened during renovations a few years ago. Wits its cracked and blinded mirrors, elaborate chandeliers and old-timey wallpaper, it recalls the decadence of past epochs when it was the domain of the city's elite while the common folks hit the planks in the ballroom downstairs. Alfred Döblin set a scene in his novel *Berlin Alexanderplatz* here, as did Tom Cruise's movie *Valkyrie* nearly a hundred years later.

For a schedule of upcoming Sonntagskonzerte check the website or call ahead. It's possible to make reservations but there are no assigned seats, so come early. Also note that for a few weeks in summer, performances take place outdoors against the glorious backdrop of the Bodemuseum (p89) on Museumsinsel (if weather permits).

REDEFINING THE ARTS

Contemporary dance meets medieval music, poetry meets pop, painting meets digital. Radialsystem V (Map pp150-1; ☎ 2887 8850; www.radialsystem. de; Holzmarktstrasse 33; ⊕ Ostbahnhof) is a creative space that defies definition, and intentionally so. Set up in a gorgeously converted early 20th-century riverside pump station for the Berlin waterworks, this progressive cultural centre blurs the boundaries between music, dance, fine arts, new media and other art forms to nurture new forms of creative expression that are greater than the sum of its parts. Ideas here 'radiate' out in all directions, attracting artists and the public from within and beyond Berlin. Nice waterfront cafe-bar from 10am (noon on weekends).

DEUTSCHES SYMPHONIE-ORCHESTER

☎ 2029 8711; www.dso-berlin.de, in German; tickets €9-35

The DSO, led by German Ingo Metzmacher, started life in 1946 and was financed by the USA until 1953. Like the Berliner Symphoniker, it has no permanent venue, although it primarily performs at the amazing Berliner Philharmonie (opposite).

HOCHSCHULE FÜR MUSIK HANNS EISLER Map p76-7

☎ 688 305 700; www.hfm-berlin.de; Charlottenstrasse 55, Mitte; ⊕ Stadtmitte

The gifted students at Berlin's top-rated music academy populate several orchestras, a choir and a big band, which collectively stage as many as 400 performances annually, most of them in the recently converted Neuer Marstall (p91), where the Prussian royals once kept their coaches and horses. Most events are free or low-cost.

KONZERTHAUS BERLIN Map pp76-7

☎ tickets 203 092 101; www.konzerthaus.de; Gendarmenmarkt 2, Mitte; tickets €10-99; ⊕ Stadtmitte, Französische Strasse

One of Berlin's top classical venues is home of the renowned Konzerthausorchester, which gives about 100 concerts per season. Others, including the Rundfunk-Sinfonieorchester Berlin, also perform in its four rooms, including the lavish Grosser Saal (Great Hall). Visiting international artists, thematic concert cycles, contemporary music and performances for children and teens complete the schedule.

DANCE

With independent choreographers and youthful companies consistently promoting experimental choreography, Berlin's independent dance scene continues apace, despite state funding cuts in recent years. Though there are few dedicated venues, many theatres now include dance performances in their programmes; check listings. In the mainstream, classical ballet is performed at the Staatsoper Unter den Linden (p253) and the Deutsche Oper (p253), while more modern interpretations crop up at the Komische Oper (p253) and the Hebbel am Ufer (p255).

DOCK 11 Map pp156-7

☎ 448 1222; www.dock11-berlin.de, in German; Kastanienallee 79, Prenzlauer Berg; ⊕ Eberswalder Strasse

For cutting-edge, experimental dance, there are few better places in town than this unpretentious space tucked into an old factory. Many productions are original works developed inhouse as a result of courses and workshops offered throughout the week.

SOPHIENSAELE Map pp102-3

☎ 283 5266; www.sophiensaele.com, in German; Sophienstrasse 18, Mitte; tickets €8-13; Ⓡ Hackescher Markt, ⊕ Weinmeisterstrasse

Back in the 1990s, Sascha Waltz transformed the Sophiensaele into Berlin's number-one spot for experimental and avant-garde dance. Since then, the emphasis has edged back towards theatre and performance art, but you can still expect to find some of the city's most exciting dance events here.

CINEMAS

Celluloid fans are well catered for in Berlin with movies showing in indie art houses, tiny neighbourhood screens and ultra-deluxe, stadium-style megaplexes. Ticket prices vary accordingly from a low of €5 to a high of €13 for 3-D blockbusters. Almost all cinemas also add a sneaky *Überlängezuschlag* (overrun supplement) of €0.50 to €1.50 for films longer than 90 minutes. Seeing a flick on a *Kinotag* (film day, usually Monday or Tuesday) or before 5pm can save you a couple of euros.

Mainstream Hollywood movies are dubbed into German, but a growing number of

MOVIES UNDER THE STARS

Alfresco screenings are a popular summertime tradition with classic and contemporary flicks spooling off in various *Freiluftkinos* (outdoor cinemas) around town. Come early to stake out a good spot and bring pillows, blankets and snacks. Films are usually screened in their original language, with German subtitles, or in German with English subtitles.

Freiluftkino Insel in Cassiopeia (Map pp150-1; ☎ 5471 3247; www.freiluftkino-insel.de; Revaler Strasse 99; tickets €6; ☽ Mon, Thu & Sun; ☻ ☒ Warschauer Strasse) Free blanket rental.

Freiluftkino Friedrichshain (Map pp150-1; ☎ 2936 1629; www.freiluftkino-berlin.de, in German; Volkspark Friedrichshain; tickets €6.50; ☽ daily mid-May–mid-Sep) In the open-air amphitheatre inside the park.

Freiluftkino Kreuzberg (Map pp140-1; ☎ 2936 1628; www.freiluftkino-kreuzberg.de; Mariannenplatz 2; tickets €6.50; ☽ daily late Apr–late Aug) In the courtyard of Künstlerhaus Bethanien.

theatres also show movies in their original language, denoted in listings by the acronym 'OF' *(Originalfassung)* or 'OV' *(Originalversion)*; those with German subtitles are marked 'OmU' *(Original mit Untertiteln)*.

ARSENAL Map p112

☎ 2695 5100; www.arsenal-berlin.de; Sony Center, Potsdamer Strasse 21, Tiergarten; adult/child €6.50/3; ☻ ☒ Potsdamer Platz
This artsy twin-screen cinema is the antithesis of popcorn culture, with a bold, daily-changing global flick schedule that hopscotches from Japanese satire to Brazilian comedy and German road movies. Many films have English subtitles.

BABYLON Map pp140-1

☎ 6160 9693; www.yorck.de, in German; Dresdner Strasse 126, Kreuzberg; tickets €5.50-7.50; ☻ Kottbusser Tor
One of 12 Berlin cinemas making up the Yorcker family of broad-appeal, art-house screens, Babylon screens only movies in the original language.

BABYLON BERLIN Map pp102-3

☎ 242 5969; www.babylonberlin.de, in German; Rosa-Luxemburg-Strasse 30, Mitte; adult/child €6.50/4; ☻ Rosa-Luxemburg-Platz
Not to be confused with the Kreuzberg Babylon, this bi-screen art house is in a fantastic protected 1920s building by New Objectivity master Hanz Poelzig and is one of the best indies in town. Programming ranges from new German films to international art-house flicks, silent movies and themed retrospectives, plus concerts and readings. Parents get a chance to catch a flick with their tots in tow at 11am on Wednesdays during '*Kinderwagenkino*' (pram cinema).

CENTRAL KINO Map pp102-3

☎ 2859 9973; www.kino-central.de, in German; Rosenthaler Strasse 39; adult/child €6.50/4; ☻ Weinmeisterstrasse
Tucked away in the Hackesche Höfe, this handy little cinema features well-picked art-house fare, with films in their original language and German subtitles.

CINEMAXX POTSDAMER PLATZ Map p112

☎ 01805 2463 6299; www.cinemaxx.de, in German; Voxstrasse 2, Tiergarten; adult €5.50-8, child €5; ☻ ☒ Potsdamer Platz
This state-of-the-art multiplex, part of a national chain, is the primary venue of the Berlinale (p17) international film festival. A lavish foyer with a 13m-long stainless-steel slide leads to 19 screens showing mostly Hollywood blockbusters. Promotions target specific groups: Men's Night, for instance, presents testosterone flicks and two-for-one beers. Ladies Night comes with sparkling wine.

CINESTAR ORIGINAL & IMAX 3D Map p112

☎ 2606 6400; www.cinestar.de, in German; Potsdamer Strasse 4, Tiergarten; adult/child €9/7.50; ☻ ☒ Potsdamer Platz
This is a pricey but state-of-the-art cinema with big screens, comfy seats and ear-popping surround-sound. It shows the latest Hollywood blockbusters, all in English, all the time, plus some cool 2-D Imax flicks.

HACKESCHE HÖFE KINO Map pp102-3

☎ 283 4603; www.hoefekino.de; Hackesche Höfe, Rosenthaler Strasse 40/41, Mitte; tickets €6.50-8; ☒ Hackescher Markt
This indie art house in the heart of Mitte specialises in European feature films,

international documentary and indie films from the US. Nearly all are screened in the original language with German subtitles.

KINO INTERNATIONAL Map pp150-1

☎ 2475 6011; www.yorck.de, in German; Karl-Marx-Allee 33, Mitte; tickets €5.50-8; ⊕ Schillingstrasse

With its camp 1960s cavalcade of glass chandeliers, glitter curtains and parquet floor, the Kino International is a show in itself, and also hosts regular club nights. Monday is 'MonGay' (tickets €6.50) with gay-themed classics, imports and previews.

LICHTBLICK KINO Map pp156-7

☎ 4405 8179; www.lichtblick-kino.org, in German; Kastanienallee 77, Prenzlauer Berg; adult/concession €5/4.50; ⊕ Eberswalder Strasse

With space for 32 cineastes, there's not a bad seat in Berlin's smallest cinema, run by a collective and known for its eclectic programming of fine retrospectives, political documentaries, Berlin-made movies and global art-house fare. Luis Buñuel is honoured with a special filmic line-up every year on his birthday on 22 February.

MOVIEMENTO Map pp140-1

☎ 692 4785; www.moviemento.de, in German; Kottbusser Damm 22, Kreuzberg; tickets €5-7.50; ⊕ Hermannplatz

Berlin's oldest cinema (since 1911), this three-screen cult venue was briefly owned by Tom Tykwer (director of Run Lola Run) in the '80s and shows primarily new German film and original-version international classics. It's also one of the venues of the Porn Film Festival (p19). The Sunday brunch (€6.50, 10am to 4pm) is also popular.

NEUE KANT Map pp124-5

☎ 319 9866; www.kantkino.de, in German; Kantstrasse 54, Charlottenburg; tickets €6.50-8; ⊕ Wilmersdorfer Strasse

Founded in 1912, this venerable venue took on a different persona as a concert stage for punk and new wave greats like Nina Hagen, Siouxie and the Banshees and U2 in the '80s. When threatened with bankruptcy in 2001, a group of industry professionals, including director Wim Wenders, banded together to rescue the venue. It now screens a mix of popular and art-house fare from Europe.

OPERA & MUSICALS

Not many cities afford themselves the luxury of three state-funded opera houses, but then opera has been popular in Berlin ever since the first fat lady loosened her lungs, and fans can catch some of the biggest and best performances in the country here. This interest, however, has never translated into a great public passion for musicals, and there's no equivalent of London's West End here.

DEUTSCHE OPER Map pp124-5

☎ 3438 4343; www.deutscheoperberlin.de; Bismarckstrasse 35, Charlottenburg; tickets €14-120; ⊕ Deutsche Oper

Berlin's humungous opera house (nearly 1900 seats) was founded by local burghers in 1912 as a counterpoint to the royal opera (today's Staatsoper, below) on Unter den Linden. Since 2005 it's been led by its first-ever female boss, Kirsten Harms, who's dusted off its image and enjoys generating the occasional controversy with provocative productions. All operas are performed in their original language.

KOMISCHE OPER Map pp76-7

☎ 4799 7400; www.komische-oper-berlin.de; Behrenstrasse 55-57, Mitte, box office Unter den Linden 41, Mitte; tickets €10-72; ⊕ Französische Strasse

Musical theatre, light opera, operetta and dance theatre are the domain of Mitte's high-profile central venue. Productions are drawn from many periods and all are sung in German.

NEUKÖLLNER OPER Map pp140-1

☎ 688 9070; www.neukoellneroper.de, in German; Karl-Marx-Strasse 131-133, Neukölln; tickets €12-23; ⊕ Karl-Marx-Strasse

Definitely not your upper-crust opera house, Neukölln's refurbished prewar ballroom has an actively anti-elitist repertoire ranging from intelligent musical theatre to original productions to experimental interpretations of classic works. Many productions pick up on contemporary themes or topics relevant to Berlin.

STAATSOPER UNTER DEN LINDEN Map pp124-5

☎ 2035 4438, tickets 2035 4555; www.staatsoper -berlin.de; Bismarckstrasse 110, Charlottenburg; tickets €5-160; ⊕ Deutsche Oper, Ernst-Reuter-Platz

While its permanent digs on Unter den Linden (Map pp76-7) are getting a facelift (probably until 2013), you'll have to travel to the Schiller Theater in Charlottenburg for performances by the grande dame of Berlin's opera companies. Daniel Barenboim still directs the high-calibre productions, which are all sung in their original language.

THEATER AM POTSDAMER PLATZ
Map p112

☎ 259 2290, tickets 01805 4444; www.stage -entertainment.de; Marlene-Dietrich-Platz 1, Tiergarten; ticket price varies; Ⓢ Ⓡ Potsdamer Platz

Big-name touring musicals (such as *Dirty Dancing*) are showcased at this up-in-lights location, designed by none other than star architect Renzo Piano. Inside, there's seating for 1800 and a sense of occasion.

THEATER DES WESTENS Map p128

☎ 319 030, tickets 01805 4444; www.theater-des -westens.de, in German; Kantstrasse 12, Charlottenburg; ticket prices varies; Ⓢ Ⓡ Zoologischer Garten

The same company in charge of Theater am Potsdamer Platz (above) also puts on German-language versions of big-name West End or Broadway productions, hosting both touring and home-grown companies. Acoustics are ok but the cheaper seats in the nose-bleed section tend to have lousy views.

THEATRE

Get ready to smell the greasepaint and hear the roar of the crowd; with over 100 stages around town, theatre is the mainstay of Berlin's cultural scene. Add in a particularly active collection of roaming companies and experimental outfits and you'll find there are more than enough offerings to satisfy all possible tastes.

Many theatres are closed on Mondays and from mid-July to late August. Box offices generally keep at least office hours on days without performances. Good seats are often available on the evening of the performance itself, with unclaimed tickets sold 30 minutes before curtain. It's also fine to buy spare tickets from other theatregoers, though you should make sure they're legit. Some theatres offer discounts of up to 50% for students and seniors. Prices quoted below are full price.

The area around Friedrichstrasse and the Kurfürstendamm are Berlin's main drama drags; check www.berlin-buehnen.de (in German) and local listings magazines for smaller, experimental theatres around town.

BERLINER ENSEMBLE Map pp76-7

☎ 2840 8155; www.berliner-ensemble.de, in German; Bertolt-Brecht-Platz 1, Mitte; tickets €5- 30; Ⓢ Ⓡ Friedrichstrasse

The company founded by Bertolt Brecht in 1949 is based at the neo-baroque theatre where his Threepenny Opera premiered in 1928. Since 1999, it's been helmed by artistic director Claus Peymann who keeps the master's legacy alive while also peppering the repertory with works by Schiller, Beckett and other European playwrights. Quality is high, tickets are cheap.

DEUTSCHES THEATER Map pp76-7

☎ 2844 1225; www.deutschestheater.de, in German; Schumannstrasse 13a, Mitte; tickets €4-45; Ⓢ Oranienburger Tor

Max Reinhardt's old theatre is still Berlin's top stage and has reeled in numerous thespian awards, including Theatre of the Year in 2008. Now under the leadership of Ulrich Khuon, the focus is both on classical and bold new plays that reflect the issues and big themes of today. Plays are also performed in the smaller Kammerspiele (Map pp76-7) next door and at Box + Bar (Map pp76-7), an 80-seat space with cocktail bar that presents edgy and experimental fare (tickets €4 to €16).

ENGLISH THEATRE BERLIN Map pp140-1

☎ 691 1211; www.etberlin.de; Fidicinstrasse 40, Kreuzberg; tickets €18; Ⓢ Platz der Luftbrücke

Berlin's oldest English-language theatre has charted the evolution and trends in international theatre for more than two decades. Its extensive repertory consists of classics, physical theatre and comedy, performance art and works by emerging writers and directors. On Tuesdays, tickets are half price.

GRIPS THEATER off Map p112

☎ 397 4740; www.grips-theater.de, in German; Altonaer Strasse 22, Tiergarten; tickets €18; Ⓢ Hansaplatz

The Grips is the best, and best-known, of Berlin's youth stages, producing high-quality topical and critical plays that are suitable for older children and teenagers. The regular productions of director Volker Ludwig's highly successful U-Bahn musical *Linie 1* are a definite highlight.

HEBBEL AM UFER (HAU) Map pp140-1
☎ 2590 0427; www.hebbel-am-ufer.de; box office Hallesches Ufer 32, Kreuzberg; tickets €11-18; Ⓤ Hallesches Tor

A pack of pit bulls mills about the seats. The audience has gathered on the stage. An upside down world? No, just another performance at Hebbel am Ufer, one of Berlin's most avant-garde and adventurous theatre venues. After a merger in 2003, there are three nearby stages: HAU 1 (Stresemannstrasse 29), HAU 2 (Hallesches Ufer 32) and HAU 3 (Tempelhofer Ufer 10).

MAXIM GORKI THEATER Map pp76-7
☎ 2022 1115; www.gorki.de, in German; Am Festungsgraben 2, Mitte; tickets €10-32; Ⓤ Ⓢ Friedrichstrasse

The smallest and least subsidised of the state-funded theatres, the Gorki was founded in 1952 as a key proponent of the Soviet-created, and thus highly ideologically charged, style of Socialist Realism. Naturally, it's mellowed a lot since and now habitually stages contemporary interpretations of the classics as well as plays dealing with local and regional themes. Quality tends to be high thanks to artistic director Armin Petras.

PUPPENTHEATER FIRLEFANZ
Map pp102-3
☎ 283 3560; www.puppentheater-firlefanz.de, in German; Sophienstrasse 10, Mitte; adult €7-13, child €5-8; Ⓤ Weinmeisterstrasse

Traditional puppets and marionettes play to crowds of all ages here, next to the Hackesche Höfe.

SCHAUBUDE BERLIN Map pp156-7
☎ 423 4314; www.schaubude-berlin.de, in German; Greifswalder Strasse 81-84, Prenzlauer Berg; adult €6-12.50, child €4; Ⓢ Greifswalder Strasse

Not just for the kiddiewinks – the professional puppeteers here take their art

seriously, and evening shows are generally aimed at adults (performances range from *Punch and Judy* to *Faust*).

SCHAUBÜHNE AM LEHNINER PLATZ
Map pp124-5
☎ 890 023; www.schaubuehne.de; Kurfürstendamm 153, Wilmersdorf; tickets €6-38; Ⓤ Adenauerplatz

West Berlin owes any cutting-edge theatrical credentials to this former 1920s cinema, rescued from bland obscurity under the forceful leadership of director Thomas Ostermeier, since joined by playwright Jens Hillje. Expect an ambitious and wide-ranging programme, with some performances featuring English subtitles.

THEATERDISCOUNTER Map p96
☎ 2809 3062; www.theaterdiscounter.de; Klosterstrasse 44, Mitte; tickets €13; Ⓤ Ⓢ Alexanderplatz

Now in permanent digs on the 2nd floor of the former East Berlin telephone exchange near Alexanderplatz, this indie troupe constantly works on its own productions and pushes the envelope when it comes to theatrical format. Plays have minimal rehearsal times, a rapid turnover and tickets are cheap. Apparently this cash 'n' carry model works, as Theaterdiscounter has quickly become a one-stop shop for brand-new experimental plays.

VOLKSBÜHNE AM ROSA-LUXEMBURG-PLATZ Map pp102-3
☎ 2406 5777; www.volksbuehne-berlin.de; Rosa-Luxemburg-Platz, Mitte; tickets €10-30; Ⓤ Rosa-Luxemburg-Platz

Nonconformist, radical and provocative: performances at the freshly renovated 'People's Stage' are not for the squeamish. And it's been that way pretty much since the early 20th century when early theatre-reformer directors Max Reinhardt and Erwin Piscator were at the helm. Since 1992, the stage has been led by enfant terrible Frank Castorf who regularly tears down the confines of the proscenium stage with Zeitgeist-critical productions that are somehow both populist and elitist all at once.

GAY & LESBIAN BERLIN

top picks

- Berghain (p260)
- GMF@Weekend (p261)
- Lab.oratory (p261)
- Heile Welt (p259)
- Klub International (p261)
- Propaganda@Goya (p261)
- SchwuZ (p262)
- Zum Schmutzigen Hobby (p260)

What's your recommendation? www.lonelyplanet.com/berlin

Berlin's legendary liberalism has spawned one of the world's biggest, most divine and diverse GLBT playgrounds. Anything goes in 'Homopolis' (and we *do* mean anything!), from the highbrow to the hands-on, the bourgeois to the bizarre, the mainstream to the flamboyant.

The closest that Berlin comes to a 'gay village' is Schöneberg (Motzstrasse and Fuggerstrasse especially), where the rainbow flag has proudly flown since debauchery first flourished in the 1920s. There's still lots of partying going on, but it's all pretty old-school and trendier types and anyone under 35 will likely feel more comfortable elsewhere. Current hipster central is Kreuzberg, which teems with excellent drinking dens, especially along Oranienstrasse and Mehringdamm. Across the river, Friedrichshain has fewer gay bars but some of the key clubs like Berghain/Panorama Bar and Lab.oratory. Prenzlauer Berg also has a few hotspots but locales are fairly spread out across the entire neighbourhood.

Generally speaking, Berlin's gayscape runs the entire spectrum from mellow cafes, campy bars and cinemas to saunas, cruising areas, clubs with darkrooms and all-out sex venues. In fact, sex and sexuality are entirely everyday matters to the unshockable city folks and there are very few, if any, itches that can't be quite openly and legally scratched. As elsewhere, gay men have more options for having fun, but grrrrls – from lipstick lesbians to hippie chicks to bad-ass dykes – won't feel left out either.

Except for the hardcore places, gay spots get their share of opposite-sex and straight patrons, drawn by gay friends, the fabulousness of the venues, abundant eye candy and, for women in gay bars, a laid-back atmosphere.

Note that in Germany www.gayromeo.com is the gay dating site of choice.

SIGHTS

SCHWULES MUSEUM Map pp140-1

☎ 6959 9050; www.schwulesmuseum.de; Mehringdamm 61, Kreuzberg; adult/concession €5/3; ☾ 2-6pm Wed-Mon, to 7pm Sat; ⊕ Mehringdamm
Museum, archive and community centre all in one, the nonprofit Gay Museum is a great place to learn about the milestones over the last 200 years in Berlin's queer history. Enter via the courtyard behind Melitta Sundström (p260).

SHOPPING

PRINZ EISENHERZ Map p136   Books

☎ 313 9936; www.prinz-eisenherz.com, in German; Lietzenburger Strasse 9a, Schöneberg; ☾ 10am-8pm Mon-Sat; ⊕ Wittenbergplatz
The 'Prince' is *the* source for gay lit, nonfiction and mags in many different languages. There's even a respectable lesbian section here, plus DVDs, postcards, calendars, erotic picture books and guides.

FRONTPLAY Map p96   Clothing & Accessories

☎ 4431 9366; Rosa-Luxemburg-Strasse 3, Mitte; ☾ noon-8pm Mon-Fri, 11am-7pm Sat; ⊕ Weinmeisterstrasse, ⊕ ⓡ Alexanderplatz

With its neatly edited line-up of labels – Ben Sherman, Fred Perry, Merc, New Balance – this popular store will have you looking sharp from head to toe in no time. There's a second branch in Schöneberg (Map p136; ☎ 6270 4270; Motzstrasse 25; ⊕ Nollendorfplatz).

BRUNO'S Map p136   Erotica

☎ 6150 0385; www.brunos.de, in German; Bülowstrasse 106, Schöneberg; ☾ 10am-10pm Mon-Sat, 1-9pm Sun; ⊕ Nollendorfplatz
This gay-themed supermarket is the go-to place for books, magazines, toys, tools and DVDs for men only. There's a smaller branch stocking the essentials in Prenzlauer Berg (Map pp156-7; ☎ 6150 0387; Schönhauser Allee 131; ⊕ Eberswalder Strasse).

LA LUNA Map pp156-7   Erotica

☎ 4432 8488; www.laluna-toys.de, in German; Dunckerstrasse 90, Prenzlauer Berg; ☾ noon-8pm Mon-Fri, to 6pm Sat; ⊕ Eberswalder Strasse
This store quite literally puts 'babes in Toyland', but don't expect the PG variety. Browse around neatly arranged dildos, vibes, edible massage oils, chocolate body paint and other toys to tickle your fancy – or whatever.

GAY MEMORIALS

The gay community suffered tremendously under the Nazis. Male homosexuals were humiliated, socially ostracised and made to wear pink triangles on their clothing. About 54,000 were imprisoned and 7000 tortured and murdered in concentration camps. For decades after WWII, these victims were excluded from public cultural commemoration and reparation payments. But in June 2008, the spotlight was finally trained on their plight with the unveiling of the Denkmal für Homosexuelle NS Opfer (Memorial for Homosexual Nazi Victims; Map p112; Ebertstrasse, Tiergarten). It's a 4m-high, solitary, off-kilter concrete cube by the Danish-Norwegian artist duo Michael Elmgreen und Ingar Dragset. Through a small window, you can look at a looped video showing two men kissing tenderly. After lesbian and feminist organisations complained, this was expected to be rotated with another video featuring women, possibly some time in 2010.

Other memorials include the pink-granite triangle (Map p136) on the south facade of Nollendorfplatz U-Bahn station in Schöneberg, and a plaque at Konzentrationslager Sachsenhausen (Sachsenhausen Concentration Camp; p287).

DRINKING
SCHÖNEBERG

HAFEN Map p136 — Bar
☎ 211 4118; www.hafen-berlin.de, in German; Motzstrasse 19; ⏰ from 8pm; ⊖ Nollendorfplatz
The friendly Harbour has been a great stop to dock for more than two decades. On Mondays, quizmaster Hendryk tests your trivia knowledge with his hilarious Quiz-O-Rama shows (in English on the first Monday of the month).

HEILE WELT Map p136 — Bar
☎ 2191 7507; Motzstrasse 5; ⏰ from 6pm; ⊖ Nollendorfplatz
Chic yet laid-back, the 'Perfect World' gets high marks for its communicative vibe, high flirt factor and handsome laddies (and the occasional lady). It's a great whistlestop before launching into a raunchy night, but gets packed in its own right the higher the moon rises in the sky.

TOM'S BAR Map p136 — Bar
www.tomsbar.de; Motzstrasse 19; ⏰ 10am-6am; ⊖ Nollendorfplatz
Erotic artist Tom of Finland inspired the name of this been-here-forever bar, although you don't have to look as buff as his subjects to feel comfortable. It's cruisy, with most people tempted to check out the action in the labyrinthine darkroom. On Mondays drinks are 2-4-1.

CAFÉ BERIO Map p136 — Cafe
☎ 216 1945; www.cafe-berio.de; Maassenstrasse 7; ⏰ 8am-midnight Sun-Thu, to 1am Fri & Sat; ⊖ Nollendorfplatz
Watch the pretty boyz on parade from your perch on the pavement terrace of this bi-level coffeehouse while nibbling cake as sweet as the gooiest love letter. Around for over half a century, its low-key, flirty and an enduring gay fave.

KREUZBERG & NORTHERN NEUKÖLLN
Also see Möbel Olfe (p226).

BIERHIMMEL Map pp140-1 — Bar
☎ 615 3122; Oranienstrasse 183, Kreuzberg; ⏰ 1pm-3am; ⊖ Kottbusser Tor
Bierhimmel is an essential lesbigay hangout in Kreuzberg. The decor is more stylish than over-the-top, making this a good place to start off the evening before moving on to saucier places (like Roses, see below).

ROSES Map pp140-1 — Bar
☎ 615 6570; Oranienstrasse 187, Kreuzberg; ⏰ from 9pm; ⊖ Kottbusser Tor
The ultimate in camp and kitsch, Roses is a glittery fixture on the lesbigay Kreuzberg booze circuit. Drinks are cheap and the bartenders pour with a generous elbow, making this a popular wrap-up spot for hard-party nights.

SILVERFUTURE Map pp140-1 — Bar
☎ 7563 4987; www.silverfuture.net; Weserstrasse 206; ⏰ from 6pm; ⊖ Hermannplatz
Dressed in rich purple, burgundy and silver, this hipster lesbian bar is as charmingly over-the-top as a playful grope from your favourite drag queen. There's Madonna on the jukebox, Polish and Czech beer in the

fridge and enough smiling faces for a dependably good time. Draws a mixed crowd at the weekend.

MELITTA SUNDSTRÖM Map pp140-1 Cafe
☎ 692 4414; Mehringdamm 61; ⊙ from 1pm; ⊙ Mehringdamm

Melitta is named for a famous Berlin singer, writer and queen who died of AIDS in 1993. The cheerful cafe is busy at all hours but never more so than on Saturday nights when it's a preferred fuelling-up stop for parties at SchwuZ (p262) down in the cellar.

FRIEDRICHSHAIN

GROSSE FREIHEIT Map pp150-1 Bar
www.gay-friedrichshain.de/grosse-freiheit-114, in German; Boxhagener Strasse 114; ⊙ 10pm Tue-Sun; ⊙ Frankfurter Tor

Ahoy captain! Named for a lane in Hamburg's red-light district where the Beatles once cut their teeth, Grosse Freiheit is a safe harbour for just a drink and meet-up or to disappear into the good-sized darkroom. The fabulous nautical decor looks just like most '80s films portrayed gay bars. Best day: 2-4-1 Wednesdays. DJs get toes tapping on weekends.

HIMMELREICH Map pp150-1 Bar
☎ 7072 8306; www.himmelreich-berlin.de, in German; Simon-Dach-Strasse 36; ⊙ from 7pm Mon-Fri, from 2pm Sat & Sun; ⊙ ⊙ Warschauer Strasse

Proving all those stereotypes about gays having good taste, this smart red-hued cocktail bar cum retro-style lounge makes most of the competition look like a straight guy's bedsit. Tuesdays are women-only and, just as at Grosse Freiheit, drinks are 2-4-1 on Wednesday.

PRENZLAUER BERG
Also see Marietta (p228).

GREIFBAR Map pp156-7 Bar
☎ 444 0828; www.greifbar.com, in German; Wichertstrasse 10; ⊙ 10pm-6am; ⊙ ⊙ Schönhauser Allee

Men-Film-Cruising: Greifbar's motto says it all. This Prenzlauer Berg staple draws a mixed crowd of jeans, sneakers, leather and skin sniffing each other out below the big-screen video in the comfortable bar before

retiring to the sweaty play zone in the back. Beer's half-price on Mondays.

STILLER DON Map pp156-7 Bar
☎ 445 5957; www.stillerdon.de, in German; Erich-Weinert-Strasse 67; ⊙ from 8pm; ⊙ ⊙ Schönhauser Allee

A relic from the GDR days, 'Quiet Don' is anything but on Mondays when boy pals kick off the evening with beer, peanuts and flirty chat before moving on to business at Greifbar (left).

ZUM SCHMUTZIGEN HOBBY
Map pp156-7 Bar
www.ninaqueer.com, in German; Rykestrasse 45, Prenzlauer Berg; ⊙ from 6pm; ⊙ Senefelderplatz

Local trash drag deity Nina Queer presides over this louche den of kitsch and glam with decor, clientele and goings-on that aren't for the faint-of-heart (check out the porno wallpaper in the men's room). On Wednesdays at 9pm it's standing-room only for Nina's 'glamour trivia quiz'.

CLUBBING

BERGHAIN Map pp150-1
www.berghain.de, in German; Am Wriezener Bahnhof, Friedrichshain; cover €14; ⊙ Sat; ⊙ Ostbahnhof

Take off your shirt and head to this vast post-industrial techno-electro hellhole filled with studly queer bass junkies. With three floors of dark and hidden corners, including labyrinthine darkrooms, there's plenty of space for mischief. See p232 for the full scoop.

top picks

GAY PARTY WEEK

- Monday Fag Bar@Monster Ronson's (p227) Stiller Don (above) and Hafen (p259)
- Tuesday Cookies (p233)
- Wednesday Marietta (p228), Shade Inc@nbi (p234) and Zum Schmutzigen Hobby (above)
- Thursday Möbel Olfe (p226), Chantals House of Shame (opposite)
- Friday SchwuZ (p262)
- Saturday SchwuZ (p262), Berghain (above), also see the boxed text opposite
- Sunday GMF (opposite), Pork@Ficken 3000 (opposite) and Cafe Fatal@SO36 (p237)

PARTY PLANNER

Some of the best club nights are independent of the venues they use and may move around, although most have some temporary residency. Berlin's scene is especially fickle and venues and dates may change at the drop of a hat, so make sure you always check the websites or the listings magazines for the latest scoop. Most of these parties are geared towards men.

- **Shade Inc** (☾ from 10.30pm Wed) The long-running Berlin Hilton club night (they apparently got sued by the eponymous hotel chain) has recast itself as Shade Inc but still brings chatty boyz to small and low-tech **nbi club** (p234) for extended electro-rock dance-a-thons.

- **Café Fatal** (www.cafefatal.de, in German; ☾ 7pm-2am Sun) All comers descend on **SO36** (p237) for the ultimate rainbow tea dance that goes from 'strictly ballroom' to 'dirty dancing' in a flash. If you can't tell a waltz from a foxtrot, come at 7pm for free lessons.

- **Chantals House of Shame** (www.siteofshame.com, in German; ☾ from 11pm Thu) Trash diva Chantal's louche lair (currently at **Bassy Club**, p231) is a beloved institution, not so much for the glam factor than for the over-the-top transvestite shows and the hotties who love 'em.

- **Girls Town** (www.girlstown-berlin.de; ☾ 2nd Sat of every other month) This busy and buzzy girl-fest graces the vintage **Kino International** (p253) with down-and-dirty dance music in the foyer and cocktails-with-a-view in the upstairs bar.

- **L-Tunes** (www.ltunes.de, in German; ☾ 10.30pm last Sat of the month) Lesbians get their groove on with Pink, Madonna and Melissa Etheridge in the dimly lit dancing pit of **SchwuZ** (p262).

- **Gayhane** (www.so36.de, in German; ☾ last Sat of the month) Geared towards gay Muslims but everyone's welcome to rock the kasbah when this 'homoriental' party takes over **SO36** (p237) with Middle Eastern beats and belly dancing.

- **GMF** (www.gmf-berlin.de, in German; ☾ 11pm Sun) Currently at **Weekend** (p235), Berlin's premier Sunday club is known for excessive SM (standing and modelling) with lots of smooth surfaces – and that goes for both the crowd *and* the setting. Predominantly boyz, but girls OK.

- **Horse Meat Disco** (www.tapeberlin.com; ☾ usually 2nd Sat of the month) This London import energises a mostly male crowd with disco-tastic dance tunes during its monthly residency at industrial-glam **Tape Club** (p235).

- **Irrenhaus** (www.ninaqueer.com, in German; ☾ 3rd Sat of the month) The name means 'insane asylum' and that's no joke. Party hostess with the mostest, trash queen Nina Queer puts on nutty, naughty shows at **Geburtstagsclub** (Map pp156-7; Am Friedrichshain 33, Friedrichshain) that are not for the faint-of-heart. Expect the best. Fear the worst.

- **Klub International** (Map pp150-1; ☎ 690 4087; www.klub-international.com; Karl-Marx-Allee 33, Mitte; ☾ 1st Sat of the month) Up to 1500 boyz-to-men come out to the glamorous **Kino International** (p253) to work three sizzling dance floors presided over by trash tranny royalty like Biggy van Blond, Nina Queer and Ades Zabel.

- **Pet Shop Bears** (www.myspace.com/petshopbears; ☾ last Fri of the month) The club du jour attracts a Butt Magazine-type international crowd of lean but hairy 30- and 40-somethings who come for kicking electropop. At Berghain Kantine, next door to legendary **Berghain** (opposite).

- **Pork@Ficken 3000** (www.ficken3000.com, in German; cover €3; ☾ 10pm Sun; Urbanstrasse 70; ⊕ Hermannplatz) A bit of a down-at-heel sex club during the week, Ficken 3000 truly hits its stride on Sundays for this edgy polysexual arty-trash party. Dancing upstairs, orgy downstairs.

- **Propaganda@Goya** (Map p136; www.propaganda-party.de, in German; Am Nollendorfplatz; ☾ Fri; ⊕ Nollendorfplatz) In a sexy old theatre, this New York–style house and electro party-and-a-half draws fashionable see-and-be-scenesters with its buff and bronzed go-go dancers, big sound and gyrating on two dance floors.

- **SpyClub** (www.spyclub.de; ☾ 4th Sat of the month) Dress up! is the motto and they mean it, so get your glam on to get past the door standing between you and Berlin's most fashionable house and electro party at **Cookies** (p233).

CLUB CULTURE HOUZE Map pp140-1

☎ 6170 9669; www.club-culture-houze.de; Görlitzer Strasse 71, Kreuzberg; cover varies; ☾ Wed-Mon; ⊕ Görlitzer Bahnhof

Drop your clothes (and inhibitions) at the door of this legendary sex party palace with hot 'n' heavy themes like 'Naked Sex' Mondays to 'Fist Factory' Fridays (although most fetishes are welcome most of the time). Adventurous hets and bis are more than welcome to get in on the action on Wednesdays, Thursdays and Sundays.

LAB.ORATORY Map pp150-1

www.lab-oratory.de, in German; Am Wriezener Bahnhof, Friedrichshain; ☾ Thu-Sun; ⊕ Ostbahnhof

Part of the Berghain complex, this well-equipped 'lab' has plenty of toys and rooms for advanced sexual experimentation in what looks like the engine room of an aircraft carrier. Party names like Yellow Facts, Naked Sex Party and Pump Electro Tits leave little to the imagination. Hedonism pure. Note that entry is usually restricted to between 10pm and midnight. Also, skip the aftershave or run the risk of getting rejected.

SCHWUZ Map pp140-1
☎ 629 0880; www.schwuz.de, in German; Mehringdamm 61, Kreuzberg; cover €3-8; ☺ Wed, Fri & Sat; ⊕ Mehringdamm

This queer institution has defied the odds and stayed popular even after 30 years in business. Fortify yourself at Melitta Sundström (p260), then drop down to the cellar to flirt with friendly locals over a high-energy mix of retro hits, glam pop, alt-rock and whatever else makes you move those feet. A good place to ease into the scene. Lesbians take over during L-Tunes (p261).

CINEMAS

From September to May, Cinemaxx Potsdamer Platz (p252) also runs homo-themed movies during their monthly Gay Filmnacht (www.gay-filmnacht.de) for boys and L-Filmnacht (www.l-filmnacht.de) for lesbians.

MON-GAY@KINO INTERNATIONAL
Map pp150-1
☎ 2475 6011; www.yorck.de, in German; Karl-Marx-Allee 33, Friedrichshain; tickets €6.50; ☺ 10pm Mon; ⊕ Schillingstrasse

Homo-themed classics, imports and previews take over the Kino International (p253), where the GDR film elite once held its movie premieres. Come early for cocktails at the campy '60s-style bar.

XENON Map p136
☎ 7800 1530; www.xenon-kino.de, in German; Kolonnenstrasse 5-6, Schöneberg; tickets €4-6, child €3; ⍟ Julius-Leber-Brücke

Berlin's second-oldest cinema lacks fluffy leather seats and surround-sound but its homo-themed repertory is decidedly progressive with lots of juicy imports and themed retrospectives. Incongruously, kiddie films are shown in the afternoons.

FESTIVALS & EVENTS

LEATHER & FETISH WEEK
www.blf.de
☺ Easter

Europe's largest party for the leather, rubber, sportswear, skin and military fetish crowd whips tens of thousands of fans out of the dungeons and into the streets of Berlin. Six days of wild partying include the crowning of the 'German Mr Leather' and culminate in Snax, an insane sex party that takes over Berghain (p260) and Lab.oratory (p261) for 24 hours of full-on mayhem.

LESBISCH-SCHWULES STRASSENFEST
☎ 2147 3586; www.regenbogenfonds.de
☺ mid-Jun

A warm-up for the Christopher Street Day (CSD), this huge gay and lesbian street fair spreads across Schöneberg for one weekend. A highlight is the outrageous 'Wild Sofa' talk show, which puts local politicians and entertainers in the hot seat.

GAY NIGHT AT THE ZOO
☎ 2147 3586; www.gay-night-at-the-zoo.de
☺ mid-Jun

One night a year, the resident tigers, monkeys and elephants at the Berlin Zoo get quite an eye- and earful when throngs of lesbigay merrymakers invade for swinging music, drinks at the Penguin Bar and smooching beneath the lampions.

CHRISTOPHER STREET DAY
☎ 2362 8632; www.csd-berlin.de
☺ late-Jun

Come out and paint the town pink. No matter what your sexual persuasion, everybody's welcome at this huge pride parade featuring floats filled with writhing naked torsos, transvestites strutting their stuff in campy costumes and more queens than at a royal wedding. The route of the parade varies but always ends at the Siegessäule.

TRANSGENIALER CSD
http://transgenialercsd.wordpress.com
☺ late-Jun

Berlin's 'lefties' organise this alternative CSD, which culminates in a big party on

Heinrichplatz. It doubles as a demonstration against homophobia, discrimination, racism, gentrification, war and various other causes.

LADYFEST BERLIN
www.ladyfest.net
🕑 mid-Sep
The Berlin edition of this community festival brings out creative and artistic feminists, lesbians and their friends for four days of music, art, performance and workshops around the city.

FOLSOM EUROPE
www.folsom-europe.com
🕑 Sep
This cavalcade of latex, leather, traps, whips and chains takes over the Schöneberg gay quarter for one weekend (the first weekend in September) of kinky partying. Mostly for men, but with a growing contingent of lesbians.

LESBEN FILM FESTIVAL BERLIN
☎ 852 2305; www.lesbenfilmfestival.de
🕑 Oct
For about 20 years, Berlin's Lesbian Film Festival has given international filmmakers – professional to amateur – a platform to showcase their work.

HUSTLABALL BERLIN
☎ 8939 8213; www.hustaball.de/berlin
🕑 Oct
Flag the date for this weekend of debauched partying in the company of porn stars, gorgeous go-gos, crooning trash queens, stripping hunks and about 3000 other men who love 'em.

VERZAUBERT
www.verzaubertfilmfest.com, in German
🕑 Nov
Prepare to be 'enchanted' (English for *verzaubert*) by the best of international queer cinema. Both new and established international talents get screen time here.

SLEEPING
All Berlin hotels are, of course, open to gays but places listed here are especially geared to scene crawlers.

AXEL HOTEL Map p136   Hotel €€
☎ 2100 2893; www.axelhotels.com/berlin; Lietzenburger Strasse 13/15, Schöneberg; r €70-180; ◉ Wittenbergplatz
Boho meets Bauhaus in this black-and-gold designer hotel that cheekily bills itself as 'hetero-friendly' but is squarely aimed at the gay community. Thoughtful extras include condoms in the nightstand, transparent red plexiglass separating bed- and bathroom and a huge outdoor Jacuzzi in the rooftop gym. In summer, the Skybar is the perfect launch pad for a tour of the Schöneberg queer quarter.

GAY HOSTEL Map p136   Hostel €
☎ 2100 5709; www.gay-hostel.de; Motzstrasse 28, Schöneberg; dm €22-25, s/d €48/56; ◉ Nollendorfplatz; 🛜
It's a hostel, so you know the drill. Except that this one is in the heart of Queertown and open to gay men only. Rooms (all with shared bathrooms) are bright and contempo and come with lockers; private rooms also have flatscreens. The communal kitchen and lounge provide plenty of mingling opportunities. Also offers free wi-fi and coffee.

ENJOY BED & BREAKFAST Map p136 B&B €
☎ 2362 3610; http://ger.ebab.com; Nollendorfplatz 5, Schöneberg; s/d from €20/40; 🕑 reservations 4.30-9.30pm; ◉ Nollendorfplatz
This private room-referral service caters specifically for gays and lesbians. It is affiliated with Mann-O-Meter (p264). The website has all the details.

FURTHER RESOURCES
MEDIA
Blattgold (www.blattgold-berlin.de, in German) This is a monthly publication with tips and listings for women, available at women-oriented cafes and venues.

Blu Magazine (www.blu.fm, in German) Print and online magazine with searchable, up-to-the-minute location and event listings.

L-Mag (www.l-mag.de, in German) Bimonthly magazine for lesbians.

Out in Berlin (www.out-in-berlin.de) Published by the Siegessäule folks, this English/German booklet and website is an indispensable guide to the queer scene in town. It's usually available at the Berlin Tourist Info (p316) offices.

Siegessäule (www.siegessaeule.de, in German) This weekly freebie magazine is the bible for all things gay and lesbian in Berlin.

ORGANISATIONS

Lesbenberatung (Lesbian Support Centre; Map p136; ☎ 215 2000; www.lesbenberatung-berlin.de, in German; Kulmer Strasse 20a, Schöneberg; ☼ 10am-5pm Mon, Wed & Fri, 10am-7pm Tue & Thu; ◉ ⊕ Yorckstrasse) Resource centre with psychological and social support, a cafe, lesbo mags and party info.

Mann-O-Meter (Map p136; ☎ 216 8008; www.mann-o-meter.de, in German; Bülowstrasse 106, Schöneberg; ☼ 5-10pm Tue-Fri, 4-8pm Sat & Sun; ◉ Nollendorfplatz) One-stop information centre. Also operates a hotline (☎ 216 3336; ☼ 5-7pm daily) to report attacks on gays.

Schwulenberatung (Gay Support Centre; Map pp124-5; ☎ 2336 9070; www.schwulenberatungberlin.de; Mommsenstrasse 45, Charlottenburg; ☼ 9am-8pm Mon-Fri; ◉ Adenauerplatz)

TOURS

Berlinagenten (☎ 4372 0701; www.berlinagenten.com) Customised gay-lifestyle tours (nightlife, shopping, luxury, history, lifestyle and culinary).

WEBSITES

Berlin Gay Web (http://berlin.gay-web.de, in German) General portal to all things gay in Berlin.

Berlin Tourist Office (www.visit-berlin.de) Has an excellent section with up-to-date GLBT travel info. Click on the 'Berlin for' tab.

Discodamaged (www.discodamaged.net) Excellent 'underground' clubbing and lifestyle site with party schedule and A-Z listings.

Gay Berlin4u (www.gayberlin4u.com) Info on gay bars, clubs, shops, hotels, apartments and more.

Girl Ports (www.girlports.com/lesbiantravel/destinations/berlin) Lesbian travel magazine.

SLEEPING

top picks

- Honigmond Garden Hotel (p270)
- Hotel Art Nouveau (p274)
- Hotel Askanischer Hof (p273)
- Hotel de Rome (p268)
- Mandala Hotel (p272)
- Meininger Hotel Prenzlauer Berg (p278)
- Propeller Island City Lodge (p274)
- Hotel Amano (p271)
- Wombat's City Hostel Berlin (p272)
- Circus Hotel (p271)

SLEEPING

Berlin boasts around 110,000 beds and more are scheduled to come online. You can sleep in a former bank, boat or factory, in the home of a silent-movie diva, in a 'flying bed' and even a coffin. Standards are high, and fierce competition keeps prices low compared with other capital cities.

Accommodation listings in this chapter are organised by neighbourhood and then by budget, from most to least expensive. Most of our recommendations are midrange options, which generally offer the best value for money. Expect clean, comfortable and decent-sized rooms with at least a modicum of style, a private bathroom and TV. Our selection also includes a few top-end hotels, which have an international standard of amenities and perhaps a scenic location, special decor or historical ambience. Budget places are generally hostels and other simple establishments where bathrooms may be shared.

ACCOMMODATION STYLES

Berlin offers the full gamut of places to unpack your suitcase. Of course, if you enjoy the anonymity and predictability of an international chain (or simply want to use up those frequent flyer miles), you'll find just about all of them – from Holiday Inn to Ritz-Carlton – in the German capital. But, quite frankly, that would be a shame, because Berlin has a wonderful range of lodging options that better reflect the city's verve and spirit.

Berlin's hostel scene is as vibrant as ever and consists of both classic backie hostels with alternative flair and modern 'flashpacker' hostels catering to lifestyle-savvy city-breakers. The cheapest beds in big dorms cost just €9, but spending a little more may get you a smaller dorm or even a private room, often with ensuite, or even a small apartment with a kitchen.

Of late, hostels have been facing competition from budget designer hotels, which feature contemporary design and minimal amenities at low prices. The fast-growing Motel One chain is the best known contender in town. In response, several hostel owners,

HOLIDAY FLATS

For self-caterers, indie types, families and anyone in need of extra privacy, a short-term furnished-flat rental may well be the cat's pyjamas. We only have space to list a few candidates, but you'll find lots more at www.be-my-guest.com, or www.homeaway.com, a no-fee searchable platform that lets you communicate directly with the owner to ask questions and/or make a reservation.

- Berlin Lofts (Map pp72-3; ☎ 0151 2121 9126; www.berlinlofts.com; Stephanstrasse 60, Tiergarten; apt €120-200, three-night minimum; ⊖ Ⓡ Westhafen, ⊖ Birkenstrasse) Rents huge lofts in handsomely converted historic buildings (including an old smithy and a bi-level horse barn) near the Hauptbahnhof (main train station). Kommune 1, the first politically-motivated student commune, formed in 1967, once lived in one of the apartments.
- Brilliant Apartments (☎ 8061 4796; www.brilliant-apartments.de; apt from €86) Seven stylish and modern units (named for precious stones) with full kitchens that sleep up to six and are located on Oderberger Strasse or Rykestrasse, both hip drags in Prenzlauer Berg that put you close to everything.
- IMA Loft Apartments (Map pp140-1; ☎ 6162 8913; www.imalofts.com; Ritterstrasse 12-14, Kreuzberg; apt €55-170; ⊖ Moritzplatz) These uncluttered, contemporary apartments are part of the IMA Design Village, an old factory shared by design studios and a dance and theatre academy. They sleep from one to four and include free wi-fi.
- Miniloft Berlin (Map pp102-3; ☎ 847 1090; www.miniloft.de; Hessische Strasse 5; apt from €90; ⊖ Naturkunde-museum) Eight stunning lofts in an architect-converted building, some with south-facing panorama windows, others with cosy alcoves, all outfitted with modern designer furniture and kitchenettes. Near the Natural History Museum and across from the national headquarters of the Green Party.
- Roof Apartments (☎ 6951 8833, 0173 542 3607; www.roof-berlin.com; 1-/2-bedroom apt from €80/105, two-night minimum) Three quiet, darling apartments, in historic buildings on leafy Christburger Strasse and off Greifswalder Strasse, mix classic and modern features (retro radio, acrylic chairs) and come with lots of imaginative design touches and thoughtful amenities such as an orange press or fluffy robes.

including Circus and Meininger, have opened their own versions. Design-minded travellers with deeper pockets can choose from plenty of lifestyle and boutique hotels as well as *Kunsthotels* (art hotels), which are either designed by artists and/or liberally sprinkled with original art.

Nostalgic types seeking unique 'Old Berlin' flavour should check into a charismatic B&B, called *Hotel-Pensions* or simply *Pensions*, which are especially prevalent in the western district of Charlottenburg. They typically occupy one or several floors of a historic residential building and offer local colour and personal attention galore. Amenities, room size and decor vary; many have been updated and feature wi-fi, cable TV and other mod cons.

Also increasingly popular among short-term visitors are stays in furnished flats that give you the benefit of space, privacy and independence, making them especially attractive to families and self-caterers.

Many properties set aside rooms or entire floors for nonsmokers; these are identified with the nonsmoking icon ⊠ in this book. Those offering a guest terminal for public internet access are indicated by the internet icon ▣; places with wi-fi carry the ⊚ icon. Hotels with wheelchair-accessible rooms are identified with the ⟐ icon.

LONGER-TERM RENTALS

If you're planning to stay in Berlin for a month or longer, renting a room or an apartment might be the most sensible option. The online platform www.zwischenmiete.de might yield some options, or try the following agencies:

Exberliner Flat Rental (☎ 4737 2964; www.exberliner
.net) English-speaking flat-finding service affiliated with the expat-oriented *ExBerliner* magazine.

HomeCompany (Map pp72-3; ☎ 194 45; www.home
company.de; Bundesallee 39-40, Wilmersdorf;
🄶 Kurfürstendamm) Long-term apartment rentals and flat-shares throughout Berlin.

WHERE TO STAY

Berlin's public transportation system puts you within easy reach of everything, so you don't have to be too fussy about where to stay. However, if you enjoy being within walking distance of the trophy sights, find a place in Mitte or around Potsdamer Platz, although you'll pay for the privilege. The high-end international chains cluster around Gendarmenmarkt and Potsdamer Platz, while their smaller arty cousins and a few hostels prefer the quiet side streets north of Unter den Linden and in the Scheunenviertel. North of here, Prenzlauer Berg is cheaper, yet quite close to the Mitte action.

In the western part of town, Charlottenburg and Wilmersdorf offer good value for money but are quite far from the main sights and happening districts. Because of the area's relative proximity to the trade-fair grounds, many hotels here cater primarily to business travellers. Kreuzberg and Friedrichshain are ideal if you want to stay within stumbling distance of the hottest bars and clubs.

RESERVATIONS

Berlin has lots of beds, but the best ones often sell out, so make reservations, especially around major holidays (p309), cultural events (p16) and trade shows. Most properties accept reservations by phone, fax and the internet. Then of course there are all the usual international booking engines, from Expedia to Travelocity. Locally, try Berlin Tourism (☎ 250 025; www.visitberlin.de), which books rooms at partner hotels for free and with a best-price guarantee. For last-minute bargains check www.hrs.de. For hostels, try www.gomio.com, www.hostels.com, www
.hostelworld.com or www.hostel-berlin.de. For holiday flats try www.be-my-guest.com in addition to those listed opposite.

ROOM RATES

Berlin's room rates are low compared with other European capitals. A night in a four- or five-star hotel averages €150 compared with €380 in London and €360 in Paris. Unless noted, we've quoted the price range for a standard double room with private bathroom to give you an idea of cost. Reviews also indicate whether breakfast is included in the rate or whether an extra (optional) per-person charge applies.

PRICE GUIDE

The following breakdown is a rough guide and refers to one night in a double room with private bathroom, outside of major events, holidays or trade-show periods.

€€€	over €160
€€	€70 to €160
€	under €70

Different prices apply to single or family rooms, where available. We do not – in fact cannot – take into account seasonal fluctuations, promotional discounts, jacked-up rates during high-demand periods, rates available through online booking engines and so on. Many hostels give slight discounts in the winter months (November to February).

HISTORIC MITTE

ADLON KEMPINSKI Map pp76-7   Hotel €€€
☎ 226 10; www.hotel-adlon.de; Unter den Linden 77; d €320-520, breakfast €39; ⊕ ® Brandenburger Tor; Ⓟ ☒ ☒ ⌨ ⌂ ☂ 묘 ৬

Close to embassies, the government quarter and just about everything else, the Adlon has been Berlin's most high-profile defender of the grand tradition since 1907. The striking lobby is a mere overture to the full symphony of luxury awaiting in spacious, amenity-laden rooms and suites, even if the decor is old-fashioned in a regal sort of way. The fantastic Adlon Day Spa (p314), gourmet restaurants and the Felix Clubrestaurant (p233) add a bit of 21st-century spice to the mix. See p82 for historical background on the Adlon.

HOTEL DE ROME Map pp76-7   Hotel €€€
☎ 460 6090; www.hotelderome.com; Behrenstrasse 37; d from €215, breakfast €25; ⊕ Hausvogteiplatz, 묘 100, 200, TXL; Ⓟ ☒ ☒ ⌨ ☂ 묘 ৬

If you have coin, set up shop at this delightful alchemy of historic and contemporary flair. A Rocco Forte property, it was originally a 19th-century bank HQ where the former vault is now the pool/spa area and the directors' offices (with wartime-era shrapnel wounds, 5m-high ceiling and Bebelplatz views) are now the luxury suites. Great cocktails in the Bebel Bar (p221). Kids under 12 stay free.

top picks

HISTORIC CHARMERS

- Adlon Kempinski (above)
- Hotel Askanischer Hof (p273)
- Hotel Bogota (p274)
- Hotel-Pension Dittberner (p274)
- Hotel-Pension Funk (p275)

SOFITEL BERLIN GENDARMENMARKT
Map pp76-7   Hotel €€€
☎ 203 750; www.sofitel.com; Charlottenstrasse 50-52; d €180-270, breakfast €30; ⊕ Französische Strasse; Ⓟ ☒ ☒ ⌨ ৬

This cocoon of quiet sophistication has 92 rooms and suites that are a flawless interplay of marble, glass and light, even if some are a tad twee. Same goes for the bathrooms and the top-floor spa, although no complaints about the latter's fantastic views. Cute touches: the rubber ducky and the string by the bed you can pull to request a lullaby.

ADINA APARTMENT HOTEL BERLIN
Map pp76-7   Apartment Hotel €€
☎ 200 7670; www.adina.eu; Krausenstrasse 35-36; apt €105-255; ⊕ Stadtmitte, Spittelmarkt; Ⓟ ☒ ☒ ⌨ ⌂ 묘

With its tasteful, modern design and 125 roomy apartments with good-sized kitchens, Adina is a good choice for families, anyone in need of elbow room, and self-caterers. (There's a supermarket just a minute's walk away). Smaller studios without kitchens are also available. Staff are friendly and the pool and sauna are perfect for soothing sore muscles at the end of the day.

ARCOTEL JOHN F Map pp76-7   Hotel €€
☎ 405 0460; www.arcotel.at; Werderscher Markt 11; r €110-280, breakfast €18; ⊕ Hausvogteiplatz; Ⓟ ☒ ☒ ⌨ ☂ ৬

This urbane lifestyle hotel pays homage to John F Kennedy with plenty of whimsical detail, including hand-carved rocking chairs (because the President used one to combat a bad back) and curvaceous lamps inspired by Jackie's ball gown. Rooms are smartly dressed in black, white, silver and dark zebrano wood and feature plenty of mould-breaking extras.

COSMO HOTEL BERLIN Map pp76-7 Hotel €€
☎ 5858 2222; www.cosmo-hotel.de; Spittelmarkt 13; d €120-193; ⊕ Spittelmarkt; Ⓟ ☒ ☒ ⌨ ☂ ৬

If style and design matter to you, you'll feel quite Piccadilly in this newish boutique hotel in a ho-hum location but within walking distance of the big sights. The silver-red lobby with its extravagant lamps and armchairs sets the tone. The cheaper rooms don't fit a ton of luggage (get a deluxe category or junior suite if you need

top picks

ARTSY ABODES

- Arte Luise Kunsthotel (below)
- art'otel berlin mitte (right)
- Hotel Concorde Berlin (p273)
- Hotel Art Nouveau (p274)
- mitArt Hotel & Café (p270)
- Propeller Island City Lodge (p274)

more space), but the comfy beds are veritable 'dream machines' and the blackout shutters helpful if you're fighting jetlag.

ARTE LUISE KUNSTHOTEL
Map pp76-7 Hotel €€

☎ 284 480; www.luise-berlin.com; Luisenstrasse 19; d €100-210, with shared bathroom €80-110, breakfast €11; Ⓤ Ⓢ Friedrichstrasse;

One of Berlin's most unique places to unpack your bags is this 'gallery with rooms'. Each unit reflects the vision of different artists, who receive royalties whenever it's rented. One has a bed built for giants (room 107), another puts you in the company of astronaut suits (310) or inside a boudoir-red 'Cabaret'. Cash-strapped art fans should enquire about the smaller, bathless rooms. Courtyard rooms are quieter.

MITTE – ALEXANDERPLATZ AREA

RADISSON BLU HOTEL Map p96 Hotel €€€

☎ 238 280; www.radissonblu.com/hotel-berlin; Karl-Liebknecht-Strasse 3; d €155-340, breakfast €25; 🚌 100, 200, TXL; Ⓟ

At this swish and super-central contender, right next to Museumsinsel (Museum Island), you will quite literally 'sleep with the fishes', thanks to the Aquadom, a 25m-high tropical aquarium (p95) in the lobby. Streamlined design radiates urban poshness in the 427 rooms and throughout the two restaurants and various social nooks. Flat screens and coffee- and tea-makers are among standard amenities, as is free wi-fi and access to the 24/7 spa area with pool, steam room, sauna and fitness equipment.

ALEXANDER PLAZA Map p96 Hotel €€

☎ 240 010; www.hotel-alexander-plaza.de; Rosenstrasse 1; d €125-180, breakfast €12; Ⓢ Hackescher Markt; Ⓟ

This 92-room boutique hotel in a sensitively restored historic fur-trading house retains such period details as a mosaic floor and a stucco-adorned floating stairway. Rooms are good-sized, neutral-hued and business-oriented but do get some style from Vitra chairs and Tolomeo lamps. Kick back in the sauna or borrow a bike for a day of cardio-sightseeing.

ART'OTEL BERLIN MITTE Map p96 Hotel €€

☎ 240 620; www.artotels.de; Wallstrasse 70-73; d incl breakfast €90-160; Ⓤ Märkisches Museum; Ⓟ

This boutique hotel wears its 'art' moniker with a justified swagger: more than 400 works by renowned contemporary German artist Georg Baselitz decorate its 109 rooms and the public areas. Fans of cutting-edge Italian design will also be happy here, especially in the suites with their extra-cool bathrooms; those on the 6th floor even have small balconies for rewinding the day's events against a panorama of the historic harbour and the 368m-high Fernsehturm (TV Tower).

PARK INN BERLIN-ALEXANDERPLATZ
Map p96 Hotel €€

☎ 238 90; www.parkinn-berlin.de; Alexanderplatz 7; d €80-210, breakfast €18; Ⓤ Ⓢ Alexanderplatz; Ⓟ

Views, views, views! Berlin's tallest and second-largest hotel has got them. Right in the belly of Alexanderplatz, this sleek tower is honeycombed with 1012 rooms (some rather snug) sporting panoramic windows, soothing earth tones, flat-screen TVs and noiseless air-con. For superb sunsets, snag one facing the Fernsehturm. In fine weather, the 39th-floor panorama terrace with bar and lounge chairs is tailor-made for starring in your very own 'king of the world' scene.

MOTEL ONE BERLIN-ALEXANDERPLATZ Map p96 Hotel €€

☎ 2005 4080; www.motel-one.de; Dircksenstrasse 36; s/d €69/84, breakfast €7.50; Ⓤ Ⓢ Alexanderplatz; Ⓟ

If you value location over luxury, this fast-growing budget designer chain makes for

top picks

ROOMS WITH A VIEW

- Adlon Kempinski (p268)
- Grand Hyatt (p272)
- Park Inn Berlin-Alexanderplatz (p269)
- Radisson Blu Hotel (p269)
- Ritz-Carlton Berlin (p272)

an excellent crash pad. Smallish rooms come with up-to-the-minute touches (flat-screen TVs, granite counters, massage showerheads, air-con) that are normally the staple of posher players. The lobby comes to life as a breakfast area and bar, and in summer there's even a small garden chill zone. Completely nonsmoking, this is the most central of eight Motel One properties. Check the website for other locations around the city.

CITYSTAY HOSTEL Map p96   Hostel €

☎ 2362 4031; www.citystay.de; Rosenstrasse 16; dm €17-21, s/d with bathroom €55/64, linen €2.50; Ⓜ Ⓡ Alexanderplatz, 🚌 100, 200, TXL; ✗ 🖵 🛜

Inside an immaculately restored 1896 department store, Citystay scores on three counts: location, service and design. Plank-floored rooms with high ceilings sleep one to eight; not all have ensuite bathrooms but the down-the-hall showers are lockable and clean. Welcome touches: top security (you need a key card to enter), a lift, and the 23/7 restaurant-bar with courtyard tables. It's on a quiet street yet only a hop, skip and jump from Alex, Museumsinsel and the buzzy Scheunenviertel.

MITTE – SCHEUNENVIERTEL

CASA CAMPER Map pp102-3   Hotel €€€

☎ 2000 3410; www.casacamper.com; Weinmeisterstrasse 1; r/ste €185/335; Ⓜ Weinmeisterstrasse; Ⓟ ✗ 🖵 🛜 ♿

Camper has long been synonymous with sensible yet fashionable footwear, but of late the Spanish label has translated the concept to the hospitality industry. The 51 rooms pack a lot of design cachet and come with day-lit bathrooms and ultra-comfy beds. Minibars are eschewed for a

top-floor lounge that serves breakfast and 24/7 complimentary hot and cold drinks and snacks.

HOTEL HONIGMOND Map pp102-3   Hotel €€

☎ 284 4550; www.honigmond-berlin.de; Tieckstrasse 12; d incl breakfast €145-235; Ⓜ Oranienburger Tor; Ⓟ ✗ 🛜 ♿

This delightful hotel scores a perfect 10 on our 'charmometer', not for being particularly lavish but for its familiar yet elegant ambience. Rabbits frolic in the garden, the restaurant is a local favourite and rooms sparkle in restored glory. The nicest are in the new wing and flaunt their historic features – ornate stucco ceilings, frescoes, parquet floors – to maximum effect.

HONIGMOND GARDEN HOTEL

Map pp102-3   Hotel €€

☎ 2844 5577; www.honigmond-berlin.de; Invalidenstrasse 122; d incl breakfast €125-165; Ⓜ Naturkundemuseum; Ⓟ 🖵 🛜

Never mind the busy thoroughfare, this well-managed 20-room guesthouse is an utterly sweet retreat. Before even reaching your comfortable, antique-filled room, you'll be enchanted by the garden with koi pond, fountain and old trees – in short, a great oasis for making dinner plans after a day of gallery-hopping. In the main building, the clubby lounge comes with internet access, an honour bar and magazines, and is tailor-made for trading tips with your fellow guests.

THE WEINMEISTER BERLIN-MITTE

Map pp102-3   Hotel €€

☎ 755 6670; www.the-weinmeister.com; Weinmeisterstrasse 2; d €150-220; Ⓜ Weinmeisterstrasse; Ⓟ ✗ 🖵 🛜 ♿

Behind its shiny golden facade, this sassy new bastion of style and glamour curries favour with creative types from fashion, music and film. Even if you don't run with this crowd, you'll likely appreciate the big rooms with their premium king-size beds, tactile furnishings and progressive hi-tech touches such as iMacs replacing TVs.

MITART HOTEL & CAFÉ

Map pp102-3   Hotel €€

☎ 2839 0430; www.mitart.de; Linienstrasse 139-140; d incl breakfast €110-180; Ⓜ Oranienburger Tor; ✗ 🛜 ♿

If you like to 'sleep with an original', book into this 'hotel gallery' whose 33 rooms are decorated with changing canvasses by up-and-coming Berlin artists. The owners go the extra mile when it comes to being green by using only natural materials, organic food, eco-minded cleaning products and other measures. Amenities are not really what you'd expect for the price, but the location and dedication to the arts and the environment mean that the place does get bonus points.

ARTIST RIVERSIDE HOTEL & SPA
Map pp102-3   Hotel €€

☎ 284 900; www.great-hotel.de; Friedrichstrasse 106; d €95-185, breakfast from €6; ❸ 🚇 Friedrichstrasse; 🅿 ✕ 🖥 🖵 🛜 ♿

If you like a hotel with a flair for the dramatic, this plush riverside place is your stage. Behind a rather tacky mirrored facade awaits an eccentric and colourful fantasy world with rooms available in five levels of comfort, from plain-Jane singles to a fanciful suite with a bronze bathtub. The in-house day spa is perfect for unwinding. Brazilian chocolate massage, anyone?

ARCOTEL VELVET Map pp102-3   Hotel €€

☎ 278 7530; www.arcotel.at; Oranienburger Strasse 52; d €90-265; ❸ Oranienburger Tor; 🅿 ✕ 🖥 🖵 🛜 ♿

This magnet wows the lifestyle crowd with edgy custom design from the street-level lounge to the swank penthouse suites. Digs are flooded with light, boldly coloured and smartened up with such mould-breaking perks as hi-tech window vents, open bathrooms and blackout blinds – perfect for sleeping off that hangover. Noise-sensitive? Avoid rooms overlooking the adjacent Kunsthaus Tacheles backyard. Rates include continental breakfast.

FLOWER'S BOARDING HOUSE MITTE
Map pp102-3   Serviced Apartments €€

☎ 2804 5306; www.flowersberlin.de, in German; Mulackstrasse 1; apt for one person €89-133, extra person €12; ❸ Weinmeisterstrasse, Rosa-Luxemburg-Platz; 🅿 ✕ 🛜

Self-caterers won't miss many of the comforts of home in these breezy, nonsmoking apartments whose heart-of-Scheunenviertel location makes them quite a steal. Choose from three sizes – L, XL and XXL – the latter being a split-level unit sleeping up to six and letting you peer out over the Scheunenviertel rooftops. Units come with full kitchens;

top picks

HOSTELS

- Circus Hostel (p278)
- East Seven Hostel (p279)
- Meininger Hotel Berlin Prenzlauer Berg (p278)
- Raise a Smile Hostel (p276)
- Wombat's City Hostel Berlin (p272)

rates include free wi-fi and a small breakfast (rolls, coffee, tea) you pick up at reception, which is staffed from 9am to 6pm.

CIRCUS HOTEL Map pp102-3   Hotel €€

☎ 2839 1433; www.circus-berlin.de; Rosenthaler Strasse 1; d €80-100, apt from €110, breakfast €4-8; ❸ Rosenthaler Platz; ✕ 🖥 🛜

With this stylish outpost, the Circus crew has upped the ante once again. There are lots of progressive touches to make life on the road as comfortable as possible, from the personalised welcome letter to the library stocked with Berlin books and, of course, good-sized and stylish rooms with ensuite bath. You can rent all sorts of equipment, including an iPod, DVD, laptop, bicycle, rollerblades and even a Smart Car. Green credentials range from rooftop solar panelling to energy-efficient windows; to reduce wastage, there are no toiletries in the bathrooms (although they're available for free at the reception). The onsite restaurant Fabisch is named for the Jewish family that used to operate a men's clothing store in the building. A small exhibit in the basement of the hotel chronicles their story.

HOTEL AMANO Map pp102-3   Hotel €€

☎ 809 4150; www.hotel-amano.com; Auguststrasse 43; r from €79, breakfast €11; ❸ Rosenthaler Platz; 🅿 ✕ 🖥 🖵 🛜 ♿

A top contender in the budget designer hotel category, Amano was an instant hit with style-minded wallet-watchers. After the generous lobby dressed in brushed copper walls and cocoa-hued banquettes, the ship-cabin-sized rooms are a bit of a let-down (get an apartment for more elbow room), but at this price it's hard to find a hotel that's cleaner or more central. Luxuriously appointed rooftop lounge for post-sightseeing unwinding.

WOMBAT'S CITY HOSTEL BERLIN

Map pp102-3   Hostel €

☎ 8471 0820; www.wombats-hostels.com; Alte Schönhauser Strasse 2; dm €15-24, d €58-70, apt with kitchen €80-100, breakfast €3.70; ⊙ Rosa-Luxemburg-Platz; ⊠ ▢ ▨ ⅏

Wombat's knows how to do hostelling right. From backpack-sized in-room lockers to individual reading lamps and a guest kitchen with dishwasher, the attention to detail here is impressive. Spacious rooms with bathrooms are as de rigueur as freebie linen and a welcome drink, best enjoyed with fellow party pilgrims in the 7th-floor Wombar.

BAXPAX DOWNTOWN Map pp102-3   Hostel €

☎ 2787 4880; www.baxpax.de/downtown; Ziegelstrasse 28; dm €10-21, linen €2.50, s/d from €29/54, breakfast €5.50; ⊙ Oranienburger Tor, ▨ Oranienburger Strasse; ⊠ ▢ ▨ ⅏

From 'backie dorm' for 50 to smaller dorms and private rooms with ensuite bath and even chic apartments, BaxPax caters for all sorts of penny-wise travellers. This makes for an interesting mix of ages and backgrounds in the cafe with fireplace, the courtyard lounge with stylish pods for chilling or the rooftop terrace. Retire to modern, spacious rooms and dorms outfitted with flat-screen TV, a table and bedside reading lamps. The spot-on location is another asset. Note that prices may increase during special events and major holidays.

POTSDAMER PLATZ & TIERGARTEN

MANDALA HOTEL Map p112   Suite Hotel €€€

☎ 590 050 000; www.themandala.de; Potsdamer Strasse 3; ste €270-580, breakfast €27; ⊙ ▨ Potsdamer Platz; ℗ ⊠ ▨ ▢

How 'suite' it is to be staying at this swank and ultra-discreet retreat, a place of casual sophistication and unfussy ambience. Six types of suites, ranging from 40 to 101 sq metres, are available, each outfitted for maximum comfort and ideal working conditions, in case you're here to ink that deal. Bonuses include Michelin-starred Facil (p205) and a sexy hotel bar.

RITZ-CARLTON BERLIN Map p112   Hotel €€€

☎ 337 777; www.ritzcarlton.com; Potsdamer Platz 3; d €205-400, breakfast €38; ⊙ ▨ Potsdamer Platz; ℗ ⊠ ▨ ▢ ▨ ⅏ ⅏

Only a discreet logo reveals that you've arrived at one of Berlin's most popular full-on luxury addresses. The 302 rooms and suites exude effortless sophistication through a neutral-hued colour palette, classical furnishings and watercolours by German artist Markus Lüpertz. Expect all the trappings of a big-league player, including the delightful Desbrosses (p205), a luxurious spa, and a clubby bar where Robbie Williams has been known to check out the 400 varieties of schnapps.

GRAND HYATT Map p112   Hotel €€€

☎ 2553 1234; www.berlin.grand.hyatt.com; Marlene-Dietrich-Platz 2; d €205-340, breakfast €32; ⊙ ▨ Potsdamer Platz; ℗ ⊠ ▨ ▢ ▨ ⅏

Sure, it's a swank celebrity haunt but you don't need to be Madonna to sleep, eat or party at this consistently cool designer temple a whiff away from theatres and the casino. The moment you step into the lavish, cedar-clad lobby, you sense that it's luxury all the way to the breathtaking rooftop pool. Rooms are dressed in drama and luxury and perfect for planning tomorrow's sightseeing attack or spend-a-thon.

MÖVENPICK HOTEL BERLIN

Map p112   Hotel €€€

☎ 230 060; www.moevenpick-berlin.com; Schöneberger Strasse 3; d €110-265, breakfast €22; ▨ Anhalter Bahnhof; ℗ ⊠ ▨ ▢ ▨ ⅏

This snazzy hotel cleverly marries bold contemporary design with the industrial aesthetic of the historic Siemenshöfe, making it a chic base of operations for both the suit brigade and city-breakers. Rooms vamp it up with Philippe Starck lamps and sinks, glass cube walls and furniture made from sensuous olive wood. Tip: the top-floor Atelier Rooms come with cool freestanding tub.

CHARLOTTENBURG & NORTHERN WILMERSDORF

LOUISA'S PLACE Map pp124-5   Hotel €€€

☎ 631 030; www.louisas-place.de; Kurfürstendamm 160; ste €135-595, breakfast €20; ⊙ Adenauerplatz; ℗ ⊠ ▢ ▨ ▨ ⅏

Louisa's is the kind of place that dazzles with class not glitz, a discreet deluxe hideaway, perfect for sharp dressers tired of anonymous big-city hotels. We know of few properties that put more emphasis on customising guest services. It'll even send you a pre-arrival questionnaire asking for your likes and dislikes! Suites here are huge, the spa heavenly and the library palatial.

HOTEL CONCORDE BERLIN
Map p128   Hotel €€

☎ 800 9990; www.concorde-hotels.com /concordeberlin; Augsburger Strasse 41; d €160-350; ⊕ Kurfürstendamm, ⬚ M19, M29; P ☒ ☒ ▣ 🛜 ♿

If you like designer boutique hotels but value the amenities of a big-city property, the Concorde should fit the bill. Designed by Jan Kleihues, from the curved limestone facade to the door knobs, it channels New York efficiency, French lightness of being and Berlin-style unpretentiousness. The 311 rooms and suites are supersized, warmly furnished and accented with quality prints by contemporary German artists.

HOTEL Q! Map p128   Hotel €€€

☎ 810 0660; www.loock-hotels.com; Knesebeckstrasse 67; d €105-215, breakfast €20; ⊕ Uhlandstrasse; P ☒ ☒ ▣ 🛜

No fancy marquee here, only an innocuous grey facade to indicate your arrival at this hot-spot popular with *Wallpaper* readers. Corners are eschewed, from the tunnel-like crimson lobby to the sexy rooms, some with pod chairs and L-shaped sofas, others with tubs right next to the bed. Note that the cheapest ones are tiny. Nice touch: the spa with 'sandroom' for relaxing. For that extra air of exclusivity, the bar is open only to members and hotel guests.

SAVOY HOTEL Map p128   Hotel €€

☎ 311 030, reservations toll free 0800 7286 9468; www.hotel-savoy.com; Fasanenstrasse 9-10; d €146-277, breakfast €18; ⊕ ⬚ Zoologischer Garten; ☒ ☒ 🛜 ▣

History streams through this hotel as strongly as the Thames does through London. In business since 1929, there's something comfortably stuffy about this intimate grand hotel that writer Thomas Mann called 'charming and cosy' and Talking Head's David Byrne considered 'friendly and helpful'. Rooms come in six categories of comfort and exude a pleasant, lived-in feel. All sport the gamut of mod cons you'd

expect from a hotel of this pedigree. Kids under 12 stay free in parents' room.

ELLINGTON HOTEL Map p128   Hotel €€

☎ 683 150; www.ellington-hotel.com; Nürnberger Strasse 50-55; d €130-270, breakfast €19; ⊕ Augsburger Strasse; P ☒ ☒ ▣ 🛜 ♿

Duke and Ella gave concerts in the Badewanne (bathtub) jazz cellar and Bowie and Prince partied in the Dschungel night club, then the lights went out in the '90s. Now the handsome 1920s building has been resuscitated as a high-concept jewel that wraps all that's great about Berlin – history, innovation, elegance, the art of living – into one attractive package. Rooms are stylishly minimalist, and the restaurant, Duke (p206), gets the nod for its Sunday jazz brunch. One child under 12 is allowed to stay free in their parents' room.

KU'DAMM 101 Map pp124-5   Hotel €€

☎ 520 0550; www.kudamm101.com; Kurfürstendamm 101; d €120-250, breakfast €15; ⬚ Halensee; P ☒ ☒ ▣ 🛜 ♿

If it were in Mitte, this sassy lifestyle hotel would be hipster central. But, alas, it's kinda out there in the far west, albeit close to the trade-fair grounds. Still, you may want to make the trip out to experience the edgy design that's stylishly minimalist without sacrificing comfort. Don't skip breakfast, served in an airy 7th-floor lounge with a feast of views. Children under 12 stay free in parents' room.

BLEIBTREU BERLIN Map p128   Hotel €€

☎ 884 740; www.bleibtreu.com; Bleibtreustrasse 31; d €120-200, breakfast €17; ⊕ Uhlandstrasse; ☒ ▣ 🛜 ♿

On a leafy avenue, the stylish Bleibtreu pioneered sustainable hospitality long before everyone else jumped on the bandwagon. Furniture made from untreated oak, virgin wool carpets and walls daubed with organic paint are among the thoughtful features. Rooms don't fit a ton of luggage but, heck, the minibar is free and breakfast is available all day in the on-site deli. Children under 12 stay free in parents' room.

HOTEL ASKANISCHER HOF
Map p128   Hotel €€

☎ 881 8033; www.askanischer-hof.de; Kurfürstendamm 53; d incl breakfast €117-150; ⊕ Adenauerplatz; ☒ 🛜

ASLEEP IN THE TWILIGHT ZONE

It is only fitting that Berlin's most original hotel takes its name from a novel by the master of imagination, Jules Verne. Each of its 32 rooms is a journey to a unique, surreal and slightly wicked world, spawned by the vision of artist-composer-owner Lars Stroschen. To be stranded on Propeller Island City Lodge (Map pp124-5; ☎ noon-8pm 891 9016; www.propeller-island.de; Albrecht-Achilles-Strasse 58; r for 1 person €69-115, extra person €15, breakfast €7; 🔵 Adenauerplatz; ✖) means waking up on the ceiling (in the Upside-Down Room), in a comfortable prison cell (Freedom Room) or inside a kaleidoscope (Mirror Room). The only aspect this place shares with other hotels is that each room has a bed or two. Except here it's a rotating round bed, a 'flying' bed, one that's suspended on ship's rope or a ziggurat platform, in a lion's cage or inside a coffin. It took Lars, who designed and crafted every piece of furniture and accessory, some six years to finish this creative tour de force, mostly using recycled materials. There are sinks wrought from metal beer barrels, faucets made from heater valves and table bases carved from tree trunks. Absent are any of the usual hotel trappings: no telephone, no room service, no pillow treats. Instead, each room has an audio-system playing 'sound sculptures' composed by – who else? – Lars himself.

If you're after character and vintage flair, you'll find heaps of both at this 17-room jewel with a Roaring Twenties' pedigree. An ornate oak door leads to a quiet oasis where no two rooms are alike but all are filled with antiques, lace curtains, frilly chandeliers and timeworn oriental rugs. The quaint Old Berlin charms make a popular setting for fashion shoots.

CASA HOTEL Map p128 Hotel €€
☎ 280 3000; www.hotel-casa.de; Schlüterstrasse 40; d incl breakfast €115-180; 🔵 Uhlandstrasse, Adenauerplatz; 🅿 ✖ 📶 🛜
Take an aging hotel, gut it, apply vision and money and end up with a modern-design abode for fashion-forward travellers without a trust fund. Fresh colour accents brighten the 29 comfortable rooms, which mix custom-designed furniture with pieces by Philippe Starck. The swivelling flat-screen TV and free wi-fi are handy tech touches. Breakfast is served until a hangover-friendly noon.

HOTEL OTTO Map p128 Hotel €€
☎ 5471 0080; www.hotelotto.com; Knesebeckstrasse 10; d €100-220, breakfast €13; 🔵 Ernst-Reuter-Platz; 🅿 ✖ 🛜
Otto would be just another city hotel catering to the business brigade were it not for the fall-over-backwards staff and thoughtful extras such as unlimited bottled water and a rooftop lounge where you're free to fill up on coffee, tea and cake at no extra cost. Rooms are fairly functional but enlivened by splashes of colour. Note that those in the 'standard' category really are tiny, so spend a few extra euros for a little more legroom.

HOTEL ART NOUVEAU
Map p128 Hotel-Pension €€
☎ 327 7440; www.hotelartnouveau.de; Leibnizstrasse 59; d incl breakfast from €96; 🔵 Adenauerplatz; 🅿 ✖ 🛜
A rickety birdcage lift drops you off with belle époque flourish at one of Berlin's finest boutique pensions. The 22 rooms (all non-smoking) skimp neither on space nor charisma, and offer a blend of youthful flair and tradition. The affable owners are fluent English-speakers with a knack for colour and a penchant for sourcing fantastic pieces of art and furniture. Nice touches: the honour bar for feeding late-night cravings. Children under six stay free.

HOTEL-PENSION DITTBERNER
Map p128 Hotel-Pension €€
☎ 881 6485; www.hotel-dittberner.de; Wielandstrasse 26; d incl breakfast €97-133; 🔵 Adenauerplatz; ✖ 🛜 ♿
Travel back in time aboard a century-old lift that deposits you at this friendly pension with its treasure-trove of old furniture, plush rugs and armloads of paintings, lithographs and posters. The location is great for city explorations, while free wi-fi makes keeping in touch with the folks back home a snap.

HOTEL BOGOTA Map p128 Hotel €€
☎ 881 5001; www.bogota.de; Schlüterstrasse 45; d incl breakfast €90-150, without bathroom €64-77; 🔵 Uhlandstrasse; 🅿 ✖ 🛜
One of our favourite budget picks in the west, the Bogota comes with a high charm quotient and oozes vintage flair from every nook and cranny. Helmut Newton studied with fashion photographer Yva here in the

1930s and to this day the rambling landmark hosts glam-mag photo shoots. Room sizes and amenities vary greatly, so ask to see a few before settling in.

HOTEL-PENSION FUNK
Map p128   Hotel-Pension €€

☎ 882 7193; www.hotel-pensionfunk.de; Fasanenstrasse 69; d incl breakfast €82-129; ◉ Uhlandstrasse, Kurfürstendamm; ✗ 🛜

This little pension in the 1930s home of silent-movie siren Asta Nielsen has been riding on the coat-tails of its Golden Age glamour image for decades. Although showing some wear and tear, it's still a good choice if you value old-fashioned charm. Rooms vary quite significantly, so if size matters bring up the subject when booking. There are also cheaper ones with shared bathroom or in-room shower and shared toilet.

FRAUENHOTEL ARTEMISIA
off Map pp72-3   Hotel €€

☎ 873 8905; www.frauenhotel-berlin.de; Brandenburgische Strasse 18; d €78-108, breakfast €8.50; ◉ Konstanzer Strasse; ✗ 🛜

Named after a 16th-century Italian woman artist, this was the first hotel in Germany to cater exclusively for the x-chromosome set (plus boys to age 14). Owners Manuela and Renata have recently expanded their friendly and communicative hospitality zone to 19 rooms, each equipped with modern furniture and changing art. In summer breakfast is served on the rooftop terrace, which is also great for sunbathing and meeting fellow guests.

SCHÖNEBERG

For lodging options specifically geared to the lesbigay market, see p263.

ARCO HOTEL Map p136   Hotel €€

☎ 235 1480; www.arco-hotel.de; Geisbergstrasse 30; d incl breakfast €70-117; ◉ Wittenbergplatz; 🖥 🛜

On a residential street, near the famous KaDeWe department store, this gay-friendly hotel rents 23 pleasant, if rather generic, rooms with all major mod cons. It's nothing special but still a good value-for-money pick, at least if you're not too picky or a space-craver. On balmy days breakfast is

best enjoyed alfresco in the lovely back garden dotted with mature trees.

BERLINER BED & BREAKFAST
Map p136   B&B €

☎ 2437 3962; www.berliner-bed-and-breakfast .de; Langenscheidtstrasse 5; d without bathroom €55; ◉ Kleistpark

Owner Andreas has poured his heart and money into his little B&B in an 1895 building with high ceilings and polished plank floors. Stretch out comfortably in six rooms, each cheerfully decorated in a different theme (eg Asia, Pop, Oriental). Rates include breakfast, which you're free to prepare anytime in the guest kitchen and enjoy in the candy-striped communal room with its many plants and old furniture.

KREUZBERG & NORTHERN NEUKÖLLN

HOTEL RIEHMERS HOFGARTEN
Map pp140-1   Hotel €€

☎ 7809 8800; www.riehmers-hofgarten.de; Yorckstrasse 83; d incl breakfast €138-155; ◉ Mehringdamm; ✗ 🖥 🛜

Take a lovely old building, infuse it with a generous dose of style, stir in a touch of trendiness and you'll get one killer cocktail of a hotel. Close to Viktoriapark and Bergmannstrasse, Riehmer's has large double French doors leading to mostly spacious, high-ceilinged rooms that are modern but not stark. If you're staying Friday and Saturday, you can add Sunday night for only €69.

WINTER'S HOTEL Map pp140-1   Hotel €€

☎ 3198 6180; www.winters.de; Hedemannstrasse 11-12; d €110; ◉ Kochstrasse; 🅿 ✗ 🖥 🛜

Although it caters mostly to the business brigade, this hotel in a historical building should also meet the needs of leisure travellers. Budget-minded types will definitely appreciate the weekend rates, which can be as low as €59. Rooms are quite stylish, although in a rather stark charcoal-and-white colour scheme, and have hip touches such as wall-mounted flat-screen TVs and laptop-sized safes. Bonus points for being in a quiet spot, yet close to the infamous Checkpoint Charlie.

HOTEL JOHANN Map pp140-1   Hotel €€
☎ 225 0740; www.hotel-johann-berlin.de;
Johanniterstrasse 8; d €95-105; ⊖ Prinzenstrasse,
Hallesches Tor; ✗ 🖥 🛜 🕭

Everything drops into place as smoothly as
a bead of oil slides down a scallion in this
33-room hotel that consistently tops the
popularity charts thanks to its eager-to-
please service and gorgeous rooms; some
still sport historic touches such as scalloped
ceilings and exposed brick walls. The small
garden is perfect for summery breakfasts,
while happening Bergmannstrasse and the
Jüdisches Museum (Jewish Museum) are
just quick strolls away.

36 ROOMS HOSTEL Map pp140-1   Hostel €
☎ 5308 6398; www.36rooms.com; Spreewaldplatz
8; dm €14-20, s €35-38, d €50-56, linen €2.50;
⊖ Görlitzer Bahnhof; ✗ 🖥 🛜 🕭

Floorboards, cosy furniture and wooden
windows (overlooking a park if you get the
right room) are among the vintage touches
of this charmer in a 19th-century town-
house in the heart of Kreuzberg. The major
sights are a U-Bahn or bike ride away, but
instead you'll be within stumbling distance
of cool bars, breakfast spots, kebab joints,
the park and a public indoor swimming
pool. Women-only dorms available.

RIVERSIDE LODGE HOSTEL
Map pp140-1   Hostel €
☎ 6951 5510; www.riverside-lodge.de; Hobrechtstrasse 43; dm €21-22, d €52, linen €3, breakfast
€4; ⊖ Schönleinstrasse; ✗ 🖥 🛜

This sweet little nautical-themed, 12-bed
hostel is as warm and welcoming as an old
friend's hug thanks to its wonderful owners, Jutta and Liane. Both avid travellers,
they have created a cosy, communicative
hostel close to the Landwehrkanal and its
happening cafes and restaurants. In the
large dorm, beds can be curtained off for
extra privacy.

RIXPACK HOSTEL Map pp140-1   Hostel €
☎ 5471 5140; www.rixpack.de; Karl-Marx-
Strasse 75; dm Sun-Thu €10-20, Fri & Sat €13-24;
⊖ Rathaus Neukölln; ✗ 🖥 🛜

Bucking the designer-hostel trend, the
newish Rixpack is your classic low-fi backie
with communal kitchen, bunk beds, shared
facilities and free coffee and internet. In the
heart of Neukölln, it's perfect for getting
ahead on the latest bar/gallery/shop in this

grittily hip district, even if the blockbuster
sights are quite far away (the U-Bahn stops
right outside, though).

FRIEDRICHSHAIN

HOTEL 26 Map pp150-1   Hotel €€
☎ 297 7780; www.hotel26-berlin.de; Grünberger Strasse 26; d incl breakfast €90-120;
🚊 Warschauer Strasse, 🚋 M10 Grünberger
Strasse; 🅿 ✗ 🖥 🛜 🕭

Set back from the street and with a lovely
garden out back, this architect-owned hotel
in a revamped factory sparkles in cheery
citrus colours that instantly put you in a
good mood. Clear lines and blonde-wood
furniture dominate both public areas and the
rooms. Hotel 26 also has a lot going on in the
eco-department with such things as natural soaps, filtered water and a cafe serving
mostly sustainable and organic products.

EAST-SIDE HOTEL Map pp150-1   Hotel €€
☎ 293 833; www.eastsidehotel.de; Mühlenstrasse
6; d incl breakfast €80-120; ⊖ 🚊 Warschauer
Strasse; 🅿

The East-Side's white-and-butter-yellow
classical facade is a bit of a tease because
its 36 rooms really are a meditation on
minimalism. The best thing about the
place, quite frankly, is being just steps from
the East Side Gallery (Berlin Wall remnant),
the Spree River with its beach bars, the
Kreuzberg and Friedrichshain fun zones
and the O2 World arena. Single rooms are
tiny but face the river.

MICHELBERGER HOTEL
Map pp150-1   Hotel €€
☎ 2977 8590; www.michelbergerhotel.com;
Warschauer Strasse 39/40; d from €60, breakfast €8;
⊖ 🚊 Warschauer Strasse

The ultimate in creative crash pads,
Michelsberger pushes the envelope when
it comes to the DIY aesthetic that's increasingly invading hotel design. The 119 rooms
in the former factory range from functional
to cheeky to kitsch, are big enough for love-
birds or rock bands and are close to public
transport, the East Side Gallery, beach bars,
big clubs and other essential fun zones.

RAISE A SMILE HOSTEL
Map pp150-1   Hostel €
☎ 0172 855 6064; www.raise-a-smile-hostel
-berlin.com; Weidenweg 51; dm/d from €9/38;

🚉 Warschauer Strasse, 🚇 M10 Bersarinplatz; ✕ 🖥 🛜 ♿

This charity-run African-themed hostel donates 100% of all profits to children's projects in Zambia. Elephants, zebras, giraffes and big cats watch over guests in smallish dorms and private rooms with shared facilities. With only 19 beds total, it's definitely not a party hostel, but the kind of place conducive to banding up with fellow travellers.

OSTEL Map pp150-1   Hostel €

☎ 2576 8660; www.ostel.eu; Wriezener Karree 5; dm/d/apt €9/61/120; 🚉 Ostbahnhof; 🅿 ✕ 🖥 🛜

Fancy a stay on the set of *Good Bye Lenin*? Book a bed in this unusual hostel, which resuscitates socialist GDR charm with original furnishings sourced from flea markets, grannies' attics and eBay. Style police alert! With portraits of Honecker and other party apparatchiks peering down on you, you can stay in a pioneer-room dorm, a '70s holiday apartment, a prefab flat or the bugged Stasi suite. Tip for clubbers: it's close to lots of hot party spots, including Berghain/Panorama Bar (p232).

EASTERN COMFORT HOSTELBOAT

Map pp150-1   Hostel €

☎ 6676 3806; www.eastern-comfort.com; Mühlenstrasse 73-77; dm €16, d 1st-/2nd-class

€58/78, linen & towels €5, breakfast €4; 🅾 🚉 Warschauer Strasse; ✕ 🖥 🛜

Moored on the Spree River right by the East Side Gallery, this floating hostel puts you within staggering distance of party-hearty Kreuzberg and Friedrichshain. Cabins are carpeted and trimmed in wood, but pretty snug (except for 'first-class'); all but the dorms have their own shower and toilet. The 18 doubles and triples in the Western Comfort boat across the river (check-in at Eastern Comfort) cost €50 and €60, respectively. On Wednesdays, the hostel hosts the English-language Boat Party (p227).

GLOBETROTTER HOSTEL ODYSSEE

Map pp150-1   Hostel €

☎ 2900 0081, toll-free reservations 0800 2665 2233; www.globetrotterhostel.de; Grünberger Strasse 23; dm €9-22, s €29-39, d with shower €46-57, breakfast €3; 🚉 Warschauer Strasse, 🚇 M10 Grünberger Strasse; ✕ 🖥 🛜

Young, social types give high marks to this eastside hostel that puts the 'fun' in funky and is a great launching pad for in-depth nightlife explorations. Clean rooms sport pine beds, lockers and artsy styling: here a vertigo-inducing ceiling swirl, there a bright orange flower-power homage or a giant puzzle. Guest kitchen, backyard and onsite pub are all great socialising zones. Prices include linen.

QUIRKY SLEEPS

For other unique ways to spend the night in Berlin, check out our reviews of Ostel (above), Propeller Island City Lodge (p274) and Eastern Comfort Hostelboat (above).

- Alte Bäckerei Pankow (off Map pp72-3; ☎ 486 4669; www.alte-baeckerei-pankow.de; Wollankstrasse 130, Pankow; s/d/tr & q €35/70/80; 🚉 Wollankstrasse; ✕) Yesteryear is now in this small rooftop apartment in a 19th-century bakery. Bedrooms and sitting rooms are furnished country-style and the bathroom has a deep wooden tub. The building also houses a childhood museum, and fresh bread is still baked between 3pm and 6pm Tuesday and Friday.

- Das Andere Haus VIII (off Map pp72-3; ☎ 5544 0331; www.dasanderehaus8.de; Erich-Müller-Strasse 12, Lichtenberg; s €40-45, d €60-65; 🚉 Rummelsburg; 🅿 ✕ 🛜) At this 19th-century former waterfront jailhouse you'll be sleeping in one of five 'cells' that are snug but warmly furnished and come with private baths; some even have bay views. Best of all, they don't throw away the key.

- Gästehaus Euroflat (Map pp140-1; ☎ 6003 1532; http://berlin-rooms.eu; Alexandrinenstrasse 118, Kreuzberg; s €40-50, d €50-60; 🅾 Hallesches Tor; ✕ 🖥 🛜) No need to be religious when staying at this congenial guesthouse attached to a former church. The five rooms won't win style awards but neither are they monastic, and guests are free to refuel with free coffee or tea in the kitchen, lobby and garden.

- Yes Residenz (Map pp156-7; info@yes-berlin.de; www.yes-berlin.de; Fehrbelliner Strasse 84, Prenzlauer Berg; one person €55, extra person €11; ✕) Fancy sleeping in a tent on camping beds and taking showers from a watering can without roughing it in the woods? In this teensy yet undeniably unique mini-apartment, you can just do that. Architect Julian Marhold has created a charmingly unique space, complete with forest wallpaper, right in a regular Berlin building, so you can have your Hansel and Gretel moment without leaving town.

PRENZLAUER BERG

ACKSELHAUS & BLUE HOME
Map pp156-7   Hotel €€

☎ 4433 7633; www.ackselhaus.de; Belforter Strasse 21; apt incl breakfast €110-180; ◉ Senefelderplatz; ✗ ⤢

This charismatic contender on a pretty residential street in the city centre brings 'sexy' back to the bedroom in 10 units spread over two 19th-century buildings. Themed from naughty to nautical, elegant to eastern, each sports a small living room and kitchenette. Breakfast is served until 11am (until 12.30pm at the weekends).

HOTEL KASTANIENHOF
Map pp156-7   Hotel €€

☎ 443 050; www.kastanienhof.biz; Kastanienallee 65; r incl breakfast €103-138; ◉ Rosenthaler Platz; ℗ ✗ ▭ ⤢

This charmer puts you right onto Kastanienallee with its many cafes and restaurants, although the hotel design itself has more of a traditional bent. Family-owned and with fall-over-backwards staff, it has 35 rooms, including themed ones decorated with historical photos, paintings and information about Berlin landmarks. Bikes for hire at a small fee.

HOTEL APARTMENTHAUS ZARENHOF
Map pp156-7   Apartment Hotel €€

☎ 802 0880; www.apartmenthaus-zarenhof.de; Schönhauser Allee 140; apt €80-160, breakfast €11; ◉ Eberswalder Strasse; ✗ ▭ ⤢ ♿

A homage to Nicholas II, the last Russian tsar, this chic hotel has rooms that are daubed in regal reds and blues but have otherwise arrived in the 21st century (think plasma TVs, free wi-fi). Most of the 54 units come with kitchenettes and small balconies wrapped around a central courtyard. Breakfast is a gut-buster, featuring such Russian specialities as *blinis* (pancakes) and even caviar.

HOTEL GREIFSWALD
Map pp156-7   Hotel €€

☎ 442 7888; www.hotel-greifswald.de; Greifswalder Strasse 211; d €65-75, breakfast €7.50; ▤ 100, ▥ M4 to Hufelandstrasse; ℗ ⤢

This 30-room hotel, tucked into a back building away from tram and traffic noise, has a serious rock pedigree. The teensy lobby doubles as a veritable hall of fame for former guests, including Mitch Ryder

and Steppenwolf. Rooms are handsome, if rather generic, but it's the awesome breakfast spread – served until 1pm – that gets our thumbs up.

MYER'S HOTEL
Map pp156-7   Hotel €€

☎ 440 140; www.myershotel.de; Metzer Strasse 26; d €78-228, breakfast €12.50; ◉ Senefelder Platz; ✗ ▨ ⤢ ♿

This 41-room boutique hotel combines the elegance of your rich uncle's mansion, the cheerful warmth of your parents' home and the casual comforts of your best friend's pad. Rooms are classically furnished with rich woods and sheathed in soothing colours. Unwinding spots include the 24-hour lobby bar, the light-filled gallery lounge, the spanking-new sauna and steam room and the bucolic garden.

MEININGER HOTEL BERLIN PRENZLAUER BERG
Map pp156-7   Hostel-hotel €

☎ 6663 6100; www.meininger-hotels.com; Schönhauser Allee 19; dm €18-21, s/d €52/68, breakfast €5.50; ◉ Senefelderplatz; ✗ ▨ ⤢ ♿

Run with panache and professionalism, this top-flight hotel-hostel combo is ideal for savvy nomads seeking plenty of comforts without dropping buckets of cash. A lift whisks you to mod rooms and dorms (all with attached bathrooms) with plenty of space, quality furnishings, flat-screen TVs and even blackout blinds to combat jetlag (or hangovers). Other assets: the all-day cafe-bar, guest kitchen and spot-on location close to sights, eats and parties. Check the website for the other four Berlin locations, including new ones at the Hauptbahnhof and on Oranienburger Strasse. Rates include linen.

CIRCUS HOSTEL
Map pp156-7   Hostel €

☎ 2839 1433; www.circus-berlin.de; Weinbergsweg 1a; 3- to 8-bed dm €19-25, s/d €53/70, without bathroom €43/56, 2-/4-person apt €85/140; ◉ Rosenthaler Platz; ✗ ▭ ⤢ ♿

In business since 1997, this hostel still fires on all cylinders, especially after a recent makeover. Clean, cheerfully painted rooms, abundant showers and competent, helpful staff are among factors that keep it at the top of the hostel heap. Stay in dorms, private rooms (some with ensuite baths) or one of 10 penthouse apartments with kitchen and terrace. The downstairs cafe serves inexpensive breakfasts, drinks and small meals, while the basement bar puts on different activities nightly. Upmarket touches include laptop and iPod rentals, laptop-sized in-room lockers with integrated electrical plug and a staff-written touch-screen Berlin guide in the lobby. To download a free self-guided city tour, go to www.circus-berlin.de/bustour.

EAST SEVEN HOSTEL Map pp156-7 Hostel €
☎ 9362 2240; www.eastseven.de; Schwedter Strasse 7; dm €13-21, s €30-37, d €42-50, linen €3; ⓔ Senefelder Platz; ⊠ ▯ ⌂ ♿
Friendly and fun, this small hostel is within strolling distance of hip hangouts and public transport. Cultural and language barriers melt quickly over a barbecue in the idyllic back garden, spaghetti dinner in the modern kitchen (with dishwasher!) or

chilling in the retro lounge. Come bedtime, retreat to comfy pine beds in brightly painted dorms or private rooms (baby beds are available).

LETTE'M SLEEP Map pp156-7 Hostel €
☎ 4473 3623; www.backpackers.de; Lettestrasse 7; dm €17-28, tw without bathroom €49, apt with bathroom €69; ⓔ Eberswalder Strasse; ⊠ ▯ ⌂ ♿
A textbook boho hostel: friendly, earthy, casual and a little chaotic. It's right on hip Helmholtzplatz, perfect for plunging into local nightlife. Dorms sleep three to seven and have a sink, lockers and table, while twins come with a small fridge. There are also four apartments with their own kitchens, although the communal kitchen-lounge is more conducive to chilling and hooking up with fellow globetrotters. Free coffee and tea.

EXCURSIONS

EXCURSIONS

Often overlooked amid the tumult and excitement of Berlin, the states and regions surrounding the German capital offer some unique attractions in their own right. The palaces and gardens of Potsdam or the swampy Spreewald ('Spree Forest') are good examples, while Dresden and Leipzig in Saxony are remarkable cities with their own style and character. Good rail links make most of the excursions here an easy day trip or overnight stay.

PARKS & PALACES

Few places in Germany can compete with the pomp and splendour of historic Potsdam (right), a superbly civilised break from the bustle of Berlin. Easily reached on local transport, it's an essential day trip for anyone with a few hours to spare.

ARCHITECTURE

Despite the notoriously heavy bombing at the end of WWII, the centre of Dresden (p291) is a treasure-trove of architectural gems, including the splendid Semperoper. Just walking around the Altstadt (old town) should satisfy most building buffs. Further classical treats can be found in Leipzig (p296).

WATERWAYS

The Spreewald (p290) is a great place to get out onto the many miles of canals, rivers, nature trails and marshes that dot the landscape around Berlin.

DINING & NIGHTLIFE

Sippers, suppers and boppers will have good times in Leipzig (p299), home of Goethe's old local, Auerbachs Keller, and in the buzzy Neustadt district of Dresden (p295).

PILGRIMAGES

No need to be Lutheran to appreciate Lutherstadt-Wittenberg (p300). Anyone interested in the man and the Reformation should find plenty to see here.

ACOUSTICS

For a special musical treat in the idyllic setting of ancient monasteries, score tickets early for the summer concerts at Chorin Monastery (p289) and Kloster Zinna (p289), the latter having the additional attraction of being on Germany's longest inline skating and cycling trail.

DAY TRIPS

POTSDAM

Potsdam, on the Havel River just southwest of Greater Berlin, is the capital and crown jewel of the state of Brandenburg. Scores of visitors are drawn to the stunning architecture of this former Prussian royal seat and to soak up the elegant air of history that hangs over its parks and gardens. A visit to this Unesco World Heritage site is essential if you're spending any time in the region at all.

No single individual shaped Potsdam more than King Friedrich II (Frederick the Great), the visionary behind many of Sanssouci's fabulous palaces and parks. In April 1945, Royal Air Force bombers devastated the historic centre, but fortunately many palaces escaped with nary a shrapnel wound. When the shooting stopped, the Allies chose Schloss Cecilienhof for the Potsdam Conference of August 1945 to decide Germany's fate.

Potsdam was also the centre of Germany's film industry from the very early days of the medium when the UFA studio was based here. After reunification, the dream factory was resurrected as Studio Babelsberg and is now involved in such international blockbusters as *Inglourious Basterds* and *The Reader*.

TRANSPORT: POTSDAM

Direction 24km southwest

Travel time 40 minutes

Car Take the A100 to the A115

Train Regional trains leaving from Berlin-Hauptbahnhof and Zoologischer Garten take only 25 minutes to reach Potsdam Hauptbahnhof; some continue on to Potsdam-Charlottenhof and Potsdam-Sanssouci, which are closer to Park Sanssouci than Hauptbahnhof. The S7 from central Berlin makes the trip in about 40 minutes. You need a ticket covering zones A, B and C (€2.80) for either service.

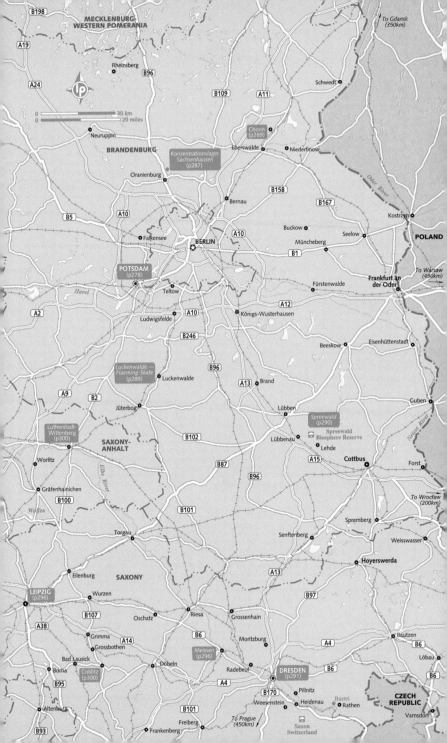

POTSDAM

0   500 m
0   0.3 miles

Information

Sanssouci Visitors' Centre (☎ 0331 969 4200; www.spsg .de; An der Orangerie 1; 🕐 8.30am-6pm Mar-Oct, 8.30am-5pm Nov-Feb)

Tourist office Brandenburger Tor (☎ 0331 275 580; Brandenburger Strasse 3; 🕐 9.30am-6pm Mon-Fri, to 4pm Sat & Sun Apr-Oct, 10am-6pm Mon-Fri, 9.30am-2pm Sat & Sun Nov-Mar)

Tourist office Potsdam Hauptbahnhof (☎ 0331 275 580; Bahnhofspassagen, next to platform 6, Babelsberger Strasse 16; 🕐 9.30am-8pm Mon-Sat, 10am-4pm Sun)

Park Sanssouci

Park Sanssouci is the oldest and most splendid of Potsdam's many gardens, anchored by Frederick the Great's favourite summer retreat, Schloss Sanssouci. It's open from dawn till dusk year-round and dotted with numerous palaces and outbuildings that all have different hours and admission prices. A one-day pass valid at all Potsdam palaces is €19 (concession €14) and available only at Schloss Sanssouci. A day pass to all palaces except Sanssouci is €14 (concession €10) and sold at any of them and at the Sanssouci Visitors' Centre (see Information, above).

The palaces are fairly well spaced – it's almost 2km between the Neues Palais (New Palace) and Schloss Sanssouci. Free maps are available at the tourist office. Cycling is officially permitted all along Ökonomieweg and Maulbeerallee.

SCHLOSS SANSSOUCI & AROUND

The biggest stunner, and what everyone comes to see, is Schloss Sanssouci (☎ 0331 969 4200; www.spsg.de; adult/concession incl audioguide €12/8 Apr-Oct, €8/5 incl tour or audioguide Nov-Mar; 🕐 10am-6pm Tue-Sun Apr-Oct, to 5pm Nov-Mar), the celebrated rococo palace designed by Georg Wenzeslaus von Knobelsdorff in 1747. Only 2000 visitors a day are allowed entry, so arrive early and avoid weekends and holidays. For guaranteed admission, shell out €27 for the 3½-hour Potsdam Sanssouci Tour, which leaves from the tourist offices (above) at 11am from Tuesday to Sunday (Friday to Sunday only November to March).

Favourite rooms include the circular Bibliothek (library), with its cedar panelling and gilded sunburst ceiling; the Konzertsaal (Concert Room), playfully decorated with vines, grapes, seashells and even a cobweb where spiders frolic; and the domed Marmorhalle (Marble

top picks

POTSDAM

- Schloss Sanssouci (left)
- Park Sanssouci (left)
- Chinesisches Haus (p286)
- Neues Palais (p286)
- Holländisches Viertel (p286)

Hall), an elegant symphony in white Carrara marble.

The ladies-in-waiting resided in the Damenflügel (Ladies' Wing; adult/concession €2/1.50; 🕐 10am-6pm Sat & Sun May-Oct), added under Friedrich Wilhelm IV in 1840. In the eastern wing is the Schlossküche (palace kitchen; adult/concession €3/2.50; 🕐 10am-6pm Tue-Sun Apr-Oct), whose *pièce de résistance* is a giant, wood-fired 'cooking machine'.

Schloss Sanssouci is flanked by the Bildergalerie (Picture Gallery; ☎ 0331 969 4181; adult/concession €3/2.50; 🕐 10am-5pm Tue-Sun May-Oct), which brims with paintings by Rubens, Caravaggio, van Dyck and others, and the Neue Kammern (New Chambers; ☎ 0331 969 4206; adult/concession incl tour or audioguide €4/3; 🕐 10am-6pm Tue-Sun May-Oct), a former orangery and guesthouse where the festive *Ovidsaal* ballroom is a highlight.

ORANGERIESCHLOSS & AROUND

Maulbeerallee is the only road cutting straight through Park Sanssouci. North of it are a number of buildings, starting in the east with the Historische Mühle (☎ 0331 550 6851; adult/child with tour €3/2, without tour €2.50/1.50; 🕐 10am-6pm daily Apr-Oct, 10am-6pm Sat & Sun Nov & Jan-Mar), a functioning replica of an 18th-century windmill.

Next up is the elegantly ageing Orangerie (Orangery; ☎ 0331 969 4280; tour adult/concession €4/3; 🕐 10am-6pm Tue-Sun May-Oct, 10am-6pm Sat & Sun Apr), a 300m-long Renaissance-style palace used as a guesthouse for visiting royalty. The tower (admission €2) delivers some nice park views, but otherwise the most interesting room is the Raphaelsaal, featuring 19th-century copies of the painter's masterpieces.

From the Orangerie, a tree-lined path forms a visual axis to the temple-like Belvedere auf dem Klausberg (☎ 0331 969 4206; admission €2; 🕐 10am-6pm Sat & Sun May-Oct), which offers delightful park views. En route, you'll pass the Drachenhaus (Dragon House, 1770), a small Chinese palace with a pleasant café-restaurant.

NEUES PALAIS

At the far western end of the park, the vast Neues Palais (New Palace; ☎ 0331 969 4200; adult/concession with tour or audioguide €6/5; ⏱ 10am-6pm Wed-Mon Apr-Oct, to 5pm Nov-Mar) has made-to-impress dimensions and about a dozen splendid rooms. The most memorable are the Grottensaal (Grotto Hall), a rococo delight with shells, fossils and baubles set into the walls and ceilings; the Marmorsaal, a large banquet hall of Carrara marble with a wonderful ceiling fresco; and the Jagdkammer (Hunting Chamber), with lots of dead furry things and fine gold tracery on the walls. Frederick the Great's private apartments (Königswohnung; adult/concession €5/4; ⏱ 10am, noon, 2pm & 4pm Wed-Mon Apr-Oct) can only be seen on guided tours.

PARK CHARLOTTENHOF

South of the Neues Palais, Park Charlottenhof was laid out under Friedrich Wilhelm IV and now blends smoothly with Park Sanssouci. It gets a lot fewer visitors, partly because it lacks the blockbuster sights. Still, the small neoclassical Schloss Charlottenhof (☎ 0331 969 4228; tour adult/concession €4/3; ⏱ 10am-6pm Tue-Sun May-Oct) was modelled after a Roman villa and is actually considered one of Karl Friedrich Schinkel's finest works.

Schinkel, aided by his student Ludwig Persius, also dreamed up the nearby Römische Bäder (Roman Baths; ☎ 0331 969 4225; adult/concession €3/2.50; ⏱ 10am-6pm Tue-Sun May-Oct), a picturesque ensemble of Italian country estates and Roman villas. The setting is pleasant, but don't go out of your way to come here.

A same-day combination ticket for both sites is €5/4 per adult/concession.

CHINESISCHES HAUS

The Chinesisches Haus (Chinese House; ☎ 0331 969 4225; admission €2; ⏱ 10am-6pm Tue-Sun May-Oct) is one of the most photographed buildings in the park, largely because of the gilded sandstone figures with oriental dress shown sipping tea, dancing and playing musical instruments. Inside the domed pavilion is a precious collection of Chinese and Meissen porcelain.

Altstadt

Moving into old town Potsdam, the baroque Brandenburger Tor (Brandenburg Gate) on Luisenplatz is actually older than its more famous cousin in Berlin.

Bounded by Friedrich-Ebert-Strasse, Hebbelstrasse, Kurfürstenstrasse and Gutenbergstrasse, is the very picturesque Holländisches Viertel (Dutch Quarter). It consists of 134 gabled red-brick houses built for Dutch workers who came to Potsdam in the 1730s at the invitation of Friedrich Wilhelm I. It now houses all kinds of galleries, cafés and restaurants; Mittelstrasse is especially scenic.

Southeast of the GDR-era Platz der Einheit looms the great neoclassical dome of Schinkel's Nikolaikirche (☎ 0331 270 8602; ⏱ 9am-7pm Mon-Sat, 11.30am-5pm Sun), built in 1850, complemented by an obelisk and a small pavilion on the old market square. The tower can be climbed.

Further west is the exotic Dampfmaschinenhaus (Pump House; ☎ 0331 969 4225; Breite Strasse 28; tour adult/concession €2/1.50; ⏱ 10am-6pm Sat & Sun May-Oct), the former palace waterworks were built to look like a Turkish mosque complete with an authentic minaret.

Neuer Garten

The winding lakeside Neuer Garten (New Garden), laid out in natural English style on the western shore of the Heiliger See, is another fine park in which to relax. Right on the lake, the neoclassical Marmorpalais (Marble Palace; ☎ 969 4550; tour adult/concession €5/4; ⏱ 10am-6pm Tue-Sun May-Oct, 10am-4pm Sat & Sun Nov-Apr) has a stunning interior characterised by a grand central staircase, marble fireplaces and stucco ceilings. The most fanciful room is the upstairs Orientalisches Kabinett, which looks like a Turkish tent.

Further north, Schloss Cecilienhof (☎ 0331 969 4200; adult/concession with tour or audioguide €6/5; ⏱ 10am-6pm Tue-Sun Apr-Oct, to 5pm Nov-Mar) is a rustic English-style country manor completed in 1917 for crown prince Wilhelm and his wife Cecilie. The palace is most famous for being the site of the 1945 Potsdam Conference where Stalin, Truman and Churchill (and later his successor Clement Atlee) hammered out Germany's postwar fate.

Pfingstberg

For the best view over Potsdam and surrounds, head up to the beautifully restored Belvedere Pfingstberg (☎ 0331 2005 7930; adult/concession €3.50/2.50; ⏱ 10am-8pm Jun-Aug, to 6pm Apr, May, Sep & Oct, to 4pm Sat & Sun Mar & Nov). Just below the palace is the 1801 Pomonatempel (admission free; ⏱ 3-6pm Sat & Sun mid-Apr–Oct), a small pavilion that was0 Karl Friedrich Schinkel's very first architectural commission.

Babelsberg

Babelsberg is synonymous with film making. The mighty UFA began shooting flicks here in 1912 and, by the 1920s, was producing such blockbusters as Fritz Lang's *Metropolis* and *The Blue Angel* with Marlene Dietrich. After WWII, it became the base of the East German production company DEFA, and today cameras are rolling in what is called Studio Babelsberg.

For visitors, the main reason to come here is the attached Filmpark Babelsberg (☎ 721 2750; www.filmpark.de; enter on Grossbeerenstrasse; adult/child 4-14/concession/family €20/13/16/60; 10am-6pm Apr-Oct), a movie-themed amusement park with live shows (great stunt show!), a 4D cinema and a few pokey rides. A highlight is the guided tram ride where you'll be whisked past working soundstages to the studio back-lot and such outdoor sets as 'Berlin Wall' and 'Berlin Street'. The Filmpark is about 4km east of Potsdam's city centre and served by bus 601.

Eating

Pfeffer & Salz (☎ 0331 200 2777; www.pfefferundsalz potsdam.de, in German; Brandenburger Strasse 46; pizza & pasta €7-15, mains €18-24; 11am-11pm) In a street of tourist traps, this Italian eatery stands out for its authenticity. All noodles are home-made daily, the antipasti selection is mouth-watering and the pizza comes crispy-hot from the wood-fired oven.

Loft (☎ 0331 951 0102; www.restaurant-loft.de, in German; Brandenburger Strasse 30/31; mains €8-15; 10am-midnight Mon-Sat, 10am-10pm Sun) Fine views, bright surroundings and a lovely terrace make this a favourite place to enjoy decent food ranging from pasta to steaks.

Maison Charlotte (☎ 0331 280 5450; www.maison charlotte.de, in German; Mittelstrasse 20; mains €12-22; noon-11pm) This enchanting bistro may be in the Dutch Quarter but it's so fantastically French you half expect to see the Eiffel Tower out the door. Oysters and foie gras make appearances, but so do more rustic offerings such as *croques* (toasts) and Flammkuche (French pizza).

Uhlmann's Restaurant (☎ 0331 7304 0253; www .uhlmanns-restaurant.de; Jägerstrasse 38; mains €10.50-18.50; 5-10pm Wed-Sun) In an 18th-century pottery workshop, this is a luscious port of call for modern German fare. Most of the meats (schnitzel, steak) and fish, such as pike perch and *matjes* (herring), on the menu are sourced locally.

Ristorante Massimo (☎ 0331 8171 8982; Mittelstrasse 18; mains €10-18; noon-2.30pm & 6-10pm Mon-Fri, noon-10pm Sat & Sun) Next to Maison Charlotte, Massimo specializes in robust southern Italian *cucina*. From wafer-thin carpaccio to mounds of linguine with lobster, and locally sourced roast lamb with rosemary potatoes, it's all lip-smacking good.

Meierei Potsdam (☎ 0331 704 3211; www.meierei -potsdam.de, in German; Im Neuen Garten 10; snacks €3-8, mains €7.50-13.50; 11am-11pm Mon-Fri, 10am-11pm Sat, 10am-11pm Sun) Near Schloss Cecilienhof, this brewpub is especially lovely in summer when you can count the boats sailing on the Jungfernsee from your beer-garden table. The hearty Berlin-style dishes go well with the delicious suds brewed on the premises.

Getting Around

A great way to get around Potsdam is by bike, which can be hired from Potsdam per Pedales (☎ 0331 748 0057; per day from €8.50; 9.30am-7pm May-Sep) at Potsdam Hauptbahnhof.

KONZENTRATIONSLAGER SACHSENHAUSEN

Built by prisoners imported from another *Konzentrationslager* (KZ; concentration camp) Sachsenhausen Concentration Camp opened in 1936 just outside Berlin as a so-called model camp or, to quote Himmler, a prototype of a 'modern, ideal and easily expandable' camp. By 1945 about 220,000 people, mostly men, from 22 countries had passed through its gates. Initially it held mostly political prisoners but over time their ranks were swelled by gypsies, gays and, after the *Kristallnacht*

TRANSPORT: KZ SACHSENHAUSEN

Direction 35km north

Travel time One hour

Car Take the A10 towards Prenzlau, exit at 'Birkenwalder' and go along the B96 to Oranienburg, then follow the signs to the memorial.

Train The S1 makes the trip from central Berlin (eg Friedrichstrasse) to Oranienburg in about 45 minutes. RE trains leaving from Hauptbahnhof need about 25 minutes. From Oranienburg station, it's about a 20-minute walk: turn right onto Stralsunder Strasse, right on Bernauer Strasse, left on Strasse der Einheit and right on Strasse der Nationen. Alternatively, bus 804 makes the trip twice hourly. Get off at 'Gedenkstätte'.

pogroms of 1938, Jews. After 1939, POWs, mostly from the Soviet Union, were brought here as well. Tens of thousands died here from hunger, exhaustion, illness, exposure, medical experiments and executions. Thousands more succumbed during the death march of April 1945, when the Nazis evacuated the camp in advance of the Red Army. There's a memorial plaque to these victims as you approach the camp, at the corner of Strasse der Einheit and Strasse der Nationen.

After the war, the Soviets turned the tables on the Nazis by turning the camp into Speziallager No 7 (Special Camp No 7) and imprisoning some 60,000 of them. About 12,000 are believed to have died of malnutrition and disease before it was dissolved in 1950. Soviet and GDR military continued using the grounds for another decade until the camp became a memorial site in 1961. Updated many times since, today's memorial delivers a predictably sobering experience.

Information

Although the memorial site is open daily, we recommend that you don't visit on a Monday when all of the indoor exhibits are closed. No food is available at the site, although there's a vending machine offering hot drinks in the Neues Museum.

Memorial & Museum Sachsenhausen (☎ 03301 200 200; www.stiftung-bg.de; admission free; ⏰ 8.30am–6pm mid-Mar–mid-Oct, to-4.30pm mid-Oct–mid-Mar) Unless you're on a guided tour, stop by the Visitors Centre to pick up a leaflet (€0.50) or, better yet, an audio guide (€3, including leaflet) to fully get a grasp on this huge site.

Memorial & Museum

The approach from the visitors' centre to the camp entrance takes you past photographs taken during the death march and the camp's liberation. Just beyond the perimeter is the Neues Museum (New Museum), which has exhibits on the history of the memorial site since GDR days as well as on the Oranienburg concentration camp, the precursor to Sachsenhausen set up in 1933 in a nearby disused brewery. Both are only moderately interesting and could easily be skipped.

You're now in front of Tower A, the entrance gate, cynically labelled, as at Auschwitz, *Arbeit Macht Frei* (Work Sets You Free). Beyond here is the roll-call area with barracks and other buildings fanning out beyond. Off to the right are two restored barracks that illustrate the abysmal living conditions prisoners were subjected to. Barrack 38 has an exhibit on Jewish inmates, while Barrack 39 graphically portrays daily life at the camp. The prison, where famous inmates included would-be Hitler assassin Georg Elser and the theologian Martin Niemöller, is next door.

Another famous prisoner was Soviet master forger Salomon 'Sally' Sorovitsch, who was brought to Sachsenhausen to produce counterfeit foreign currency with the goal of undermining the Allied economies. Millions of fake British pounds ended up in circulation but the US dollar proved too difficult to copy. The building where the operation took place once stood behind Barrack 39. The story was retold in the Austrian movie *The Counterfeiters*, which won an Academy Award in 2008.

Moving towards the centre you'll reach the former Prisoners' Kitchen with exhibits from key moments in the camp's history as well as reproduction instruments of torture and the original gallows that stood in the roll-call area; in the cellar you'll see heart-wrenching artwork scratched into the wall by prisoners. The most sickening displays, though, deal with the nearby Station Z, the site of unspeakable mass murder. It consisted of an execution trench, a crematorium and a gas chamber. More than 10,000 Soviet POWs were executed here by being shot in the back of the neck through a hole in the wall while ostensibly being measured for a uniform. Bullets were then retrieved and reused.

Tours

Nonprofit Mosaic Tours (☎ 0176 8754 5620; www .mosaic.de; adult/student €12/10; ⏰ 10am Tue & Sat

DETOUR: THE GREAT SKATE

Inline skating is popular in Germany and its eldorado is Flaeming-Skate (www.flaeming-skate.de), a 210km smooth asphalt trail that winds through forest, meadows and picturesque villages. It's Germany's longest, with side-trails adding to the fun of exploration. The heart of the area is in Luckenwalde, some 50km south of Berlin on the train line to Lutherstadt-Wittenberg. There are numerous skating routes, from easy 10km jaunts for beginners to thigh-burning day trips. All are well signposted, making navigating a snap. The website has full details, also in English. Of course, if you're not skating, you can just as easily explore the region by bicycle.

A good place to hire skates and protective gear is Sportmarkt Luckenwalde (☎ 03371 611 030; Breite Strasse 5, Luckenwalde; per day/weekend/week €8/15/25; ⏰ 9am-6pm Mon-Fri, 9am-12.30pm Sat) Also in Luckenwalde, Hotel Märkischer Hof (☎ 03371 6040; www.skatemekka.com; Poststrasse 8; bikes per day €7; s/d €55/70; mains €4.50-10, ⏰ bike rental 9am-10pm) has a good-sized fleet of bicycles for rent. The restaurant serves salads and flavoursome mains, and rooms here will give you a good night's sleep, should you decide to stay.

One interesting place to skate or cycle to is Jüterbog, with the 12th-century Kloster Zinna (Zinna Monastery; ☎ 03372 439 505; www.jueterbog.eu; Am Kloster 6; adult/concession €5/3.50; ⏰ 10am-5pm Tue-Sun). The classical Kloster-Zinna-Sommermusiken (☎ 03372 4650; www.kloster-zinna-sommermusiken.de; tickets €7.50-16) concert series is held here from mid-June to late August. The museum sells tickets.

Regional trains make hourly trips to Luckenwalde or Jüterbog from Berlin-Hauptbahnhof (€5.10, 40 minutes). Drivers should follow the B101.

year-round, also Thu & Fri May-Oct) specialises in Sachsenhausen tours and donates all net proceeds to charity, including the Friends of the Sachsenhausen Memorial Museum. Tours meet at the foot of the TV Tower, next to the Alexanderplatz S-Bahn station. No reservations are necessary.

The English-language walking tour companies Berlin Walks, Insider Tour and New Berlin Tours, all described in the Directory chapter (p313), also operate guided tours of Sachsenhausen several times weekly.

CHORIN

Plenty of people make the day trip from Berlin to the tiny village of Chorin. Their destination: the renowned Kloster Chorin (Chorin Monastery; ☎ 033366 703 77; www.kloster-chorin.com, in German; Amt Chorin 11a; adult/concession/family €4/2.50/10; ⏰ 9am-6pm Apr-Oct, 9am-4pm Nov-Mar), a romantically ruined monastery near a little lake and surrounded by a lush park. Some 500 Cistercian monks laboured over six decades starting in 1273 to erect what is widely considered one of the finest red-brick Gothic structures in northern Germany. The monastery was secularised in 1542 and fell into disrepair after the Thirty Years' War. Renovation has gone on in a somewhat haphazard fashion since the early 19th century.

Enter the complex through the ornate step-gabled western facade that leads to the central cloister flanked by the monastic quarters. To the north looms the church with its sleekly carved portals and elongated lancet windows. Both cloister and church are an enchanting setting for classical summer concerts. On weekends from June to August, top talent performs during the Choriner Musiksommer (☎ 03334 657 310; www.musiksommer -chorin.de; tickets €7-24). A shuttle bus connects Chorin train station and the Kloster before and after concerts. Make ticket reservations as early as possible or hope for no-shows on the day of performance.

If you need to stay or just fancy a bite, steer towards the lakeside Hotel Haus Chorin (☎ 033366 500; www.chorin.de; Neue Klosterallee 10; s €39-69, d €59-89; P ⊠). The kitchen uses organic ingredients in some dishes, and claims to be the world's first 'honey restaurant' where all dishes contain the sweet stuff (mains €9-16).

TRANSPORT: CHORIN

Direction 60km northeast

Travel time 1½ hours

Car Follow the A11 to exit 'Britz' and follow the signs towards Chorin via the B2.

Train Chorin is served hourly by regional trains from Berlin-Hauptbahnhof (€7.70, 40 minutes) roughly every hour. Trains are often met by bus 912, which takes you within a five-minute walk of the monastery. Alternatively, it's a 2.5km walk along a marked trail through the woods, or rent a bike at the station for €8.50.

FURTHER AFIELD
SPREEWALD

The Spreewald, a unique lacework of channels and canals hemmed in by forest, is the closest thing Berlin has to a backyard garden. Visitors come here in droves to punt, canoe or kayak on more than 970km of waterways, hike countless nature trails and fish in this Unesco biosphere reserve. Although it can be seen on a day trip, spending the night definitely has its rewards.

The Spreewald is famous for its gherkins – over 40,000 tons of cucumbers are harvested here every year! Lübben and Lübbenau, the main tourist towns linked by a 13km trail along the Spree River, often drown beneath the tides of visitors vying for rides aboard a *Kahn* (shallow punt boat), once the only way of getting around in these parts. To truly appreciate the Spreewald's unique charms, hire a canoe or kayak or get yourself onto a bike or walking trail. Bikes can be hired from Spreewaldradler/Vitalpunkt (☎ 035603 158 790; bikes per day €8-17) right at the Lübben train station.

The Spreewald is also home base to large numbers of Germany's Sorbian minority (see the boxed text, right).

Information

There are frequent buses between Lübben and Lübbenau on weekdays.

Lübbenau tourist office (☎ 03542 3668; www.spreewald-online.de; Ehm-Welk-Strasse 15; ☺ 9am-7pm Mon-Fri, 9am-4pm Sat Apr-Oct, 11am-3pm Sun May & Jun, 11am-4pm Jul-Sep, 10am-4pm Mon-Fri Nov-Mar)

Spreewaldinformation Lübben (☎ 03546 3090; www.luebben.de; Ernst-von-Houwald-Damm 15; ☺ 10am-6pm Apr-Oct, to 4pm Mon-Fri Nov-Mar)

TRANSPORT: SPREEWALD

Direction 80km southeast

Travel time Up to two hours

Car Take the A100 to the A113 to the A13. Exit at Duben, turn left and follow the B87 to Lübben.

Train Regional trains serve Lübben (€9.10, one hour) and Lübbenau (€10.40, 1¼ hours) every one to two hours from Berlin-Hauptbahnhof and Friedrichstrasse en route to Cottbus.

THE SORBS

The Spreewald region is part of the area inhabited by the Sorbs, Germany's only indigenous minority. Numbering just 60,000, this group descends from the Slavic Wends, who settled between the Elbe and Oder Rivers in the 5th century in an area called Lusatia (Luzia in Sorbian).

Lusatia was conquered by the Germans in the 10th century, subjected to brutal Germanisation throughout the Middle Ages and partitioned in 1815. Lower Sorbia, centred on the Spreewald and Cottbus (Chośebuz), went to Prussia, while Upper Sorbia, around Bautzen (Budyšin), went to Saxony. The Upper Sorbian dialect, closely related to Czech, enjoyed a certain prestige in Saxony, but the Kingdom of Prussia tried to suppress Lower Sorbian, which is similar to Polish. The Nazis, of course, tried to eradicate both.

Since German reunification interest in the culture has been revived through the media and colourful Sorbian festivals such as the *Vogelhochzeit* (Birds' Wedding) on 25 January and a symbolic *Hexenbrennen* (witch-burning) on 30 April.

Lübbenau

Pretty Lübbenau has a model-village air and a forest of signs pointing to hotels, restaurants and other businesses. Behind the tourist office, the Haus für Mensch und Natur (☎ 03542 892 10; Schulstrasse 9; admission free; ☺ 10am-5pm daily Apr-Oct, Sat & Sun Nov-Mar) has exhibits and information about the Spreewald Biosphere Reserve. If you're interested in the region's cultural history, visit the Spreewald-Museum (☎ 03542 2472; Am Topfmarkt; adult/concession/family €3/2/5; ☺ 10am-6pm Tue-Sun Apr–mid-Sep, to 5pm mid-Sep–Oct) inside a historic brick building that's gone through stints as a courthouse, jail and town hall.

Several operators offer pretty much the same punt boating tours, including the popular three-hour trip to Lehde (adult/child €11/5.50), a completely protected village known as the 'Venice of the Spreewald'. Here you'll find the wonderful Freilandmuseum (☎ 03542 2472; adult/concession/family €3/2/5; ☺ 10am-6pm Apr–mid-Sep, to 5pm mid-Sep–Oct), an open-air museum of traditional Sorbian houses and farm buildings. Lehde is also reached via an easy 30-minute walking trail.

The main embarkation points are the Kleiner Hafen (☎ 03542 403 710; www.spreewald-web.de; Spreestrasse 10a), about 100m northeast of the tourist office, and the more workmanlike Grosser Hafen (☎ 03542 2225; www.grosser-spreewaldhafen.de; Dammstrasse 77a), 300m southeast. Buy tickets at the embarkation points or from the captain. Bootsverleih Francke (☎ 03542 2722; Dammstrasse 72) rents canoes and kayaks for up to four people for €3 to €8 for one hour (additional hour €2 to €5) or €12 to €31 per day, depending on size.

Lübben

Compared to Lübbenau, tidy Lübben feels more like a 'real' town and has a history going back at least two centuries further than its neighbour. Activity centres on the Schloss and the adjacent harbour area, both about 1.5km east of the train station. The compact Schloss (☎ 03546 187 478; www.schloss-luebben.de, in German; Ernst-von-Houwald-Damm 14; adult/concession €4/2; ☻ 10am-5pm Tue-Sun Apr-Oct, 10am-4pm Wed-Fri, 1-5pm Sat & Sun Nov-Mar) contains a progressively presented regional history museum; look for the interactive town model and a 2m-long medieval executioner's sword. The real highlight, though, is a (free) wander around the Schlossinsel, an artificial archipelago with gardens, a leafy maze, playgrounds, cafes and the harbour area where you can board punts for leisurely tours (adult/child from €8/4). If you'd rather go at your own speed, rent a canoe or kayak from Bootsverleih Gebauer (☎ 03546 7194; www.spreewald-bootsverleih.de, in German; Lindenstrasse 18; per 2 hours from €8).

Eating & Sleeping

Stadtbrauerei Babben (☎ 03542 2126; www.babben-bier.de, in German; Brauhausgasse 2, Lübbenau; mains €5-10, s/d €39/46; ☻ from 5pm mid-Mar–Oct; P ✗) Brandenburg's smallest brewery makes a mean pilsner and seasonal beers, all of them unfiltered, unpasteurised and therefore always fresh. The menu features casual pub eats; upstairs are four cosy rooms for spending the night.

Pension Am Alten Bauernhafen (☎ 03542 2930; www.am-alten-bauernhafen.de, in German; Stottoff 5, Lübbenau; s/d from €32/49; P ✗) Charmingly decorated, large rooms and a fantastic riverside location make this big, family-run house a fine base of operation. The owner couple grows their own organic vegetables and make many of the breakfast products themselves.

Hotel Lindengarten (☎ 03546 4172; www.spreewald-luebben.de; Treppendorfer Dorfstrasse 15, Lübben; s/d €51/71; P ✗) This family-run hotel is a class act all around and has bright and airy rooms, youthful flair and a nice restaurant that serves tapas and regional fare. Rooms are discounted November to March.

Spreewaldhotel Stephanshof (☎ 03546 272 10; www.hotel-stephanshof.de, in German; Lehnigksberger Weg 1, Lübben; s/d €65/90; P ✗ ☏) About a 10-minute walk north of central Lübben, this modern riverside hotel has its own boat landing, a regional restaurant and bike rentals. Some rooms have balconies and there are discounts November to March.

Hotel Schloss Lübbenau (☎ 03542 8730; www.schloss-luebbenau.de; Schlossbezirk 6, Lübbenau; s €68-78, d €108-138, lunch mains €10-16, dinner €13-25; P ✗) Check in at this handsome palace for a surprisingly reasonable splurge with all the class you can handle amid lovely park surroundings. The restaurant here is your only fine-dining option in Lübbenau.

Goldener Löwe (☎ 03546 7309; www.goldenerloewe-luebben.de, in German; Hauptstrasse 14, Lübben; mains €4-11; ☻ 10am-10pm Mon-Fri, 11am-10pm Sat & Sun) This old-fashioned restaurant is an ambience-laden purveyor of regional fare, including a fish platter featuring eel, perch and carp. In summer, enjoy your meal in the beer garden.

DRESDEN

There are few city silhouettes more striking than Dresden's. The classic view takes in a playful phalanx of delicate spires, soaring towers and dominant domes belonging to palaces, churches and stately buildings that's inspired many artists, most notably the Italian Canaletto.

The Saxon capital was called the 'Florence of the north' in the 18th century, when it was a centre of artistic activity presided over by the cosmopolitan Augustus the Strong (August der Starke) and his son Augustus III. Their vision produced many of Dresden's iconic buildings, including the Zwinger, the Frauenkirche and the Hofkirche. Given the near-total destruction of the city by Allied bombers in 1945, it's a miracle some of these monumental edifices are here today at all.

But Dresden is a survivor and there is no more potent symbol of its people's

TRANSPORT: DRESDEN

Direction 200km south

Travel time Two hours

Car Take the A113 to the A13, which runs all the way to Dresden.

Train IC trains make the trip to Dresden from Berlin-Hauptbahnhof (€37) in 2½ hours every two hours.

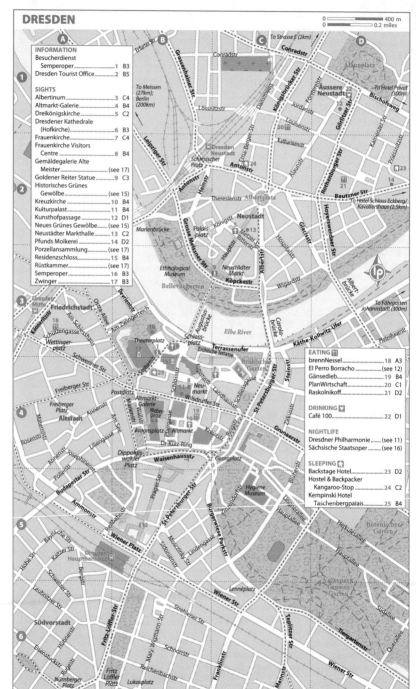

DRESDEN

0 — 400 m
0 — 0.2 miles

determination than the resurrected Frauenkirche. Although the city has been around for eight centuries, it is also forward-looking and solidly rooted in the here and now. There's some great new architecture, a constantly evolving arts and cultural scene, and zinging pub and nightlife quarters.

Information

Besucherdienst Semperoper (☎ 0351 491 1705; Schinkelwache, Theaterplatz 2; ☻ 10am-6pm Mon-Fri, 10am-5pm Sat & Sun) Tickets and tours.

Dresden tourist office (☎ 0351 5016 0160; www.dresden-tourist.de; Kulturpalast, Schlossstrasse; ☻ 10am-7pm Mon-Fri, to 6pm Sat, to 3pm Sun Apr-Dec, 10am-6pm Mon-Fri, to 4pm Sat, to 2pm Sun Jan-Mar) Also houses the central ticket office.

Altstadt
FRAUENKIRCHE

The domed Frauenkirche (Church of Our Lady; ☎ 0351 6560 6100, tickets 0351 6560 6701; www.frauenkirche-dresden.de; admission free; ☻ 10am-noon & 1-6pm Mon-Fri, limited hr on weekends) has literally risen from the city's ashes. The original graced Dresden's skyline for two centuries before collapsing two days after the February 1945 bombing. The East Germans left the rubble as a war memorial, but after reunification a grassroots movement to rebuild the landmark gained momentum. It was reconsecrated in November 2005.

A spitting image of the original, it may not bear the gravitas of age but that only slightly detracts from its festive beauty inside and out. Audioguides (€2.50) provide detailed information and the dome (adult/concession/family €8/5/20; ☻ 10am-6pm Mon-Sat, 12.30-6pm Sun Mar-Oct, to 4pm Nov-Feb) can be climbed for sweeping city views. The galleried interior is also a wonderful place for concerts, meditations and services. Check the website for the current schedule or stop by the Frauenkirche Visitors

top picks

DRESDEN

- Albertinum (right)
- Frauenkirche (above)
- Grünes Gewölbe (right)
- Kunsthofpassage (p295)
- Pfunds Molkerei (p295)

Centre (Galeriestrasse cnr Wilsdruffer Strasse; ☻ 9.30am-6pm Mon-Sat) in the Kulturpalast.

RESIDENZSCHLOSS & GRÜNES GEWÖLBE

The highlight of the neo-Renaissance Residenzschloss (Taschenberg 2) is the must-see Grünes Gewölbe (Green Vault), a real-life 'Aladdin's Cave' with a bonanza of precious objects wrought from gold, ivory, silver, diamonds and other materials. There's so much of it, two separate 'treasure chambers', both in the palace west wing (enter from Sophienstrasse), are needed to display everything.

The Neues Grünes Gewölbe (New Green Vault; ☎ 0351 4914 2000; www.skdmuseum.de; adult/concession/child under 16 €10/7.50/free; ☻ 10am-6pm Wed-Mon) presents some 1000 objects in 10 modern rooms on the upper floor. Key sights include a frigate fashioned from ivory with wafer-thin sails, a cherry pit with 185 faces carved into it, and an exotic ensemble of 132 gem-studded figurines representing a royal court in India. The artistry of each item is simply dazzling. To avoid the worst crush of people, visit during lunchtime.

A further 3000 items are exhibited below in the show-stopping Historisches Grünes Gewölbe (Historical Green Vault; ☎ tickets & information 0351 4914 2000; www.skdmuseum.de; adult/child under 16 incl audioguide €10/free; ☻ 10am-7pm Wed-Mon). Admission is by timed ticket and visitor numbers are limited to 120 per hour. Advance tickets (€2 service fee) are available online and by phone, and about a third are sold at the palace box office on the day.

ALBERTINUM & BRÜHLSCHE TERRASSE

In 2010, the Albertinum (☎ 0351 4914 2000; www.skdmuseum.de; enter from Brühlsche Terrasse or Georg-Treu-Platz; adult/concession/child under 16 €8/6/free; ☻ 10am-6pm) reopened after a lavish makeover following damage caused by the epic 2002 flood. The state-of-the-art (and flood-proof) building now houses paintings and sculpture from the Romantic period to the present: from the moody landscapes of Caspar David Friedrich to the bold musings of Gerhard Richter.

West of the Albertinum is the Brühlsche Terrasse, a spectacular promenade above the Elbe. Nicknamed the 'Balcony of Europe', it's a must for strolling, with expansive views of the river and the opposite bank.

ZWINGER

The sprawling Zwinger (☎ 0351 4914 2000; www .skdmuseum.de, Theaterplatz 1) is among the most ravishing baroque buildings in all of Germany. Charming portals lead into the vast fountain-studded courtyard framed by buildings festooned with sculpture. Atop the western pavilion stands a tense-looking Atlas, while opposite is a cutesy carillon of 40 Meissen porcelain bells, which emit a tinkle every 15 minutes.

The Zwinger now houses several museums. The most important is the Gemäldegalerie Alte Meister (Old Masters Gallery; adult/concession/child under 16 €10/7.50/free; ☺ 10am-6pm Tue-Sun), which features masterpieces including Raphael's *Sistine Madonna*. Admission here is good for the Rüstkammer, a grand collection of ceremonial weapons, and the Porzellansammlung, a dazzling assortment of Meissen classics and East Asian treasures.

SEMPEROPER & HOFKIRCHE

One of Germany's most famous opera houses, the Semperoper (☎ 0351 491 1705; www.semperoper.de; Theaterplatz 2) has gone through multiple incarnations. The original burned down a mere three decades after its 1841 inauguration. When it reopened in 1878, the neo-Renaissance jewel entered its most dazzling period, which saw the premieres of works by Richard Strauss, Carl Maria von Weber and Richard Wagner. Alas, WWII put an end to the fun, and it wasn't until 1985 that music again filled the grand hall. Guided tours (☎ 0351 796 6305; www .semperoper-erleben.de; adult/concession/family €8/4/18) are offered daily (the 3pm tour is in English) but

exact times depend on the rehearsal and performance schedule. Call or check the website for details.

The big pile that stands next to the opera house is the baroque Dresdener Kathedrale (☎ 0351 484 4712; Schlossplatz; admission free; ☺ 9am-6pm Mon-Tue, to 5pm Wed-Thu, 1-5pm Fri, 10am-5pm Sat, noon-4pm Sun), more colloquially known as the Hofkirche (Court Church). Aside from brimming with centuries of treasure, including a lavish rococo pulpit, its crypt contains the heart of Augustus the Strong.

ALTMARKT

The Altmarkt area was once the historic heart of Dresden but postwar reconstruction was heavily influenced by a socialist aesthetic as exemplified by the squat Kulturpalast (☎ 0351 486 60; www.kulturpalast-dresden.de; Schlossstrasse 2), home to the Dresdner Philharmonic Orchestra (opposite) and the tourist office. The starkness is tempered by street-side cafes, the sparkling Altmarkt-Galerie shopping mall and the late baroque Kreuzkirche (☎ 0351 496 5807; www .kreuzkirche-dresden.de, in German; Altmarkt; admission free, tower adult/child €2.50/1; ☺ 10am-6pm Mon-Sat, noon-6pm Sun), which hosts services and concerts accompanied by its world-famous boys' choir, the 700-year-old Kreuzchor. Free 15-minute organ recitals take place at 3pm on Tuesday and Thursday.

Neustadt

Across the Elbe, the Neustadt was largely untouched by the wartime bombings. After reunification, it became the centre of the city's alternative scene and still teems with

A BRIDGE TOO FAR

The Saxon heartland, with Dresden at its centre, represents one of the richest cultural tapestries in all of Germany. This fact obviously didn't escape the Unesco officers in charge of designating new World Heritage sites, who in 2004 welcomed a 20km section of the river valley, the Dresdner Elbtal, including Dresden's matchless baroque magnificence, into their exalted club.

But only five years later, in June 2009, the Elbtal joined the most exclusive (and most embarrassing) Unesco club of all. After Oman's Arabian Oryx Sanctuary, Dresden became only the second place on earth (and the first in the developed world) to have its World Cultural Heritage status revoked. The reason? The construction of the controversial four-lane Waldschlösschenbrücke (bridge) across the river, spoiling the breathtaking scenery. This followed a 2005 referendum, in which Dresden residents voted in favour of building a new bridge across the Elbe in order to relieve bottleneck traffic. Despite Unesco's (and the German government's) best efforts at hammering out a compromise solution, even offering to pay for a tunnel as an acceptable alternative, city leaders remained unmoved. Preparatory construction work on the bridge began in 2007.

Unesco has suggested the city may get the chance to submit a new nomination in the future, but with different boundaries. Dresden's officials will no doubt be eager to regain Unesco-listed status, which not only brings prestige and tourists, but also much-needed federal cash.

interesting bars, restaurants and clubs. The first thing that catches the eye after crossing Augustusbrücke is the Goldener Reiter (1736) statue of Augustus the Strong. This leads to the tree-lined pedestrian mall of Hauptstrasse and eventually to the Dreikönigskirche (☎ 0351 812 4102; An der Dreikönigskirche; admission free; 9am-6pm Mon-Fri, 10am-6pm Sat, 11am-4pm Sun), which houses some lovely Renaissance artworks, including the *Dance of Death* frieze. Across Hauptstrasse, the Neustädter Markthalle, a gorgeously restored old market hall (enter on Metzer Strasse), is filled with stalls selling everything from Russian groceries to kid's wooden toys. There's also a supermarket.

Hauptstrasse culminates at Albertplatz with its two striking fountains representing turbulent and still waters. North of here, the Äussere Neustadt is a spidery web of narrow streets, late-19th-century patrician houses and hidden courtyards, all chock full of pubs, clubs, galleries and one-of-a-kind shops. A highlight here is the Kunsthofpassage (enter from Alaunstrasse 70 or Görlitzer Strasse 21), a series of five whimsically designed courtyards each reflecting the vision of a different Dresden artist.

About 1km east of Albertplatz is 'the world's most beautiful dairy shop', Pfunds Molkerei (☎ 0351 808 080; www.pfunds.de; Bautzner Strasse 79; admission free; 10am-6pm Mon-Sat, to 3pm Sun). Founded in 1880, it's a riot of hand-painted tiles and enamelled sculpture. The shop sells replica tiles, wines, cheeses and, of course, milk. Not surprisingly, the cafe-restaurant upstairs has a strong lactose theme.

Eating

Raskolnikoff (☎ 0351 04 5706; www.raskolnikoff.de, in German; Böhmische Strasse 34; mains €5-14; 10am-2am) This beloved bohemian cafe behind a tatty facade has a menu sorted by compass direction (borscht to quiche Lorraine to smoked fish). There's a sweet little beer garden out back and basic guestrooms start at €40.

brennNessel (☎ 0351 494 3319; www.brennnessel-dresden.de, in German; Schützengasse 18, Altstadt; mains €7-12; 11am-midnight; V) This superb vegetarian place with a woodsy interior and leafy cobbled courtyard is a favourite hangout for off-duty Semperoper musicians. Lots of wholesome and creative casseroles, pasta dishes and salads to choose from.

Gänsedieb (☎ 0351 485 0905; www.gaensedieb.de, in German; Weisse Gasse 1, Altstadt; mains €8-17; 11am-11pm) Worth a gander in the Weisse Gasse, the 'Goose Thief' serves hearty schnitzels, goulash and steaks alongside a full range of Bavarian Paulaner beers. The name was inspired by the fountain outside.

El Perro Borracho (☎ 0351 803 6723; www.elperro.de, in German; Alaunstrasse 70, Kunsthof, Neustadt; tapas from €3.30; 10.30am-2am) Almost blocking an entrance to the Kunsthofpassage, this buzzy eatery is a great place to enjoy a glass of Rioja and a platter of tapas on the cobblestoned courtyard when the mercury heads north.

PlanWirtschaft (☎ 0351 801 3187; www.planwirtschaft.de, in German; Louisenstrasse 20, Neustadt; mains €7-14; 9.30am-1am Sun-Thu, to 2am Fri & Sat) Only fresh, organic ingredients sourced from local butchers and farmers make it into the international potpourri of dishes at this long-time favourite. There's a romantic courtyard for balmy days.

Drinking & Nightlife

Fährgarten Johannstadt (☎ 0351 459 6262; Käthe-Kollwitz-Ufer 23b; 10am-1am Apr-Oct) East of the Altstadt, and occasionally too close to the flood-prone Elbe for its own good, this idyllic beer garden pulls great ales and does a mean barbecue.

Café 100 (☎ 0351 273 5010; Alaunstrasse 100; 6pm-2am) Wine lovers should make a beeline for this candle-lit pub, with its romantic cavernous cellar and 250 wines on the menu. It's a great place for first dates.

Dresdner Philharmonie (☎ 0351 486 6866; www.dresdnerphilharmonie.de) The city's renowned orchestra performs mostly at the Kulturpalast (opposite) on Altmarkt. Also check the listings magazines for concerts at the Hofkirche, the Dreikönigskirche, the Kreuzkirche and the Frauenkirche.

Sächsische Staatsoper (☎ 0351 491 1705; www.semperoper.de) Dresden is synonymous with opera, and performances at the spectacular Semperoper are brilliant. They practically always sell out, so purchase your tickets online as early as possible or hope for returns.

Strasse E (www.strasse-e.de; Werner-Hartmann-Strasse 2) Dresden's high-octane party zone is in an industrial area between Neustadt and the airport. Venues cover the sound gamut, from disco to dark wave, electro to pop. Take tram 7 to Industriegelände.

Sleeping

Hostel & Backpacker Kangaroo-Stop (☎ 0351 314 3455; www.kangaroo-stop.de; Erna-Berger-Strasse 8-10; dm €12.50-16.50, s/d/tr €33/40/53, apt €74-88; breakfast €5, linen €2; P ⊠ 💻) With an Australian theme

DETOUR: MEISSEN

Straddling the Elbe some 25km upstream from Dresden, Meissen is famous around the world for its china, easily recognised by its trademark insignia of blue crossed swords. Production started in 1710 in the mighty Albrechtsburg (palace; ☎ 03521 470 70; www.albrechtsburg-meissen.de; Domplatz 1; adult/concession €4/2; ☀ 10am-6pm Mar-Oct, 10am-5pm Nov-Feb), atop a ridge above the compact old town with its cobbled lanes, dreamy nooks and idyllic courtyards. Next to the palace looms Meissen's medieval cathedral (☎ 03521 452 490; Domplatz 7; adult/concession €2.50/1.50; ☀ 10am-6pm Mar-Oct, 10am-4pm Nov-Feb), a Gothic masterpiece with stained-glass windows and delicately carved statues decorating the choir. Views from up here are extraordinary.

Most Meissen visitors are magnetically drawn to the Museum of Meissen Art (☎ 03521 468 233; www.meissen .com; Talstrasse 9; adult/concession/family €8.50/4.50/18.50; ☀ 9am-6pm May-Oct, 9am-5pm Nov-Apr), in an Art Nouveau villa adjacent to the actual porcelain factory about 1km southwest of the Altstadt. It's worth braving the crush (and the waiting) to witness the astonishing artistry and craftsmanship that makes Meissen porcelain truly unique. A 30-minute tour (with English audioguide) takes you through four studios where you can observe live demonstrations of vase throwing, plate painting, figure moulding and the glazing process. This helps you gain a better appreciation for the 3000 pieces, displayed chronologically, of the main exhibit.

To reach Meissen, simply hop on the S-Bahn from Dresden (€5.50, 40 minutes).

---

throughout, this superb hostel has one building for backies and another for families. Extras include a huge communal kitchen and free internet.

Hotel Privat (☎ 0351 811 770; www.das-nichtraucher -hotel.de; Forststrasse 22; s €54-69, d €69-94; P ☒ ▯) This small, family-run hotel in a quiet residential district has Saxon charm galore and 30 good-sized rooms, some with alcoves and balconies. Tobacco is definitely a no-no here, even in the garden.

Backstage Hotel (☎ 0351 8887 777; www.backstage -hotel.de; Priessnitzstrasse 12; s/d from €75/85, breakfast €6.50; P ☜) A cool converted factory on the edge of Neustadt where rooms, each designed and furnished by local artists and craftsmen, will blow your mind but not your budget. One has a four-poster made entirely of bamboo; others have swirling Gaudi-esque bathrooms. Reception open from 7am to 6pm.

Hotel Schloss Eckberg/Kavaliershaus (☎ 0351 809 90; www.schloss-eckberg.de; Bautzner Strasse 134; Schloss s/d €160/225, Kavaliershaus s/d €97/135; P ☒ ▯) You'll feel like royalty when arriving at this romantic estate set in its own riverside park east of the Neustadt. Rooms in the historic Schloss are pricier and have more flair, but the modern Kavaliershaus has almost as many amenities and the same dreamy setting.

Kempinski Hotel Taschenbergpalais (☎ 0351 491 20; www.kempinski-dresden.de; Taschenberg 3; s €280-370, d €320-400, ste €500-900; P ☒ ☒ ▯ ☜ ☒) This restored 18th-century mansion certainly prickles with wow factor, with views over the Zwinger, incredibly quiet corridors and Bulgari toiletries. In winter, the courtyard turns into an ice rink.

LEIPZIG

Always an independent-minded entity, Leipzig became known as the *Stadt der Helden* (City of Heroes) for its leading role in the 1989 'Peaceful Revolution'. Residents organised protests against the communist regime in May of that year; by October, hundreds of thousands were taking to the streets, placing candles outside the Stasi headquarters and attending peace services at the Nikolaikirche. By the time the secret police started pulping their files, Leipzigers were partying in the streets, and sometimes it seems they haven't stopped since.

Leipzig also stages some of the finest classical music and opera in the country, and its art and literary scenes are flourishing. It was once home to Bach, Schumann, Wagner and Mendelssohn, and to Goethe, who set a key scene of *Faust* in the cellar of his favourite watering hole. The university still attracts students from all over the world and has turned out several Nobel laureates.

Leipzig's centre lies within a ring road that traces the town's medieval fortifications. To

TRANSPORT: LEIPZIG

Direction 160km southwest

Travel time 1¼ hours

Car Leipzig lies just south of the A14 and east of the A9 Berlin–Nuremberg road; it's best to leave your vehicle in one of the car parks outside the Altstadt.

Train Regular ICE trains link Leipzig and Berlin-Hauptbahnhof (€43).

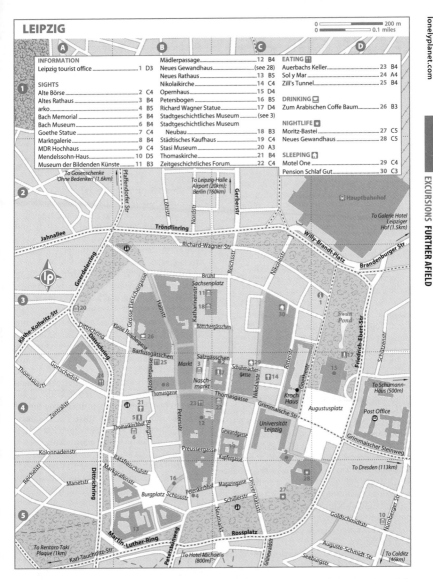

0 ————— 200 m
0 ————— 0.1 miles

INFORMATION		
Leipzig tourist office	1	D3

SIGHTS		
Alte Börse	2	C4
Altes Rathaus	3	B4
arko	4	B5
Bach Memorial	5	B4
Bach Museum	6	B4
Goethe Statue	7	C4
Marktgalerie	8	B4
MDR Hochhaus	9	C4
Mendelssohn-Haus	10	D5
Museum der Bildenden Künste	11	B3

Mädlerpassage	12	B4
Neues Gewandhaus	(see 28)	
Neues Rathaus	13	B5
Nikolaikirche	14	C4
Opernhaus	15	D4
Petersbogen	16	B5
Richard Wagner Statue	17	D4
Stadtgeschichtliches Museum	(see 3)	
Stadtgeschichtliches Museum		
Neubau	18	B3
Städtisches Kaufhaus	19	C4
Stasi Museum	20	A3
Thomaskirche	21	B4
Zeitgeschichtliches Forum	22	C4

EATING 🍴		
Auerbachs Keller	23	B4
Sol y Mar	24	A4
Zill's Tunnel	25	B4

DRINKING 🍷		
Zum Arabischen Coffe Baum	26	B3

NIGHTLIFE 🎭		
Moritz-Bastei	27	C5
Neues Gewandhaus	28	C5

SLEEPING 🛏		
Motel One	29	C4
Pension Schlaf Gut	30	C3

reach the centre from the Hauptbahnhof, cross Willy-Brandt-Platz and continue south along Nikolaistrasse to Grimmaische Strasse. A couple of blocks west, the central Markt is dominated by the Renaissance Altes Rathaus, one of Germany's most stunning town halls. Inside, the moderately interesting Stadtgeschichtliches Museum (City History Museum; ☎ 0341 965 130; www.stadtgeschichtliches-museum-leipzig.de; Markt 1; adult/concession/child under 16 €4/3/free; ☉ 10am-6pm Tue-Sun)

chronicles the twist and turns in Leipzig's history. Temporary exhibits are displayed in a Neubau (Annexe; Böttchergässchen 3; adult/concession/child under 16 €3/2/free; ☉ 10am-6pm Tue-Sun).

Opposite the town hall, the Marktgalerie is one of the shiny new shopping complexes that have popped up throughout central Leipzig in recent years. These modern malls continue the tradition spawned by the historic Mädlerpassage, easily among the world's most

top picks

LEIPZIG

- Bach Museum (right)
- Nikolaikirche (below)
- Stasi Museum (opposite)
- Thomaskirche (right)
- Zeitgeschichtliches Forum (below)

beautiful shopping arcades. A mix of neo-Renaissance and Art Nouveau, it opened as a trade hall in 1914 and was renovated at great expense in the early 1990s. Today it's home to shops, restaurants, cafes and, most notably, Auerbachs Keller (opposite). There are statues of Faust, Mephistopheles and some students at the northern exit; according to tradition you should rub Faust's foot for good luck.

Next door, the engrossing Zeitgeschichtliches Forum (Forum of Contemporary History; ☎ 0341 222 20; www.hdg.de/leipzig, in German; Grimmaische Strasse 6; admission free; ☺ 9am-6pm Tue-Fri, 10am-6pm Sat & Sun) depicts the history of the GDR from division and dictatorship to resistance and post-reunification blues.

Immediately opposite is the Naschmarkt (snack market) which is dominated by the Alte Börse, an ornate former trading house from 1687, and a statue of Goethe. North of the Naschmarkt, Sachsenplatz is anchored by an edgy glass cube housing the Museum der Bildenden Künste (Museum of Fine Arts; ☎ 0341 216 990; www.mdbk .de, in German; Katharinenstrasse 10; adult/concession permanent exhibit €5/3.50, temporary exhibit from €6/4, combination ticket from €8/5.50; ☺ 10am-6pm Tue & Thu-Sun, noon-8pm Wed), which has a well-respected collection of paintings from the 15th century to today. Highlights include rooms dedicated to native sons Max Beckmann and Neo Rauch, the latter a chief representative of the New Leipzig School.

East of Naschmarkt, the Nikolaikirche (☎ 0341 960 5270; www.nikolaikirche-leipzig.de; Nikolaiplatz; admission free; ☺ 10am-6pm Mon-Sat & during services 9.30, 11.15am & 5pm Sun) has Romanesque and Gothic roots but now sports a striking neoclassical interior with palm-like pillars. More recently, the church played a key role in the non-violent movement that led to the downfall of the East German government. In 1982 it began hosting 'peace prayers' every Monday at 5pm and in 1989 it became the chief meeting point for peaceful demonstrators.

Carry on east through the Theaterpassage to reach Augustusplatz, Leipzig's cultural hub. The behemoth on your left is the functional 1950s-era Opernhaus (Opera House; ☎ 0341 126 1261; www.oper-leipzig.de; Augustusplatz 12), backed by a little park with a pond and a statue of Richard Wagner. Opposite the opera, the boxy Neues Gewandhaus is the home base of the world-famous Gewandhaus Orchestra, which was founded in 1743 and is one of Europe's oldest civic orchestras. Next door is the landmark MDR Hochhaus (1970), a surprisingly attractive high-rise with a viewing platform and restaurant on top.

Follow Grimmaische Strasse west past the university, turn left on Universitätsstrasse and look for the entrance to the Städtisches Kaufhaus (Universitätsstrasse 16), the site of the city's first cloth exchange (Gewandhaus) and later the inaugural concert hall of the Gewandhaus Orchestra.

Exit the Städtisches Kaufhaus, head south on Neumarkt, then turn right on Peterskirchhof and you'll come to arko (ex-Café Richter; ☎ 0341 960 5235; Petersstrasse 43; ☺ 9.30am-8pm Mon-Fri, 10am-6pm Sat), the oldest coffee retailer in town (since 1879). This fabulous and eclectic building, with its golden iron spiral staircase, is worth a gander; the luscious beans are wonderful too.

From here head north on Petersstrasse, a major shopping street, then follow the glass-covered Petersbogen arcade to Burgplatz lorded over by the 114m-high tower of the neo-baroque Neues Rathaus. With more than 600 rooms, it's one of the world's largest town halls.

From Burgplatz, walk up Burgstrasse to the 13th-century Thomaskirche (St Thomas Church; ☎ 0341 222 240; www.thomaskirche.org; Thomaskirchhof; admission free; ☺ 9am-6pm), where Johann Sebastian Bach, who worked as a cantor here from 1723 until 1750, is buried. All of Bach's children were baptised in the church, as were Richard Wagner and Karl Liebknecht. The church is also home of the world-famous St Thomas Boys' Choir, founded in 1212. Services at 6pm on Fridays and 3pm on Saturdays are accompanied by the choir. The church steeple can be climbed for great views (adult/child under 12 €2/free, ☺ 1, 2 & 4.30pm Sat, 2 & 3pm Sun).

Outside the church is the Bach Memorial (1908), showing the composer standing against an organ, while opposite is the newly expanded and updated Bach Museum (☎ 0341 913 7202; www.bach-leipzig.de; Thomaskirchhof 16; adult/concession/child under 16 €6/4/free; ☺ 10am-6pm Tue-Sun).

MUSICAL FOOTNOTES

Besides Bach, two other renowned composers have museums dedicated to them in Leipzig: Felix Mendelssohn-Bartholdy, who lived (and died) in Mendelssohn-Haus (☎ 0341 127 0294; www .mendelssohn-stiftung.de; Goldschmidtstrasse 12; admission €3.50; ⌚ 10am-6pm, concerts 11am Sun); and Robert Schumann, who spent the first four years of his marriage to Leipzig pianist Clara Wieck in what's now the Schumann-Haus (☎ 0341 393 9620; www.schumann-verein.de; Inselstrasse 18; adult/concession €3/2; ⌚ 2-5pm Mon-Fri, 10am-5pm Sat & Sun, concerts 5pm Sat).

On Ferdinand-Rhode-Strasse you'll also find a plaque dedicated to the little-known Japanese composer Rentaro Taki (1879–1903). Taki was the first Japanese artist to study music in Europe – where else but at the Leipzig Conservatory?

The interactive exhibit lets you follow in the footsteps of the composer and gives you a peek at original Bach scores and letters, an organ console from a local church that Bach himself examined and played, and an iron chest that once belonged to the family. In one room you can walk around and press buttons to customise the instrumentation of a Bach chorale, while in another one you'll learn how to date a Bach manuscript.

Back on the ring road, the chilling Stasi Museum (☎ 0341 961 2443; www.runde-ecke-leipzig .de; Dittrichring 24; admission free; ⌚ 10am-6pm) is in the former Leipzig headquarters of the East German secret police, a building known as the Runde Ecke (Round Corner). The all-German displays on propaganda, preposterous disguises, cunning surveillance devices, Stasi recruitment among children, scent storage and other chilling machinations reveal the GDR's all-out zeal when it came to controlling, manipulating and repressing its own people.

Information

Leipzig tourist office (☎ 0341 710 4265; www.lts-leipzig .de; Richard-Wagner-Strasse 1; ⌚ 9.30am-6pm Mon-Fri, 9.30am-4pm Sat, 9.30am-3pm Sun)

Eating

Auerbachs Keller (☎ 0341 216 100; www.auerbachs-keller -leipzig.de, Mädlerpassage; mains €12-25; ⌚ 11.30am-midnight) Founded in 1525, Auerbachs Keller was Goethe's old hang-out and even inspired a scene in *Faust*. It's cosy and touristy, but the food's actually quite good and the setting memorable.

Zill's Tunnel (☎ 0341 960 2078; www.zillstunnel.de; Barfussgässchen 9; mains €10-15; ⌚ 11.30am-midnight) Empty tables are a rare sight at this outstanding restaurant offering a classic menu of robust Saxon dishes. Sit on the outside terrace, in the rustic cellar, or in the covered 'tunnel' courtyard.

Sol y Mar (☎ 0341 961 5721; www.solymar-leipzig.de, in German; Gottschedstrasse 4; mains €5-14; ⌚ from 9am; Ⓥ) The soft lighting, ambient sounds and lush interior (including padded pods for noshing in recline) make this a relaxing place to dine. There's lots of choice for non-carnivores.

Gosenschenke 'Ohne Bedenken' (☎ 0341 566 2360; www.gosenschenke.de, in German; Menckestrasse 5; mains €6-16; ⌚ noon-1am) This historic Leipzig institution, backed by the city's prettiest beer garden, is *the* place to sample *Gose*, a local top-fermented beer often served with a shot of liqueur. The menu has a distinctly carnivorous bent. Take tram 12 to Fritz-Seger-Strasse.

Drinking & Nightlife

Zum Arabischen Coffe Baum (☎ 0341 961 0061; www .coffe-baum.de, in German; Kleine Fleischergasse 4; ⌚ 11am-midnight) Hosting six different eateries, Leipzig's oldest coffeehouse is as stuffy as your grandma's attic, but the cakes and meals are excellent and there's a free coffee museum to boot.

Moritz-Bastei (☎ 0341 702 590; www.moritzbastei .de; Universitätsstrasse 9) This classic student club occupies a warren of historic cellars below the old city fortifications. Daytime readings, large-screen football, theatre and live and club music – it all happens here most nights and on some days.

Neues Gewandhaus (☎ 0341 127 0280; www .gewandhaus.de; Augustusplatz 8) Led by Ricardo Chailly since 2005, this is one of Europe's finest and oldest orchestras, with a tradition harking back to 1743 – Felix Mendelssohn was one of its conductors.

Sleeping

Pension Schlaf Gut (☎ 0341 211 0902; www.schlafgut -leipzig.de; Brühl 64-66; s €30-48, d €43-61; Ⓟ ⌧) You decide the level of comfort at this modular sleep station. The base rate buys the room; small extra fees are charged for TV, kitchen use, daily cleaning, parking and breakfast.

Motel One (☎ 0341 337 4370; www.motel-one.de; Nikolaistrasse 23; r €59, breakfast €7.50; Ⓟ ⌧ ⌧ 📶)

If you like your design minimalist, your TVs flat-screen, your colour schemes edgy but your budget unsqueezed, you'll love this hotel right opposite the Nikolaikirche. The 194 rooms have nothing you don't need, the staff are efficiently charming and the location is unsurpassed.

Galerie Hotel Leipziger Hof (☎ 0341 697 40; www .leipziger-hof.de; Hedwigstrasse 1-3; s €69-175, d €87-195; P ⊠ 🖳 🛜) Leipzig's most unique place to unpack your bags is this 'gallery with rooms', which brims with originals created by local artists since 1989. It's a first-rate stay, yet relatively affordable, as is the restaurant.

Hotel Michaelis (☎ 0341 267 80; www.hotel -michaelis.de; Paul-Gruner-Strasse 44; s €79-149, d €99-179; P ⊠ 😵 🖳) Close to the Karl-Liebknecht-Strasse hipster mile and the city centre, this well-run place gets a big thumbs up for its 62 handsome rooms, well-respected restaurant (with a very pleasant leafy terrace) and original art collection.

LUTHERSTADT-WITTENBERG

As its full name suggests, Wittenberg is first and foremost associated with Martin Luther (1483–1546), the monk who triggered the German Reformation by publishing his 95 theses against church corruption in 1517. Sometimes called the 'Rome of the Protestants', its many Reformation-related sites garnered it the World Heritage Site nod from Unesco in 1996. As a result, Wittenberg's popularity has steadily grown since reunification and – like it or not – even a nascent Luther industry has developed. 'Hier stehe ich. Ich kann nicht anders' (Here I stand. I can

TRANSPORT: LUTHERSTADT-WITTENBERG

Direction 100km southwest

Travel Time 40 to 75 minutes

Car Take A10 to A9 in the direction of Leipzig. Exit at 'Coswig' and follow B187 to Lutherstadt-Wittenberg.

Train Regional trains zip out to Wittenberg from Berlin-Hauptbahnhof (€20.30) in about 1¼ hours but ICE (€29) and IC (€22) trains make the trip in 40 minutes; be sure to board for 'Lutherstadt-Wittenberg' – there's another place called Wittenberge west of Berlin.

do no other), Luther had declared after being asked to renounce his Reformist views at the Diet of Worms. Today, you can buy souvenir socks bearing the same credo.

Germany's most important museum devoted to Luther is the Lutherhaus (☎ 03491 420 30; www .martinluther.de; Collegienstrasse 54; adult/concession €5/3; 🕑 9am-6pm daily Apr-Oct, 10am-5pm Tue-Sun Nov-Mar) in the former family home. Through an engaging mix of accessible narrative, spot-lit artefacts, Cranach paintings and interactive multimedia stations, you'll learn about the man, his times and his impact on world history. Highlights include Cranach's Ten Commandments in the refectory and an original room furnished by Luther in 1535.

Did he or didn't he nail those 95 theses to the door of the Schlosskirche (Castle Church; ☎ 03491 402 585; Schlossplatz; admission free; 🕑 10am-6pm Mon-Sat, 11.30am-6pm Sun, to 4pm Nov-Easter)? We'll never know for sure, for the original portal was

DETOUR: COLDITZ

High on a crag above the sleepy town of Colditz, some 46km southeast of Leipzig, is the imposing Schloss Colditz (☎ 034381 437 77; www.schlosscolditz.com; Schlossgasse 1; adult/concession/family €6/4/15; 🕑 10am-5pm Apr-Oct, 10am-4pm Nov-Mar), a Renaissance palace that gained lasting fame as Oflag IVC, a WWII-era, high-security prison for Allied officers, including a nephew of Winston Churchill. Most inmates had already escaped from less-secure camps and been recaptured. Some 300 made further attempts, and 31 actually managed to flee. The would-be escapees were often aided by ingenious self-made gadgetry, including a glider fashioned from wood and bed sheets, and a homemade sewing machine for making bogus German uniforms. Most astounding, perhaps, is a 44m-long tunnel below the chapel that French officers dug in 1941–42, before the Germans caught them. You can see some of these contraptions, along with lots of photographs, in the small but fascinating Fluchtmuseum (Escape Museum; ☎ 034381 449 87; adult/ concession €3/2; 🕑 10am-5pm Apr-Oct, to 4pm Nov-Mar) within the palace. Several inmates wrote down their experiences later, of which Pat Reid's The Colditz Story is the best known account.

Getting here without your own wheels is a bit tricky but can be done. On weekdays bus 690 runs hourly to Colditz from Leipzig, or alternatively take a train to Bad Lausick and catch bus 613 from there. At weekends catch the train to Grossbothen then change to bus 619. The one-way trip takes between 90 minutes and two hours and costs €6. The town is at the junction of the B107 and B176 roads between Leipzig and Chemnitz.

destroyed by fire in 1760 and replaced in 1858 with a massive bronze version (1858) inscribed with the theses in Latin. Luther himself is buried inside below the pulpit, opposite his friend and fellow reformer Philipp Melanchthon.

If the Schlosskirche was the billboard used to advertise the forthcoming Reformation, the twin-towered Stadtkirche St Marien (Town Church of St Mary; ☎ 03491 403 201; admission free; ⏰ 10am-6pm Mon-Sat, 11.30am-6pm Sun Easter-Oct, to 4pm Nov-Easter) was where the ecumenical revolution began, with the world's first Protestant worship services in 1521. It was also here that Luther preached his famous Lectern sermons in 1522, and where he married ex-nun Katharina von Bora three years later. The centrepiece is the large altar, designed jointly by Lucas Cranach the Elder and his son. The side facing the nave shows Luther, Melanchthon and other Reformation figures, as well as Cranach himself, in biblical contexts.

How would you like to study grammar and algebra in a building where trees sprout from the windows and gilded onion domes balance above a rooftop garden? This fantastical environment is everyday reality for the 1300 pupils of Wittenberg's Hundertwasserschule (Hundertwasser School; ☎ 881 131; Strasse der Völkerfreundschaft 130; tours adult/concession €2/1; ⏰ 10am-5pm), designed by eccentric Viennese artist Friedensreich Hundertwasser. You can view the exterior any time, but tours of the interior wait for at least four participants before they start. Ring ahead for tours in English. The school is a 20-minute walk northeast of the centre. From the Markt, head east on Jüdenstrasse, turn left into Neustrasse and continue into Geschwister-Scholl-Strasse. Turn left into Sternstrasse, right into Schillerstrasse, and the school is at the next intersection on the left.

The Wittenberg tourist office (☎ 03491 498 610; www.wittenberg.de; Schlossplatz 2; ⏰ 9am-6pm Mon-Fri, 10am-3pm Sat & Sun Apr-Oct, 10am-4pm Mon-Fri, 10am-2pm Sat, 11am-3pm Sun Nov-Mar, closed Sat & Sun Jan & Feb) is on Schlossplatz.

Eating & Drinking

Brauhaus Wittenberg (☎ 03491 433 130; Im Beyerhof, Markt 6; mains €4-12; ⏰ 11am-11pm) This place – with a cobbled courtyard, indoor brewery and shiny copper vats – thrums with the noise of people having a good time. The menu is hearty but also features smaller dishes for waist-watchers. Upstairs are a few simple rooms with air-con (singles/doubles €50/70).

Café de Marc (☎ 03491 459 114; Pfaffengasse 5; mains €5-12; ⏰ 10am-6pm Tue-Sun) This French cafe with its unpretentious literary vibe is a delightful find for breakfast, java jolts or a refined calvados. When the sun's out, the idyllic courtyard is the place to be.

Sleeping

Stadthotel Wittenberg Schwarzer Baer (☎ 03491 420 4344; www.stadthotel-wittenberg.de; Schlossstrasse 2; s €56-65, d €69-85; P X ⏰) The modern rooms in this 500-year-old, heritage-listed building (no lift) are light, airy and clean-smelling, with wooden floors and cork headboards. Staff are on the ball, too.

Alte Canzley (☎ 03491 429 190; www.alte-canzley.de; Schlossplatz 3-5; s €70-125, d €84-139; P X 💻) The nicest place in town for our money is in a 14th-century building opposite the Schlosskirche. Each of the eight spacious units are furnished in dark woods and natural hues and named for a major historical figure. The vaulted downstairs harbours Saxony-Anhalt's first certified organic restaurant (dishes €4 to €17).

When Berliners have to be somewhere else, they're most likely to walk or use public transport or bicycles to get there. In fact, many of them don't even own a car and those who do don't use it for every trip. So when in Berlin, do as Berliners do: it's smarter, cheaper and saves you from looking for that elusive parking spot. Getting to the city is easy as well. Flights, tours and rail tickets can be booked online at www.lonelyplanet.com /travel_services.

AIR

Lufthansa and practically all other major European airlines and low-cost carriers (including Air Berlin, easyJet, Ryanair and Germanwings) operate direct flights to Berlin from throughout Europe. With few exceptions, travel from outside Europe involves a change of planes in another European city such as Frankfurt or Amsterdam.

Your best friend in ferreting out deals is the internet. Start by checking out fares at www.expedia.com, www.travelocity.com or www.orbitz.com, then run the same flight request through meta-search engines such as www.sidestep.com, www.opodo.com or www.kayak.com. If you're not tied to any particular travel dates, use the flexible-date search tool to find the lowest fares, or consult www.itasoftware.com.

Many airlines now guarantee the lowest fares on their own websites, so check these out as well. To get the skinny on which low-cost airlines fly where, go to www.whichbudget.com and then book your tickets through the airline's website.

THINGS CHANGE...

The information in this chapter is particularly vulnerable to change. Check directly with the airline or a travel agent to make sure you understand how a fare (and ticket you may buy) works and be aware of the security requirements for international travel. Shop carefully. The details given in this chapter should be regarded as pointers and are not a substitute for your own careful, up-to-date research.

Airports

Berlin has two international airports, reflecting the legacy of the divided city. The larger one is in the northwestern suburb of Tegel, about 8km from the city centre. The other is in Schönefeld (off Map pp72-3), about 22km southeast in the former East Berlin. For information about either, go to www.berlin-airport.de or call ☎ 0180 500 0186.

If all goes according to plan (big if!), Berlin will finally get its own major international airport some time in 2012, as Schönefeld is being expanded into Berlin Brandenburg International (BBI). Tempelhof, Berlin's historical city airport, was closed in late 2008 and reopened as a park two years later (see p145).

BICYCLE

Flat as a pancake, Berlin is tailor-made for two-wheeling. From students to lawyers, nannies to nuns, locals of all ages and walks of life love getting from A to B by bicycle. In fact, the number of cyclists has more than

SMART TRAVEL

Flying has become second nature in this era of low-cost airlines and few of us stop to consider using alternative travel methods and doing our bit for the environment. Yet, depending on where you're based, getting to Berlin without a plane is easier and more comfortable than you might think. Coming from London, for instance, you could be in Berlin in as little as nine hours by taking the Eurostar to Brussels and then catching a high-speed train with a change in Cologne. From other cities, including Warsaw, Vienna, Munich and Paris, there are direct overnight trains as well as frequent day-time connections. For the full low-down, check out Rail Europe (www.raileurope.com) or, if in the UK, call ☎ 0871 880 8066.

Buses are slower and less comfortable, but they're another option, especially if you're travelling at short notice or live in an area poorly served by air or train. Eurolines (www.eurolines.com) is the umbrella organisation of 32 European coach operators whose route network serves 500 destinations in 30 countries, including Berlin.

GETTING INTO TOWN

Tegel

Tegel airport (TXL) is connected to Mitte by the JetExpressBus TXL (30 minutes) and to Zoologischer Garten in Charlottenburg by express bus X9 (20 minutes). Bus 109 also serves the western side of the city but is slower and useful only if you're headed somewhere along Kurfürstendamm (30 minutes). Tegel is not directly served by the U-Bahn, but both bus 109 and X9 stop at Jakob-Kaiser-Platz (U7), the station closest to the airport. Each of these trips costs €2.10.

Taxi rides cost about €20 to Zoologischer Garten and €23 to Alexanderplatz and should take between half an hour and 45 minutes. There's a €0.50 surcharge for trips originating at the airport.

Schönefeld

Schönefeld airport (SFX) is linked twice-hourly by AirportExpress trains to Zoologischer Garten (30 minutes), Friedrichstrasse (23 minutes), Alexanderplatz (20 minutes) and Ostbahnhof (15 minutes). Note that these are regular regional RE or RB trains designated as AirportExpress in the timetable. S9 trains run more often but are slower (40 minutes to Alexanderplatz). The S45 line goes straight to the trade-fair grounds.

Trains stop about 400m from the terminals, which are served by a free shuttle bus every 10 minutes. Walking takes about five to 10 minutes.

Buses 171 and X7 link the terminals directly with the U-Bahn station Rudow (U7), with onward connections to central Berlin. The fare for any of these trips is €2.80 (ABC tariff).

A cab ride to central Berlin averages €40 and takes about an hour.

---

doubled in the last decade to 400,000 riders daily, accounting for 12% of total traffic in the city. And after pumping €2.5 million into expanding the bike lane system, the city now has 130km of dedicated paths in the streets or on the pavements, with 30km more to come by 2011.

There are even eye-level miniature traffic lights at intersections. Still, it pays to keep your wits about you (and preferably a helmet on) when negotiating city streets. Getting a tyre caught in tram tracks is particularly nasty. The website www.bbbike.de is a handy route planner.

Of course it's far more relaxing to pedal around the leafy suburbs. Grunewald, for instance, a forest with many lakes, is a great getaway. Or follow the course of the former Berlin Wall along the marked Berliner Mauerweg (p83). For more ideas, drop by the office of the bicycle club ADFC (Map pp156-7; ☎ 448 4724; www .adfc-berlin.de, in German; Brunnenstrasse 28; ☼ noon-8pm Mon-Fri, 10am-4pm Sat). Staff here are a wealth of information and also sell books and maps. For guided bike tours, see p311.

Bicycles (Fahrräder) may be taken aboard designated U-Bahn and S-Bahn cars (though not on buses) for the price of a reduced single ticket (see the table, p305). Deutsche Bahn charges €4.50 for a bike ticket (Fahrradkarte) on regional RE, RB and IRE trains and €9 on long-distance trains (IC, EC, NZ; reservations required). Bikes are not allowed on high-speed ICE trains.

Hire & Purchase

Many hostels and hotels rent bicycles to their guests or can refer you to an agency. Expect to pay from €6 per day and €35 per week. A minimum cash deposit and/or ID is required. There are now lots of bicycle rental places. For a handy list by neighbourhood, see www.adfc .de (link to Service, then Fahrradverleih).

One reliable outfit is Fahrradstation (Map pp140-1, Map pp124-5, Map pp76-7, Map pp102-3; ☎ central reservations 0180 510 8000; www.fahrradstation.de). They're a bit pricier (from €15 per day or €50 per week) but offer quality bikes, and have English-speaking staff and six branches throughout central Berlin. Alternatively, try Little John Bikes (☎ 7889 4123; www.little-john-bikes.de, in German) with branches in Schöneberg, Mitte and Kreuzberg. In Prenzlauer Berg, Lila Bike (Map pp156-7; ☎ 4209 3446; www .berlin-citytours-by-bike.de; Schönhauser Allee 41; ☼ 10am-8pm mid-Mar–Oct) has a good reputation.

If you want to buy a used bike, you could try the Mauerpark flea market (p196), www .zweitehand.de or www.craigslist.de.

BUS

Berlin's 'central' bus station, ZOB (off Map pp72-3; Masurenallee 4-6; ⊖ Kaiserdamm, 및 Messe Nord/ICC), is anything but. In fact, it's in deepest western Berlin, next to the trade-fair grounds, about 4km west of Zoologischer Garten station.

Tickets are available from travel agencies in town and from the on-site ZOB Reisebüro (☎ 301 0380; ☼ 6am-9pm Mon-Fri, 6am-8pm Sat & Sun). The main operators are BerlinLinienBus (☎ 861 9331; www.berlinlinienbus.de) and Gulliver's (☎ 311 0211; www.eurobusexpress.de) with departures for destinations throughout Europe. Both companies offer discounts to students and people under 26 and over 60.

Backpacker-oriented hop-on, hop-off service Bus About (Map p96; ☎ +44 (0)8450 267 514 in the UK; www.busabout.com) stops at the Citystay Hostel in Mitte.

CAR & MOTORCYCLE
Driving

Driving in Berlin is more hassle than it's worth, especially since parking is expensive and hard to find. Since 1 January 2008, all vehicles (yes, that includes foreign ones) entering the environmental zone (defined as the area bounded by the S-Bahn rail ring) must display a special sticker (*Umweltplakette*). Drivers caught without one will be fined €40. For the full scoop on how and where to obtain one, see www.berlin.de/sen/umwelt/luftqualitaet/de/luftreinhalteplan/download/touristeninfo_en.pdf.

Hire

All the big internationals maintain branches at the airports, major train stations and throughout town. The best rates are usually available through the central reservation offices listed here, but if you don't like the price, try calling a local branch to see if they have any special promotions.

Avis (☎ 01805 217 702; www.avis.com)

Budget (☎ 01805 244 388; www.budget.com)

Europcar (☎ 01805 8000; www.europcar.com)

Hertz (☎ 01805 333 535; www.hertz.com)

Local outfits may not have the newest vehicles or the biggest fleets, but prices are generally lower. For weekend rentals, reserve at least a couple of days ahead. One small but reliable local company is Das Hässliche Entlein (Map pp124-5; ☎ 0180 343 3683, 2100 5682; www.die-ente.de, in German; Lietzenburger Strasse 29; ☺ 9am-6pm Mon-Fri; Ⓜ Ⓡ Augsburger Strasse) in Charlottenburg. Daily rentals start at €18, including full insurance, VAT and unlimited kilometres; new cars start at €20. Make reservations as early as possible because they only have a smallish fleet.

If you get 'Harley hunger', head to Classic Bike (Map pp124-5; ☎ 616 7930; www.classic-bike.de; Salzufer 6; ☺ 9am-7pm Mon-Fri, 10am-3pm Sat Apr-Sep, 10am-6pm Mon-Fri, 10am-3pm Sat Oct-Mar; Ⓡ Tiergarten). Daily (24-hour) rates range from €80 to €135.

Taking your rental vehicle into an Eastern European country, such as the Czech Republic or Poland, is often a no-no; check in advance if you're planning a side trip from Berlin.

LOCAL TRANSPORT

Berlin's extensive and efficient public transport system is operated by BVG and consists of the U-Bahn (underground, subway),

S-Bahn (light rail), buses and trams. In this book the nearest station or stop is noted in each listing. For trip planning and general information, call the 24-hour hotline at ☎ 194 49 or go to www.bvg.de.

Tickets

Bus drivers sell single tickets and day passes, but all other tickets must be purchased before boarding, either from orange vending machines (with instructions in English) located in any U- or S-Bahn station or from any kiosk or shop bearing the BVG logo.

All tickets, except those bought from bus drivers, must be validated (stamped) at station platform entrances. For route maps, swing by BVG offices in such major stations as Zoologischer Garten, Alexanderplatz and Friedrichstrasse.

Since buying tickets is on the honour system, a small army of inspectors sporadically swoops down to keep people honest. Anyone caught without a valid ticket escapes only with a red face and a €40 fine payable on the spot.

Fares

The network is divided into fare zones A, B and C with tickets available for zones AB, BC or ABC. Unless you're venturing to Potsdam or Schönefeld airport, you need the AB ticket, which is valid for two hours.

If you're taking more than two trips in a day, a day pass *(Tageskarte)* will save you money. It's valid for unlimited rides on all forms of public transport until 3am the following day. The group day pass *(Kleingruppenkarte)* is valid for up to five people travelling together. For short trips, buy the *Kurzstreckenticket*, which is good for three stops on the U-Bahn and S-Bahn or six on any bus or tram; no changes allowed. The weekly pass *(Wochenkarte)* is transferable and entitles you to take along another adult and up to three children aged six to 14 for free after 8pm Monday to Friday and all day Saturday, Sunday and holidays.

Children aged six to 14 generally qualify for reduced *(ermässigt)* rates, while kids under six travel for free.

Ticket type	AB (€)	BC (€)	ABC (€)
single	2.30	2.70	3
reduced single	1.40	1.80	2.10
day pass	6.30	6.60	6.80
group day pass	15	15.30	15.50
7-day pass	27.20	28	33.50

Bus & Tram

Buses run frequently between 4.30am and 12.30am. From Sunday through Thursday, night buses take over the remaining hours, running roughly every 30 minutes. Buses N2, N5, N6, N8 and N9 follow more or less the routes of the U-Bahn lines U2, U5, U6, U8 and U9. Night buses don't run on Friday and Saturday night, when U-Bahn service is available 24/7. Nightline route maps are available from BVG offices and are also displayed at bus stops and on station platforms.

Trams only operate in the eastern districts. The M10, N54, N55, N92 and N93 offer continuous service nightly.

S-Bahn & Regional Trains

S-Bahn trains make fewer stops than U-Bahn ones and are therefore handy for longer distances, but they don't run as frequently. Denoted as S1, S2 etc in this book, they operate from around 4am to 12.30am and all night on Friday, Saturday and public holidays.

Destinations further afield are served by RB and RE trains. You'll need an ABC or Deutsche Bahn ticket to use these trains.

U-Bahn

The most efficient way to travel around Berlin is by U-Bahn, designated U1, U2 etc in this book. Trains operate from 4am until about 12.30am and throughout the night on Friday, Saturday and public holidays (all lines except the U4).

TAXI

You'll find taxi ranks at the airports, major train stations and throughout the city. Flag fall is €3.20, then it's €1.65 per kilometre up to 7km and €1.28 for each kilometre after that. Taxis can also be ordered on ☎ 443 322, 210 202 or 263 000. There's no surcharge for night trips but bulky luggage costs an extra €1 per piece. A ride from Alexanderplatz to Zoologischer Garten costs about €13. For a nifty fare calculator or to order a cab online, see www.taxi-in-berlin.de.

For short trips, you can use the €4 *Kurzstreckentarif* (short-trip rate), which entitles you to ride for up to 2km. It is only available if you flag down a moving taxi and request this special rate before the driver has activated the regular metre. If you continue past 2km, regular rates apply to the entire journey.

Tip taxi drivers around 10%.

TRAIN

Berlin is well connected by train to other German cities and destinations such as Prague, Warsaw and Amsterdam. Most German trains are operated by Deutsche Bahn (DB; ☎ reservations & information 118 61, toll-free automated timetable 0800 150 7090; www.bahn.de).

Hauptbahnhof

The futuristic glass canopy of Berlin's swanky central train station (Map pp76-7) shelters five floors of tracks and services. North- and southbound trains depart from the bottom floor, while east- and westbound trains, as well as the S-Bahn, run from platforms on the uppermost level.

The station has great infrastructure but its open-plan layout can be confusing. Buy tickets in the *Reisezentrum* (Travel Centre) located between tracks 14 and 15 on the 1st upper floor (1F) and 1st lower floor (B1). The latter also has a EurAide (p316) desk.

The left-luggage office (€4 per piece per 24 hours) is behind the Reisebank currency exchange on level 1F, opposite the *Reisezentrum*. Other services include a 24-hour pharmacy, a Berlin tourist office (p316), a supermarket (☷ 6am-11pm Mon-Sat, 8am-10pm Sun) and other stores open

daily from 8am to 10pm. The TXL bus to Tegel airport leaves from Europaplatz (exit north entrance).

Other Stations

While all long-distance trains converge at the Hauptbahnhof, some also stop at Spandau (off Map pp72-3), Ostbahnhof (Map pp150-1), Gesundbrunnen (Map pp72-3) and Südkreuz. Of these, Ostbahnhof has the second-best infrastructure.

Tickets

Tickets are sold online (www.bahn.de), at the *Reisezentrum* ticket counters and, for shorter distances, through vending machines. Tickets sold on board (cash only) incur a service fee of €3 to €8 unless the station where you boarded was unstaffed or had a broken vending machine.

Seat reservations for long-distance travel are highly recommended, especially if you're travelling on a Friday or Sunday afternoon, around holidays or in summer. They can be made up to 10 minutes before departure by phone, online or at ticket counters. The cost is €4.50 per person or €9 for groups of up to five people; if bought online the cost drops to €2.50 and €5, respectively.

BUSINESS HOURS

Shops may set their own hours but typical core times are from 10am to 8pm Monday to Saturday. Some malls, supermarkets and department stores stay open until 9pm or 10pm, while small boutiques tend not to open until noon and close as early as 6pm or 7pm weekdays and 4pm Saturdays. See the boxed text, p214, for where to stock up on basic supplies after hours and on Sundays.

Banking hours are from 8.30am to 4pm Monday to Friday, with most branches staying open until 5.30pm or 6pm on Thursday. Post office core hours are 9am to 6pm Monday to Friday and 9am to 1pm on Saturday, although this varies slightly between branches.

Travel agencies and other service-oriented businesses unlock their doors from 9am to 6pm weekdays and until 1pm or 2pm on Saturday. Public servants, on the other hand, often put down their pencils as early as 1pm on Friday. Some museums are closed on Monday but stay open late one evening a week, usually Thursday.

For restaurant hours, see p199. Bars generally open around 6pm while clubs open their doors at 11pm or midnight but don't kick into high gear until 1am or 2am.

CHILDREN

(Tiny) hands down, travelling to Berlin with tots can be child's play, especially if you keep a light schedule and involve the kids in the day-to-day planning. Lonely Planet's *Travel with Children* offers a wealth of tips and tricks on the subject.

There's plenty to keep the tykes occupied, from zoos to kid-oriented museums to magic and puppet shows. Parks and imaginative playgrounds abound in all neighbourhoods, but especially in family-heavy Prenzlauer Berg. On hot summer days, a few hours spent at a public outdoor pool or a lakeside beach will go a long way towards keeping kids' tempers cool. For more ideas, see the boxed text, p131, as well as our list of favourite playgrounds (p153), ice-cream parlours (p216) and kid-friendly eateries (p205).

Baby food, infant formula, soy and cow's milk, disposable nappies (diapers) and the like are widely available at chemists (drugstores) and in supermarkets. Breastfeeding in public is practised, although most women are discreet about it.

Children enjoy a wide range of discounts for everything from museum admission to bus fares and hotel stays, although the cut-off age can be anything from six to 18. At hotels, ask for family rooms with three or four beds; practically all hotels can provide rollaway beds or cots, although there may be an extra charge.

Babysitting

Ask staff at your hotel for a referral, or try one of the following agencies, all of which have English-speaking personnel:

Babysitter Express (☎ 4000 3400, 160 9722 0665; www.babysitter-express.de; per hr €11-13.50) Can send someone at short notice, often within the hour. Calls are only accepted until 10pm.

Kinder-Hotel (Map pp102-3; ☎ 4171 6928; www.kinder insel.de; Eichendorffstrasse 17, Mitte; ⏱ office 10am-4pm Mon-Fri; ⓔ Naturkundemuseum) Offers 24-hour day care in 17 languages for kids aged from zero to 14. Hourly fees are €13, overnight stays (14 hours) cost €69.

Welcome Kids (☎ 0177 310 8456, 4699 1802; www .welcome-kids.de; prices vary) Provides child care in your hotel or takes kids out on excursions; for children aged five months to 15 years.

CLIMATE

Berlin has a continental climate, meaning summers can be scorching and winters bitingly cold. If you're after pleasant weather, the best months tend to be May, June, September and October, although packing your brolly is a good idea any time of year. If

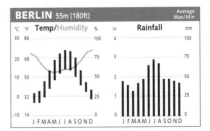

the sun's out, life moves outdoors instantly, even in January when you see Berliners sipping their latte al fresco huddled below heaters or bundled into thick blankets (provided by the cafe).

CUSTOMS REGULATIONS

Most articles that you take to Germany for your personal use don't incur duty and tax. If you're over 15, you may also bring in other products up to a value of €300 if arriving by land or €430 if arriving by sea or air. The limit for those under 15 is €175. The following allowances apply to duty-free goods purchased in a non-EU country by people over 17.

Alcohol 1L of strong liquor or 2L of less than 22% alcohol by volume plus 4L of wine plus 16L of beer.

Tobacco Either 200 cigarettes or 100 cigarillos or 50 cigars or 250g of loose tobacco.

DISCOUNT CARDS

Cutting costs while exploring Berlin is as easy as identifying the TV Tower on the skyline. If you're a full-time student, the International Student Identity Card (ISIC; www.isic.org) is your ticket to savings on airline fares, travel insurance and many local attractions. The Euro<26 youth card (www.euro26.org) grants similar savings and benefits to anyone under 30. These cards can be bought online or from student unions, hostelling organisations and youth-oriented travel agencies.

The following are Berlin-specific discount cards that will help you stretch your travel euros even further, regardless of age:

Berlin WelcomeCard (www.visitberlin.de/welcomecard; per 2/3/5 days for public transport fare zones AB €16.90/22.90/29.90, for zones ABC €18.90/25.90/34.90) Entitles you to unlimited public transport and up to 50% discount to 140 attractions and tours. The ABC fare zone extends to Potsdam and Schönefeld airport. Available online, at the Berlin Tourist Info offices (p316), U-Bahn and S-Bahn ticket-vending machines, from bus drivers and at many hotels.

CityTourCard (www.citytourcard.de; per 2/3/5 days zones AB €19.50/21.90/28.90, for zones ABC €17.90/23.90/33.90) Works on the same scheme as Berlin WelcomeCard and is a bit cheaper, but offers fewer discounts. Available online, at some hotels and from U-Bahn and S-Bahn vending machines.

Museumspass Berlin (adult/child €19/9.50) Unbeatable deal for museum-lovers. Buys admission to about 70 Berlin museums on three consecutive opening days, including such blockbusters as the Pergamon and the Neues Museum. Sold at the Berlin Tourist Info offices (p316) and all participating museums.

ELECTRICITY

Standard voltage in Germany is 220V, 50Hz AC. Plugs are the continental type with two round pins. Your 220V appliances may be plugged into outlets (if necessary with an adaptor), but their 110V cousins (eg from North America) need a transformer. Most shavers and laptops work on both 110V and 220V. For more information, see www.kropla.com.

EMBASSIES

Most embassies and their consular divisions can be reached by telephone from 8am or 9am until 5pm or 5.30pm Monday to Friday. Walk-in office hours are usually limited to the morning, but afternoon appointments are possible; call for details. For additional foreign missions in Berlin, check the website of the German Foreign Office (www.auswaertiges-amt.de, link to 'English', then 'Addresses').

Australia (Map p96; ☎ 880 0880; www.germany.embassy.gov.au; Wallstrasse 76-79, Mitte; Ⓜ Märkisches Museum)

Canada (Map p112; ☎ 203 120; www.kanada-info.de; Leipziger Platz 17, Tiergarten; Ⓜ Ⓢ Potsdamer Platz)

Czech Republic (Map pp76-7; ☎ 226 380; www.mzv.cz/berlin; Wilhelmstrasse 44, Mitte; Ⓜ Mohrenstrasse)

France (Map pp76-7; ☎ 590 039 000; www.botschaft-frankreich.de; Pariser Platz 5, Mitte; Ⓜ Ⓢ Brandenburger Tor, Ⓑ 100, TXL)

Ireland (Map pp76-7; ☎ 220 720; www.embassyofireland.de; Jägerstrasse 51, Mitte; Ⓜ Hausvogteiplatz)

Italy (Map p112; ☎ 254 400; www.ambberlino.esteri.it; Hiroshimastrasse 1, Tiergarten; Ⓑ 200)

Japan (Map p112; ☎ 210 940; www.de.emb-japan.go.jp; Hiroshimastrasse 6, Tiergarten; Ⓑ 200)

Netherlands (Map p96; ☎ 209 560; www.niederlandeweb.de; Klosterstrasse 50, Mitte; Ⓜ Klosterstrasse)

New Zealand (Map pp76-7; ☎ 206 210; www.zembassy.com/germany; Friedrichstrasse 60, Mitte; Ⓜ Stadtmitte)

Poland (off Map pp72-3; ☎ 223 130; www.berlin.polemb.net; Lassenstrasse 19-21, Charlottenburg; Ⓢ Grunewald)

Russia (Map pp76-7; ☎ 229 111 029; www.russische-botschaft.de; Unter den Linden 63-65, Mitte; Ⓜ Ⓢ Brandenburger Tor, Ⓑ 100, TXL)

Spain (Map p112; ☎ 254 0070; www.spanischebotschaft.de; Lichtensteinallee 1, Tiergarten; Ⓑ 100)

Switzerland (Map pp76-7; ☎ 390 4000; www.eda.admin.ch; Otto-von-Bismarck-Allee 4a, Mitte; Ⓜ Bundestag, Ⓑ 100)

UK (Map pp76-7; ☎ 204 570; www.britischebotschaft.de; Wilhelmstrasse 70, Mitte; Ⓜ Ⓢ Brandenburger Tor, Ⓑ 100, TXL)

USA (Map pp76-7; ☎ 830 50; www.usembassy.de; Pariser Platz 2, Mitte; ⓢ ⓡ Brandenburger Tor, 🚌 100, TXL)

EMERGENCY

For emergency assistance call the police (☎ 110) or fire department/ambulance (☎ 112). Other useful phone numbers and addresses:

ADAC Car Breakdown Service (☎ 0180 222 2222)

American Hotline (☎ 0177 814 1510) Despite the name, this is a crisis hotline and referral service for all English-language speakers.

BVG Public Transport Lost & Found (Map p136; ☎ 194 49; Potsdamer Strasse 180/182; ⏱ 9am-6pm Mon-Thu, to 2pm Fri; ⓢ Kleistpark)

Call-a-Doc (☎ 01805 321 303) Free, nonemergency medical advice and physician referral.

Deutsche Bahn & S-Bahn Lost & Found (☎ 0900 199 0599; ⏱ 8am-8pm Mon-Sat, 10am-8pm Sun) For items lost on RE, RB, S-Bahn and other DB trains.

Emergency Dental Referrals (☎ 8900 4333; ⏱ after 8pm Mon-Fri, 24hr Sat & Sun)

Emergency Medical Referrals (☎ 310 031; ⏱ 24hr)

Municipal Lost & Found (Map pp140-1; ☎ 902 773 101; Platz der Luftbrücke 6, Tempelhof airport; ⏱ 8am-3pm Mon & Tue, 1-6pm Thu, 8am-noon Fri; ⓢ Platz der Luftbrücke) Entrance is on the right side of the former airport terminal.

HOLIDAYS

Shops, banks and public and private offices are closed on the following *gesetzliche Feiertage* (public holidays):

Neujahrstag (New Year's Day) 1 January

Ostern (Easter) March/April – Good Friday, Easter Sunday and Easter Monday

Christi Himmelfahrt (Ascension Day) 40 days after Easter, always on a Thursday

Maifeiertag (Labour Day) 1 May

Pfingsten (Whitsun/Pentecost Sunday & Monday) May/June

Tag der Deutschen Einheit (Day of German Unity) 3 October

WI-FI ACCESS

Practically all hostels, most hotels and many cafes and bars offer wireless surfing (called W-LAN in German), either for free or for a small fee. The entire Sony Center (p111) at Potsdamer Platz is a free public hotspot. The website www.hotspot-locations.com can help you pin down others.

Reformationstag (Reformation Day, Brandenburg state only) 31 October

Weihnachtstag (Christmas Day) 25 December

Zweiter Weihnachtstag (Boxing Day) 26 December

INTERNET ACCESS

Berlin is well connected to cyberspace, so getting online either with your own laptop, through a public terminal or at an internet cafe should be a snap. Public libraries offer free computers and sometimes wi-fi access, but the downsides may include time limits, reservation requirements and queues. Internet access is also available at slightly seedy telephone call shops, which cluster near train stations. Generally speaking, internet cafes in Berlin have about the lifespan of a fruit fly, but here are a couple that were in business at the time of writing:

InternetWork (Map pp156-7; ☎ 4401 7483; Gaudystrasse 1, Prenzlauer Berg; ⏱ noon-midnight)

Netlounge (Map pp102-3; ☎ 2434 2597; Auguststrasse 89, Mitte; ⏱ noon-midnight)

Fat Tire Bike Tours (p311), below the TV Tower, offers all-you-can-surf for €1.99. Also look for coin-operated laptops by Sidewalk Express (www.sidewalkexpress.com; per hr €2), usually found in malls (eg Potsdamer Platz Arkaden, Alexa) and inside Dunkin' Donuts, Burger King or Point Shop To Go convenience stores in train stations (eg Friedrichstrasse, Alexanderplatz). See the website for the full list of locations.

For useful trip-planning websites, flip to p20.

LEGAL MATTERS

By law, you must carry photo identification such as your passport, national identity card or drivers licence. The permissible blood-alcohol limit is 0.05%; drivers caught exceeding this amount are subject to stiff fines, a confiscated licence and even jail time. If you are arrested, you have the right to make a phone call and are presumed innocent until proven guilty. If you don't know a lawyer, contact your embassy (opposite) for a referral.

MAPS

Besides the handy pull-out map included with this book, you might want to pick up a larger city map such as those published by ADAC, RV Verlag or Falkplan, especially if you're planning an in-depth exploration of the outer

THE LEGAL AGE FOR...

Being served beer or wine in a pub: 16
Buying cigarettes: 18
Driving a car: 18
Sexual consent: 14 (with restrictions)
Voting in an election: 18

districts. Look for them at bookshops, petrol stations, newsagents and tourist offices.

MEDICAL SERVICES

The standard of healthcare in Germany is excellent, and with nearly 9000 doctors and dentists in Berlin alone you're never far from medical help. The US and UK consulates are among those that can provide you with lists of English-speaking doctors.

If you are a citizen of the EU, the European Health Insurance Card (EHIC) entitles you to reduced-cost or free medical treatment for illness or injury, though not for emergency repatriation home. Check with your local health authorities for information on how to obtain an EHIC. Non-EU citizens should check if a similar reciprocal agreement exists between their country and Germany, or if their policy at home provides worldwide healthcare coverage.

If you need to buy travel health insurance, be sure to get a policy that also covers emergency flights back home. While some plans pay doctors or hospitals directly, note that many healthcare providers may still demand immediate payment from nonlocals. Most do not accept credit cards. Except in emergencies, call around for a doctor willing to accept your insurance.

There are no vaccinations required to visit Germany.

Emergency Rooms

Charité Campus Benjamin Franklin (off Map pp72-3; ☎ 844 50; www.charite.de; Hindenburgdamm 30; ⓡ Botanischer Garten) In Steglitz in southern Berlin.

Charité Campus Mitte (Map pp76-7; ☎ 450 50; www .charite.de; Schumannstrasse 20-21; Ⓞ Oranienburger Tor, Ⓞ ⓡ Hauptbahnhof) The most central of the big hospitals.

Charité Campus Virchow-Klinikum (Map pp72-3; ☎ 450 50; www.charite.de; Augustenburger Platz 1; Ⓞ Amrumer Strasse) In the Wedding district in northern Berlin.

Zahnklinik Medeco (Dental Clinic; Map p112; ☎ 2309 5960; www.medeco.de, in German; Stresemannstrasse

121; ⊙ 7am-9pm; Ⓞ ⓡ Potsdamer Platz) Check the website for other branches around town.

Pharmacies

German chemists (drugstores, *Drogerien*) do not sell any kind of medication, not even aspirin. Even over-the-counter *(rezeptfrei)* medications for minor health concerns, such as a cold or upset stomach, are only available at a pharmacy *(Apotheke)*. For more serious conditions, you will need to produce a prescription *(Rezept)* from a licensed physician. If you take regular medication, be sure to bring a full supply for your entire trip, as the same brand may not be available in Germany.

The names and addresses of pharmacies open after hours (on a roster) are posted in every pharmacy window, or call ☎ 011 41.

MONEY

Euros come in seven notes (five, 10, 20, 50, 100, 200 and 500 euros) and eight coins (one and two euro coins, and one, two, five, 10, 20 and 50 cent coins). At press time the euro had lost a bit of strength. See the exchange-rate table on the inside front cover for some guidelines or check currency converter sites such as www.xe.com or www.oanda.com.

You can exchange money at airports, some banks and currency exchange offices. Cash is still king in Germany and you can't really avoid carrying at least some notes and coins, say €100 or so, on you at all times. The easiest way to get cash is from ATMs linked to international networks such as Cirrus, Plus, Star and Maestro. Check with your bank or credit-card company about fees. Credit cards

COME ON BABY, LIGHT MY FIRE

After years of foot-dragging, a total smoking ban in all gastro establishments was to take effect in Berlin on 1 July 2008. But less than a month later, Germany's highest court ruled the sweeping ban unconstitutional. Now smoking is again allowed, but only in single-room bars and clubs that are smaller than 75 sq metres, don't serve anything to eat and keep out customers under 18. Huh?

Never mind, it's as absurd as it sounds, which explains the current state of 'anarchy'. Some places allow smoking, others don't, at some you can puff away after 10pm, at others in certain areas only. In short, Berlin-style laissez-faire at its finest!

are becoming more widely accepted in central Berlin, but it's best not to assume that you'll be able to use one – always inquire first. The emergency hotline to report the loss or theft of any credit or debit card is ☎ 116 116.

For an overview of what things cost in Berlin, see p20.

Changing Money

Currency exchange offices are called *Wechselstuben*. You'll find them at airports and major train stations. Reisebank (www.reisebank .de), for instance, has branches at Zoologischer garten (Map p128), Hauptbahnhof (Map pp76-7), Ostbahnhof (Map pp150-1) and Bahnhof Friedrichstrasse (Map pp76-7), while Euro-Change (www.euro-change.de) is located at Zoologischer Garten (Map p128), Alexanderplatz station (Map pp76-7) and Friedrichstrasse 80 (Map pp76-7). Reisebank keeps slightly longer hours (at least until 8pm); on Sundays your only bets are the offices at the airports.

NEWSPAPERS & MAGAZINES

Berliners are news junkies who support five daily local newspapers, including the mainstream *Der Tagesspiegel* (www.tagesspiegel.de) and *Berliner Morgenpost* (www.morgenpost .de), the left-leaning *Berliner Zeitung* (www .berlinonline.de/berliner-zeitung) and *taz* (www.taz.de), and the tabloid-style *BZ* (www .bz-berlin.de). *Zitty* (www.zitty.de), *Tip* (www .tip-berlin.de) and *Prinz* (www.prinz.de), in that order, are the dominant listings mags, although the free *030* (www.berlin030.de) is popular as well. Another freesheet, the *Siegessäule* (www.siegessaeule.de), is required reading for gays and lesbians. *ExBerliner* (www .exberliner.de) is a well-written, English-language magazine largely catering to expats, with features, essays and listings. International dailies and periodicals are widely available at large newsstands and in bookshops. Most cafes have piles of mags for their patrons to enjoy.

ORGANISED TOURS

Bicycle Tours

Companies listed here are excellent and operate English-language tours. Reservations are recommended. The walking tour company Insider Tours (p313) also runs bike tours.

Berlin on Bike (Map pp156-7; ☎ 4373 9999; www.berlinon bike.de; Knaackstrasse 97; tours incl bike €18, with own bike €13; ◷ Mar-Oct; ◉ Eberswalder Strasse) runs a general city tour, neighbourhood tours and an excellent Berlin Wall tour from Court 4 of the Kulturbrauerei. Discounts are available.

Fat Tire Bike Tours (Map p96; ☎ 2404 7991; www .fattirebiketoursberlin.com; Panoramastrasse 1a; tours incl bike & insurance adult/student €20/18; ◉ ◉ Alexanderplatz) offers city tours year-round as well as themed tours (Third Reich, Berlin Wall) and a Potsdam tour (adult/student €38/36, including transportation and admission to Cecilienhof) from April to October. Tours leave from the TV Tower main entrance.

Boat Tours

A lovely way to experience Berlin on a warm day is from the deck of a boat, cruising along the city's rivers, canals and lakes. Tours range from one-hour spins around Museumsinsel (from €8) to longer trips to Schloss Charlottenburg and beyond (from €16). Most tours offer live narration in English and German and sell refreshments on board. Small children usually travel for free; those under 14 and seniors get 50% off. The season runs roughly from April to October.

Berliner Wassertaxi (☎ 6588 0203; www.berliner -wassertaxi.de, in German) Departures from Museumsinsel (Map pp76-7 & Map p96).

Reederei Bruno Winkler (☎ 349 9595; www.reederei winkler.de) Departures from Reichstagufer/Friedrichstrasse (Map pp76-7), Schlossbrücke Charlottenburg (Map pp124-5), Märkisches Ufer (Map p96) and Spreebogen (Map pp72-3).

Reederei Riedel (☎ 693 4646; www.reederei-riedel.de) Departures from Märkisches Ufer (Map p96) and Ludwig-Erhard-Ufer (Map pp76-7).

Stern & Kreisschiffahrt (☎ 536 3600; www.sternundkreis .de) Departures from Jannowitzbrücke (Map p96), Reichstagufer/Friedrichstrasse (Map pp76-7) and Schlossbrücke Charlottenburg (Map pp124-5).

Bus Tours

You'll see them everywhere around town: colourful buses (often open-topped double-deckers in summer) that tick off all the key sights on two-hour loops with basic taped commentary in eight languages. You're free to get off and back on at any of the stops. Buses depart roughly every 15 or 30 minutes between 10am and 5pm or 6pm daily. BBS Berliner Bären Stadtrundfahrt (☎ 3519 5270; www.sight seeing.de) and Severin + Kühn (☎ 880 4190; www .berlinerstadtrundfahrten.de) both offer 24-hour tickets costing €20. Tempelhofer Reisen (☎ 752 4057; www.tempelhofer.de) charges €15 for tickets good on the day of issuance only. Traditional city tours where you don't get off the bus, combination boat and bus tours as well as trips to Potsdam, Dresden and the Spreewald are also available. For details, call, check the websites or look for flyers in hotel lobbies and at the Berlin Tourist Info offices (p316).

Speciality Tours

Berlinagenten (☎ 4372 0701; www.berlinagenten.com; 4-course dinner tours per person €175 for groups of two, less for bigger groups) Get under the skin of Berlin's lifestyle scene with clued-in guides who whisk you off the beaten track and into unique bars, boutiques, restaurants and clubs, and even private homes. For an insider's primer on the culinary scene, book the Gastro-Rallye, where you'll enjoy one course each at four restaurant stops. Advance booking required.

Berliner Unterwelten WWII Bunker Tour (Map pp72-3; ☎ 4991 0517; www.berliner-unterwelten.de; most tours adult/concession €9/7; ⏱ English tours 11am Thu-Mon, German tours noon, 2pm & 4pm Thu-Mon) Explore Berlin's dark and dank underbelly by picking your way past hospital beds, war-time helmets and filter systems on a 90-minute tour of WWII-era underground bunkers below the Gesundbrunnen U-Bahn station. Five other tours, including one of a WWII air-raid tower, are also offered. Buy tickets at the company's kiosk in the south hall of U-Bahn station Gesundbrunnen (facing Brunnenstrasse).

Fritz Music Tours (☎ 3087 5633; www.musictours-berlin .com) Berlin music expert Thilo Schmied gives you the lowdown on Berlin's legendary music history – from Iggy and Bowie to U2 and Rammstein, cult clubs to the Love Parade, along with news about who's rocking the city right now – on a dynamic 2½-hour bus tour (€19; in English 12.30pm Sunday, in German 12.30pm Saturday; reservations required). Tours meet in front of the Adlon Kempinski (p268) hotel. Fritz also offers: two-hour walking tours (€12; in English 4pm Friday, in German 2pm Wednesday and Sunday) leaving from the tourist office in the Kultur-

brauerei (Map pp156-7; Schönhauser Allee 36-39); private minibus tours (per person €45, by arrangement); and monthly tours of the Hansa Studios (p112; €10-20, depending on the number of participants). Reservations are required for all tours.

Sta* Tours Berlin (☎ 3010 5151; www.sta-tours.de; for groups of up to 6, per person €35; ⏱ by appointment) If you're a German-film buff, first visit the Museum für Film & Fernsehen (p112), then let celluloid expert Birgit Wetzig-Zalkind take you on two-hour van tours of the places where Billy Wilder, Leni Riefenstahl, Nastassja Kinski, Horst Buchholz, Marlene Dietrich and other legends lived and played.

Trabi Safari (Map pp140-1; ☎ 2759 2273; www.trabi-safari.de; Zimmerstrasse 97; 1/2/3/4 passengers per person €60/40/35/30; ⏱ Kochstrasse) Spend an hour exploring classic Berlin sights or the city's 'Wild East' from behind the wheel – or as a passenger – of a GDR-made Trabant (Trabi for short). Live commentary (in English by prior arrangement) is piped into your car. The two-hour Wall Ride (one to two people €79, three to four people €89) takes you to the East Side Gallery and other wall-related stops. There's a second office in the Domaquaree (Map p96; Karl-Liebknecht-Strasse 5; ⏱ 🚉 Alexanderplatz).

Videobustour (☎ 4402 4450; www.videobustour.de; 2-2½ hour tours adult/concession €19.50/16.50) This ingenious tour company brings the past into the present by showing you historical footage and photographs on a TV screen as you ride by Berlin's famous landmarks in an air-con bus. There's a general sightseeing tour as well as the Filmstadt Berlin tour, which takes you to famous film locations (Good Bye, Lenin!, Lives of the Others) and shows you excerpts from the movie while your guide regales you with anecdotes and fascinating trivia. The regular tours are in German and leave from Unter den Linden 40. English tours are available upon request.

Self-Guided Tours

Also see the boxed text, below, for a self-guided bus tour.

HAVE A BLAST ON THE BUS!

One of Berlin's best bargains is a self-guided city tour aboard public buses 100 or 200, whose routes check off nearly every major sight in the city centre for the price of an AB ticket. You can even get on and off within the two hours of the ticket's validity period as long as you continue in the same direction. If you plan to explore all day, a Tageskarte (day pass) is your best bet.

Bus 100 travels from Bahnhof Zoo (Zoo Station) to Alexanderplatz, passing by the Gedächtniskirche, Tiergarten (with the Siegessäule), the Reichstag, the Brandenburger Tor (Brandenburg Gate) and Unter den Linden. German readers can get details at www.bus100.de.

Bus 200 also starts at Bahnhof Zoo, but takes a more southerly route via the Kulturforum and Potsdamer Platz before hooking up to Unter den Linden. Without traffic, trips take about 30 minutes. There's no commentary, of course, but you can pick up a map and information leaflet from the BVG information kiosk (Map p128) on Hardenbergplatz outside Zoologischer Garten. Buses get crowded, so be wary of pickpockets. To get a seat on the upper deck, it's best to board at either terminus, ie Zoologischer Garten or Alexanderplatz.

Jewish Berlin iGuide tour of Jewish sites in the Scheunen-viertel. Available at the Anne Frank Zentrum (p105).

Mauerguide (Wall Guide) GPS-guided tours of the Berlin Wall; for details, see the boxed text, p82.

Mitte Schritte (www.urban-sounds-to-go.de) Dynamic audio tour of 14 major sights in the Mitte district, put together by a duo of locals. Available at the ausberlin store (p184; Karl-Liebknecht-Strasse 17; per person €7.50; ☽ noon-7pm, last rental 5pm).

Walking Tours

Several walking tour companies run English-language introductory spins that take in both blockbuster and offbeat sights, plus themed tours (eg Third Reich, Cold War, Sachsen-hausen, Potsdam). Guides are fluent English speakers, well informed, sharp-witted and keen to answer your questions. Tours don't require reservations – just show up at one of the central meeting points. Since these change quite frequently, it's best to look for the companies' flyers (eg in hostels, hotels or the tourist offices) or to contact them directly. Some tours are free (well, the guides work for tips, so give what you can) but most cost between €10 and €15. Companies include:

Alternative Berlin (☎ 0162 819 8264; www.alternative berlin.com) Free tours with a funky-punky twist, plus the '666 Anti-Pubcrawl'.

Berlin Walks (☎ 301 9194; www.berlinwalks.de) The first English-language walking tour company founded after the fall of the Wall is still running strong.

Brewer's Berlin Tours (☎ 0177 388 1537; www.brewers berlintours.com) Home of the epic all-day Best of Berlin tour (foot massage not included) and shorter free tour.

Insider Tour (☎ 692 3149; www.insidertour.com) Also does bike tours and a pub crawl.

New Berlin Tours (☎ 5105 0030; www.newberlintours .com) Pioneered the concept of the 'free tour' and the (in) famous pub crawl and also offers 'alternative berlin' tour.

POST

You can buy stamps at post offices (see p307 for standard hours); some branches also have vending machines outside that can be accessed 24/7. Within Germany, postal rates are €0.45 for standard-sized postcards and €0.55 for letters up to 20g. Mail sent to other European destinations costs €0.65 and €0.70, respectively, while rates to the rest of the world are €1 for postcards and €1.70 for letters up to 20g. A surcharge applies to oversized items.

Letters sent within Germany take one to two days for delivery; those addressed to destinations within Europe or to North America take four to six days, and to Australasia five to seven days.

Check www.deutschepost.com for post office locations throughout Berlin. Here's a selection of convenient branches:

Charlottenburg (Map p128; Joachimstaler Strasse 7; ☽ 9am-8pm Mon-Fri, 10am-8pm Sat; 🅿 🚇 Zoologischer Garten)

Mitte (Map p96; Rathausstrasse 5; ☽ 8am-7pm Mon-Fri, 9am-4pm Sat; 🅿 🚇 Alexanderplatz)

Potsdamer Platz (Map p112; inside Potsdamer Platz Arkaden, Alte Potsdamer Strasse 7; ☽ 10am-9pm Mon-Sat; 🅿 🚇 Potsdamer Platz)

SAFETY

Travellers will rarely get tricked, cheated or conned simply because they're tourists. In fact, Berlin is one of the safest and most tolerant of European cities. Walking about at night, even for women alone, is not usually dangerous. Of course, this doesn't mean that there are no rotten apples ready to poison the statistics, so keep your wits about you just as you would at home. Spiked drinks in bars and clubs do happen, so don't leave yours out of sight. Always carry enough cash for a cab ride back to the hotel.

The most headline-grabbing crimes are racial or homophobic attacks, but these are actually quite rare and mostly confined to areas with little if anything to lure travellers. The eastern district of Lichtenberg, for instance, is plagued by neo-Nazi activity, while ethnic gangs occasionally cause trouble in parts of Neukölln and Wedding. Seriously nervous Nellies should quiz hotel staff or call local police about particulars.

Homeless punks accosting you for cash with their dogs looking on are a nuisance but not really dangerous – just ignore them. The same goes for the impecunious types standing near U-Bahn entrances trying to sell you used tickets for a few cents. Don't fall for it – it's illegal and most likely the ticket is no longer valid.

SPORTS & ACTIVITIES

Beach Volleyball

Bump, set and spike at Beach Mitte (Map pp102-3; ☎ 0177 280 6861; www.beachmitte.de, in German; Caroline-Michaelis-Strasse 8; court per hr €10-16; ☽ 10am-midnight Apr-Sep; 🚇 Nordbahnhof), a huge urban beach volleyball complex with 60 courts and a beer garden for post-workout socialising. Book courts early, especially for evenings and weekends.

Cycling

See p302 for information about cycling in and around Berlin.

Running

Berlin offers great running terrain in its many parks. Flat and spread out, Tiergarten is among the most popular and convenient, although the Grunewald in Wilmersdorf/ Zehlendorf is even prettier. The trip around the scenic Schlachtensee is 5km. The park of Schloss Charlottenburg is also good for a nice, easy trot. More challenging is Volkspark Friedrichshain, which has stairs, hills and even a fitness trail.

Skating

Exploring the city in the company of thousands of other skate enthusiasts is both fun and great for socialising and going local. In Berlin, a couple of organisations take over city streets in the warmer months, usually from May to September. Skate by Night (http:// berlin.skatebynight.de, in German; per person €2; 8.30pm Sun; Alexanderplatz) is a weekly organised roll-through that starts and ends on Alexanderplatz. Check-in starts at 7pm and kick-off is at 8.30pm. Routes vary. There's also Berlinparade (www.berlinparade.de), which organises free biweekly 20km to 27km runs (usually at 8pm on Tuesdays) that double as a demonstration for skaters' rights. Check the website for exact dates. A great place to skate on your own, with kilometres of smooth surface, is the new Tempelhofer Park (pp140-1) on the former airfield of Tempelhof Airport.

X-Games aficionados head to the Skatehalle Berlin (Map pp150-1; 2936 2966; www.skatehalle-berlin.de, in German; Revaler Strasse 99; day pass €5; 2-8pm Mon, 2pm-midnight Tue, Wed & Fri, 2pm-10pm Thu, noon-midnight Sat, noon-8pm Sun, reduced hours May-Oct; Warschauer Strasse), which has the biggest halfpipe in Germany along with curbs, ledges, funboxes, a 3.5m wall ride and other fun zones. It's part of the RAW Tempel complex in Friedrichshain.

For skate hire, try Ski-Shop Charlottenburg (Map pp124-5; 341 4870; www.ski-shop-charlottenburg.de, in German; Schusterhrusstrasse 1, Charlottenburg; day rate fitness/ speed skates €8/20; 11am-7pm Mon-Fri, 10am-3pm Sat; Richard-Wagner-Platz).

Spas

Adlon Day Spa (Map pp76-7; 301 117 200; www.adlon-day-spa.de; Behrenstrasse 72; facials/massages from €50/45; 9am-8pm Sun & Mon, 9am-10pm Tue-Sat; Brandenburger Tor) Earth, wind, fire and water – these are the magic words at this exclusive spa, where massages, wraps, scrubs and facials are calibrated to achieve your chosen goal, be it melting away stresses or getting red-carpet ready. Pampering is taken to seriously luxe levels here in minimalist, off-white treatment rooms for both girls and boys.

Liquidrom (Map pp140-1; 258 007 820; www.liquidrom-berlin.de; Möckernstrasse 10; 2hr/4hr/all day session €17.50/20.50/22.50; 10am-midnight Sun-Thu, 10am-1am Fri & Sat; Anhalter Bahnhof) Any time is a fine time to feel your daily cares slip away at a stylishly minimalist day spa that's the perfect mood enhancer on a rainy day. There are a couple of saunas, dipping pools and lounge areas, but the star of the show is the darkened domed hall where you float in a saltwater pool while being showered with soothing sounds and psychedelic light projections. Pure bliss.

Sultan Hamam (Map p136; 2175 3375; www.sultan-hamam.de; Bülowstrasse 57; 3/5hr session €16/21; noon-11pm; Yorckstrasse) An exotic Arabian Nights flair embraces you at this traditional Turkish bathhouse, which has an exotically tiled sauna, steam and relaxation rooms. For an extra treat, book a soapy scrub and a kese (full body peel with silken gloves) costing €13 each. Mondays are men only, Tuesday to Saturday women only and Sunday it's open to both.

SPORTS CALENDAR

- Berliner Sechstagerennen (www.sechstagerennen-berlin.de, in German; Jan) Pedal power is king at this six-day-long series of indoor cycling races that has brought the world's elite to Berlin for nearly a century.
- Ladies German Open (www.german-open.org; May) The world's top tennis players come to the Spree for this very popular event that serves as a warm-up for the French Open.
- ISTAF (Internationales Stadionfest; www.istaf.de; early Sep) This annual track-and-field meet brings the world's best athletes to the Olympiastadion.
- Berlin Marathon (www.berlin-marathon.com; Sep) Sweat it out with the other 50,000 runners or just cheer 'em on during Germany's biggest street race that has seen nine world records set since 1977.

Spectator Sports

Alba Berlin (Map pp150-1; ☎ 01805-570 011; www.alba berlin.de; O2 World arena; tickets €10-64; ⓡ Ostbahnhof) Berlin's top basketball team competes hard on a European level and has a solid winning record. Since the 2008 season, fans have flocked to the new O2 arena for home games.

Eisbären Berlin (Map pp150-1; ☎ 9718 4040; www .eisbaeren.de; O2 World arena; tickets €18-57; ⓡ Ostbahnhof) Fervent ice-hockey fans ensure that every home game of the Polar Bears practically explodes with atmosphere, especially since the team has been national champion in 2005, 2006, 2008 and 2009.

Hertha BSC (off Map pp72-3; ☎ 01805 189 200; www .herthabsc.de; Olympiastadion; tickets €9.50-35.50) Much to the dismay of loyal fans, Berlin's main football (soccer) team was relegated from the Bundesliga (premier league) to the second division for the 2010/11 season. Home games are played at the Olympic Stadium. For public training times call ☎ 01805 189 200. Tickets are usually still available on game day.

Swimming

Berlin has plenty of public pools to get you wet. For the full lowdown, see www.berliner baederbetriebe.de (in German). Opening hours vary widely by day, time and pool, so call ahead before setting out. Indoor pools close in summer (usually May to September). Many facilities also have saunas, which generally cost between €10 and €15. For details about the Badeschiff pool moored in the Spree River, see p147.

There's also swimming in lakes, including the Krumme Lanke, the Schlachtensee, the Tegeler See and the Müggelsee (off Map pp72-3). For information on water quality, call ☎ 9022 9555 or check www.berlin.de/badegewaesser/ detail (in German).

Kinderbad Monbijou (Map pp102-3; ☎ 282 8652; Oranienburger Strasse 78; adult/child €4/2.50; ☽ from 10am or 11am-7pm; ⓡ Hackescher Markt, Oranienburger Strasse) Kids get to splash around in a shallow pool or swoosh down slides while their parents relax on the ample lawn at this public pool in a little Scheunenviertel park.

Sommerbad Olympiastadion (off Map pp72-3; ☎ 6663 1152; Osttor, Olympischer Platz 1; adult/concession €4/2.50; ☽ 7am-8pm May-early Sep; Ⓞ ⓡ Olympiastadion) Do your laps in the 50m pool built for the 1936 Olympic athletes.

Stadtbad Neukölln (Map pp140-1; ☎ 6824 9812; Ganghoferstrasse 3; adult/concession €4/2.50; ☽ 9am-8pm Sep-May; Ⓞ Rathaus Neukölln, Karl-Marx-Strasse) This gorgeous bathing temple from 1914 wows swimmers

with mosaics, frescoes, marble and brass. There are two pools (20m and 25m) and a Russian-Roman bath.

Strandbad Wannsee (off Map pp72-3; ☎ 803 5450; www.strandbadwannsee.de, in German; Wannseebadweg 25, Zehlendorf; adult/concession €4/2.50; ☽ 10am-6pm mid-Apr–late Apr, 10am-7pm Mon-Fri, 8am-8pm Sat & Sun May–mid-Jul, 9am-8pm Mon-Fri, 8am-9pm Sat & Sun mid-Jul–Aug, 10am-7pm Sep; ⓡ Nikolassee, then walk or ⎔ 118, 218, 318) One of Europe's largest lakeside lidos with 1km of sandy beach and plenty of infrastructure. Often gets packed.

TAXES & REFUNDS

Prices for goods and services include a value-added tax (VAT), called *Mehrwertsteuer*, which is 19% for regular goods and 7% for food and books. If your permanent residence is outside the EU, you can have a large portion of the VAT refunded, provided you shop at a store displaying the 'Tax-Free for Tourists' sign and obtain a tax-free form for your purchase from the sales clerk. At the airport, show this form, your unused goods and the receipt to a customs official before checking your luggage. The customs official will stamp the form, which you can then take straight to the cash refund office at the airport.

TELEPHONE

German phone numbers consist of an area code (☎ 030 for Berlin) followed by the local number, which can be between three and nine digits long. From landlines, numbers dialled within Berlin don't require the area code.

If calling Berlin from abroad, first dial your country's international access code, then 49 (Germany's country code), then 30 (dropping the initial 0) and the local number. Germany's international access code is 00.

Faxes can be sent from and received at most hotels, photocopy shops and internet cafes (p309).

For important and useful phone numbers, see the inside front cover.

Mobile Phones

Mobile (cell) phones operate on GSM900/ 1800. If your home country uses a different standard, you'll need a multiband GSM phone in Germany. If you're staying for a while and have an unlocked multiband phone, getting a prepaid SIM card with a local number might work out cheaper than using your own network. Cards are available at any telecommunications store (eg T-Online, Vodafone, E-Plus or O2), although cards sold through discount supermarkets such as Aldi and Lidl offer the best rates.

Calls made to German mobile phone numbers are charged at higher rates than those to landlines, but incoming calls are free.

Phonecards

Most public payphones only work with Deutsche Telecom (DT) phonecards, available in denominations of €5, €10 and €20 from post offices, newsagents and tourist offices.

For long-distance and international calls, prepaid calling cards issued by other providers tend to offer better rates. Look for them at newsagents and telephone call shops. There may be a connection fee and a surcharge for calls made from payphones.

TIME

Clocks in Germany are set to central European time (GMT/UTC plus one hour). Daylight-saving time kicks in on the last Sunday in March and ends on the last Sunday in October. The use of the 24-hour clock (eg 6.30pm is 18.30) is common.

TOILETS

If you feel the urge, finding a toilet in Berlin isn't usually terribly difficult. The city centre is littered with free-standing public pay toilets that are barrier-free and self-cleaning. Occasionally, you'll also see historic *pissoirs*, although these are usually equipped with urinals only. Toilets in shopping centres, some cafes and restaurants and public venues are often attended by a cleaner who either charges a flat fee (say, €0.50) or expects a small tip.

TOURIST INFORMATION

The local tourist board, Berlin Tourismus Marketing (BTM; www.visitberlin.de), operates five walk-in offices and a call centre (☎ 250 025; ⊙ 9am-8pm Mon-Fri, 10am-6pm Sat & Sun) whose multilingual staff field general questions and make hotel and ticket bookings. From April to October the branches at Neues Kranzler Eck, Brandenburger Tor and Alexa Shopping Mall keep extended hours.

Berlin Tourist Info Alexa Shopping Mall (Map p96; Grunerstrasse 20, ground fl, near Alexanderplatz; ⊙ 10am-8pm Mon-Sat; ◉ ℞ Alexanderplatz)

Berlin Tourist Info Brandenburger Tor (Map pp76-7; south wing; ⊙ 10am-7pm; ◉ ℞ Brandenburger Tor)

Berlin Tourist Info Hauptbahnhof (Map pp76-7; Europaplatz north exit; ⊙ 8am-10pm; ◉ ℞ Hauptbahnhof)

Berlin Tourist Info Humboldtbox (Map pp76-7; Schlossplatz; ⊙ 10am-6pm; ☒ 100, 200, TXL)

Berlin Tourist Info Neues Kranzler Eck (Map p128; Kurfürstendamm 21; ⊙ 10am-8pm Mon-Sat, to 6pm Sun; ◉ Kurfürstendamm)

EurAide (Map pp76-7; www.euraide.de; Hauptbahnhof; ⊙ 10am-7pm May-Jul, 11am-6pm Mon-Fri Aug-Apr, closed Christmas–mid-Feb; ◉ ℞ Hauptbahnhof) Inside the Reisezentrum on the lower level (B1), this helpful office is staffed with English speakers who can assist with all train-related issues (rail passes, tickets) and other travel-related topics.

TRAVELLERS WITH DISABILITIES

Overall, Berlin caters quite well for the needs of the disabled, especially the wheelchair-bound. You'll find access ramps and/or lifts in many public buildings, including train stations, museums, concert halls and cinemas. Newer hotels have lifts and rooms with extra-wide doors and spacious bathrooms. The Mobidat nonprofit assesses the accessibility of cafes, restaurants, hotels, theatres and other public spaces and makes the information available via an online databank at www.mobidat.net; alternatively call ☎ 7477 7115.

Most buses and trams are wheelchair-accessible and many U/S-Bahn stations are equipped with ramps or lifts. For trip planning assistance, contact the BVG (☎ 194 19; www .bvg.de). Many stations also have grooved platforms to assist blind passengers. Seeing-eye dogs are allowed everywhere. The hearing impaired can check upcoming station names on displays installed in all forms of public transport.

Some car-rental agencies offer hand-controlled vehicles and vans with wheelchair lifts at no extra charge, but you must reserve them well in advance. In parking lots and garages, look for designated disabled spots marked with the wheelchair symbol.

If your wheelchair breaks down, call Rollstuhlpannendienst at ☎ 0180 111 4747 or 0177 833 5773 for 24-hour assistance. The same company also offers wheelchair rentals.

VISAS

Most EU nationals only need their national identity card or passport to enter, stay and work in Germany. Citizens of Australia, Canada, Israel, Japan, New Zealand, Poland, Switzerland and the US are among those who need only a valid passport (no visa) if entering as tourists for a stay of up to three months within a six-month period. Passports must be valid for at least another four months from the planned date of departure from Germany.

Nationals from other countries need a so-called Schengen Visa, named after the 1995 Schengen Agreement that abolished passport controls between Austria, Belgium, Denmark, Finland, France, Germany, Iceland, Italy, Greece, Luxembourg, the Netherlands, Norway, Portugal, Spain and Sweden. In late 2007 the following nine countries joined the agreement: Czech Republic, Estonia, Hungary, Latvia, Lithuania, Malta, Poland, Slovakia and Slovenia. Switzerland joined in late 2008.

You must apply for the Schengen Visa with the embassy or consulate of the country that is your primary destination. It is valid for stays of up to 90 days. Legal residency in any Schengen country makes a visa unnecessary, regardless of your nationality. For full details, see www.auswaertiges-amt.de or check with a German consulate in your country.

WOMEN TRAVELLERS

Berlin is remarkably safe for women to explore, even for solo travellers. Going alone to cafes and restaurants is perfectly acceptable, even at night. It's quite normal to split dinner bills, even on dates, or for a woman to start talking to a man. In bars and nightclubs, solo women are likely to attract some attention, but if you don't want company, most men will respect a firm 'no, thank you'. If you feel threatened, protesting loudly will often make the offender slink away with embarrassment or spur others to come to your defence. Unfortunately, drinks spiked with so-called 'date-rape drugs' are a potential problem in some bars and clubs, so don't leave your drink unattended.

If assaulted, call the police (☎ 110) or, if you prefer, a women's crisis hotline (☎ 251 2828, 615 4243, 216 8888) whose staff members are trained to help you deal with the emotional and physical trauma associated with an attack. Note that none are staffed around the clock. Don't get discouraged, and try again later.

WORK

Non-EU citizens cannot work legally in Germany without a residence permit *(Aufenthaltserlaubnis)* and a work permit *(Arbeitserlaubnis)*. EU citizens don't need a work permit but they must have a residence permit, although obtaining one is a mere formality. Since regulations change from time to time, it's best to contact the German embassy in your country for the latest information.

Citizens of Australia, New Zealand and Canada aged between 18 and 30 may apply for a Working Holiday Visa, entitling them to work in Germany for up to 90 days in a 12-month period. Contact the German embassies in those countries for details.

If you're not looking for a full-time job but simply need some cash to replenish your travel budget, consider babysitting, cleaning, English tutoring, tour guiding, bar tending, waiting tables, yoga teaching, donating sperm or perhaps nude modelling for art classes. You won't get rich, but neither will you need a high skill level, much training, or fluent German.

Start by placing a classified ad in a local newspaper, listings guide or the English-language magazine *ExBerliner*. Other places to advertise include noticeboards at universities and local supermarkets. You could also scour the postings on www.craigslist.de, but it pays to have a good 'bullshit detector'.

LANGUAGE

German belongs to the West-Germanic branch of the Indo-European language group (along with English) and is spoken by over 100 million people throughout the world, including Austria and parts of Switzerland. There are also ethnic German communities in neighbouring Eastern European countries, such as Poland and the Czech Republic.

High German is the official and 'standard' form of the language, though most people also speak a local or regional dialect. The same is true in Berlin, though only a small number of Berliners speak pure Berlinisch.

You'll find that locals appreciate travellers trying their language, no matter how muddled you may think you sound, and learning even a few phrases will enrich your travel experience. If you want to learn more German than we've included here, pick up a copy of Lonely Planet's comprehensive *German* phrasebook, or, for shorter trips, *Fast Talk German*. Lonely Planet iPhone phrasebooks are available through the Apple App store.

SOCIAL
Meeting People
Hello.
Guten Tag.
Goodbye.
Auf Wiedersehen.
Please.
Bitte.
Thank you (very much).
Danke (schön).
Yes./No.
Ja./Nein.
Do you speak English?
Sprechen Sie Englisch?
Do you understand (me)?
Verstehen Sie (mich)?
Yes, I understand (you).
Ja, ich verstehe (Sie).
No, I don't understand (you).
Nein, ich verstehe (Sie) nicht.

Could you please …?
Könnten Sie …?
 repeat that
 das bitte wiederholen
 speak more slowly
 bitte langsamer sprechen
 write it down
 das bitte aufschreiben

Going Out
What's on …?
Was ist … los?
 locally
 hier

this weekend
dieses Wochenende
today
heute
tonight
heute Abend

Where are the …?
Wo sind die …?
 clubs
 Klubs
 gay venues
 Schwulen- und Lesbenkneipen
 restaurants
 Restaurants
 pubs
 Kneipen

Is there a local entertainment guide?
Gibt es einen Veranstaltungskalender?

PRACTICAL
Numbers & Amounts
1	eins
2	zwei
3	drei
4	vier
5	fünf
6	sechs
7	sieben
8	acht
9	neun
10	zehn
11	elf
12	zwölf
13	dreizehn

14	vierzehn
15	fünfzehn
16	sechzehn
17	siebzehn
18	achtzehn
19	neunzehn
20	zwanzig
21	einundzwanzig
30	dreizig
40	vierzig
50	fünfzig
60	sechzig
70	siebzig
80	achtzig
90	neunzig
100	hundert
1000	tausend

Days

Monday	Montag
Tuesday	Dienstag
Wednesday	Mittwoch
Thursday	Donnerstag
Friday	Freitag
Saturday	Samstag
Sunday	Sonntag

Banking

I'd like to …
Ich möchte …
  cash a cheque
  einen Scheck einlösen
  change money
  Geld umtauschen
  change some travellers cheques
  Reiseschecks einlösen

Where's the nearest …?
Wo ist der/die nächste …? (m/f)
  automatic teller machine
  Geldautomat (m)
  foreign exchange office
  Geldwechselstube (f)

Post

I want to send a …
Ich möchte … senden.

fax	ein Fax
parcel	ein Paket
postcard	eine Postkarte

I want to buy a/an…
Ich möchte … kaufen.

aerogram	ein Aerogramm
envelope	einen Umschlag
stamp	eine Briefmarke

Phones & Mobiles

I want to make a …
Ich möchte …
  call (to Singapore)
  (nach Singapur) telefonieren
  reverse-charge/collect call (to Singapore)
  ein R-Gespräch (nach Singapur) führen

I want to buy a phonecard.
Ich möchte eine Telefonkarte kaufen.

Where can I find a/an …?
Wo kann ich … kaufen?
I'd like a/an …
Ich hätte gern …
  adaptor plug
  einen Adapter für die steckdose
  charger for my phone
  ein Ladegerät für mein Handy
  mobile/cell phone for hire
  ein Miethandy
  prepaid mobile/cell phone
  ein Handy mit Prepaidkarte
  SIM card for your network
  eine SIM-Karte für Ihr Netz

Internet

Where's the local internet cafe?
Wo ist hier ein Internet-Café?

I'd like to …
Ich möchte …
  check my email
  meine E-Mails checken
  get internet access
  Internetzugang haben

Transport

What time does the … leave?
Wann fährt … ab?

boat	das Boot
bus	der Bus
train	der Zug

What time's the … bus?
Wann fährt der … Bus?

first	erste
last	letzte
next	nächste

What time does the plane leave?
Wann fliegt das Flugzeug ab?
Where's the nearest metro station?
Wo ist der nächste U-Bahnhof?
Are you available? (taxi)
Sind Sie frei?

Please put the meter on.
Schalten Sie bitte den Taxameter ein.
How much is it to …?
Was kostet es bis …?
Please take me to (this address).
Bitte bringen Sie mich zu (dieser Adresse).

FOOD

For more detailed information on food and dining out, see p197.

breakfast	Frühstück
lunch	Mittagessen
dinner	Abendessen
snack	Snack

Can you recommend …?
Können Sie … empfehlen?

a bar/pub	eine Kneipe
a cafe	ein Café
a coffee bar	eine Espressobar
a restaurant	ein Restaurant
a local speciality	eine örtliche Spezialität

What's that called?
Wie heisst das?
Is service included in the bill?
Ist die Bedienung inbegriffen?

EMERGENCIES

It's an emergency!
Es ist ein Notfall!
Call the police!
Rufen Sie die Polizei!
Call a doctor!/an ambulance!
Rufen Sie einen Artzt!/Krankenwagen!
Could you please help me?/us?
Könnten Sie mir/uns bitte helfen?
Where's the police station?
Wo ist das Polizeirevier?

HEALTH

Where's the nearest …?
Wo ist der/die/das nächste …? (m/f/n)

(night) chemist	(Nacht) Apotheke (f)
dentist	Zahnarzt (m)
doctor	Arzt (m)
hospital	Krankenhaus (n)

Symptoms

I have (a) …
Ich habe …

diarrhoea	Durchfall
fever	Fieber
headache	Kopfschmerzen
pain	Schmerzen

GLOSSARY

You may encounter the following terms and abbreviations while in Berlin.

Bahnhof (Bf) – train station
Berg – mountain
Bibliothek – library
BRD – Bundesrepublik Deutschland (abbreviated in English as FRG – Federal Republic of Germany); see also *DDR*
Brücke – bridge
Brunnen – fountain or well
Bundestag – German parliament

CDU – Christliche Demokratische Union (Christian Democratic Union), centre-right party

DDR – Deutsche Demokratische Republik (abbreviated in English as GDR – German Democratic Republic); the name for the former East Germany; see also *BRD*
Denkmal – memorial, monument
Dom – cathedral

ermässigt – reduced (eg admission fee)

Fahrrad – bicycle
Flohmarkt – flea market

Flughafen – airport
FRG – Federal Republic of Germany; see also *BRD*

Gasse – lane or alley
Gästehaus, Gasthaus – guesthouse
GDR – German Democratic Republic (the former East Germany); see also *DDR*
Gedenkstätte – memorial site
Gestapo – Geheime Staatspolizei (Nazi secret police)
Gründerzeit – literally 'foundation time'; early years of German empire, roughly 1871–90

Hafen – harbour, port
Hauptbahnhof (Hbf) – main train station
Hof (Höfe) – courtyard(s)

Imbiss – snack bar, takeaway stand
Insel – island

Kaiser – emperor; derived from 'Caesar'
Kapelle – chapel
Karte – ticket
Kiez(e) – neighbourhood(s)
Kino – cinema
König – king
Konzentrationslager (KZ) – concentration camp

Kristallnacht – literally 'Night of Broken Glass'; Nazi pogrom against Jewish businesses and institutions on 9 November 1938

Kunst – art

Kunsthotels – hotels either designed by artists or liberally furnished with art

Mietskaserne(n) – tenement(s) built around successive courtyards

Ostalgie – fusion of the words Ost and Nostalgie, meaning nostalgia for East Germany

Palais – small palace

Palast – palace

Passage – shopping arcade

Platz – square

Rathaus – town hall

Reich – empire

Reisezentrum – travel centre in train or bus stations

Saal (Säle) – hall(s), large room(s)

Sammlung – collection

S-Bahn – metro/regional rail service with fewer stops than the U-Bahn

Schiff – ship

Schloss – palace

See – lake

SPD – Sozialdemokratische Partei Deutschlands (Social Democratic Party of Germany)

SS – Schutzstaffel; organisation within the Nazi Party that supplied Hitler's bodyguards, as well as concentration camp guards and the Waffen-SS troops in WWII

Stasi – GDR secret police (from Ministerium für Staatssicherheit, or Ministry of State Security)

Strasse (Str) – street

Tageskarte – daily menu; day ticket on public transport

Tor – gate

Trabant – GDR-era car boasting a two-stroke engine

Turm – tower

Trümmerberge – rubble mountains

U-Bahn – rapid transit railway, mostly underground; best choice for metro trips

Ufer – bank

Viertel – quarter, neighbourhood

Wald – forest

Weg – way, path

Weihnachtsmarkt – Christmas market

Wende – 'change' or 'turning point' of 1989, ie the collapse of the GDR and the resulting German reunification

BEHIND THE SCENES

THIS BOOK

This 7th edition of *Berlin* was researched and written by Andrea Schulte-Peevers. Andrea has worked on all seven editions of the book. She co-authored the 1st edition with David Peevers, the 4th and 5th editions with the late Tom Parkinson, and the 6th edition with Anthony Haywood and Sally O'Brien. This guidebook was commissioned in Lonely Planet's London office, laid out by Cambridge Publishing Management Ltd, and produced by the following:

Commissioning Editors Clifton Wilkinson, Anna Tyler

Coordinating Editors Monique Choy, Thomas Lee

Coordinating Cartographer David Kemp

Coordinating Layout Designer Paul Queripel

Senior Editor Katie Lynch

Managing Cartographer David Connolly

Managing Layout Designer Celia Wood

Assisting Editors Charlotte Harrison

Assisting Cartographer(s) Jennifer Johnston, Enes Basic

Cover Research, lonelyplanetimages.com

Internal Image Research Aude Vauconsant, lonelyplanet images.com

Indexer Amanda Jones

Project Manager Melanie Dankel

Language Content Annelies Mertens

Thanks to Lisa Knights, Michelle Glynn, Bruce Evans, Yvonne Kirk, Branislava Vladisavljevic, Carol Jackson, Lyahna Spencer

Cover photographs Sculptures on the National Monument, Kreuzberg, David Peevers (top); Paul-Löbe-Haus, Thomas Winz (bottom)

Internal photographs All images are copyright of the photographer unless otherwise indicated. Many of the images in this guide are available for licensing from Lonely Planet Images: www.lonelyplanetimages.com

THANKS
ANDREA SCHULTE-PEEVERS

A heartfelt *danke schön* to Miriam Bers, Jörg Buntenbach, Stefan Danziger, Alisa Ehlert, Frank Engster, Arne Krasting, Thilo Schmied, Christian Taenzler, Alexander Vogel, Anne Wilson and Ron Wilson for helping me ferret out Berlin's finest and funnest spots. My good friend Henrik Tidefjärd deserves special applause for his never-flagging inspiration, enthusiasm and passion for Berlin. Big thanks to Caroline Sieg for giving me the gig in the first place and then for braving crazy friends, mad cab rides and long nights on the town in the name of friendship and research. My colleague Tom Masters deserves his own medal for so generously sharing his unique insights on Berlin. Kudos to the LP team responsible for producing such a kick-ass book. And as always, deep thanks to David, my loyal companion in life.

THE LONELY PLANET STORY

Fresh from an epic journey across Europe, Asia and Australia in 1972, Tony and Maureen Wheeler sat at their kitchen table stapling together notes. The first Lonely Planet guidebook, *Across Asia on the Cheap*, was born.

Travellers snapped up the guides. Inspired by their success, the Wheelers began publishing books to Southeast Asia, India and beyond. Demand was prodigious, and the Wheelers expanded the business rapidly to keep up. Over the years, Lonely Planet extended its coverage to every country and into the virtual world via lonelyplanet.com and the Thorn Tree message board.

As Lonely Planet became a globally loved brand, Tony and Maureen received several offers for the company. But it wasn't until 2007 that they found a partner whom they trusted to remain true to the company's principles of travelling widely, treading lightly and giving sustainably. In October of that year, BBC Worldwide acquired a 75% share in the company, pledging to uphold Lonely Planet's commitment to independent travel, trustworthy advice and editorial independence.

Today, Lonely Planet has offices in Melbourne, London and Oakland, with over 500 staff members and 300 authors. Tony and Maureen are still actively involved with Lonely Planet. They're travelling more often than ever, and they're devoting their spare time to charitable projects. And the company is still driven by the philosophy of *Across Asia on the Cheap*: 'All you've got to do is decide to go and the hardest part is over. So go!'

OUR READERS

Many thanks to the travellers who used the last edition and wrote to us with helpful hints, useful advice and interesting anecdotes:

Úrsula Ávalos, Benjamin Ducke, Yusuf Esiyok, Robert Gardham, Philip Gatter, Michalis Kalamaras, Kim Lockwood, Katerina Pintova, Juergen Rolfs, Daniel Schaumann, N Wiedenhof

ACKNOWLEDGMENTS

Many thanks to the following for the use of their content:

Globe on title page ©Mountain High Maps 1993 Digital Wisdom, Inc.

lonelyplanet.com

SEND US YOUR FEEDBACK

We love to hear from travellers – your comments keep us on our toes and help make our books better. Our well-travelled team reads every word on what you loved or loathed about this book. Although we cannot reply individually to postal submissions, we always guarantee that your feedback goes straight to the appropriate authors, in time for the next edition. Each person who sends us information is thanked in the next edition and the most useful submissions are rewarded with a free book.

To send us your updates – and find out about Lonely Planet events, newsletters and travel news – visit our award-winning website: lonelyplanet.com/contact.

BEHIND THE SCENES

Notes

Notes

Notes

INDEX

A

Abbado, Claudio 43
accessories, see Shopping subindex
accommodation 265-79, see also Gay & Lesbian Berlin & Sleeping subindexes, individual neighbourhoods
  costs 267-8
  flats 266
  gay & lesbian travellers 263
  longer-term rentals 267
  reservations 267
  styles 266-7
Achilles, Daniel 203
Achtung Berlin 17
activities, see sports
air travel 302
  to/from airport 303
Alexanderplatz, see Mitte – Alexanderplatz Area
All Nations Festival 18
ambulance 309
antiques, see Shopping subindex
apartments, see Sleeping subindex
Apparat 46
aquariums 95-6
architecture 52-7
  baroque 53-5
  Bauhaus 42, 56, 118
  GDR era 57-8
  Gründerzeit 26, 55-6

Historicism 55-6
housing 55, 56, 58, 59, 61
Modernism 56
Nazi monumentalism 57
Renaissance 53
area codes 315, see also inside front cover
Art Forum Berlin 19
art galleries 242-5, see also Shopping & Sights subindexes
arts 37-52, 242-5, 249-55, see also Arts subindex
  dance 51-2, 251
  fashion 245-6
  festivals 17, 18, 19
  graffiti 244-5, **243**
  music 43-7, 246-8, 250
  private collections 80
  sculpture 40-3, 242-5
  street art 244-5, **244**
  visual arts 40-3, 242-5
ATMs 310

B

Baader, Andreas 34
babysitters 307
Bach, Johann Sebastian 298-9
Badeschiff 147, **7**
bags, see Shopping subindex
ballet 51-2
bars 220, 258, **9**, see also Drinking & Gay & Lesbian Berlin subindexes
basketball 315
bathrooms 316
Bauhaus 42, 56, 118
B&Bs, see Sleeping subindex
beach bars 224, **7**
beach volleyball 313-14
bears 97
Beate Uhse Erotikmuseum 130, **6**
Beckmann, Max 42
beer 18, 221
beer gardens, see Drinking subindex

Behrens, Peter 56, 58
Berlin Air Show (ILA) 18
Berlin Airlift 32
Berlin Biennale 18
Berlin Fashion Week 16, 18
Berlin Hi-Flyer 146
Berlin Marathon 19
Berlin Music Week 19
Berlin Secession 41
Berlin Wall 33, 35, 82-3, 106, **4**
  cycling tour 178-80, **179**
Berlin Zoo 126-7, 133
Berlinale 17
Berliner Bierfestival 18
Berliner Gauklerfest 18-19
Berliner Liste 19
Berliner Philharmoniker 43, 116
Berliner Schule 42
Berlinisch dialect 66
Ber-Mu-Da 20
Bers, Miriam 244
bicycle travel 287, 302-3, see also cycling tours
Bismarck, see von Bismarck, Otto
Boat Party 227
boat travel 287, 290, see also tours
Bonaparte, Napoleon 24-5
books 25, 37-40, 41, see also literature
bookshops 184, see also Shopping subindex
Bowie, David 45, 137
BPitch Control 46
Brandenburger Tor 81, 179, **4**
Braun, Eva 30-1, 84
breakbeat 46
Brecht, Bertolt 44, 50, 107, 254
Britspotting 17
Brussig, Thomas 39, 40
buildings, see Sights subindex
Bundesrepublik Deutschland 32
Buntenbach, Joerg 246
bus travel 302, 303-4, 305, see also tours

business hours 307, see also inside front cover
  restaurants 199-200
  shops 182, 214

C

cabaret 51, 52, 238-9, see also Nightlife subindex
cafes 220, 258, see also Drinking & Gay & Lesbian subindexes
car travel 304
casinos 239
cathedrals, see Sights subindex
cell phones 315-16
cemeteries, see Sights subindex
central Berlin **72-3**
Charlottenburg & Northern Wilmersdorf 121-34, **124-5, 128**
  accommodation 272-5
  drinking 223-4
  food 206-8
  shopping 188-9
  transport 126
  walking tour 132-4, **133**
Checkpoint Charlie 33, 144, 180, **10**
chemists 310
children, travel with 131, 153, 205, 307, see also Sights subindex
Chorin 289
Christmas markets 20
Christopher Street Day 262, **6**
churches, see Sights subindex
cinema 47-9, 251-3, see also Arts, Gay & Lesbian Berlin & Sights subindexes
  film festivals 17, 19, 47, 263
Classic Open Air Gendarmenmarkt 18
classical music 43, 250-1, see also Arts subindex
  festivals 17, 19, 289
climate 16, 307-8

INDEX

GREENDEX

GOING GREEN

It seems like almost everyone is going 'green' these days. But how can you know which businesses really are ecofriendly and which are simply jumping on the bandwagon? All of the following sights and attractions, activities, tour operators, restaurants, shops, lodgings and even transportation have been hand-picked by our authors because they act in harmony with sustainable tourism goals. Some are locally owned and operated, others are actively involved in resource conservation, but whatever their speciality, all are committed to lowering their impact on the environment. We want to keep developing our sustainable tourism content. If you think we've omitted somewhere that should be listed here, or if you disagree with our choices, email us at talk2us@lonelyplanet.com.au and set us straight for next time. For more information about sustainable tourism and Lonely Planet, see www.lonelyplanet.com/about/responsible-travel.

EATING

b.alive 213
Fresh 'N' Friends 214
Kollwitzplatzmarkt 195
Majakowski Gasthaus 218
Natural'Mente 207
Ökomarkt Chamissoplatz 207
Witty's 209

EXCURSIONS

Alte Canzley 301
Hundertwasserschule 301
Mosaic Tours 288
Pension Am Alten Bauernhafen 291
PlanWirtschaft 295

SHOPPING

Kollwitzplatzmarkt 195, 207
Trippen 187

SIGHTS

Freilichtmuseum Domäne Dahlem 163
Museumsdorf Düppel 164

SLEEPING

Bleibtreu Berlin 273
Circus Hostel 278
Circus Hotel 271
Hotel 26 276
Miniloft Berlin 266
mitArt Hotel & Café 270
Raise a Smile Hostel 276

MAP LEGEND

ROUTES

Tollway
Freeway
Primary
Secondary
Tertiary
Lane
Under Construction

Mall/Steps
Tunnel
Pedestrian Overpass
Walking Tour
Walking Tour Detour
One-Way Street
Unsealed Road

TRANSPORT

Bicycle path
Ferry
Metro
Bus Route
S-Bahn

Rail
Rail (Underground)
Tram
U-Bahn

HYDROGRAPHY

River, Creek
Water

Canal

BOUNDARIES

Wall

AREA FEATURES

Airport
Area of Interest
Building
Campus
Cemetery, Christian
Cemetery, Other

Forest
Land
Mall
Market
Park
Sports

SYMBOLS

Information

Monument
Museum, Gallery
Ruin
Point of Interest
Zoo, Bird Sanctuary

Embassy/Consulate
Hospital, Medical
Information
Police Station
Post Office, GPO

Shopping

Shopping

Eating

Eating

Sights

Christian
Jewish

Drinking

Drinking

Nightlife

Nightlife

The Arts

Arts

Sleeping

Sleeping

Transport

Airport, Airfield
Bus Station
Parking Area
Taxi Rank

Published by Lonely Planet Publications Pty Ltd
ABN 36 005 607 983

Australia (Head Office)
Locked Bag 1, Footscray, Victoria 3011,
☎03 8379 8000, fax 03 8379 8111,
talk2us@lonelyplanet.com.au

USA 150 Linden St, Oakland, CA 94607,
☎510 250 6400, toll free 800 275 8555,
fax 510 893 8572, info@lonelyplanet.com

UK 2nd fl, 186 City Rd, London, EC1V 2NT,
☎020 7106 2100, fax 020 7106 2101,
go@lonelyplanet.co.uk

MIX
Paper from
responsible sources
FSC
www.fsc.org
FSC™ C021741